Business Law
Principles, Documents, and Cases

Business Law
Principles, Documents, and Cases

JOHN R. GOODWIN, J.D.
Professor of Business Law
West Virginia University

 1976

U.C.C., C.C.P.A., and O.S.H.A. text, revised

RICHARD D. IRWIN, INC. Homewood, Illinois 60430
Irwin-Dorsey Limited Georgetown, Ontario L7G 4B3

Revised Edition

4 5 6 7 8 9 0 K 5 4 3 2 1 0 9 8

ISBN 0-256-01781-6
Library of Congress Catalog Card No. 75-28948
Printed in the United States of America

LEARNING SYSTEMS COMPANY—
a division of Richard D. Irwin, Inc.—has developed a
PROGRAMMED LEARNING AID
to accompany texts in this subject area.
Copies can be purchased through your bookstore
or by writing PLAIDS,
1818 Ridge Road, Homewood, Illinois   60430.

To
MATTHEW,
MARK,
LUKE,
JOHN, JR.,
ELIZABETH ANN,
and
BETTY LOU

Note

1. This book was designed to provide authoritative information in regard to college level *Business Law*. It is understood that the publisher is not engaged in rendering legal services.

2. The legal documents in the book are representative of those used in Virginia and West Virginia. However, legal requirements and procedures vary from state to state and therefore these documents might not meet all legal requirements of another state. This is true even where the name of a state appears upon them.

3. Where statutes are quoted, the masculine pronoun is used. This is due to the fact that legislatures, state and federal, draft laws in that manner. However, it is clear that these laws apply to both male and female.

Otherwise, masculine pronouns are used only where reference is made to a male person.

4. All quotes from the Uniform Commercial Code, were taken from *West Virginia Code*, Chapter 46, "Uniform Commercial Code," and not from the uniform draft.

J.R.G.

Preface

This is a college level book for use in Business Law, Commercial Law, and Legal Environment of Business courses. The book was first published in 1972. Since that time it has been reprinted many times and has been used in scores of universities and colleges throughout the United States.

Those who used the first edition will be pleased to note that the basic format of the book – which has been so popular with students – has been maintained. Also, new subjects have been added including bailments, sales contracts, consignments, life insurance, the Occupational Safety and Health Act (O.S.H.A.), and the Fair Credit Billing Act.

The purpose of this text is to acquaint the student with the modern legal setting of business – and the relationship of that setting to one's personal affairs – in a meaningful and accurate manner. This main purpose has been divided into three more specific objectives. The first of these is to convey an understanding of the nature of law and the part that it plays in the regulation of modern business as well as one's life; the second is to emphasize that law, the courts, and the legal system, in the final analysis, exist for the citizen as an employer, employee, taxpayer, and consumer; and the third is to accomplish the first two objectives in a readable, informative, and understandable manner.

The first edition has been favored with a considerable amount of success. A large measure of the credit for this must go to Dean Jack T. Turner and the faculty of the College of Business and Economics at West Virginia University, who for so many years now have provided encouragement, suggestions, and a most welcome free hand, thus permitting a text to be developed that has come to be known as an innovation in a traditional subject.

This new edition represents almost two decades of study and of teaching at the undergraduate level of a major university. If it continues to meet its objectives, the effort that it has taken to produce it will have been most worthwhile.

Acknowledgments

Acknowledgments are due many persons and firms who made contributions to this new edition.

First, a word of thanks to the ten undergraduate students who volunteered to serve as student editors on one of the first drafts of the book.

Consents of many firms, banks, journals, and individuals were required to permit the forms, documents, news items, photographs, and other materials to be reproduced. Thanks are in order to the board of directors of the National Association of Business Law Teachers, Inc., publishers of the *Business Law Review* and the *Business Law Letter,* and the editors of the *American Business Law Journal* and *The Advocate* for permission to reprint portions of the many articles, case reviews, and other materials written for those publications by the author; to C. Glenn Zinn, Executive Vice President of the Farmers' and Merchants' Bank, Morgantown, West Virginia, for permission to reproduce many documents used by that bank; to Clay Miller of Casto and Harris, Inc., Spencer, West Virginia, printers, for permission to reproduce the "Fictitious Enterprises, Inc.," corporate documents; to Goes Lithographing Company, Chicago, Illinois, for permission to reprint documents furnished by it to the business community and legal profession; to Kenneth Smith, Production Manager, United Press International, New York, for permission to reprint UPI news items; to Joseph F. Kiich, BankAmericard Center, New York, for permission to reprint the charts found in the chapter on credit cards; to Massachusetts Mutual Life Insurance Company for permission to use its sample policy and mortality table in the *Student Workbook;* to James W. Thompson, Public Relations Manager, Card Division, American Express Company, New York, for permission to reproduce the credit card and charge slips; to the Secretary of State of West Virginia, for permission to reproduce the U.C.C.1. forms; to the Louisiana National Bank, Baton Rouge, Louisiana, for permission to reproduce their "picture check"; to Darl J. Phillips, U.S. Postal Service, for assistance in material that relates to U.S. mailing practices and procedures; to Duke Nordlinger Stern for helpful suggestions on credit cards and text content; and to C. Vincent Townsend, Jr., who screened the entire manuscript for grammatical errors, which led to considerable improvement.

Special thanks must go to three people whose criticisms, encouragements, and suggestions have done more to shape the new edition than any other persons. They are listed in alphabetical order.

Richard L. Begin, of Thomas College, Waterville, Maine, one of the first adopters of the first edition, has made valuable comments and suggestions. In addition, he has made a substantial written contribution on arbitration.

Myron L. Erickson, College of Administration and Public Affairs, University of Missouri, Columbia, one of the reviewers of the original manuscript, saw the potential and made his views known in splendidly written critiques. He served in this capacity for the new edition and is credited with the material on ownership of property as well as the new data on small claims courts.

Bernadine Meyer, Duquesne University, another of the first adopters of the text, has done much to preserve the morale of the author, and she is probably unaware of this. Her enthusiasm filtered down the "student grapevine" that runs between the Duquesne and W.V.U. campuses and provided a constant source of encouragement to the author. In addition, Dr. Meyer made a substantial written contribution through her excellent reviews prepared for the publisher.

Extra special thanks must go to my wife, Betty Lou Goodwin, who did the typing for the new edition and who kept good spirits and an even temper during 18 months when the author literally vanished into stacks of books, research materials, desks, typewriters, court documents, critical reviews, and endless correspondence.

Finally my thanks must go out to the thousands of business law students at West Virginia University, who over the years served as a "sounding board" and a captive audience when technical material was being reduced to understandable form. At times they shouldered a formidable burden, but in the end always expressed their gratitude for having played a part in the process.

Morgantown, West Virginia   JOHN R. GOODWIN
January 1976

Contents

tion of a Lawyer: *The Employment Contract. Conflicting Interests. Supporting the Client's Cause.* Paralegal Laypersons. What Do Lawyers Do? *Counseling. Negotiating. Representing Lenders. Litigation.* Form of Legal Services: *Prepaid Legal Services.* Fees and Costs: *Are Legal Fees Tax Deductible?* Termination of the Relationship.

part two
The Laws of Business

"Notice"? Actual Notice. Constructive Notice. Legal Notices. Notchel Notice. Notices of Pending Marriages. Notice under O.S.H.A. Rule against "Remoteness" in Vesting: *Rule against Perpetuities. Rule against Accumulation.* Reasonableness. Fictions. Courts and Military Personnel. Many Other Policies.

Does It Work? Who Is Served? A Strange Thing Occurs. Why This Result? Subrogation. The Hit-and-Run Accident. Liability versus No Fault: *What Has Been Suggested?*

part three
Consumers and Credit

U.C.C.: *Express Warranties. Implied Warranties.* The U.C.C. Provision in Operation.

part four
Business

Characteristics of a Corporation. Classification of Corporations: *Ecclesiastical Corporations. Lay Corporations. Eleemosynary Corporation. Civil Corporation. Sole and Aggregate. Domestic–Foreign. Profit–Nonprofit. Public–Private. Close–Open. Parent–Subsidiary. Dejure–Defacto. Regular and Conglomerate. Merger Distinguished from Consolidation. A Corporation Not Taxed as a Corporation.*

appendixes

indexes

part one
Law

Introduction

Familiarity with the law and the commercial codes, and with those agencies available at the state and local as well as the national level can do much to reduce the vulnerability of each of us in today's hostile environment.
—*Alfred A. Smith, Virginia Commonwealth University*

During recent years, the environment or setting within which business must function in the United States, has undergone a dramatic and frequently drastic alteration. The big change can be attributed primarily to a "legislative avalanche" of commercial laws at both state and federal levels. All states with the exception of Louisiana have adopted the Uniform Commercial Code (U.C.C.), a uniform and extensive body of commercial laws by which those in business must be guided. At the federal level, Congress enacted the Consumer Credit Protection Act (C.C.P.A.) and the Occupational Safety and Health Act (O.S.H.A.), providing further laws that concern and affect business. Many other federal and state business laws have been adopted.

In addition to these new laws, the traditional principles of business law remain predominant—although frequently altered by legislation and court rulings. Considered together, these laws—old, new, and a mix of both—provide a staggering body of guidelines that constitute a major factor in the operation of business. In addition, these guidelines make up a legal framework in which we must live and work as employee, consumer, and citizen.

This makes it mandatory that those in business—as well as the rest of us—have an understanding of the nature of this legal framework. This understanding must include knowledge of the history of law; how law was created in former times; how it is created now; how it was used to meet the needs of our nation over the past 200 years; how in many instances it failed to meet those needs; and how it must be utilized to meet our needs in the future.

Included will be the need to develop our human resources; conserve our energy supplies; develop new sources of energy and protect our environment and our natural resources. In this way we can preserve our nation for ourselves, our children, and our children's children as well.

An important part of this understanding can begin with this study of business law.

Coverage:	A discussion of the controls that are placed upon society.
What to Look For:	An understanding of the constant interplay between law and society.
Application:	Relate this chapter to the next criminal prosecution that you read about.

1 Society and Controls— An Introduction

"There are always those dissatisfied after every revolution, as Señor Keogh knows better than anyone from his own country." Which was hitting pretty low. "Just as there are always those who will reject any kind of authority if they can. In the area of Mojada, the people enjoy complete freedom from state control. Taxes are not collected for no tax collector can operate. There is no law, no justice, because no police officer can live there. They have even rejected the church. Three priests during the past eighteen months. Two murdered and one found wandering in the desert, stripped of his clothes, beaten half to death. Quite out of his mind."

— *Hungarian Janos*[1]

Most of us have had no formal contact with "law" in our earlier years and therefore we lack a common "base" upon which an advanced study may be undertaken. This is unfortunate because law welcomed us into the world in the form of our birth certificates and will affect us in countless ways during the balance of our lives—and even beyond as we will see.

Therefore we need a common topic with which to begin and experience tells us that this is best supplied by an examination of the "environment" or "surroundings" within which law, business, and the laws of business must function. It is here that law is created, defined, redefined,

---

[1] James Graham, *The Wrath of God* (New York: Dell Publishing Co., 1973), with permission.

4

and applied—and it is known as a "society." So let's begin by an examination of "society."

WHAT IS A "SOCIETY"?

A society is an aggregate of all of those persons, their customs and purposes, businesses, associations, and others, as may relate to the common interest and purpose of a life of its members free from fear, want, and war.

As the population of the earth grows larger, accompanied by perpetual demands for a better life, the complexity of society increases necessarily. From ancient times until the present the need for systems of control within an organized society was apparent in order to achieve the objectives of that society. Controls have come in the form of religious sanctions, the laws of nature—and human-made law. In more recent times, the impact of custom and ethics has come to the front.

How does the system of controls work? Is it possible to reduce the subject to simple terms to examine it? The following simplified example has been prepared as one answer to these important questions.

THE GOLD FRAME OF SOCIETY

Assume for purposes of discussion that the society in which we live has been placed in a large picture frame much as one frames an oil painting. The word "society" appears inside the frame. Since one of the principal functions of law is the "maintenance of society," the word "law" is added to each side of the frame. The words "custom," "religion," "morals," and "ethics" are also printed on the frame at various places indicating that they are all part of the "framework" that preserves society. (See Figure 1-1.)

FIGURE 1-1
The Gold Frame of Society

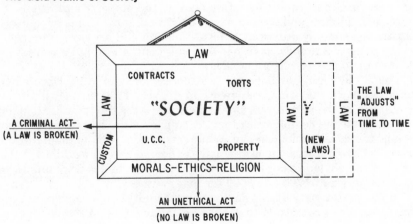

If one "breaks a law," the act pierces the legal portion of the frame and results in a person and that act standing "outside the law" and society. In short, one who breaks the law is an "outlaw." It is now the duty of law, through the prosecuting attorney, police agencies, and the courts, to correct the breach in the frame. The arrest, subsequent indictment, trial, verdict of guilty, and imprisonment of the offender enables the legal branch to close the breach, correct the unlawful act, and preserve the status of society and the framework that surrounds it. If one violates an obligation to another that is merely moral and not legal, then the moral aspects of society have been breached. The same is true with ethical and religious sanctions. As will be discussed, society does not respond to this type of breach as it does when a law is broken.

As the needs and demands of society change, what may have been treated as unlawful at one time, may become a lawful act. When this happens, the framework of law is expanded outwards to encompass a new area into which society moves and functions. For example, the state may declare that the sale of liquor by the drink is unlawful and those who sell liquor by the drink would be breaking the law. The state by its law-making body (its legislature) may subsequently declare sale of liquor by the drink to be lawful. Thus, a subsequent sale would be legal, expanding the legal framework of society. As society expands, so must the law. One creates the other and they maintain each other.

Business can only operate within a framework protected by law, and property can only exist within an organized civilization. The land upon which primitive persons walked still has the characteristics in modern America that it had in ancient times. In the strict sense, it is still the same property. But, from a legal point of view, it has taken on very different characteristics. It is now property in the legal sense. This means that it is titled in the name of a person, a business, an organization, or the state — and the owner is protected by law in a system of courts. If possession of property is wrongfully taken from one at the expense of another or if taken without "due process of law," or if it is taken for public use "without just compensation," the party injured has a "cause of action." He or she may turn to the court for adjustment of the property interests.

Morals, religion, and ethics are samples of other pressures or controls, but these generally do not have legal sanction and are not enforceable in the courts. But they have had and will continue to have a great influence upon the development of law.

The "Gold Frame of Society" in America today is quite large when compared with the same framework in the year 1790. At that time, the population of the nation was small, the states were few, and life had not yet taken on the complexities that accompany a nuclear, mass-production-oriented, technological age. While law was needed to maintain the society of 1790, it was not as extensive or complex in its workings as it is today. As an obvious example, the laws of motor vehicles were unknown in the America of 1790 — or 1890 for that matter.

In our preliminary discussion, we pointed out that laws were not the only pressures or controls that have an influence upon the conduct of members of an organized society. The effect of morality as it acts upon the conscience has at times been an effective control over one's conduct. An example will illustrate the point.

Many years ago, a resident of the New England Coast provided care for an ailing sailor for some 30 days prior to the sailor's death. Upon learning of this charitable act, the parents of the sailor promised to pay the New England resident the sum of $50 for the care provided. As happens so often when promises are made under emotional stress, payment was not made and suit for legal enforcement of the promise followed. After reviewing the facts, the court was forced to apply the legal rule that "past consideration will not support a present promise." In other words, what had been given in exchange for the promise to pay (the care of the sailor) had occurred *before* the promise was made. Therefore the promise was unenforceable at law. While there was a *moral* duty to pay, there was no legal duty and the case was dismissed. However, many persons would keep their promise in such a situation and make payment because of the "moral duty" to do so.

This illustrates that what is moral is not necessarily legal. Fireworks are legal in the State of Virginia and illegal in West Virginia, but are not immoral in either state. Gambling, on the other hand, is illegal in some states and legal in others; if it results in the loss of a wage-earner's salary, it is immoral even if the loss occurs in a state where gambling is legal.

The impact of morals upon the development of the law can be illustrated by the case in which one farmer sold another a dead horse. The horse had been propped up against a fence located several hundred yards from where the transaction had been consummated. The buyer failed to examine the horse and as a consequence, paid $50 for a dead animal. The case eventually came up for hearing before a judge who said among other things, "If you were under age, I would give you relief, but this isn't the case. You know it is the practice in this county to look at the teeth of a horse before buying it, and you chose to ignore this custom." The court held that the buyer was not entitled to recover. In short, "caveat emptor" (let the buyer beware). This maxim summarizes the rule that a purchaser must examine, judge, and test for oneself. It was immoral for the seller to take advantage of the buyer under these circumstances, yet it was not illegal. During ensuing years as the complexity of merchandise confronting the buyer increased, the warning to the buyer to beware has started to change to "caveat venditor"[2]—let the seller beware.

The horse case above is a good example also, of how custom plays a part in the development of law. At this point, it is helpful to pause for a moment and compare morals and ethics and constitutional law as we will be discussing it, with religion.

Religion concerns our relationship to Divinity, to worship and submission to mandates of superior beings. In its broadest sense, it includes all beliefs in superior beings who exercise power over human beings by power in some form. In its strict sense, it is not the same as law in the

---

[2] In Roman law, the maxim or rule casting the responsibility for defects or deficiencies upon the seller of the goods.

constitutional form. However, the concerns of future punishments and for rewards in the future tend to place controls upon each of us as we pursue our goals in society. Yet these controls, when they in fact exist, are not the same as rules and mandates laid down by our constitutions and laws. Nor are they like morals and ethics.

An excellent example of the interplay of law and morals, as well as the defining and redefining of law, can be found in a study of the Eighteenth Amendment to the U.S. Constitution and its aftermath. It is examined here briefly.

EIGHTEENTH AMENDMENT

On June 4, 1919, the following Amendment to the United States Constitution was proposed by Congress and offered to the states for ratification:

> One year from the ratification of this article the manufacture, sale, or transportation of intoxicating liquors within, the importation thereof into, or the exportation thereof from the United States and all territory subject to the jurisdiction thereof for beverage purposes is hereby prohibited.

The states responded rapidly and on August 26, 1920, the Amendment was ratified and became the Eighteenth Amendment to the United States Constitution. It has been known since as the "Prohibition Amendment" or the "Volstead Act."

FIGURE 1–2

From the author's collection.

What followed has become part of the folklore of America. From the day the law became effective, Americans simply did their drinking underground. "Speakeasies," "bathtub gin," and "roadhouses" sprang into existence and these words became part of the American language.

Criminal interests quickly saw ways to "cash in" on a new market and did so by the smuggling, unlawful manufacture, and sale of alcoholic beverages.

Enforcement of the law was delegated to the Treasury Department, Internal Revenue Service—and try to enforce it they did. The raids by U.S. agents accompanied by underworld plays for power and the open flaunting of the law by the citizens, earned for that decade, (1920-1930), the apt name of the "Roaring Twenties."

Could liquor be consumed legally during the years that the Amendment was in effect? As it turns out, there was a way it could be done. Examine Figure 1-2. Prescription blanks were furnished to medical doctors. The neighborhood drug stores stocked liquor for "medicinal purposes"; a simple combination of both permitted "legal drinking"—an interesting and little-known footnote in the history of the United States.

On February 20, 1933, Uncle Sam gave up. On that date, Congress proposed the Twenty-first Amendment and it was declared ratified on December 5, 1933—just nine months later. This Amendment simply stated that "The eighteenth article of the amendment to the Constitution of the United States is hereby repealed."

REVIEW QUESTIONS

1. Explain briefly the role of law as it relates to society, as you understand that role.
2. What would the "lawmaking" body be in the average American family? What type of "laws" are created there?
3. What is the basic difference between what is "legal" and what is "moral?"
4. Try to think of a way in which a business person could be unethical and yet not break the law.
5. True or False. An act that is illegal is usually immoral.
6. "Morality points toward high idealism—law toward what will work." What does this mean to you?
7. State one reason why the old doctrine of "caveat emptor" is being replaced by "caveat venditor."
8. New laws tend to lag behind the need for them. Frequently a series of disasters will occur before lawmakers move to correct the problems. How can you relate this fact to simple human nature?
9. You own a Honda 125 motorcycle. The state has enacted a law requiring that all cyclists and passengers wear goggles and helmets. Why might you resent this law?
10. A prosecuting attorney waged a "crack-down" on Bingo games claiming that this was a form of gambling and thus illegal. Proceeds from the Bingo games were used to fund the volunteer fire departments in the county. What are the legal, moral and practical implications of this situation? (The prosecutor was defeated in an attempt at reelection.)

Words and Phrases

Write out briefly what they mean to you.
1. Past consideration.
2. Caveat emptor.
3. Repealing a law.
4. Laws of nature.
5. "Looking a horse in the mouth."

Coverage:	A look at the origins and sources of law.
What to Look for:	The ways that law is created and reasons for its creation.
Application:	You will play a part in the law-making process in the future.

2 What *Is* "Law"?

In Chapter 1, it was pointed out that there are a variety of controls that regulate the affairs of the members of our society as they pursue their personal as well as business goals. In this chapter, we will begin an examination of law as one of those controls.

One court said

>   That which is laid down, ordained or established; a rule or method according to which phenomena or actions co-exist or follow each other. That which must be obeyed and followed by the citizens, subject to sanctions or legal consequences, is the law.[1]

Webster's Twentieth Century Dictionary states that law is

>   . . . all the rules of conduct established and enforced by the authority, legislation, or custom of a given community or other group.

A close examination of the two definitions discloses that the situations that could be described by them would be virtually limitless. For example, they could be used to define the system of brutal power over the people that existed in Nazi Germany. They could be used to define the gentle control that a Cub Scout leader exercises over the young Scouts. In short, the definitions disclose a timeless problem that arises when one attempts to define "law" – it is impossible to define in one way and one way only.

When we were young, the "law" was the police officer who issued speeding tickets on the interstate. Or perhaps it was that mysterious thing that our parents made reference to as they prepared their income tax returns. Or maybe it was an act of those "ignorant city council members" who ordered the curb painted yellow in front of the house.

As we grew older, the "law" took on new meaning as we discovered

---

[1] *Koenig* v. *Flinn*, 258 N.Y. 292, 179 N.E. 705 (1932).

11

that there were regulations in school, in church, and at the movie house. The law became something more to us as we learned that certain stores are closed on Sunday; that a letter with "postage due" would not be given to us without payment of the amount due; and that we were not permitted to cross at an intersection until the light said "walk."

In our daily lives, we continue to experience and sense the "law" as we learn more about it, and sometimes we "feel it." Witness the motorist passing through town at 2 A.M. who patiently waits for a stop light to turn green before driving through the deserted intersection.

As we read the daily newspapers or watch the news on TV, we discover that there have been new rulings by the Supreme Court; that changes have been made in the income tax laws; that new regulations have been imposed by city ordinances; and that the legislators at the current session of lawmaking at the state house have been active. It is not uncommon to find that over 50 percent of the type content in newspapers relates to legal or court matters.

If we inquire further, we suddenly discover that "law" is about us at all times and that it is much more than the activities of lawyers and the courts. For example, discipline administered to a grade school student, the yellow light that blinks at the construction site at midnight, the draft card and the driver's license that we carry, and the common understanding that the buyer pays the freight on glass bottles that are "seconds," are all products and subjects of the "law."

One must conclude that law is all pervading and omnipresent just as religion and science. It is complex, varied, hard to understand and sometimes strange in the application. Rather than making further attempts to define law, let us find the answers to three preliminary and important questions: (1) From where does law come? (the subject of the balance of this chapter); (2) How does it appear to different persons? (Chapter 3, "Looking at Law—An Overview"); and (3) What part does it play in the regulation of society?

FROM WHERE DOES LAW COME?

The earth is a most remarkable planet and provides us with all of the material items that we need as a human race—although as we have discovered in recent years, its resources are not without limit. The earth gives us an amazing variety of food products; it gives us pasture lands for our animals; wood for our lumber; clay for our bricks; and gold and diamonds for our rings. It provides the flowers that grace our gardens— as well as the litter that disgraces our roadsides.

The earth gave us what may be thought of as a system of law but only as it relates to the "laws of nature." There is regulation in the length of a day and the seasons of the year. There is order and system in the cycle of life of all living things whether human, plant life or animal. But the earth never gave us a system of laws in the broad sense—that is, a legal system designed for the control and preservation of society—and it is to this type of law that we now direct our attention.

What has been produced as law by people has traditionally lacked the grace and beauty of the laws of nature. This has been true because of the setting in which law has been created: a setting in which people created law to regulate people. Such law has always carried with it a tendency on the part of those who are regulated to resist, resent, ignore, or in many instances to attempt to overturn what was created. We cannot alter the growing season of wheat, but we can go to city council and raise thunder about the increase in garbage fees.

Perhaps in time we will create a more just, expedient, and updated system of laws that will take a place beside the fabulous discoveries in medicine, the advances in the social sciences, and the developing beauty of the human arts. This is a worthwhile goal for all of us to seek.

Next, how is "law" created? Traditionally, law has been created in one of six ways.

1. Common Law

The systems, rules, and sanctions that developed in ancient times represent an important source of law. As one studies the subject in detail, an awareness follows that our modern legal system is just as it was 6,000 years ago—only the form of it and those to whom it applies have changed.

2. From the People

One of the basic ideas of the government formulated by the drafters of the United States Constitution, was that when the people create rules to govern themselves, that creation is the "supreme law" of the land and continues to be so until the people amend or repeal it. The result of these acts of the people are called "constitutions."

Constitutions. A constitution is the fundamental law of a state or nation and may be written, as the U.S. Constitution, or unwritten as in England. It establishes the basic rules by which internal life is to be organized and operated, and sets forth the limits of power of those who exercise the governmental functions.

The U.S. Constitution grew out of a "grant of powers" to the federal government. At the same time, the states "reserved" to themselves all other powers. What in fact was granted and what was not, has been a subject for debate for two centuries. Many persons feel that the federal government has moved into areas of power that were never contemplated in the beginning. Others argue that there should be free adaptation of federal power as the needs of the people change. In all probability these arguments will continue for many years.

The Tenth Amendment to the U.S. Constitution reads as follows: "The powers not delegated to the United States by the Constitution, nor prohibited by it to the States, are reserved to the States respectively, or to the people." For example, the federal government was expressly given the power to "regulate commerce between the states." By this grant of power the authority to regulate "interstate commerce" was clearly given to the federal government. Since no mention was made of it, the power to regulate *intrastate* commerce (wholly within a state) was reserved to the states.

In addition to the U.S. Constitution, which regulates us as a nation, each state has it's own constitution.

The States.   Each state has at the fountainhead of its legal system a state constitution. Many of these have been patterned after the U.S. Constitution and most have followed the Bill of Rights, the first ten amendments, very closely. For example, the Fourth and Eighth Amendments to the U.S. Constitution were copied into the Constitution of West Virginia with the exception of one word.

Distinguished from Statutes and Charters.   A statute is a law created by representatives elected by the people. A charter, on the other hand, is a grant of powers from a government which was created by the people. That is, the people create a constitution by the "ratification process," thus creating the state. The state then operates through laws created by the representatives of the people elected for that purpose. The state issues charters to corporations and cities for the purpose of transacting business. (See Figure 2–1.)

FIGURE 2–1

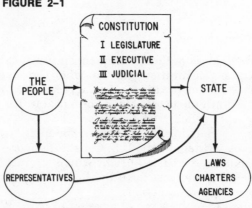

The Final Word.   The drafters of the U.S. Constitution, or the state constitutions for that matter, did not intend to bind future generations to the literal words that they wrote. Looking back, we know that it was not possible for those of the late 1700s to envision a world of the 1970s. It was this fact that John Marshall, Chief Justice of the United States Supreme Court, referred to when he wrote,

> We must never forget that it is a constitution that we are expounding, intended to endure for ages to come, and consequently, to be adapted to the various crises of human affairs.[2]

_____
[2] *McCullough* v. *Maryland,* 4 Wheat 316, 4 L.Ed. 579 (1819).

This concept has been widely used since 1819 to place different interpretations upon the constitution as conditions change.

Interpretation. The Eighth Amendment to the U.S. Constitution states: "Excessive bail shall not be required, nor excessive fines imposed, nor cruel and unusual punishments inflicted." Assume for a moment that it is 1800, and Sam Brown has been accused of stealing. Bond is being set so he may work on his farm until his hearing. Since Sam lives from the earth and rarely earns cash, would bail of $1 be excessive? It could well be in the year in question. Assuming that Sam pleads guilty or is found guilty after trial, would a fine of $10 be excessive—or punishment by ten strokes from a whip be cruel and unusual? The fine might be excessive by court interpretation, but the punishment might not have been "cruel and unusual" at that time.

Contrast the plight of Sam Brown with that of John Smith, who was arrested in 1976 for stealing merchandise worth $65. After arrest and preliminary hearing, he was placed under $2,000 bond. Is that excessive? If he is convicted and sentenced to imprisonment in the state penitentiary for one to ten years, is that "cruel and unusual"? The answer to both questions is "not today." Bail of $50,000 is not unusual in armed robbery cases, and in murder cases the courts generally set bond at a very high figure.

Are the Courts "Rewriting" the Constitution? The courts have been accused of taking from the people their natural right when they place new meanings upon the written word of constitutions. But the answer is that constitutions were written in general language for that very reason. In short, constitutions are the supreme law of the land or the state—but they are not the final word. A third and constant source of law is that of the "lawmakers."

3. Actions of the Representatives of the People

When the representatives of the people enact law, these acts are called "legislation." At the federal level the acts are referred to as "acts of Congress," at the state level, "statutes," and at the municipal level, "ordinances." The result is "law" in the sense in which it is being discussed.

The Legislative Concept. It was recognized early that a government in the United States as envisioned could not function if all of those governed had a right to take a direct part in the making of the laws that governed them. This process is called a "democracy"—and has not been successful in other nations historically. Instead, the form chosen was a "republic"—a government in which those governed elect those who make the laws for that purpose.

How Does It Work? For purposes of simplicity, an incident of lawmaking in a small city will be examined. The city has a population of 40,000 persons. It was granted a charter from the state in 1922, and formed its government under the power of the grant from the state.

For many years the city has been divided into seven "wards." Each of the wards elects two representatives to city hall. The terms of office are staggered to assure that at least seven persons are in office at all times. Those elected are called "councilmen" or "councilwomen." (At the federal level they would be "congressmen" or "congresswomen," or "United States senators;" at the state level, "delegates" or "representatives" and state senators.)

A Law Is Born.   One morning, the postal carrier in the first ward noticed that a utility company had opened First Street and had uncovered their utility line. Barricades had been erected and yellow lights had been installed to warn motorists at night. Approaching the work site, the carrier noticed that two small children were standing at the edge of the barricade watching what was taking place within the opening.

Two employees of the company were welding a section of pipe using an arc welder. The arc was exposed to the eyes of the children. The carrier realized that the exposure was dangerous, and told the children to move away and warned them not to watch the arc. After gaining the attention of the workers, it was pointed out what had taken place, but they ignored this. After all, they had more to do than chase children from their work area.

Later, the postal carrier called the incident to the attention of the representative of that ward. At the next council meeting, the matter was referred to the Ordinance Committee for study. The committee decided that an ordinance should be prepared prohibiting open arc welding in the city unless the arc was covered by a shield. The committee made its report to council and a motion was made and carried that the ordinance be prepared by the city attorney. The following week, the attorney brought to council "An Ordinance to Regulate the Use of Open Arc Welders and Providing Penalties for the Violation Thereof."

The ordinance was read by the chairperson of the Ordinance Committee. Following this "first reading," a motion was made that it pass to second reading. The votes in favor of this motion were sufficient to approve the motion. The city clerk then ran a legal notice informing the public that a public hearing would be held on the proposed law. The notice specified the nature of the law and the time and place of the hearing.

The Public Hearing.   At the public hearing, those who opposed the pending law were given a chance to voice their objections and those in favor of it were also heard. Following the hearing, a motion was made that the ordinance pass to the third reading. This is the alternative stage in lawmaking and the ordinance could be amended or tabled if the lawmakers should so decide. It passed by the required vote. The following week it was presented for the third reading at which time it passed, and is now binding upon those who use arc welders in that city.

In certain situations where the city lawmakers are in unanimous agreement, an ordinance may be read three times at one sitting, thus creating an "instant law." However, there are moral and ethical overtones in allowing this to happen — even though it is legal. For example, it takes from the citizens the right to be heard in a public hearing at the second reading. (This procedure should only be used in legislative bodies to meet emergencies.) But a new law is worthless unless it is placed into effect.

The New Law in Operation. It is customary for the lawmakers to spell out the effective date of the law and it may be "from the date of passage" or at some future date. (Federal laws usually become effective 60, 90, or 120 days after passage. Title III of the Consumer Credit Protection Act, Garnishment, became effective over one year after passage.)

Once our city ordinance is in effect, a violator can be arrested by city police and taken to the city police court for a hearing. The police court has "jurisdiction" or power to enforce the law since it was created by the city lawmaking body. Upon conviction, the fine set forth in the ordinance may be imposed.

When new laws are in effect and someone violates the law out of ignorance, it is not unusual for the court to impose a warning rather than a fine. The judges are given wide discretion in matters such as these.

Is the "Arc Law" Legal? The acts of lawmakers do not always meet the approval of their constituents and the new law may be subjected to a court test. These tests usually follow an arrest and conviction of violating the law. Under our system, a court has the power to declare the new law unconstitutional. In the case discussed, no appeal was taken and the law is well observed.

The procedure discussed is basically the same at the state and federal levels. The lawmakers carry different names; the public hearings are handled with more formality and committees are used to stop or "bottle up" pending legislation – but the process is the same.

The New Law Is Clear—Or Is It? After a legislative body acts, the question of "What did the lawmakers mean?" often arises. When it does, it becomes the job of a court to decide what was meant by the law – a process referred to as "court interpretation."

An Example. A state enacted a "statute" as follows: "Commodity X shall not be sold within 300 feet of a church or school." The legislature, in its collective wisdom, had decided that commodity X should not be sold near schools or churches. These laws are common in all states and cover a variety of items including alcoholic drinks and pornographic materials. This particular statute had not been subjected to a court case until Jones came along.

What Does the Law Mean? Business person Jones, who had a store directly across the street from a church, decided that if he sold commodity X, his earnings would increase. He applied for a license but was turned down because he would violate the law if he sold the item since the church was only 100 feet from his store. Jones appealed to the county circuit court – and lost. He then appealed to the state supreme court.

The High Court Interprets. The court docketed the case (put it on its schedule for hearing) and arguments were heard on the question of "What did the legislature intend when it enacted the statute?" The court held that the legislature meant that the 300 feet should be measured as a person would walk after leaving a church or school. Jones obtained the license. Examine Figure 2–2.

Example 2. A store owner applied for a permit to sell commodity X and was refused since the place of business was back to back with the Salvation Army building. Should the permit be issued? The permit was issued after the court held that the Salvation Army was not a "church or school" within the meaning of the law.

FIGURE 2–2

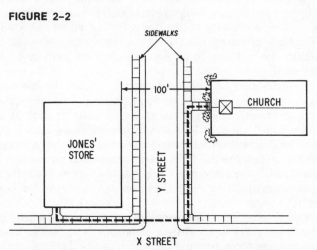

The dotted line indicates how the 300 feet was to be measured.
By court interpretation, 100 feet became more than 300 feet.

Example 3. A store owner in a southern town applied for a permit to sell commodity X and the store was within 100 feet of the front door of a grade school. The state had the 300-foot law as set out above. The supreme court of that state held that commodity X could be sold on Saturday and Sunday since school was not in session on those days, it being the intention of the lawmakers to prohibit sale only when children were in school.[3]

Did These Courts Legislate? In the examples cited, the courts expanded the statute to mean things that possibly the lawmakers did not intend. Court interpretation is an important source of law and will be discussed later.

Uniform Legislation. Each state in the United States has a lawmaking body that is independent of the other states. As a result of this, the laws in our 50 states vary widely. For many years it has been recognized that this is not desirable, especially where the laws of business are concerned.

---

[3] *State* v. *Willie Smith* 265 N.C. 173, 143 S.E.2d. 293 (1965).

A number of years back, a movement was started toward the end of realizing uniformity in state laws.

A National Conference. A National Conference of Commissioners on Uniform State Laws was established to promote uniformity in state laws; to draft "model acts"; and to promote uniform decisions in the courts in the various states. A "model" act is one created to be used as a pattern by the lawmakers; a "uniform" act is one that is intended to be adopted without change.

The Most Notable Uniform Law. The most notable effort of the national conference has been the development and promotion of the Uniform Commercial Code, which has been adopted by all of the states except Louisiana. For selected portions of the Uniform Commercial Code, see Appendix A.

A fourth and important source of law is found in the decisions of courts.

4. Decisions of Courts—A Common Law Role

The commodity X cases discussed make it clear that the rulings of courts tend to expand or alter the acts of lawmakers. While legislation is a constant source of law, court decisions are still a primary and important source, and create the "common law."

The Common Law.[4] It is customary to refer to court decisions as "cases," which make up what is called the "common law"—meaning that cases are law in common to the people of that jurisdiction. Legislation is created by lawmakers while common law is created by the courts.

How Does It Work? A case is tried in a court and a conclusion is reached. The rulings in the case become binding upon lower courts and all of the citizens in the same jurisdiction under the principle of "stare decisis"—"let the decision stand." This causes disputes to be settled out of court. For example, if the lawyers learn that an attack upon the building code of a city usually fails in court, they will discourage their clients from bringing similar suits in the future. Thus "precedent"—prior case decisions—tend to create stability among the members of society. Yet this stability must still be tempered with some flexibility.

Once Decided, Does That Settle It? The doctrine of stare decisis serves as a guide for the lawyer in advising clients. But blind adherence to the doctrine is not good business. Therefore, the courts have the power to distinguish prior cases, modify them, or overrule them—that is, they can adhere to prior case decisions, or they can follow them in part or not at all. Thus, the court has the power to make the common law flexible so that it can be applied in common sense form at different times.

For example, Doctor Smith located a medical office on Z Street. Leading from the back of the office was a 10-foot easement that extended to

---

[4] The phrase "common law" also has other meanings such as the body of law that developed in England, and customs and usages of a people.

X Street. (See Figure 2–3) The prior owner of the property had bought it from John Calhoun in 1878. In the deed from Calhoun was the following provision:

> There is expressly conveyed with the above described realty, a 10-foot easement to X Street, said easement to run to the use of the Grantee, his heirs, executors, administrators and assigns. This easement is granted, however, with the express condition that both sides of the easement be closed by a suitable fence together with a gate at X Street.

The fence had been gone for many years and the gate had not been maintained since the turn of the century.

FIGURE 2–3

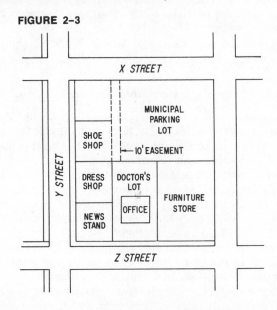

The City Steps In. The city acquired the real estate behind the doctor's office and proceeded to build a parking lot, blocking access to the easement. The doctor filed suit, asking that the easement be declared in force and valid. The city defended, citing cases that held that where a "condition" existed as in this deed, the easement was lost by failure to meet the terms of the condition.

How Did the Court Rule? The judge said this:

> It is true that there have been cases decided in this jurisdiction in which such conditions have been held to be "conditions subsequent" – in other words, since the condition was not met, the easement was lost. Normally this law would be binding upon us. However, what was the reason for the provision requiring the fence and gate in the 1878 deed? In that year, the tract of land was part of a farm. The purpose was to keep chickens, cows, pigs, and other animals from getting under the wheels of the carriages going in and out of the property now owned by the doctor. The need for the fence and gate has not existed for over 70 years. If I adhere to the cases cited

by counsel for the city, I would be imposing upon a modern situation a standard of another century — and I am not inclined to do that. It is the judgment of the court that the easement is valid. The city shall remove obstructions from the easement so that the doctor and future owners may have access to the same. The city is free to pursue those remedies under eminent domain as provided by law.

The city did not condemn the right-of-way for public use. The parking meters were removed and the doctor uses the easement daily — thanks to the refusal of a modern judge to be bound by rulings of earlier judges that had no application here.[5]

A fifth source of law is found independent of judges and courts.

5. Acts of Administrative Agencies

The drafters of the U.S. Constitution created three branches of government: the legislative branch (Article I of the U.S. Constitution); the

FIGURE 2–4

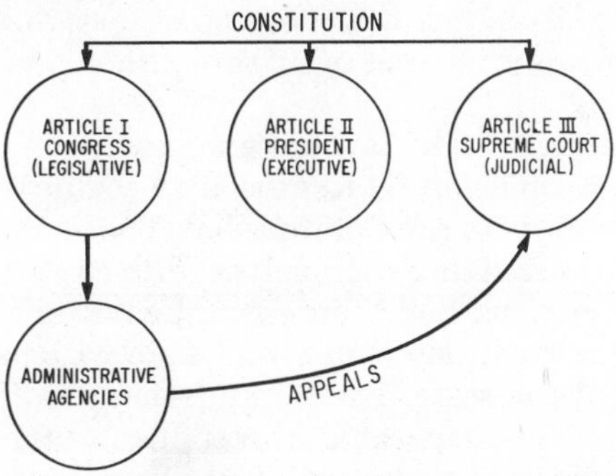

executive branch (The President, Article II); and the judicial branch (The Supreme Court, Article III.) They gave no consideration to a "fourth branch" of government — the title frequently used to describe administrative agencies. See Figure 2–4. In spite of this fact, a growing source of law is found in the rules and regulations created by administrative agencies.

Administrative agencies are groups, committees, or boards, created by act of a lawmaking body. Thus they are "creatures of statute." Once they are created, they have those powers that are set forth in the statute that created them, and can usually issue subpoenas, conduct hearings, and issue rulings which have the force and effect of law. The number of administrative agencies have been on the increase in recent years.

The Commissions Are Many. At the federal level, the commissions include the Federal Aviation Agency, the Federal Trade Commission, the

---

[5] It should be observed that the doctrine of stare decisis has no application in "equitable" as distinguished from "legal" actions. In the former, a judge renders a decision based upon what is "right" or "just" and therefore is not bound by precedent. In the latter, the judge is bound by precedent.

Federal Communications Commission, and many more. At the state level are found mental institutions, drug control agencies, public service commissions, and police departments. Agencies are widely used at the municipal level with examples being parking authorities, water commissions, human rights commissions, boards of zoning appeal, and many others.

Are the Agencies Legal? This question has been raised many times, but the courts have upheld the agencies for two reasons: first, they are created by the legislative branch of government; and second, an appeal to the courts is permitted from the rulings of agencies. Examine Figure 2–4 again.

A helpful way to gain insight into administrative agencies is to examine a situation that arises constantly and see how one state met this problem by the creation of an agency.

State X Has a Problem. For many years, State X had neglected its streams and rivers. Vast industrial complexes had located along the waterways and used them as sewers for wastes. In addition, the cities used the rivers and streams to dispose of human and other wastes. As time passed, it became obvious that something had to be done about these conditions.

The Legislature Acts. The lawmakers enacted legislation creating a "Clean Streams Commission." After the law became effective, the governor appointed members to the Commission. These members met, organized, and began familiarizing themselves with the objectives they were to meet. The Commission had been given the power by the law to create its own rules and regulations which was done with assistance from the Attorney General of the state. The Commission then went into action.

They turned to the colleges and universities of the state, seeking advice from those trained in water pollution abatement. One person in the engineering department at the state university was particularly helpful. The professor had been writing and speaking for years on pollution abatement, and now opinions were being sought by an agency that had the power to tackle the problem.

The Agency Acts. One September morning, the mayor of Anytown received a letter from the Clean Water Commission. The letter read (in part) as follows:

> Dear Mayor:
>   You are hereby notified that on the 3rd day of November a hearing will be held in the council chambers for the purpose of determining if your city is polluting Crystal River. You may appear and present evidence that would prove to this commission that you are not doing so.

The Day of the Hearing. On the day of the hearing, the mayor and members of city council were present at city council chambers. Yost, an attorney hired by the Commission, came into the room accompanied by a person carrying a steno-mask recording machine.

At the scheduled time, Yost called the meeting to order. He then asked those who intended to testify, to state their names and addresses for the record.

A Witness Is Called.   As it turned out, only one witness was called and this was the chemist hired by the Commission. After being sworn, the chemist testified as follows:

Q. What is your occupation?

A. I am a research chemist for Capital Industries.

Q. What are your duties with Capital Industries?

A. I operate a chemical laboratory in which we examine, analyze, and record results from samples taken from chemical products of Capital Industries.

Q. What is the purpose of your work?

A. To determine the bacteria count in the samples analyzed to be used as a guide at the production level.

Q. What degrees do you hold?

A. I hold a B.S., M.S., and a Ph.D., all in chemistry from State University.

Q. Upon what was your doctoral dissertion based?

A. Water pollution abatement. (Specific questions were then asked about the study and its results.)

Q. Have you done other writing?

A. Yes.

Q. State the topics written about. (These were spelled out in detail.)

Q. Have your articles been used by others in scientific studies?

A. Yes. (Explanations given.)

Q. Have you had occasion to analyze samples of water in order to determine bacteria count?

A. Yes, many times.

Q. Have the results of your tests been checked by others?

A. Many times.

Q. Have your findings been substantiated as being accurate?

A. Yes, they have.

Q. I direct your attention to Commission's Exhibit A and ask you if you can identify it. (See Figure 26-1.)

A. Yes, this is a map of Anytown showing Crystal River as it flows by the corporate limits.

Q. Is this map accurate and does it clearly show what it was designed to show?

A. Yes, it does.

Q. I now offer Commission's Exhibit A into evidence. (There was no objection, so the map became a part of the record in the proceedings. If there had been some legal objection, such as the map not being accurate, it might have not been admitted into evidence, or if it were, this defect might have formed the basis of an appeal.)

Q. Did you take a water sample from Crystal River, at the point marked *A* on Exhibit A?

A. Yes, I did.

Q. Did you take samples from points *B* and *C* as marked on Exhibit A?

A. Yes, I did.

Q. What did you do with these samples?

A. I labeled them, isolated them, and then analyzed them for bacterial count.

The testimony of the chemist continued until it was established that as the river flowed by the city the bacteria count increased with the count being the highest in the sample taken from below the city. The Commission thus established a "prima facie" case that the city was polluting the river—or was adding to the pollution. By "making a case," the burden shifted to the city to rebutt the presumption raised by the evidence. The city had no way to defend and did not offer testimony. The meeting was adjourned.

The Second Letter. In three weeks, the mayor received a letter which read in part as follows:

> Dear Mayor:
>
> At the hearing held in council chambers in November of this year, it was established that Anytown was polluting the waters of Crystal River, in violation of the Clean Streams Law of this state. You are hereby ordered to cease and desist polluting the waters of Crystal River.

The mayor called a special session of city council and laid the matter before them. They were faced with two options: comply with the order or face the penalties of fine and imprisonment as provided by the regulations of the Clean Waters Commission. (They complied.)

A Law Is Born. The action of the Commission resulted in the creation of "law." Other cities in the state began taking action to treat their sewage—and not another formal hearing was required to force compliance.

Commissions and Courts. Once an administrative agency has ruled, those who are affected have the right to appeal to the courts. In practice, however, the courts are reluctant to override the rulings of administrative agencies. The judges view the situation as follows: "The hearing was held and all parties had the right to present evidence. The ruling issued was based upon the findings of experts. You are asking me to substitute my judgment for the judgment of the experts. I am not inclined to do so."

This obvious reluctance of the courts to override the rulings of administrative agencies, seems to give the agencies more power than the other three branches of our government. This prompted governmental leaders to search for ways to exercise control over the agencies. Precedent was found in Sweden in the "ombudsman" concept (pronounced *AHM-boods-man*).

The Ombudsman. In 1809, the Swedish Parliament created the "ombudsman"—the title derived from the Swedish word "umboo" meaning "agent." The job of the first "Justitieombudsman," called "JO" for short, was to act as a "watchdog" over administrative agencies. Today, the JO cannot interfere with decision making of agencies, but can hear complaints and when warranted, ask the official involved to justify his or her actions. In most of the modern cases handled by the Swedish JO, 90 percent are closed by explaining to the complaining citizen that what the agency did was justified.

The JO makes an annual report to Parliament and this is probably the JO's biggest weapon. The heads of administrative agencies in that nation do not want their names appearing on lists before lawmakers who have the power to wipe out their commission by an act of Parliament.

In America. The JO concept has been carried into America in recent years and Hawaii became the first state to create the office of an ombudsman. Nassau County, Long Island, New York, created an "Office of Citizen Redress" and a similar office was created at San Diego, Califor-

nia, but the latter two were local offices only. The growing list of griev-
ances by citizens against administrative agencies will assure that the
JO concept or its equivalent will find widespread acceptance in the
United States as a "safety valve" on the "fourth branch" of our three-
branch government.

A type of administrative action is encountered in "executive orders."

Executive Orders. A little known source of law is found in the "executive orders" made by the governors of the states from time to time, as
well as the President of the United States.

Executive orders stem from "executive privilege" and encompass
matters that are within the realm of power of the executive as distinguished from the power of the legislature.

These orders are a unilateral exercise of power in which neither the
legislative branch of government nor the public have any control. However, these orders often affect the public in one form or another.

At the federal level, the only requirement for executive orders is that
they be published in the *Federal Register*—an obscure federal publication with limited circulation. When notice of an executive order is published there, it has the same legal effect as if the notice had been published in all newspapers in the United States.

6. Agreement of Parties

The sixth source of law is found independently of the lawmakers and
the courts. It comes into operation when two or more persons or firms
enter into an agreement that spells out their future course of conduct.
The agreement is a "contract," and it governs the relationship of the parties as it relates to the subject matter of the contract. If one party refuses
to honor the agreement, the other has recourse to the courts. Therefore,
those who create contracts create "law" in the broad sense.

REVIEW QUESTIONS

1. If a constitution were drafted today for the United States, how could we pro-
    vide for conditions that will exist in 2176?
2. Will our present living conditions appear primitive 100 years from now? Our
    laws? (The 19th century seems quaint to us now.)
3. The "arc law" case was an example of how a law was created at the city level.
    Apply the procedural steps to the creation of a statute at the state level.
4. Examine the transcript in the pollution case and see if you can identify the
    steps taken by the examiner. First, the witness was identified. The steps that
    followed displayed a clear pattern. Remember, the examiner is "proving a
    case."
5. Is the Swedish JO simply another agency that has been created to watch other
    agencies—which in turn will need watching itself?
6. A state law provides that "firearms shall not be fired across public roads."
    By interpretation, what might "firearms" be construed to include? How about
    "public roads"? Would this include private roads that are used by the public?
    What other interpretations are possible?

7. Name one problem that might confront a legislature when considering the adoption of a "uniform law."
8. Write out one explanation of the "common law."
9. True or False. A binding contract is a form of "legislation."
10. Write out three features of a constitution: a charter.

Words and Phrases

Write out briefly what they mean to you.

1. Ombudsman.
2. Statutory interpretation.
3. Public hearing.
4. The laws of nature.
5. Contract.

Coverage:	A look at law from the viewpoint of the lawyer, the citizen, and the judge.
What to Look for:	The parts or segments into which law can be divided.
Application:	As additional chapters are read, classify them into the headings discussed in this chapter.

3 Looking at Law—An Overview

An early writer suggested that law cannot be observed in segments by calling it a "seamless web." The thought carried by this idea is accurate, but if accepted literally it would mean that law can never be looked at in parts. If this were true, then one who seeks a nonprofessional understanding of the law would be at a handicap and the "labyrinth of the law" and our "temples of justice" would continue to be shrouded in mystery. Only those who were willing to devote their lives to a ritualistic study would become acquainted with the blind lady who holds the sword and scales (See Figure 14–10.): a lady sometimes referred to as the "jealous mistress." (This phrase is descriptive of law as practiced by the lawyer.) As strange as it may sound, this view is expressed frequently—and even in legal circles—but it is rejected here. While the "web" may be "seamless," it has segments and a look can be had at the parts if one cares to do so. To achieve this purpose, the look will be taken through the eyes of three persons: the lawyer, the citizen, and the judge.

THE LAWYER

One who engages in the practice of law tends to view law as being "substantive" or "procedural"—and all parts of the practice fall neatly under one heading or the other. That which is "an essential part or constituent or relating to what is essential"[1] is "substantive"—the substance of the law. "That which prescribes a method of enforcing rights or ob-

---

[1] *Barker* v. *St. Louis County*, 340 Mo. 986, 104 S.W.2d. 371 (1937).

taining redress for their invasion"[2] is procedural, or the machinery by which a law suit is carried forward.

An Example. X was injured in a car accident at a four-way stop intersection and now seeks the services of an attorney in an attempt to recover damages. The lawyer will be interested first in the substantive law of the state as it relates to intersections. In the typical state code, once a motorist stops at a four-way intersection, the motorist can proceed provided that no other car is doing the same thing. Once in the intersection, it becomes the duty of all others to yield. In this example, the lawyer may conclude that "a cause of action" exists — that is, a claim exists for which legal action can be brought.

After the decision is made to take the case, the lawyer will begin to use the machinery of the court. The first step is to prepare and file a "complaint." The defendant will be "served" (be given notice) with process. The procedural steps will then continue until the case is settled out of court or matures for trial on the court "docket" (schedule of cases). These procedures will be covered in detail in later chapters.

THE CITIZEN

Law as viewed by the citizen falls under two headings: "private law" and "public law." Private law governs the rights and duties between individuals as they pursue their goals in society, while public law regulates the enforcement of rights and duties between individuals and the state.

As a general principle, those who live in each state are not concerned (en masse) with whether A performs a contract with B. But whether the contract promises are kept or not *is* of concern to B and others who may be involved in the contract. Therefore, a contract is part of "private law." Whether the promises contained in the contract are kept or not is a personal matter between the parties to the agreement.

Now assume that A murders B and A is at large. The violation that has occurred is against *society itself* and not merely against one person. As long as the killer is at large, there will be a threat to society. The public has every right to expect that public funds be used to apprehend and bring the accused to trial for the offense. Therefore, murder and other criminal acts are classified under "public law" and this is true whether the victim of the crime is a leading citizen in the community or a vagrant who is passing through town.

Private Law—Property, Contract, and Tort

Private law can be divided into three headings: property (a subject of contract), contract, and tort. Property law relates to the ownership and transfer of land, fixtures, personal effects, buildings, and other property permanently affixed to the earth. Contracts involve duties created by voluntary agreements between the parties, expressly or impliedly. Torts

---

[2] Ibid.

arise out of conduct not initially anticipated and is not closely related to business. However, torts often rise in the *conduct* of a business and involve duties between individuals. Torts will be discussed in detail here.

Each person has rights protected by law which create corresponding duties on all of us not to invade those rights. Included are the right to be free from bodily harm, the right to keep good reputations, the right to enjoy the privacy of one's home, the right for one's home and other property to be free from destruction and the right to conduct business without interference from others. If these rights are invaded and damage results, the injured person can bring an action for the wrong committed. The action "sounds in tort."

The word "tort" comes from the Latin word "torquere," which means "to twist" or "twisted." It is a wrong independent of contract and in-

FIGURE 3–1

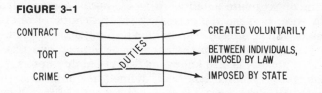

volves a violation of some duty owing the injured party. The duty does not exist by agreement of the parties but rather arises by operation of law. See Figure 3–1.

Most tort actions arise out of one of six types of actions:

1. Recklessness. Conduct in disregard of the safety of others is involved. An example would be speeding in a school zone. The *intention* to cause harm is not the legal test and in many recklessness cases, one did not actually intend to injure another. But the legal test is *reasonable forseeability* that harm might result to others from such conduct.

2. Intentional Harm. Intentional injury to another is a tort. An example is assault and battery, which is an attack upon another accompanied by blows that causes injury. Other examples include "false imprisonment" libel, slander, assault only, and trespass. Intentional harm can also be a crime if the act committed is prohibited by law. Therefore, one wrongful act may be both a tort and crime in some instances.

3. Negligence. Negligence has been defined as

> . . . the omission to do something which a reasonable person, guided by those ordinary conclusions which ordinarily regulate human affairs, would do, or something which a reasonable and prudent person would not do . . .[3]

and is the most common basis for tort actions.

The definition of negligence makes it clear that a tort can arise from an "omission"—that is, one fails to do something that a "reasonable person" would have done under the same circumstances. In that event, one

---

[3] *Schneider* v. *C. H. Little Company,* 184 Mich. 315, 151 N.W. 587 (1915).

would be guilty of negligence for the failure to act. For a further discussion of the "reasonable person" concept, see Chapter 12. Negligence can also be classified as "gross" or "simple." The legal effects are usually more severe for the former than the latter.

4. Dangerous Instrumentality. When a person uses an item that is "inherently dangerous," liability may arise even though the greatest amount of care is exercised in its use. For example, explosives are widely used in construction work. An action in tort would arise by the reckless or negligent use of explosives – or liability can also arise where these elements are *not* present. A contractor who is shooting a ditch may use small charges and cover the blast area with a "fly mat." The contractor may clear the area and take all precautions that a reasonable, prudent person would take. If, after taking all of these precautions, damage results to another by virtue of the blast, an action in tort would lie under the doctrine of "absolute liability." It would not be a good defense if the contractor were to plead the extreme care and caution exercised. Fire, wild animals, and acid have been held to be dangerous instrumentalities and injury that results from their use or ownership can result in tort liability. This process is also known as "strict liability in tort."

5. Nuisance. Nuisance has been defined as "annoyance; anything which essentially interferes with the enjoyment of life and property."[4] A nuisance might be public in nature, or it may be private in that it only injures one person.

If in the conduct of a business, dust or other dirty material is deposited upon the property of another, an injunction – a "legal order" from a court – may be sought to prohibit such deposit and may be coupled with a suit for damages. The conduct of businesses such as slaughter houses, refineries, smelters, and other industries that cause smell and noise may give rise to actions in tort.

6. Trespass. Trespass has been defined as "doing an unlawful act or a lawful act in unlawful manner to the injury of another person or property."[5] Not all cases of trespass give rise to an actionable tort. A trespass lacking in *intention* usually does not form the basis of an action in tort. For example, a boat tied to the dock is torn loose during a storm, drifts downriver, and comes to rest in the front yard of a lower riparian owner. If damage results to the property when the boat is removed, the landowner will be entitled to payment. But the recovery for the damages would not be for the "tort" committed. Rather, it would be in "bailment." By this we mean that the lower land owner became a "bailee" of the boat – although an "involuntary bailee" – and is thus entitled to be compensated for damages caused by the "bailment." This subject is developed in detail in Chapter 19.

If however, one should recklessly drive a motor vehicle through another's lawn, a trespassing warrant could be sworn out by the injured

---

[4] *Holton* v. *Northwestern Company*, 201 N.C. 744, 161 S.E. 391 (1931).
[5] *Waco Cotton Oil Mill* v. *Walker*, 103 S.W.2d. 1071 (1937).

party. This would then be a "criminal action" and would place a duty upon the state to take appropriate action against the offender.

Contrasted against the classification of private law is that of public law.

Public Law

As the name implies, the public has an interest in this type of law and it includes constitutional, administrative and criminal law.

Constitutional Law. If the U.S. Supreme Court lays down a new rule on the use of wiretaps in obtaining evidence for use in criminal trials, "constitutional" and thus public, law is involved.

Administrative Law. If a state Public Service Commission creates new rules to regulate public transportation, "administrative" and thus public, law is involved.

Constitutional and administrative law have been discussed previously and will not be covered further here.

Criminal Law. It is the responsibility of the state to prosecute those who commit crimes, thus criminal law is also "public." The attorney for the state is often called the "prosecuting" or "district" attorney. If a federal crime is being prosecuted, it will be handled by a United States Attorney.

In both instances, public funds are used to carry forth the prosecution. These actions are styled *"People* v. *the Accused," "State* v. *the Accused,"* or *"The United States* v. *the Accused"* as the case may be. It is not proper to speak of the state or federal government as being the "plaintiff." A plaintiff is one who brings a private civil suit as distinguished from a criminal prosecution by the state or federal government.

Types of Crimes. Crimes may be "common law" or they may be "statutory." Those acts that are prohibited by statutes of the states or federal government, are "statutory crimes." All others would be common law crimes because they were prohibited by the common law. For example, in some states, murder is not a statutory crime. Rather it is prohibited by the common law. For this reason, indictments often have to be drafted in common-law language and they sound strange to the layperson. In drafting such indictments, minor errors often cause the court to throw out the indictment—spoken of as "quashing" the indictment. However, today the greatest percentage of crimes are statutory.

Degrees of Crimes. Crimes include misdemeanors, felonies, and treason. Violations of city ordinances are not crimes "per se" and have been called "petty offenses" or "public torts." The offender is usually punished in the municipal court and subjected to a fine plus costs.

Misdemeanors are crimes punishable by fine or imprisonment in a county jail or both. Stealing less than $50 or goods of a value of less than $50, is a misdemeanor in some states. Other examples include assault, public drunkenness, disturbing the peace, making threats, reckless driving, hazardous driving, and "joy riding."

Felonies are crimes punishable by death or imprisonment in a state penitentiary. Stealing more than an amount set by statute is a felony in each state. Other examples include murder, rape, arson, armed robbery, and breaking and entering.

Treason is the "highest type" of crime and "consists of levying war against them (the States) or giving aid or comfort to their enemies,"[6] referring to the enemies of the United States. A conviction requires the testimony of at least two witnesses to the same act and one charged with treason is entitled to trial by jury. The Constitution permits conviction by a confession in open court, but it is unlikely that this will ever occur. A conviction for treason usually carries a death penalty.

Looking at the law from the point of view of the lawyer and the citizen, leaves undiscussed one important classification of the law: that of "law" as it is compared with "equity." As a rule, the judges are keenly interested in knowing if a matter pending before them is in law or in equity. If it is a law matter, a jury is usually required. If it is a matter in equity, a jury is usually not permitted.

AS THE JUDGE VIEWS LAW

To suggest that the judge, who most often is a lawyer, does not look at law in the same manner as a lawyer would be inaccurate.

But on many occasions, judges are required to look at a matter pending before them, and ask a realistic question: "Is this a 'legal' or 'equitable' matter?" Some background is helpful in understanding this.

Following the Norman Conquest, a "writ system" was used in the courts of England. A "writ" was a document issued by the courts, designed to cover a specific situation. A prospective litigant was required to fit the case into one of the established writs and if this could be done, litigation was started and the matter was disposed of by the court. The writs were broken into the classifications "ex contracto" (in contract) and "ex delicto" (in tort) a classification widely used today, as we have seen.

In the simplest sense, the writ system was one of finding the right "pigeon-hole"; and it prevailed for many centuries and has left a mark upon the American legal system. But it had one great failing: the two basic categories were not broad enough to encompass all of the matters that came before the courts. If A borrowed farm tools from B but refused to return them, the action would be in "detinue." If C rode a horse through the garden of D causing damage, the action would be in "trespass." If an executor of an estate refused to account to the heirs, an action in "account" was used. But what if one wanted to challenge a will, or obtain a divorce, or rescind a contract, or obtain an injunction? Under the common-law writs, this type of relief was not obtainable.

As time went by, the courts began to consider matters that were not covered by the writs and usually did so for matters of "conscience" rather

---

[6] U.S. Constitution, Article III, Section 3.

than for matters of "law." For example, A sold a painting to B, who paid for it in full. Later, A refused to deliver the painting and B refused the offer of the return of the money. There was no writ available to B because these facts did not fit the established writs. But why *shouldn't* A deliver the painting? A judge who reasoned this way might order A to deliver the painting because "it was the right thing to do." In short, it was the "equitable" thing to do. The body of rules that grew from such court action came to be known as "equity"—the sibling of "law." And therein lies the problem for the judge who looks at a pending case. If the matter was an "equitable" one at common law, then it is a case for the judge to decide and a jury is not permitted. If it is a legal matter, a jury may be required.

About one half of the states have adopted rules of civil procedure—usually based upon the Federal Rules of Civil Procedure. In those states, the distinction between law and equity has allegedly been abolished and all cases are called "civil actions." But curiously enough, *all* of our courts still recognize the distinction and honor the age-old matters of equity by disposing of them without a jury.

When a court enters an order in equity, called a "decree," the person to whom it is directed is expected to obey. If it is not obeyed, the person is in "contempt" and may be fined or imprisoned.

Normally, a suit for damages (dollars) is a legal matter and will be heard on the law side of the court. Frequently, a court that takes jurisdiction in equity also awards money damages. In a recent case, timbercutter B began taking timber from A's farm. A insisted that B stop, but B refused and A sought an injunction. After bond was posted, the judge ordered B to stop cutting until the question of the ownership of the timber could be decided. At first, B refused to obey and was imprisoned until B agreed to tell the workers to stop—which only took 15 minutes after B was jailed. At a subsequent hearing, B failed to prove ownership of the timber and could not produce the necessary written document. The court made the injunction permanent and awarded A $3,000 for damages done to the farm.

Turning from the classifications, one final matter must be developed in some detail. In many business law textbooks tort law is treated under a single heading that carries that name. However, the decision was made here to treat tort law in relationship with those other branches of law to which it relates. This necessarily results in some diminution of the discussion of torts. To overcome this, the balance of this chapter is devoted to tort principles as these are being applied in the modern business setting. To facilitate this discussion, three topics of general interest have been selected for discussion.

TORT PRINCIPLES IN APPLICATION—SOME EXAMPLES

Law is evolutionary, not revolutionary, in most instances. Because of this, law is constantly being refined, redefined, and expanded as the years go by. This has happened in tort law in three specific areas. For want of a better title, these areas have been referred to as "Who Owns the Sky?"; "Tort Liability for Mental Injury"; and "Spring Guns in Iowa."

Who Owns the Sky?

At common law, the owner of real property owned everything from the center of the earth to the heavens. It was a common-law trespass for a tree, wire, or eave of a house to be extended over the land of another. Interesting problems arose when aircraft began to use the space above the land of others. If the courts had tried to perpetuate common-law property rights, flights by commercial and military aircraft would have been impossible. As it turned out, as long as aircraft maintained a decent level of altitude, no one complained and the question of "who owns the sky" did not arise. But when low-level flights were made over private property causing noise and loss of enjoyment of one's property, the cases went to court.

The Supreme Court of Ohio declared that there is a taking of property in the constitutional sense when flights of aircraft are so low and frequent as to interfere with the enjoyment and use of the land. The court said

> ... We think that a person's residence is for his use for which he is entitled to have compensation whenever he can prove a direct and immediate interference with that use.[7]

Thus, as a general, modern rule, when low-level flights cause direct interference with one's private property, an action in tort will lie under the theory of trespass over the land or nuisance growing out of the interference that is caused.

Tort Liability for Mental Injury

The rule that came to America from the common-law courts of England, was that mental injury which was not accompanied by "impact" could not form the basis for an action in tort.[8] To be recoverable at law, damages must first, be the proximate result of the injury complained of, and second, be definite and not the product of speculation. Under this two-part rule, damages for mental suffering were not allowed at common law as an independent cause of action. There had to be some other injury accompanying the mental injury.

One state court stated that damages for mental and emotional disturbances caused by the tort of another can only be recovered in two types of cases. First, where mental disturbances accompany or follow physical injury to the plaintiff, caused by impact upon the happening of the tort; or second, where there is no impact on the plaintiff at the time of the tort, but such injury afterwards results as a casual effect of nervous shock, which was the proximate result of the tort.[9]

---

[7] *State* v. *City of Columbus*, 3 Ohio St. 2d 154, 209 N.E. 2d. 405 (1965).

[8] Lord Wensleydale in *Lynch* v. *Knight*, 9 H.L.C. 577,598, 11 Eng. Rep. 854 (1861).

[9] *Monteleone* v. *Co-Operative Transit Company*, 340, 36 S.E.2d., 475 (1945).

Another case from the same state illustrates the second class of cases. The defendant wrongfully and violently assaulted the plaintiff's father within her sight and hearing, causing fright to the plaintiff. The defendant was not aware of the plaintiff's presence. Defendant was found guilty. The upper court permitted the jury verdict in the lower court to stand. The court stated, "Why should the defendant be allowed to shock plaintiff's nervous system anymore than he should be allowed to inflict injury by physical contact?"[10]

In a "slight impact" case,[11] (meaning that the fright complained of had been accompanied by some contact although slight) the court raised a warning, however, by stating that in the absence of a relationship between physical injury caused by impact and mental condition on which suit was brought, mere impact (here a cut on the cheek) does not authorize recovery of damages for nervous shock or emotional injury.

It would seem reasonable that if a cause of action in tort exists regardless of the mental suffering, compensation for mental suffering that proximately follows should be allowed,[12] but it has taken the courts a long time to adopt this view.

The New York position of "no recovery in the absence of impact," was laid down in the case of *Mitchell* v. *Rochester Ry.*[13] A two-horse carriage suddenly turned and stopped near the sidewalk where the plaintiff was standing. The plaintiff ended up between the heads of the horses and fainted. She had not been touched by the horses or the vehicle and recovery was denied. This case remained the law in New York until 1961 when in the case of *Batella* v. *State*[14] Burke, J., speaking for a majority of one, stated that fraudulent accidents and injuries are just as easily feigned in the slight impact cases[15] and other exceptions wherein New York permits a recovery, as in the no impact cases it has heretofore shunned.[16] "The ultimate result is that the honest claimant is penalized for reluctance to fashion the facts within the framework of the exceptions." In the *Batella* case, A had entered a ski lift chair and the attendant failed to secure and lock the safety belt to protect A, who became hysterical on descent. Severe injury to A resulted from the fright. The case illustrates that the law undergoes gradual change in relation to our changing society and the changing needs of society.

The possession of a peaceful mental state free from injury will in time be accepted as a proper subject for legal protection in all of the courts just as freedom from bodily harm is now recognized as a legitimate matter to sue upon in the courts. As one judge said, "Wounding a man's feelings is as much actual damages as breaking his limbs."[17]

---

[10] *Lambert* v. *Brewster*, 97 W. Va. 124, 125 S.E. 244 (1924).

[11] *Monteleone* v. *Co-Operative Transit Co.*, supra.

[12] *Kennedy* v. *Chesapeake & Ohio R. Co.*, 68 W.Va. 589, 70 S.E. 359 (1911).

[13] 151 N.Y. 107, 45 N.E. 354 (1896).

[14] 10 N.Y.2d. 237, 176 N.E.2d. 729 (1961).

[15] *Jones* v. *Brooklyn Heights R.R.*, 23 App.Div. 141, 49 N.Y.S. 914, where plaintiff recovered from "fright" caused by being hit in the head with a small light bulb.

[16] *Newton* v. *New York N.H. & H.R.*, 106 App.Div. 415, 94 N.Y.S. 825 (1905).

[17] *Head* v. *Ga. Pac. Ry.*, 79 Ga. 358 (1887).

Tort liability for mental injury is going to be extended into another area that is just beginning to develop. Do we have the right to be free of the mental anguish placed upon us by collection agencies who call us late at night, or bill collectors who threaten "to tell the boss?" The threatening letter "bombardment" that accompanies the use of the computer in bill collecting, where it causes severe mental injury, will be looked at carefully by the courts.

A Case Example. Miss Florence Long owed Beneficial Finance the sum of $1,484.90 and was not able to make payments on the debt. The company tried to collect by sending agents to her home. In addition, the company dunned her at her place of employment and placed numerous calls to her friends and neighbors.

After eight months of this, Miss Long suffered a heart attack—brought on as she claimed by the harrassment of the finance company. The company knew of the heart attack but continued their collection efforts. After suffering a second heart attack, Miss Long brought suit against the finance company for "mental distress and tortious conduct."

Upon motion to dismiss, the court held that Miss Long did have a cause of action in tort for infliction of mental distress—even though the distress was caused in the attempt to collect a lawful debt.[18]

The Trend Continues. The Superior Court of Fairfield County, Conn., has permitted recovery to parents for mental injury and shock caused by seeing their child killed in an automobile accident caused by the negligence of the defendant.[19]

The Court of Appeals of New York permitted a passenger to recover for a skin rash caused by psychic trauma suffered during the hijacking of an airplane by Arab terrorists. However, the court denied recovery for those who did not suffer some physical, objective bodily injuries.[20]

It should be observed that the last case, which was decided after the Connecticut case, does not indicate a liberalizing trend. Perhaps that court was influenced by the prior positions that have been taken by the courts.

The final topic, "Spring Guns in Iowa," raises important warnings for those in business.

Spring Guns in Iowa

A most unbelieveable case arose in an Iowa court—and it involved a would-be burglar who was shot in the ankle by a "spring gun"—a gun rigged to a line designed to cause the gun to fire if a door to a building was opened. The incident involved both a tort and a crime with results that few persons could have predicted. The United Press International release tells the story.

---

[18] *Long* v. *Beneficial Finance Co.* 330 N.Y.S. 2d. 664 (1972).

[19] *D'Amicol* v. *Alvarez Shipping Co. Inc.*, 326 A. 2d. 129 (1973).

[20] *Rosman* v. *Trans World Airlines*, 314 N.E.2d 848, 358 N.Y.S. 2d. 97 (1974).

EDDYVILLE, Iowa (UPI)—Last November, an all-woman jury awarded a $30,000 judgment to an admitted intruder who was severely wounded by a shotgun blast into his right leg while he was prowling an unoccupied farm house.

Edward Briney of Eddyville, population 1,000, had rigged a trapgun in his home early in the summer of 1967 to cope with thieves.

The device was successful. On July 16 of that summer, Marvin Katko, now 30, was shot by it; he first was charged with breaking and entering, pleaded innocent; the charge was reduced to larceny in the nighttime, he pleaded guilty, paid a $30 fine and was released.

Then he filed suit, a personal injury claim, against Briney, 53, and his wife Bertha, 49. His right leg is now $2\frac{1}{2}$ inches shorter than the left. He sought $60,000; the claim was reduced to half that amount by the jury.

To pay part of the judgment, 80 acres of a 120-acre farm estate belonging to Mrs. Briney was sold at a forced auction for $10,000. Included on the estate was the vacant farm home in which Katko was shot.

The Brineys have since appealed the Mahaska County District Court jury's verdict to the Iowa Supreme Court. A decision is not expected for at least six months, according to Katko's attorney, Garold Heslinga of nearby Oskaloosa.

Whatever the jury ruled, Iowans, including several state legislators, now are debating, sometimes bitterly, over the extent to which a man may act in defense of his property.

Some people believe Briney had every right to set the booby trap, and even go so far as to say he would have been justified if Katko had been killed. Others feel Briney went too far and acted maliciously to be setting the trap.

There is nothing specific in Iowa law on this type of case. Both Heslinga and Briney's attorneys, H. S. Life and Bruce Palmer of Oskaloosa, say the case was based on old English common-law principles which say force may be used to protect property—but no greater force than is reasonably necessary.

To the Brineys, however, there is no question. They feel they had the right to protect their property in any manner essential to getting the job done.

"I should think we would be allowed to protect our property, particularly since there is so much of that kind of thing going on," says Mrs. Briney, adding that there have been many instances of abandoned dwellings broken into around the area in recent years.

Heslinga feels the whole case is "pretty much cut and dried." However, he feels it all boils down to "human rights versus property rights" pointing to the Judeo-Christian ethic that "life is more valuable than property rights."

The tall, lean, graying, pipe-smoking Heslinga, 46, also has some very definite opinions on the "many, many" persons that have written him hate mail and criticizing him for being Katko's counsel.

"These are the law and order nuts," he says, "who somehow justify this type of violence."

Briney's attorneys refused to talk about the case unless they were guaranteed their opinions would be kept in confidence.

Life, 77, has an office right across the street from Heslinga's. All he would say publicly is that he is a firm believer in the right to defend life and property and that Iowa's law is not clear on the situation.

"The Iowa Supreme Court will have to decide whether we are changing the basis of our law—that man has a right to defend his home," he says.

Most of the jurors in the case refused to talk about the case because they say they have been the targets of abusive calls and letters, both from former friends and from strangers. Those that would talk would only talk on the condition they remain anonymous.

One juror says most of the people who strongly feel the Brineys were treated unfairly do not know the facts of the case and did not sit through the court hearing.

The juror said Briney had openly admitted, and the court transcript confirmed it, that he had wanted to aim the gun so it would hit someone in the stomach and only lowered it so it would hit a person between the ankle and knee after his wife had convinced him to lower it.

"This wasn't just protection of property," the juror said. "He (Briney) had to pry the boards off the window to look in and see if anyone was caught in the trap—that's not protection."

On February 9, 1971, the Supreme Court of Iowa, in an opinion by Chief Justice Moore, upheld the judgment in the court below holding that a property owner may not protect personal property in an unoccupied, boarded-up farm house against trespassers and thieves, by the use of a spring gun capable of inflicting death or serious injury. (See 183 N.E. 2d 657 (1971).)

But the Briney–Katko escapade did not end there. Under the heading of "The Thief's Revenge," *Newsweek* for June 9, 1975, had the following report. After discussing the case in detail, *Newsweek* continues:

Rent: Then a flood of sympathetic letters and contributions poured in to farmer Briney from 39 states and even Vietnam, where a U.S. soldier's wife wrote, "it makes me feel my husband is fighting for the wrong government." To help Briney pay the judgment, three of his neighbors purchased one-quarter of his land for a modest $10,000, allowing him to rent it for taxes and bank interest.

But as the value of good Iowa soil rose over the years, this particular flame of human kindness flickered lower. Last year, Briney's three neighbors first offered to sell the land back to him—but at a price he could not afford. They then kicked him off the land and sold it for a fat profit. Charging that his erstwhile benefactors held the land effectively in trust for him, Briney has now sued them. He wants either the right to buy the land back at the original price or to collect $14,000, which he claims represents the increase in value of the land. But since Briney still owes Katko for part of the judgment, he has assigned his rights to the convicted thief. Next fall, victim and robber will go to court hand in hand against the good Samaritans.

Briney v. *Katko* v. *others,* is a good example of law as contrasted with "reality."

California Agrees with Iowa. The California Supreme Court has concluded that there is no privilege to use a deadly mechanical device to prevent burglary of a dwelling house in which no one is present. The court confirmed a conviction for assault that arose out of a spring gun shooting of a teenage boy who attempted to gain entry to the defendant's garage.[21]

---

[21] *People* v. *Ceballos,* 116 Cal. Rptr. 233, 526 P. 2d 241, (1974).

At the turn of this century, spring guns were offered on the market as a commercial product. Examine Figure 3-2. This device was attached to a door frame or window by screws. The arm contains a hole that was wired to the door or window. The arm can be cocked by pulling against its spring and a .32 caliber rimfire cartridge can be inserted. The bullet would fire in the direction it was pointed when the door or window was opened. These were marked "burglar alarms" and you can see in the photo that "patent's have been applied for." Needless to say, this type of activity today will lead to an assault or perhaps murder charge.

FIGURE 3-2
A Spring Gun

From the author's collection.

REVIEW QUESTIONS

1. Name an "equitable matter" not found in the chapter.
2. *Should* mental injury form the basis for recovery in tort? Why?
3. From your own experience, give an example of an injunction.
4. What is the name of the prosecuting attorney in your home county?
5. What is the name of the United States Attorney in your home district?
6. How would you explain the distinction between crime and tort to one of your younger family members?
7. If an action "sounds in tort," it means what?
8. The six types of torts in the text all have one thing in common. What is it?
9. Why is administrative law classed as public rather than private law?
10. At common law, "no writ — no remedy" meant what?

Words and Phrases

Write out briefly what they mean to you.
1. "Jealous mistress."
2. "Seamless web."
3. A cause of action.
4. Intention.
5. Nuisance.

Coverage:	An introduction to basic legal terms and topics.
What to Look for:	The ways in which law serves as a means of control.
Application:	Relate the items here to the classifications of law in Chapter 3.

4 Some Legal Basics both in and out of Court

The purposes of this chapter are twofold: First, to acquaint the reader generally with legal topics of importance to those in business, and second, to set forth terms that must be understood before further meaningful study may be undertaken.

As these terms and topics are covered, an effort should be made to gain enough understanding of them so that, if requested, a simple definition could be given. Some of the items have been encountered in previous chapters and will be covered in depth in subsequent chapters. The chapter is divided into "general legal topics and terms," and "terms and topics of our courts."

GENERAL LEGAL TOPICS AND TERMS

1. Tort

A tort is a personal private wrong committed upon another's person, reputation, or property by the "tort feasor"—the one who commits the wrong. If two or more persons unite in the commission of a wrong, or where independent acts of more than one person result in an injury to another, they are said to be "joint tort feasors." Torts are most commonly caused by the failure of the wrongdoer to use due care—called "negligence." The commission of a tort involves a breach of a duty imposed by law. An example would be the duty that each of us has not to harm another.

2. Crime

A crime occurs when there is a breach of a duty owed to the community or the state. A crime can be of a lesser offense called a "misdemeanor," which includes petty thefts and simple assault, or it can be of a more serious type such as murder, arson, rape, or armed robbery, which are "felonies." The most severe type of crime is "treason" which is a crime against the nation itself. It consists of ". . . levying War against (the United States), or in adhering to their Enemies, giving them aid and Comfort."[1] Examples of treason in modern times include desertion from military duty in the face of the enemy and providing enemies of our nation with secrets to military weapons. There is historical precedent for the crime of treason, one example being "conspiracy against the Pharoah" found in the laws of ancient Egypt.

It is the responsibility of the state, and the federal government, to do two things: First, to prevent crimes through the use of adequate police agencies and research into the causes of crime; and second, to provide a means by which those who commit crimes can be prosecuted. Thus, criminal prosecutions are handled by public attorneys called prosecutors, district attorneys, and United States Attorneys. Criminal cases are brought in the name of the state or the United States, as the case may be. A prosecution by a state against John Doe for armed robbery would be styled "*State* v. *John Doe*," or "*Commonwealth* v. *John Doe.*"

A tort and a crime may arise out of one occurrence and when they do, double lawsuits may follow. If X negligently kills Y while driving under the influence of alcohol, a tort and a crime have both been committed. The estate of Y can sue in tort for the loss to the estate of future earnings. In most states, the amount that can be recovered in a civil action for a "wrongful death" is limited by statute. The sum is as low as $10,000 in some states and as high as $100,000 in others. (It should be noted that while the sum for wrongful death is limited, there is generally no limit upon the amount of money that can be recovered for negligent *injury* to a person who survives.) The state may also prosecute X for the wrongful death of Y. This means that the prosecuting attorney of the state where the death occurred, could present the matter to a grand jury for consideration. If the grand jury believes that there was "probable cause" that the death was in fact a criminal act, they could indict (charge) X with the crime of wrongful death. The burden would then be on the state to convince a petit jury (trial jury) that X was guilty "beyond a reasonable doubt." If the petit jury convicts X, the judge may sentence X to a jail or prison term and also set a fine that must be paid to the court. A typical "wrongful death" statute provides for imprisonment not to exceed one year and a fine not to exceed $1,000 or both in the discretion of the court.

---

[1] United States Constitution, Article III, Section 3.

3. Contract

A contract is a voluntary agreement entered into between two or more persons that creates duties and corresponding liabilities between those persons. A "breach of contract" results when one breaches (fails to honor) duties voluntarily assumed. On the other hand, a tort action arises when there is a breach of a duty imposed by law—such as negligently causing personal injury to another. A criminal action arises when there is a breach of a duty owed to the state or nation. These basic distinctions are of importance to an understanding of our legal system. (See Figure 3–1.)

A contract situation comes into being as one makes an "offer" to another, and the other "accepts" as provided by law. The result is a "contract." Many contract situations will be identified in the chapters that follow.

4. The Uniform Commercial Code[2]

An extensive grouping of laws of business are found in the Uniform Commercial Code. The U.C.C. is a product of the National Conference of Commissioners on Uniform State Laws. The significance of the U.C.C. to one in business is so great that it cannot be ignored in any study of law. Yet the complexity of it makes an effort to study it as a single law an almost complete waste of time. To help overcome this dilemma, key provisions of the U.C.C. are incorporated throughout the text where they find application. In addition, four articles of the U.C.C. are treated in depth:

Article 2.   Sales, Chapters 14 and 20.
Article 3.   Commercial Paper, Chapters 29, 30, 31, and 32.
Article 8.   Investment Securities, Chapter 54.
Article 9.   Secured Transactions, Chapter 37.

The ten articles of the U.C.C. are:

Article 1.   General Provisions (including definitions).
Article 2.   Sales.
Article 3.   Commercial Paper.
Article 4.   Bank Deposits and Collections.
Article 5.   Letters of Credit.
Article 6.   Bulk Transfers.
Article 7.   Warehouse Receipts, Bills of Lading and other Documents of Title.
Article 8.   Investment Securities.
Article 9.   Secured Transactions; Sales of Accounts, Contract Rights and Chattel Paper.
Article 10.   Effective Date and Repealer.

---

[2] This is a state law and all states but one have adopted it. See the Introduction for a fuller discussion.

It should be noted however, that the precise content of the U.C.C. will vary from state to state.

5. The Consumer Credit Protection Act[3]

Many laws have been enacted in recent years to aid the consumer in credit transactions. The most notable of these is the Consumer Credit Protection Act, called the C.C.P.A.: It is a federal law. This means that it was enacted by Congress and is to be applied throughout the states.

The C.C.P.A. contains 6 divisions:

Title I.   Truth in Lending and Credit Advertising.
Title II.   Extortionate Credit Transactions.
            National Commission on Electronic Transfers.
Title III. Garnishment.
            Fair Credit Billing Act.
Title IV.   National Commission of Finance.
            1974 Amendments.
Title V.   General Provisions.
            Equal Credit Opportunity Act.
Title VI.   The Fair Credit Reporting Act.

All of these titles will be examined in detail in Part Three of the text.

6. Occupational Safety and Health Act (O.S.H.A.)[4]

While workmen's compensation laws (see Chapter 44) were created to *compensate* employees who were injured while "on the job," O.S.H.A. was created to *prevent* on the job injuries and deaths.

Under this federal law, employers have a legal obligation to provide all employees a safe place in which to work. The law makes provisions for standards which must be applied in the various work areas, and provides an elaborate nationwide network of inspectors and regional offices for enforcement of the law. This topic is covered in detail in Chapter 45.

7. Commercial Paper

Article 3 of the U.C.C. covers the law of commercial paper, the most common types being checks, notes, and bills of exchange. These documents are widely used in commercial practice as a means of paying debts or of creating a debt obligation so that credit may be extended. The main characteristic of commercial paper is that it is "negotiable," meaning that it can move freely in the commercial setting, much like a $20 bill.

8. Investment Securities

Article 8 of the U.C.C. contains the laws that regulate the issuance of the principal types of investment securities, stocks and bonds. These

---

[3] P.L. 90–321: 82 Stat. 146 et seq., Act of May 29, 1968.
[4] U.S. Code Annot. Title 29, Chapter 15.

are treated as being negotiable under the U.C.C. but the article does *not* regulate the sale of securities upon the market. (This is the function of the Securities and Exchange Commission (SEC) which is a federal administrative body.)

9. Property

The great percentage of business contracts (excluding employment agreements) involve property. Property is "real" – everything affixed to the earth itself, or "personal" – all other property. Whether something is "realty" or "personalty" can be of importance to the rights of one who lays claim to it.

10. Secured Transactions

Article 9 of the U.C.C. is closely related to Article 2, Sales, because, through the machinery of Article 9, one can obtain funds for the buying and selling of all types of consumer and industrial goods – and "security" is involved. "Security" is of importance because of a simple principle: those who have funds to lend will not do so unless they have assurance that the loan will be repaid promptly and at the agreed rate of interest. The assurance is given by "security" or "collateral" in a form that will permit recovery by the lender in the event of default. In real estate loans the security used is a deed of trust or mortgage which pledges real estate; that is, upon default the land can be sold to pay off the debt. Where personal property is involved, a "security interest" is given in personal property – often the item purchased with the loan. It is the latter activity that Article 9 governs.

Turning now from general legal business matters, it next becomes important to begin getting acquainted with basic court matters.

GENERAL COURT TOPICS AND TERMS

1. Courts

The basic institution of the American legal system is the court itself. Courts provide the forum in which disputes can be settled. America has a dual system – state courts and federal courts. This resulted from the grant of certain powers to the federal government and the reservation of all others to the states.

2. Lawsuits

Disputes are settled in the courts through lawsuits. The person who brings a "civil action" is called the "plaintiff." The person against whom it is brought is called the "defendant." In the case of a "criminal prosecution," there is no plaintiff but the accused is called the "defendant."

In "courts of record," a record is made of the proceedings in the courtroom, both in and out of the hearing of the jury. The reporter who makes a record uses a steno-machine, a voice recording method, or the shorthand method. If one of the parties to litigation in a court of record desires to appeal to the next higher court, a "transcript" of the proceedings is mandatory. If one fails to have a record made, there is no way that an appeal can be taken. Procedures for appeals (or writs of error, as the case may be) are spelled out in state statutes, constitutions, and the federal laws. In addition, the courts themselves usually create their own local trial rules.

3. Juries

There are two basic types of juries: grand juries and petit juries. The function of grand juries is to find "probable cause" in criminal matters, not guilt or innocence which is the job of petit (or trial) juries. The grand jury listens to preliminary evidence and decides if there is reason to believe a formal accusation (indictment) should be made. If so, a "true bill" is returned. If not, a "not true bill" is returned. Grand juries are made up of different numbers of persons, depending upon the state involved. One state provides that a grand jury shall be made up of not less than 14 nor more than 16 persons, who are citizens of the county wherein the jury is called to serve. Historically and traditionally, petit juries have had 12 members.

However, there is no legal (in the absence of a statute) or constitutional reason why a *petit* jury must have 12 members. The state of Florida and the federal courts use a six person jury and other states will follow this practice in the future. In many courts, attorneys in civil actions agree to let a number less than 12 hear and decide a case.

The petit jury is a "fact finding" body. That is, it establishes the facts that are in controversy as distinguished from decisions of "law" which is the job of the judge (court).

Trial juries hear and decide both civil and criminal matters. In criminal cases, they will find the defendant "guilty" or "not guilty"—a finding of fact. In some states after a finding of guilt, the jury will set the penalty. In civil cases the jury decides "fault" and sets "damages." In a civil case if the jury does not find fault, they will find the defendant "not guilty."

In only a few types of civil cases are the parties *not* given the right to trial by jury and the cases "in equity" provide the most common example. In most criminal trials, the cases are heard and decided by the jury.

4. Cases

In early centuries, court proceedings and rulings were seldom reduced to written form. Because of this, the law was passed from one generation to another by memory or custom. It can be assumed that a ruling in a court in 2000 B.C. became altered in the telling 1000 years later.

During these early centuries, suitable material upon which the written word could be placed, simply was not available. In time, paper as we know it today, became available and "scribes" and writers began to record cases decided in the courts. In 10th century England, the Royal Writs and Decrees were being recorded on "sheepskin." (See Figure 14–8.)

Ultimately the printing press was developed and the appeal court's rulings or "opinions," or "cases," were printed and bound into numbered and indexed volumes and made available to the public. This process, however, is essentially a product of the last century and this one.

Today. The case reporting system has developed to a point where the lawyer, or citizen, can find any appellate case decided in the United States in the past 150 years. However, it must be remembered that state *trial* court cases do not appear in printed form in the reporter system. These cases are preserved in local circuit court offices and it is difficult to find them except on a local, word of mouth basis. An exception is found in the trial courts of the federal system – the Federal District Courts. The judges of these courts reduce their more important rulings to writing. These are printed in the *Federal Supplement*.

Researching Law. Cases are used by lawyers and other persons, who want to establish legal authority to support a point or position. Once a case is found to support that position, the "citation" is "Shepardized."[5] This will lead to every appellate case in the United States that was involved with the same issue. Under the Shepard system it is possible to tell at a glance whether the ruling in the original case has been "overruled," "distinguished," or "modified." This is helpful in practice because if one discovers that the cases have been going against one's position, that person can look for a new approach to the matter at hand.

Researching law is a proper subject for study and most law schools include this as one of the required subjects. The layperson in turn can make use of law school libraries by visiting them and becoming familiar with the systems in use. Law students are particularly helpful to the visitor to a law library. They make constant use of the library in their studies and are usually quite willing to share their newly learned skills with others.

The "citation" of a case must be understood before use can be made of it in the library. Three samples follow: a state criminal citation, a state civil citation, and one from the Supreme Court of the United States.

A State Criminal Case. *"State* v. *Boles*, 147 W.Va. 674, 130 S.E.2d. 192 (1963)." This citation tells us that one by the last name of Boles was tried in West Virginia, in 1963, and took an appeal. (This is assumed since the state has no right to appeal if an accused is found "not guilty.") The case can be found in vol. 147 of the *West Virginia Reports* beginning on p. 674. Or it may be found in vol. 130 of the *South Eastern Reporter, Second Series,* beginning on p. 192. This was a criminal prosecution since the word "State" appears as a party. In other states this may be

---

[5] *Shepard's Citations* is a research tool published by a Colorado corporation.

"The Commonwealth," "State of Florida," or the like. In federal criminal prosecutions the style would be *"United States of America* v. *The Accused."*

A State Civil Citation. *"Peco. Inc.,* v. *Hartbauer Tool & Die Co.,* 262 Ore. 573, 500 P.2d. 708, 11 *U.C.C. Rep.* 383, (1965)." This was a civil action in the state of Oregon between the parties named. One cannot tell from the citation which one was the "plaintiff"—the one who started the suit. This is true since the appellate courts usually style the case by placing the name of the "appellant" (the one who took the appeal) first—but not always.

The case can be found in vol. 262 of the *Oregon State Reports* starting on p. 573. It can be found in the *Pacific Reporter, Second Series,* vol. 500 beginning on p. 708. It can also be found in vol. 11 of the *U.C.C. Reporter* at p. 383. It was decided in 1965.

A Federal Citation. *"Moose Lodge No. 107,* v. *Irvis,* 407 U.S. 163, 92 S. Ct. 1965, 32 L.Ed. 2d 627, (1972)." This case can be found in the *United States Supreme Court Reports,* vol. 407 at p. 163; in the *Supreme Court Reporter,* vol. 92 at p. 1965, and in *Lawyers Edition,* vol. 32 Second Series, at p. 627. This was a civil rights case brought by Irvis, a black, against the Moose Lodge No. 107 at Harrisburg, Penn. The Lodge had refused to serve Irvis in its restaurant.

As might be expected, "cases" are used in most of our law schools today as a means of studying "law." This concept is not new. Christopher C. Langdell, Dane Professor of Law at Harvard University, introduced the case system in 1869–70. This is a method whereby the law is studied inductively by using cases that have been decided in the courts.

This system has carried into the study of law in some schools of business administration and it is not uncommon to find business law texts that make wide use of cases as a supplement to the text material. However, in recent years, many persons and institutions have begun to complain that too much case study by the undergraduate is a serious duplication of law school study. Also it is now generally accepted that case study without a suitable background of basic principles is a waste of time. However, cases are encountered in the text material here. Some are in the language of the court that announced the decision, but most are in "ABC" form as part of the narrative. Case "citations" are provided by footnote should the student want to read the entire case.

5. Legal Documents

The laws of business are placed to use by the "papers of the law." And while these documents are most often prepared by lawyers, they are almost always used by the businessperson and citizen. They are frequently used in court action.

These documents may be classified into "contractual," "litigating," "disclosing," "devising," and "securing" documents. An order for shoes accepted by the factory is a contractual document. The complaint filed in a civil action for personal injury is a litigating document. The disclosure form given to a borrower at the time of closing of a bank loan is a disclosing document. A will whereby a person makes provisions for one's family upon death is a devising document. The deed of trust or mortgage given to secure a real estate loan is a securing document. These and many other legal documents will be examined in the following chapters.

6. Rules of Evidence

Over the centuries, certain rules of trial have developed which have become traditional in the courts. Each rule has an established reason for its existence and usually relates to an attempt to achieve fairness during the trial. Following are samples of rules of evidence:

It is the policy of trial courts to stop lawyers from asking "leading questions" of witnesses. A leading question is one that suggests the answer desired or is framed in such a manner that it can be answered "yes or no." That type of question is considered to be unfair to the other party because it gives the witness a hint of the answer desired. Following is a sample of a leading question followed by an example of how the question should be asked in court.

Plaintiff's Attorney: After you left the automobile, you began experiencing pain. Is that true?

Plaintiff's Attorney: Following the accident, what, if anything, happened?

A timely objection to the first question would result in the judge sustaining the objection and the witness would not be permitted to answer the question in the form in which it was first asked.

Another important rule prohibits "hearsay" evidence. This is evidence in which a witness does not testify from personal knowledge but rather relies upon a statement that was made by another person. The rule extends to both oral and written statements. In short, a witness cannot say what A said about B, or what A wrote upon a piece of paper about B. The person who spoke or wrote the statement is not before the court and was not under oath when the statement originated. If possible, the person who made the statement will be called as a witness, placed under oath, and questioned about what was said. In many cases, the rule is used to create injustices — but the reason for it is clear. There are exceptions such as confessions, spontaneous declarations (such as what a person said immediately following an accident), and admissions made by a party to a suit.

Another rule of evidence, the "parol evidence rule" is based upon a simple principle: If A and B agree upon terms to a contract, and these are reduced to writing and signed by both, neither will be permitted to "vary or alter" the terms of the contract later by parol (oral) testimony. The policy reason for the rule makes sense. The exceptions are narrow and are limited to such things as typographical errors ($1,000 instead of $10) or fraud on the part of one party. The rule makes it mandatory that a contract be read carefully before it is signed to make certain that it contains the terms orally agreed upon.

Other rules of evidence are used in the courts but the above are representative.

7. Motions

Under rules of parliamentary procedure, one who seeks action upon an issue does so by a "motion" to the presiding officer. It is usually made orally and, once made, requires that the request be ruled upon. The same procedure was adopted in trial courts centuries ago, and once a motion is made, the judge must rule at that time or "reserve ruling" to some future time. Quite frequently, motions and rulings on them are made out of the hearing of the jury. At the pretrial stage, motions are made in writing and a copy is delivered to the opposite counsel. The "moving party" then sets a date for a hearing upon the motion.

8. Evidence

Evidence as it relates to a jury trial comes from one single source, the words of a person upon the witness stand spoken while under oath. This is true whether the evidence originates in a photograph, a deed, a will, other documents, or an oral statement. Before a jury can see or hear what is on a document, a "proper foundation" must be laid by a witness on the stand. Getting papers, photos, and statements made by others admitted "into evidence" is one of the arts of a jury trial.

Evidence is proof which tends to give reason for a jury to believe that a fact is or is not as represented. It can be "direct" or circumstantial. In the former, it is in such form to lead a jury to believe the fact in issue. In the latter, it is not direct, but when considered with the surrounding facts and circumstances, tends to lead the minds of a jury to the conclusion that the fact does exist – even though there is no direct proof of it. Proving a case by circumstantial evidence is difficult in civil cases – and almost impossible in a criminal case. The reason is found in the degree of proof required.

9. Degree of Proof

For one to prevail in a lawsuit whether as a plaintiff or the state, the burden of proof must be carried in a manner provided by law. The amount or extent of proof is different in a civil action than it is in a criminal prosecution. In a civil case, whether it is a contract or tort action, the degree of proof required is by a "preponderance of the evidence," and this does not mean the one who has the greater number of witnesses or the longest testimony from the stand. Rather, it has to do with the quality and reliability of the evidence as it comes to the minds of the jury members. Following is an instruction of a court that defines "preponderance of the evidence":

The court instructs the jury that a "preponderance of the evidence" means the evidence which has the greater weight and is the most convincing in the minds of the jurors.[6]

To draw a parallel with a football game, it is proof that overcomes the defense by at least one more point than a tie.

In criminal prosecutions, the degree of proof is "beyond a reasonable doubt"—a burden that goes far beyond 51 percent. The burden is upon the state to prove guilt to this degree. There is no requirement that the accused prove innocence. The reasons for the requirement are historical and should be considered against the conditions that existed in the colonies under Crown rule. The following instruction was taken from a criminal case and illustrates how the courts give force to the requirement:

The court instructs the jury that the Commonwealth must prove this case beyond all reasonable doubt. That means that the Commonwealth must prove every material element beyond a reasonable doubt, which constitutes the alleged crime. It is not sufficient that the jury may believe guilt probable or more probable than innocence; sufficient or probability of guilt, however strong, will not authorize a conviction. The evidence must be of a character as to produce a moral certainty of guilt to the exclusion of all reasonable doubt. Nor may the jury speculate or go outside of the evidence and consider what they think might have taken place, that they are to try this case and confine it to the evidence as given by the witnesses introduced. And if that evidence when considered along with the evidence of the defense, does not convince the jury beyond all reasonable doubt as to every material element of the guilt of the accused, then the jury must find the accused not guilty.[7]

A close reading of this instruction makes it clear that the burden upon the state is a heavy one—and that is how the drafters of the U.S. Constitution intended it to be.

10. Cross-Examination

When either party in a trial places a witness upon the stand and asks questions, this is referred to as "direct examination." When counsel for the opposite party questions that same witness, it is called "cross-examination." The right to cross-examine witnesses developed slowly in the law.

Today, it is a protected right in civil and criminal cases and in administrative proceedings as well. The purpose of cross-examination is to permit the opposite party to test what has just been stated. In many cases, one who testified falsely on direct examination can be unmasked on cross. Or, if a person testified on direct in a positive, convincing manner, cross-examination may cause the witness to qualify or change what was said on direct. Cross-examination has been referred to as the "truth finder" in a jury trial—and it is that in many cases.

---

[6] *Burks* v. *Webb*, 199 Va. 296, 99 S.E.2d. 629 (1957).

[7] *Kuckenbecker* v. *Commonwealth*, 199 Va. 619, 101 S.E.2d 523 (1958).

However, the experienced trial lawyer does not cross-examine unless something can be gained by it. A witness who is cross-examined may be able to qualify or clear up a point that was not clear on direct. This is one of the hazards of asking questions. It is a dangerous process and most attorneys prefer to "lead" the witness on cross—which is permitted. A question that frequently proves fatal is to ask an adverse witness (one of the other side of the case, or one who has become hostile) "why?" The question has ruined the chances of a recovery in many contract and tort cases because it gives the adverse witness the right to explain in full any previous answer given.

REVIEW QUESTIONS

1. How would you explain to your younger brother or sister the distinction between murder and a "wrongful death"?
2. Why would the "case study" of law be popular in the law schools?
3. What was the effective date of the U.C.C. in the state where you attend school? How can you find out?
4. There are two broad classifications of negotiable paper under the U.C.C. In what two articles are they found?
5. True or False. A finances a mobile home at the bank. The security interest that the bank takes is provided by the workings of Article 9.
6. If a witness saw X remove something from Y's office, and Y says that someone took $1,000 from the office, would this be "probable cause"?
7. For an example of two types of stock certificates, see Figures 54–2 and 54–3. Remember these documents are treated as being negotiable—but they are *not* commercial paper.
8. List five items that are personal property but which can be converted to real property.
9. Examine the case citations found in the index.
10. Examine the index for a list of legal documents in the text.

Words and Phrases

Write out briefly what they mean to you.
1. "Beyond a reasonable doubt."
2. "A preponderance of the evidence."
3. Parol evidence.
4. Evidence.
5. Circumstantial evidence.

Coverage:	An in-depth look at the attorney-client relationship.
What to Look for:	The severe restraints that are imposed upon the activities of lawyers.
Application:	Think in terms of the effect these restraints might have on a business case in court.

5 Lawyers, Paralegal Laypersons, Clients, and Legal Services

Before the Bar can function at all as a guardian of the public interests committed to its care, there must be appraisal and comprehension of the new conditions, and the changed relationship of the lawyer to his clients, to his professional brethren and to the public.

—Justice Harlan Fiske Stone

One who would gain an understanding of the nature of law and the part that it plays in the regulation of society must, at some point in time, study the relationship between lawyers and clients. A good way to begin is by making an examination of the regulations that lay down the standards by which a lawyer is expected to practice the profession.

THE CODE OF PROFESSIONAL RESPONSIBILITY

Following the turn of this century, the American Bar Association, then in embryo stage, recognized the need for a body of written rules, or "canons" by which the conduct of the members of the legal profession could be regulated. Precedent was found in two principal sources. In 1854, George Sharswood had published *Professional Ethics,* an early but sound attempt to set forth acceptable professional guidelines. This

52

was followed by the *Code of Ethics* which was adopted by the Alabama Bar Association in 1887. Using these as a guide, and drawing upon the experience of more recent years, the ABA drafted and in 1908 adopted the *Canons of Professional Ethics.*

The *Canons* defined legitimate areas in which the lawyer could function, and set forth rules by which services were to be provided. The hope was expressed at the time that not only the client but society in general would benefit from the guidelines.

These canons served well for over 50 years and were looked to as patterns for codes of legal conduct in other nations. But the march of American progress through the first half of this century, brought with it vast changes in the structure of our society as well as in the legal environment of business. It was growing more apparent each year that the canons were no longer in tune with a modern America. Against this background, the American Bar Association took action.

On August 14, 1968, the president of the ABA appointed a committee to examine the old rules and to make suggestions for changes. After extensive study, the committee concluded the *Canons* could not be updated by amendment. They found that new guidelines were required to bring the practice of law into the framework of the society of the latter part of the twentieth century.

Out of this effort came the *Code of Professional Responsibility* which was formally adopted by the ABA on January 1, 1970. The *Code* has been accepted by our states and lays down the standards by which one is expected to practice law. Principal parts of the *Code* have been incorporated in the following material.

THE LAWYER AND DUTIES

The attorney-client relationship is a personal one and is unique in many ways. The attorney is in a "fiduciary" relationship with the client. The word "fiduciary" comes from Roman law and when used as a noun, means "a person holding a high position of trust and confidence." When the relationship comes into being, countless duties arise on the part of the lawyer and these often conflict with duties owed to others.

A lawyer's duties to the client include "zealous representation within the bounds of law"[1] and, the lawyer ". . . may urge any permissible construction of the law favorable to the client . . ."[2] However, one cannot assert a position during trial that is frivolous.[3] Furthermore, duty to the client does not permit the lawyer to ignore the rights of others, and the lawyer is cautioned to ". . . treat with consideration all persons involved in the legal process and to avoid the infliction of needless harm."[4]

In addition, ". . . the duty to the client and to the legal system are the

---

[1] Canon 7, EC 7-1.
[2] Canon 7, EC 7-4.
[3] Canon 7, EC 7-4.
[4] Canon 7, EC 7-10.

same: to represent the client zealously within the bounds of law."[5] In addition, being an officer of the court, the lawyer owes duties to the court, the state, society in general, and to the nation. The lawyer must always be aware of these duties and take care not to violate them. In practice, these duties often come into conflict with each other and when they do, an impossible situation arises. The Smith case will illustrate.

Mrs. Smith Loses an Eye

Mrs. Smith was employed as a helper in a hospital kitchen. On the day in question, she was seated near a high shelf containing cooking utensils including an iron skillet resting on the top shelf. Inside the skillet was a smaller iron cook pan. Mrs. Smith was preparing vegetables and did not notice Mrs. Jones who walked up beside her. Mrs. Jones removed the skillet from the shelf and the pan within fell, striking Mrs. Smith on the left side of the head.

Mrs. Smith testified later that she had been knocked unconscious by the blow. Several weeks following the incident, she began experiencing flashes of light in her right eye and the condition persisted. The doctor concluded that Mrs. Smith had become "industrially blind" in the right eye, meaning that the vision was severely constricted. The effect was similar to that of one with normal vision who looks into a room through a key hole. The doctor concluded that the condition was permanent.

Mrs. Smith applied for workmen's compensation benefits, claiming the blow had caused the blindness. If an award was granted, it would be a $33\frac{1}{3}$ percent permanent-partial disability award fixed by the statutory law of that state. Mrs. Smith did not have to prove damages as she might in a tort case—only that the incident caused the injury.

At the hearing before the workmen's compensation examiner, the ophthalmologist who had treated Mrs. Smith testified that in his medical opinion, the blow caused the condition to the eye. But he qualified his opinion by stating that it was based upon the fact that Mrs. Smith had been unconscious for ten minutes. If she had *not* been unconscious, then in his opinion the blow had not caused the blindness.

Mrs. Jones, who had been subpoenaed (called) for the hearing, was examined prior to the hearing by Mrs. Smith's lawyer. He asked her this question: "How long was Mrs. Smith unconscious after she was struck on the head?" Mrs. Jones replied in a surprised and convincing voice, "Unconscious? Why she didn't even stop peeling potatoes!"

The case illustrates the kinds of problems that face the lawyer in practice. If Mrs. Jones was called to the stand to testify, the case would obviously have been ruined. If Mrs. Jones was *not* called, many of the *Canons* of ethics would have been violated.

Such conflicts are difficult to avoid—and impossible to resolve within the bounds of the *Canons* when they arise. Perhaps situations such as this are one of the reasons why the legal profession has been subjected to criticism for centuries.

---

[5] Canon 7, EC 7–19.

CRITICISM OF THE LEGAL PROFESSION

Over the years, there have been many sensational exposes of lawyers who looted estates or "sold their clients short under the table." In recent years, there has been further publicity about lawyers who have been held by appeal courts to be incompetent to handle criminal defense cases. We cannot make excuses for these acts and shortcomings. Even the writers in older days, voiced their disapproval of the legal profession. Witness Shakespeare in *Hamlet* in the graveside scene, and the second part of King Henry VI, in which he wrote: "The first thing we do, let's kill all lawyer's."[6] Also witness the works of Charles Dickens in which he satirized and criticised the legal profession with abandon.

WASHINGTON (UPI)—Mrs. X hired a lawyer to represent her in a divorce case. He sent her a bill for $15,000.

She paid $7,500. He demanded the rest. She sought the advice of the disciplinary agency of his state bar association. Investigation determined that the lawyer's services were worth $3,000 at most.

The agency negotiated the return of $4,500. Should the lawyer be let free to overcharge the next client who might not report his complaint?

How should the discipline of the nation's 350,000 lawyers be financed? Should investigations be confined to sworn complaints?

How can discipline be administered in small towns where lawyers and judges are on a first-name basis?

These questions are being tackled by a special American Bar Association (ABA) committee headed by retired Supreme Court Justice Tom C. Clark.

The group has just released a 253-page preliminary report on the problems of bar discipline and how they can be solved. Since the committee was appointed in 1967, it has conducted hearings in New York, Washington, Miami, Denver, San Francisco, Boston, Dallas and Chicago.

It heard stories like that of Mrs. X.

The hearings alone moved several states, notably Pennsylvania and Michigan, to start working on improved disciplinary machinery.

The Clark group would like its recommendations, if adopted in final form at the ABA's annual convention next August, turned over to a national conference on disciplinary enforcement. This body would assist state and local bars in setting up more effective programs.

The Clark committee recommended a centralized program in each state, with a professional staff to carry it on.

It also approved the creation of a national discipline data bank which is scheduled to begin operating April 1 in Chicago. The purpose is to keep records so that a lawyer disciplined in one place cannot easily move elsewhere and hang out his shingle again.

Source: The *Morgantown Post*, February 25, 1971.

---

[6] Act IV, sc. II . . Jack Cade replies: "Nay, that I mean to do." Part II, Act 4, sc. 2. (If one reads the scenario in full one will discover that Shakespeare was not criticising lawyers but was recognizing that a totalitarian form of government would be impossible unless the lawyers were disposed of.)

The accompanying news item provides an example of the concern about the profession today.

But one should reserve judgment before making a blanket indictment of the profession. Evaluation and experience in working with and knowing members of the legal profession should be used as the basis for judgment. The profession is made up of an overwhelming proportion of intelligent, honest practitioners who are often the best friends and advisers that a business person and citizen can have. And the legal profession, perhaps more than any other, routinely removes from its ranks those who are considered unfit to practice law as indicated in an article from a state bar news letter. The names and places have been altered. The clipping speaks for itself.

Lawyer's License Annulled on Tax Evasion Conviction

The Supreme Court of Appeals on June 30 annulled the license of David C. Day to practice law in the State.

The court's action was based on the entry of a plea of nolo contendere to one count of an indictment charging evasion of income tax, and his being adjudged guilty and convicted by the judge of the United States District Court for the Northern District of the State, following which a sentence and fine was imposed by the judge.

The annullment proceeding was instituted by the Committee on Legal Ethics of the State Bar through transmission of the records of the U.S. District Court to the Supreme Court of Appeals.

The Supreme Court in its opinion revoking Day's license, restated its holding in former cases that "a conviction of a charge of wilfully attempting to evade and defeat income taxes in violation of the provision of Section 7201, Internal Revenue Code, . . . is a conviction involving moral turpitude."

The By-Laws of the State Bar imposes upon any court before which an attorney has been qualified a mandatory duty to annul the license of such attorney to practice law upon proof that he had been convicted of any crime involving moral turpitude.

Losing one's license to practice law is "easy," as illustrated. Obtaining it in the first place is another story.

BECOMING A LAWYER

One can only generalize about admission to law schools because the requirements vary. Two requirements are fundamental, however: an undergraduate degree from an acceptable college or university and a satisfactory score on the Law School Admission Test (LSAT). Other requirements vary from school to school and it has been observed in recent years that interviews and "projections of probable success and service to the community" are replacing mere academic credentials.

Upon admission, the student is introduced to a world of "torts," "contracts," "stare decisis," books, cases, and perpetual class discussion and analysis which spans three years of intensive study. Time does not permit specialization in the law schools, and one who would become a specialist must do so by study after graduation.

After graduation, one must pass the bar exam, which may require 6 to 12 months additional study. After completion of the "bar" the applicant is screened by the "committee on admissions." The committee may refuse admission for many reasons. Once refused, the applicant has little chance to practice law because the courts are reluctant to substitute their judgment for the judgment of a bar committee. Once admission is gained, the lawyer can "hang out the shingle"—although this is a figure of speech only. The shingle must be conservative in size and be placed flat against a wall. After admission to practice, the lawyer is supervised by the bar, the courts and those served. The inescapable conclusion is that membership in a bar is not a right but a privilege that is guarded by the members of the profession—as it should be.

Lawyers have been prohibited from advertising their services and the business person is frequently faced with the problem of deciding who should handle the matter at hand. However, in light of recent U.S. Supreme Court cases, this will change.

SELECTION OF A LAWYER

Traditionally, lawyers have been selected by asking for recommendations from friends, business associates, law professors, or by consulting the various legal directories. These methods are still effective. But because of specialization in the practice of law other means must be resorted to such as the legal referral systems in use in most cities. After one selects a lawyer, it is customary to enter into an arrangement for fees and costs.

The Employment Contract

The lawyer in America can refuse any employment offered—although he or she cannot escape "court appointments" in criminal cases. Once employment is accepted, a contract comes into being between the attorney and client.

Most lawyers prefer that the agreement be reduced to writing—although it does not have to be. In personal injury cases it is routine to use a written contract which contains the fee arrangement. This helps to avoid controversy later when settlement is reached. See Figure 5-1, for an example. This contract contains provisions for a "contingent fee" which will be discussed later.

Conflicting Interests

Upon assuming a client's cause, it is the duty of the lawyer to do all within the principles discussed to advance the purposes of that cause.

FIGURE 5-1

John Sterling
Attorney at Law
1300 Silver Avenue

Dear Client:

   If your case is settled before suit is filed, my fee will be 25% of the total settlement. After suit is filed, my fee will be 33$\frac{1}{3}$% of any settlement or payment made after jury verdict. This will be true whether or not the case is tried in court. If an appeal is taken from a jury verdict and it is sustained by the Supreme Court of this state, my fee will be 50% of the final sum obtained.

   Settlement will be made only with your approval.

I acknowledge receipt of

$_____ suit fees. These

fees will be adjusted at the

time of settlement.

RETAINER AGREEMENT

   I hereby employ John Sterling, Attorney at Law, to render legal services on my behalf against _____,

_____ for injuries

or other claims sustained by me on the _____ day of _____,

19___, as a result of _____.

   I agree to pay 25% of any settlement obtained in this case before suit is filed; 33$\frac{1}{3}$% of any settlement or verdict after suit is filed or 50% of any verdict if sustained in the Supreme Court of this state.

   Dated this _____ day of _____, 19___.

John Sterling	Client

This could not be accomplished if the attorney would represent another person, or another cause, adverse to that of the client. It would be unprofessional for an attorney to represent a wife who is seeking a divorce and, at the same time, accept employment from her husband who desires the marital relationship to continue. To contend for one would require opposition to what the other desires. The question of who is right or wrong would have no bearing upon the situation.

Supporting the Client's Cause

   How far should the attorney go? The *Code* states that questionable transactions, false claims, and arguments concerning the personal belief of the attorney of the client's cause must be avoided.[7] On the other hand, the client is entitled to the benefit of every legitimate means available under law to advance the cause. For this reason, the attorney must

---

[7] Canon 7, EC 7-4.

avoid areas in which he or she is not qualified.[8] In addition, the attorney cannot limit liability for incompetence.[9] In cases of doubt, co-counsel should be used or the employment declined.

Representing those accused of crimes is difficult, but the attorney is not to let fear of criticism from the bar, bench, or public prevent the exertion of all reasonable efforts on behalf of the client. Concern for public image must not stop the lawyer from advancing the client's cause to the utmost of training and ability. The lawyer must represent the client "zealously."[10] But in spite of the *Code,* an attorney is not expected to blindly support an unjust or immoral cause or a frivolous defense. In such cases, the lawyer may withdraw from the employment. In addition, if the client refuses "fair settlement" when offered, the lawyer may also withdraw.

Turning from the *Canons,* it next becomes important to examine a relationship that has just begun to develop and which exists *within* the usual attorney-client relationship. This is the "paralegal" movement.

PARALEGAL LAYPERSONS

In order to provide legal services in a more expeditious and economical manner, many lawyers and law firms are using "legal laypersons" or "legal assistants." It was found that laypersons – both male and female – fit well in the practice of law. This is not unlike "paramedics" who have proven their worth for several years..

The legal assistant movement began for a good reason. The practicing lawyer of 1900 was far ahead of other professionals, such as medical doctors, in individual income. By 1971 this was reversed and the legal practitioner was so inundated with trivial matters that the lawyer simply did not have the time to utilize talents in the way they should be used. And it was discovered that many of these duties could be delegated to assistants, freeing one to pursue the more important matters and issues of the practice of law.

The legal assistant is now being used in the large firms, but the greatest field of opportunity lies with the small firms and single practitioners. The demand for business students is particularly great, because the principles of management, finance, and even marketing, can be applied to law office operations.

Do the "Canons" Permit This?   Canon 3, EC 3–6, states: "A lawyer often delegates tasks to clerks, secretaries, and *other laypersons.* Such delegation is proper if the lawyer maintains a direct relationship with clients, supervises the delegated work, and has complete professional responsibility for the work product. This delegation enables the lawyer to render legal services more economically and efficiently." (Emphasis added.) Just what type of services do paralegals perform?

---

[8] Canon 6, EC 6–3.
[9] Canon 6, EC 6–6.
[10] Canon 7, EC 7–1.

Some Specific Examples. Lawyers who do trial work use paralegals to perform duties such as the following:

1. To prepare information needed to take depositions and interrogatories. The former are oral statements and the latter are written. Both are given under oath.
2. To "Shepardize" case decisions and do basic legal research. (See previous chapter for definition of "Shepardize.")
3. To assemble facts needed for interviews.
4. To collect data needed in the preparation of pleadings.
5. To conduct on-the-scene investigations of accident cases.

Lawyers in real estate practice delegate many duties to assistants. Examples include:

1. Determining taxes due on real estate so they may be prorated at closing.
2. Assembling tax receipt records.
3. Preparing settlement sheets for closings.
4. Scheduling closings.
5. Follow-up work on land transfers.

The general practitioner uses legal assistants to prepare corporate minutes, file motions with court clerks, check on trial schedules, and do routine jobs that were formerly performed by the lawyer. For example, one of the most time-consuming activities of the lawyer in some states is to attend the "calling of the docket." There is absolutely no reason why this simple function must be done by a lawyer.

It can be expected that the paralegal movement will find growth in the coming years. With this growth will come a developing body of case law that will arise out of their activities. Turning now from legal laypersons, lets examine the final topic of the chapter.

The final discussion is concerned with the types of legal services that are available and the ways in which the costs for these services are established and paid. The discussion is intended to be broad enough to include the services of the paralegal working under the supervision of counsel. The fees for the paralegal's services would be part of the overall legal fees charged.

WHAT DO LAWYERS DO?

Lawyers engage in a variety of events as they represent their clients, and the types of activities are endless. However, the functions of lawyers can be classified into four principal headings for purposes of discussion: (1) counseling, (2) negotiating, (3) representing lenders, and (4) litigation.

Counseling

Counseling requires knowledge of the law. It may consist of advice no more spectacular than "don't do it," or it may be advice contained in a written opinion developed after months of research and analysis. A lawyer who is "a wise counselor," is learned, experienced, and extremely valuable.

Negotiating

A lawyer frequently engages in negotiation. The lawyer may represent a union during the contract phase with employers, work out a property settlement in a pending divorce, or seek an adequate out-of-court settlement for an injured client. This function of the lawyer is important to clients and the courts because the cases that are settled out of court are not added to the backlog of cases. Lawyers have been particularly successful in negotiations involving contracts of athletes. Until their services were utilized, the "stars" were paid relatively low sums. With their services, the salaries for sports figures have risen into the hundreds of thousands of dollars per year – called "six figure contracts."

Representing Lenders

Lawyers represent banks who loan money to others for personal, business, or other uses. The lawyer must know the law of "security" and will prepare the documents by which the lender will find protection in the event of default by the debtor.

Litigation

The litigation function includes preparation of a case for trial; taking it through the preliminary stages and to a jury if negotiations for settlement fail. The trial of cases before a judge or jury is an art not easily acquired. Neither is the art of appeal, which is also a litigation function.

FORM OF LEGAL SERVICES

Legal services are available in a variety of forms. As it turns out, the ability to pay fees and costs often determines the form in which services are available. To begin with, many companies hire lawyers as employees.

House Counsel. Most larger companies have legal departments that are staffed by "kept counsel." These lawyers are hired on a salary basis and perform exclusive services for their employers. Many of these companies will permit the lawyers to handle legal matters for employees under company guidelines. It is not uncommon to find such lawyers moving from the legal department into positions in top management.

Medium size companies and many labor unions, are provided legal services on a "retainer" basis.

Annual Retainers. A lawyer who provides services on this basis, is paid a sum annually to make services available if they are needed. The retainer might be as low as $100 per year or as high as $100,000 per year.

While *a lawyer on retainer* is *not* an employee of the client, the retainer obligates the lawyer to give preferential services should they be required. In some instances no services are required at all in a given year.

Federal, state, and local governments provide civil and criminal legal services to those who qualify. These services are normally only available to those in lower income brackets.

Services Provided by Government. Civil legal service plans are provided in many of our cities and counties. These plans are labeled "Legal Aid Societies," "Neighborhood Legal Services," "Judicare," or some similar name. They provide services to qualified persons and assist them in landlord-tenant problems, contract disputes, and consumer complaints.

Where crimes are involved, legal services are provided by "Public Defenders" or "court appointments." The accused must file a "paupers affidavit" stating that the accused is without funds to hire counsel before these services will be made available.

A rapidly growing source of funds for legal services is provided by "prepaid legal services" plans.

Prepaid Legal Services

In the early 1970s, studies by the American Bar Association uncovered a startling fact: The Americans who were doing without legal services were those in the $5,000 to $15,000 per year income brackets! The poor were adequately provided for and so were the rich — but those in the middle income bracket were not.

The ABA funded a program to see how legal services could be made available to those in the middle income bracket. The original plan was started in Shreveport, Lousisiana, and has become known as the "Shreveport Plan." It was an instant success.

The prepaid plans take two forms: "open panels" in which the client can choose the lawyer and "closed panels" in which the client cannot.

Under these plans, the participants make payments into a fund, ranging from $1.75 to $9.50 per month. In return the participant is provided legal services on an annual basis. The following annual legal service is typical under prepaid plans:

1. Six hours of advice and consultation.
2. One will.
3. Two other legal documents plus services in such matters as bankruptcy; divorce; adoptions and real estate transfers.

Many plans provide "maximums" in dollars per year and most provide "deductibles." This means that the client will pay the first $10 or $20 for certain services.

These plans are much the same as Blue-Cross and other medical plans and are widely accepted today, particularly in labor unions.

At the time of the inception of the Shreveport Plan, employees could not bargain for prepaid legal services under the Labor Management Relations Act (Taft-Hartley Act) because the language in the act was not broad enough to cover legal services. Late in 1973, Congress by specific law[11] authorized prepaid legal services as a fringe benefit subject to collective bargaining. Also the law made the employee contributions tax deductible.

Some of the original adopters of prepaid legal services include Utah Credit Union League, labor unions in California, Vantage Corp. in Dallas and District Council 37 of the State, County and Municipal Employees Union of New York. There are now thousands of such plans throughout the United States.

FEES AND COSTS

Where house counsel and annual retainers are involved, the fees and costs are paid out of business revenue. The government-financed programs are funded out of local, state or federal revenues—and sometimes a combination of them. The prepaid plans are paid for out of contributions from the employees and are usually deducted from wages. Fees for legal services that are contracted for privately, are based upon "flat," "hourly," or "contingent" rates. (See Figure 5–2 for a sample of the cost of legal fees in 1803).

FIGURE 5–2

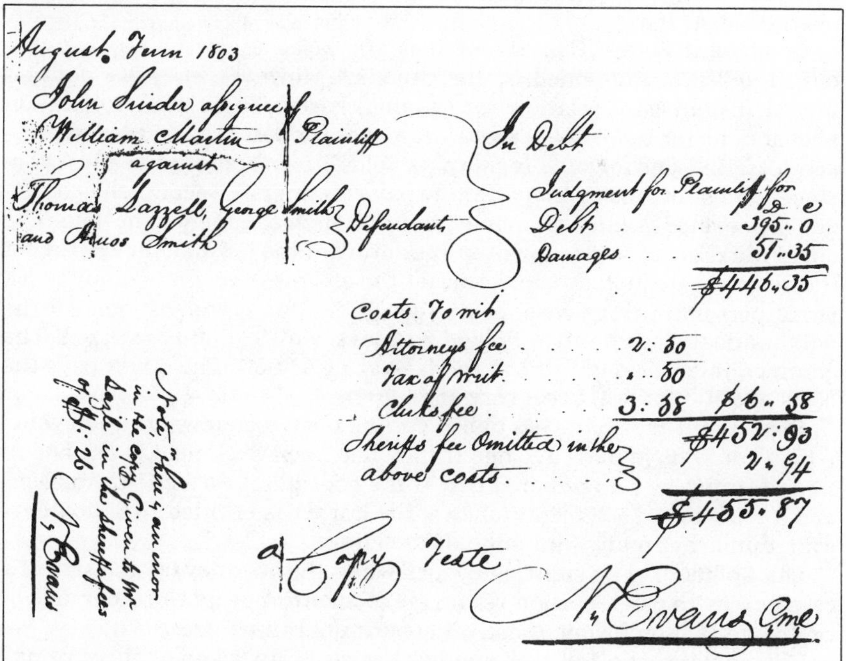

August Term 1803
John Snider assignee of William Martin — Plaintiff
against
Thomas Lazzell, George Smith and Amos Smith — Defendant
In Debt
Judgment for Plaintiff for

	$	c
Debt	395	0
Damages	51	35
	$446	35

Costs. To wit

Attorneys fee	2: 50	
Tax of writ	. 50	
Clerks fee	3: 58	$6. 58
		$452: 93
Sheriffs fee omitted in the above costs		2. 94
		$455. 87

A Copy Teste
N. Evans Cmc

Note, there is an error in the copy given to Mr. Lazzle in the sheriffs fees of $1: 26
N. Evans

From the author's collection.

[11] S.1423

Flat Fees. For many years, local bar associations created and made available to their members "Minimum Bar Fee Schedules." These contained suggested fees for standard services. In the early 1970s, these schedules came under attack as a form of price fixing in violation of the Sherman Anti-Trust Act. One challenge was in Virginia in *Goldfarb* v. *Virginia State Bar*,[12] in which the court held that schedules of fees were unconstitutional.

However, in June 1974, the Court of Appeals for the Fourth Circuit held that the Virginia State Bar Association is a quasi-official body and thus immune from such suits. The court also held that the legal profession is exempt from anti-trust regulations. The U.S. Supreme Court was then asked to pass on the issue. In June 1975, the Supreme Court held that fee schedules were a form of price fixing and thus unlawful. (See *Goldfarb* v. *Virginia State Bar*, 43 *U.S. Law Week* 4723 (1975).

Most bar associations had abandoned the fee schedules after the 1973 Virginia ruling, but a reminder of them exists in the "flat fees." These are fees that have become so standardized that most lawyers in the same locale make identical charges for them. Samples include preparation of deeds, options, contracts, wills, name changes, and adoptions.

Hourly Rates. Hourly rates are in widespread use for legal services including those under the prepaid plans. Rates run from $30 per hour up. In many instances this is the most inexpensive way in which to be charged legal fees.

Contingent Fees. Contingent fees are based upon the recovery obtained and are sanctioned by the canons.[13] However, they are not permitted in domestic relations or criminal cases. Their widest use is in civil actions for recovery of money damages for personal injury and property loss. Reasons for such fees are twofold. First, there is a need for them since many persons cannot afford to pay "retainers." Second, the contingent fee provides the *res* (money) out of which the fee will be paid. The client must understand, however, the nature of the fee and know whether the costs are deducted before or after the attorney fee. For example, in a small personal injury case, court fees, including compensation for the witness doctor, come to $300 and a recovery of $3,000 is realized. The contract calls for one third to the lawyer or $1,000. The client pays the costs of $300 for a net recovery of $1,700.

Contingent fees have led to bad feelings between lawyers and clients which could have been avoided if they had been explained in the beginning. It must be remembered that if the contract is on a one-third basis, and a recovery of $300,000 follows, the lawyer is entitled to $100,000 — something that many find difficult to believe.

Fee Splitting. Fee splitting occurs when the attorney on one side of a case agrees to pay a portion of the fee to an attorney on the other side in exchange for some concession and is criminal in nature.

The *sharing* of a fee with another lawyer is lawful on a "forwarding"

---

[12] 355 F. Supp. 491, E.D. Va. (1973.)

[13] Canon 2, EC 2–20.

basis provided the services of the other attorney are sought after full disclosure to the client, and does not result in more fees than if only one lawyer was involved. It is customary for attorneys to work on a one-third "forwarding fee," being one third of the one third that might be recovered in a personal injury case. Forwarding fees are not "fee splitting." It should be observed that fee sharing will never be with the lawyer on the *opposite* side of a case. It will always be with a lawyer who will work with the one who is sharing the fee. Forwarding fees are widely used in real estate and contract work where work must be done in another state but the client wishes to use the services of the homestate lawyer. One final matter is of importance to one in business.

Are Legal Fees Tax Deductible?

This question is difficult to answer because it will vary from situation to situation. However, legal fees fall into one of three categories and sometimes one fee can be divided into two or even three of these groupings.

1. Some fees are "ordinary and necessary" business expense. Under Section 162 (a) of the Internal Revenue Code, these fees are deductible in the year in which they are incurred.
2. Other fees must be "capitalized" (added to the capital value of a business). These must be depreciated under Section 167 (a), or taken as a depletion allowance under Section 611 (a). This means that only a portion of certain fees can be deducted each year and this continues each year for the life of the value of the services. In some instances, deductions are deferred until the item is sold that was improved by the services. At that time the fees would be allowed as a deduction against income realized.
3. In many instances legal fees are not deductible at all. This is true when they are simply "personal living expenses."

In any event, as we incur legal fees, we should make careful note of why the fees were incurred and make this information available to our accountant. The final decision on deductibility should be left up to the C.P.A. or accountant.

TERMINATION OF THE RELATIONSHIP

The courts have held that in the attorney-client employment agreement, there is an implied right on the part of the client to discharge the attorney at will. Therefore, the client has the power to terminate the relationship at any time—and without notice. On the other hand, it is clear that the attorney may only withdraw for good cause. And even then, a lawyer cannot withdraw under circumstances that might leave the client legally unprotected—even for the shortest period of time. The lawyer must give full notice so the client has an opportunity to obtain counsel to "cover." The lawyer—even when being fired—must make every effort to prevent even the smallest harm being done to the client's cause.

REVIEW QUESTIONS

1. A reasonable prediction would be that the contingent fee contracts will come under fire in the near future. Based upon the attacks on the minumum bar fee schedules, why might this happen?
2. The Uniform Commercial Code provides that judges may refuse to enforce contracts that they find to be "unconscionable." Might someone raise this point of law in reference to contingent fee contracts?
3. How might clients in the future be *injured* if contingent fees are eliminated?
4. How might future clients *benefit* from it?
5. True or False. *The Code of Professional Responsibility* was written to protect the lawyer and legal assistants.
6. Zero Corporation purchased a warehouse for $98,000 and paid their lawyer $3,000 for services in relation to the purchase. Is this most likely a "current business expense" or one that must be depreciated over the life of the building?
7. Give an example of how you think a "deductible" in prepaid legal services would work.
8. True or False. A "closed panel" under a prepaid plan permits the client to select the lawyer.
9. What business reason can be suggested for the use of "house counsel"?
10. Does the *Goldfarb* attack upon bar fee schedules indicate dissatisfaction with legal fees? (Goldfarb is a lawyer and a member of the Virginia Bar. In the course of buying a house, he had been quoted an identical fee by over a dozen lawyers).

Words and Phrases

Write out briefly what they mean to you.
1. "Res."
2. Contingent fee contract.
3. Refusing clients.
4. "Day in court."
5. Fiduciary relationship.

Coverage:	A look at the regulations that guide the judge on the bench.
What to Look for:	The restrictions placed upon judges.
Application:	How might these restrictions affect a business contract case in court?

6 Those Who Judge

Thou shalt not wrest judgment; thou shalt not respect persons, neither take a gift; for a gift doth blind the eye of the wise, and pervert the words of the righteous.

—Deuteronomy XVI:19

The word "court" is often used to mean "judge." The traditional opening statement to the judge, "May it please the court," illustrates the point. A judge is a public officer appointed or elected to preside over and administer law in some court of justice. The judge is charged with control of court proceedings and has the power to make decisions on questions of law. In addition, the judge has a wide area of discretion. The grant of certain powers to the federal government and the reservation of others to the states created a double system of courts in America. This resulted in a dual system of judges. The areas of jurisdiction (power) of federal and state judges are therefore separate and distinct although their duties and responsibilities are similar—and there are quite a large number of judges in some states.

The U.S. Census Bureau has reported that there are 41,000 persons in the United States for each major trial judge. In Vermont, there is one judge for each 13,000 persons. In South Carolina, North Carolina, and Massachusetts, there is one for every 100,000 population. The largest percentage of these would be state and not federal judges.

FEDERAL JUDGES

Federal judges are appointed by the President of the United States and confirmed by the U.S. Senate. Controversy often arises out of these appointments. The political character of the person under consideration may form the basis for acceptance or rejection of the appointment. Or concern about a "shift in power" may come into issue, when one is being considered for an appeals court.

Federal judges must be residents and citizens of the United States and the appointment system makes it mandatory that they be qualified by training, reputation, and experience. The term of office and the source of their compensation is found in Article III, Section I of the U.S. Constitution:

> ... The Judges, both of the supreme and inferior Courts, shall hold their office during good Behavior, and shall, at stated Times, receive for their services, a Compensation, which shall not be diminished during their continuance in Office.

The appointment amounts to a lifetime job in most instances. However, retirement at a specific age is under current discussion.

Circuit Riders

Judges of the federal district courts and the federal courts of appeal are called upon from time to time to sit on other courts. Sickness or disability may make this necessary. In some cases, federal judges may disqualify themselves from hearing a case.

The geographical area in which a federal judge may sit is not restricted by state boundaries since the federal system extends throughout the states. However, the federal courts have specific geographical areas and these follow state lines or are wholly contained within a state—at least at the present time.

STATE JUDGES

State constitutions and statutes spell out the qualifications of state judges. One state constitution provides:

> They (State Supreme Court Judges) shall be elected by the voters of the State and hold their office for a term of twelve years, unless sooner removed ...

A residency requirement of five years prior to seeking office, a minimum age of 30 years, and a term of office of eight years are typical provisions. As to whether judges must be lawyers or have legal training, an interesting situation exists.

Law schools as we know them today did not exist during the early years of America and one studied law by reading under the guidance of an older lawyer—an apprentice system of sorts. As a result of this, there was no requirement that a judge be a lawyer, or for that matter, trained in law. The rule still prevails in most states and a degree in law or legal training is not prerequisite to holding the office of state judge. However, as a practical matter, the great majority of state judges are competent attorneys and experienced trial lawyers.

Removal of a judge from office must be for good cause and a full hearing is required. Removal cases are rare and few are found in the law books. Vacancies on state courts are filled by the governor, or other designated official or political body, and the new judge serves until the next election. State trial judges, as distinguished from appellate or state supreme court judges, are elected by the voters of the circuit, district, or county over which they will preside. States with larger populations or those that have special courts in larger cities may have different provisions.

A judge may decide that it would be improper to hear and decide a given case. Reasons, such as personal friendship with a person who stands accused of a crime in court; or personal interest in the pending litigation; or fear of not being able to remain impartial in the trial of a certain case, are often cited. In these instances, the judge will make arrangements for another judge to handle the trial in the other judges court—called "removal." However the new judge would have the right to refuse to hear the case if the judge felt it would be improper to do so. Guidelines for removal are provided by statute and notice to the parties involved and the court to which removal is sought are required.

A situation involving "removal" must be distinguished from a "change of venue."

CHANGE OF VENUE

A "change of venue" (location of the trial) is frequently requested by one accused of a crime. Reasons often cited include prejudice against the accused or unnecessary and prejudicial publicity. Whether the motion is granted is in the discretion of the judge to whom it is directed. If granted, the case is sent to another state court for trial. If the motion is refused, the accused often appeals to a higher court on these grounds.

Turning from the requirements of becoming a federal or state judge, it next becomes important to examine the rules and standards by which judges are expected to carry out their judicial responsibilities on—as well as off—the bench.

THE CODE OF JUDICIAL CONDUCT

On July 9, 1924, the American Bar Association adopted the *Canons of Judicial Ethics.* For over one-half century these 34 canons served well, yet it became obvious that they were not tuned to a society of the 1970s.

At the annual meeting of the ABA held at San Francisco in August, 1972, the *Code of Judicial Conduct* was adopted.

The *Code* provides the basis for the following discussion.

The judge is reminded of the high nature of judicial responsibilities and is told that the courts exist to create justice both speedy and careful. The warning is given to avoid

> ... falling into the attitude of mind that the litigants are made for the courts instead of the courts for the litigants.

The judge is urged to hear both sides of a matter because "qui aliquid statuerit, parte inadita aequum lecit dixerit, haud aequum fecerit"—he who determines any matter without hearing both sides, though he may have decided right, has not done justice. The judge should be temperate, attentive, patient, and impartial.[1] The judge must study the law and make a diligent effort to determine the facts before rendering a decision of law.

If the question to be decided is one for jury determination (a question of fact), the judge must be certain that the parties have an opportunity to present the facts to the jury so that the decision will be fair. The judge is reminded to be courteous to the attorneys who practice in court, especially those who are young and inexperienced. The judge is told to make certain that clerks and other officers of the court (attorneys are officers of the court) are courteous to those who have business in the court, whether they be jurors, witnesses, or litigants. A judge must support the United States Constitution and the constitution of the state and in so doing should ". . . uphold the integrity and independence of the judiciary."[2]

The influence that a judge's decisions may have upon the development of law cannot be ignored. A current decision must be made with one eye on heritage but with the other on posterity. The judge ". . . may engage in activities to improve the law, the legal system, and the administration of justice,"[3] but must guard against allowing a personal consideration in a given case to be used as a reason to disregard general law that is binding on the court. Such practice could result in the unsettling of settled principles and cause damage far beyond the immediate controversy since others in the future may be affected.

Politics. Most state constitutions and the *Code,*[4] prohibit a judge from becoming involved in politics. The prohibition extends to political speeches, soliciting funds for political purposes, and endorsing candidates for political office. A judge cannot accept a place on a political committee or engage in partisan activities. However, campaigning for elections as judge is not prohibited because it is necessary. The judge does not lose the right to state personal views on political questions and does not have to surrender rights and opinions as a citizen. Nevertheless, this happens in actual practice.

Social Circles. A judge cannot live in seclusion, yet "over activity" in social relations causes problems that overlap into other restrictions discussed. Therefore, while encouraged to maintain active membership in the bar association, judges are told to avoid social or business relationships that might lend suspicion in litigation to the end that decisions of the court might be questioned.

Practice Law? Most states prohibit their judges from engaging in the practice of law (with some exceptions). The constitution of one state provides:

> No judge during the term of office, shall practice the profession of law or hold any other office, appointment or public trust, under this, or any other

---

[1] *Code of Judicial Conduct,* The American Bar Association, Canon 3.

[2] Ibid., Canon 1.

[3] Ibid., Canon 4.

[4] Ibid., Canon 7.

government, if the acceptance shall vacate the judicial office. Nor shall the judge, during continuance therein, be eligible to any political office.[5]

Some states do not have such restrictions and the canons recognize that some counties or cities, especially where inferior courts are involved (courts of petty jurisdiction), may not be able to pay adequate compensation to a judge. In this type of situation, the practice of law is permitted because it is necessary. In cases where the judge practices law a position of "great delicacy" arises and the judge must scrupulously avoid conduct that utilizes, or appears to utilize, the judicial position to further personal professional success.

Other Prohibitions. Writing or lecturing upon the subject of law is not prohibited unless those activities disturb the judicial duties, which always come first. A judge may receive compensation and reimbursement of expenses for the quasi-judicial and extra-judicial activities permitted by the *Code*, if the source of such payments does not give the appearance of influencing the judge in judicial duties or otherwise give the appearance of impropriety.

Investments in businesses which become involved in litigation in court are forbidden and investments made prior to election must be disposed of within a reasonable time after taking office. The position cannot be used for speculation of any nature and relationships that arouse suspicion of judgment or impartiality in carrying out judicial duties must be avoided.

Dispatch and Discipline. "Prompt and convenient discharge" of the business of the court is required. The judge should not tolerate negligence and carelessness by clerks and others who assist in the judicial process. Occasionally, the conduct of attorneys who practice before the court becomes unprofessional. When this happens, the judge must criticize those who engage in such misconduct and in extreme cases refer the matter to the proper disciplinary committee of the local bar or state bar. The Judge may also cite the attorney for contempt of court if the circumstances warrant the action.

Court proceedings must be conducted in a manner that reflects the importance and seriousness of the matter at hand, no matter how trivial it may seem to some. A judge should avoid interference with the conduct of the trial through inquiry or statements which might influence the outcome of the case. However, the judge may intervene in order to expedite the trial or clear up questions, but undue influence or impatience must be avoided.

Retirement. Judges, as other human beings, become tired and "out of touch" as age increases. One suggestion is to require that all judges state and federal, retire by the age of 70 – a rule in effect in some 20 states by statutory law.

What about Cameras in the Courtroom?

A judge should prohibit broadcasting, televising, recording, or taking photographs in the courtroom and areas immediately adjacent, during

---

[5] West Virginia Constitution, Article VII, Section 16.

sessions of court or recesses between sessions, except that a judge may authorize: (*a*) the use of electronic or photographic means for the presentation of evidence, for the perpetuation of a record, or for other purposes of judicial administration; (*b*) the broadcasting, televising, recording, or photographing of investitive, ceremonial, or naturalization proceedings; (*c*) the photographic or electronic recording and reproduction of appropriate court proceedings under the following conditions; (1) the means of recording will not distract participants or impair the dignity of the proceedings; (2) the parties have consented, and the consent to being photographed or recorded has been obtained from each witness appearing in the recording and reproduction; (3) the reproduction will not be exhibited until after the proceeding has been concluded and all appeals have been exhausted; and (4) the reproduction will be exhibited only for instructional purposes in educational institutions.[6]

OTHERS WHO JUDGE

A "judge," in the simplest sense, is a member of society who is chosen by one means or another, to pass judgment upon others within that society. And many persons outside of our conventional courts are "judges" within this meaning. Samples include bankruptcy judges, "small claims" judges, police judges, mayors as judges, and justices of the peace—called "magistrates" in some states.

New Federal Judges

In October 1964, Congress gave the Supreme Court of the United States the power to create new procedural provisions for the Bankruptcy Act. After nearly a decade of study, new rules were enacted and became effective October 1, 1973.

From the time of the enactment of the original Bankruptcy Act of 1898, those who administered the law in the federal courts were known as "referees." In these courts, lawyers and others have been uncertain of the status of the referees and the amount of courtesy that should be extended to them. They were simply not treated as being judges.

Under the new rules, the old referees are now judges and they are called "Judges in Bankruptcy." This change came about primarily to enhance the prestige of the office.

Small Claims Judges

In an effort to erase some of the court log-jam, small claims courts have been developed in the larger cities. The Los Angeles system is typical. There the plaintiff files a claim with the court clerk and a summons is issued ordering the defendant to appear.

The judge calls the case at the designated time. The defendant may

---

[6] *Code of Judicial Conduct*, Canon 6.

appear, but in many instances does not. The court asks the plaintiff to explain the complaint. Since the vast majority of the cases heard in the Los Angeles Small Claims Court involve minor auto accidents, a large "road board" and model cars are available for the plaintiff to show the judge what happened. If the defendant appears, the defendant has a turn to explain. While witnesses may be called, the proceedings are informal. The judge listens to both – if present – and renders an opinion in the form of a "judgment." Either party may appeal – but most do not. These courts dispose of cases that might otherwise go into circuit court. The judges of such courts are usually appointed and in a few instances, are members of the bar assigned to the duty for a prescribed period of time. The court is limited in jurisdiction to the sum of $200, meaning that the judge has no power to hear and decide matters where more than that amount is involved.

The Trend Continues.[7] Small claims courts are proliferating and a number of states are considering them on a statewide basis. Also, several states have already instituted these on a statewide basis. For example, the state of Michigan has established a small claims court within each district court, which has a limited jurisdiction as to amount, which was originally $300 but was being considered for an increase several years ago. In the small claims court the filing fee is substantially reduced and the clerk of the district court has an obligation to aid a plantiff in filling out the complaint, which does not have to be in legal terminology. It can be simply a running commentary of the case as the plantiff sees it. Additionally, no lawyers are allowed to represent clients in a small claims court. Therefore each party must represent themself. However, because no trial by jury is permissible and because no representation is allowed, either party has the right to have a case removed to the regular court docket. This may frustrate the purpose of a small claims court, since the defendant may remove to the regular docket, consequently retaining an attorney to represent her or him. However, it is felt that the majority of minor cases within this limited jurisdiction will remain within the small claims court, and it has to date served to reduce court congestion at the district level as well as providing a forum for the lower income individual to obtain relief through the court system. However, it is administered through the regular court system and the district judge is also the small claims judge. The judge is not bound by rules of evidence as would be required in the regular court docket. It is also an informal procedure and the hearing frequently will take place in the judge's chambers rather than in the regular courtroom, with the judge asking whatever questions are appropriate and necessary to ascertain the facts and make a legal decision. Also the decision of a small claims court is final, with no right to appeal. This of course applies only if both parties have submitted to the jurisdiction of the small claims court, either by voluntarily appearing or by failing to file an answer and thereby losing by default. (Michigan

---

[7] The author extends thanks to Myron L. Erickson, the University of Missouri, for the following information on small claim courts in the state of Michigan.

varies in this respect from the Los Angeles court where an appeal is permitted.)

Police Judges

Most cities maintain a police court, headed by a police judge, who hears and decides law infractions that arise in the city. A police judge spends a lot of time hearing and disposing of parking fines, city traffic violations, assault and battery cases, and minor theft cases where city police make the arrests. The typical police judge holds another full-time job; is appointed by the city manager or mayor; is not a lawyer; and holds court early in the morning or late in the evening to gear the sessions to changes of police shifts so that the patrol officers involved may be present to testify. The proceedings are informal but may take on aspects of a regular trial if the defendant has counsel who calls witnesses to testify. One who is arrested by city police may demand that the case be transferred to the county circuit court. The only good reason for such a move is to obtain a trial by jury. But a word of caution is in order: In the majority of cases, the accused fares better in a police court than in a county circuit court. The fees are less, the fines are smaller, there is no prolonged delay and publicity is normally avoided.

Mayors as Judges

In many incorporated towns and cities, the mayor serves as a part-time judge and hears and decides town legal matters. Most states permit mayors to levy fines up to a set amount and to imprison for short periods of time, such as 30 days. Appeals from mayor's courts are usually to the county circuit court. In unincorporated towns there is no way that a mayor's court can be maintained because there is no way that taxes can be collected with which to pay the mayor's salary.

Justices of the Peace

The justice of the peace evolved from the early English system where "squires" had jurisdiction in portions of the "shires" and "hundreds." Today, the squire is elected in the district of the county where the office is to be located. Different states have different titles for this type of "judge," such as "magistrate," or "borough squire."

The jurisdiction of the squire is limited to a prescribed sum of money ($300 is typical) and in criminal matters the squire may imprison up to one year. In some states (Maryland, for example) the squire may perform marriages. The typical squire is a part-time person, untrained in law, and in some cases with no experience at all for the job.

Litigants may have their case tried by a jury in this court if demanded and if the required fees are paid in advance.

In many states the justice of peace courts are "constitutional" because they are provided for in the state constitution. Police courts are almost always "statutory courts," created by state law or by city ordinance.

As a rule, a justice of the peace court, although a constitutional court, has no criminal jurisdiction unless there is "enabling legislation." Therefore, the state legislature could abolish criminal jurisdiction by an act of the lawmakers, thus reducing the jurisdiction of the J.P. courts.

The system has been under fire in recent years and some states have abolished the office. Other states have limited the power of the J.P. One state recently made it unlawful for a J.P. to collect accounts for businesses. The "evil" found in the J.P. court is that the squire operates on a "fee basis." That is, the J.P. is paid no salary and must "find guilt" in order to be paid. This tends to make one partial or biased. Of the 33 states that still maintain the J.P. system, 28 compensate the "squire" out of fees collected from the cases heard. In addition, the trial lawyers frequently complain of the quality of the preliminary hearings their clients receive in the J.P. courts. Many of these "judges" seem to be disinterested in the proceedings before them and routinely bind the accused over to the grand jury of the county. Many times this occurs when the J.P. should have dismissed the charges in this court.

In the states that still maintain the J.P. system, interested persons are advocating that the J.P. be replaced with some other system. The one most frequently mentioned is based upon the "magistrate system" in use in the federal courts as the accompanying news item—fictionalized— illustrates.

In spite of the criticism of the J.P. system, they still serve useful functions. They issue "peace warrants," "distress warrants" for the collection

---

First Magistrate to Take Oath Soon

NEXT TOWN—A modernization of the first level of the federal judicial system will take place next month when Maryanne Martin becomes the state's first U.S. magistrate.

U.S. District Court Judge Michael Rogers, in announcing Martin's appointment, set in motion a restructuring operation that will replace the 178-year-old U.S. commissioner system with one composed of formally trained and salaried magistrates.

Judge Rogers also plans to appoint four part-time magistrates to serve the 31-county area in the jurisdiction of the northern district court.

A spokesperson for the U.S. District Court said federal judges Frank Jury and Nancy Day were still studying ways of implementing the new system.

The magistrates, who must be attorneys, can be assigned additional duties designed to ease the caseloads of the federal court system. Also the magistrates are given authority to preside over cases that can carry fines up to $1,000 and jail terms of one year.

Previously, commissioners were allowed to handle only cases involving up to a $500 fine and a six-month imprisonment.

Martin, a former U.S. attorney, will serve an eight-year term with offices here.

of past due rent, and handle countless small claims matters. Any whole-sale abolishment of the J.P. system must be accompanied by something to take its place. One frequently mentioned possibility is to replace the J.P. with arbitration panels.

Arbitration Panels

Many courts of general jurisdiction are using arbitration panels to assist in disposing of the civil backlog. The system in use in Allegheny County, Pennsylvania, is representative, if not typical. On the day that the civil docket is called, the docket room in the Pittsburgh courthouse is jammed with litigants and lawyers. As each case is called, responses such as "plaintiff is present" and "defendant is present" are heard in the crowded room. If no appearance is made, the case is continued. If both parties are present, they are given a choice: trial by jury in three to five years—or by a three-person panel that will arbitrate the matter the same day. If both sides agree to arbitration, the case is assigned to a hearing room. The arbitrators are three members of the local bar, serving for that day. The hearing is brief, yet formal rules of procedure are followed. After the hearing, the panel renders an "award" which states how they decided the case. Either party may appeal within a designated time period.

Arbitration is compulsory in Allegheny and Philadelphia Counties in Pennsylvania where civil disputes of under the sum of $1,000.00 are involved. This "jurisdictional amount" varies from county to county in that state. Arbitration works well in the courts in Pennsylvania and provides one solution to the growing backlog of civil cases in our courts. Arbitration *cannot* be used to hear and decide criminal cases, however.

REVIEW QUESTIONS

1. How could the change of one person on a nine-person court alter the policies and the decisions of that court?
2. Do you know of recent appointments to judgeships?
3. Does your state use the J.P. system?
4. Does your state have small claims courts?
5. True or False. A judge may refuse to hear a case if the judge's relative will be called as a witness.
6. True or False. The U.S. Constitution states that federal judges shall receive compensation "during their natural lifetimes."
7. Give two reasons why judges should be elected and not appointed.
8. Give two reasons why they should be appointed and not elected.
9. State one argument for voluntary retirement of judges at a set age and one against it.
10. Can you see a constitutional issue where mayors are paid salaries out of fines that they collect? What is it? Why isn't this a "civil rights" matter rather than a constitutional issue?

Words and Phrases

Write out briefly what they mean to you.
1. Courts of limited jurisdiction.
2. Arbitration.
3. "Social circles."
4. Fee system.
5. Decorum in court.

Coverage:	Introduction to courts.
What to Look for:	The functions of the personnel of the court.
Application:	All business legal situations must be viewed with a knowledge of what can happen if suit is filed.

7 Courts—An Introduction

Darrow's mapped route for the trial had reached dead end—in a legal and educational dump. He had argued that the Butler Act violated freedom of speech and religion. The judge had overruled him. He had planned to show that the Act was too vague to be valid because the theory of evolution and the Bible both required interpretation. He had also planned to show that the Act was not a reasonable exercise of the police power because the evidence of evolution was overpowering. The judge had blocked both those roads. So Darrow sought to by-pass the road blocks by opening a new road. He bulldozed it, ruthlessly. Arthur Hays later implied that the events of Monday, July 20, were unpremeditated. Actually Darrow had written the script in his 55 questions about Genesis, addressed to Bryan and printed in the Chicago Tribune *on July 4, 1923.*

—Ray Ginger, Six Days or Forever?

An exhaustive treatise of the American court system would fill many volumes, require years to complete, and when completed, would be obsolete. That type of study is beyond our objective here, which is to present a concise, up-to-date, yet thorough, picture of the American court system—in a simplified manner. The material that follows will provide a satisfactory foundation upon which further study may be undertaken.

First, examine the drawing of Typical State, U.S.A., Figure 7–2.

The state has 41 counties; Capital City is located in Capital County in

---

[1] Ray Ginger, *Six Days or Forever?* (New York: Signet Books, The New American Library of World Literature, 1958), p. 129. (See Figure 7–1).

FIGURE 7-1
The Rhea County Courthouse, Dayton, Tennessee, Site of the "Scopes Monkey Trial" in July, 1925.

Photo by the author.

the southern part of the state. The seat of government, including the governor's mansion, the state legislature, and the state supreme court, is located there. Anytown is located in King County and it is the second largest city in the state. Crystal River flows between Anytown and Next Town, and is a "navigable" river; that is, a body of water wide enough and deep enough to afford a useful channel for commerce.

The eastern boundary of Typical State is the western edge of Big River. This means that the boundary of the state to the east extends across the river. The question of where the state boundary line is located can become of importance in litigation. For example, if A, while swimming in Big River, is struck by B, who negligently drives a motorboat, Typical State or the federal courts of that state would probably *not* have jurisdiction to hear the case since the negligent act occurred in another state.

The legislature created 30 "judicial circuits" in the state and has provided that a full-time judge shall preside over each. The counties that contain Anytown and Capital City have large concentrations of population; therefore, each is a judicial circuit within itself. Since the outlying counties are sparsely populated, the legislature combined certain counties to form larger circuits. Therefore, the state has 31 principal state courts—one in each of the 30 circuits plus the supreme court at Capital City. Each county has justice of the peace courts.

FIGURE 7-2
Typical State, U.S.A.

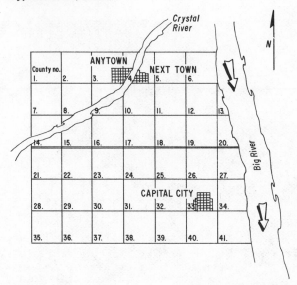

The heavy line across the center of the state, which follows county boundaries, is the dividing line between the two federal district courts located within the state. They are called "The United States Federal District Courts for the Northern and Southern Districts" of the state. Each district is presided over by a federal judge. These judges are "circuit riders" since they travel to different towns in their districts. It is not uncommon for the federal government to have several courtrooms in one district. The courtrooms are customarily located in U.S. post offices or other federal buildings. This permits suits to be filed and arraignments (all federal) to be held close to where the parties to the dispute reside or where a suspect is arrested on a federal charge.

An understanding of the court makeup of the fictitious state makes it easier to examine similar facts in other states. The state of West Virginia has been chosen for comparison as being a representative compromise between large and small states (see Figure 7-3).

While West Virginia has 55 counties, it only has 29 judicial circuits. Fourteen counties make up single judicial districts, while the balance are combined with one or more counties to form the other 15 circuits. Each circuit is presided over by at least one judge—while some of the more densely populated circuits have more than one. For example, some of the circuits have both civil and criminal judges who operate separate courts.

The state contains two federal district courts, one for the northern and one for the southern district. The heavy dotted line is the dividing line between the two districts and follows county lines. The federal judge in

FIGURE 7-3
Map, West Virginia Judicial Circuits

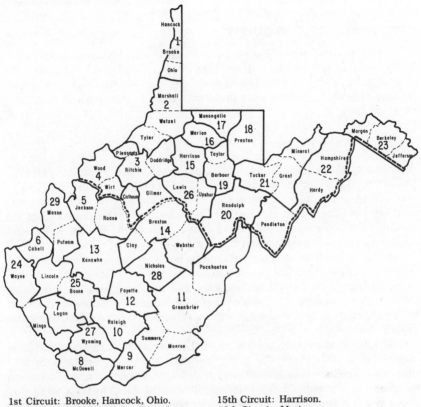

1st Circuit: Brooke, Hancock, Ohio.
2d Circuit: Marshall, Tyler, Wetzel.
3d Circuit: Doddridge, Pleasants, Ritchie.
4th Circuit: Wirt, Wood.
5th Circuit: Calhoun, Jackson, Roane.
6th Circuit: Cabell.
7th Circuit: Logan.
8th Circuit: McDowell.
9th Circuit: Mercer.
10th Circuit: Raleigh.
11th Circuit: Greenbrier, Monroe, Pocahontas,
    Summers.
12th Circuit: Fayette.
13th Circuit: Kanawha.
14th Circuit: Braxton, Clay, Gilmer, Webster.

15th Circuit: Harrison.
16th Circuit: Marion.
17th Circuit: Monongalia.
18th Circuit: Preston.
19th Circuit: Barbour, Taylor.
20th Circuit: Randolph.
21st Circuit: Grant, Mineral, Tucker.
22d Circuit: Hampshire, Hardy, Pendleton.
23d Circuit: Berkeley, Jefferson, Morgan.
24th Circuit: Mingo, Wayne.
25th Circuit: Boone, Lincoln.
26th Circuit: Lewis, Upshur.
27th Circuit: Wyoming.
28th Circuit: Nicholas.
29th Circuit: Mason, Putnam.

Note: The heavy dotted line separates the two federal district courts.

the northern district travels to different parts of the district. For example, the judge holds court in Fairmont, Elkins, Wheeling, Clarksburg, and other West Virginia cities. The state has a "roving" federal judge who hears and decides cases in both the northern and southern districts. This judge is able to lift the burden when the dockets become overcrowded.

Next it is helpful to become acquainted with those who operate the courts.

PERSONNEL OF THE COURTS

A working understanding of the judicial system requires some familiarity with those who make it operate—both directly and indirectly. We tend to assume that judges and lawyers run the system and this is not so. A large number of persons are involved—even in the smallest court in a rural county.

1. Clerk of the Court

Each court—federal, state, trial, appellate, police, or small claims— has a person designated as the "clerk" of the court. The clerk may have a specialized name such as "recorder," "circuit clerk," "master," "trustee" or other—but the duties are similar. The functions of the clerk's office are twofold: first, to receive and process the papers of the lawsuits; and second, to index and preserve court records for future use.

Once a suit is filed, all original papers, such as motions, notices, memorandums of law, and the like, are deposited with the clerk, who "clocks" them in, files them in appropriate files, and indexes them for reference. In the case of "orders," the judge must sign them before they are entered. When appeals are taken, the clerk prepares and forwards all papers to the proper court.

The citizen is usually not aware of the operation of the clerk's office. Since the records there are public records, they may be examined by those who are interested. To illustrate: A business person who has reason to believe a debtor has been sued can obtain the facts quickly from this office. Such information may prove valuable in making a decision about future dealings with that debtor. A few records are "privileged"—that is, not open for public inspection, such as adoptions—and divorce cases in some states.

In most states, the clerk plays an active part in the election process. It is the clerk's duty to prepare ballots, both regular and absentee, and coordinate the election with the county court. In courts in which the judge is elected by popular vote, the clerk also runs for office. In the federal system where judges are appointed, the clerk is appointed—often by the judge.

2. Clerk of the County Court

It is easy to confuse the "clerk of the county court" with the "clerk of the circuit court." In some states different names are used and Pennsylvania provides a good example. That state has done away with the "county court" and has replaced it with the "Common Pleas Court." The clerk of that court is called the "Prothonotary." Pennsylvania also has an "Orphans Court." The clerk is called the "Registrar of Wills"—an interesting comparison of terms. This tells us that the name of the clerk does not necessarily indicate the type of work that a particular clerk performs.

Regardless of the names, they are best distinguished from the clerks of the trial and appellate courts by the duties they perform. The clerk keeps the records of the county *other* than the court records. Found here will be deeds, deeds of trust, mortgages, birth and death records, marriage records, discharge papers of veterans, financing statements filed in secured transactions, plats, estate records, indexes to and charters of corporations, and many more. The clerk's office is a storehouse of material for one who has the ability to use it. The records here are true citizens' records—because they are the records of the citizens. Lawyers make wide use of the office in doing title searches for clients and in settling estates—and so do citizens. Most "family trees" can be traced from the county court records.

The clerk's office is the first stop for one who wants to know the credit standing of another. The records here will disclose judgments, tax liens, unsettled estates, tax assessments, and many other matters routinely inquired into by business persons. The office is a prime source of data for local and national credit bureaus.

The clerk is usually elected for a term provided by statute. There is no comparable office in the federal system since it would be pointless for the federal government to duplicate what has already been recorded here. (However, the federal government has been filming data from county court records and storing it at a central location.) The filing and recording procedures are perpetual and great care is used to assure that the records are recorded properly and indexed accurately.

The clerk has personal duties such as preparing ballot boxes for elections and coordinating with the proper persons for the creation of voting precincts. The clerk also maintains the voting records in the county. One other nonpublicized function of some clerks is to receive petitions in lunacy matters and to coordinate such hearings between the proper officials.

All courts, large and small must be financed in some manner. This important function is carried out by the "taxing and budgeting" authorities.

3. The Assessor or Tax Officer

The assessor is an elected county official who, through field agents and office staff, performs two basic functions: makes estimates of the value of real and personal property owned by citizens in the county, or area of jurisdiction, and levies taxes upon the property. The tax rates are based upon percentages allowable in the state in question. Figure 7–4 illustrates the procedure.

The assessor has the power to increase evaluations, which results in an increased tax levy. The assessor provides the basis upon which taxes are collected thus playing a direct part in the court process. But the levies

FIGURE 7–4

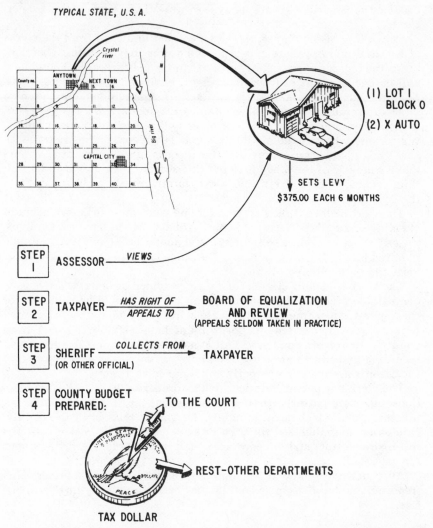

TYPICAL STATE, U.S.A.

(I) LOT I
BLOCK 0

(2) X AUTO

SETS LEVY
$375.00 EACH 6 MONTHS

| STEP 1 | ASSESSOR —— *VIEWS* |

| STEP 2 | TAXPAYER —— *HAS RIGHT OF APPEALS TO* → BOARD OF EQUALIZATION AND REVIEW (APPEALS SELDOM TAKEN IN PRACTICE) |

| STEP 3 | SHERIFF (OR OTHER OFFICIAL) —— *COLLECTS FROM* → TAXPAYER |

| STEP 4 | COUNTY BUDGET PREPARED: — TO THE COURT — REST-OTHER DEPARTMENTS |

TAX DOLLAR

are of little value if the taxes are not collected. This duty falls upon the chief executive officer of the county—the sheriff—or some other elected or appointed official.

4.   The Sheriff

The Saxon word "shire" signified an indefinite number of "hundreds," later called counties. The word "reeve" is the Saxon word for "bailiff." At common law the sheriff was the "bailiff" of the county, and the "viscount" of the Anglo-Normans. As time passed, the bailiff of a county, the "shire reeve," became known simply as the "sheriff."

The office of the sheriff was the King's representative in old England. It is probably the oldest office still in operation in the United States today. The first sheriffs offices were established in the colonies of Maryland and Virginia in the 1630s. The National Association of County Officials tells us that there are 3,099 sheriffs in the United States today and of that number, 3,088 were elected to office.

Many of the duties of the sheriff are related to court functions such as service of "process," service of subpoenas upon witnesses and jurors, and protection of the court when in session.

In addition, the sheriff provides police service for the county; maintains the county jail, and in general serves as the "chief conservator of the peace" for the jurisdiction.

In many states, and counties in those states, the sheriff or those who work through that office—collect taxes that are levied by the assessor. In some states the sheriff is paid a percentage of the taxes collected above a certain amount due. This can be lucrative in populated areas but at the same time, serves as an incentive to keep tax collections as high as possible.

In the role as tax collector, the sheriff takes part in the maintenance of the judicial system. This is true because part of the tax dollars collected is budgeted to the court. The budgeting is done by "county commissioners"—or some similar panel of administrative officials. In many states these commissioners are known as the "county court."

5. County Court

The internal affairs of the counties in various states are managed by a body often called the "county court." This court is presided over by "county commissioners" and must be distinguished from a county trial court. It is fundamentally administrative in nature—although it may perform quasi-judicial functions. The duties of county commissioners include maintenance of county schools, rest homes, and bridges. They receive and admit to probate the wills of those who die in the county, and administer the estates of those who pass away without a will.

Once tax assessments are set, the commissioners sit as a board of "equalization and review." Those who have complaints about tax assessments, real or personal, are given an opportunity to protest. Notice of the right to protest is given by direct notice when assessments have been increased, and by legal notice of publication otherwise. Examine Figure 7-5. This is an actual copy of a notice of increase of tax assessment. It speaks for itself.

The typical citizen does not understand that there is a right of review; and during a usual 30-day session, as few as 15 persons out of 100,000 may appear to protest their tax assessments—which are often lowered following the protest. Tax assessment adjustments are frequently made for the following reasons: an error is made in transferring figures: the

FIGURE 7–5

Glenvale County Court
Glenvale, New York

Certified Mail   January 1, 19___
Return Receipt Requested

Dear Property Owner:

As required by Law, the County Court is meeting as a Board of Review and Equalization during the month of February, 19___, for the purpose of reviewing and equalizing the assessment made by the Assessor.

The objective of this review is to provide equality and uniformity in assessed valuations between individual properties so that each property owner, in proportion to the value of property, pays only the fair share of the ad valorem property tax—no more; no less.

The following adjustment to the assessed valuation placed upon your property is required in order to comply with this statutory provision:

Block 3, Lot No. 6, Hess Addition—Shaker Heights

(Land Book Description of Property)

Assessor's Valuation		*Adjusted Valuation*	
Land	$ 1,100	Land	$ 1,700
Buildings	$27,000	Buildings	$28,800
Total	$28,000	Total	$30,500

Please be advised that the Law also provides that if any person fails to apply for relief at this meeting, that person shall have waived the right to ask for correction in the assessment for the current year as fixed by the County Court, except on appeal to the Circuit Court.

Very truly yours,

Tom Jackson
President, Glenvale County Court

---

assessment is too high when compared with similar properties in the same neighborhood; and the assessment is too high when compared with the market value of the property involved.

The commissioners serve as the budget officers of the county. In this capacity, they play a direct role in the court system since they estimate income and then decide what portion of the income will be spent to pay the judge, court costs, and others in the court system.

In rural areas of the nation, the tax "base" or the tax dollars collected, is so small that a full-time court, as well as other county functions, cannot be maintained. Even in the most populous areas of the country, the tax base is limited—thus the yield will always be limited.

A new addition to court personnel—and not always the most popular with judges and lawyers—is the "court administrator."

6. Court Administrators

In recent years, many state and all federal courts have been using the services of "court administrators." These are non-lawyer personnel trained in the administration of court activities. This has opened up new career opportunities for non-lawyers, much like paralegal laypersons.

The administrators regulate the activities of the courts and juries by scheduling and rescheduling trials as required. They coordinate with the lawyers; arrange for continuances, and manage the dockets of the courts. Their activities must not be confused with the conduct of trials in which they take no part. Many administrators use the computer for scheduling and for calling jury panels. Their services have proven to be valuable in the courts where they are used.

The federal government initiated the administrator program under the insistence of the Chief Justice of the United States Supreme Court. Schools are now available for this training.

An unofficial member of the "court family" is the "notary public."

7. Notaries Public

In ancient Rome a "notarius" was one who was skilled in shorthand writing or reporting. Their services were called upon by the courts and lawmaking bodies when they were in operation. In addition, the notarius prepared deeds, wills, and other legal documents which the Romans used in the conduct of their business and personal affairs.

The term "notary" was adopted in England in the early years of the common law and was used to identify one who was a writer of short documents and instruments. The word "public" was added in time, indicating a public official. The notary came to America as part of the English colonies and has survived to become part of the judicial system in this nation.

Today, a notary public is a public officer who is commissioned by the governor of the state where the notary operates. The commission is for a prescribed number of years and the expiration date is spelled out upon documents "notarized." (In Germany, the commission of a notary is for life.) One who applies to become a notary must be over a prescribed age, of good moral character, and be recommended by persons of good standing in the community. One state requires that recommendations be given by the sheriff, the judge, and the clerk of the county or circuit court of the county in which the notary will operate.

After the commission is granted, the notary may begin performing duties, which include administering oaths, attesting affidavits, deeds, and other documents. The notary will perform other official duties such as protesting notes or marine losses where required.

The function of the notary as a certifying witness becomes important when legal documents are involved in court action. For example, a properly executed affidavit will be accepted by a court as being true—and if the facts contained therein are not denied, it will form the basis for a motion for summary judgment—that is, the court may enter judgment without further trial. However, *in trial,* an affidavit cannot be used unless the person who gave it is called so the other side will have an opportunity to cross-examine that person.

A document that is notarized is "sworn" and has higher legal standing than one that carries a mere signature. A sample acknowledgment used on a deed is illustrated. (For an example of a deed, see Chapter 24.)

OLIVET, MICHIGAN
COUNTY OF OLIVET:

I, John Eagle, a Notary Public in and for the County in the state aforesaid, do hereby certify that Frank Fisher, Jr., and Elaine Fisher, husband and wife, whose names are signed to the above deed dated the 6th day of March, 1976 have this day before me in my said County, acknowledged the same.
Given under my hand this 6th day of March, 1976
My Commission expires February 21, 1979.

S/S John Eagle
Notary Public

The persons who signed and "acknowledged" the document, did so in the presence of the notary and in the notary's area of jurisdiction. The acknowledgment would be defective if taken out of the area in which the notary is commissioned. Some states issue commissions that are effective statewide, but most are limited to a single county.

REVIEW QUESTIONS

1. The notice of increased tax assessment in this chapter was sent by registered mail, "return receipt requested." Do you know what this means? Why was it mailed in this manner?
2. Define a "navigable river."
3. True or False. The court structure in a given state will vary with the makeup of the federal district courts.
4. Assume that a *federal district court* includes part of Ohio and ten counties in Pennsylvania. What problems would be created in the trial of cases in that court? (There are plans to realign the federal courts in just this fashion.)
5. Refer to Figure 7–5. Give two probable reasons why the value of the real estate was *increased.*
6. The courts are hesitant to interfere with the judgment of assessors who place values on property for tax purposes. Why?
7. True or False. The "prothonotary" in Pennsylvania is comparable to the "circuit clerk" in Virginia.
8. Name other functions of a notary that you know of.

9. Are notaries listed in the yellow pages? If not, how can you find one?
10. Name one use that a student would have for the services of a notary.

Words and Phrases

Write out briefly what they mean to you.
1. "Navigable river."
2. Judicial circuits.
3. "Clerks have different titles."
4. Financing the court.
5. The notary's role in court.

Coverage:	The "geography" of the courts.
What to Look for:	How the courts are laid out.
Application:	Make certain you understand how the courts are organized in your state.

8 Courts—A Closer Look

Highlands County Court House at Sebring, Florida

WHAT IS A "COURT"?

A "court" is a "body in government to which the administration of justice is delegated. A body organized to administer justice, and including both judge and jury."[1] The words "court" and "judge" or "judges" are used in statutes as being synonymous. When used with reference to orders made by the court or judges, they are to be so understood. But how did our courts develop in the first instance?

NATURE OF THE COURT FUNCTION

Down the dark corridors of ancient time, people lived in a wilderness surrounded by beasts and winged creatures that rendered prolonged

---

[1] *State* v. *Caywood,* 96, Iowa 367, 65 N.W. 385 (1895).

existence impossible. Under such conditions, only the most fundamental laws of nature were in use—"survival of the fittest" being paramount. It was impossible for one to contemplate a formal system of law and courts. Such a system waited for more recent centuries, as the human race moved from the wilderness into the early ages.

As we began to coexist under more civilized circumstances, a simple fact became obvious: One person has difficulty existing with another without disputes—in some form—arising between them. Therefore, one of the needs of early civilization was a forum in which disputes could be settled as they arose. The result was the beginning of the development of a court system.

Today, just as in ancient times, courts exist in anticipation of disputes and provide means whereby disputes can be settled efficiently, impartially, and fairly—at least in theory. Unfortunately, our courts are not efficient; some judges are not impartial; and a few are plainly unfair.

Our courts and legal system today are not in "full bloom" and final form. Rather, they are merely serving at this time, and the need to upgrade both the law and its application in the courts is as pressing today as it was 5,000 years ago.

The same will be true in the future as new generations see the system through eyes that will judge on the basis of other times and circumstances. Perhaps in time disputes will fade and the need for courts will decrease to only an occasional need, thus bringing us closer to a dream shared by all—a world without conflict. But until that time, our courts shall continue providing the forum in which disputes can be settled efficiently or inefficiently, impartially or partially, fairly or unfairly.

It is helpful to become acquainted with basic terms that are used in the courts.

Some Terminology

"Jurisdiction" has to do with the "power" that a court may exercise in a given case. A court may have "limited jurisdiction," such as a justice of the peace court, which can hear civil matters only up to set dollar limits or a divorce court which can only hear and decide divorce matters.

A court may have "unlimited jurisdiction," indicating that its power to act is not limited to money amounts or subject matter.

"Venue" is the geographical area over which a court has jurisdiction. The problem of "proper venue" confronts the practicing attorney frequently. A "change of venue" is the process of taking a case from one court to another. Motions requesting a change of venue are often made in criminal prosecutions. They are based upon such claims as extreme hatred toward the defendant in the community or excessive pretrial publicity.

"Trial courts" must be distinguished from "appellate courts." In the former, juries are found while in the latter, judges alone hear and decide cases. At the trial level, witnesses are called and testimony is heard. At the appellate level, the court proceeds upon the "record" taken in the

FIGURE 8-1

Hughes, William

Judge Kiger: Your objection is overruled, and the confession may be admitted into evidence.

Mr. Laurita: I offer it now, Your Honor.

Q. I hand you this statement, Lt. Hughes, and ask you if it is in exactly the same condition as when you took it?

A. Yes, sir.

Mr. Laurita: Your Honor, I ask that this statement be admitted into evidence as State's Exhibit Number 1.

Judge Kiger: It may be admitted into evidence.

State's Exhibit Number 1 Admitted in Evidence

Mr. Eagle: Show my exception, please.

Judge Kiger: And the defendant is given his exception.

Mr. Laurita: Lieutenant Hughes, I hand you State's Exhibit Number 1 and ask you to read the statement to the jury.

A. Of course. This statement was taken at eleven-fifty, on the evening of July 1, 1975. "I, Joe Dingle, make this statement of my own free will, after having been informed of my rights. On the night of June 30, 19__, I . . ."

---

court below. State trial courts become appellate courts when appeals are taken from rulings of justices of the peace or police judges. But they are not appellate courts in the strict sense because cases brought up from the lower courts or tribunals are heard "de novo"—from the beginning.

The "record" includes the transcript of testimony of the witnesses called to testify as well as motions made by the lawyers. The record is taken by the court reporter and the method used varies from court to court. Some court reporters use the shorthand method, while others use stenographic machines or "face mask" type recording devices. Figure 8-1 is an actual page taken from a criminal prosecution.

Courts that make records—in whatever form—are "courts of record." Recording is expensive—particularly when transcripts (copies) are needed for appeal purposes. Transcribing records is time-consuming. Since these must be typed word for word, the reporter often runs months behind. This is one of the causes for delays in appeals. Some courts are experimenting with recording trials by video tape. Thus, an appeal court could not only hear but see what took place at the trial as the accompanying news item illustrates. But under present practices, appellate courts work with typed or printed words. In many instances, the attorney making an appeal—in an effort to cut costs—does not have enough of the record transcribed. The appellate court does not get a full picture of what happened below and an appeal may not be granted. This seldom happens when appeals are taken by lawyers who are skilled in appellate procedure. A good trial lawyer is not always a good appellate lawyer because two en-

Videotape Use Grows in Courts

SAN FRANCISCO (UPI)—The day may be coming when baliffs will intone "roll 'em" instead of "order in the court."

Videotape is beginning to play a more and more important part in court trials. At a recent trial in San Francisco, all testimony was presented via videotape over closed-circuit television.

Last March, the testimony of William "Whispering Bill" Pifer was taped for the murder trial in Martinez, Calif., of Bill Moran, a member of the Hell's Angels motorcycle gang. Pifer, suffering from throat cancer, died three days before the tape was used in the trial.

Similar experiments have been conducted in Colorado, Florida, Georgia, Kentucky, Missouri, New York and Vermont under supervision of the National Center for State Courts in Denver.

In some cases all testimony was pre-recorded; in some, only that of certain witnesses. Sometimes entire trials were put on tape for future viewing by appellate courts.

The center believes videotaping will save time for jurors, witnesses and others involved in the actual trial. And, it points out, shorter trials are cheaper for the taxpayer.

Pittsburgh Press, Jan. 20, 1974.

tirely different endeavors are involved. In the former, the lawyer attempts to control the "findings of fact" of a jury: in the latter, the lawyer seeks to control the ruling of the appellate judges—a "ruling of law."

Next it is important to see how our courts are organized. As it turns out, we have a double system of courts and we are the only nation in the world in which this is true.

A DUAL SYSTEM OF COURTS

Our nation has a double system of courts which exist concurrently within each state. This came about when our original 13 colonies granted restricted powers to the "federal" government, while at the same time, reserving all legal powers not granted, to themselves, as was discussed previously.

From this came the federal system of courts—while the state courts developed independently of them.

Source of Power for Federal Courts

The United States Constitution states:

> The judicial power of the United States shall be vested in one supreme court, and in such other inferior courts as the Congress may, from time to time ordain and establish.[2]

---

[2] U.S. Constitution, Article III, Section 1.

Thus the creation of the federal court system was delegated to the legislative branch of government—namely, Congress. The broad sweep of this constitutional provision gave Congress wide powers to create "courts." It should be noted that it does *not* contain limits upon how many or what types might be created.

Jurisdiction. The Constitution specifies the types of cases in which the power of the federal courts shall extend. The jurisdiction of the federal courts ". . . shall extend to all Cases, in Law and Equity . . ."[3] involving the following;

1. Constitutional rights of the individual.
2. Laws of the United States.
3. Treaties between the United States and other countries.
4. Cases affecting ambassadors, consuls, and other public ministers.
5. All cases of admiralty and maritime jurisdiction.
6. Controversy in which the United States is a party.
7. Controversy between two or more states.
8. Controversy between the state and citizens of another state.
9. Controversy between citizens of different states.[4]
10. Controversies between citizens of the same state claiming land belonging to different states.
11. Controversies between a state and citizens thereof and foreign states and citizens.

All of the above have one thing in common: none of them involve any matter that could be construed to be a pure internal matter of one state. If it was, the federal courts would not have jurisdiction and the resolution of the dispute would be the sole function of the state.

Some Examples. Assume that A lives in Indiana and B is a resident of Kentucky. A injures B in an auto accident in Kentucky. If B can in good faith claim that the injuries and property damages will exceed $10,000, B may (at B's option) file suit against A in the federal district court in Kentucky. This is "diversity jurisdiction" because the place of residency of the parties is "diverse" to each other. The sum of $10,000 is a "jurisdictional amount" established to keep smaller cases out of the federal courts. This figure has been raised from $3,000 in just a few years. Since the sum of money is jurisdictional, as it is increased, the number of civil cases that can be brought in federal court is reduced. If both parties to litigation are from the same state, then a suit between them may be brought in a state court, but not in a federal court. Other examples of federal and state jurisdiction follows.

Sam Thompson of Louisville, Kentucky, a black, was arrested for dancing in a public restaurant and fined $10 in police court. He attempted to appeal the conviction in the state system but under Kentucky law, no appeal is provided from a fine of $10. Sam, who complained that his constitutional rights had been violated, appealed directly to the

---

[3] U.S. Constitution, Article III, Section 2.

[4] For an example of how the federal courts treat this, see *Burns* v. *Anderson*, 502 F. 2d. 970, 5th Cir. (1974).

Supreme Court of the United States, invoking "constitutional jurisdiction." The high court accepted the case, heard the matter, and reversed the police court of Louisville.

Cases involving federal income tax evasion are tried in federal courts — state income tax evasion cases in the state courts.

The kidnap-murderer of the infant son of Charles Lindbergh, was tried in a state court (New Jersey). Because of that unfortunate incident, kidnaping (where state lines are involved) has become a federal crime by act of Congress. The accused assassin of President John F. Kennedy would have been tried in a state court because killing the president did not break a federal law at that time. Cases involving the tampering of federal juries are tried in federal courts. The reverse is true if a state jury is involved. The federal government has jurisdiction over admiralty and maritime matters. Therefore, Crystal River and Big River in the fictitious state are under federal jurisdiction. State lines are involved since the rivers flow through more than one state. In addition, the rivers are "navigable"—that is, commerce-bearing ships and vessels may travel upon the rivers and through the different states. Because of this federal jurisdiction, locks and dams on navigable streams, rivers, and other bodies of water are constructed, maintained, and guarded by the U.S. Corps of Engineers—a federal agency.

An interesting and important question arises when one begins to think about our sea coasts and the oceans beyond. This is especially so in these times of off-shore drilling for gas and oil. What courts have jurisdiction over these waters?

Jurisdiction over Off-Shore Waters. How far beyond a nations coast line may it's courts claim jurisdiction? At common law the distance was three miles—being the maximum range of muzzle loading cannon. But today, nations are claiming 12, 24, and up to 200 miles with Russia opting for the latter. The United States has long favored a 12 mile limit.

International conferences have been directed to a resolution of this conflict, the most notable having been held in 1958, 1960, and the Caracas, Venezuela, conference in 1974.

Ocean waters beyond those limits claimed would be "international waters" and international law would apply.

Turning from the question of jurisdiction, just how are the federal courts organized?

Organization of the Federal Courts

Federal cases usually begin in the federal district courts (trial courts). The federal district judges hear cases and conduct trials that range from criminal prosecutions for federal firearms violations to civil actions for money damages. Appeals are taken to the Court of Appeals that contains the district court where the trial was held. There are 11 U.S. courts of appeals, with the District of Columbia being number 11. (There is no state court in the District of Columbia for a simple reason: It is not a state.) (See Figure 8-2.)

The states of California, Oregon, Washington, Nevada, Idaho, Arizona,

FIGURE 8-2

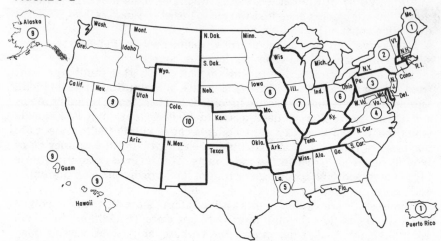

Note: The Canal Zone is part of the 5th Circuit. The 11th Circuit is located in the District of Columbia.

and Montana make up the 9th U.S. Court of Appeals; the 7th Circuit includes Wisconsin, Illinois, and Indiana. The courts of appeals do not cross the borders of any state—although more than one state is found within all of them but one. A close examination of the map permits one to learn the makeup of the other courts of appeals. This alignment of federal courts may be changed soon. If it is, the map will have to be adjusted accordingly.

The federal district courts are wholly contained within each state. However, consideration is being given to crossing state lines to include more populous areas of certain states. The principal reason for this would be to permit a more equitable distribution of the case load among federal judges.

Twenty-four states have more than one federal district court within their boundaries. Of these, 13 have two districts in each state. Three states—New York, Texas, and California—are each divided into four district courts. Pennsylvania, North Carolina, Georgia, Florida, Alabama, Tennessee, Illinois, and Oklahoma have three districts. All other states, plus Puerto Rico, the Canal Zone, and Guam, have a single federal district court within their boundaries. When Alaska and Hawaii became states, they were added to the 9th Circuit and each is a single district.

A National Court of Appeals

Serious study is being given to the creation of a federal "National Court of Appeals." The principal reason suggested for this is to ease the case load of the U.S. Supreme Court and to permit case decisions in the courts of appeals to be standardized.

As it is now, appellate lawyers in the federal courts "shop" for jurisdictions that are favorable to their points of view. For example, the 2d Circuit in New York City is considered to be one that is likely to hand down more innovative decisions and is sought by some for that reason — and avoided by others for the same reason.

Most cases that start in the federal district courts end at the court of appeals level and this fact is not widely known. Contrary to popular belief, there is no absolute right of appeal to the Supreme Court of the United States. (The Thompson case is not an exception since it originated in a state court, not a federal court.) Due to the manner in which cases

FIGURE 8-3

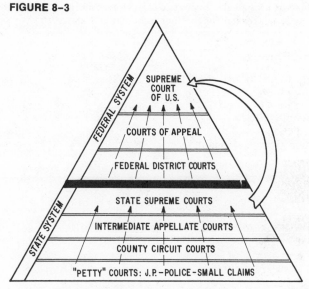

Note: The arrows indicate the appeal "flow."

are heard before the high court, only a limited number are accepted for decision each year. It has been the policy of the court to allow issues to develop at the court of appeals level until these issues take on major proportions — or until the rulings become so inconsistent that uniformity is desired. The high court will then accept a representative case and consolidate all similar cases for decision. This procedure was followed in the desegregation, reapportionment, and obscenity cases. See Figure 8-3 for the route of appeals in the state as well as in the federal systems.

From the State to the Federal System. The defendant can appeal from the final decision of the highest court of the state if the Constitution or laws of the United States are in question. The appeal would be direct to the Supreme Court of the United States.

REVIEW QUESTIONS

1. At common law, the "core" was a central place in a community where disputes were heard and settled. Might this be the origin of the word "court"?
2. Transcripts have traditionally been typed double space. What practical reason can you think of for this being done?
3. Distinguish "venue" (pronounced *"ven-you"*) from "jurisdiction."
4. Have you read recently of a motion for a "change of venue"? If so what was the reason cited?
5. A change of venue is usually sought only in criminal cases. Explain why.
6. How could a case arise involving Item 4 under "jurisdiction" – "Cases affecting ambassadors, consuls, and other public ministers."?
7. Could a J.P. fine an ambassador for speeding?
8. If the J.P. did so, would the fine be likely to be upheld?
9. Which court of appeals covers the largest geographical area?
10. Can you give a reason for the fact in question 9 above?

Words and Phrases

Write out briefly what they mean to you.
1. "Appeal flow."
2. Reservation of powers.
3. Power of courts.
4. Jurisdiction.
5. "Venue giving defendant."

Coverage:	An examination of procedures used in courts.
What to Look for:	How "procedures" are distinguishable from "substantive law."
Application:	Assume that you are the plaintiff in a contract action. How do these procedures affect your case?

9 Procedures in Courts

In this chapter, the "procedures" that are followed in *state* courts will be examined. It must be understood at the outset that almost everything discussed has application in the federal courts as well. This is true because the material is based upon state "Rules of Civil Procedure." Since these rules are patterned after the "Federal Rules of Civil Procedure," an examination of one is essentially an examination of the other.

STATE COURTS

The source of power—or jurisdiction—of the 50 state court systems is found in the 50 state constitutions. One state constitution contains the following provision:

> The judicial power of the State shall be vested in a Supreme court of appeals, in circuit courts and the judges thereof, in such inferior tribunals as are herein authorized and in justices of the peace.

This provision permits the creation of higher courts as well as "J.P." courts. Therefore, in this state the J.P. court is "constitutional." These courts are "county based" and one county may have more than one J.P. court.

The language of the provision is *not* broad enough however, to create just any type of court. For example, there might be a question whether small claims courts could be created in that state. These courts are of relatively recent origin while the above provision is 100 years old. Therefore, a legal question arises: may that state create a court of recent origin, out of a constitutional provision that is 100 years old? The words "as are herein authorized" causes the problem in the above provision.

JURISDICTION

The "power" or "jurisdiction" of the courts in a state includes all matters at law where the amount in controversy exceeds a set sum or is less than a set sum; cases in equity, and cases involving crimes and misdemeanors. The circuit courts have appellate jurisdiction by appeal or "writ of error" from courts of lower jurisdiction. They are charged with supervision and control of proceedings before justices of the peace or magistrates and other inferior tribunals. Such supervision is generally carried out by writs of "mandamus" – which commands a public official to *do* an act that under law the official is supposed to do but fails to do – and "prohibition" – which commands a public official to *stop* doing an act that the official should not be doing.

The state courts function as provided by law and as long as they operate within their guidelines, actions taken are valid. But if the courts act otherwise, their actions will be a nullity for "lack of jurisdiction." But "jurisdiction" of a court includes more than mere "powers"; it encompasses "jurisdiction over the "subject matter" as well as "jurisdiction over the person," as follows.

OBTAINING JURISDICTION

All state courts have power to hear and determine personal injury cases. But a court in state A has no power to hear a personal injury case that happened in state B where both the plaintiff and defendant are in state B. Why? No jurisdiction over the subject matter *or* the person. Let's examine this principle in more detail.

Over Subject Matter

There are four basic ways by which a court can obtain jurisdiction over subject matter. First, the laws of the state can give the court jurisdiction. For example, the laws of all states give circuit judges the power to permit adoptions, grant divorces, and change names: thus, they have these powers by law. A justice of the peace cannot hear and grant an adoption because the J.P. does not have this power in any state, thus state law can *limit* jurisdiction. Second, if the subject matter is located within the boundaries of the court, its mere presence gives the court jurisdiction over it. If a debtor's house is located in county B, the court of that county, after suit is brought and judgment obtained, may order the house sold to satisfy the judgment. Third, if the subject matter *happens* within the boundaries of the court, this gives the court jurisdiction. For example, if a car wreck occurs in county A, the circuit court of the county has power to hear and decide the case. A fourth way occurs when a person moves into a state and remains there for a period of time. For example, the Nevada courts have power to grant divorces to persons from other states, if such persons move to Nevada and reside there for six weeks "with the intention of becoming a permanent resident."

However, it is not enough for a court to have jurisdiction over subject matter; it must also have jurisdiction over the person or persons involved.

Over the Person

If a car wreck occurs in Capital County the circuit court of that county has power over the subject matter—namely, the accident because it happened there. A personal injury suit may be brought in that court by the complaining party, but if the matter stops at this point, the court is powerless to take action. Why? Because the court lacks jurisdiction over the person of the defendant until the defendant is "served" with notice as provided by law. Procedures vary in obtaining such jurisdiction, but the following is representative.

"Process" Created

In a state that follows procedures based upon the federal rules, the clerk of the court prepares a summons which is attached to a copy of the complaint. (See Figures 9-1 and 9-2.)

FIGURE 9-1

SUMMONS
CIRCUIT COURT OF CHULA VISTA, CALIFORNIA 92012

Norman Roe and
ABC Insurance Company,
     a Corporation   , Plaintiffs

          v.   Civil Action No. 1000

     James E. Doe   , Defendant

To the above-named Defendant:
IN THE NAME OF CALIFORNIA:
    You are hereby summoned and required to serve upon JOHN EAGLE, plaintiff's attorney, whose address is 1300 University Avenue, Chula Vista, California, an answer, including any related counterclaim or defense you may have, to the complaint filed against you in the above styled civil action, a true copy of which is herewith delivered to you. You are required to serve your answer within 20 days after service of this summons upon you, exclusive of the day of service. If you fail to do so, thereafter judgment, upon proper hearing and trial, may be taken against you for the relief demanded in the complaint and you will be thereafter barred from asserting in another action any claim, cross complaint, or defense you may have which must be asserted in the above styled civil action.
Dated: January 2, 1976.

                                  s/s Jean Friend
                               CLERK OF COURT
                               s/s Bobbie Dawson
                               DEPUTY CLERK

FIGURE 9-2

IN THE CIRCUIT COURT OF CHULA VISTA, CALIFORNIA 92012

Norman Roe and
ABC Insurance Company,
_____a Corporation_____ , Plaintiffs

v.   Civil Action No. 1000

_____James E. Doe_____ , Defendant

C O M P L A I N T

1. On the 28th day of October, 1975, in a public highway called Route 7, in Chula Vista near Grand Company, Defendant James E. Doe, by and through his agent, duly authorized, negligently drove a motor vehicle owned by said Defendant and operated for his benefit by his authorized agent, into and against an automobile owned and operated by the Plaintiff Norman Roe upon said highway.

2. As a result of said negligence, Plaintiff Roe's automobile was damaged to the extent of $1,057.95. Roe was the insured under a policy insuring his automobile against loss by collision, with $50.00 deductible, issued by Plaintiff ABC Insurance Company, and Plaintiff paid to Norman Roe the sum of $1,007.95 and is subrogated to his rights in that sum as set out on Exhibit A, attached and made a part hereof by reference.

3. As a further result of said negligence, Norman Roe was violently thrown about, striking the inside of his automobile, and suffered severe injuries to his person including a whiplash; was hospitalized and incurred medical bills; suffered pain of mind and body; lost work and wages and further suffered the damage to his car as set out above.

WHEREFORE, Plaintiffs, demand judgment against the Defendant in the sum of Five Thousand ($5,000) Dollars.

PLAINTIFFS by Counsel

_____s/s John Eagle_____

John Eagle—Attorney for Plaintiffs
Southwestern Avenue,
Chula Vista, California 92010

The complaint and summons is called "process" and must be "served" upon the defendant.

The Sheriff—or Process Server—Acts

After the documents are delivered to the proper office (in duplicate) along with the fee for service of process, the sheriff, usually through a deputy or "process server," takes up the search for the defendant. In smaller communities, the server knows the defendant and knows where to find him or her. If not, a quick look at the city directory, or the tax rolls, provides an address. Different options are now open to the "process server."

Defendant Submits

In many cases a phone call will result in the defendant coming to the office to accept service. Most servers try this in lieu of serving at one's place of employment. On rare occasions, the defendant is in jail, thus providing the server with a "captive defendant."

FORMS OF SERVICE OF PROCESS

Personal Service

If possible, the server will personally hand "process" to the defendant. If this is done within the county, the court has jurisdiction over the defendant at that moment. Some states require that the server make some statement such as: "This is a summons. You have been sued by John Doe." In other states, there is no such requirement. The purpose of the procedure being discussed is to give the defendant notice of the suit and thus an opportunity to defend. In one case, a process server drove up beside the defendant's car at a stop light. The defendant rolled up the window and locked the doors, making it clear that the defendant was not going to accept any papers. The server tossed the papers onto the hood of the defendant's car, who drove off as the light changed. The papers were scattered about the highway and the defendant did not return for them. A judge ruled that the defendant had been served personally and had no reason to complain of the judgment entered by default. Personal service is preferred by plaintiff's lawyers. It removes doubts that sometimes arise where other forms of service are used.

Substitute Service

Often the server does not find the defendant at the residence. Since the fee for service is small, the server is reluctant to try later. In such instances the server may serve a "substitute," which, if done properly, will bind the defendant. Most states require that the substitute be over a certain age (16 in one state) and a member of the defendant's family. It is usually a statutory requirement that the server inform the substitute of certain facts. In a recent case the following conversation took place at the defendant's front door:

Server: Is John Doe here?
Young woman: No.
Server: Who are you?
Young woman: I am John Doe's niece.
Server: How old are you?
Young woman: Eighteen.
Server: John Doe has been sued in the circuit court of this county. These papers must be given to him by you when he comes home. Do you understand?
Young woman: Yes.

The niece failed to give the papers to Doe thus he knew nothing of the suit at that time: Judgment was taken by default and Doe's wages were attached. When Doe saw the 25 percent deduction from his pay-check, he inquired and for the first time, learned of the suit. Doe consulted an attorney who after an examination of the facts brought a writ of prohibition to stop the wage attachment. The writ claimed the attachment had not been done according to law. At the hearing, the judge ruled that the niece was not a member of Doe's family within the meaning of the statute since she lived in another town and was only visiting on the day of service. This is a good illustration of why plaintiff's lawyers prefer personal service.

Posting

A process server often fails to find the defendant home, or if home, will not answer the door. The server cannot enter by force because this would be a trespass and would render the server subject to suit. The server may "post" process on the "front door of the usual place of abode" and this is good service in most states. In earlier days the papers were nailed to the door using the butt of a six-shooter as a hammer—today cellophane tape is in vogue.

This method of posting is also hazardous. To illustrate, in a recent case, the question of jurisdiction arose on another writ of prohibition to stop a wage attachment. The evidence disclosed that the deputy had attached process to apartment 123—but the defendant lived in apartment 124. The judgment and wage attachment were ruled unlawful.

Posting is sometimes used in cases where a defendant leaves the county near the time suit is brought. The court obtains power if the posting is proper—even though the defendant never returns to the "usual place of abode." The theory is that the owner of the building, a mail carrier, or other person will see the papers and inform the defendant of the suit. In practice, the defendant often does not know of the suit—but it doesn't matter if the posting is done properly.

Service by Mail

In some states, process can be served by mail—usually by registered letter, "return receipt requested," as discussed previously.

Alaskan law permits process to be served by mail. The legislature of that state felt this was necessary in view of the inaccessible roads and long distances of travel—often by plane—that would otherwise be required. Defendants in Alaska are also allowed to defend by mail—and many do so without the assistance of counsel.

REACHING A NONRESIDENT DEFENDANT

Two principal methods of service of process are available to reach one who is not living in the state where suit is brought, publication and long-arm statutes.

Publication

All states have statutes that permit service of process under limited circumstances, by the publication of "legal notices." This means of service is limited, however, to cases where the "subject matter" is before the court. Publication as a means of "service" is used in divorces, settlement of estates, and partition of land cases where the defendant is out of the state or unknown. For an example of a legal notice, see page 143. Also see any issue of a daily newspaper in "general circulation." Publication as it is discussed here should be distinguished from "publication" discussed on page 144, under Notchel Notice.

The second means of serving a nonresident is more powerful than publication.

Long-Arm Statutes

A serious problem has been caused by the nonresident who travels into a state, causes a loss—such as a car wreck—and then returns to another state. The nonresident may be a corporation acting through agents, or an individual. The problem is the same. If jurisdiction can be obtained in federal court under diversity rules, the problem is avoided.

But what if the plaintiff has an auto damaged in the sum of $800 or $1,000 by a nonresident and has suffered only slight personal injury? Federal jurisdiction is out because of the $10,000 jurisdictional amount. If suit is filed, personal, substitute, or posting service cannot be used. Publication will not work because the plaintiff is seeking money damages. The only possibility would be for the plaintiff to go to the defendant's state and sue there. This is economically impossible in small cases. Because of this type of situation, most states have enacted "nonresident statutes," referred to as "long-arm statutes." The phrase "long arm" indicates that the court can "reach out" and obtain jurisdiction over the defendant.

How Do the Statutes Operate? Assume that a resident of Arizona is driving to the east coast and the trip plan is through Wheeling, West Virginia. As soon as the traveler crosses the West Virginia border, a legal event takes place—the nonresident appoints the Secretary of State as agent for the purpose of receiving service of process whether a nonresident is aware of this or not. This happens automatically by operation of the laws of West Virginia. (Some states use the State Auditor.) These statutes are justifiable in that it is part of what one must give to use the highways.

Upon entering the Wheeling Tunnels, the nonresident strikes John Doe's auto from the rear, causing $800 property damage and a slight whiplash injury. The investigating officer issues a citation to the negligent driver who then pays a $24 fine to a J.P. and returns to Arizona in due course. Is Doe caught in the problem of not being able to recover damages? Not at all. John Doe's lawyer prepares and files the lawsuit and posts a "statutory" or "cost" bond. See Figure 9–3 for an example.

FIGURE 9–3

STATUTORY BOND

John Doe

v.

Arizona Traveler

Know all men by these presents:

That we, John Doe, principal and Southern Surety Company, Inc., surety, are held and firmly bound to West Virginia in the penal sum of One Hundred Dollars ($100.00), which well and truly to be paid we bind ourselves, our heirs, etc., jointly and severally, firmly by these presents.

Witness our hands and seals this the 30th day of January, 1976.

The condition of the above obligation is such that, whereas, John Doe has this day filed a complaint in the office of the Clerk of the Circuit Court of Ohio County, West Virginia, for the institution of an action in which John Doe is plaintiff and Arizona Traveler (and others) are defendants:

Now, therefore, if the plaintiff fails to prevail in said action and will reimburse the defendant or cause him or her to be reimbursed, the necessary expense incurred in and about the defense of the action then this obligation to be void,; otherwise to remain in full force and effect.

John Doe   (SEAL)

Joe Agent   (SEAL)

Binding Agent for Southern
Surety Co., Inc.

Acknowledged before and approved by me this 30th day of January, 1976.

Jean Friend

Clerk

Upon payment of the fee ($2.00 in West Virginia), the clerk sends "process" to the Secretary of State. Upon receipt of this, the Secretary of State accepts service on behalf of the defendant. At that moment, the court has jurisdiction over the defendant. The Secretary of State mails process to the defendant by registered mail. The defendant must answer within a designated time limit (30 days in West Virginia) or face judgment by default. In practice, the system works well and former injustices are avoided. However, after judgment is obtained, it does not mean that it will always be collected.

Most states have long-arm statutes of the type discussed and these find wide application in business cases, tort or contract, and can be used against nonresident corporations as well. For a list of states that have such statutes, see Chapter 52. (*Creditors* have attempted to use long-arm statutes to reach out of state *consumer* debtors. Can they be used for this purpose? An FTC law judge has held that they cannot.)[1]

---

[1] *In re Spiegel, Inc.,* F.T.C. Dkt. No. 8990 (Jan. 31, 1975).

REVIEW QUESTIONS

1. Distinguish a "statutory" from a "constitutional" court. Why is the distinction important?
2. What happens if the defendant fails to answer the summons and complaint in Figures 9-1 and 9-2?
3. Explain "substitute service."
4. Under what conditions will the bond in Figure 9-3 be released?
5. Do you understand how the "long-arm" statutes work? If not, ask.
6. Many "fly by night" organizations form a partnership and then cross state lines to transact business. Can you give one reason why this is done?
7. Is it fair for the federal courts to use the $10,000 minimum to keep out small personal injury cases? What arguments can be made *for* this policy?
8. Why were limits placed upon the courts that could be created in the provision at the beginning of this chapter under "State Courts"?
9. Why is "jurisdiction" so important under our legal system?
10. True or False. "An act of a court that lacks jurisdiction is a nullity for all practical purposes."

Words and Phrases

Write out briefly what they mean to you.
1. Long-arm statute.
2. "Dismissed for lack of jurisdiction."
3. Service of process.
4. Cost bonds.
5. Publication.

Coverage:	The nature and function of juries used in the courts.
What to Look for:	The ways in which the use of juries cause delays in trials.
Application:	You are considering bringing a contract suit against another business person. Look for reasons why you should attempt to compromise out of court.

10 Juries

Proude felt depressed and a little apprehensive. All the lids he had raised to expose the turmoil of dark lives in his time. If he stretched out a hand or lifted his head and sniffed when the wind was right, it was there, around the corner, through a doorway, roiling all the time. You never thought of it coexisting because then how could you enjoy the cool sanity of your own life? So this trial was a farce. All those jurors lived in the light, as did all the witnesses and lawyers and the court stenographer and deputies and reporters and the waitresses at the Long Arm. To properly come to a verdict the jury ought to be told: The victim comes from the dark world which you know nothing about. The defendant lives there too and in order to judge him you have to know something about that place. You were told of a woman who was dreadfully mauled and killed and you think of it happening where you live but it isn't like that. What you want to do is put this man away so you can forget about such things. That would not be justice. Justice has to come from understanding.

—Benjamin Siegel, The Jurors[1]

Since ancient times, panels of persons selected from an organized society have been used to hear evidence and pass judgment upon other members of that society. The panel selected was sworn (jurati) to inquire into the facts. In time, the panel came to be known as the "jurati"

---

[1] From Benjamin Siegel, *The Jurors*. (New York: Dell Publishing Co., 1972), with permission.

—the sworn—or "jury," as used today. The jury came to be part of the tradition of the courts. When the U.S. Constitution and its first ten amendments were drafted, mention of trial by jury was made in three places. And from the Constitution a legend began to grow: that the right to trial by jury is "guaranteed" by the Constitution. As a result, the "right to trial by jury" has become wrapped in an aura of respect—and in the mind of the uninformed almost approaches a point of reverence. But just what does this "right" mean as set forth in the U.S. Constitution?

IS THE "RIGHT" THERE OR NOT?

Three sections of the U.S. Constitution must be examined. Article III, Section 2 of the U.S. Constitution states, in part:

> The Trial of all Crimes, except in Cases of Impeachment, shall be by Jury; and such Trial shall be held in the State where the said Crimes shall have been committed . . .

The Sixth and Seventh Amendments that follow were part of the "Bill of Rights" proposed by Congress on September 25, 1789, and declared ratified on December 15, 1791.

> *Sixth Amendment.*
>
> In all criminal prosecutions, the accused shall enjoy the right to a speedy and public trial, by an impartial jury of the State and district wherein the crime shall have been committed . . .
>
> *Seventh Amendment.*
>
> In Suits at common law, where the value in controversy shall exceed twenty dollars, the right of trial by jury shall be preserved, and no fact tried by a jury, shall be otherwise re-examined in any Court of the United States, than according to the rules of the common law.

WHAT DOES THE CONSTITUTION SAY?

First, it is clear that one accused of a crime has a right to trial by jury and the Constitution makes it clear where the trial shall be carried out. However, in criminal cases where the accused pleads guilty, the accused waives the right to a jury trial. If the waiver is made "knowingly," the right to trial by jury is gone. Thus, in criminal matters, the accused is guaranteed a jury trial—but it is not forced if not wanted. Now, how about civil matters?

Civil Cases

A close reading of the Seventh Amendment permits several conclusions to be made. First, it does *not* guarantee the right to trial by jury, it merely *preserves the right as it existed at common law.* Therefore, if a matter before a court was not heard by a jury at common law, it cannot be heard by a jury now. In short, all matters in "equity" were heard without a jury—and are heard without a jury now. Some examples include will contests, contract rescission cases, divorces, adoptions, name changes, and many other civil matters. In addition, under the Federal Rules of Civil Procedure, and under procedural rules of many states, the right to trial by jury—where it in fact exists—can be lost by failure to demand it.

The right to a jury trial is limited in fact to very few civil cases. In practice, civil trials by jury achieve little in the way of clearing court dockets and in fact add to the congestion. The following data was taken from the docket of a circuit court in a county with a population of 75,000 persons.

Civil actions carried over from previous year	609
New civil actions started within the year	582
Cases settled out of court	281
Cases disposed of by judge (by hearings and/or motion of judge for being on the docket too long)	257
Cases tried by jury	13
Cases carried forward to next year	640

The 13 cases tried by jury cost the county over $8,000 in jury fees. An examination of the verdicts in the 13 cases disclosed that the total verdicts recovered by plaintiffs was less than the cost to the county. The jury trials contributed little toward solving the increasing backlog of cases in that county. Of the 281 cases settled out of court, 30 had been scheduled for jury trial and were apparently settled for that reason. But even by adding the 30 to the 13 trials, it can be seen that the jury contributed little in disposing of cases. These figures are representative of the situation in other courts. During the year in which the above figures arose, the court had before it a total of 1,191 cases, 191 more than were handled in an average year in *all* of the 13 colonies—an interesting historical fact.

Federal Juries

In examining the material involving state juries, both "grand" and "petit," one must be aware that the federal system also has "grand" and "petit" juries. The functions are similar—but the cases pivot upon the type of jurisdiction, federal or state. Those who serve on federal juries come from the geographical area occupied by the court in question, and the federal courts cover large areas of the state. Jury panels are selected by persons appointed for that purpose, usually called "jury commissioners." In the past, there was a tendency for federal jury commissioners to select jurors only from the metropolitan areas. This resulted in a jury made up predominantly of businesspersons, executives, and professional persons. Such juries were labeled "blue ribbon juries." Recent court rulings have ordered this practice to be discontinued and working persons, housewives, as well as business persons, executives, and professionals, are widely used on federal juries.

TYPES OF JURIES

Most juries, federal and state, fit into one of five categories: coroner's juries, justice of the peace juries, eminent domain commissioners, petit juries, and grand juries. A sixth type exists in the military court martial juries.

1. Coroners and Their Juries

State laws require that each county court or other appropriate body appoint a person to serve in the capacity of a coroner. In heavily populated counties, a medical doctor is selected. In smaller counties, a county official serves, often a justice of the peace. It is the duty of the coroner to investigate deaths that have resulted from unlawful means, or which *might* have resulted from unlawful means. It is customary for the coroner to be called to the death scene whether it be a case of murder, wrongful death on a highway, or an apparent suicide. The coroner has the power to declare the death "accidental" or "self-inflicted"—and the matter is summarily disposed of in most cases. If the coroner is not certain, or if there are suspicious circumstances, the coroner has the power to call an "inquest."

Panel Called. The coroner issues subpoenas for the prescribed number of panel members—six being representative. It is the duty of those called to hear evidence and, in some cases, view the body of the deceased. After preliminary investigation, the jury will issue an "inquisition" or report in form provided by law. The finding may be "accidental death." If so, the matter is considered closed—unless new evidence arises later. If the coroner's jury finds that death was caused by a crime of a known person, or unknown persons, the report is forwarded to the prosecuting attorney and sheriff of the county. Warrants then follow, arrests are made, and criminal prosecutions follow.

In many larger cities, coroners and their inquests are being replaced by licensed medical examiners.

2. Justice of the Peace Juries

Most states by statute permit juries to be used in J.P and magistrate courts. However, the request for a jury must be timely made and accompanied by the statutory fee to be paid to the jurors.

3. Eminent Domain Commissioners

The state has the power to take private property for public use. However, the taking cannot be done except by "due process of law," followed by payment of "just compensation." The power has been widely exercised in recent years as a part of urban renewal and construction of the interstate highway system.

How Does It Work?   First, a determination is made of the real estate needed for the project. Surveys and other preliminary work follow. A governmental representative will go to the landowners whose land—and often homes—are to be taken. An offer will be made for the property involved. The sum offered is usually arrived at by an examination of prices received on the open market for similar property in the same vicinity. If agreement is reached, payment is made and the matter is treated as a sale and purchase. If agreement is not reached, the courts are used.

"Freeholders" Called.   The number of commissioners used will vary, but five is representative. The court will summon the commissioners who must be landholders (freeholders) in the county where the realty in question is located. Expert witnesses are called by both the landowner and the state to establish the price that the state should pay. The experts usually disagree on value. The commissioners make a determination of the price by their "verdict" or finding. Either party has the right to a trial by a petit jury if not satisfied with the findings of the commissioners. The following occurred recently in an East Coast condemnation suit:

Offered by state initially (a commercial property was involved)	$160,000.00
Commissioners award (landowner appealed)	175,000.00
Petit jury award (!) (the state paid)	314,000.00

4.   Court Martial Juries

The armed forces of the United States have a system of military justice to regulate the affairs of the members of the service while on active duty. By court decision, jurisdiction of military tribunals is limited to criminal matters and petty disciplinary matters that occur while one is on active duty and while still a member of the armed forces. A soldier who commits a crime within a state is subject to the laws of that state as well as military law, and could in some cases face dual punishment. In practice, the military defers to a civilian court when it takes jurisdiction over an offense caused by one in the service.

The Panel.   A court martial panel is made up of not less than five nor more than ten military personnel chosen from a command *other* than the one of which the accused is a member. Civilian counsel can be used for defense purposes, and, while procedures are different from those followed in a civilian court, the taking of evidence is similar. A "law officer" presides over the hearing and serves in a capacity similar to that of a trial judge. One member of the jury is designated as the "president" and plays the role of a "second presiding officer."

If the accused in a military court is facing a possible death penalty, a verdict of guilt must be unanimous. If the possible sentence is ten years or more, a three-fourths vote for guilty is required. Offenses involving lesser penalties require a two-thirds vote of the jury—a variation from the requirement in criminal cases in civilian courts.

THE "BIG" JURIES

The most publicized juries in the American system and the most misunderstood are the "grand" juries and "petit" juries. Both are used in the federal and state court systems.

5. Grand Juries

The name given to this type of jury brings to one's mind a suggestion of importance or superiority. To that extent the title tends to mislead. Nevertheless, the word is used in the U.S. Constitution and no doubt had a precise meaning to the drafters since "grand inquests" were held at common law. The provision follows:

> No person shall be held to answer for a capital or otherwise infamous crime, unless upon a presentment or indictment of a Grand Jury . . .[2]

Article III of the U.S. Constitution, which vests judicial power in federal government, does not mention "grand" juries. Therefore, the grand jury system is part of our constitutional law because of the above provision which is found in the Bill of Rights.

Historical Reason For. To understand the reason for the creation of a system of grand juries, one must have some understanding of the conditions that existed in the American colonies prior to the American Revolution. The King of England, George III, by comparison with previous kings, was a weak monarch. His choice of representatives in the colonies left much to be desired and they outraged the Americans by their acts. Increased taxation and perpetual duty acts became intolerable to the business community. On the colonial court scene, the situation had deteriorated. It was not uncommon for one accused of committing a crime against the crown to be tried summarily under harsh British procedure, or to be shipped to England for trial. In either case, the most fundamental principles of fairness were denied and especially so if an ocean stood between an accused and the accused's witnesses. Many of the complaints of the colonists are spelled out specifically in the Declaration of Independence. For these reasons, it was logical for the drafters of the U.S. Constitution and the first ten amendments, to avoid those matters they so bitterly complained of in those days. Thus, specific mention was made in the Fifth Amendment of the requirement of a "grand" jury—something that existed in the colonies only as a matter of choice on the part of the king.

What Is a Grand Jury? A grand jury is a body of persons, in specified number, who are subpoenaed to appear in court, federal or state, at a designated time and place. The number of persons required varies. In

---

[2] U.S. Constitution, 5th Amendment.

New York, 23 are used; in Virginia, not less than five nor more than seven are required. Another state requires the panel to consist of 16 persons, but 15 can act as a jury if only 15 show.

Function. A grand jury is a "board of inquiry." The jury decides if there is "probable cause" that a crime has been committed. In short, a grand jury serves as a "buffer panel" between an accused and the state.

Terms. Most state and federal courts operate by a "term system" in which the grand jury meets at designated times. A person who is "bound over to the next term of the grand jury" may face one or two months delay before action will be taken in the case. The reason for the bail or bond system is to prevent hardships to the accused caused by the delay. In rural areas, a grand jury may be called infrequently because of a lack of matters to present to them. Or, if called, they may adjourn for lack of matters to consider.

The Panel Is Called. A grand jury is summoned by the use of subpoenas, a "request" from the court for them to appear for service. These are issued by the clerk's office and are served by the sheriff. The subpoena states the time and place where the juror is to report. Jurors may be excused upon showing good cause. Otherwise, grand jury duty is usually accepted as a necessary public service.

Grand Jury Meets. On the "return" day of the subpoenas, the court will ask the clerk to call the names of the jurors. If those who have reported are fewer than required by law, the court will order the jury commissioners to produce additional jurors. It is not uncommon for persons to be taken from the streets to serve. Once the requisite number are present, the court will have the jurors sworn and will, by questions to them, determine if they are qualified to serve. It is important that they be over 18 years of age, residents of the county and be without criminal records. If mistakes are made in the empaneling of a grand jury, a subsequent conviction may be reversed because of defects in the panel.

The Prosecutor Steps In. Once the court has determined that the panel members are qualified, the judge may give them a statement of their duties and powers. Following this, the jury retires to a suitable room along with the prosecutor, or the district or state's attorney. In the federal system, the United States attorney conducts the hearings.

Secrecy. At common law in the proceedings against the regicides of King Charles, the king's counsel had the right to privacy before the "grand inquest." The same policy is followed today. Many objections have been raised by those who argue that the accused should have a right to be present. The courts have uniformly rejected the argument – but a change may be seen in the future.

What Takes Place? For discussion purposes, assume that Joe Smith has been arrested on a grand larceny charge. After a preliminary hearing, he was released on bond. The prosecutor is now before the grand jury:

Prosecutor: Ladies and gentlemen, the next matter to be considered is the case of *State* v. *Joe Smith.* I call as a witness, Trooper Brown. (Brown enters and is sworn – or he may have been "presworn" with the other witnesses.) State your name, age, and occupation.

Trooper: My name is John Brown. I am 32 and I am a member of the Department of Public Safety.

Prosecutor: Is that the State Police?

A: Yes.

Q: On the night of September 25, of this year, did you make an arrest?

A: Yes.

Q: Where?

A: At Jones Corporation.

Q: Who did you arrest?

A: Joe Smith.

Q: Tell the jury why you went to Jones Corporation and what you found Joe Smith doing.

The proceedings continue until the jury is satisfied that enough evidence has been heard to conclude that a crime has *probably* been committed. The degree of proof before a grand jury is less than in a regular trial and an experienced prosecutor can present 25 to 40 cases to a jury in a short time. If the jury is not convinced that a crime probably occurred, they may refuse to "indict." In that event, no formal charge is made. If a jury is convinced, they "indict" by returning the indictment—sometimes called a "true bill."

Nature of Indictment. An indictment *is not a finding of guilt*—only a finding that there is probable cause to believe a crime has been committed. Following the indictment, if the accused has not been arrested previously, a warrant is issued and the police agencies will arrest the accused.

Special Grand Juries. The states have laws permitting special grand juries to be called to make inquiry into general matters rather than to look at individual cases. Juries have been called to investigate fraudulent voting practices in a community, the nature and extent of local gambling and its influence, corruption in local government, and causes of student unrest on the campuses. In many cases, a special grand jury uncovers enough evidence to permit them to believe that certain persons may have committed a crime and indictments follow.

Abuses. Unfortunately, the grand jury system lends itself to corrupt practices. Threats of all types have been made upon the lives of grand jurors if they indict "so and so." Cases are on record of jurors being bribed if they "do not indict so and so." In some instances, state's attorneys have used their power before a grand jury to punish or "get at" certain persons for personal reasons. It is the responsibility of the court and society to make certain that these abuses do not occur.

But if they do, there is also a duty to see that those responsible are punished. A special grand jury can be called to investigate the practices as well as the procedures of the prosecutors—and prior grand juries as well. In some states, judges and even magistrates, can find "probable cause" and thus place one in position to be tried for the alleged crime. (In states that follow this procedure, the accused is allowed to be present; to have counsel; to cross-examine witnesses and to present evidence on his or her behalf.)

6. Petit Juries

The juries that hear cases and render verdicts in the federal as well as the state court systems, are by tradition, made up of 12 persons but in some courts four, six or eight are used.

Today, these juries are called "petit juries" to distinguish them from "grand juries." They are also referred to as "trial juries." It is the function of petit juries to hear evidence from witnesses upon the witness stand, and after instructions from the judge, to decide upon a verdict.

In many of our states, the petit – or trial – jury, not only finds guilt in criminal cases, but also determines the sentence that will be imposed. In other courts, a new jury is called to decide the penalty.

How Are They Selected? A panel of "jury commissioners," often only two persons, begins the selection of a jury by compiling a list of 300 names or more. The commissioners cannot place persons on the list as a "favor," and neither can those interested in serving request that their names be added. In most states, either act is a misdemeanor.

Great power is vested in the commissioners. In the past, it was not uncommon to find that certain ethnic groups or races or women were "systematically excluded" from the list. This meant that these persons would never have a chance to serve on a jury. Many convictions have been reversed by higher courts where it has been demonstrated statistically that certain persons or groups had been eliminated from the jury rolls.

The panel is screened by the clerk or a deputy to find if those named are qualified. It is not uncommon to find that some members of the first list have moved or are deceased. Once these names are removed, the clerk establishes that the others on the list are over the proper age, without criminal records, and are voters of the county or district and reside therein.

Under provisions of Public Law 92–269,[3] those over the age of 18 years are eligible to serve on federal juries. The same is true in Pennsylvania and most other states by virtue of state legislation.

Panel Called. Once the first day for jury trial is fixed, the clerk will call a panel by use of summons or subpoenas. In courts where only one case is tried at a time, 50 jurors are usually sufficient. In larger courts, proportionally more will be required depending upon the number of trials being conducted at the same time. The panels are selected at random from the larger group.

Must I Serve? Those who receive a summons to report for jury duty are often distressed by the call. A wage earner will be concerned about what jury service will cost in lost wages. While jurors are paid in all courts, the sum is small compared to modern wages. In a representative state, a juror is paid $8 per day plus mileage to the courthouse. Many union employees earn that much per hour. A housewife with small children to care for may be hard pressed if forced to hire a babysitter. The professional may be in a hopeless conflict with obligations in private practice. And there is the person who has religious convictions about

---

[3] Effective October 31, 1973.

passing judgment upon another. In a few instances, there are those who have no reason to object other than they simply do not want to serve. How can such conflicts and hardships be reconciled?

A Duty to Serve. First, it is the duty of each mature person in an organized society to respond to the call for jury service. And this will continue to be so as long as trial by jury is part of our court process. Common sense tells us that if each citizen had an absolute right to *refuse* to serve, the system would not operate. On the other hand, a blind refusal of a court to exempt or excuse certain persons would result in unreasonable losses and hardships to them.

Exemptions. Most states list by law those who are exempt from jury service. The following statute is typical:

> 5265. (2) *Exemptions and Disqualifications.* — The following persons shall be exempt but not disqualified, from serving on juries: Licensed practicing attorneys, licensed practicing physicians and dentists, registered practicing pharmacists, postmasters, all persons employed in the actual care and conveyance of the mails of the United States, officers of any court, justices of the peace, constables, all state, county and federal officers, all officers and employees of the department of public safety, all officers and members of the national guard while in actual service, all telegraph operators actually engaged as such in any office in this State, ministers of the gospel, superintendents, officers and assistants of hospitals, prisons and jails, conductors and engineers of railways, the members of any regularly organized fire or police department in any city, town or village, all persons in the army or navy or volunteer force of the United States, all professors, tutors and pupils of institutions of learning while such institutions are actually in session; and the following persons shall be disqualified from serving on juries: Idiots, lunatics, paupers, vagabonds, habitual drunkards, and persons convicted of infamous crimes.

Excuses. Most courts are liberal in excusing persons for cause who are not otherwise exempt. However, the morning the panel is to report is the wrong time to ask to be excused. The best time is as soon after receiving a jury summons as possible. Jurors are excused for such reasons as death in the family, illness of members of the family, bad health of the juror, and others.

Jury in the Box. Once a sufficient number of qualified jurors are present in the courtroom, the clerk will "call the roll." Those who attend v. ill be paid for the day — whether they are seated on a jury or not. The clerk calls 20 names of persons who take their place in the jury box. Extra chairs are provided for the extra persons.

"Jurati." After the panel members are seated, they are sworn and then asked qualifying questions by the court. The following are representative:

> Are you all over the age of 18 years and citizens of this state? Do you reside in this judicial district? Have any of you been convicted of an infamous crime? Are any of you employees of this state or any state agency?

Once the panel is "settled," the court will generally permit counsel to ask questions of the panel.

Alternate Jurors. While the traditional petit jury is made up of 12 persons, it is not uncommon to see juries in criminal cases, or lengthy civil cases, in which the panel is 14 or 16 persons. The extras are known as "alternates." They have been selected just as the basic 12, and have heard the evidence from the beginning of the case. But they will only join in the final deliberations if one of the first 12 becomes disabled or dies during the course of the trial. In that event, the first alternate moves into the jury and the trial continues. In cases of short duration—one to five days—alternates are seldom used.

Striking the Jury. Once the jurors are in the box—and extras if alternates are to be used—the "striking" begins. This is the first time that the parties to the litigation will have a voice in which persons will hear the case. In civil cases, the plaintiff and defendant alternate strikes. This means that of the 20 persons in the box, the plaintiff will eliminate the first one. The defendant follows until each has struck four persons. The remaining 12 make up the jury. If alternates are used, the process is continued as to the extra persons.

The striking of a jury requires two things: first, that counsel be familiar with each person who makes up the larger panel. The lawyer should know where each juror works, religious affiliation, type of personal life led and other pertinent facts. This information is often prepared by paralegal personnel. Second, counsel for both sides must use care to avoid striking one who would have been struck by the other.

In criminal prosecutions, the state is limited in strikes by law, for example two, and must strike first. The defendant then has a choice of who goes off the panel afterwards. This is often helpful to the accused.

Most states and the federal courts, permit "peremptory" or "no cause" challenges. Before these are used, challenges for "cause" are also permitted. By using the latter, the former can be reserved for later use because a challenge for cause removes one from a panel and still preserves the peremptory challenges for later use.

The Jury in Operation. A jury that hears a civil or criminal case lives a "jury life" of isolation. Under the rules of procedure and rules of evidence, only certain matters can be heard by the jury. A trial is often a frustrating experience for jurors and they frequently complain because they did not hear evidence that they wanted to hear. Most courts will not permit a juror to take notes. The theory is that, if permitted, the juror would have an advantage over the other jurors during deliberation. The logic of this is questionable. Some judges will permit jurors to ask questions during trial. But this happens infrequently since most jurors, like students in class, choose to remain silent. In certain cases, a jury may lose the right to decide a case—even after they have spent many hours hearing evidence. This can happen in two ways: a "directed verdict" or a "mistrial."

Directed Verdicts. Judges have the power to "take a case from a jury," and when this happens the judge instructs the jury to retire, select a foreman, and return with a verdict for the party designated. It often happens when the judge feels that the evidence does not present a "question of fact" for the jury. Therefore, the judge decides the case based upon the controlling law. In practice, courts direct a fair number of verdicts during a normal court docket. When a verdict is directed, it usually means that the losing party failed in the proof or had a weak case in the beginning.

Mistrials. During a jury trial, certain matters may occur that will prompt the judge to declare a mistrial. When this happens, the jury is excused and the matter is carried over to a future docket. For example, if the plaintiff mentions before the jury that the defendant's insurance adjuster contacted the plaintiff, the judge will almost always declare a mistrial. Or if a juror comes up missing after part of the evidence is in, and there are no alternates, a mistrial will be declared.

Once the evidence is completed—and assuming the judge permits the case to go to the jury—the court instructs the jury (called "charging the jury" in federal courts).

If the lawsuit is a contract matter, the instructions would be based on principles of contract law.

In practice, instructions tend to confuse a jury—just as they confuse one who reads them. There is a move underway to create uniform instructions to make them easier for jurors to understand. But until changes are made, instructions will continue to be part of the court system, confusion and all. After the court instructs the jury, and closing arguments of counsel are completed, the jury begins its deliberations.

Deliberations. Upon retiring to the jury room, the jury selects a foreman. The jury is entitled to deliberate in secret and intrusion upon their privacy is a misdemeanor in most states. Any attempt to influence their decision is a felony. In criminal trials, where extreme penalties may be involved, juries are isolated and kept that way until a verdict is reached.

One with trial experience will admit that there is no way to decide what juries base their verdicts upon. In personal injury cases, the typical jury seems to have a sense of right and wrong and will usually favor the innocent party. But on the question of the amount of damages, no guidelines can be established. One thing is certain, however, juries do not run a "giveaway" game. High verdicts are rare unless serious injuries are involved. The large verdict cases have made headlines, yet in every such case the plaintiff is paralyzed or otherwise incapacitated for life.

Empirical studies have been made on verdicts in various types of cases. The results provide helpful guidelines for placing a dollar value upon a case. For example, A negligently drives an auto so that it strikes the auto of B from the rear. Property damage to B's car is $300 and B suffers a "whiplash" injury. In such cases, the plaintiff wins 90 percent of the time and the average verdict nationwide is $3,000. The case has a "dollar tag" of $2,700 or $3,000 × 90 percent.

In some states before a jury can convict one of a criminal charge, the jury must be in unanimous agreement. In some states a prescribed number less than the entire panel can return a verdict of "guilty." In Wisconsin for example, a $5/6$ths vote of a jury is all that is required for conviction.

In civil cases, less than unanimous vote can decide an issue – provided that the parties have agreed to this in advance. If the jury cannot agree, they are said to be "deadlocked." In such cases, the judge usually takes action.

Deadlocked Jury. If a jury announces that they cannot agree upon a verdict, the judge will have them brought in for some "gentle persuasion." The following is from a court record:

> Ladies and gentlemen of the jury. I am aware that arriving at a verdict is not always an easy job. If you like, I will reinstruct you. In any event, the dispute in this case must be settled sometime by a jury, and it might as well be you. It is 7 P.M. and I am going to the restaurant for supper. You will retire to consider your verdict and I will see how you are doing when I return.

In earlier common law years when a jury was deadlocked, they were loaded into an ox-cart and driven around the village, foodless. The townsfolk would toss a rock or two and verbally lash them for their refusal to reach a verdict. Forcing verdicts must be done in a more subtle manner today. But in some cases all efforts to force a verdict fail and the judge must again step in.

Hung Jury. When it becomes apparent that a jury will not return a verdict, the judge will declare them to be a "hung jury." When this happens, the panel is dismissed and the case remains undecided. This happens frequently in cases that require testimony over an extended period of time. The more evidence a jury hears, the more likely they are to disagree when it comes time to deliberate.

It is common knowledge that juries sometimes use the "quotient verdict" to reach a decision.

Quotient Verdicts. If a jury decides the plaintiff should recover, it then becomes a matter of "how much." A technique used is to have each juror to write down the dollar sum the plaintiff should recover. These 12 figures are totalled and divided by 12. The average is the verdict returned – a "quotient verdict." As reasonable as this procedure may sound, it is unlawful in many courts. The argument against it is that the verdict arrived at is not a verdict of the jury but rather a compromise of 12 verdicts. It is not uncommon for the losing defense lawyer to rummage through the waste baskets in the jury room searching for evidence that the verdict was arrived at in this manner. If this can be established, a motion to set aside the verdict is usually successful.

Once the jury has arrived at a verdict, the court reconvenes for the purpose of receiving the verdict.

Announcing Verdict. Verdicts are announced in open court. In criminal cases, the accused must be present to hear the reading of the verdict. In civil cases, it is not necessary for the parties to be present. The following is typical.

> *Judge:* Mr. Foreman, have you arrived at a verdict?
> *Foreman:* Yes, we have, Your Honor.
> *Judge:* Will you give us that verdict?
> *Foreman:* We, the jury, find . . .

(The verdict is then recorded by the clerk of the court.)

Judge: The clerk will read the verdict to the jury—Harken unto your verdict.
Clerk: We, the jury, find . . .
Judge: So say you all?
Jury: (Nods of assent.)
Judge: The jury is excused until tomorrow morning at 9:30.

In some cases, the attorney for the losing party will ask the court to "poll" the jury. Each juror is then asked individually if that is his or her verdict. In cases where one juror was pressured into a verdict, the juror often uses this opportunity to make it known. If one juror indicates that the verdict was forced, the court will refuse to accept the verdict and declare a mistrial or make the jury resume deliberations. Once the verdict is fixed, it is entered on the order books of the court and the appeal period begins running.

Posttrial Motions. The usual motion made following a verdict is to have the verdict set aside, but there are others. Such motions must be based upon matters from the trial. In rare cases the court on its own may set the verdict aside, but in most cases will not for a simple reason: If error had occurred during the trial, the judge would not have permitted the case to go to the jury.

If the motion to set aside is overruled, then the appeal period begins to run. The losing party must then take timely steps for appeal—or be bound by the verdict.

This look at the operations of a petit jury demonstrates that the system is full of possibilities for delay. In addition, the jury is often confused and quite often their verdicts are wrong. But until changes are made, the procedures discussed here will be followed when the citizen is successful in obtaining the "right to trial by jury."

THE FUTURE?

Two suggestions are currently being studied to solve the increasing backlog in jury trials. The first is that the number of jurors be reduced from 12 to six—or less. The second is to permit a verdict to be returned where the majority of the panel is in favor of a verdict, but a minority of the jury disagrees. For example, four votes out of a panel of six would permit a verdict to be returned.

There is precedent for both suggestions. Florida uses a six-person jury and the constitutionality of the jury of that state has been upheld by the U.S. Supreme Court. There is no constitutional requirement that a jury contain 12 persons, nor is there any requirement in the Constitution that a verdict be unanimous.

On June 21, 1973, the United States Supreme Court in the case of *Colgrove* v. *Battin*,[4] held that a local federal rule providing for a six member jury in civil cases, is consistent with the Seventh Amendment. In addition, the court held that the constitutional requirement that the right

---

[4] 413 U.S. 149 (1973).

to trial by jury be preserved in suits at common law, is not violated by the use of a six-member jury.

States that follow rules of procedure based upon the federal rules, permit the parties in civil litigation to agree in advance that less than a unanimous verdict may be returned by the jury.

Another suggestion has been to eliminate the jury entirely and permit the judges to hear and decide civil cases. Studies have disclosed that judges who preside over jury cases are in agreement with the verdicts as to liability in almost 100 percent of the cases. But they would have allowed the plaintiff more money damages than the jury did. A more serious problem will develop if an effort is made to do away with the jury in criminal cases. New York State attempted to eliminate jury trials where one is charged with a crime that is punishable by less than one year in jail. The U.S. Supreme Court declared that law to be unconstitutional.

REVIEW QUESTIONS

1. Have you seen a jury trial in operation? If not, make it a point to do so in the future.
2. Name ways in which trial juries are restrained by rules of 200 years ago.
3. How could the computer be used in the selection of juries?
4. Make one suggestion of how the jury system could be improved. Might "professional juries" be one answer?
5. True or False. The American jury system will probably be changed in the future.
6. Explain why the Seventh Amendment "preserves" the right to trial by jury in certain cases.
7. What is the necessity of having coroner's juries?
8. In practice, the J.P. jury can be used to create an injustice. Can you give a reason why?
9. There is sentiment for abolishing the grand jury system. Give an argument for and against this.
10. How could a prosecuting attorney use a grand jury to maliciously cause injury to another?

Words and Phrases

Write out briefly what they mean to you.
1. Alternates.
2. "Striking."
3. Quotient verdicts.
4. Mistrial.
5. Jury commissioners.

Coverage:	Ways that controversies can be settled without litigation.
What to Look for:	How the techniques discussed can be used in business.
Application:	Think in terms of using one of these techniques to settle your contract dispute.

11 Avoiding Court

Discourage litigation. Persuade your neighbors to compromise whenever you can. Point out to them how the nominal winner is often a real loser—in fees, expenses, and waste of time.
—Abraham Lincoln, Notes for a Law Lecture, July 1, 1850.

The legal system is characterized by two predominant features: delay and expense. Add to this the bad feelings that accompany lawsuits, and one comes to the conclusion that other means of settling controversies should be sought. This is especially so in business, big or small, where the publicity that accompanies litigation is undesirable. The business person cannot afford the reputation of being one who constantly brings suit against customers and clients. Resort to the courts *can* become mandatory but should be delayed until other methods of settling are attemped. There are six widely used techniques: compromise, substitute performance, substitution of debtors, arbitration, mediation, and "composition."

1. Compromise

When two or more persons adjust their differences by mutual agreement for the purpose of avoiding a lawsuit, or ending one in progress, it is called a "compromise and settlement." The principal feature is that each balances the hope of winning in court against the danger of losing there. Such agreements are favored by law if fairly made.[1]

From a strict legal point of view, a mere offer to compromise is not enough. There must be acceptance of the offer, and mere silence of the

---

Davis v. *Lilly*, 96 WVa. 144, 122, S.E. 444 (1924).

FIGURE 11-1

Litigation	Compromise
B Sues A for $20,000. B Obtains Judgment of $15,000.	Defendant A Pays Plaintiff B $8,000 to Compromise and Settle Out of Court.

Features
 1. Two to five years in court.
 2. Destruction of good will.
 3. Expenses:
    Attorney.................. $5,000.00
    Doctor..................... 500,00
    Misc....................... 100.00
    Net........................ $9,400.00
	Features
	 1. B is paid now.
	 2. No publicity.
	 3. Preservation of good will.
	 4. Net $8,000.

other party is not enough. If acceptance follows, there is a binding contract and courts will not disturb the contract unless there has been fraud, duress, or the like. The "consideration" (the reason for enforcing promises) is found in each giving up the right to test the matter in court. That is sufficient "payment" to support the promises to settle. If either refuses to perform as promised, that person can be sued for breach of contract.

If a matter in court is compromised and settled, a court order will be prepared and entered, dismissing the suit as being "fully compromised and settled" and "with prejudice," meaning that the suit can never be brought again.

A Guide to Consider. While each dispute must be examined upon its facts, a rule of thumb is suggested in determining how to work out a compromise. In the following example the plaintiff is demanding $20,000 while the defendant has offered $3,000.

Plaintiff————————————— Area ———→Demands $20,000
                                                     of
Defendant Offers———→$3,000   Compromise

This is typical in personal injury cases. An attempt should be made to agree upon a sum in the area designated as "the area of compromise." It may be $4,000 or it may be $14,000, but both figures have one thing in common: Both parties are doing something that they do not want to do. That is, the plaintiff is taking less than was demanded and the defendant is paying more than was offered. The ancient Egyptians stated, "A bad compromise is better than a good lawsuit," and this advice is timely today. Figure 11-1 compares a compromise with litigation. (B has been injured by A in a car accident.)

2. Substitute Performance

Frequently, one owes another a sum of money and cannot pay it, but the debtor has goods or services to substitute for the debt. For example, A owes B $500 and is unable to pay B since A is out of work. A is a painter by trade and offers to paint B's store in exchange for the debt. If B accepts the offer, and if A performs the work, the debt is settled. In legal terms the substitution of services or goods for a debt is called "accord," the tender of substitute performance, and "satisfaction," the completion of the substitution. It is not uncommon in business for debts to be settled in exchange for sign painting, truck repairs, or a new roof job. The legal effect of the substitute performance, once completed, is that it bars the original contract or cause of action.

3. Substitution of Debtors

When creditor A agrees to substitute Debtor C for Debtor B, Debtor B is released and the debt is paid. Where a substitution of debtors occurs, it is called a "novation." An example will illustrate.

Texas Company Vanishes. For three years Supply Company sold drilling supplies to Texas Company. The terms of sale were "30 days net." Texas Company paid on time and purchased from $3,000 to $10,000 in supplies each month. One Monday morning, Supply Company discovered that Texas Company had packed its inventory and drilling equipment and had disappeared! Supply Company was carrying an accounts receivable balance of $5,000 with Texas Company at the time. The accountant for Texas Company was without explanation of what had happened. Upon inquiry, the accountant admitted that the company had funds due them for work performed but the amount Texas Company owed others was substantial—the debts being more than what was due the company.

A debtor of Texas Company agreed to pay $5,000 of its debt to Supply Company. All that was requested was a receipt from Texas—which the accountant gave. Supply Company gave Texas Company a receipt for $5,000 and the books were changed to reflect the exchange. Had Texas Company been forced into involuntary bankruptcy, the $5,000 would have been demanded by the trustee in bankruptcy. However, no bankruptcy followed, the accountant worked out settlements with other creditors, and the matter was closed. (Texas Company is still missing.)

Distinguished from "Garnishment." Novation should be distinguished from "garnishment." (See Chapter 36). In the latter, money in the hands of a third party that is due to the debtor is "garnished," or "suggested." The garnishment must be preceded by court action with judgment entered against the debtor. The court then orders the third party to surrender to the judgment creditor what it owes to the debtor, under legal guidelines.

Therefore in garnishment, a court is used. In a novation, there must be a voluntary agreement between all concerned and no court is involved. In the Texas case there was agreement by Texas Company—through its agent, the accountant.

4. Arbitration

The procedure by which parties to a dispute submit the matter to a panel of laypersons, or even one person, for decision, is called "arbitration." The procedure is widely used in the settlement of fire insurance claims and labor disputes. The citizen is aware of its use, particularly during labor disputes. One little-known fact is that arbitration was widely used in the American colonies due to the inaccessibility of conventional courts. To illustrate, in Pennsylvania, William Penn's laws of 1682, provided for the appointment of three "Common peacemakers" in each precinct. These peacemakers were given power to arbitrate disputes and their decisions were to stand "as judgments of the Courts of Justice."[2]

Today, arbitration clauses are used in construction contracts, sales agreements and collective bargaining contracts. The *form* of these clauses should be left up to the lawyer to draft. For example, should the rules of evidence control proceedings under them and do the arbitrators have to submit "findings of fact" with their decisions?

Statutes.   Many states have statutes that spell out the procedures to be followed in arbitration. The statutes "are supplementary to and not exclusive of the common law." In short, the common-law provisions are changed only to the extent of the changes in the statutes. All other common-law provisions are in effect. In states without statutes, the common-law rules of arbitration control.

Unlawful?   It has been argued that arbitration is unlawful. If courts are provided as the forum for settling disputes, why should the parties be able to create their own tribunal (arbitration) and submit a case to it? The answer is found in two facts: first, the final decision of arbitration, called the "award," *is* recognized by the courts. The award can be filed in court in most states, and if no appeal is taken, it can be enforced just as any other judgment or order of the court. Second, as a general rule, parties to the arbitration cannot agree that the award shall be final and that neither will go to court. This is against public policy because such an agreement would in fact "oust the jurisdiction" of the courts. Therefore, either can take a case to court after the dispute is submitted to arbitration.

But it must be pointed out that arbitration *can* be binding in certain situations.

Binding Arbitration.   In collective bargaining agreements involving the federal statutes, arbitration is final and binding.[3] In some states, by statutory law, an arbitrator's award involving collective bargaining agreements of municipal employees, is subject to court review. But in some states, Maine for example, the review must be limited to questions of law — not fact. Therefore, in such states the arbitration award is binding.

The Seattle Plan.   The Seattle–King County Bar Association of Washington, has approved an arbitration program designed to help relieve the congestion in Superior Court there.

Under this plan, specified types of cases can be voluntarily submitted by the parties to a single arbitrator whose decision will be final. The ar-

---

[2] Edwin B. Bronner, *William Penn's Holy Experiment* (New York: Columbia University Press, 1962), p. 36.

[3] *United Steelworkers of America* v. *American Manufacturing Co.*, 363 U.S. 564, (1960); *United Steelworkers of America* v. *Warrior & Gulf Navigation Co.*, 363 U.S. 574, (1960).

bitrator is chosen from a list of experienced trial lawyers and serves without pay. This duty is rotated between a list of lawyers chosen for that purpose.

Outside of the exceptions noted, in most states, the losing party still has recourse to the courts – provided that one acts within time periods provided by law for appeals.

At Common Law. Two types of arbitration were known at common law. First, "submission in pais" in which there was no suit pending but the parties agreed to arbitrate, and second, submission when a suit was pending. In the second situation, the procedures were carried out in court by notice to "show cause," making it in effect a court procedure. By the rules of common law, an arbitrator was an agent. Therefore, the authority of the agent could be terminated anytime prior to the award – even during the hearing. The statutes have modified this rule and today, one who agrees to arbitration cannot discharge the arbitrators.

Who Can Submit to Arbitration? Any person or corporation that is capable of making a binding contract may submit a controversy to arbitration. For example, an attorney may submit a client's cause to arbitration in a circuit court, *if* the client is an adult, *if* the client agrees, and *if* it is done in open court. Municipal corporations, partners, and other contracting agencies may submit matters to arbitration – provided those involved are in agreement.

What May Be Submitted? Personal demands of all kinds including tort claims, contract disputes, and partnership problems may be submitted. The trial of public crimes, however, cannot be arbitrated because of the constitutional requirement of trial by jury in criminal cases.

How Is It Carried Out? First, the arbitrator, or panel of arbitrators, is chosen. In many cases, the parties have agreed to use one person who will hear the matter, decide the issue, and enter an award. Professional arbitrators are available and can be hired on an hourly basis. In other cases a panel is used, quite often three persons. The following illustrates how arbitrators are selected and how the hearing is conducted.

A Dispute Arises. A merchant contracted with a contractor to install floor tile in the merchant's store. The contract contained a clause that stated that in the event a dispute arose, the parties agreed to submit the matter to arbitration under the rules of the American Arbitration Association – the national organization. A further provision stated that neither party waived the right to go to the court once the matter had been submitted to arbitration. Arbitration was made a "condition precedent" to the right to go to court, that is, "arbitrate first and then sue."

Within a week after the installation, the store owner noticed that the tile was coming loose at different parts of the store. The store owner refused to pay the balance due and, at the same time, the contractor was demanding payment – a good example of how business persons get into court.

Notice Is Given. The contractor sought legal advice and her attorney examined the contract. Since arbitration had been made a condition precedent to suit, the contractor was told to first arbitrate the matter.

A letter was prepared by the lawyer and sent to the store owner advising of the following:

1. The dispute was to be submitted to arbitration the coming Thursday at 7 P.M.
2. The hearing was to be held in a certain room at the municipal building (prior permission had been granted by the mayor).
3. The contractor had named an attorney to represent her.
4. The store owner was to name his representative.
5. The two representatives were to select a third party prior to the hearing date.

At the Hearing.   At the designated time and place, both parties were present along with three arbitrators. The store owner had selected an attorney and the two lawyers had in turn selected a local banker as the third party, injecting a neutral element into the panel.

The attorney who gave the notice called the meeting to order. The parties told their versions of the problem and each was questioned by the panel. This required 20 minutes. After the testimony was complete, the panel excused the parties so that they could discuss the matter in private. In the closed session, each attorney tried to impress the banker with their client's point of view. The banker, however, felt there was not enough information to decide which way to vote, and suggested that they take a look at the floor. After a short walk to the store, the panel discovered two things: asphalt instead of vinyl plastic tile had been used, and the tile had been laid on the old wooden floor with only tar paper cemented under it.

The panel questioned the parties again and each made an admission: The contractor had insisted that underlayment board be used but the store owner did not want to use it because of the additional cost; and the store owner had intended that plastic tile be used but the contractor had substituted asphalt. It was these two facts that caused the floor to come loose and the panel concluded that both parties should carry part of the blame—and burden.

The Award.   During a second brief session, the following "award" was written and signed by all three members of the panel.

After identifying the contract and other facts, the award continued:

It is the finding of the undersigned that the parties to the dispute shall do as follows:

1. The contractor shall remove the asphalt tile and install $\frac{1}{4}$" hardboard underlayment. The hardboard is to be paid for by the storeowner.

2. The contractor shall purchase vinyl plastic tile and install the same as per the original contract.

3. The storeowner shall pay the contractor the amount set forth in the original contract in addition to the cost of the underlayment board.

4. The parties shall divide the costs of the arbitration between them equally.

The award was given to the local circuit clerk, who accepted it and placed it in a file as required by statute. The ten-day appeal period began running. Either party had the legal right to place the matter in court as an appeal from the award.

What Happened?   Neither party appealed and their duties as spelled out in the award became fixed. The work was completed promptly, and all costs were paid. Today the parties to the dispute are friends, the floor in the store is wearing well, and one lawsuit had been avoided.

Features of Arbitration.   The incident discussed points out advantages that follow from the good faith use of arbitration. Outside of the three panel members, no one was aware of the dispute, thus harmful publicity was avoided. The good will between the parties was preserved—and, in this case, enhanced. The entire proceeding from the time of notice until the decision took one week—a far removal from the unbelievable delays that occur in court. The total cost was reasonable under the facts ($150); the arbitrators applied common sense to the situation. In short, features of arbitration include privacy, preservation of goodwill, quick determination, low cost and common-sense interpretation of the law—most of which simply are not found in our courts today.

5. Mediation

Under Old English statutory law,[4] where questions arose between merchants relating to quality of goods, improper shipments and the like, the dispute was referred to "mediators of questions." The statute provided that a panel of six laypersons would, upon taking oath, examine the dispute and settle it. The parties to the dispute had to agree to submit the matter, however. This had some of the characteristics of arbitration, yet it was not precisely the same. Out of this law came a modern counterpart, known as "mediation."

Definition.   The word mediation means "interposition" or "intervention" and is the act of some third party who comes between parties in a dispute in an attempt to encourage them to settle their differences.

Mediation is found internationally when a representative of one nation attempts to encourage other nations who are in a dispute, to compromise their differences. Wars are sometimes prevented in this manner.

Mediation is widely used in attempts to settle labor disputes in the United States, and the one who performs this function is known as a "mediator."

6. Compositions

In ancient times a "composition" was a sum paid in satisfaction of an injury or other wrong committed by one person against another. If the injured person died, the payment was made to the decedents' family. The purpose of the composition was to avoid vengeance against the wrongdoer. In time the composition became part of the common law and today, it is found in two principal areas.

Composition of Creditors.   Debtor A is insolvent and cannot meet obligations due creditors. The creditors and debtor A enter into an agreement in which each creditor agrees to accept a sum smaller than the

---

[4] 27 Edw. III St. 2, c. 24.

amount due in satisfaction of the entire sum. Since the creditors will be owed varying sums of money, the distribution will be on a "pro rata" (to share or divide) basis. A composition of creditors is a contract and requires that *adequate consideration*[5] be present. This is supplied by the mutual promises to give up a portion of the sum due.

A composition of creditors is distinguishable from an "accord" in that the accord is usually made with just *one* creditor who accepts payment by some different means. In the composition, all creditors join in the agreement.

But as may be expected, it is unusual to find unanimous agreement among creditors in such circumstances. Some will not want to compromise the sum due to them. Can they be forced to do so?

Compositions in Bankruptcy.   One who petitions for relief in bankruptcy court (federal), can ask to be permitted to retain all assets upon the condition that partial, pro rata payments be made to the creditors. Thus a composition in bankruptcy is a matter of law and does *not* depend upon agreement between the creditors. By the use of the "composition," many businesses have been spared the agonies of straight bankruptcy.

REVIEW QUESTIONS

1. Distinguish a "novation" from "garnishment."
2. Identify a lawsuit that you know of that might have been settled if it had been submitted to arbitration.
3. In older times, merchants frequently engaged in a system of "barter" – the exchange of goods. How does "barter" square up with "accord and satisfaction"?
4. How could novation be used between a car manufacturer, a steel producer, and an assembly plant, all of which do business with one another?
5. True or False. Arbitration may provide one solution to the court congestion.
6. Distinguish "arbitration" from "mediation." How are they related?
7. Give an example of the use of mediation on an international basis. Use a current example in the news.
8. Normally, an arbitration award is not treated as being final – at least at the outset. Why?
9. Distinguish a "judgement creditor" from an ordinary "creditor." Does one have an advantage over the other? If so, what is it?
10. True or False. A "compromise" that is carried out to completion is a binding contract.

Words and Phrases

Write out briefly what they mean to you.
1. The award.
2. Choosing an arbitrator.
3. Novation.
4. "Arbitration is unlawful."
5. "Area of compromise."

---
[5] See Chapter 14.

part two
The Laws of
Business

Coverage:	The material is developed in detail and it must be examined carefully.
What to Look for:	The reader should try to see the relationship between the items discussed even though they appear unrelated.
Application:	These "policies of the law" will provide a better understanding of the nature of law and the legal system.

12 Policies of the Law

As civilization emerged from the Dark Ages, certain relationships began to develop between the members of society and the law that regulated those within that society. These relationships did not appear in easily recognizable form, especially at first. Rather, over the centuries they developed through a perpetual interplay of law and society. These relationships are "policies of the law"—although it can be argued that they are in reality the law itself.

The policies discussed in this chapter all find application in the laws of contract, regulation of trade, tort, and other major topics, and it has become traditional to study them in those settings. Such treatment is legitimate and useful, but often one who completes a course in "business law" or "commercial law" fails to realize that many of the rules, customs, and usages of law have common origins which have grown out of a "policy" or trend or established course of conduct. One who gains this awareness is better able to understand the nature of our legal system and the part that it plays in the regulation of business and society. This chapter was prepared with the thought that perhaps this objective could be attained by the reader by treating major policies of the law under a single heading. Now a look at some of those policies as found in practice.

RECORDING

At the time of the Norman Conquest, writs, grants from the Crown, and other important legal documents were being created and preserved, usually in rolls, and filed at appropriate points. Indexes to the documents were maintained so they could be located, although the system was inaccurate and poorly developed. As time passed and recording systems were developed, the older documents were destroyed, or scattered, although many can be found today in the collections of those who keep and preserve such documents. (See Figures 14–8 and 14–9.)

Today, in each county of the United States, a central office is found where a variety of documents will be "on record." In larger urban areas, many of these have been computerized. In smaller communities the records are typed or photocopied and filed in loose-leaf binders. Regardless of the system, the public is presumed to know what is on record there. The function of recording, then, is to place the public on notice, and it is a major policy of the law.

An Example

A offers to sell a mobile home to B for $5,000. In the office of the clerk of the county court of that county is an index to "Financing Statements." Opposite the name of A is the following notation: "Bank XYZ, file number 123." In another file in the clerk's office is an envelope that carries the number "123." Inside the envelope is a "financing statement" covering the mobile home that A is attempting to sell to B.

The financing statement is a "notice document" and tells B that Bank XYZ has a "security interest" in the mobile home. If B purchases the mobile home, B will be subject to the interest of the bank. If A defaults on the payments to the bank, the bank will foreclose, repossess the mobile home from B, sell it for the highest price obtainable, and sue A for any deficiency. (For a discussion of repossession and sale, see Chapter 37). B would be left to seek remedies against A, and would be $5,000 wiser because of it. B would also have a better understanding of what "recording" means.

Other Documents

Birth and death records, real estate mortgages or deeds of trust, corporation charters, deeds, wills and real estate plats are examples of other documents that are placed on record. Also, recording offices maintain indexes to judgments, pending suits, tax liens, and other data that involves one's credit standing.

The clerk of each court maintains records of court action including suits, pending suits, summary proceedings, name changes, and others. The divorce and adoption files are "privileged" and cannot be opened for public inspection. In most of our states, it is virtually impossible for those who have been adopted to trace their biological parents. Only three states, Alabama, South Dakota, and Virginia have laws that permit limited access to adoption records.

In other states, the adoption records can only be examined with permission of the court—which is seldom given. In the other 47 states, the birth records are changed so that the adopting parents appear on the birth certificate as natural parents.

Otherwise, the records of the counties and the courts are "public record" and are available for inspection by any interested person. The recording offices are storehouses of information available to the business person and to the citizen. The careful person will orient oneself to what is on record and will use the data by personal examination or through the services of a lawyer.

Another major policy of the law is that "limitations must be placed on the filing of suits."

LIMITATIONS ON ACTIONS

An old principle of the common law was that "all disputes must in time be settled." From this came statutory laws which provide time periods within which an action or suit may be brought against another, commonly called "statutes of limitations." Time periods are also provided within which certain legal rights become fixed. Following are examples from one state. When a person is missing for seven years, it is presumed that person is dead. If one holds adverse possession of realty under "color of title" for ten consecutive years (and meets other conditions as spelled out by law), that person acquires legal title. If one fails to file a claim against an estate within six months, the right to file is lost. If one is not prosecuted for a misdemeanor within two terms of court following indictment, that person is free. And many other periods of limitation are found in the state laws.

The most important to the citizen and to anyone in business are the periods of limitations that are placed upon actions in tort and contract. Examine Figure 12–1.

Limitations in Tort

If one negligently causes injury to another, an action must be brought within a specified time period. A typical statute provides that if loss to property arises in "tort," an action must be started no later than one year from the date of loss. If bodily injury is involved, the period of limitations is extended to two years.

Limitations in Contract

Three types of contracts are recognized: oral contracts, written contracts, and sales contracts under the U.C.C. The state mentioned previously has the following periods of limitation on contracts: oral agreements, five years; written contracts, ten years; and U.C.C. sales agreements, four years. Failure to sue within the prescribed time periods may result in a substantial contract loss.

FIGURE 12–1
Periods of Limitations

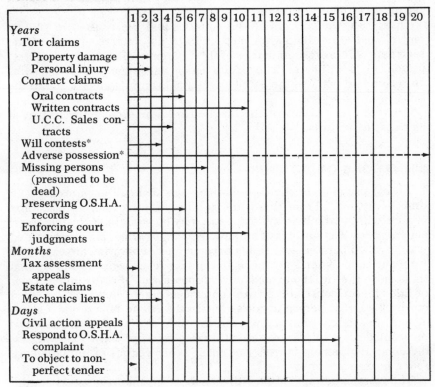

* Note: Periods of limitation will vary from state to state. In addition, the periods will begin running at different times depending upon the facts. The broken line after adverse possession indicates that this time period is more than ten years in some states.

Tolling of the Statutes

All states have laws that permit the "tolling" or "holding" of the period of limitations under prescribed circumstances. For example, the ten-year period on a negotiable instrument such as a note (which is a contract) would not run until ten years after the last payment was made on the note. If one leaves a state in which a contract obligation is owed, the time out of the state is not counted toward the period of limitation. Or if one becomes incapacitated in some manner, a court may stop the running of the statute of limitations during the time of disability. This happened in the *Lacy* case, and this in itself, is a major policy of the law.

> *Lacy* v. *Ferrence.*[1] Roger Wendell Lacy filed his petition in the Superior Court of Grady County against Dr. John A. Ferrence, reciting personal injuries allegedly sustained on April 30, 1962, as the result of the negligence of one of the defendant's employees while acting within the course of his

---

[1] 222 Ga. 635, 151 S.E.2d 763 (1966).

employment. His petition, later amended, also alleged that because of the serious brain injury thereby received, the plaintiff immediately, on the day of the injury, became insane so as to render him incapable of conducting his business affairs and of filing this action, and that such insanity continued until December 1, 1963. This suit was filed on December 30, 1964.

The defendant moved to dismiss the petition upon the ground that it affirmatively showed that the suit was barred by the statute of limitations. This motion was denied. The trial resulted in a verdict for the plaintiff, after which the defendant's motions for judgment notwithstanding the verdict and for new trial were also denied.

Upon review, the Court of Appeals reversed the denial of the motion to dismiss.

The substance of the ruling of the Court of Appeals complained of was that, notwithstanding the plaintiff's alleged insanity from the injury on April 30, 1962, until December 1, 1963, his petition did not allege any facts showing why he could not have filed suit within the five-month period between the removal of his insanity on December 1, 1963, and the expiration of the two-year statutory limitation on April 29, 1964, and in the absence of such showing, his temporary mental incapacity would not excuse his failure to bring the action within the applicable period of limitation.

We regard this ruling as contrary to the import of statutes which toll, in favor of persons under disability, the time limitations for the bringing of actions.

The statute of limitations applicable to the action here is Code 3–1004: "Actions for injuries to the person shall be brought within two years after the right of action accrues . . ."

Tolling the running of that two-year limitation are the following provisions: "Infants, idiots, or insane persons, or persons imprisoned who are such when the cause of action shall have accrued, shall be entitled to the same time after the disability shall have been removed, to bring an action, as is prescribed for other persons" (Code 3–801); and "If either of the foregoing disabilities shall happen after the right of action shall have accrued, and shall not be voluntarily caused or undertaken by the person claiming the benefit thereof, the limitation shall cease to operate during its continuance." (Code 3–802.)

These two provisions recognize certain circumstances which require the postponement of the running of such limitations and the suspension of their running. They stop the clock during the specified disabilities.

In the case at bar, the plaintiff's allegations are that he became insane due to serious brain injury. His allegations as to insanity are sufficient. The fact that the plaintiff also alleged that he was physically incapacitated did not lessen the effect of the allegations as to insanity.

Under such circumstances, time did not begin to run against him until the removal of his insanity on December 1, 1963, and from that date he had the full two years to bring his action.

Why he did not sue on some date between the removal of his insanity on December 1, 1963, and the expiration of two years from the date of his injury on April 29, 1964, is immaterial. The law gave him the benefit of two years time exclusive of the duration of his insanity in which to sue. He was not required, in order to avoid dismissal, to allege any explanation of why he did not sue earlier. Such a requirement would cause him to have less than two years opportunity, as a sane person, to protect and assert his right of action.

For the reasons stated, the judgment of the Court of Appeals is Reversed.

The policy of placing limitations on actions is grounded in fairness. The exception to the rule which permits "tolling" is also based on "what is right." In short, the law announces that "you have a legal right to sue — but you must do so within a stated time period."

A related policy of the law makes another announcement: "Seek your contract rights and the law will uphold those rights. But in certain situations you must be able to prove those rights by producing a written and signed document. If you fail, the law cannot assist you." This policy finds statutory backing in the "statute of frauds."

STATUTE OF FRAUDS, 1677

Three centuries ago, a statute was enacted in England that has had a profound effect upon the laws of every state of the Union. The statute was titled "A Statute for the Prevention of Frauds and Perjuries." This law has been adopted completely or in modified form in all of our states. It is also found in four important parts of the U.C.C. It is interesting to note that it has all but been abandoned in England where it originated.

Background

At first there were no trials in England in the form in which they are conducted today. Rather, there was resort to the Ordeals with corresponding reliance upon "divine intervention." Later, when the courts became refined enough to start taking testimony rather than burning, clubbing, or drowning people, the rule was adopted that the party in interest in the litigation could not testify. Since one could profit by failing to tell the truth, it was believed that anything that person said would have no value as evidence. In time, a party to a civil or criminal action was permitted to testify at trial, but as was feared in the beginning, those who testified did not always tell the truth.

There were countless opportunities to profit by the use of perjured testimony. For example, the wife of a deceased man might testify that certain promises had been made to her by the decedent which might divert funds from other heirs. How could it be proven that the promises had *not* been made? Or a merchant who was owed a sum of money by B might testify in court that the father of B had promised to pay the debt for the son. While it would be a question of fact for a jury, nevertheless, upon proof of the debt of the son, a jury would be inclined to believe that the promise had been made by the father. In short, perjured testimony became a serious problem and the lawmakers began a search for a solution.

Solution to the Problem

The device chosen was a simple one: In designated areas, the person suing would be required to prove the case by the production of some "note or memorandum" signed by the one who had made the promise. If

FIGURE 12-2
Is It "In" or "Out" of the Statute?

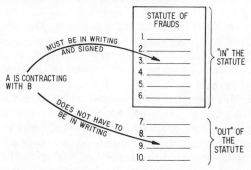

the writing could not be produced, the proof failed and the case would be dismissed upon motion, a procedure which exists today.[2] Examine Figure 12-2.

The original act covered six areas:

1. Contracts for the Sale of Real Estate. A contract for the sale or purchase of real estate, or an interest therein, must be in writing and signed by the person "to be charged." This means the one who is to sell and the one who is to buy.

Witness the effect of the statute: If A and husband promise to sell their home to B and wife for a stated price, the promise cannot be enforced by *either* of the parties unless it has been reduced to a written contract. For a further discussion of a real estate contract, see Chapter 25. Therefore, oral promises for the sale of realty are risky for both parties. The interested parties must have real estate contracts prepared in writing and executed.

2. Contracts in Consideration of Marriage. If A promises half of his estate to B if she will marry him, the promise cannot be enforced – even if it had in fact been made – unless B can produce the promise in writing and signed by A.

3. Promises to Pay the Debts of Another. It is not uncommon for one person to promise to pay the debt of another. But in many instances, the one making the promise has a change of heart and later refuses to perform. If the promise was not made in writing and signed, it cannot be enforced. Therefore, it is good business practice to keep a blank note or two on hand and when one promises to pay the debt of another, it can be reduced to writing.

4. Promises of Executors. Frequently, creditors of a deceased person become concerned about whether the estate will be sufficient to pay the estate obligations. In many cases executors are confident that funds are

---

[2] Modern courts have held that a check can meet the requirements of a signed writing, as well as a business letterhead that contains the business name but is not signed. *Associated Hardware Supply Co.,* v. *Big Wheel Distributing Company,* 355 F.2d. 114 (3rd Cir. 1966).

sufficient and will make a statement such as, "Of course you will be paid; if there isn't enough to pay you, I will pay it myself." This promise is unenforceable unless it is made in writing—and executors (or administrators) seldom make such promises in writing. The evil that existed at common law was the false claim by a disgruntled creditor that such a promise had been made by the executor. There was thus a fraudulent way to recover in court even though one could not be paid from the estate of the deceased person.

5. Contracts that Cannot Be Performed within One Year. The law requires any contract that cannot be performed within one year to be in writing and signed. The courts have made exceptions to this part of the statute of frauds. For example, an employment contract between A and B for two years is not covered since if A died within the first year, the contract would be ended. But as a practical matter, all long-term contracts should be in writing and signed. Leases are covered by this provision. For example, a lease for a student apartment for two years must be in writing and signed by the tenant and landlord. If it is not, the landlord can evict the student with a month's notice—and the student can quit with a month's notice. This is true no matter how clear the oral agreement may have been between them.

6. Sales Provision. In the original statute of frauds, contracts for the sale of goods in excess of 10 pounds sterling had to be in writing. The modern counterpart is found in the Uniform Commercial Code as follows:

(1) Except as otherwise provided in this section a contract for the sale of goods for the price of $500 or more is not enforceable by way of action or defense unless there is some writing sufficient to indicate that a contract for sale has been made between the parties and signed by the party against whom enforcement is sought or by his authorized agent or broker. A writing is not insufficient because it omits or incorrectly states a term agreed upon but the contract is not enforceable under this paragraph beyond the quantity of goods shown in such writing.

(2) Between merchants if within a reasonable time a writing in confirmation of the contract and sufficient against the sender is received and the party receiving it has reason to know its contents, it satisfies the requirements of subsection (1) against such party unless written notice of objection to its contents is given within ten days after it is received.

(3) A contract which does not satisfy the requirements of subsection (1) but which is valid in other respects is enforceable

(a) if the goods are to be specially manufactured for the buyer and are not suitable for sale to others in the ordinary course of the seller's business and the seller, before notice of repudiation is received and under circumstances which reasonably indicate that the goods are for the buyer, has made either a substantial beginning of their manufacture or commitments for their procurement; or

(b) if the party against whom enforcement is sought admits in his pleading, testimony or otherwise in court that a contract for sale was made, but the contract is not enforceable under this provision beyond the quantity of goods admitted; or (*c*)   with respect to goods for which payment has been made and accepted or which have been received and accepted.[3]

This provision of the Uniform Commercial Code has caused, and will cause, problems, as the Garrison case illustrates.

> *Garrison* v. *Piatt*.[4] Suit was filed upon a contract for the purchase of a house trailer for a sum in excess of $500. The defendant demurred (objected) on the ground that the face of the petition showed that the contract was oral and thus in the Sales Statute of Frauds.[5] The demurrer was sustained on the basis stated (meaning the plaintiff could not present evidence or question the defendant on trial as no trial would be allowed) and the plaintiff appealed.
>
> An unusual question was thus presented to the Georgia court for decision: When a petition (complaint in other states) upon its face discloses that the oral contract sued upon is in the Sales Statute of Frauds, does a demurrer lie to give the defendant the benefit and protection of the statute?
>
> The court answered this question in the negative, reversing the lower court, reasoning as follows: Under the prior statute of frauds for the sale of goods,[6] a party sued on an oral contract could admit the contract and still retain the benefit of the statute.[7]
>
> Under the Uniform Commercial Code, such a contract is otherwise enforceable ". . . if the party against whom enforcement is sought admits in his pleading, testimony, or otherwise in court that a contract for sale was made . . ." as to the quantity of the goods admitted.[8] The court continued, "It is the intent of this change in the statute of frauds, that if, after the petition is filed, the person charged admits the contract, the statute of frauds as a defense shall not be available to the party charged; but on the contrary the case thus made shall be determined on the merits without reference to the statute of frauds."
>
> The court reasoned further that since such a contract can become enforceable by admissions of the party charged *only in the case itself* (emphasis added), it would be contrary to the intention and purpose of the statutory change to permit the sustaining of the demurrer since this would deny the plaintiff ". . . his opportunity of determining in a trial whether the making of the contract would be admitted and thus made enforceable for the first time . . . It follows, therefore, that a petition upon such a contract which is valid in other respects is not demurrable because it shows on its face that it is within the statute of frauds; this for the reason that the demurrer admits the facts pleaded (for the purpose of the demurrer only) and the demurrer, thus admitting the contract, is ineffective to set up the benefit of the statute of frauds." (Judgment was reversed).

As the court points out, the defendant can no longer admit a sales contract, even in a demurrer, and still claim the statute as a defense. However, as stated in the comments, Uniform Commercial Code (U.L.A.) 2–201, ". . . the contract is thus not conclusively established. The ad-

---

[3] U.C.C., 2–201.

[4] 113 Ga. App. 94, 147 S.E.2D 374 (1966).

[5] U.C.C. 2–201(3)(*b*). Other statutes of frauds are found in the U.C.C. 1–206, sale of personal property beyond $5,000; 8–319, securities; and 9–203, security agreements.

[6] Ga. Code 20–401(7).

[7] *Douglass* v. *Bunn*, 110 Ga. 159, 165, 35 S.E. 339 (1900).

[8] Ga. Code 109A–2–201(3)(*b*), U.C.C. 2–201(3)(*b*).

mission so made by the party is itself evidential against him of the truth of the facts so admitted and of nothing more; as against the other party, it is not evidential at all."

Under the rule of this case, the statute *could be used to commit fraud,* thus returning the matter to the place it occupied in the years prior to 1677.

Another major policy of the law involves the principle of "notice," and it is directly related to "recording" which was discussed above.

NOTICE

Before legal, binding steps may be taken against another, or before the legal rights of another may be changed or disturbed, that person is entitled to "notice" of what is taking place so that steps can be taken to protect those rights. This is a major policy of our law and its origin can be traced deep into history. The policy is so well grounded that it is common to refer to the civil and other procedural requirements in the federal and state courts as being a system of "notice pleading."

What Is "Notice"?

Notice has been defined as ". . . information, an advice, or written warning, in more or less formal shape, intended to apprise a person of some proceedings in which his interests are involved, or informing him of some fact which it is his right to know and the duty of the notifying party to communicate."[9] Yet notice is more than that because it also includes ". . . knowledge of facts which would naturally lead an honest and prudent person to make inquiry."[10]

The way that notice is given in law varies with the circumstances. The following are examples:

Actual Notice

One has actual notice of something when one knows of it in fact. When Sheriff A hands a summons and complaint to B, B has actual notice that B has been sued. This type of notice is referred to as "express" notice as contrasted with "implied" notice.

If one has express knowledge about fact A, it may be inferred or implied that one also has knowledge about how fact A relates to fact B. This process in law is called a "presumption" and is treated as being actual notice although it is called implied notice.

Constructive Notice

In many legal situations the courts will hold that a person has knowledge of a fact when the truth is that person knows nothing about it. One

---

[9] *Black's Law Dictionary,* 4th ed.
[10] *Bank of Lincoln* v. *Martin,* 277 Ill. 629, 115 N.E. 721, 729 (1917).

is said to have "constructive notice" of the fact. For example, each person of legal capacity is presumed to have constructive notice of all legal documents filed or recorded in public offices. Another common way of giving notice is through notices in newspapers.

Legal Notices

Frequent use is made of "legal notices" published in a newspaper of general circulation within the jurisdiction of the court before which a matter is pending.

In the following legal notice, the defendants have been placed upon notice of the suit as well as the steps that they must take to defend. If they fail to take action and file an answer, the court has power to enter an order to grant the relief sought by the plaintiffs.

The business person must screen the legal notices each day. It cannot be assumed that counsel will do this because the attorney may not recognize the matter as being one that relates to a client.

For example, a notice of a judicial sale of an auto repossessed from A may prevent a sale of merchandise to A at a time when it is doubtful that A's credit standing is still satisfactory. Or a legal notice that specifies the time period in which a claim against the estate of a deceased

---

ORDER OF PUBLICATION

IN THE CIRCUIT COURT OF KING COUNTY, TYPICAL STATE, SAMUEL E. AMY and DONALD KEY, Plaintiffs, v. WENDELL WATER AND EMY WATER, Husband and Wife, WOOD LUMBER COMPANY, a Corporation, STEVE RICE and EMILY RICE, Husband and Wife, THE FIRST SAVING AND TRUST COMPANY, AGENT, Anytown, Other State, AND ALL OTHER UNKNOWN CREDITORS OF WENDELL WATER and EMY WATER, Husband and Wife, Defendants.

The object of the above styled Civil Action is to determine priorities among lien creditors of Wendell Water and Emy Water, husband and wife, and to sell the following real estate if necessary to satisfy same:

Situate in Key District, King County, and more particularly bounded and described as follows:

(Description follows here.)

It appearing by affidavit filed in this action that the First Saving and Trust Company, Agent, are nonresidents and further that there might be other lien creditors who are not residents of this State who might have an interest in the real estate that is the subject matter of this suit who are unknown to the Plaintiffs; it is ordered that each of them serve upon John Eagle, of Counsel for the Plaintiffs, whose address is 177 Campus Avenue, an answer or other defenses to the complaint filed in this action on or before November 1, 197– otherwise judgment by default will be taken against them at any time thereafter. A copy of said Complaint can be obtained from the undersigned Clerk at her Office.

Entered by the Clerk of said Court October 6, 197–.

Jean Lowe
Clerk of Court

PUBLISHER'S CERTIFICATE
LEGAL NOTICE

Typical State,
County of King

I, John R. Mur, General Manager of THE ANYTOWN NEWS, a newspaper of general circulation published in the City of Anytown, County and State aforesaid, do hereby certify that the annexed

Samuel E. Amy et al.

was published in the said THE ANYTOWN NEWS once a week for 2 consecutive weeks, commencing on the 12th day of October, 197- and ending on the 19th day of October, 197-.

I also certify that the same was duly posted on the 12th day of October, 197- at the front door of the Court House of said county, as provided by law.

The publisher's fee for said publication is $50.40.

Given under my hand this 19th day of October 197-.

s/s John R. Mur   (SEAL)
General Manager,
The Anytown News

Subscribed and sworn to before me this 19th day of October, 197-
s/s Frank Fisher, Jr.

Notary Public of King County.

My commission expires on the 7th day of November, 1982.

---

person must be filed may enable one to collect a debt that might otherwise be lost.

Other matters that are the subject of legal notices include requests for bids on contracts and materials; notice of dissolution of corporations; requests for rezoning; announcement of paving assessments; applications for "certificates of convenience and necessity" from the public service commissions, and many others.

One of the forerunners of the legal notice was the "notchel" notice.

Notchel Notice

In older times in the shires in England, it was the practice of husbands who were married to "spendthrift" wives, to publish a public notice to the following effect: "To whom it may concern: I will not be responsible for debts contracted by my wife after this date. Signed, Husband." Of course, rich wives could do the same thing to husbands.

Such an ad or notice was called a "notchel" notice and the wife or husband was said to be "notchelled" by it. The practice is followed today but the legal effectiveness of it is open to question. It does have practical value depending upon the circumstances. In the strict sense it is not a true legal notice because it is seldom related to court activity.

Notices of Pending Marriages

English common law required that a notice of a pending marriage be posted at the church during regular service on three consecutive Sundays before the marriage. When this was done, the "banns were posted" and those who had objections could make them known.

This principle developed first in medieval Swiss law and is used today in China, our New England states, and in other nations.

Notice under O.S.H.A.

Employers covered by the Occupational Safety and Health Act, must post a summary of all job injuries, illnesses, and deaths, at the job site once each year. This notice must be posted by February and remain in place for 30 days. This provides notice to all of the employees of the nature and type of injuries and deaths of the previous year. This presumably will aid in reducing job losses in the future. (For a further discussion of O.S.H.A., see Chapter 45).

RULE AGAINST "REMOTENESS" IN VESTING

It has long been a policy of the common law to prohibit persons from taking legal steps during their lifetimes that would withdraw property from commerce for extended periods of time after their deaths. This has come to be known as the "Rule against remoteness in vesting," and is a major policy of law.

This ancient policy of the law has been given statutory backing in most of our states. These statutes are commonly known as the "rule against perpetuities" and the "rule against accumulations," and are classic examples of "statutes of limitations."

Rule against Perpetuities

The common-law rule was that no interest in property was good unless it would "vest" (become the property of another) within a measurable period of time. The "measuring stick" was "no later than 21 years, plus the period of gestation (9 months) after some life in being at the time of the creation of the interest." To illustrate, if A desires to control property beyond A's life, A can do so for the period of A's life and on beyond—but not to exceed 21 years, 9 months. By the end of that time the property must vest in (that is, legal title and right to control) some other person.

Various states have different time periods. For example, Idaho provides for 25 years after lives in being for real property, but places no limitation on personal property. Minnesota provides for 20 years after 2 lives in being for real property and 21 years for personal property.

The rule is nicely illustrated by the fact that leases of real property seldom exceed "99 years." A lease for a longer time period might be held to violate the rule and be declared invalid.

Rule against Accumulation

As a "partner" to the above rule, all states have rules that prohibit income to accumulate beyond designated time periods. In other words, income must vest in another within that time period.

Over 40 of our states use the "21 years plus lifetime in being" rule. Michigan sets 33 years as an outside limit after death, Alabama ten years. Wisconsin permits accumulations of income "as directed" by the testator of a will.

The practical effect of both rules is to assure that property returns to the stream of commerce at some forseeable point in time.

Three final policies of the law will be discussed briefly. Two are "tools of law" applied by courts in settling disputes. The first is an intangible standard by which certain "measurements" can be made. The second is a tool sometimes applied to create a situation that in fact never existed at all. The third was designed to protect military personnel. First, the "measuring standard."

REASONABLENESS

The word "reasonable," means proper or just. A "reasonable person" is one who is governed and guided by reason in that person's acts. In law, reasonableness is used as a test to establish standards in given situations. Once established, the court, through instructions to a jury, can permit a dispute to be decided as a question of fact based upon this standard.

To illustrate, assume that A did work for B, but there was no agreement on wages. If B refuses payment, upon suit being brought, B would be expected to pay A a "reasonable sum" for services rendered. To determine that sum, evidence would be heard from which the amount could be established. It then becomes a question of fact to be determined by a jury.

The "reasonable person" standard is frequently used to establish whether what one did in a given situation was what a reasonable person would have done under similar circumstances. For example, A is confronted by a "sudden emergency," such as B's auto blocking a road at night. A injures B in an attempt to avoid the collision. If the acts that A took were those that could be expected from "a reasonable person faced with similar circumstances," then A may be absolved from blame for B's losses. On the other hand, if A did *not* react as a reasonable person would have been expected to, A might be found guilty of negligence, and be forced to pay damages.

The reasonableness test has been applied to establish just rates for public service companies; to establish a fair market value; to determine what constitutes reasonable notice and many other similar items. It is a versatile unit of measure. Its mere existence as a policy of the law, tends to discourage unreasonable acts by those who know of its existence.

Another tool available to the courts is the "fiction."

FICTIONS

A *fictio* in Roman law was an assumption or supposition of law. From its use developed an ancient maxim: *fictio cedit veritati fictio juris non est ubi veritas*—"Fiction yields to truth. Where there is truth, fiction of law does not exist." That is, if facts are present, there is no need for fictions. To illustrate, if A and B in fact create a trust,[11] a bailment,[12] or a contract,[13] then "fiction yields to truth" and the facts control.

But in law, conditions arise in which there is "no truth." In these situations the courts resort to fictions if their use is justified.

To Illustrate. Z makes a forced landing on the farm of Y. Y becomes a "bailee" of the airplane and has legal duties as to its care until Z can have it removed. In truth there was no bailment yet a court may hold that there was one just the same.

Distinguished from "Presumptions." A presumption is an inference which is *probably* true, and which the law will apply for the purpose of arriving at a certain conclusion. In a "fiction" something known to be false is assumed to be true.

Not the Same as an Estoppel. In an "estoppel" a person is prohibited from asserting a fact that is inconsistent with one's own acts. It is not the same as a fiction. In an estoppel, one is "stopped" from denying something inconsistent with what has in fact been done—a fiction is something that does not exist—yet a court says that it does.

One final example of a policy of law protects military personnel at times when they are not able to be in civilian courts.

COURTS AND MILITARY PERSONNEL

The American Colonies and later the States, had repeated occasions when men and women of suitable age were needed for military service. One who was called to military duty was frequently isolated from the courts by distance and lack of suitable transportation. If such a person were involved in litigation at the time of call to the military, that person might be at a severe legal handicap, and especially so if that person were a defendant in a suit for damages.

Quite early in the history of our nation, the courts adopted a policy of providing assistance to military personnel under such circumstances by permitting continuances or delays until the military person was able to be present and take active part in the trial. Today, this policy finds statutory backing in the Soldiers' and Sailors' Civil Relief Act of 1940,[14] and its amendments. The *Starling* case illustrates how the courts lend substance to the policy in practice.

---

[11] *See* chapter 28.
[12] *See* chapter 19.
[13] *See* chapter 15.
[14] 50 U.S.C.A. App. 521.

Starling v. *Harris*.[15] This is an appeal from the judgment of the trial court continuing in effect until further order of court a stay in proceedings previously granted upon application of the defendant under the Soldiers' and Sailors' Civil Relief Act. *Held:*

The record in this case discloses that the original stay was granted upon the verified application of the defendant showing among other things that he was a member of the United States Army stationed in Korea, that he could not obtain leave to attend court, and that his presence was essential to a proper defense to this action in tort arising out of an automobile collision to which there were no eyewitnesses other than the parties and to which action the defendant claimed a good defense; and there being no evidence produced on the subsequent hearing to show any change in circumstances of the defendant, it cannot be said that the trial court abused its discretion in continuing the stay until further order of court even though the original application contained the statement that the defendant "expects to be available in March, 1966 to defend this case."

Order affirmed — meaning that all court procedures were halted until the soldier had a full opportunity to be present.

MANY OTHER POLICIES

There are many other policies of law and as one proceeds into further study, an effort should be made to recognize these and to relate them to the discussion here. Other examples include prohibitions against restraint of trade; contractural protection of those under age; protection of those under mental disability; and limits on the amount of interest that can be charged by a lender.

REVIEW QUESTIONS

1. The father of a teenage boy has promised a merchant that on payday he will pay a $50 debt owed by his son. What should the merchant do?
2. In one sentence, describe the policy reason for placing limitations on actions.
3. Clip three legal notices from a newspaper, read them, label them, and place them in your notes.
4. What practical effect might the $500 goods statute of frauds have upon a dealer who sells mobile homes on time?
5. True or False. The tolling provisions of limitations on actions were created to benefit the debtor.
6. Does it strike you as being unusual that the rules against perpetuities and accumulations are centuries old? Can you think of what might have prompted the rules to be developed?
7. Distinguish a "fiction," a "presumption," and an "estoppel" in terms of their legal effects.
8. Examine the limitations chart, Figure 12–1. What is the rationale behind some periods being so short — and some so long?
9. Americans are the world's best record keepers. Name as many ways as you can in which a business person can make use of legal documents that are on "record."

---

[15] 114 Ga. App. 282, 151 S.E.2D 163 (1966).

10. Examine U.C.C. 2–201 (under **6. Sales Provision**). You are dealing in used cars. This statute places a legal duty upon you. What is it?

Words and Phrases

Write out briefly what they mean to you.
1. Constructive notice.
2. Implied notice.
3. Statute of limitations.
4. Statute of frauds.
5. Tolling.

Coverage:	An introduction to the contract.
What to Look for:	The different ways in which a contract can come into being.
Application:	The majority of this book is involved directly or indirectly with contracts. Keep this in mind as other chapters are studied.

13 Basics of Contract

A contract is a "blueprint for the future," created to cover a specific event or undertaking, voluntarily made by the parties involved and which they recognize may be enforced in court if either refuses to perform. In most contracts, specific promises are made and it is from these promises that the contract is created.

The contract is widely used in business as a regulatory device. That is, when A and B make binding promises to each other, each has a right to rely upon the promise of the other, and each tends to do what was promised. If not, the law provides a remedy, or way to allow one to be compensated for the breach of the other. Therefore, each is inclined to perform as promised and is thus regulated to that degree.

The principles of tort and crime are regulatory in nature also, but as was mentioned previously, are distinguishable from contract because the contract is a *voluntary arrangement* between A and B. Never in practice will A consent to being injured by B and never will C agree to be robbed by D.

SOME CONTRACT FACTS

As the material develops, certain facts become apparent about contract law. It is helpful to see these facts at the outset because they tend to make one curious about the reason for them. Some basic facts about contracts are set out below.

1. A contract is an agreement.
2. Most contracts arise out of promises.
3. The promises that create a contract do not have to be stated expressly.

4. A court may find that a contract exists in situations in which a contract was not intended at the outset.
5. In some cases, it is cheaper to breach (break) a contract than it is to keep the promise made.
6. It is possible for A to be bound in a contract with B, in which B can hold A to the contract but A cannot hold B.
7. Most oral agreements are legally binding contracts.
8. Some contracts must be in writing and signed or they cannot be enforced.
9. An insurance policy is a contract.
10. A student attending a state university is in a contract with the state.
11. When one consumes a meal at a restaurant and pays for it, that person has entered into a contract that has been fully performed or "executed."
12. The overwhelming majority of the countless contracts entered into yearly are fully performed without objection on the part of either party.

There are many other interesting contract facts, but these are representative.

Next, it is important to identify what may be thought of as the "contract setting" and then to identify legal promises as they are contrasted with social promises.

Assume that A and B are seated at opposite ends of a library table reading books. Neither are in a contract setting as it relates to the other. But they are both in a contract setting or "posture" with the library. If A checks out a book, A promises to return it at the end of two weeks and if not, promises to pay "damages" at the rate of 10 cents per each day the book is late. A does not make these promises orally, but A makes them just the same. The library promises to let A take the book out if A keeps the promise, and there is a binding contract between them.

Back at the table, A looks at B and says "hello." B waves to A and asks if A will stop at the drugstore for a coke after the library closes. The two parties are in a "social setting" and if A promises to go to the drugstore with B and then refuses later, there is nothing the other can do about it.

After returning the book to the shelf, A says to B, "I am in need of money and I'll sell you my Honda 250 for $375." The statement is made in good faith and suddenly casts A and B into a "contract setting." But observe the nature of the setting at this point. The offer of A places no duty upon B—not even the duty to reply. This illustrates the voluntariness required in a contract. But B does reply, "I'll take it—here is $10. I'll give you the balance tomorrow." There is a contract between the two, but since both A and B are under the age of 18, the contract has a self-contained problem called "voidability" which will be discussed later.

The simplified example above distinguishes social from legal promises and points out that contract making requires what may be thought of as a "stage" or "scene," which is often difficult to recognize in the operation of a business and one's everyday affairs. When the "stage is set," if you will, a contract may result and the stage is most often set by an "offer" or promise.

Contract making is an essential part of the business community of any nation. It is by the contract that banks can safely lend money to a manufacturer. It is by the contract that the manufacturer can be assured that production will not be halted due to a shortage of goods; it is by the contract that one hires employees; and it is by the contract that manufactured goods find their way to the ultimate buyer or consumer. The law of contract is the primary law as it relates to business—and it is probably the oldest.

HISTORICALLY

The origins of contract principles have been lost in the fading horizons of the beginnings of civilization. Historians tell us that the ancient Egyptians made wide use of the contract over 6,000 years ago. As the centuries passed, contract principles became established in the merchant courts and finally developed into a separate body of recognizable law in England sometime following the Norman Conquest. By the time of American independence, contract principles were in full bloom and little material change has been made since that time. An examination of some of the lawbooks of the 1790s will bear this out. Therefore, our modern contract principles have their roots in ancient times and even the basic classifications of contract are very old.

CLASSIFICATION OF CONTRACTS

Contracts can be classified as being valid, voidable or void, express or implied, and bilateral or unilateral.

Valid, Voidable, or Void

A valid contract is one that has been brought into being by parties who are competent and which is fully enforceable in court. A voidable contract is one that is "cancellable" by one who has a reason recognized by law for canceling the contract. Other examples will follow, but the best example is the power that one under a statutory age (usually 18) has by law to cancel or avoid certain contractual obligations. So if C sells a motorboat to D, who is under the age of 18, in most states D could demand the return of the money if the contract had been executed, or could refuse to make the payments if the contract was executory—that is, not yet performed. In all states D would have to return the boat to C, or make it available to C.

A contract that is "void" is one that is no longer treated as having legal effect.

Express or Implied

An express contract can be oral or written but it has been "expressed" by the parties—that is, the parties clearly intended a contract to come into being. An implied contract is one in which nothing was expressly stated by the parties, yet a contract resulted from their acts, or a court says that there was a contract in order to prevent one from being unjustly injured. Two examples follow.

Implied in Fact. When A and B conduct themselves in such a manner that there is a contract in fact between them, it is not necessary that either of them expressly state that they are in a contract. For example, A begins painting B's house by accident, and B observes this and says nothing because B wants the house painted. Once the painting is completed, B would be under a contract obligation to pay A a reasonable sum for painting the house. If B refuses, A could sue on the implied contract and the jury would decide the sum that B should pay. The judge would guide the jury in making this determination by the use of the "court's instructions" — statements of the applicable law. As one court stated:

> A contract for sale of personal property, as other contracts not required to be in writing, need not necessarily be express but may be implied from facts and circumstances which create an obligation on part of one to pay for goods or services received from another.

Contracts Implied in Law. While contracts implied in *fact* are true contracts, contracts implied in *law* — called "quasi contracts" — are imposed by law and are not true contracts. Such contracts are treated as contracts *for the purposes of remedy only*. They will not be used by the court as a substitute for a contract implied in fact — or an express contract. They are based upon the equitable principle that one should never enrich oneself at the expense of another.

To Illustrate. In a contract for services in which no agreement had been reached on payment, the law will imply that a "reasonable compensation" had been agreed upon — even though it in fact had not been. Where property is transferred without agreement for payment, the law implies a promise to pay a reasonable value.

The one providing the services or property, is entitled to recover on a "quantum meruit"[1] or "quantum valebant"[2] basis. The measure of the amount due becomes a question of evidence of the value of the services or property.

As a practical business matter, however, it is always best to agree on a price for services or property. This is true because it takes court action for a contract to be implied in law.

The next classification is that of bilateral, as contrasted with unilateral, contracts.

Bilateral or Unilateral

A bilateral contract is one in which there is a positive "contractual move" on the part of both parties. In essence, there is a promise from both parties. For example, Zero Corporation orders 1,000 units of commodity X and does this by use of a purchase order. The order form states

---

[1] "As much as one deserved."

[2] "As much as they were worth."

the price per unit and the shipping conditions, and in contract language, is an "offer" and becomes legally effective when received by the manufacturer. The manufacturer sends an acknowledgment which states the approximate date of shipping. As soon as the acknowledgment form is received, the contract is in full force—and it is a bilateral contract. That is, there are promises going from each party to the other.

A unilateral contract, in comparison, is one in which one person has made a promise, but has made it in such form that it is clear that the offeror—(the one making the offer)—wants *performance* rather than a *promise* in return for it. In that form the situation can be dangerous for the other party—and for a legal reason. The following example will illustrate.

Unilateral Uncertainty. A says to B, "Paint my warehouse and I'll pay you $1,000." A specifies the type of paint; the completion date; and states that B must pay for all supplies and labor. B begins work immediately. A close examination of the facts discloses that there is no contract and there will not be one until B completes the work. While A has made an offer, B must complete the painting before B has legally "accepted" the offer. B completes 75 percent of the painting and A suddenly announces, "I revoke my offer." See Figure 13–1.

FIGURE 13–1
"I revoke!"

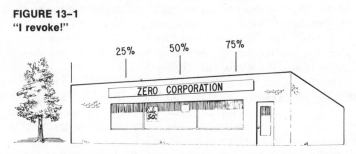

It has been a basic rule of contract for centuries that one who makes an offer may revoke it at any time before it is accepted. The principle again illustrates the voluntariness of the contract. Since there is no legal obligation on the part of anyone to ever make an offer, once it is made the one who made it should be able to take it back before it is accepted. This is the danger in the unilateral situation.

One can argue that since B had completed 75 percent of the work that B should be given a reasonable chance to complete the work and the courts are beginning to accept this view as an exception to the rule. But look at the situation from the other point of view. What if B had completed only 25 percent and decided not to continue? Could A have sued B for breach of contract? The answer is clearly "no"—because there was in fact no contract.

A business law text published in 1876[3] contained a curt warning:

---

[3] Theophilus Parsons, *Laws of Business*, (Hartford, Conn.: S. S. Scranton & Co., 1876).

"Never enter into a unilateral contract." The advice is as good today as it was then. In the Weikert case that follows, the problems inherent in a unilateral situation are illustrated.

Weikert v. *Logue*.[4] The plaintiff, Mary Elizabeth Logue, individually and doing business as Lenox Personnel, seeks $1,450 as compensation for services performed in obtaining employment for the defendant, Phillip H. Weikert, with the Burroughs Corporation, basing her claim on the arranging of an interview and a referral after the defendant had signed a writing captioned "Contract with Lenox Personnel" which states that Lenox Personnel is licensed, bonded, and operated under Georgia law, and regulated by a division of the State Labor Department, and which provides that:

> If I accept a position with any firm or person to whom you have sent me within six months of such interview, or if any prospective employer to whom I have been referred by your company should refer me to some other firm or employer, then such referral shall be considered as due to your efforts and I agree to pay the fees as herein stipulated.

This is followed by provisions covering the computation and payment of fees. The defendant admits the execution of the writing, and that he accepted employment with Burroughs Corporation, but he denied that the plaintiff "acquired or aided in the acquisition of employment." The defendant moved for a summary judgment, contending that the writing is not an enforceable agreement upon which the plaintiff may bring an action. No matter outside the pleadings was submitted and the trial court denied the motion, from which the defendant appeals.

As the writing does not, in itself, impose any obligation on Lenox Personnel to do anything, it is nothing more than an offer to make use of the services of Lenox Personnel, in return for a fee if employment is obtained resulting therefrom, and as such, standing alone fails to create any enforceable obligation. But the plaintiff alleges, in effect, that she did accept this offer by providing the contemplated services, which the defendant used, resulting in his employment with the Burroughs Corporation. One may accept an offer by doing the acts contemplated by an offer, thus creating an enforceable contract, and where, as here, the defendant denies that the plaintiff performed these acts, whether the offer was accepted in this manner is a matter of proof and a question for the jury.

Judgment affirmed.

REVIEW QUESTIONS

1. Apply the facts of the warehouse painting case to the *Weikert* case and see how an innocent party could have been injured.
2. Why *should* there be a difference between legal and social promises?
3. Explain why a contract is regulatory in nature.
4. Is it fair for one to revoke an offer before it is accepted?
5. True or False. A voidable contract is good until it is avoided.
6. List the contracts that *you* have been involved in.
7. You are on the board of directors of Flash Shopping Mall, Inc. Your new mall is due to start soliciting tenants soon. List five provisions that you want your lawyer to draft into your leases.

---

[4] 121 Ga. App. 171, 173 S.E.2d 268 (1970).

8. Create a fact situation that involves a unilateral contract. How can it be converted to a bilateral contract?
9. There are case decisions holding that if one is in good faith attempting to perform in a unilateral contract situation, the other person should be "estopped" to revoke before the other has a reasonable opportunity to complete the performance. Why might a court *hesitate* to rule this way?
10. In the *Weikert* case, what disposition was made of the case?

Words and Phrases

Write out briefly what they mean to you.
1. Contracts implied in law.
2. Revocation.
3. Promises.
4. "Contract setting."
5. Unilateral contract.

Coverage:	The requirements of a binding contract.
What to Look for:	The ways in which these requirements are met.
Application:	Contract making is a perpetual matter in any business.

14 Forming a Contract

In business, the contract is used in an almost informal manner and it is seldom that contract problems arise. Outside of the lawyer's office, little attention is paid to the technical steps of the construction of a contract. When A sends B $500 as a down payment for an equipment order, A rarely equates the payment to the contract requirement of "consideration." Or when B orders 1,000 pairs of shoes from D, B will almost never ask, "Is this contract I am entering into legal and is there mutuality?"

In spite of this, one who would increase one's knowledge of law and the part that it plays in the regulation of business and one's personal affairs, should examine these technical requirements to broaden the scope of that understanding. This chapter was designed to serve that purpose.

To begin with, it must be understood that we have two distinct bodies of contract principles. First are the "traditional" rules that have evolved over the centuries. These find the widest application in the purchase, sale, and lease of real estate. Second are the "U.C.C. contract rules" designed to cover the "sale" of "goods" between "merchants." This second class of principles have developed in this century—although based upon age-old rules. This dual body of principles came about because traditional rules did not work well in settling contract disputes that arose between merchants in the sale of goods.

It is helpful to begin by examining the requirements of a binding contract, comparing each with traditional as well as sales principles. (Sales contracts will be examined in further detail in Chapter 20.)

There are six legal requirements needed to create a binding contract: (1) offer, (2) acceptance, (3) mutuality, (4) consideration, (5) legality or legal purpose and (6) competent parties. If all elements are present, there is a binding contract. If one or more are missing, there is not. (See Figure 14-1.)

FIGURE 14–1

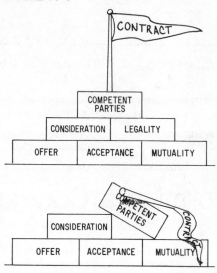

UNDER THE U.C.C.

The formation of a contract under the U.C.C. has been simplified and the preciseness of the formal requirements is lacking. Article 2–204(1), U.C.C., tells us that:

> A contract for the sale of goods may be made in any manner sufficient to show agreement, including conduct by both parties which recognizes the existence of such a contract.

Therefore, under the U.C.C., as it is applied to the "sale of goods," a contract can arise from not only what the parties say, but also from what they do.

As the elements of a conventional contract are examined, the applicable provisions of the U.C.C. will be compared with them. This permits one to compare the strictness of basic contract requirements with the liberality of the U.C.C. rules.

OFFER

The one who makes an offer is called the "offeror"—the one to whom it is made, the "offeree." An offer is a question that is put by one to another, and it relates to the future. It may be oral or it may be in writing. In either event, it will specify what the one making the offer is willing to do if the other is willing to do what is specified. An offer must be "communicated," that is, it must come to the mind of the one to whom it is made. It must be made in good faith and not under strain or in jest. It must also be definite enough that the one to whom it is made understands it.

Examples

A frantically offers $10,000 to anyone who saves A's child from a burning building. B saves the child but A refuses to pay. The court holds the offer was not legally effective because at the time it was made, A was almost insane with fear for the safety of the child and therefore no binding contract resulted.

A car dealer offers a certain model car for "1,300 bananas." A buyer attempts to purchase the car by use of the fruit named. (This actually happened, but it was never court tested.) A court would probably hold the offer to fail because as it reads it was in jest—or at least not made in "good faith" as it related to bananas.

The U.C.C.

The U.C.C. tempers the harshness of these requirements. Article 2-204(3), U.C.C., states:

> Even though one or more terms are left open, a *contract for sale* does not fail for indefiniteness if the parties have intended to make a contract and there is a reasonably certain basis for giving an appropriate remedy. (Emphasis added.)

Not all business communications are offers because frequently the businessperson wants merchandise before the public, but wants to reserve the making of the contract for a later time. The most common examples of this are found in newspaper and magazine advertisements.

Advertisements

A typical supermarket or chain store ad contains some type of phrase such as "subject to prior sale," "prices subject to change," "we reserve the right to limit quantities." In stock "offerings" as found in business magazines, these words are encountered: "This is not an offer for sale. The offer is made by prospectus only." These are steps taken to prevent the ad from being a legal offer. In the absence of qualifying words, an advertisement is still held not to be an offer, but a "mere invitation to stop in and negotiate." However, care is always in order when drafting ads and a good rule of thumb is, "Never use the word *offer* in an advertisement." This becomes important when an advertisement appears with the wrong price on an item.

Mistakes in Ads. It is a fairly common occurrence in business for mistakes to be made in advertisements. Two samples noted recently were:

FIGURE 14–2

"This week only, Sealy Posturepedic Mattresses, 49¢ each" and "4' x 8' Mahogany panels, 9½¢ each" (see Figure 14–2)!

When these errors occur, a legal question arises: Was the ad an "offer"? If it was, then as each customer tenders the purchase price, a contract results. If not, then the tender is an *offer by the customer* and there is no contract until the seller accepts.

These errors have been made in ad layouts and they have been made

FIGURE 14–3

by printers. If it was made clear in the ad that the ad was *not* an offer, then no harm has been done.

However, when faced with such a situation, the seller has other options to consider. Perhaps the seller will decide to sell at the lower price but limit quantities. Or the seller may offer a compromise price to buyers after explaining what happened. If a person does not want to sell at the erroneous price, that person should retract the ad by another notice and post a corrected copy at the doors of the business.

To guard against such errors and the inconvenience they cause, it is good practice to include in ads such words as "We reserve the right to change prices without notice," or "We reserve the right to limit sales," or other qualifying language. This makes it clear that an offer was *not* intended (examine Figure 14-3).

Pictures in Ads

Once an offer is made and acceptance follows, the terms of the ad become part of the terms of the contract. That is, specifications in the ad as to size, quality and type, will be treated by the court as part of the contract. But what if the ad is accompanied by a picture and the picture varies from the terms of the ad? The U.C.C. states that there is an express warranty (promise) that the goods will conform to the photo.[1] In a New York case, the court held that an advertisement that contained a picture of a skating rink, was covered by the above U.C.C. provision. Since the rink sold conformed to the word description in the ad – but not the picture, there was a breach of an express warranty by the seller.[2] Photos or illustrations used in advertisements should conform strictly to the word description.

Ads are similar to "bids" in their legal setting.

Bids

State University has obtained approval from its Board of Regents to construct a sports arena. After architectural plans are prepared, the school advertises for bids from contractors. As the bids are made, the offer is made by the *bidder* and the university may accept any one of the offers – or it may reject all of them.

Auctions

At an auction sale the offer is made by the one who bids and the acceptance follows when the auctioneer "knocks down" or accepts the highest bid. Auctions of "goods" are specifically covered by Article 2 of the U.C.C.[3] and guidelines are provided. If goods are put up for sale in *lots*, each lot is subject to a separate sale.

Normally, the acceptance is made upon the "fall of the hammer or

---

[1] U.C.C., 2-313 (1).

[2] *Rinkmasters, Inc.* v. *City of Utica,* 348 N.Y.S.2d, 940, 13 U.C.C. Rep. 797 (1973).

[3] U.C.C., 2-328.

in other customary manner." If a bid is made while the hammer is falling, the auctioneer can accept the bid – or reopen the bidding.

Auction sales can be "without reserve" or "with reserve." In the latter, the goods offered can be withdrawn anytime until the auctioneer announces completion of sale. If the goods are offered "without reserve," once bids are called for, the article or lot cannot be withdrawn unless no bid is made within a reasonable time.

In either type of reserve, a *bidder* may retract a bid anytime before announcement of the completion of the sale. However, a retraction does *not* revive any previous bid. An auction is a clear example of the offer and acceptance process in operation.

Another example of an offer is found in "tickets."

Tickets as Offers

When we purchase a ticket to the movie, or park our car at the parking lot, we seldom pay attention to the piece of paper handed to us. But that

FIGURE 14–4

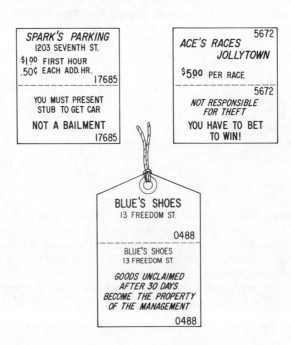

piece of paper often contains legal terms that bind us because it is an offer. By accepting it, we have accepted the terms of the offer.

To illustrate, examine Figure 14-4, items A, B, C, and D. In item A, the only liability of the theater owner is to return the price of admission: In item B, the parking lot has made it clear that they have not received the parked auto in a "bailment" situation. (For a complete discussion of bailments, see Chapter 19). In item C, what happens if the auto *itself* is stolen? Item D gives title to the (bailed) goods to the store owner if not reclaimed. For the legal authority for this, see Chapter 19.

Figure 14-5 is a ticket from an Atlantic City parking lot. Examine it closely and decide what the terms mean' to one who parks a car there.

Another type of offer is found in rewards that are offered by private citizens as well as business organizations.

Rewards

Rewards are offers made by a person or firm who wants in return certain information or the return of some lost or stolen item or arrest of a certain person. The one making the reward offer is the offeror—the one who meets the terms of the offer is the offeree. Acceptance occurs at the time that the conditions of the offer are met.

Rewards are often used to assist in the apprehension of those who commit crimes—and they have been used for centuries. See Figure 14-6.

Rewards are used in business as well. The reward in Figure 14-6 was offered for business reasons. It should be noted in that offer that before there could have been an acceptance and thus a contract to pay the reward sum, *all* of the conditions of the offer must have been met. In the event of an arrest but no subsequent conviction, the terms of the offer would not have been met.

After an offer is made, regardless of *how* it is made, how long does it remain in effect?

Effective How Long?

After a legal offer is in being, it does not stay in being forever. If it is an oral offer, it usually ends when the one to whom it was made departs. It can end by being revoked (withdrawn) by the one who made it. It ends if rejected (refused) by the one to whom it is made. If A says to B, "I'll sell you my watch for $50," and B replies, "I'll give you $25," the offer is ended because B has, in effect, rejected the offer and has made a new offer, called a "counteroffer." An offer also ends if the death or insanity of the offeror occurs before acceptance; or if illegality of purpose should come into being; or it can simply lapse after a passage of an unreasonable length of time. What a "reasonable length of time" would be is a question of fact for a jury. It could be as short as a few seconds if the commodity offered is fluctuating in price on the market.

The U.C.C. Article 2-206(2) states:

> Where the beginning of a requested performance is not a reasonable mode of acceptance, an offeror who is not notified of acceptance within a reasonable time may treat the offer as having lapsed before acceptance.

FIGURE 14–5

Fleetwood Auto Park
Adjoining Fleetwood Hotel
TENNESSEE AVE. Near BOARDWALK
184 S. TENNESSEE AVE.   ATLANTIC CITY, N. J.

13-488

CLAIM CHECK

TERMS AND CONDITIONS

Cars driven by our employees solely at owner's risk.   Not responsible for fire or theft.
Not responsible for any valuables, merchandise or clothing, etc. left in the car at time of parking or storing same.   Our storage charges are for the motor vehicle left with us only.   Our attendants cannot verbally change any of these conditions.

13-488

Date

Fleetwood Auto Park

Lic.

Owner

Address

Name of Car

IN   2:45

OUT   3:45

**AMOUNT
PAID**

1.00

FIGURE 14–6

$750 REWARD!

Wells, Fargo & Co. will pay

$250 each for the arrest and conviction of the three men who robbed the Silver City bound stage, near Boise City, on the 10th inst.

AN ADDITIONAL

reward of ONE-FOURTH will be paid on all treasure recovered.

Wm. B. MORRIS,

Agent.

Boise City. Nov. 10th. 1875.

From the Author's Collection.

In short, under conventional and U.C.C. contract rules, if one desires the benefits that may flow from an offer, that person should accept in due course. Otherwise, the "reasonable time" rule may cancel the offer.

Because of the fact that an offer can "expire" rapidly, it is desirable to have a means of keeping an offer in force and in such form that it cannot be withdrawn for a stated period of time. An offer that takes this form is called an "option" and becomes irrevocable for the stated period of time.

Regular Option

Steve B. Amos offered John Eagle a commercial building in Anytown, for the sum of $86,000. Eagle was not certain that he could arrange the financing, but rather than risk a delay, asked Amos for an "option to buy." Amos agreed and an option (which is a contract) was created as shown.

Once an option is signed, it becomes a contract and cannot be revoked for the time period stated. This gives the option holder the opportunity to arrange financing. If financing cannot be arranged, the option money is forfeited as damages. In the option (over) the option money was very low. Some persons granting options, require as much as 10 percent of the purchase price or the equivalent of the rental for the time period of the option.

THIS OPTION, Made this 5th day of January, 1975, by and between Steve B. Amos and Susan Ann Amos, husband and wife, parties of the first part, and John Eagle and Elizabeth Mary Eagle, parties of the second part.

WITNESSETH:

That for and in consideration of the sum of Two Hundred ($200.00) Dollars paid to the parties of the first part by the parties of the second part, the receipt of which is hereby acknowledged, the parties of the first part, their heirs or assigns, do hereby give and grant to the parties of the second part, their heirs and assigns, the exclusive right or option to purchase any-time within sixty days (60) from the date of this option, all that certain lot or parcel of real estate together with the buildings and improvements thereon, situated in the Fourth Ward of the City of Anytown, Estate District, King County, Typical State, and more particularly bounded and described as follows:

Beginning at the point of intersection of the Southeasterly line of State Avenue with the Northeasterly line of Eagle Avenue and traveling along State Avenue N. 41° 57′ E. 54.58 feet to a point; thence S. 48° 35′ E. 65.71 feet to a point; thence S. 39° 25′ W. 12.1 feet to a point; thence N. 48° 31′ W. 22.88 feet to a point; thence S. 41° 21′ W. 34.04 feet to a point on the North-easterly line of Eagle Avenue; thence with the line of Eagle Avenue, N. 48° 35′ W. 45.66 feet to the point of beginning, and being the same real estate conveyed to the parties of the first part by Deed dated the 20th day of May, 1960, and of record in the office of the Clerk of the County Court in Deed Book 600 at page 375, for the consideration or sum of Eighty Six Thousand ($86,000.00) Dollars payable in full at the time of the exercising of this Option. If the parties of the second part exercise this option within said sixty-day period, then the closing will be in accordance with standard prac-tices in the area.

It is expressly provided that if the parties of the second part do not exer-cise this option within the sixty-day period, for reasons other than those having to do with the title, said option money is to be retained by the parties of the first part as liquidated damages.

WITNESS the following signatures and seals:

s/s Steve B. Amos	(SEAL)
Steve B. Amos	
s/s Susan Ann Amos	(SEAL)
Susan Ann Amos	
s/s John Eagle	(SEAL)
John Eagle	
s/s Elizabeth Mary Eagle	(SEAL)
Elizabeth Mary Eagle	

In most cases the option would be acknowledged and placed on record to prevent a sale to third parties during the option period.

U.C.C. Options. The U.C.C. contains an option provision as it relates to the sale of goods and it is found in Article 2–205:

> An offer by a merchant to sell goods in a signed writing which by its terms gives assurance that it will be held open is not revocable, for lack of con-sideration (money), during the time stated or if no time is stated for a rea-

sonable time, but in no event may such period of irrevocability exceed three months. . . .

Both types of options must be in writing, but only the regular option must be accompanied by option money—there is no need for any in the U.C.C. option. It should be observed that the U.C.C. option only applies to "merchants"—not to individuals who are not merchants.

Review

There are definite rules that relate to the first step in contract making —the making of the offer. These rules are a matter of form and many things can end an offer including the making of a counteroffer. The following chart provides a review of the timing of an offer, a revocation, a rejection and a counteroffer.

	Made by	*Effective When*
Offer......................	Offeror	Received by Offeree
Revocation..............	Offeror	Received by Offeree
Rejection	Offeree	Received by Offeror
Counteroffer...........	Offeree (Initially)	Received by Original Offeror (Now the Offeree)

ACCEPTANCE

An acceptance is some act or promise or other indication from the offeree that he or she wants the benefit of the offer and is willing to be bound in a contract in order to obtain it.

It could be an act where the promise was unilateral. It could be the signing of the option above or it could be the nod of the head in a face-to-face situation.

One must accept an offer with the actual intention of accepting, and seldom does this requirement cause problems in practice.

However, a related problem arises from time to time in certain contract situations and it involves an offer made by the offeror—and silence by the offeree.

Silence

In a few cases, due to custom or prior usage, silence can constitute an acceptance, but the general rule is that it does not. We cannot force our offers on others. The U.C.C. recognizes the impact of customs in Article 2-208(1):

> Where the contract for sale involves repeated occasions for performance by either party with knowledge of the nature of the performance and opportunity for objection to it by the other, any course of performance accepted or acquiesed in without objection shall be relevant to determine the meaning of the agreement.

When Does Acceptance Become Effective?

The time that the acceptance becomes effective can be very important because it is usually at that time the contract becomes legally binding. Three general rules have developed.

Rule 1

The offer is sent by mail; the acceptance is sent by mail and the offeror does not say when it is to be effective. The acceptance is effective when *sent* and not when received. The legal reason for this is that the offeror chose the U.S. Postal Service as agent and when the acceptance was placed with the agent it was the same as if the offeror had received it personally. This rule is dangerous and can be guarded against by the use of Rule 2.

Rule 2

The offer is sent by mail and the offeror states, "The acceptance must be sent by telegram and is not effective until it is received in my office." The restriction controls and the condition must be observed, thus avoiding the dangers of Rule 1.

Rule 3

The offer is sent by mail; the acceptance is sent by telegram and the offeror is silent. The acceptance is effective when *received* by the offeror and not before because the offeree chose a different agency of communication.

The U.C.C. rule removes the strictness from the above rules. Article 2–204(2) states:

> An agreement sufficient to constitute a contract for sale may be found even though the moment of its making is undetermined.

The U.C.C. goes a step further and permits the acceptance to vary from the terms of the offer—a fatal move under normal contract rules. Article 2–207, U.C.C., states:

> (1) A definite and seasonable expression of acceptance or a written confirmation which is sent within a reasonable time operates as an acceptance even though it states terms additional or different from those offered or agreed upon, unless acceptance is expressly made conditional on assent to the additional or different terms.
>
> (2) The additional terms are to be construed as proposals for addition to the contract. Between merchants such terms become part of the contract unless:
>
> (a) The offer expressly limits acceptance to the terms of the offer;
> (b) They materially alter it; or
> (c) Notification of objection to them has already been given or is given within a reasonable time after notice of them is received.

(3) Conduct by both parties which recognizes the existence of a contract is sufficient to establish a contract for sale although the writings of the parties do not otherwise establish a contract. In such case the terms of the particular contract consist of those terms on which the writings of the parties agree, together with any supplementary terms incorporated under any other provisions of this Act.

While the U.C.C. provision is difficult to grasp without close study, it's general meaning is clear. The practical effect of this material change in contract principles is obvious—but it only applies between merchants.

MUTUALITY

Mutuality, or the agreement, must be present as the third requirement of a binding contract and normally comes into being where there has been a legally effective offer and acceptance. If A offers B one of two cars and B accepts, thinking he or she is buying the other car, the "minds did not meet" and mutuality would be lacking. It can be thought of as diagramed in Figure 14–7.

FIGURE 14–7

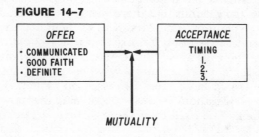

Case Example

Sas prepared the following offer: "Dear Lucas, I hereby offer to sell you my house on Z Street for $25,000. I reserve the right to sell anytime before your acceptance arrives at my office." The offer was sent by mail and arrived at Lucas' home at 9 A.M. on Monday. Lucas wanted to purchase the house and knew that if he answered by mail it would take two days before Sas received the acceptance. (Rule 1 above is of no help to him. Why?)

Lucas immediately went to the telegraph office and sent an acceptance, believing that this was the quickest means available. This was at 9:10 A.M. The telegraph company negligently failed to send the acceptance until 4:41 P.M. that same day. The telegram was received by Sas at 6:03 P.M.—but he had sold the house to another at 3:30 P.M. There is no contract between Sas and Lucas, and Lucas' only recourse is a tort action against the telegraph company for negligence.

The fourth and sometimes important requirement in a conventional contract is the requirement of "consideration."

CONSIDERATION

In contract law, consideration is the "reason for enforcing promises" and it usually takes the form of money—but it can be supplied in other ways as the church case illustrates.

Church Case

Mrs. X fell down an unlighted stairway at her church. The church carried liability insurance and the adjuster stopped at her home one evening and made the following promise: "If you do not file suit, my company will pay you $1,500.00." This was a promise for a unilateral act—a promise in exchange for the act of *not* filing suit. To say it another way, it was a promise in exchange for doing nothing.

Mrs. X did what was requested; the statute of limitation expired barring her from ever filing suit against the church—and the insurance company refused to pay. Mrs. X filed suit, claiming that she had accepted the offer of the adjuster and therefore there was a contract between her and the insurance company to pay her $1,500.00. The company conceded that the three elements (offer, acceptance, and mutuality) were present—but defended on the grounds that there was no "consideration." In other words, they were claiming that Mrs. X gave them nothing in exchange for the promise, *because churches are immune from suit in Kansas*—the state where the case arose. Since Mrs. X had no right to sue in the beginning, she in fact gave up nothing when she did not file suit—because her case would have been dismissed on motion. The court said "Yes, there is consideration, because she gave up the right to go to court and find out she had no right to be there." The court upheld the $1,500 contract.[4]

The case illustrates that in law the question of "adequacy" is not important. It is just a question of whether there is or is not consideration in the legal sense.

Courts have found legal consideration in many unusual cases and have held the following to be sufficient to support contract promises:

1. Bringing one a "rose in June."
2. Giving up smoking.
3. Paying a $500 obligation with $300 worth of groceries.
4. Payment of $1.00 for a valuable tract of land.
5. "Love and affection."

Consideration and the U.C.C.

It is apparent that the U.C.C. is moving sharply away from consideration in its traditional setting. For example, a U.C.C. option not to exceed three months is effective if in writing, even though there is no consideration. In addition, a court may refuse to enforce a sales contract if after a

---

[4] *Ralston* v. *Mathew*, 173 Kan. 550, 240 P. 284 (1952).

hearing the court finds it to be "unconscionable" and even though all of the elements of contract are present. There are other provisions of the *Code* that point toward a trend of abolishing "consideration" and replacing it with "good faith"—a requirement of the code. Article 1-203 states:

> Every contract or duty within this Act imposes an obligation of good faith in its performance or enforcement.

Consideration and Real Estate

In contracts for the sale of real estate, it is practice nationwide, to require the buyer to "bind the deal" by the payment of a sum of money. It can be as little as $1.00 as mentioned or it may be as much as one third of the purchase price. The amount makes no difference at law.

Such consideration is usually called "hand" or "earnest" money. In the usual realty sale, if the sale is not consumated and there is no fault on the seller, the hand money is retained as liquidated damages. An example of a realty contract is shown earlier in this chapter (see "Regular Option").

Is Consideration Necessary?

Consideration in the conventional sense is peculiar to Anglo-American law.

Scotland has flatly rejected it as part of their contract principles. The German courts merely look to the intention of the parties. The French Civil Code as well as Roman law simply speaks of "causa"—the purposes of making a contract.

It is reasonable to assume that in time, under the guidelines established by the U.C.C., consideration will cease to be a major part of our contract law.

COMPETENT PARTIES

The requirement of competent parties is fulfilled by the parties themselves being of contractual competence and capacity at contract time.

However, if they are not, the contract is "voidable" at the election of the one under the disability—that is, it can be set aside by that person.

Examples of incompetent parties include those under the statutory age provided by law—currently 18 in most states—those who are adjudicated insane, and in some cases, those under the influence of alcohol or narcotics. The careful business person simply does not deal with incompetent persons—or if one does, proceeds with caution and legal advice.

LEGALITY

The final requirement seldom becomes an issue because most contracts are for legal purposes. But if they are not, an essential element is lacking and the so-called contract would not be enforceable in court. For example, a contract to pay for services by a lawyer who is not admitted to practice in that state would be illegal.

For further insight into the conventional contract, examine chapter 22, "Introduction to Property."

In drafting a contract, the lawyer often asks the following question: Should the contract be "sealed"? As it turns out, some contracts do *not* have to be sealed; some *should* be and some *must* be. Just what *is* a "seal" on a contract?

Seals and Sealed Instruments

Since early times, a "seal" was some impression made on a wax wafer or other substance affixed to a written document. We have been told of the king or queen's ring used to "seal" royal writs and documents that came before him or her. See Figure 14–8 upper left, for an example of an

FIGURE 14–8

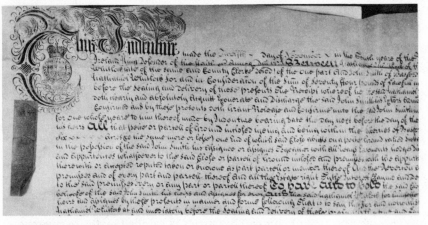

From the author's collection.

early English seal. This document is dated November 12, 1723, and conveys land in Nottingham Forest in England.

For another example, see Figure 14–9 lower left. This seal was affixed to a Virginia land grant, dated 1785, and was signed by Patrick Henry who was Governor of Virginia at that time.

The devices most frequently used in early times were metal disks with suitable words carved within them. See Figure 14–10. This seal was used in Monongalia County, Virginia, beginning in 1803. The seal was carved in silver and was found in a deserted cabin in the Old Dominion.

Legal Effect. When one places a seal on a legal document – regardless of the form – that document has greater legal force than it would have

FIGURE 14–9

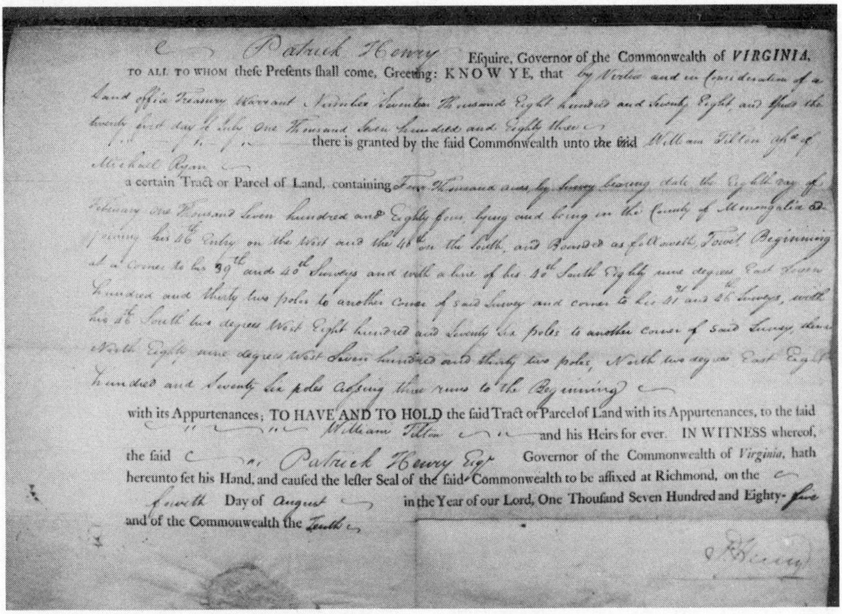

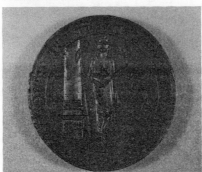

Patrick Henry Esquire, Governor of the Commonwealth of VIRGINIA,
TO ALL TO WHOM these Presents shall come, Greeting: KNOW YE, that by Virtue and in Consideration of a Land office Treasury Warrant Number Seventeen Thousand Eight hundred and Seventy Eight, and issued the twenty first day of July One Thousand Seven hundred and Eighty three
there is granted by the said Commonwealth unto the said William Tilton ass[ignee] of Michael Ryan
a certain Tract or Parcel of Land, containing Four Thousand acres by Survey bearing date the Eighth day of February One Thousand Seven hundred and Eighty four lying and being in the County of Monongalia adjoining his 46 Entry on the West and the 48 on the South, and Bounded as followeth, to wit, Beginning at a Corner to his 39th and 40th Surveys and with a line of his 40th South Eighty nine degrees East Seven hundred and thirty two poles to another Corner of said Survey and corner to his 41 and 26 Surveys, with his 26 South two degrees West Eight hundred and Seventy six poles to another corner of said Survey thence North Eighty nine degrees West Seven hundred and thirty two poles, North two degrees East Eight hundred and Seventy six poles crossing three runs to the Beginning
with its Appurtenances; TO HAVE AND TO HOLD the said Tract or Parcel of Land with its Appurtenances, to the said William Tilton and his Heirs for ever. IN WITNESS whereof, the said Patrick Henry Esq Governor of the Commonwealth of Virginia, hath hereunto set his Hand, and caused the lesser Seal of the said Commonwealth to be affixed at Richmond, on the fourth Day of August in the Year of our Lord, One Thousand Seven Hundred and Eighty-five and of the Commonwealth the Tenth
P. Henry

From the author's collection.

had without it. This is true because common law judges "jealously protected sealed documents" – just as modern judges do.

Affixing a seal to a legal document gave it a dignity of its own, and the common law courts considered the presence of the seal forceful enough to do away with the need to prove that "consideration" had in fact been present. In addition, the sealed instrument was not merely *evidence* of the obligation, it was *treated as being the obligation itself.* To say it another way, the presence of a seal operated as an "estoppel"

FIGURE 14–10

From the author's collection.

and a party to the instrument could not raise the defense of lack of consideration nor could that party question the facts surrounding the execution of the document.

The common law effect has been dissipated somewhat over the years, but it is still very much in evidence.

Today. Some states by statute, have abolished the need for a seal in the transfer of real estate. Others maintain the requirement. Most states require that a deed that is being notarized out of the state have the seal of the notary affixed. In addition, all promissory notes are sealed.

Some Modern Examples. All notaries have a seal which they use on papers that they notarize. This lends considerable "solemnnity" to the notorization. See Figure 14–11.

FIGURE 14–11

In the case of notes (negotiable instruments) the signature lines are usually printed in one of the two following forms:

```
_____ (SEAL)
_____ (SEAL)

_____ (L.S.)
_____ (L.S.)
```

"L.S." is an abbreviation of *"locus segilli"* – the "location of the seal." This tells us that mere type or a typewriter can provide the seal on such instruments.

Under the U.C.C. The seal and its common law operation retained enough impact upon modern lawyers to prompt the drafters of the U.C.C. to state in Article 2.:

> "The affixing of a seal to a writing evidencing a contract for sale or an offer to buy or sell goods does not constitute the writing a sealed instrument and the law with respect to sealed instruments does not apply to such a contract or offer."[5]

However, the seal does have other modern effects in various states, depending upon state law. A Connecticut case illustrates.

---

[5] U.C.C., 2–203.

American Fin. Co. v. Lawlor.[6] In this case a borrower had signed a note for a loan and the printed word "SEAL" followed his signature. Twelve years later the finance company sued on the instrument.

In Connecticut a note that is *properly* sealed can be collected in court within a 17 year time period. Unsealed notes can only be collected within six years.

Here, the evidence established that the borrower did not know what the word "seal" after his name meant and therefore he had not adopted the seal as his own. As a result, the case was dismissed because the six year statute of limitations had expired. (A word of caution, however: Many courts have held just the opposite.)

The result in this case could have been avoided if the effect of the seal had been explained to the borrower. The company would have done well to have had the borrower acknowledge in writing that he understood the effect of the seal.

One final subject must be considered in the formation of contracts, and it is a direct outgrowth of worldwide shortages of materials and energy.

SHORTAGE CONTRACTS

The business person must be careful not to become bound in contracts in which the performance may be impossible later because of shortages of materials or inavailability of transportation for delivery.

To avoid this contingency, contracts must be drafted with provisions that spell out the rights of the parties in the event of delays in shipment or shortages. Contracts that are based upon "requirements" should contain provisions on how output and requirements can be adjusted downward in the event of shortages. It is practice in business today, to avoid "boilerplate"—that is, contracts that are so strict that no variation is permitted from them.

REVIEW QUESTIONS

1. What is your general impression of the difference between conventional and U.C.C. contract principles?
2. Why would a church carry liability insurance when it is immune from suit?
3. In the "1,300 banana" case, the car dealer let the car go for approximately $50 worth of fruit. Can you think of a reason why the dealer did this?
4. What might happen if an ad was stated in such a way that it was in fact a legal offer?
5. True or False. An offer lasts until it is revoked by the offeree.
6. Joe Doe purchased a $10,000 life insurance policy. What "consideration" is provided by Doe? The insurance company?
7. Options are offers that cannot be revoked for the stated time periods. Why are they also binding contracts?
8. True or False. Since we have a double set of contract principles, there are likely to be overlaps in practice.

---

[6] CV6.718–5267 AP, Conn. C.P. (1973).

9. Explain why a "counteroffer" is, in law, a completely new "offer."
10. The law of agency (see Chapter 41) regulates the activities of one who acts through another. Do you understand why the U.S. Postal Service can be an "agent?" If not, ask.

Words and Phrases

Write out briefly what they mean to you.
1. Mutuality.
2. Competency.
3. "Inviting offers."
4. Rules of acceptance timing.
5. Consideration.

Coverage:	An examination of situations in which the contract-making steps fail.
What to Look for:	The specific instances in which this occurs.
Application:	Think of business situations where these matters could arise.

15 What Does *Not* Make a Contract?

Traditionally, business law textbooks have emphasized the structural requirements of the contract. However, it is becoming increasingly evident that the parts of a valid contract may not be the most important feature of contract law as it affects one in business. In reality, business persons are not confronted with the intricacies of contract law except in two situations: first, where there has been a breach by one party or the other; and second, where one party contests the validity of an existing contract. This second aspect of contracts is the subject matter of this chapter.

SOME DEFINITIONS

A "valid contract" is a contract that possesses the legal quality of being enforced against one or all of the parties to the agreement. This category may include contracts which are classified as "voidable."

A "voidable contract" is one which, although it is valid, is for some reason not enforceable against all of the parties involved.

A "void contract" is one which is defective to the point that the courts will give it no legal effect whatsoever. In short, it is no contract at all, and therefore the phrase "void contract" is a redundancy.

Finally, an "unenforceable contract" is one which, as the term implies, cannot be enforced, in whole or part, because it is voidable or void, or otherwise defective.

VOIDABLE CONTRACTS

The majority of defective agreements are those which, although valid, cannot be enforced by or against all of the parties involved. Examples

177

of voidable contracts include those involving a minor (or other party deemed legally incompetent to contract) and those involving fraud or mistake.

At common law those who were incompetent were permitted to avoid their contracts, even though the same incompetents were allowed to enforce the same contracts against all *competent* parties to the agreement. It was argued that, if incompetent persons were held to *their* agreements, the "floodgates" would be opened to the unscrupulous who would take advantage of them.

The Infant as an Incompetent

Although the term "infant" may have acquired a more limited meaning in the past hundred years, the law still regards anyone as an infant until the age of "majority" – 18 years of age in most states. One who is not yet 18 is a legal incompetent and is considered not to have the mental power and free will to enter into a valid contract. The rule of infancy is not a restriction on the rights of underage persons, but rather it is a protection for those persons. For example, in most cases when a minor enters into a contract with an adult, the minor can elect not to be bound by the contract and suffer no penalty. The minor can, however, compel compliance on the part of the adult. The ability of the infant to rescind the contract is limited by exceptions, but the applications far outweigh the exceptions.

Perhaps the greatest limitation on the infant's ability to avoid a contract with an adult rests in the concepts of "disaffirmance and ratification." The accepted rule is that when an infant enters into a contract with an adult, the power to disaffirm the agreement extends until majority – 18 for example – and then for a "reasonable time" thereafter. The failure of a minor to disaffirm within a reasonable time after reaching majority will generally constitute a "ratification" or an "affirmance" of the contract. Although a minor can disaffirm while still a minor, she or he cannot effectively ratify or affirm the contract until she or he has reached majority. One major exception to this rule is that an infant can *neither* disaffirm nor ratify a contract involving real estate until majority – at least as far as the legal title is concerned. The infant could disaffirm as far as the sum of money paid was concerned and have it returned.

Necessities. The most important exception to the law of contracts regarding minors is that the minor cannot escape liability under a contract for necessities. The theory is that the minor would have to purchase "necessities" in order to sustain one's self, and therefore should not have the power later to say that he or she did not want them. However, an infant can only be held in "quasi-contract" for the *reasonable value* of the "necessities." For goods or services to be considered within the scope of this exception, they must be *necessary* to the infant's continued well-being and healthy existence.

A Problem of Mathematics. One problem at common-law was more mathematical than legal: When does one age end and the next begin in calculating birthdays? The common-law rule—which remains today—was that a person attains the next year of age on the day *before* the birth date. For the purposes of the law, then, a party who enters into a contract on the 365th day of his or her 17th year will be treated as being age 18 relative to the contract.

What about the Parents?   The alleged rule that a parent is liable for the debts of a child seems to have gained prominence in today's society. A parent is *seldom liable* for a child's debts. The situations in which a parent will be held liable include: (1) If the child incurs a debt while acting as agent of the parent, the parent will be liable just as any principal in an agency relationship because the debt is the debt of the parent; (2) if the parent joins in the contract with the child and is a party to the contract, the parent may be held liable since the debt is the debt of both and (3) if the parent has failed to provide the child with the necessities of life, third parties may ask a court to hold the parent liable for debts incurred by the child in providing those necessities. This would be an "agency by necessity" and the parent would be the principal.

How about the Business Person?   Business persons today cannot afford to cease doing business with those under the age of 18, but just what is the alternative in such a situation? For instance, if a minor buys an auto and wrecks it, the only obligation in most states is the return of the auto to the seller—regardless of condition and the infant is entitled to the money back. What can the seller do? The answer is simple: require an adult to co-sign all contracts with minors. If the minor later disaffirms, the third party will have recourse against the adult.

Getting an adult to co-sign a contract with a minor is not always easy, but it is the only way the third party can be protected under law. All of this is fine, but how do *courts* deal with infants?

How Courts Deal with Infants

Courts are often called upon to render judgments that affect the rights of infants. For example, a court may order the interest of an infant in real estate sold, or enter an order permitting a sum of money to be paid to an infant in settlement of a tort claim. Just how does a court carry out these actions?

Summary Proceedings

All courts have by statute or common law, procedures by which infants rights can be determined and judgment entered in relation to them. (It should be observed that we are talking about rights of the infant and not rights of third parties *against* the infant.) The procedures vary but they are "summary" in nature. That is, they are carried forth with dispatch and strict adversary procedures are not followed.

To Illustrate.   Assume that J. Strahan, a 16-year-old, is injured in an automobile while riding as a "guest passenger" with W. Brown. The injuries included a broken arm and contusions. Medical and doctor bills were incurred as a result of them. The injuries were caused by the negligence of Brown in the operation of the car. The insurance carrier of Brown has agreed to pay Strahan the sum of $6,000.00 in settlement of all claims arising out of the accident.

What Now? The insurance company will *not* pay the money to Strahan. Why? She is an infant and would not be bound by the release that she might sign. She would have until the age of majority in which to repudiate the settlement and file suit for a larger sum. The insurance company will not pay the money to Strahan's parents. Why? Because it is not their money. If they would spend it, Strahan could still demand payment at a later date. Because of these facts, procedures are provided by which a settlement can be made now which will both bind and protect the infant.

How Is It Done? A petition is prepared that sets forth the pertinent facts. The petition requests that a "guardian ad litem" (called other things in different states) be appointed to represent the infant. If the judge is convinced by the petition that the proceedings will be in the best interests of the infant, the judge will order the petition filed, appoint a guardian and set a day for the hearing.

Prior to the hearing, the guardian ad litem will investigate the facts and file an answer stating whether or not the settlement will benefit the infant. If the answer is favorable to the settlement, then the hearing will proceed at the scheduled time.

At the Hearing. Medical testimony will be offered to establish the nature and extent of the injury. The probability of future medical problems will be examined. The guardian at litem will testify to the findings and the infant will also testify as to whether or not he or she is in agreement with the settlement.

If the court is satisfied that the settlement is in the best interests of the infant, an order will be entered to that effect. In most instances, the insurance company will pay the costs of the proceeding. The attorney representing the infant will be paid out of the infant's proceeds. The judge usually sets this figure. The money can then be paid in trust for the infant to be used for medical and other expenses. In some states the balance must be held for the infant until majority.

Other Forms of Legal Incompetence

Throughout legal history, the concern for the incompetent has not been restricted to minors. Generally, all classes of incompetents have been allowed to avoid contracts within a reasonable time after attaining the competency they lacked at the time the contract was made. Although a wide variety of incompetency situations exist in legal theory, only three will be discussed: insanity, intoxication, and corporate incompetency.

Insanity. Generally, an insane person will not be held liable for contracts entered into while insane. In order for this rule to apply, however, the person must have been adjudicated insane by a court of appropriate jurisdiction. When a person is adjudicated insane, an administrator or guardian is appointed. It is the duty of that person to carry out obligations under preinsanity contracts. The only preexisting contracts which are discharged by subsequent insanity are those which would require the personal services of the person who has become insane.

The rationale behind the insanity rule is the same as behind all incompetency situations: one who does not have control of one's own will and reasoning ability does not have the mental state of mind necessary to enter into a valid contract.

Intoxication. An intoxicated person will not be held liable for contracts entered into while intoxicated. The problem here arises in determining the actual state of intoxication, and determining whether or not the person was under the influence of alcohol to such a degree as to restrict reasoning ability and will power. If the person did not have full control of reasoning ability and will power the contract is voidable. (The intoxication rules also apply to those who may be under the influence of drugs or narcotics at the time contracts are entered into. Many cases have been decided in favor of those who signed releases in hospitals while heavily sedated, for example.)

Ratification. Even though contracts entered into by the insane or intoxicated are not enforceable against the incompetent party, that party can enforce them against other parties to the contract. To do this, the incompetent party must, in effect, ratify the original, voidable agreement. In so ratifying, the party who was incompetent gives up the right to disaffirm later. In order for the ratification to be valid, however, the person so doing must have attained competency. For instance, a person who was insane cannot ratify a voidable contract until adjudicated sane. One who was intoxicated must have attained sobriety before the contract can be affirmed.

Corporations as Incompetents. A unique type of incompetence involves a corporation contracting beyond the scope of its corporate powers. The powers of a corporation are defined in chapter 53 and a corporation is limited by those definitions. If a corporation officer enters into a contract which the charter does not authorize, the contract is voidable at the option of the corporation. However, if the other contracting parties have relied on the agreement in good faith and to their own detriment, the courts will use estoppel to compel the corporation to honor the contract. In such situations, the stockholders can then bring an action against the officers who exceeded their authority in entering into the agreement.

Other Classes of Voidable Contracts

Duress and Undue Influence.[1] The law protects innocent parties from contracts created by duress or undue influence by allowing them to avoid these contracts. Duress robs one of the free will to contract because a refusal to contract at that point will cause that person to incur the

---

[1] "Duress" means some unlawful constraint used upon one that forces that person to do some act that might not otherwise have been done. "Undue influence" means an improper persuasion by which the free will of another is overpowered so that that person does not act freely.

threatened physical or pecuniary damage. For example, a contract brought on at gunpoint will not be enforced since the victim did not have the "free will capacity" at the time of the agreement.

The same is true with undue influence, and the same remedies are available to the party who was the victim of undue influence.

Generally courts will allow the victim to disaffirm contracts brought on by fraud. The fraud itself must meet specific requirements, however.

Fraud as a Defense to a Contract.   For fraud to have the effect of invalidating an agreement, it must be an intentional misrepresentation of a past or present material fact upon which one party relied in good faith to that persons detriment.[2] Therefore, even though a misrepresentation is intentional, relief will not be granted unless it can be shown that the fraud was concerned with a material element in the contract, and that the victim relied on it in good faith to one's detriment. If all conditions are met, the victim may avoid the contract or hold the other party to the agreement, whichever the victim prefers.

Mistake as a Means to Avoid a Contract.   As a general rule, a mistake as to the terms of a contract will not be sufficient grounds to allow the avoidance of the contract. Therefore, it is essential that the parties be certain of all the facts, conditions, and consequences of any contract they enter into. As a rule of thumb, once a person signs an agreement, the courts will deem that person to have agreed to all of the terms contained therein.

In a few situations, however, a mistake will affect the enforceability of the agreement as discussed below.

Unilateral and Bilateral Mistakes.   When a mistake is made by only one of the parties, this will not render the contract unenforceable. The person who entered into the agreement on the basis of a mistake did so with personal risk and should bear the loss. By the same token, a unilateral mistake of law will have no effect on the enforceability of the contract, because all citizens are deemed to know the law at all times.

However, if *both* parties to the contract make the same mistake of fact, the courts will consider the contract void, since there was no agreement as to the facts. A mutual mistake as to law, however, usually will not have an effect on the contract, the same as in the unilateral situation. For instance, if A is contracting to sell a piece of real estate, and the contract calls for a "quitclaim deed," no relief will be granted just because both parties thought a "quitclaim deed" was a general warranty deed.

Bidders Beware.   The "mistake rules" come into play frequently in bidding situations. For example, ABC Building Company makes a bid to build a garage for Jones in the amount of $25,700. ABC Company had calculated the bid in the amount of $35,700, but the lower amount was submitted because of a clerical error. Despite this unilateral mistake of fact, ABC Company would be bound by the $25,700 bid provided that Jones accepts in good faith.

While it is true that courts generally will not allow the reformation of

---

[2] "Detriment" means a loss or harm suffered in person or property.

a unilateral mistake, the exception to the rule would be when the other party has reason to know a mistake has been made. The law will not allow the innocent party to take advantage knowingly of the other's mistake.

In our example, the court would have to determine that the submitted bid was so low as to put Jones on notice that a mistake had been made. If it was, then Jones would have notice of the mistake, and the contract would not be enforced. This problem of reasonable notice would not arise if, for example, the bid was for $257. Such a figure would be so obviously low as to put a reasonable person on notice.

LEGALLY UNENFORCEABLE CONTRACTS

Sometimes the courts will find that a contract cannot be enforced. Reasons for this include failure to meet legal requirements as well as those agreements that per se violate the law. The courts will not give legal sanction to something that is illegal.

Unconscionable Agreements

At common law, a contract would not be avoided simply because a person was taken advantage of, or because economic necessity placed one in an unequal bargaining position with the other. In recent years, however, this rule has been softened, and the courts will grant relief if it can be shown that the terms of a contract are so harsh—and that one party's bargaining power was so minimal—that the contract itself is "unconscionable" and should not be allowed to stand.[3]

Contracts Involving Usury

Traditionally, usury (the charging of an excessive interest rate for the loaning or forbearance of money) has been forbidden by the common law and statutory law. Today, most states cover the matter in statutes by stating that a contract involving an interest rate in excess of the limits stated shall be void at the outset and unenforceable—or void as to the excess interest. Generally, two interest rate limits are specified—the "contract rate" and the "legal rate." The contract rate is the maximum rate which may be agreed to in a loan agreement, and the legal rate is the maximum which can be charged when there is no express agreement as to the amount.

In one state, for instance, the contract rate is 12 percent, while the legal rate is 8 percent. For example, a contract in which the interest is stated at 14 percent would be usurious and unenforceable as would an attempt to assess a 9 percent interest charge where there is no agreed contract rate.

The implications of the usury statutes are far-reaching. For instance,

---

[3] U.C.C., 2–302.

when a department store assesses its debtors a 1.5 percent "service charge" on the balance at the end of each month (which equals 18 percent a year), do the usury laws come into play? Several courts have said "yes" to this question and the following is a good example:

> *State of Wisconsin* v. *J. C. Penney Co.*[4] This was an appeal by the state of a lower court decision which denied an injunction against the defendant. It had been alleged in the initial proceeding that the 1.5 percent monthly "service charge" on outstanding accounts was, in fact, usurious, since it was a charge being levied for the forbearance of money, i.e., the debt, and should be subject to the usury laws regarding interest rates for the forbearance of money. The appellate court said one must look at the substance of the transaction rather than the form. It held that because a charge is not called "interest" does not mean it is outside the statutes designed to control interest rates, and that the vital issue is whether or not the charge was levied for the forbearance of money. If so, the court said, it would come within the definition of the usury laws, and be subject to the interest limitations contained in those laws. In this case, the court said the money which was levied as a monthly service charge on the unpaid balance was within the purview of the interest statutes and should be governed accordingly. In keeping with this decision, the appellate court granted an injunction against the defendant, protecting the purchaser and others from any attempt to collect or levy the excess charge from then on.

The usury statutes are not uniform and because of this, the cases will vary. For example, in Iowa, the statute provides that no more than the "prescribed sum of value"—which is 9 percent in that state—shall be charged "upon contract founded upon any sale or loan of real or personal property."

In applying these provisions, the Supreme Court of Iowa refused to distinguish between "interest" and mere "time price" differential. This was true even though in other states, courts have held that a "time price" added to the sale of goods on credit, is *not* interest.[5]

In those states where the courts have ruled in favor of the consumer, the question then arises "can the consumers have returned to them all excess interest paid *before* the favorable court ruling?" The Supreme Court of South Dakota has said "no."[6]

As one result of the federal "Truth in Lending" law, debtors have become more conscious of rates of interest. Because of this, more usury cases should be going into the courts in the future. Truth in Lending is covered in detail in chapter 35.

"Blue Laws" and Contracts

Even though there is supposedly a separation of church and state in the United States, our laws still reflect the religious sentiments of the

---

[4] 179 N.W.2d 641 (1970).

[5] *Iowa ex. Rel. (on the relation of) Turner* v. *Yonker Brothers, Inc.*, 210 N.W.2d 550 (1973).

[6] *Rollinger* v. *J.C. Penney Co.*, 192 N.W.2d 699 (1971), reaffirmed 1974.

nation's founders. One example of this can be found in the "blue laws" (i.e., laws which prohibit the conduct of business on Sundays). More and more states are abolishing these laws each year, but where they exist, they are of concern to business. Ordinarily, a state blue law will prohibit the operation of businesses on Sundays except those which deal in food and medicine. In addition, the statute may have a provision which makes a contract entered into on Sunday a complete nullity.

The trend, however, is toward the repealing of blue laws, and many states allow the question to be decided by local governments. Where a state has the "local option" system, one city in the state may keep the blue laws while another may repeal them.

Contracts against Public Policy

Some contracts are held to be invalid because they violate what the courts label "public policy." Examples of these include contracts not to compete, contracts attempting to relieve one of personal liability, contracts in restraint of trade, and others. An example of a contract against public policy is one in which a seller of a product – or service – states that the seller will not be liable for injury or damage that may occur as the result of his or her actions. This type of contract should not be confused, however, with a release upon settlement of a disputed claim.

Another contract against public policy is the "price-fixing agreement" between competitors. The courts have uniformly held that such an agreement is in restraint of trade and therefore against public policy.

Contracts for Illegal Purposes

A contract which requires an illegal act be performed is automatically void. If, for example, a person makes a wagering contract with another, the contract will have absolutely no effect in court, even if it is signed, sealed, and notarized – unless wagering is legal in the particular jurisdiction. The reason for this is obvious: a court cannot put itself in a position to force someone to commit an illegal act in order to carry out the terms of a contract.

Even though the contract may not be illegal when made, if the law changes so that to carry out the contract would require the commission of an illegal act, the contract will be declared void.

CORPORATE VERSUS INDIVIDUAL LIABILITY IN CONTRACT

When a corporate officer executes a contract on behalf of the corporation, that person will almost never intend to incur personal liability on the contract. However, when a corporation becomes insolvent or files bankruptcy, it is not uncommon for creditors to try to hold corporate officers personally liable in contract. The following case illustrates:

BALEY, Judge.

This appeal brings into question only those matters decided by the trial court which relate to the individual defendant, George Bryant. If it is determined that there is no competent evidence that Bryant signed the August proposal of plaintiff as an individual, he would not be bound thereby. We are of the opinion that the exceptions of the defendant, Bryant, to the findings of fact and conclusions of law holding him to be individually liable under the August proposal are well taken, and the judgment entered against him must be reversed.

In its judgment the trial court recited the following pertinent findings of fact and conclusions of law:

"FINDINGS OF FACT

*   *   *   *   *

5.   On or about August 3, 1971, the plaintiff submitted another proposal dated August 3, 1971, for the installation of a smaller air conditioning system in the new plant addition at Efland, North Carolina. On August 23, 1971, George Bryant executed the acceptance of the proposal by signing his name 'George A. Bryant,' as owner as well as by signing his name 'George Bryant' as president of Converter's Yarn Sales, Inc."

"CONCLUSIONS OF LAW

*   *   *   *   *

3.   Both the defendant George A. Bryant, individually, and Converter's Yarn Sales, Inc., entered into a contract with the plaintiff for the installation of an air conditioning system for the sum of $23,539.00, and both defendants breached said contract.

4.   The plaintiff has been damaged in the amount of $5,310.00 as a result of the breach of said contract, and the defendants George A. Bryant and Converter's Yarn Sales, Inc., are liable, jointly and severally, to the plaintiff in said amount."

[1,2]   Where a jury trial is waived, the findings of fact of a trial court are conclusive if supported by any competent evidence. If such findings of fact support a proper basis for the judgment, it will not be disturbed on appeal. *Cogdill* v. *Highway Comm.,* 279 N.C. 313, 182 S.E.2d 373; *Huski-Bilt, Inc.* v. *Trust Co.,* 271 N.C. 662, 157 S.E.2d 352.

[3]   The evidence in this case disclosed a series of negotiations concerning the installation of an air conditioning system in the plant of the corporate defendant. These negotiations were conducted on behalf of Converter's by its president, George Bryant. The proposals from plaintiff in May and August were made in writing to Bryant at the company address at Efland. The instructions to terminate any contracts which were entered were issued by Bryant as president of the corporation and on its stationery and were honored by plaintiff. The cancellation notice concerning the August proposal on which Bryant was held personally liable was on corporate stationery, signed by George A. Bryant, president, and specifically set out in the body of the letter "We are requesting that you hold up on any further progress concerning the air conditioning project for Converter's Yarn Sales, Inc." At no

point in the evidence is there any indication that plaintiff was relying upon Bryant individually, but it was always dealing with him as the executive officer of the corporation. The August proposal which was an exhibit at the trial showed the following signature:

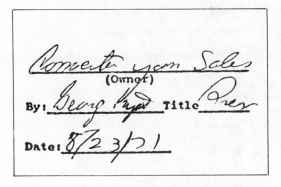

The addendum to this proposal providing for an additional fume removal system and executed the same date was also an exhibit and showed:

[4]   The intent of the parties as revealed in the transaction as a whole, and not the signatures alone, determines liability. Whitney v. Wyman, 101 U.S. 392, 25 L.Ed. 1050; Fowle v. Kerchner, 87 N.C. 49. The mere fact that Bryant signed "George A. Bryant" between the written corporate signature and his signature as president on the proposal of plaintiff and that the word "Owner" was printed on the form below his name is not sufficient evidence from which to find as a fact that he executed the contract as an individual. All the evidence concerning the negotiations and execution of the contracts supports the conclusion that plaintiff did not deal with Bryant as an individual but as the executive officer of Converter's.

The finding of fact that George Bryant executed the acceptance of the proposal by signing his name as owner is not supported by competent evidence. It would follow that the conclusion of law that Bryant, individually,

had entered any contract with plaintiff is in error, and that portion of the judgment which awards recovery against Bryant is hereby vacated.
Reversed.[7]

REVIEW QUESTIONS

1. For what reasons and to what purposes do the contractual limitations on infants and incompetents exist?
2. Will the showing of fraud *always* defeat an action on a contract?
3. When, if ever, is "mistake" a valid ground for rescission of a contract?
4. What is the rationale behind the refusal to enforce contracts that are "contrary to public policy"?
5. True or False. Restrictive employment clauses in contracts are always void.
6. List the requirements of actionable fraud; misrepresentation. How do they differ?
7. Why are infants held liable for their torts – but not always on their contracts?
8. It is a policy of the law to protect infants who enter into contracts. Explain why.
9. List one agreement that would be unlawful. Why should one in business avoid such an arrangement?
10. Distinguish a contract against public policy from one that is unenforceable.

Words and Phrases

Write out briefly what they mean to you.
1. Incompetence.
2. Fraud.
3. Usury.
4. Public policy.
5. Voidable contracts.

---

[7] *Industrial Air, Inc., of Greensboro* v. *Bryant*, 23 N.C. App. 281, 209 S.E.2d 306 (1974).

Coverage:	The legal consequences of failing to keep contract promises.
What to Look for:	Reasons why contract promises are usually honored.
Application:	The possibility of a breach of contract should always be considered at the outset.

16 Breaking a Contract

The business person must learn to distinguish damages for breach of contract from damages that arise out of tort. Contract damages arise when one breaks a binding contract promise which results in money loss to another. Tort damages come into being when one *negligently* or *carelessly* injures another or that person's property. In both types of actions, proof of the actual loss is essential. Our discussion here will be limited to contract damages.

BREACH OF CONTRACT

A breach of contract occurs when one party to a binding contract fails in whole – or part – to honor the obligation assumed at the time the contract was entered into.

Example 1. A contracted to construct a home for B for the sum of $35,000. The contract contained the specifications that A was to follow. After the house was under roof, A, who had been paid in part, walked off the job and refused to complete the house. A breached the contract.

Example 2. At the time C purchased an automobile, C gave the bank a note in the sum of $2,000 at 12 percent interest, which C promised to repay at the rate of $150 per month. The bank took security in the auto. (See chapter 37 for the documents.) C made four payments on the car and then defaulted. C too breached the contract.

In one instance, a party to a binding contract has a legal right to breach – or break – the promises. This can arise in an "anticipatory breach" situation.

Anticipatory Breach

If a party to a contract has good reason to believe that a breach of contract is going to occur, that person may take action before the breach occurs in order to protect that person's interests.

Example 3. If A knows that B will not pay for the truckload of materials that A is under contract to deliver to B, A may anticipate the breach and refuse to deliver. However, care must be used because if the information is wrong, A will be held responsible for losses caused to B by the refusal to deliver.

Once the breach of contract occurs, three important legal principles come into play. First, the one who had the contract breached must "mitigate" or "keep down" the damages of the other. Next, the loss, if any, must be "fixed" or established. Finally, a profit beyond what was anticipated originally cannot be made by the one who had the contract breached.

MITIGATION

Mitigation of damages is an essential and common-sense part of the laws of contract and can be illustrated by examples. After the contractor breached the contract on the $35,000 home in Example 1, an immediate duty fell upon the homeowner to safeguard the work that had been done. If a portion of the roof had been left uncovered, it would have to be finished at once to protect the interior of the house. If building supplies had been left outdoors where they could be damaged by the elements, they would have to be covered or brought indoors. If there was any chance that materials might be stolen or damaged by vandals, they would have to be protected.

In Example 2 where the car buyer defaulted in the payments on the car, the bank would repossess the car under its security agreement. After it was in possession of the bank or it's agent, repairs would be made if necessary to insure the highest possible money return. In addition, the sale of the car could not be delayed for an unreasonable length of time, because if it was, the car would bring less, thus violating the duty of the bank to "mitigate."

Another Example. The principle of mitigation is frequently encountered in rental contracts or leases. For example, A leases an apartment from B for $150 per month which A is to pay on the first of the month. The lease is on a month-to-month basis called a "tenancy at will." B cannot terminate the lease without giving A notice equal to one full rental period. For example, to terminate the tenancy by June 1, B would have to give notice *before* the first day of May. The reverse is true and A cannot quit without giving B the same notice. However, A breaches the contract by moving out on May 1, without giving notice. At this point, B must mitigate the damages of A. This is done by cleaning the premises if necessary and attempting to find a new tenant at once. If B finds a new renter by May 15, the only sum that B can hold A responsible for is a half month's rent and perhaps cleaning costs.

The principle of mitigation is frequently encountered in newspaper and magazine ads. For example, A contracts to have a certain ad appear in a publication once a week for 52 weeks at a cost of $100 per ad. After the second week, A cancels the ad, thus breaching the contract. The newspaper cannot continue to publish the ad and sue A for the year's rental because they did not mitigate the damages. The publishing company would be under a duty to immediately stop the ad. They could then sue for loss of profits caused by the breach.

Once one has complied with the requirement of mitigating damages, one will be concerned with "fixing" the damages.

FIXING THE LOSS

Once the contract has been breached and all reasonable steps have been taken to stop further loss to the other party, the damages should be fixed or established. In the home-construction illustration, the home-owner must hire someone to complete the work that was left unfinished and should seek bids in order to keep the costs down. Assume the builder had been paid $20,000 at the time of the breach. If the homeowner can hire one to complete the house according to the original contract for the sum of $18,000, then the damages for the breach have been established as being $3,000, the difference between the original contract price and the price that was eventually paid for the work.

In the case of the car repossession, once the car is sold, the proceeds must be applied to the obligation of the one who breached the contract. If the proceeds are less than the sum due, which happens frequently, then the bank has fixed its loss and can sue the debtor for the difference. For example, if the debtor owed $2,000 at the time of breach and the car brought $1,500 at a proper sale, the loss to the bank would be $500 and it could sue for that amount plus costs of the sale. If the car brought $2,500, which it might if it were a new car, the bank will apply the first $2,000 to the note which pays it in full; then the expenses of the sale will be deducted from the $500 and the balance will be returned to the debtor. This illustrates why every attempt must be made to receive the highest possible sum at the sale.

In the rental case, if the landlord relets the apartment on the 15th of the month at $150, then the loss has been fixed at one half of a month's rent, or $75, and the landlord can sue for that amount, plus reasonable cleaning and repairing costs.

CAN'T MAKE A PROFIT

It has long been the policy of the law to prohibit the one whose contract is breached to make a profit over what would have been made if the contract had been honored. For example, if the homeowner hires a brother to complete the building contract in Example 1, the homeowner cannot pay the brother $50,000 and expect to sue the original contractor for $15,000.

Likewise, the bank cannot sell the repossessed car to an employee for $100 and then sue the debtor for the $1,900 balance on the note. Nor can the landlord permit the premises to sit vacant or the publisher to continue to run the ad.

SUE OR NOT?

Once the damages have been established, the decision must be made whether or not to sue. If the other party has left the state – or has filed bankruptcy – the lawsuit might be a loss of time and suit fees. Many companies sue for losses even though they cannot be recovered, in order to establish the loss for income tax purposes. The small business person may decide not to sue to avoid the publicity of going to court against a former customer. It is a decision for management – not a lawyer.

PROVING DAMAGES

If suit is filed, care must be exercised to make certain that the damages can be established with precision and without speculation or guessing. If a contract suit is defended, the determination of the damages will be a question of fact for the jury. If the proof requires speculation or guessing on the part of the jury, the judge will not allow the case to go to the jury – although, the jury may be allowed to establish liability. If they do, the judge may permit them to return a verdict for a nominal sum ($1.00 for example) for the plaintiff. This happened in the following construction case.

Case Example

Business person X, entered into a contract with a contractor Y, in which Y was to construct a warehouse to certain specifications. X agreed to pay Y costs of labor and material, plus 10 percent – a "cost plus" contract. For example, if labor and material came to $200,000, X was to pay Y $220,000.

Breach of contract followed as Y refused to complete the contract. X then completed the building – but did not follow the original plan. (A lawyer would have advised X to avoid these two acts.)

At the trial, X claimed that Y could have constructed the building for $220,000 and that it cost X $320,000, and therefore X should be paid $100,000 in damages. Any verdict that a jury might return under these facts would have been sheer guessing or speculation, because there was no precise way to determine the damages. The judge instructed the jury that if they believed X should recover for the breach of contract by Y, that their verdict could not exceed $1 – which is the verdict that the jury returned.

In most construction contracts, particularly where large sums of money are involved, the parties may agree in the contract itself what the damages will be if the builder defaults. This is called "liquidated" or "established" damages.

LIQUIDATED DAMAGES

Liquidated damage clauses are widely used in construction contracts. Their purpose is to assure that the builder will complete the contract by a specified date. If not, the sum specified in the contract will be used to establish the damages, and, if reasonable, will be honored by the courts.

For example, Zero Corporation contracts with the City of Fayette to construct an airport terminal building for $500,000. The completion date is set for September 1, the following year. The contract contains the following clause:

> The parties hereto expressly agree that if Zero Corporation does not complete said terminal building by the completion date, that it shall forfeit the sum of $100.00 for each day after that date until the contract is completed.

The contractor was hit with a series of misfortunes. First, a labor dispute delayed the work three months. Next, the glass doors and windows became lost in shipment and this delayed the job another two weeks. Finally, a fire broke out at the construction site, forcing the contractor to rebuild one end of the building and roof. The contractor completed the terminal but not until January 15 of the following year. This meant that the contract was broken by 107 days, requiring the contractor to forfeit $10,700. The many misfortunes were not of the type that the contractor could legally use as an excuse for late performance.

In some contract breach suits, the defendant does not file an answer and thus the plaintiff gets "judgment by default"—that is, since the defendant did not defend within the period of limitation, right to defend is lost. But even in this situation the plaintiff must still prove the loss.

AN INQUIRY INTO DAMAGES

Following default in a contract case, the plaintiff is usually given two choices: submit the proof of loss to a jury, or permit the judge, sitting alone, to make the determination. In practice, most lawyers advise their clients to follow the latter course because it is faster and the judge is usually more capable of determining damages than a jury.

If the sum involved is a sum certain—that is a sum of money that is fixed and not in dispute—most courts will accept an affidavit in proof of the damages and a formal hearing is not required.[1]

The discussion to this point has been confined to the "legal remedy"— that is, a lawsuit in court in search of dollars—called damages. There are also remedies on the "equity" (conscience) side of the court.

REMEDIES IN EQUITY

There are two principal equity or equitable, remedies, the first of which is used more frequently than the second. They are known as "rescission" and "specific performance."

---

[1] At law, there are other types of damages including punitive damages. These are discussed at appropriate places elsewhere.

Rescission

If A breaches a contract with B, or if the contract was induced by fraud, deceit, force, or legal mistake, B may petition the court, asking that the contract be rescinded and that both parties be freed from the obligations of it. In legal terms, a successful rescission action returns the parties to the "status quo" – the place they were before they entered into the contract.

A rescission action requires the repudiation of the contract by the moving party, and refusal to be further bound by it. The word "rescission" is from the Latin "rescissio" meaning to annul, avoid, or abrogate – the meaning that the action has in equity today.

The other equitable remedy reaches a different conclusion.

Specific Performance

In some contracts, if one breaches, the remedy of damages is not acceptable to the other. This frequently arises where some "unique" or peculiar object is involved that may have value beyond the market value of the item itself. If this situation arises, a suit may be brought in equity to force the other party to specifically perform the contract obligations. If a judge believes this remedy is justified, the judge will order the other party to perform. If that person refuses, the judge may then jail that person for refusal to obey the court order. A court ordered specific performance in the following situations:

1. A promised to sell to B an 1860 Colt Army cap and ball revolver, caliber .44, serial number 51101. The sale price was to be $500 of which B paid $50 down with the balance to be paid in 30 days. The gun was in its original holster and had been carried by B's great-grandfather at the battle of Franklin, Tennessee during the Civil War. A refused to deliver and tried to return the deposit.
2. C contracted, in writing, to sell D a vacant lot that adjoined D's home. Later, C refused to honor the contract.
3. Two brothers, X and Y, were the sole stockholders in a family corporation. X contracted to sell all of his shares to Y for $100,000. Later, X refused to honor his contract.

In all of these situations money damages would have been inadequate. If B had sued for damages in the gun contract, the recovery would have been the difference between $500 – the cost – and the fair market value of the pistol (about $550) for a recovery of perhaps $50.

If D had sued for damages in the lot case, the recovery would have been measured as in the gun case. D could never recover the loss caused by losing the right to enlarge the land to D's adjoining home.

In the stock case, Y may have lost out completely if Y sued for damages because the stock was not sold on the market. Establishing the loss of profits by the breach would have been difficult at best – and perhaps impossible.

In all three illustrations the uniqueness of the subject matter permitted the court to order that the contract be performed.

REVIEW QUESTIONS

1. Is it fair for the law to protect those who breach contracts: Why?
2. What legal requirements would be forced upon a business person when a student breaches a contract in a record or book club?
3. Why are most contracts honored?
4. What practical value does a verdict of $1 have to a plaintiff?
5. True or False. A loss always results when there is a breach of contract.
6. Give an example of "mitigation" not discussed in the text.
7. Why will a court not permit a jury to speculate on the amount of damages?
8. Most construction contracts contain "liquidated damages" clauses. Why?
9. Why is "rescission" an equitable, not a legal, remedy?
10. True or False. Courts have traditionally been reluctant to decree specific performance.

Words and Phrases

Write out briefly what they mean to you.
1. Mitigation.
2. Damages.
3. Rescission.
4. Specific performance.
5. "Fixing" damages.

Coverage:	The life insurance contract.
What to Look for:	The six requirements of a conventional contract.
Application:	Begin thinking about planning your own estate.

17 Life Insurance—A Contract Application [1]

During the past 50 years, life insurance has come to the front as one of the most versatile tools that we have in the personal and business worlds. Its growth resulted from many factors, but its acceptance in estate creation, family protection, retirement planning, business buy and sell agreements, and group insurance has contributed substantially to this growth. By the use of the life insurance contract we can increase the amount of the estate that we will leave our heirs; it can be the source of funds with which one partner can buy out the share of a deceased partner; and in "close" family corporations, insurance proceeds are often used to purchase the share of a deceased stockholder thus consolidating the ownership of the business. Just what is the basic concept behind life insurance?

BASIC CONCEPT

The essence of "insurance" is the sharing of losses and the substitution of certainty for uncertainty. All forms of insurance require an accumulation of risks into one group. However, insurance differs in regard to the *nature* of the risks covered. The main difference between life insurance and other forms is in the latter, the risk insured against may or may not happen, while in life insurance the event insured against is a certainty—only the time of it happening is uncertain.

Life insurance companies have developed sound procedures for the formation of "groups" for insurance. They have established procedures

---
[1] The author extends sincere thanks to Walter S. Hopkins, Jr., Chartered Life Underwriter, Massachusetts Mutual Life Insurance Co., for technical assistance in the preparation of this chapter and for his material written contribution.

for determining who may join the group as an acceptable risk at a *standard* premium rate. This is accomplished by taking into consideration one's age, occupation, physical condition, medical history, moral fitness, financial condition, and residence, as factors in determining the *insurability* of the person being considered. Those who cannot meet the requirements (1) *may* be offered insurance at a rate different than the standard rate (a substandard or classified rate), or, (2) be refused admission as an uninsurable person. However, in true *group* insurance, insurability requirements are waived, but the premiums charged reflect this waiver.

How Are Premium Rates Established?

Insurance companies compute premium rates by utilization of the following: (1) *Mortality tables.* These tables indicate the number of persons living and dying at designated ages. Examine the *Student Workbook* for a table. (2) *Interest.* This is the rate of earnings that a company assumes that invested premiums will produce. (3) *"Loading" expense.* This is an assignment to each premium of a proportionate share of the company's operating expenses.

The methods have proven successful in providing the public with a product that has become one of the most widely held types of personal property. There are two kinds of personal property: (1) *choses (things) in possession,* and (2) *choses in action.* The former refers to *tangible* objects while the latter refers to ownership rights. The life insurance contract is a *chose in action* type of personal property. This is the principal reason why we should have an understanding of it in business law.

Nature of the Contract

The life insurance contract is an *informal, unilateral* contract in which the company is held to its promises and can be sued for failure to keep them. On the other hand, the insured cannot be sued for failure to pay premiums. *The company has no cause of action to sue a policy holder for failure to pay premiums.* In this respect, the life insurance contract is unique.

How Is the Contract Formed?

The life insurance contract involves a series of steps before it comes into being. The first is when the applicant completes an application. As a general rule, if one prepays the premium, that person is issued a "conditional receipt." This then is a contract offer and the applicant is the offeror. If the company issues a policy exactly as applied for, it has accepted the offer and the contract is in being. This constitutes the mutual assent or "mutuality."

However, if the company issues a different policy at a different premium rate, then a counteroffer has been made and there is no contract until the applicant accepts the counteroffer.

The majority of conditional receipts issued today for premiums paid in advance, are of the "condition precedent" type. This means that something must happen or be preformed before the company has a duty to perform its promises. This is simply a legal move on the part of the company to give them an opportunity to determine the insurability of the applicant before becoming bound in a contract.

Who Are Parties to the Contract?

Only the applicant and the company are parties to the contract. If the insured is not the applicant, then that person must sign a consent to being insured. This is a "third party" application. The beneficiary of the policy is *not* a party to the contract.

Legal Purpose

Since life insurance directly affects the public, public policy weighs heavily in the regulation of insurance, which at the present time is the job of the states. It follows that life insurance must be for a legal purpose. The most important requirement is that an *insurable interest* exist at the time the contract is made. However, unlike other forms of insurance, an insurable interest is *not* required at the time of loss.

Basically, an insurable interest is one that arises out of love or affection or economic factors, in that one will benefit by the *continuance* of a life, rather than benefit by the loss of it.

An Aleatory Contract

A life contract is an aleatory agreement—that is, one in which the parties can recover more in value than what those parties started with. Wagering contracts are also aleatory—but they are generally illegal. The requirement of an insurable interest removes the life contract from the gambling category.

Life insurance contracts in which there would be no insurable interest would be against public policy and thus not enforceable in court. If such contracts were permitted, it would tend to encourage one to take life for monetary gain.

Premium Payments

The consideration provided by the applicant or insured as the case may be, is the premium. While there is no legal obligation to pay them, as mentioned, failure to do so may result in lapse of the policy.

Premiums are payable in advance and may be made annually, semi-annually, quarterly, or monthly. As a general rule, the more often premiums are paid, the more they cost. Premiums should be paid promptly and one should provide some reminder of the due date so they will not be missed. A good technique is to make notes of due dates on an accessible calender.

A popular method of premium payments is by a "preauthorized check-type plan." The premiums are processed directly through the bank account of the policy owner.

Grace Periods. All policies contain a period of time after a premium is missed in which the premium can be paid and the policy continues in full force. Normally 31 days is provided. If death occurs during the grace period, the policy proceeds will be paid less the cost of the last premium.

Automatic Premium Loan Provision. When this provision is included in a policy, it gives the company the power to use cash values of the policy to pay the unpaid premium on the last day of the grace period.

Reinstatement of a Lapsed Policy

If a policy has lapsed, and if it contains a reinstatement provision, it can be reinstated within three to five years by payment of back premiums and by giving proof of insurability.

Nonforfeiture

If a premium remains unpaid at the end of the grace period and there is no automatic loan provision, another policy provision may be applied, if operative. This is the nonforfeiture provision and the policy owner may exercise one of the following options: (1) surrender the policy for its cash value, (2) elect extended term insurance, which will pay the full face amount of the policy for a limited time period, or (3) elect a reduced paid up insurance. This will pay a sum less than the face amount but for an unlimited period of time or to maturity date if it is an "endowment" policy.

In addition to the features discussed above, there are many standard or general provisions that are normally included in life contracts by requirement of state law.

STANDARD OR GENERAL PROVISIONS

Incontestable Clause

During a stated time period, two years is typical, the company may challenge the policy for reasons of fraud or material misrepresentation in the application. After the contestable period expires, the company can no longer challenge it, even if there had been fraud in the application.

Assignability

Since life insurance is personal property, it can be transferred to another *absolutely*, or *collaterally* such as pledging the proceeds of it as collateral for a loan.

This is done by a legal document called an "assignment" and renders the beneficiary subject to the assignment. The written assignment form must be filed with the company to provide notice. The company will not assume responsibility for the *validity* of an assignment.

Suicide Clause

A typical suicide provision provides that: "If the insured, whether sane or insane, commits suicide within two years from date of issue, the company will be liable only for the premiums paid, less any indebtedness, which will be paid to the beneficiary." After the time period, there are no such limitations on payment of the proceeds of the policy.

Change of Ownership

If proper forms are used, the ownership of the policy may be changed to another. However, some transfers can subject the proceeds payable on death, to the *transfer-for-value* rule of the IRS Code. This may make part of the proceeds taxable as ordinary income. Otherwise, proceeds are *not* taxable as being ordinary income.

Beneficiaries

An "irrevocable beneficiary" is one that cannot be changed without that person's permission. A revocable beneficiary can be changed without permission.

The beneficiary of a policy may be a person, a corporation, a trust or several persons. There can be a primary beneficiary and a secondary beneficiary. If a minor is a beneficiary, the proceeds will be received by a guardian or trustee and held in trust for the minor.

The use of "settlement options" in policies will permit one to set up an emergency fund reserve; establish a deferred fund for use of a child upon matriculation in a school; and can be used for many other predetermined needs.

Settlement Options

The privilege of electing options other than cash are available to the insured-owner as well as to beneficiaries. The insured-owner, for example, may place the guaranteed cash value of a policy under a life income option (one type of option available) at retirement time to supplement social security and company pension plan.

Although options will vary, the majority of policies will contain some or all of the following:

1. Interest Option. Proceeds are left with the company at a guaranteed rate of interest (typically 2.5 to 4 percent), but most companies are paying in excess of 4.5 to 5 percent on these funds. The principal is left intact, and only interest payments are paid.

2. Fixed-Amount Option. Income of a fixed amount (for example; $100 per month) is paid until the proceeds are exhausted. Interest is also credited and will serve to *extend the period of time* that payments are made.

3. Fixed-Period Option. Income of an equal amount is paid for a pre-established number of years (example: $100 a month for 10 years) at the end of which time proceeds will be exhausted. Interest credited on this option will *increase the monthly payment.*

4. Life-Income Option. This means that the proceeds will be paid in installments such as monthly during the lifetime of the insured-owner or beneficiary. This may also include a stipulated minimum number of years (usually 10 or 20) that income is to be payable, so that, if the first annuitant dies, the balance of the payments required to complete the stipulated minimum will be continued, or paid in lump sum to some other designated person. Proceeds may also be paid out in installments to two persons, such as husband and wife, during the joint lifetime, and thereafter to the survivor.

Even with the obvious value of using settlement options, not all situations can be adequately covered. One potential problem of establishing settlement options is the failure of an owner to review them periodically. Another is the inability to be flexible when circumstances change for the beneficiaries. The use of trusts, both inter vivos and testamentary,[2] are gaining popularity as a method of preserving and distributing properties and these should be considered in planning for one's estate.

Dividends on Life Insurance

Dividends paid by life insurance companies have a different meaning than attributed to other types of business where a dividend is a share of profits. Dividends are received by policyholders only from a "participating" company in which one shares in surplus funds. "Stock" life companies pay dividends to stockholders but a policy holder is *not* a shareholder in the company.

At the beginning of this chapter, we saw that premium rates were established by use of three factors: mortality, earnings, and expenses. A savings in one or more of these will mean that the premium charged was more than was needed by the company. Therefore, the excess is returned to the policyholder as a *refund of premium* called a "dividend." Under current law it is *not* reportable as income.

These dividends may be utilized in different ways, but the most common options available (by written election) to the owner of a policy are as follows: They may be (1) paid in cash, (2) applied in reduction of premiums, (3) held by the company to accumulate at interest, or (4) used to purchase paid-up additional insurance.

Upon death, or surrender of a policy, dividends remaining to the credit of the policy are payable in addition to the guaranteed values or proceeds of the policy. Note that in numbers three and four, the dividends remain with the company and, unless already encumbered by the owner, may be

---

[2] "Trusts" are legal arrangements in which property, real or personal, is held for the benefit of another. "Inter vivos" is during life and "testamentary" is created by one's will.

utilized (within company limitations) without adversely affecting the guaranteed rights of the policy.

Policy Riders

A policy rider supplements or modifies regular provisions in the contract and is attached to, and made a part of, the policy. Some of the more common types of riders follow:

Waiver of Premium (for Disability)

This is a provision that provides a type of *"insurance of continuance of insurance."* It provides that if an insured is permanently disabled, the company will *waive* any premium due thereafter during disability. Policy values and benefits continue at the *same level* as they would if the premiums were being paid by the owner. The waiting period is four to six months before benefits begin, and premiums paid during this waiting period are often refunded to the owner. Normally, disability must occur before age 60 – some companies extend this to age 65. The definition of disability will vary from company to company.

Accidental Death Benefit

This provision provides for the payment of an additional multiple (from one to four times) of the face amount of the policy, if death occurs *accidentally.* This is a *general* statement, because this provision often has exclusions and time limitations. Further, although the premium charge is reasonable, there are those who question the need to have more "cash" when death is accidental than when it is by *normal* passage. The extra premium might be better spent for additional "face amount" which pays regardless of how death occurs.

Term Riders

Most companies permit the attachment of a term insurance amount to a permanent policy. The riders can be for predetermined number of years such as five, ten, 15, 20 or to age 60, 65 or longer. Further, they can be a level term or decreasing type term. Normally, some percentage of the term is guaranteed to be convertible (can be exchanged) to permanent insurance without evidence of insurability, within a certain period of time. The premium is cheaper than a term policy issued by itself, because the basic policy will carry the "loading" expense. Therefore, this may prove for most persons a practical method of having greater protection with an element of compromise between permanent versus term insurance.

Family Insurance

Many companies will attach as a rider an agreement that provides insurance on the *family* of the insured. These are written to insure the wife or husband, and all children presently existing and future children, born or adopted. Only those children in existence at the time of issue must prove insurability—future children are covered automatically. Premiums are reasonable and coverage on the wife or husband is to age 55, 60, or 65 and that on the children to age 21 or 25. Further, the children are guaranteed the right to purchase three to five times the amount of coverage in force before expiration. (Example: the coverage is $1,000 — age 0 to age 25. At age 25, the child can buy $5,000 permanent insurance with no insurability requirements.) Most policies of this type provide that death of the insured will cause the family insurance rider to be paid-up and thus benefits continue without further payment of premiums.

Guaranteed Insurability Provision

This has developed over the past few years and is available with most companies although the benefits will vary from company to company. It essentially provides that one will have "the guaranteed ability, with no insurability requirements, to add increments of additional permanent insurance in the future as income and needs increase." Normally an insured-owner can add $10,000 each at age 25, 28, 31, 34, 37, 40 or alternately at marriage or birth of a child, if the base policy to which the rider is attached is $10,000. (Amounts available are directly proportional to the base policy amount and some companies permit as much as $25,-000 at each option time.) After initial insurability is established, it is guaranteed, normally, with the last option available at age 40.

Other riders are available and of course, extra premiums must be paid for each of them.

REVIEW QUESTIONS

1. All insurance policies have similar "contract features." Why is this so?
2. The requirement of an "insurable interest" is a policy of the law. State why.
3. Why is the tax treatment different for life insurance proceeds payable to ones estate than those paid to a named beneficiary?
4. Write out a brief statement of the insurance "pooling" concept, as used by life insurance companies.
5. Can you explain how statistics are used to help determine life insurance premiums at different ages?
6. Why would it be unfair to insure the life of one who is ill for the same premium as one in good health when both are in the same age bracket?
7. Sketch, in outline form, a $10,000 life insurance policy on yourself. Include two riders, a dividend option, and a settlement option.
8. How are you going to be certain that the premiums on your policy in question seven above are paid on time?
9. What are the dangers in allowing premium payments to go past the grace periods?
10. Agent X is trying to talk you into canceling your policy and applying for one with X's company. Name three reasons why you might not want to do this. Can you name a reason why you *might* decide to do this?

Words and Phrases

Write out briefly what they mean to you.
1. Insurable interest.
2. Dividend option.
3. Settlement option.
4. Choosing a beneficiary.
5. Nonforfeiture benefits.

Coverage:	A look at automobile insurance as its use relates to courts and contracts.
What to Look for:	Trends that are developing.
Application:	Assume that you have agents on the road as salespeople. What should you know about car insurance?

18 Automobile Insurance— A Contract Application in and out of the Courts

Two basic types of automobile insurance are in use today: liability or property damage insurance and collision coverage. Liability coverage is designed to protect a motorist who is sued by another who claims the motorist was negligent. The limits of the policy will depend upon the amount of coverage selected and the premium paid.

PROOF OF LOSS

Collision coverage is designed to provide funds to repair the car of the insured regardless of who is at fault. Most collision policies contain a "deductible" clause to prevent the insurance companies from being harrassed by small claims. For example, A has collision coverage on a new car with a deductible of $100. B strikes A's car as it is parked at the curb doing minor damage. If the damage is less than $100, the insurance company has no liability because of the $100 deductible clause; that is, A must pay the first $100. If the sum is over $100, it works as follows: After obtaining estimates, A's insurance carrier directs A to have the repairs made—usually by the garage that makes the lowest bid. If the repairs comes to $600, A is expected to pay $100 (the deductible) and the insurance carrier will pay the balance. The check will be made payable to both A and the garage. This is done to make certain that the funds are not diverted to some other use. In exchange for the payment, the carrier expects its insured to sign a "proof of loss" (Figure 18–1).

205

FIGURE 18-1

PROOF OF LOSS AND DIRECTION TO PAY

<u>VIOLET INSURANCE COMPANY</u>   CL#9720   17992
(Hereinafter Referred To As "Company")

UNDERSIGNED HEREBY EXPRESSLY AGREES THAT THE ENTIRE LOSS OR DAMAGE, OCCURRING ON OR ABOUT THE <u>8th</u> DAY OF <u>March</u>, 1976 AS SET FORTH PREVIOUSLY IN THE UNDERSIGNED'S STATEMENT OF LOSS TO PROPERTY COVERED BY POLICY NUMBER <u>9098213</u>, IS <u>$600.00</u>.

The said loss or damage did not originate by any act, design, or procurement on the part of the Undersigned nor on the part of anyone having interest in the property insured, or in the said policy of insurance; nor in any consequence of any fraud or evil practice done or suffered by the Undersigned and that no property saved has in any manner been concealed.

It is expressly understood and agreed that the furnishing of the "Proof of Loss" blank to the insured, or assistance in making up this statement by an adjuster or any person otherwise an agent of Company is an act of courtesy and is not a waiver of any rights of said Company.

In consideration of the payment, if made, of the amount set forth below by the Company, the Undersigned hereby agrees to release and discharge the Company from any and all liability under its policy for said loss and/or damage. The Undersigned further agrees upon said payment to hold the company, its successors or assigns, free and harmless from further claims for the loss described.

The Undersigned hereby directs the above described Insurance Company to pay to:

Golden Auto Shop	$600.00
1400 Daffodil Drive	$_____
	$_____

TOTAL PAYMENT (entire loss or damage, less
deductible, if applicable)..................................... <u>$500.00</u>

and agrees that such payment shall fully discharge the Company from any and all claims arising out of the above described loss.

The Undersigned hereby assigns, transfers, and sets over to the Company any and all claims or causes of action of whatsoever kind and nature which the Undersigned now has, or may hereafter have, to recover against any person or persons as the result of said occurrence and loss above described, to the extent of the payment above made; the Undersigned agrees that the Company may enforce the same in such manner as shall be necessary or appropriate for the use and benefit of the Company, either in its own name or in the name of the Undersigned, that the Undersigned will furnish such papers, information or evidence as shall be within the Undersigned's possession or control for the purpose of enforcing such claim, demand or cause of action; and further that the Company on the Undersigned's behalf may execute all receipts and releases; and endorse all checks and drafts received in payment of said loss or damage.

The Undersigned covenants that no release or settlement of any such claim, demand or cause of action has been made.

FIGURE 18-1 (continued)

The Undersigned affirms that the statements herein made are true.

Witness X s/s Joseph E. Rose   X s/s Maxwell Flower
_____
                                                         Insured

Witness Anytown, Typ. State   _____
                                                          Insured

Witness _____ hand at _____
this _____ day of _____,
19__
State of _____ss
County of _____
                                              June 29, 197–

Personally appeared <u>Maxwell Flower</u> signer of the foregoing statement who made solemn oath to the truth of same, and that no material fact is withheld of which said Company should be advised. Subscribed and sworn to before me, the day and date above written.

My Commission expires <u>February 4, 1982</u>

                                  s/s Frank Fisher, Jr. (SEAL)
                                       Notary Public

Subrogation

The proof of loss form is a contract and "subrogates" (sets over) to the insurance company the right to sue the third party. That is, the insurance company, upon payment of the loss less deductible, acquires the legal right to sue the third party to get its money back. This is called "subrogation" in practice. Many insureds believe that payment for damages by their company is unconditional. This is just not so. Because of "subrogation," the insured must not sign a release for the other party. One who does sign a release, may be sued by his own insurance company for giving away their right to sue.

In subrogation suits the insured and the company will share in the recovery to the extent of their interest, less the attorney fee. To illustrate:

Paid out by A's carrier............... $500.00 (= $\frac{5}{6}$ of $600)
Paid out by A (deductible)......... <u>$100.00</u> (= $\frac{1}{6}$ of $600)
                                $600.00

Recovered by attorney.............. $300.00
Fee to attorney (one-third)......... <u>$100.00</u>
   Balance $200.00

To carrier ($\frac{5}{6}$th of $200) $166.67
To insured ($\frac{1}{6}$th of $200)........... $ 33.33

Since the majority of accidents fall in the less than $100 damage category, the insurance company is passing off the risk of such loss to the insured, and thus the rates are much lower than they would be for coverage with no deductible. In effect, the insured bears this risk—and the cost of it—when one buys a policy with a deductible. The insurance company, of course, bears risk of loss over the limit of the deductible clause.

In practice, if A buys a new car, the one who finances the purchase will require collision coverage in an amount sufficient to cover the loan. They usually do *not* require liability or property damage coverage.

In a few instances, careless lenders, many of whom write the collision coverage, have told the insured that the "car is fully covered," meaning that the insured has collision coverage to protect the lender on its loan. The insured has sometimes interpreted this to mean that he or she also has liability coverage—which is not so. The problems that might follow are obvious.

If A buys an older model car, A may decide to waive collision coverage, to save a few dollars, and buy liability coverage only. Worse, A may decide not to purchase coverage at all, being exposed not only to other motorists, but to the state as well, under "financial responsibility" laws.

"FINANCIAL RESPONSIBILITY" LAWS

While some states have mandatory auto insurance requirements, some do not. The states that do not require insurance usually require proof of "financial responsibility," and over 30 states have such laws. If A collides with B and A is uninsured, A must prove to the state that the matter has been compromised without suit, or else post bond with a state agency in a sum at least as large as the damage done to the car of B. In short, a financial responsibility state says to a driver, "Carry insurance if you will, but if you do not and you have an accident, you must post enough bond with us to prove that you are financially responsible." However, the financial responsibility laws were dealt a setback by the United States Supreme Court in May, 1971, when it held that such laws were unconstitutional if they required a bond of one who was not at fault. In the past, A might have been parked at a curb when hit, but if uninsured, A had to post bond. Under the ruling a hearing will be required to determine fault before bond will be required of the uninsured motorist.

PREPAYMENT WITHOUT RELEASE

Some insurance companies are entering into programs of "payment without resistance" through the use of prepayment, made on their own initiative without requiring a release from the claimant (plaintiff). These are not "giveaway" programs but are only used where experience and facts show that the property damage and personal injury alleged by the claimant are "supported by law."

How Does It Work?

Some insurance companies of the one who caused the accident will settle with the person injured, with payment to be made for future medical payments up to a set sum. The injured person is then paid monthly in an effort to improve physical and mental status. Also, the defendant's company may make immediate payment for repairs to the claimant's car, and loss of wages as they arise. The companies do not ask for a release at the time of payment. Rather, a receipt is requested that simply states that sums paid will be applied against any settlement or judgment that the claimant may obtain in the future against them. The hope expressed by one company is that the program will remove fears of the claimant, lessen worry, give immediate access to medical treatment, and get the claimant back to work sooner. Delaware, Ohio, and the District of Columbia and other jurisdictions have placed their stamp of approval on the system, allowing offsets against higher judgments obtained after prepayment.

Another development in insurance coverage is to cover one who is injured by an "uninsured motorist—" but in a different fashion than under the financial responsibility laws.

UNINSURED MOTORIST COVERAGE

In many car accidents, the one who is at fault is uninsured. And not only uninsured, but frequently has little of value that can be looked to even if a judgment is obtained. Wage attachments usually fail because the defendant quits his or her job and goes to another state. This is a "judgment-proof" debtor—and a familiar person to the practicing attorney. The injured plaintiff often finds all doors closed to a recovery.

It became apparent that additional coverage was needed to provide for the person who was injured because of the carelessness of an uninsured driver. The companies began to write coverage for an additional premium and some states have made the uninsured provision mandatory in all liability policies issued. Under this coverage, the insured pays an additional premium to gain protection from those who are uninsured.

How Does It Work?

Assume that John Black has a standard liability insurance policy in effect, with $500 medical pay for himself plus uninsured motorist (U/M) coverage. On a Monday morning as he was driving to his place of employment, he approached the intersection of the main street and a side road. Without warning, Jim Smith, a 17-year-old, drove out of the side road through a stop sign and into the path of Black. The cars collided violently. Black was thrown into the steering column causing him severe injuries. His auto was damaged in the sum of $1,200. The investigating officer cited Smith for the unlawful operation of his car. Later, Smith pleaded guilty and paid a token fine. It was then discovered that Smith did not have insurance coverage. Later, Smith lost his license when he was unable to prove that he was financially able to cover the damages caused by his negligence.

In the meantime, Black was not only injured, but was without a car. Black sought the services of a lawyer, who made an attempt to settle with Black's insurance company under the U/M coverage. The company hesitated to pay because it was their information that Smith had coverage through his mother, who was the owner of the Smith car. Later, it was determined that this was not so, but in the meantime Black filed suit.

Who Is Served?

The suit was styled *John Black* v. *Jim Smith, a Minor under the Age of 18 Years*. The court appointed a "guardian ad litem" (a guardian during litigation) to defend the minor. Black's lawyer had a copy of the summons and complaint served upon Black's insurance company. This was done by having the sheriff deliver the papers to a local agent for the insurance company. The agent forwarded the papers to the proper office so that an answer could be filed. Proper service of process was also made on the infant through the guardian.

A Strange Thing Occurs

Since the insurance company for Black is going to be responsible for any judgment obtained against Smith (up to the limits of the coverage less deductible), the company must defend. They do so by filing an answer for the defendant just as if the defendant were their insured! In short, Black paid a premium for U/M insurance to protect him from the uninsured motorist, but his company will defend the one who was responsible for the accident. If the case goes to trial, Black's insurance company will try to defeat the claim of Black if possible. In many cases, the claimant does not know that the lawyer opposing him is on retainer from his own company!

Why This Result?

If the company who insured the plaintiff is given notice of the suit but fails to file an answer, judgment by default will be entered. After an "inquiry into damages," judgment for the plaintiff — which the company must pay — will be entered, less the deductible. Insurance companies as a matter of policy want to avoid this — and they are permitted to do so by law.

The insurance company will attempt to work out a settlement before suit is filed. If settlement is reached, the purpose of having the U/M coverage is realized. Assume that John Black settles with his company for $5,000. The company will pay Black $5,000 less the deductible ($300 in the Virginia's) for a net of $4,700. Black then gives the company the written right to sue the defendant in an effort to recover the $4,700. This is the "right of subrogation" as discussed previously.

Subrogation

Black's insurance company has lost $4,700 because of the negligence of the defendant. Therefore, the company will institute a suit to recover from the wrongdoer. In practice, the attempt usually fails because the defendant has little or leaves the jurisdiction once suit is filed. If settlement with the insured is reached after suit has been filed (as in our example), the original suit is dismissed "without prejudice" (meaning that it can be filed again). A new suit is instituted naming the insurance company as plaintiff, because the company is now a "party in interest." If recovery is realized, the money is distributed to the company and Black as their interests appear. For example, if full recovery is obtained in our example and, assuming the attorney had the case on a one-third basis, Black would receive $200 (his deductible less one-third). The company would recover $4,700 less one third. If no recovery is made, the company has lost the full amount.

In most uninsured motorist cases, the wrongdoer is known. But in a few cases, is not known.

The Hit-and-Run Accident

Occasionally, a motorist is struck by another who leaves the scene of the accident. If the innocent motorist has collision coverage, he or she is protected—less deductible. If he or she has medical pay, the company will pay up to the policy limits. In addition, if he or she has uninsured motorist coverage, that person may be able to recover an additional sum from the insurance company.

How Does It Work? Some states by statute permit suit to be filed against the unknown person, called a "John Doe suit," but there are "conditions precedent" to the suit. For example, the police authorities must be notified within 30 days of the accident. There are two reasons for this: first, it increases the possibility of the hit-and-run driver being found; and second, it discourages one who has been in a single car mishap to claim that another car was involved.

Once the conditions are met, suit is filed against "John Doe." The plaintiff's company is "served" and the matter goes to court like any other case. The insurance company is in a difficult position in such a suit because it must defend a person who is unknown. In practice, these cases are usually settled without hearing and the plaintiff is paid a sum agreed upon—less deductible.

A trend has been developing for many years to create "social security automobile injury" insurance. The "no fault" approach is a step in that direction.

LIABILITY VERSUS NO FAULT

During the last decade one who has followed the mounting problem of auto accidents versus insurance coverage has been impressed by one fact: No one is satisfied with the system as it exists. A moment's reflection upon U/M coverage and situations that it breeds, provides one reason for the dissatisfaction. Studies have been made and many articles have been written. All point in the same direction: Personal injury and property damage cases are not proper subjects for the courts.

What Has Been Suggested?

The studies have expressed the need for "payment regardless of fault," with limits on the amount of funds available. An analogy has been drawn between the motorist's problem and Workmen's Compensation Funds. If X employee of Zero Corporation is injured on the job, even if it is X's own fault, X cannot sue the employer. Rather, X must file a claim and in time will be paid monthly benefits based upon tables created by the legislature, and X is paid without an inquiry being made into "fault." A parallel is suggested between the situation described and the auto victim. Massachusetts and 22 other states have such laws in various forms.

REVIEW QUESTIONS

1. *Should* an insurance company be permitted to defend the person who caused the injury to it's insured in an uninsured motorist case?
2. Would it be fair to place all the blame upon the lawyers for the problems created by injuries caused by automobile collisions? (They have profited handsomely from these in the past).
3. Why should one read a "proof of loss" form before one signs it?
4. How would you explain "subrogation" to another?
5. True or False. The one who causes an accident will probably be protected in the future.
6. Distinguish "liability" from "collision" coverage.
7. Set out your own example of how a "deductible" works in practice.
8. What problem might be encountered by those who make repairs to cars that are covered by collision insurance?
9. Most repair shops now ask for a fee for making estimates—and especially when they are reasonably sure that they will not get to do the work. In the past the opposite was the truth. What social and legal changes brought this about?
10. A "proof of loss" form after it is signed is a binding contract. Why is this so?

Words and Phrases

Write out briefly what they mean to you.
1. "Prepayment without release."
2. "Fault."
3. "Subrogated."
4. John Doe.
5. Property damage coverage.

<table>
<tr><td>Coverage:</td><td>The basic principles of bailments.</td></tr>
<tr><td>What to Look for:</td><td>The legal nature of a bailment.</td></tr>
<tr><td>Application:</td><td>Think in terms of how bailments are used in business.</td></tr>
</table>

19 Bailments—A Contract Application in Business

Sir William Jones has divided bailments into five sorts, namely: Depositum, *or deposit;* mandatum, *or commission without recompense;* commodatum, *or loan for use without pay;* pignori acceptum, *or pawn;* locatum, *or hiring, which is always with reward. This last is subdivided into* locatio rei, *or hiring, by which the hirer gains a temporary use of the thing;* locatio operis faciendi, *when something is to be done to the thing delivered;* locatio operis mercium vehendarum, *when the thing is merely to be carried from one place to another.*

—Black's Law Dictionary, *4th ed.*

In the business community, buyers, sellers, consumers and others, interact in a multitude of relationships as business is transacted. These relationships most frequently arise out of contracts—and sometimes out of torts and even crimes.

One relationship frequently encountered is the "bailment"—a legal word that has precise meaning. The bailment has its roots in the common law and therefore is very old. As the material is covered the reader should keep in mind that a bailment is *not* the same as a consignment or a secured transaction. It is not like a bank deposit, personal property declared for safe keeping at a hotel, or lost property. Other rules of law cover these situations.

WHAT IS A BAILMENT?

A "bailment" is a legal relationship between one person and another, or between businesses or persons and businesses, in which one *intrusts*

213

personal property to another for a particular reason or purpose. Upon the completion of the purpose the intrusted goods must be returned to the owner of them. The one who intrusts goods is the "bailor"—the one to whom they are intrusted, the "bailee."

Some Examples

X parks a car at the race track parking lot and receives a receipt in the form of a claim check. X intends to reclaim the car after the races. This is a bailment situation.

Y leaves an auto at Zero Service Station to be washed and lubricated. This is a bailment situation.

Z takes a tuxedo to a local shop to be cleaned and pressed. This is also a bailment.

The above examples are "voluntary bailments" because they arose out of precise action and intention on the part of the bailor. However, bailments can also be involuntary.

Involuntary Bailments.   Bailments can arise where they were not contemplated at the outset. For example, D's boat is torn loose during a storm and is washed upon land of E. E is an "involuntary bailee."

F takes a pair of pants to the cleaners and forgets to remove a $5.00 bill from the pocket. The cleaner finds the $5.00 bill. The cleaner is a bailee of the pants—and an involuntary bailee of the $5.00 bill—both of which must be returned to F.

An interesting variation of the voluntary bailment is the *locatio operis faciendi* ("a letting out of work to be done").

Locatio Operis Faciendi.   A delivers grain to B, who is to grind the grain into flour and then deliver the flour to A for an agreed price. However, B accepts grain from C and D, grinds all of the grain as one lot, deposits the flour in a common container and delivers the share of each bailor out of the common mass. While the goods were "confused" (mixed) it was still a bailment.

LEGAL REQUIREMENTS OF THE BAILMENT

In general, a bailment is a relationship that is contractual and general principles of contract control. This is true whether the bailment is voluntary or involuntary. A bailment can arise out of the agreement (contract) of the parties; it can be implied from the *acts* of the parties or it can arise by operation of law. These distinctions were noted in the discussion of contract principles. (See chapter 14).

However, the bailment deviates from strict contract principles in that it can come into being in some instances even if "mutuality" or "meeting of the minds" is not present. All that is required at law is that there be *delivery* of the goods—in some form—by the bailor; *acceptance* of them by the bailee; and a legal duty on the part of the bailee to return the goods at some future time. However, a bailment can never arise if one does not know or learn that the goods are in one's possession.

Two other types of bailments are recognized at law: a "depositum"[1] and a "mandatum."[2] Both are frequently "gratuitious"—that is, for the benefit of the bailor only.

GRATUITOUS BAILMENTS

In these bailments, the bailee gains no benefit from the relationship— but the bailor does. An example of the depositum would be the storage of a lawnmower in a neighbor's garage for the winter. An example of a "mandatum" would be where A carries B's books home from school and leaves them at B's home. The first involves a "deposit"—the second a *transportation* from one place to another.

In all bailments, certain rights and liabilities fall upon the parties to the bailment.

RIGHTS AND LIABILITIES

The Bailor

The bailor has the legal right to demand return of the goods since they belong to the bailor. (This distinguishes a bailment from a sale. In a sale, the legal right to the goods is transferred to the buyer.)

If the bailee should sell bailed goods to others, the bailor has the right to reclaim those goods. If the bailee should *injure* another with the bailed goods due to negligence, this negligence generally *cannot* be imputed back to the bailor. This distinguishes a bailment from a "master-servant," "principal-agent" relationship.

Upon satisfactory completion of the bailment, the bailor has a duty to compensate the bailee—other than in "gratuitious" situations.

The Bailee

If the bailor fails to compensate the bailee for care, preservation, or repair of the goods, the bailee in most states can retain the goods as se- curity for payment. In some states, the bailee has a lien by statute. (See the "Blue's Shoes" ticket on page 162).

If third parties injure, or misappropriate goods while in the possession of the bailee, the bailee can bring legal action to restore them or their value to the bailee. At law the bailee is treated as an owner to this degree.

The bailee must use ordinary care to protect bailed goods and is re- sponsible for loss to the goods caused by the bailee's negligence. How- ever, the bailee is not an *insurer* of the goods and is not responsible for loss that is beyond control. (Most business bailees purchase "bailees in- surance" to protect them, however.)

As a general rule, not being an insurer of the goods, a bailee is not held

---

[1] A naked bailment of goods to be kept for the bailor without payment. *Black's Law Dic- tionary*, 4th ed.

[2] The contract of mandate.

responsible for loss caused by theft or "Acts of God." However, a bailee *can* be an insurer if the bailee agrees to this standard of care as part of the bailment contract.

In a gratitious bailment the bailee is held to a somewhat lesser degree of care than in a bailment for hire. A precise rule cannot be stated.

Upon completion of the bailment, or upon demand of the bailor, the bailee must deliver the goods in the condition in which received—or in an improved condition if the bailee had agreed to improve the goods.

A bailee who fails to meet these obligations, can be sued for the resulting losses. The damages of the bailor would be determined just as lossess suffered for any breach of contract.

A Bailment Case[3]

CLARK, Judge.

"Not responsible for loss or damages to vehicles or articles left in vehicles in case of fire, theft or any other cause beyond our control."

The foregoing exculpatory language was contained in a work order form which plaintiff signed at the time he delivered his 1972 Holiday Rambler trailer to defendant for the purpose of having defendant make some repairs. The quoted language was printed in a location one inch above the signature line and immediately above additional printed wording which authorized A & H Camper Sales, Inc. to render the directed service. The size and clarity of the print and its location were such that the plaintiff acknowledged "I could read it when I was signing it, if that's what you want to make clear. I could have read it if I had read the whole thing." (R. 29). During the hours of darkness that same evening or the following morning the appellant's Holiday Rambler trailer was stolen from defendant's premises. Plaintiff filed suit against defendant as bailee[4] for the value of the trailer and personalty therein, alleging the theft to have resulted from defendant's negligence. Denying negligence and relying upon the disclaimer language, defendant moved for a summary judgment after depositions had been taken of both parties. The instant appeal by plaintiff below is from judgment rendered for the bailee defendant.

[1] In the trial court emphasis was placed upon our ruling in *Brown* v. *Five Points Parking Center,* 121 Ga.App. 819, 175 S.E.2d 901. The similarity of the facts in that case to the instant situation is such that we affirm the decision below. As was stated in the *Brown* case, "It is the duty of one who contracts to read and inform himself of the contract's terms." The language of the disclaimer here was thereby effectively made known to plaintiff and was binding upon him so as to exonerate defendant as to any liability for the theft from defendant's premises.

It should be noted that the knowledge of the contractual liability limitation here attributable to plaintiff causes this case to be outside of those authorities which require such limitations to be made known to a bailor before the bailee can get the benefit of such exculpatory provision. For such cases

---

[3] *Haynie v. A & H Camper Sales, Inc.,* 132 Ga. App. 509, 208 S.E.2d 354 (1974).

[4] For charm and wit the dissenting opinion of Logan Bleckley on bailment of a hat in a barbershop in *Dilberto v. Harris,* 95 Ga. 571, 23 S.E. 112 cannot be surpassed. Paraphrasing present-day parlance: "Read it; you'll like it!"

see *Renfroe* v. *Fouche*, 26 Ga.App. 340, 106 S.E. 303; *American Laundry* v. *Hall*, 27 Ga.App. 717(1), 109 S.E. 676; *Red Cross Laundry* v. *Tuten*, 31 Ga.App. 689(1), 121 S.E. 865.

In a subsequent case, *Ellerman* v. *Atlanta American Motor Hotel Corporation*, 126 Ga.App. 194, 195, 191 S.E.2d, 295, 296, this court said "It is recognized that an ordinary bailee by contract may limit or completely exculpate himself from any liability for loss or damage to the bailed property as a result of his own simple negligence. [Cit.]" This principle was not applied there as a matter of public policy because it involved the innkeeper-guest relationship which was preempted by Code § 52–111. There is no similar public interest situation involved in the case at bar which is a common, everyday occurrence of personalty being placed in the custody of a commercial establishment and therefore governed by the general law of bailments.

[2]   Appellant urges that we should apply the "unconscionability" provision of the Uniform Commercial Code (Code Ann. § 109A–2–302) to such disclaimers. We decline to do so since bailments of this type do not come within the unfairness which should exist before courts declare an established commercial practice to be so one-sided that exculpatory clauses thereon should be declared *verboten*. (See Chapter 4 entitled "Unconscionability" in White & Summers, Uniform Commercial Code, and "The Unconscionability Offense" by Michael H. Terry and John C. Fauvre in 4 Ga.L.Rev. 469). Our reluctance to extend the "unconscionability" doctrine in the instant situation is supported by the Comments portion of the 1962 Official Text of the Uniform Commercial Code from which our Georgia statute was taken. There the drafting Commissioners stated that "The basic test is whether, in the light of the general commercial background and the commercial needs of the particular trade or case, the clauses involved are so one-sided as to be unconscionable under the circumstances existing at the time of the making of the contract . . . The principle is one of the prevention of oppression and unfair surprise and not of disturbance of allocation of risks because of superior bargaining power."

Judgment affirmed.

REVIEW QUESTIONS

1. Name two bailments not discussed in the chapter.
2. A thief hides stolen goods in a trunk of an auto parked in a parking lot. The owner of the car is *not* a bailee. Why? Could the owner become a bailee later? How?
3. Contrast an involuntary bailment to a contract implied in law.
4. Give an example of a gratuitous bailment.
5. Examine the parking receipt in Figure 14–4. Why are the words "Not a bailment" found there?
6. Distinguish the following:
    The bailee injures the bailed goods.
    The bailee injures another *with* the bailed goods.
7. It is important that one in business safeguard goods of others while they are in the business person's possession. Why?
8. Apply bailment principles to the activities of a pawnbroker.
9. Do you understand why a "secured transaction" is not a bailment? If not ask.
10. Traveler X "declares valuables" at a Holiday Inn. These are locked in a vault for the night. This is not treated as a bailment. Why?

Words and Phrases

Write out briefly what they mean to you.
1. Bailee's liability.
2. Bailee's lien.
3. Bailed goods.
4. Involuntary bailee.
5. Intrusting.

Coverage:	Contracts for the sale of goods
What to Look for:	Distinctions between sales and conventional contracts.
Application:	The procedures discussed here are relatively uniform in 49 states.

20 Sales Contracts

In the business community, the act of buying and selling "goods" between "merchants" is known as "sales." However, this simple word is used in a strict legal sense and has a precise legal meaning. At first, it is difficult to understand that this common word has a technical meaning at law.

Sales of goods are covered by Article 2 of the Uniform Commercial Code and this article is called "Sales." Article 2 is an updating of the "Uniform Sales Act" which had been prepared in 1906 by the National Conference of Commissioners on Uniform State Laws. Over the years, it had been adopted by 34 states plus Alaska and Hawaii—not then states—and the District of Columbia. It had been discovered that simple contract rules did not meet the complex problems that perpetually arose in sales. For this reason, the Uniform Sales Act was created. However, the Uniform Sales Act had been severely altered over the years by case rulings and was "out of tune" with modern sales transactions. Article 2 of the U.C.C. was designed to meet the need for a new body of sales law—and to update the Uniform Sales Act.

It is helpful to become familiar with basic terms used in Article 2.

Terminology

1. *Buyer*—a person who buys or contracts to buy goods.
2. *Good Faith*—in the case of a merchant means "honesty in fact" and the "observance of reasonable commercial standards of fair dealing in the trade."
3. *Receipt* (of goods)—taking physical possession of them.
4. *Seller*—a person who sells or contracts to sell goods.
5. *Merchant*—a person who deals in goods of the kind or otherwise by occupation holds oneself out as having knowledge or skill peculiar to the

219

practices or goods involved in the transaction, or to whom such knowledge or skill may be attributed, or an agent or broker or other intermediary who by his or her occupation holds oneself out as having such knowledge or skill.[1]

6. *Between Merchants*—a transaction with respect to which both parties are chargeable with the knowledge or skill of merchants.

7. *Goods*—all things (including specially manufactured goods) which are *movable* at the time of identification to the contract for sale, other than the money in which the price is to be paid, investment securities (Article 8) and "things in action." "Goods" also includes the unborn young of animals, growing crops and other identified things attached to realty which are to be severed.[2]

Goods must be both *existing* and *identified* before an interest in them can pass. Goods which are not existing and identified are "future" goods. A purported present sale of future goods, or of any interest therein, operates as a *contract to sell.*

There may be a sale of a part interest in existing and identified goods.

8. *Lot*—a parcel or a single article which is the subject matter of a separate sale or delivery, whether or not it is sufficient to perform the contract.[3]

9. *Commercial Unit*—such a unit of goods as by commercial usage is a single whole for purposes of sale, and division of which materially impairs its character or value on the market or in use. A commercial unit may be a single article (a machine) or a set of articles (a suite of furniture or an assortment of sizes) or a quantity (a bale, gross, or carload) or any other unit treated in use or in the relevant market as a single whole.

10. *Contract* and *agreement*—are limited to those relating to the present or future sale of goods. *Contract for sale* includes both a present sale of goods and a contract to sell goods at a future time. A *sale* consists in the passing of title from the seller to the buyer for a price.[4] A "present sale" means a sale which is accomplished by the making of the contract.

11. *Conforming*—goods or conduct including any part of a performance are *conforming* or conform to the contract when they are in accordance with the obligation under the contract.

12. *Termination*—occurs when either party pursuant to a power created by agreement or law, puts an end to the contract other than for its breach. On termination all obligations which are still executory on both sides are discharged but any right based on prior breach or performance survives.

13. *Cancellation*—occurs when either party puts an end to the contract for breach by the other and its effect is the same as that of termination except that the cancelling party also retains any remedy for breach of the whole contract or any unperformed balance.

---

[1] U.C.C. 2–104 (paraphrased in part).

[2] U.C.C. 2–107 (paraphrased in part).

[3] U.C.C. 2–105 (5) (paraphrased in part).

[4] U.C.C., 2–401.

These terms and definitions are difficult to grasp and should be reviewed as the following is developed. Turning from terminology, just what is the scope of coverage of Article 2?

Scope of Coverage

Article 2 covers sales of the following:

1. *Tangible* personal property of all types.
2. *Existing* and *identified* goods. The sales agreement of these goods can be of one of two types:
   a. An *executory* contract of sale to pass title to the goods in the future, or
   b. An *executed* contract of sale that passes title *now*.
3. *Future* goods. Such goods can only be the subject of an executory contract to pass title in the future.
4. Real property *after* it is converted to personal property.
5. Personal property that will be converted to real property up to the time that the conversion takes place.
6. The unborn young of animals. (A contract for sale of unborn animals would be an executory contract that relates to the future.)
7. Growing crops.

Article 2 does *not* cover sales of the following:

1. Sales of real property so long as it remains real property.
2. Sales of intangible personal property such as stocks, bonds and "choses in action."[5]

Turning from scope of coverage, it next becomes important to determine just how a sales contract is formed and adjusted.

FORM, FORMATION, AND ADJUSTMENT OF A SALES CONTRACT

Statute of Frauds

A contract for the *sale of goods* for $500 or more is *not* enforceable by suit or defense unless there is some *writing* to indicate that a contract of sale was made between the parties and *signed* by the one against whom enforcement is sought or that person's agent or broker.[6]

However, if there is no writing between merchants, but a writing in *confirmation* of the contract is received from the buyer or seller, this will meet the requirements of the statute of frauds. However, the one receiving the confirmation can object to its contents provided it is done in 10 days.[7]

Therefore contracts for the sale of goods for $500 or more must be in

---

[5] A personal right not reduced into possession, such as a debt due.

[6] U.C.C., 2-201 (1) (see page 140).

[7] U.C.C., 2-201 (2).

writing—or be reduced to writing eventually. But some sales contracts for goods over $500 are still valid if they fall within one of three categories:

A contract which does not satisfy the requirements of U.C.C. 2–201(1) but which is valid in other respects is enforceable (1) if the goods are to be specially manufactured for the buyer and are not suitable for sale to others in the ordinary course of the seller's business and the seller, before notice of repudiation is received and under circumstances which reasonably indicate that the goods are for the buyer, has made a substantial beginning of their manufacture or commitments for their procurement; or (2) if the party against whom enforcement is sought admits in pleadings, testimony, or otherwise in court that a contract for sale was made, but the contract is not enforceable beyond the quantity of goods admitted; or (3) with respect to goods for which payment has been made and accepted or which have been received and accepted.[8]

If a sales contract falls into any of these exceptions, a binding contract results. This is an excellent example of why conventional, strict contract rules cannot meet the complexity of sales situations.

Next, what rules are applied to determine the *terms* of the sales contract?

What Does the Sales Contract Say?

The terms set forth in the writing or writings control, and may not be varied by oral (parol) or extrinsic evidence of any agreement not set forth in the terms.

However, the terms of the contract of sale may be explained or supplemented: (*a*) by course of dealing or usage of trade[9] or by course of performance[10] and (*b*) by evidence of consistent additional terms, unless the court finds the writing to have been intended also as a complete and exclusive statement of the terms of the agreement.

Therefore, when we ask "Just what does our sales contract say?" we have three principal places to look:

1. The contract itself—if in writing.
2. The course of dealing or usage of trade customary between the buyer and seller.
3. Course of performance customary between buyer and seller.

Thus a sales contract is what the parties *say* as well as what the parties *do.*

Rather than proceeding through the numerous sections of Article 2— and becoming thoroughly confused in the process, it is much better to examine sales cases in which disputes have arisen.

The most common dispute in sales situations arise when the seller

---

[8] U.C.C., 2–201 (3) (paraphrased in part).

[9] U.C.C., 1–202.

[10] U.C.C., 2–208.

says that there was a sales contract—but the buyer sets up the statute of frauds because there had been no writing.

Sale of *D'Arc Wind*

· The seller had agreed to sell, and the buyer had agreed to buy, a boat called *D'Arc Wind*. This agreement was oral. However, the buyer had given the seller a part payment on the boat. This payment was made by check and the buyer had noted on the back what the check was for.

Later, the buyer stopped payment on the check, pleading the Sales Statute of Frauds as a defense to the contract. Suit followed.

The court looked to the official comments of U.C.C. 2–201 which state that "all that is required is that the writing afford a basis for believing that the offered oral evidence rests on a real transaction." The notation on the check was enough to do that, ruled the court.[11]

An Exception. One exception to the Sales Statute of Frauds is where the buyer *admits* in court in some manner, that there *was* an oral contract of sale. In application, this exception renders the Sales Statute of Frauds almost ineffective as the following case illustrates.

Will the Buyer Admit the Contract?

The reasoning behind the "admission" section of Article 2,[12] is simple enough: if the buyer *admits* there was a contract of sale, why should the buyer be able to escape the obligation simply because there was no writing? (In the conventional statute of frauds—this could be done). How does this exception work in practice?

In a New York case, the defendant denied the oral contract when sued, and set up the statute of frauds as a defense. However, the court said in essence, "Let the case go through the discovery stage and on to trial, because it will not be known until then whether or not the defendant will admit the oral contract in court."[13]

This subjects the defendant to the danger of lying under oath—if there had been an oral contract—or leaves the buyer free to deny it if there had not been. The court felt that this way the objective sought by the drafters of Article 2 could be realized.

The next key item in the formation of a sales contract is "acceptance."

ACCEPTANCE

When the buyer "accepts" goods in a sales situation, three legal events take place. First, the buyer loses the power to "reject" the goods as will be discussed. Second, the burden is squarely upon the buyer to prove any subsequent "breach," and third, the buyer must pay the price agreed

---

[11] *Cohn* v. *Fisher*, 10 U.C.C. Rep. 372, (N.J. Sup. 1972).

[12] U.C.C., 2–201 (3) (*b*).

[13] *Reissman* v. *J. S. O. Wood*, 10 U.C.C. Rep. 1165 (New York Civil Court, 1972).

upon. Article 2 makes it clear that acceptance can occur in one of three ways:

1. If the buyer, after a reasonable opportunity to inspect the goods, signifies in some manner to the seller that the goods are conforming, or if not conforming, that he or she is still satisfied with them, then this constitutes "acceptance."[14] Note that the goods can be "conforming," meaning that they are exactly what the buyer agreed to buy, or "non-conforming," meaning that they are *not* what the buyer wanted.

2. If the buyer receives the goods and uses them without further communication with the seller, this also is an acceptance.[15]

3. Finally, any act of the buyer that is inconsistent with the seller's ownership can operate as an acceptance.[16]

Acceptance Summary

There are three ways that goods can be accepted under Article 2:

1. The "formal" acceptance under 2–606 (1) (*a*).
2. The "acceptance by acquiescence" under 2–606 (1) (*b*), called the "automative acceptance."
3. The "inconsistent acts" acceptance of 2–606 (1) (*c*).

An Example

X, a storeowner, bought a space heater from Y, a business person. The heater did not work properly and the buyer complained. Not only that, X disconnected the heater and set it aside in a safe place. However, X made no effort to return it to the seller and in fact continued to make payments on it.

When sued by the seller for the balance of the price, the buyer said "I never accepted the heater." The court replied, "While it is true that you had the legal right to reject the heater, you did not do so." The court held that there has been an "automatic acceptance" under 2–606 (1) (b).[17] Therefore, the buyer had to pay the price for the heater.

Now, what happens if there has been a written sales contract but the seller refuses to deliver the goods. Can the buyer "force" delivery?

FORCING DELIVERY

The normal sales rule is that if the seller refuses to perform in a sales contract, the buyer *cannot* force delivery, but must sue for damages.

But the U.C.C. does provide that delivery may be forced (called "specific performance") if ". . . the goods are unique."[18] In a New York case,

---

[14] U.C.C., 2–606 (1) (*a*).
[15] U.C.C., 2–606 (1) (*b*).
[16] U.C.C., 2–606 (1) (*c*).
[17] *Southern Union Gas* v. *Taylor,* 486 P. 2d. 606, 9 U.C.C. Rep. 668 (New Mexico, 1971).
[18] U.C.C., 2–716.

the seller refused to deliver a Rolls Royce and the court ordered "specific performance" – that is, the seller must deliver the car to the buyer.[19] The U.C.C. does not limit specific performance to cases where the goods are unique, and provides that relief for nondelivery may be granted "in other proper circumstances" leaving the decision to the court.

It now becomes important to consider those situations in which there is a binding sales contract; goods are promptly shipped by the seller and received by the buyer – but the goods are "nonconforming" or otherwise defective. What can the buyer do – and what *must* the buyer do?

DEFECTIVE GOODS

When the seller delivers defective goods to a buyer, the buyer may "reject" the goods.[20] This is known as the "perfect tender rule." (A buyer who orders goods is entitled to receive what was ordered – a perfect tender.)

However, the Code does not stop here. It provides that if the buyer intends to reject the goods, two principal things must be done:

1.   The buyer must reject "within a reasonable time," and
2.   "Seasonably notify" the seller.[21]

If the buyer does not do these two things, U.C.C. 2–606 (1) (*b*) (see above), makes the failure to reject, an acceptance.

In short, the buyer rejects the goods "seasonably" – or he or she has accepted them and must pay the price.[22] Just what does "seasonable" mean and how much time is granted? The U.C.C. does not set time limits leaving this decision for a court after the pertinent facts are considered.

A Case Will Illustrate

The buyer ordered a shipment of frozen meat and this was delivered promptly at 6:00 P.M. At 7:30 P.M. – just an hour and one-half later – the buyer had completed inspection of the meat, finding that it was defective. The buyer notified the seller at 10:20 P.M. – just 250 minutes after delivery – that the meat was being rejected.

The court held that since the "goods" here were in the process of preparation for consumption, the four hour 20 minute delay in notification was *not* seasonable and that the buyer had *not* rejected in time. Therefore the buyer must pay the price.[23]

The rationale behind this decision can only be fully understood by an examination of Code provision 2–508. This section gives the seller the right to cure defects under certain conditions. So even though the seller

---

[19] *Schweker* v. *Rallye Motors,* 12 U.C.C. Rep. 1154 (New York Superior Court, 1973).

[20] U.C.C., 2–601.

[21] U.C.C., 2–602 (1).

[22] U.C.C., 2–709 (1) (*b*).

[23] *Max Bauer Meat Packer, Inc.,* v. *United States,* 458 Fed. 2d, 88, 10 U.C.C. Rep. 1056 (U.S. Court of Claims, 1972).

does not make a "perfect tender," the seller is entitled to a reasonable opportunity to "cure" the defects. The seller who is *not* informed of defects will have no way of knowing *how* to cure them. This is why the acceptance rule operates under these conditions.

Therefore, when defective goods are received, the buyer must not only seasonably notify the seller of the rejection, but must also state *why* the goods were defective.[24]

If the buyer fails to do so, the buyer is precluded from ". . . relying on that unstated defect to justify rejection or establish breach." To say it another way, in spite of the defects and the rejection, if the buyer does not state *why* so the seller can *cure* the defect, the buyer must pay the price. (However this particular provision applies only "between merchants" — not between "merchants" and "nonmerchant" buyers.)

To Illustrate. L. J. Robinson, Inc., was constructing a pool for the National Park Service. Robinson ordered certain "fill" from the seller, Arber Construction Co., Inc., and this was promptly delivered. The fill was spread as required but a few days later, government inspectors found the fill to be defective and ordered it removed. Robinson then declared the fill defective and demanded that Arber remove and replace the fill. Arber refused and suit followed.

The court stated that the failure of Robinson to discover the defects and immediately inform Arber placed the matter under 2–605. The court held that Robinson could *not* rely upon the defects in the fill because of *the failure to tell Arber what was wrong with it.*

To make it worse, when Robinson asked for *damages* as an alternative, the court held that Arber had been denied the right to "cure"[25] and therefore Robinson was precluded from relying on ". . . (the defective fill) . . . to justify rejection *or to establish breach.*"[26]

Partial Rejection

Article 2 provides that if the goods, or the tender of delivery, fail in any respect to conform to the contract the buyer may (a) reject the whole; or accept the whole; or accept any "commercial unit or units and reject the rest."[27]

In an Illinois case the buyer accepted four sets of valves that conformed to the contract — but rejected one set of flanges that did not. Upon suit by the seller, the court held this partial acceptance and partial rejection to be valid.[28]

In a similar case in North Carolina, the buyer ordered three reels of wire, type X but received one reel of type X and two reels of type Y. Again, the buyer had the right to reject part and accept part. But after

[24] U.C.C., 2–605.

[25] U.C.C., 2–508.

[26] *L. J. Robinson, Inc.* v. *Arber Construction Company, Inc.,* 292 A. 2d. 809, 11 U.C.C. Rep. 64 (D.C., 1972).

[27] U.C.C., 2–601.

[28] *Pekins Pipe* v. *Acme Valve,* 276 N.E.2d. 355 (Ill., 1971).

the two reels were rejected, the buyer tried to find transportation to return the two reels to the seller, but was not successful.

In the meantime, the two rejected reels, worth more than $9,000, were stolen. Who was to bear the loss? Under U.C.C. 2–602, the buyer "... is under a duty after rejection to hold (the goods) with reasonable care at the seller's disposition for a time sufficient to permit the seller to remove them." The court held that the buyer had met this requirement and the buyer had no further obligation with regards to the two reels which were rightfully rejected.[29]

Related to rejection of defective goods is the problem that arises when conforming goods are delivered to a buyer but too late to be used. May the buyer reject the goods under those conditions?

LATE SHIPMENT

The buyer is entitled to a "perfect tender" and may reject if the buyer does not get it. However, the buyer must give the seller a reasonable chance to *cure* the nonconformity as discussed previously. But what happens if a late delivery by its very nature *cannot* be cured?

In an Oklahoma case, the buyer had ordered calendars to be delivered on November 15. These were needed for distribution before Thanksgiving which came on November 23. The calendars were delivered on November 21. The court held this was too late. The *cure* provisions did not operate under these facts.[30]

Another serious problem in sales contracts arises when conforming goods are delivered on time—but it is discovered that the buyer is insolvent. What are the seller's rights under these conditions?

1. Where the seller discovers the buyer to be insolvent he may refuse delivery except for cash including payment for all goods therefore delivered under the contract, and stop delivery under this Article (Section 2–705).

2. Where the seller discovers that the buyer has received goods on credit while insolvent he may reclaim the goods upon demand made within ten days after the receipt, but if misrepresentation of solvency had been made to the particular seller in writing within three months before delivery the ten day limitation does not apply. Except as provided in this subsection the seller may not base a right to reclaim goods on the buyer's fraudulent or innocent misrepresentation of solvency or of intent to pay.

3. The seller's right to reclaim under subsection 2 is subject to the rights of a buyer in ordinary course or other good faith purchaser or lien creditor under this Article (Section 2–403). Successful reclamation of goods excludes all other remedies with respect to them.[31]

However, if a lien under U.C.C. 2–702 is a "statutory lien" then Section 67 c (1) (a) of the Federal Bankruptcy Act as Amended in 1966 invalidates that lien against the trustee in bankruptcy. In a Michigan

---

[29] *Graybar Elec. Co.* v. *Schook*, 17 N.C. App. 81, 193 S.E.2d 392 (N.C., 1972).

[30] *Stockard* v. *The Vernon Co.*, 9 U.C.C. Rep. 1067 (Oklahoma 1971).

[31] U.C.C., 2–702.

case, the seller delivered over $64,000 worth of goods to the buyer who was about to file bankruptcy.

Upon learning of this the buyer made its reclamation demand within the 10 day period. However, the court held that the 2–702 reclamation right was *not* effective against the trustee and the seller lost its goods.[32]

RESALE

When goods are reclaimed under the insolvency rule, or when goods are rejected wrongfully, the seller should always seek the advice of counsel before reselling the goods. This is necessary to make certain that notice and other requirements of Article 2, are met.

REVIEW QUESTIONS

1. A contract for the sale of the unborn young of animals, is not a "present sale." Explain why.
2. The material in this chapter is complex. And it must be recognized that this is only a partial coverage of Article 2. Name two reasons why sales contracts can become complex.
3. Seller X delivers nonconforming goods to Buyer Y. Explain how the *perfect tender* and *cure* rules come into play.
4. A "merchant" seller is held to a higher degree of skill and knowledge than a "nonmerchant" seller. What is the rationale behind this policy of Article 2?
5. Distinguish a "present sale" from a "contract to sell."
6. Name one business technique that a merchant seller can employ to avoid the sales statute of frauds.
7. Distinguish an "executory" from an "executed" sales contract by example.
8. Why are sales of "real estate" excluded from Article 2?
9. Explain the "ten day confirmation rule."
10. True or False. An acceptance of a sales contract can come about in more ways than one.

Words and Phrases

Write out briefly what they mean to you.
1. Acceptance under Article 2.
2. Commercial lot.
3. Perfect tender.
4. Cure.
5. Rejecting swiftly.

---

[32] *In Re Federal, Inc.,* 12 U.C.C. Rep. 1142 (Mich. 1973).

Coverage:	Sales situation in which the seller retains "title" to goods.
What to Look for:	The distinction between "sale on approval" and "sale or return."
Application:	You are considering placing goods into the hands of others on a "sale or return" basis.

21 Sales by Consignment

It is a simple business fact that most retail stores, large and small, do not pay cash for the goods they offer to the buying public. This is also true of the wholesalers who supply the retailers and the manufacturers who supply the wholesalers. Over the years, four principal methods of financing such businesses have been developed.

METHODS OF FINANCING INVENTORY

First, the seller may extend a "line of open credit" to the buyer. "Net 30 days" is common. This gives the buyer the goods in inventory and also gives 30 days in which to convert the goods to cash. A portion of the cash receipts are expected to be used to meet the 30-day obligation.

Second, the seller may "floor plan" goods to the buyer. In these instances, an arrangement is worked out with a bank or other lender who pays the seller in full for the goods. The buyer in turn makes payments to the lender as sales are made from inventory. This arrangement is widely used to offer automobiles, farm equipment, television sets, and all types of appliances to the buying public. The lender takes a "security interest" in the floor planned goods, making it a "secured transaction."[1]

Third, the seller may finance the goods and when this happens, the seller usually requires security, making it a secured transaction.

A fourth method that developed over the years, was the "consignment" or "on memorandum" situation. Here the seller delivered the goods to the buyer's inventory, but received no immediate payment for the goods. The seller "retained title" until each item was sold to others.

---

[1] U.C.C., Article 9.

229

At that time, the buyer was obligated to pay the agreed portion of the proceeds to the seller. The seller was the "consignor" – the one who made the consignment and the buyer was the "consignee" – the one who received the consignment. In effect the seller financed the inventory of the buyer – but it was *not* a secured transaction. Safety for the seller came in the fact that the goods were still the seller's – even though held by the buyer. It is in this manner that tires and batteries are offered to you at your service station today.

In the typical consignment, the consignee could return the goods to the consignor and not have any further obligation.

Two Problems

Consignments worked well in many ways, but two problems arose in their use. The first was a legal matter; the second, a practical problem.

First, if a consignee became insolvent, who got the "consigned" goods? This type of situation frequently resulted in court battles over "title to the goods." The consignor would naturally argue that "title" was never surrendered. The creditors of the consignee would argue that it had been. The case decisions went both ways.

The drafters of the U.C.C. sought to avoid the title problem, and had this to say in their comments to Article 2, Sales:

> The arrangement of (this) Article is in terms of contract for sale and the various steps of its performance. The legal consequences are stated as following directly from the contract and action taken under it without resorting to the idea of when property or title passed or was to pass as being the determining factor. The purpose is to avoid making practical issues between practical men turn upon the location of an intangible something, the passing of which no man can prove by evidence and to substitute for such abstractions proof of words and actions of a tangible character.[2]

The drafters gave this statutory backing in the following provision.

> Each provision of this Article . . . applies irrespective of title to the goods except where the provision refers to such title. . . .[3]

Second, the practical problem was that consignments misled third parties in their dealings with the consignee. For example, if the consignee displayed a large inventory, and third parties did not *know* it was consigned goods, they might attribute a financial standing to the consignee that was inaccurate and thereby be misled.

The drafters also recognized that there were two variations of consignments encountered in prior practice. The first was where the seller delivered goods "on approval" for the potential buyer to examine before deciding to buy or not. The second was the true consignment in which goods were delivered to the buyer to sell to third persons. The terms selected and used in the U.C.C. to distinguish these variations, are *"sale on approval"* and *"sale or return."*

---

[2] U.C.C., 2–101, Comments.

[3] U.C.C., 2–401.

SALE ON APPROVAL

If the goods are delivered primarily for *use*, and the buyer has the right to return them, it is a "sale on approval."

SALE OR RETURN

If the goods are delivered for resale to others, and can be returned by the consignee should the consignee decide to do so, it is a "sale or return."

The distinction can be of extreme importance to the consignor. This is true because the U.C.C. provides that:

> ... Goods held on approval *are not* subject to the claims of the buyer's creditors until acceptance; goods held on sale or return *are subject to such claims while in the buyer's possession.*[4]

As a consequence, in the event of insolvency, bankruptcy, or large judgments against the consignee, the consignor can lose goods that were delivered "sale or return."

To make the matter worse, the U.C.C. treats certain *sales on approval* as *sales or return*, making consignments even more treacherous for the consignor.

> Where goods are delivered to a person for sale and such person maintains a place of business at which he deals in goods of the kind involved, under a name other than the name of the person making delivery, then with respect to claims of creditors of the person conducting the business the goods *are deemed to be on sale or return.* The provisions of this subsection are applicable even though an agreement purports to reserve title to the person making delivery until payment or resale or uses such words as "on consignment" or "on memorandum."[5]

To gain a working understanding of these Code provisions, it is helpful to examine three common business situations: insolvency of the consignee, bankruptcy of the consignee and the effect of a "floating lien" upon the inventory of the consignee.

TO ILLUSTRATE

For purposes of illustration, assume the following facts: Furniture, Inc., a North Carolina manufacturer, has agreed to consign $20,000 of its products, to Ajax, Inc., an Illinois retail outlet. For purposes of simplicity, there is just one store of the retailer. The goods are delivered by Furniture, Inc., and are displayed as part of the inventory of Ajax.

1. Ajax Becomes Insolvent

Ajax, Inc., becomes "insolvent" meaning that it cannot meet its obligations as they fall due. Furniture, Inc., does not get immediate notice

---

[4] U.C.C., 2–326 (2) (emphasis added).

[5] U.C.C., 2–326 (3) (emphasis added).

of this because it naturally expects delays in the payments for the *sale or return* goods.

Another creditor of Ajax, Inc., files suit for $100,000 due it. This creditor gets default judgment in an Illinois court and levies execution upon the inventory of Ajax, Inc., including the consigned goods of Furniture, Inc. *The consigned goods are subject to the judgment:* Reread U.C.C. 2-326 (2).

2. Ajax Files Bankruptcy

Again, Ajax cannot meet its obligations as they fall due. A petition in bankruptcy is prepared and filed in the federal district court.

An "ex parte" hearing is held by the federal bankruptcy judge who "adjudicates Ajax, Inc. a bankrupt." At this point, the creditors of Ajax, nor the consignor, Furniture, Inc., have any idea that bankruptcy of Ajax, Inc., has become a reality. The first notice they receive is a letter from the court informing them of the "first meeting of the creditors."

At that meeting, the creditors will elect a "trustee" who will immediately "freeze" the inventory and other assets of Ajax, Inc. In due course, the assets will be liquidated (turned to cash) by the trustee.

But what about the consigned goods? They are subject to ". . . the claims of the buyer's (Ajax) creditors . . . while in the buyer's possession."[6]

Under federal law, the trustee is not only a "creditor of the buyer," but a "preferred creditor" as well and will sell the consigned goods along with the other inventory. After sale, the proceeds are distributed to the creditors of Ajax on a pro rata basis. Furniture, Inc., will share, perhaps on a ten cents on the dollar basis in the funds realized from the sale of its own goods!

But why can't Furniture, Inc., simply go to Ajax, Inc., reclaim its goods and take them back to their place of business? Or perhaps Ajax, Inc., warned them of the pending bankruptcy so they picked up the goods *before* Ajax filed its bankruptcy petition. Now, is Furniture, Inc., home free? Unfortunately, not if the trustee finds out what happened.

Under the Bankruptcy Act,[7] an act of the bankrupt that prefers one creditor over another, that occurs within four months of the filing of the petition, is a "voidable preference" and can be set aside by the trustee. See Figure 21-1.

If Furniture, Inc., refuses to return the goods upon the demand of the trustee in bankruptcy, or sells them to others in the course of their own business, the trustee has the right to sue for the value of the consigned goods.[8]

---

[6] U.C.C., 2-326 (2).

[7] Section 60 (e) (1). Bankruptcy Act as Amended in 1966.

[8] *In Re Gross Mfg. & Importing Co., Inc.*, United States Dist. Ct., D.N.J., 9 U.C.C. Rep. 355 (1971).

FIGURE 21-1
Voidable Preferences under the Bankruptcy Act

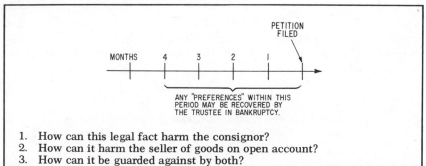

1. How can this legal fact harm the consignor?
2. How can it harm the seller of goods on open account?
3. How can it be guarded against by both?

3. The "Floating Lien"

The "floating" or "blanket" lien is a phrase that has been coined in the business and banking community, to describe a precise situation. (Assume that Ajax, Inc., is operating normally at this time.)

Ajax, Inc., is in need of working capital and one of its officers visits the loan officer at a bank. A tentative agreement is reached in which the bank agrees to loan Ajax $100,000 at 12 percent interest, repayable at $3,000 per month plus interest. However, the bank requires "security." Since Ajax does not own the building in which it does business, it agrees to give the lender a "security interest" in its inventory. The banker instructs one of its agents, generally *not* a lawyer, to do two things: first, make an appraisal of Ajax, Inc's., inventory, and second, to check the index to the "financing statements" to see if others have a security interest in the inventory.

The appraiser reports that the inventory is worth $125,000 and that no security interests are on file at the filing point.

The bank has Ajax, Inc., through an authorized agent, sign a "note" for $100,000 plus interest (see Figure 29-4 for an example) and, execute a "security agreement" (see Chapter 37 for an example). A "financing statement" is also signed (see Chapter 37 for an example).

The loan officer has Ajax, Inc., agree that the bank is not only to have a "security interest" in *present inventory*, but also in "after acquired inventory." Ajax agrees and these words are placed in the "security agreement" as well as on the face of the "financing statement."

The bank then files the "financing statement" at the correct filing point.[9] At that time the agent of the bank checks the index to the "financing statements" and reports back that the "security interest" of the bank is "perfected"[10] and also is first in "priority."[11]

---

[9] Local or central or both depending on the state. U.C.C., 9-312.

[10] U.C.C., 9-203 (1) (*b*), 9-304 and 9-304 (1).

[11] U.C.C., 9-204 (3) and (5), and 9-315.

The bank *then* disburses the $100,000 to Ajax, Inc. At this point the bank has a "blanket" or "floating" lien upon all inventory at Ajax' store *as well as inventory it will receive in the future.* (Examine Figure 21-2.)

The bank holds the note and security agreement in its files but the "security interest" flows through the filing point and attaches to the inventory of Ajax, Inc.

FIGURE 21-2
The Procedures Illustrated Create a "Blanket Lien" in Inventory While in the Store

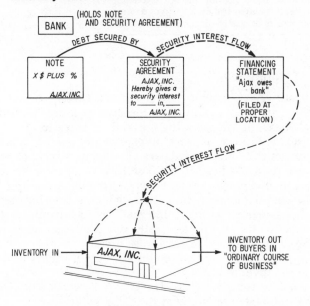

As new inventory comes in, it is subject to the lien; as inventory goes out by sale to "buyers in the ordinary course of business,"[12] the inventory is free of it.

The situation is analogous to one who stands on a bridge and looks at the water flowing by below. There is always water there, but it is never the same water because it is constantly being replaced by new water.

Ajax continues to sell from inventory, meets its obligations to Furniture, Inc., pays the bank payment on time, and all operates smoothly.

As Furniture, Inc., makes new consignments, they fall under the floating lien of the bank because they are "after acquired inventory." As the goods are sold, they move from under the lien. As long as Ajax, Inc., meets its obligations, all works well, and the floating lien is just a

---

[12] U.C.C., 9-307.

"legal relationship" that lurks in the background and perhaps is forgotten for all practical purposes.

The Inevitable Happens

Ajax, Inc., defaults on a note payment. The bank waits ten days and calls. Ajax makes an interest payment and the bank "waives the payment." But Ajax, misses the next payment. The principal balance due at that time is $90,000, and the bank "deems itself insecure."[13]

The bank calls Ajax; they stall, and the bank demands payment in full on the note. Payment isn't made and the bank forecloses on the inventory of Ajax under the provisions of its security agreement. At that time Furniture, Inc., has $30,000 in consigned goods on the floor.

The bank, through agents, advertises the sale, and auctions off *all inventory* of Ajax—including the consigned goods *plus* inventory that may have been supplied to Ajax by others on open account. The goods bring $86,000 at the sale. This is applied first to costs and attorney fees and the balance to the note. There is still a balance unpaid upon the note so the bank sues Ajax for the "deficiency." When judgment is obtained, it is called a "deficiency judgment." Where does this leave Furniture, Inc., as well as other unsecured suppliers on open account? Completely out in the cold.[14]

Looking at these examples might cause us to suffer considerable "righteous indignation" and perhaps justifiably so. And one may ask, "Just whose side were the drafters of the U.C.C. on?" As it turns out, the answer is "no one's side." Just as the above situations were created, provisions were made to avoid them. It turns out to be a case of those who comply being secure—those "who are ignorant of the law, simply have no excuse."

How can such losses be avoided?

AVOIDING LOSSES

The code gives the consignor three ways in which to protect the interest in consigned goods. (1) The consignor can comply with an "applicable sign law" and place a sign with the goods, stating who owns them.[15] The problem here is twofold: many states do not have a sign law; and second, who wants to rely upon the debtor to maintain a sign for the benefit of the consignor? (2) The consignor is protected if the consignee ". . . is generally known by creditors to be substantially engaged in selling the goods of others . . ."[16] The problem here is also apparent: this is a

---

[13] U.C.C., 1–208.

[14] It should be observed that the discussion here is one that relates to dealings between merchants. The U.C.C. limits the use of after acquired property clauses with consumers (U.C.C. 9–204–(4)) as does the FTC Improvement Act, P.L. 93–637, 93rd Cong., S. 356, January 4, 1975.

[15] U.C.C., 2–326(3)(*a*).

[16] U.C.C., 2–326(3)(*b*).

matter for determination by a jury—and in the cases decided to date, the consignor has failed to carry the burden of proof. This leaves the third means of protection and the code states:

> . . . This subsection is not applicable if the person making delivery complies with the filing provisions of the Article on Secured Transactions (Article 9). . . .[17]

The code has effectively placed consignments under Article 9.

Now What? It is clear that the filing provisions of Article 9 should be complied with in consignment situations: file to perfect the security interest,[18] file in the proper place,[19] and file the proper document.[20]

The consignor, faced with the problems discussed here—and others not mentioned—should proceed as follows in making a delivery under a consignment arrangement. First, search the records to see if there are any perfected security interests in the consignee's present inventory. If any are found, assume that they cover "after acquired property"— even if they do not. Second, prepare a financing statement and file it according to law. Third, give notice in writing to the holders of security interests—if any are found—keeping carbons of the letters. Fourth, ship the goods to the consignee. By taking the steps outlined, the consignor (lender) has complied with the provisions of both Article 2 and Article 9 — and a court *may* favor the consignor in a future contest over "who gets the goods."

REVIEW QUESTIONS

1. A seller ships you a set of encyclopedias and gives you 30 days in which to decide whether or not to keep them. Classify this consignment.
2. Are the books in question one available to your creditors *before* you decide to keep them? Why?
3. Are they available to your creditors *after* you decide to keep them? Why?
4. List two reasons why consignments have a legitimate business function.
5. List as many reasons as you can why consignments can be dangerous to the consignor.
6. Can you state a reason why the drafters of the U.C.C. treated consignments as they did?
7. "Before making large consignments, legal advice should be sought." Why is this true?
8. The "floating lien" is dangerous for both consignors and suppliers on open account. If you do not understand why, ask.
9. The words "after acquired inventory" or "after acquired property," trigger precise legal results in secured loans or transactions. State why.
10. Can you distinguish a "consignment" from a "bailment?" (In one the goods are held for sale—in the other they *must* be returned.)

---

[17] U.C.C., 2–326(3)(c).
[18] U.C.C., 9–302.
[19] U.C.C., 9–401.
[20] U.C.C., 9–402.

Words and Phrases

Write out briefly what they mean to you.
1. Dangers to consignors.
2. Floating lien.
3. Protecting the consignor.
4. Held for *sale* and not *use*.
5. Insolvency of consignee.

Coverage:	Classifications of property and forms of ownership.
What to Look for:	The "legal nature" of property as contrasted with the popular meaning of the word.
Application:	Property is the substance of almost all contracts.

22 Introduction to Property

The system of law that developed first in the American colonies and later in the states gave the modern business person two things: first, "freedom of contract"—which is considerably qualified today—and, second, the right to possess property in a private way. Both concepts are of tremendous importance in our business-oriented society and contribute substantially to the success of our economic system.

Through the use of the contract—as it relates to and controls private property—our factories, mines, manufacturing plants, and retail outlets are able to provide for us an unprecedented variety of merchandise. The markets of America are the showplaces of the world—made possible by the contract and private property.

Property in the legal sense—that is, property that is recognized as such at law—can only exist within the framework of an organized society. This is true because law can only exist as part of a society, and there must be "law" before there can be "property" in the legal sense.

Definition

One court said that property is

> . . . that which is peculiar or proper to any person; that which belongs exclusively to one; in the strict legal sense, an aggregate of rights which are guaranteed and protected by government.[1]

Here the court relates property directly to the individual and defines it as being "rights" which requires a government to back up those rights.

Another definition states that property is

---

[1] *Fulton Light, Heat, and Power Company* v. *State,* 121 N.Y.S. 536 (1909).

238

. . . ownership, the unrestricted and exclusive right to a thing; the right to possess a thing in every legal way, to possess it, to use it, and to exclude everyone else from interfering with it.[2]

Here, property is related to possession and ownership-in "every legal way."

Both definitions are broad enough to include "real" property – the earth and everything attached to it permanently – and "personal" property, all other property. A book could be filled with different definitions of property – and all would be accurate. But it would not tell us much in the end because there is much more to property than a definition. A brief look at some history will substantiate this.

Our modern system of real property law has its roots in the common-law feudal system of land tenure. A brief examination of this system makes it apparent that modern property law is almost the same as it was 1,000 years ago – only the names have changed. It should be observed that the feudal system of land tenure applied to land – not to personal property.

FEUDAL SYSTEM OF LAND TENURE

William the Conqueror introduced the feudal system into England about 1085 A.D., although some variation of it may have existed before that time. The name comes from the word "feud" meaning "an estate in land held of a superior on condition of rendering services." The right was inheritable – that is, it could be left from father to son, as long as the services were provided – or unless the land "escheated" (went back to) to the superior.

All land was held in subordination to the king or queen or designated subordinates such as nobles, lords, and vassals. The basic concept of the system was that by binding the population to the land and requiring services in return, a manageable society and political institution was created. (It can be seen that this was not a system of ownership that permitted the holding of private real property as we know it today.)

Ownership and Title

The Dominium Directum (ownership of the soil) was in the king or queen or selected subordinates. However, the Dominium Utile (possessionary title) with the right to use the land and a portion of the products and resulting profits of the soil, was in those who held "tenure." Tenure was the system of holding lands in subordination to some superior, which was the main characteristic of real property in feudal times.

Upon initial receipt of the right to use the land, or the inheritance of it, the tenure holder had to "acknowledge the tenure." This was done by a formal ceremony in which the landowner, head bared for the occasion, knelt before the lord and made a statement indicating that the land was

---

[2] Mackeld, *Rom. Law.*, Section 265.

held in subordination to the lord. This was "paying homage" and could only be done to the lord personally. In addition, the holder of the tenure had to take an oath of loyalty, and this oath was known as "fealty." With it went the duty of military service upon call by the lord—and from it came the word "fidelity."

Separation of Church and State

The churches, "the cure of souls and the right of titles," were granted tracts of land and were provided immunity from the obligations of homage and fealty—the origin of the modern separation of church and state.

Enfeoffment

It is not clear whether land could be sold to those outside of the heirship of the tenure holder. But a father could transfer ownership (qualified by the lord's ownership) to his son by the process of "enfeoffment."[3] The ceremony was held on the land and the father "symbolically delivered" the land to his son by handing him a clod of dirt or a twig from a tree. The event was attended by others who served as witnesses to the transfer. The son then became "seized" of the rights of the father, coupled with the duties to the lord.

Today, the system remains almost unchanged in principle, but the titles are different. The "monarch" has been replaced by the "state." Instead of homage and fealty, landowners are obligated to pay taxes and provide military service as provided by law. The distinction between the "ownership" of the soil and the right to use it is still valid since, in effect, we "own" in the sense that we simply have a better right to use the land than others. In the end, it could go to the state if one dies without heirs— called "escheat." We acknowledge the tenure today by taking off our hats to the tax collector rather than to the lord—but the end result is similar. The separation of church and state still continues in the traditional fashion—although the concept of immunity is finding disfavor. As one state supreme court judge said in an opinion, "Immunity breeds carelessness, liability breeds care."

The enfeoffment process is carried out today by substituting a deed for the clod of dirt. The witnesses have been replaced by the acknowledgment of a notary public. However, the common-law requirement of symbolic delivery of the land is still met by the transfer of the deed from the seller to the buyer.

A helpful way to become further oriented to the subject of property is to look at the various categories into which it can be classified.

CLASSIFICATIONS OF PROPERTY

One in business must constantly classify property and for many reasons. If it is "real" property, the written contract must be used. If it is

---

[3] "The act of investing with any dignity or possession; also the instrument or deed by which a person is invested with possessions."

"personal" property other rules must be followed. Therefore, the most important classification is that of real as contrasted to personal property.

Real Property

Property that is "real" includes the earth; everything that is affixed to it by nature, such as trees, coal, limestone, and growing crops; and everything that is affixed with the intention of it being permanently attached. For example, A pours a concrete footer and constructs a block wall upon it. The footer and wall are "real" – or "real estate." A then places a house on top of it, covering the walls with brick and installing a furnace, an air conditioner, and a water heater. All of these items are part of the "realty" because A intended them to be. A now installs wall-to-wall carpeting in the rooms. Since the carpeting is attached, it is realty also.

However, the carpet in the bathroom is *not* attached; the kitchen range, refrigerator, washer and dryer, are *not* real estate because A did not intend them to be.

In practice, there is often a "grey area" in the sale of real estate and

FIGURE 22-1

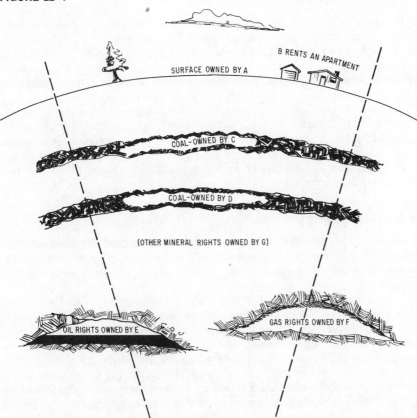

Many estates (ownership) may exist in the same parcel of land at the same time.

doubtful items must be covered in the contract of sale. For example, what about the TV antenna, the antique phone on the wall, the folding table in the kitchen, and the gymnastic equipment attached to the wall in the playroom? What is real property and what is not is extremely important in the sale of commercial property, and the contract of sale must be clear or litigation will follow.

Real property may be classified by the extent of ownership that exists in it as "fee simple" or "less than fee simple."

Fee Simple. "Fee simple" title is the best that one can own in real estate and it means that the owner owns all of the realty including mineral rights, and all easements or other estates that pertain to the realty. The phrase obviously evolved from "enfeoffment."

Less than Fee Simple. Real estate can be divided into a number of estates. When this happens, each person who owns one of the estates has a "less than fee simple" title – but is a real estate owner just the same. (See Figure 22–1)

Property that is not "real" is "personal."

Personal Property

Personal property is all property that is not "real" and includes such items as cars, boats, stock, cash, coins, wristwatches – and "rights" such as the right to be paid a debt that is due. The word "chattel" is applied to personal property and is a word of Saxon origin. A chattel is an article of personal property and it is "movable" – that is, it can be moved from one place to another.

In the feudal days in England, the amount of property that one "owned" was limited to land, personal belongings, and animals. Perhaps the word "chattel" is the origin of our word "cattle" – which are personal property.

Property can further be classified according to its physical or non-physical characteristics.

Is Property Physical?

In the early centuries, it was difficult to understand the ownership of something that was not "tangible." Because of this, property was transferred by delivery of the property itself, or by "symbolic delivery" as mentioned.

At common law an action to recover real property was called an action "in rem." The purpose of the action was to obtain the "res" or "thing" and was called a "real action." If chattels personal were stolen, an action was brought "in personum" to recover the items or, in their absence, to obtain damages against the person who took the goods. This was called a "personal action" and had to be brought against the person involved. This was true because stolen personal property was often destroyed or sold to others and could not be recovered. Real property generally cannot be destroyed – therefore, a "personal action" was not required.

The distinction between an action against the property and the person finds wide use in modern practice. If A, who lives in California, injures B in Indiana, A can be sued in Indiana and served in California by the nonresident motorist statutes. If A owns real estate in Indiana, the real estate can be proceeded against in a direct action by B in Indiana.

Property May Be Nonphysical

If one defined property as being "physical" and stopped there, many enforceable property rights would be excluded. Property can, therefore, be intangible or "incorporeal" as contrasted to "corporeal" (real). If A owes B $500, B has a property right in the $500, but the right is intangible and is called a "chose in action," "a personal right not reduced to possession, but recoverable by a suit at law."[4]

Other examples of nonphysical property include performance contracts, accounts receivable, sign privileges, water rights, easements, leases, the right to light and all types of debts.

Turning from classifications of property, let's examine the relationships that arise between persons and their real and personal property.

PROPERTY AND PERSONS

Property is always associated with human beings or corporations, thus requiring some understanding of "ownership," "title," and "possession."

1. OWNERSHIP

Ownership is the amount or degree of property interest one may have. For example, the tenant of an apartment holds a "leasehold interest" and is a property owner to the extent of the leasehold. The renter cannot be excluded from the property except under terms and conditions prescribed by law or found in the lease. (See chapter 24 for a copy of a lease.) The landlord has ownership of the apartment and holds legal title to it — but the ownership is qualified by the leasehold of the tenant.

In the case of personal property, one may own less than all of a chattel. For example, A and B, husband and wife, purchase a new automobile and have it titled in both of their names. The bank that financed the car retains a "security interest" in it to assure repayment of the loan. Each of the parties (the bank and A and B) have a property interest in the auto that is less than full ownership of it.

Forms of Ownership

One who is acquiring ownership of property, both real and personal, will naturally be concerned with the *form* of the ownership of what is being acquired. This will be determined by the manner in which the

---

[4] *Black's Law Dictionary,* 4th ed.

property is "titled." Two choices are possible in the law: sole ownership and joint ownership.

Sole Ownership.   When Jane Smith has property conveyed or titled to her in her name only, the ownership is normally hers and hers alone. Any loss that occurs will be her loss and for this reason, proper insurance must be carried in her name.

Joint Ownership.   Here, the ownership is shared with another. The most common types are "tenancies in common," the "joint tenancy," and "community property."

Tenancy in Common.   In this type of ownership, two or more persons own real or personal property by holding it in a "unity of possession" and each has the right to occupy the real estate or use the personal property in common with the co-owner(s).

To illustrate, assume that A and B own one acre of land as tenants in common. This means that A and B each own "one-half" of the entire acre but neither owns any particular one-half of it. To illustrate further, if half of the acre is going to be sold to C, A and B will share one-half in the proceeds of sale. As one court stated, they hold by ". . . distinct titles by unity of possession, neither knowing his own severally, and therefore they all occupy promiscuously."[5] Upon the death of A, A's ownership in the remaining real estate passes to A's heirs – not to B. This is one of the legal disadvantages of this form of ownership.

Joint Tenancy.   In this form of ownership, a different situation is encountered. Joint tenants have the same interest in the property that came to them by the same conveyance, starting at the same time and held by undivided possession. Upon the death of a joint tenant the property passes to the survivor(s).

The joint tenancy with the "right of survivorship" is often used in practice to give husband and wife, or two or more other persons, the form of title that permits the property to pass to the survivor, or survivors, upon the death of any of them. Title to real estate is often taken in this manner and bank accounts and stocks and bonds are frequently set up so that the benefit to them will vest in the survivor.

However, legal advice in using survivorship provisions is in order since if only one actually pays for the survivorship property, then upon the death of that person, a gift may be involved to the survivor, raising tax questions. Another form of joint ownership is found in "community property" states.

Community Property

The rule in community property states is that all property acquired by husband and wife during marriage is owned by *both* parties in equal shares no matter which one of them paid for it. This is true even though the property is titled in the name of only one of the two parties. This type of ownership has been called a "marital partnership."[6] The states that

---

[5] *Fullerton* v *Storthz Bros. Inv. Co.*, 190 Ark. 198, 77 S.W.2d. 966,968 (1935).

[6] *Mitchell* v *Mitchell*, 80 Tex. 101, 15 S.W. 705 (1891).

recognize community property laws are Arizona, California, Idaho, Louisiana, New Mexico, Nevada, Texas and Washington.

Turning from "ownership," let's examine "title."

2. TITLE

Title is the manner in which ownership is acquired. For example, Bill Jones, the owner of an apartment house, inherited it from his mother who died without a will. His title would emanate from the "statutes of descent and distribution." If he acquired title from X by deed, his title would be from the deed itself. The *quantity* of ownership that he has in the property may be qualified by other estates such as minerals, rights-of-way, and easements that were conveyed to third parties by prior owners of the realty.

In the case of personal property, "title" is the intangible status given by law to one who "owns" personal property. The location of "title" can be of key importance in business. For example, A ships goods to B and these are destroyed during transit. If B had legal title from the time of shipment, the loss is B's. If not, the loss falls on A.

Finally, ownership and title must be distinguished from "possession."

3. POSSESSION

Possession runs to the physical control of property and does not necessarily have anything to do with ownership and title. If A loans an automobile to B who uses it to take a trip, B does not have title, and B does not own the automobile. Yet, B has "possession" and has better rights to the automobile than any person except A. Possession is ". . . the detention and control or the manual or ideal custody, of anything which may be the subject of property, for one's use and enjoyment, either as owner or as proprietor of a qualified right in it, and either personally or by another who exercises it in one's place and name."[7]

It is said that "possession is nine tenths of the law." This old adage should not be taken as literally true because it would mean that the person in possession of property can only be ousted by one whose title is "nine tenths" better. But it does place "in a strong light the legal truth that every claimant must succeed by the strength of one's own title and not by the weakness of one's antagonist." However, in practice, the "possession" rule does not always come out the way it sounds. A case illustrates.

Treasure Trove? An infantry platoon leader discovered a large amount of cash while in a combat zone. After return to the U.S., he claimed it as "treasure trove" saying that he had taken possession of it and thus had superior rights to all except the true owner who could not be found.

The court held that he was not entitled to the money since at the time, he was an agent of the United States and in its employ![8]

---

[7] *Black's Law Dictionary*, 4th ed.

[8] *Morrison v United States*, 492 F.2d 1219, U.S. Court of Claims (1974).

PROPERTY CONCEPTS ARE CHANGING

The principles of real and personal property law have become rather standard. Yet as the needs of society change, the principles undergo alteration. A good example of this can be found in the "condominium" form of real estate ownership.

Condominiums

A new concept in ownership of real property was developed in the late 1950s and the early 1960s. At first this type of real estate venture had no name because there was no common law precedent for it. In time the word "condominium" was adopted and when used today is descriptive of a unique type of joint ownership in real estate.

The basic concept of the condominium is that one unit containing living or business quarters is constructed and then space within that larger unit is *sold*—not rented—to others. The result is a single unit that is owned collectively by those who purchase units within the larger unit.

The original condominium was erected at Salt Lake City, Utah, in 1960. This was a residential condominium and was called "Greystone." The unit was an unqualified success. It combined ownership with joint management, consolidation of maintenance and resulted in great economies. It was soon discovered that this type of ownership was readily accepted by financiers.

In 1963, Utah adopted a condominium law placing the promotion of the units there under statutory law. Today, almost all states have enacted such laws. In addition, Section 234 of the National Housing Act sanctions condominiums at the national level.

This type of venture offers many advantages to investors such as reduction of risks of loss; lower construction finance costs and profit margins that can be accurately controlled. For the buyers, advantages include tax shelters, part time rentals to others during periods of nonuse, consolidated recreational facilities and apartment living in single ownership form.

The concept has been extended into business and is being used by motels, shopping malls, medical buildings, and even warehouses. The concept has application in any situation, business, professional, or personal, in which ownership of space is preferable to the leasing of the same space.

REVIEW QUESTIONS

1. Why is the contract so closely tied to property?
2. Name two reasons why property can be defined in so many ways.
3. Why must property always be defined in a "legal way"?
4. What does "escheat" mean?
5. Why was the ownership of the soil in the King or Queen in olden times?
6. Explain what "tenure" was at common law. Does the word have similar meaning today?

7. What practical reasons can be stated for granting immunity to churches?
8. List three examples of real property; six of personal property.
9. What must occur before personal property can be converted to real property?
10. Distinguish a joint tenancy from a tenancy in common. (This distinction will be important to you many times in your life.)

Words and Phrases

Write out briefly what they mean to you.
1. Enfeoffment.
2. Symbolic delivery.
3. Joint ownership.
4. Community property.
5. Title.

Coverage:	An examination of how "property" may be acquired.
What to Look for:	The function of "law" in property transfers.
Application:	You are about to buy your first home.

23 Acquiring Property

Acquiring real or personal property is a "give and take" situation because what one acquires another must give up. Under our system of private ownership of both real and personal property – the legal vehicle by which the exchange is made – is the contract. In the governmental setting, it can happen other ways. For example, if A sells a watch to B, A has given up property and B has acquired it. If C fails to pay taxes and the state takes C's home for that reason, C has lost property. As one becomes more familiar with acquiring property, an awareness follows that in the end, all property is owned by someone at all times. Property may be acquired, and thus given up, by gift, by will, by inheritance, by operation of law, by forfeiture, and by sale.

GIFT

Gifts may be made of both real and personal property. In either type, the gift must be made during one's life.

The one who makes a gift is the "donor" – one to whom it is made is the "donee." If a gift is made while one is in good health, it is a gift "inter vivos" – during life. If it is made when death is anticipated, it is a gift "causa mortis" – in contemplation of death.

In some instances the law treats an inter vivos gift as being causa mortis. For example, under the federal gift law, gifts to children made within three years of death, are presumed to have been causa mortis. The estate of the decedent will be taxed as though the gifts made within the three-year period had not been made.

Legal Requirements of a Gift

The legal requirements of a binding gift are twofold. First, there must be the "intention" to make a gift, and this is usually manifested by the

248

objective acts of the donor. Second, there must be delivery. The delivery should be actual, but if this is not possible, it may be "symbolic" or "constructive" such as the delivery of a deed to the donee. Where a gift has been made, the donee has acquired property and the donor has parted with the same property. If a donor keeps control of an alleged gift, the gift fails.

Examples. A, who is facing a severe operation from which A may not survive, gives a diamond ring to B. The operation is performed the next day and A survives. The gift fails because it had been made in contemplation of death – and that contingency did not occur. If A had died, the gift would have been complete.

John Smith decides to give his farm to his son. A deed is prepared. As long as Smith retains possession of the deed, there has been no gift. When Smith hands the deed to his son, the gift has been completed. The farm has been delivered to the son "symbolically."

Bill Brown decides to give 1,000 shares of AT&T common stock to his brother Jim. Bill indorses the shares in blank (see Chapter 31), places them in his (Bill's) safety deposit box, gives Jim the duplicate key, and tells him the shares are his on Bill's death. Has there been a gift? Some courts would permit Jim to have the shares – others would not. Had Bill "delivered" the shares to Jim? How should the gift have been handled?

From a strict business viewpoint, gifts are seldom used – other than as "bonuses" or the like. They are widely used in private affairs and have been a perpetual source of litigation.

BY WILL

A will is a written, and in one instance a spoken, statement by one of what one wants done with that person's property upon death. It is different than a gift because it does not become operative until death. One who makes a will, if male, is called the "testator"; if female, the "testatrix." One who dies without a will dies "intestate" – without a will.

The states permit one over the age of 18 to write a will. A will entirely in the handwriting of the testator is a "holographic will" and will be admitted to "probate" (administration of the will) upon proof by witnesses that the will and signature are in the writing of the testator. (Some states do not recognize holographic wills, however.) If a military person, at a time when death is a possibility, tells others what she or he wants done with her or his property if death occurs, she or he has created a "nuncupative" will. If death occurs, the witnesses can swear by affidavit what they heard and the oral will may be honored.

If a will is prepared by counsel, it will be tailored to meet the client's needs; it will be witnessed by two or three adult witnesses (depending upon the state) and will usually be accompanied by an affidavit. The use of an affidavit does away with the necessity of producing the witnesses to prove their signatures – unless the will is challenged. In that event, the signatures must be proved in court by calling the certifying witnesses to testify. If they are deceased, others will authenticate *their* signatures.

A valid will requires that the testator have "testamentary capacity," that is, be of sound and disposing mind and know the consequences that accompany the execution of the will. Most "will contests" (challenges to a will) occur where wills are drafted on deathbeds or while the testator is under the influence of drugs or medication. The usual will, executed under normal conditions, is rarely upset in court. For a further discussion and a sample will, see Chapter 24.

For many years "curbstone lawyers" (who dispense free advice), have spread fallacy throughout the states and it is this: "There is no need to write a will because the law writes the best will." This saying has become part of the folklore of America—and many a widow with children has suffered because of it. The saying refers to the fact that if one dies intestate, the law will specify how the estate will pass. The law is found in the "statutes of descent and distribution." In the statute that follows, two points should be observed: First, the class of persons who occupy the top of the list, and second, the position occupied by the spouse of the deceased person.

Statutes of Descent

If one dies intestate, the laws of the state of residence will determine the distribution of real estate. A typical statute follows, in part:

> *Course of Descent Generally.* When any person having title to any real estate of inheritance shall die intestate as to such estate, it shall descend and pass in the parcenary to his kindred, male and female, in the following course:
>
> *a.* To his children and their descendants;
>
> *b.* If there be no child, nor descendant of any child, then one moiety each to his father and mother;
>
> *c.* If there be no child, nor descendant of any child, nor mother, then one moiety to the father; or, if there be no child, nor descendant of any child, nor father, then one moiety to the mother; and in either case the other moiety, or if there be no child, nor descendant of any child, nor father, nor mother, the whole shall go to the wife or husband of the intestate and to the intestate's brothers and sisters and the descendants of brothers and sisters;
>
> *d.* If there be no child, nor descendant of any child, nor mother, nor wife or husband nor brother or sister, nor descendant of any brother or sister, then the whole to the father; or, if there be no child, nor descendant of any child, nor father, nor wife or husband, nor brother, nor sister, nor descendant or any brother or sister, then the whole to the mother.
>
> *e.* And if there be no child, nor descendant of any child, nor father, nor mother, nor wife or husband, nor brother, nor sister, nor descendant of any brother or sister, then one moiety shall go to the paternal and the other to the maternal kindred in the following course:
>
> *f.* First to the grandfather and grandmother one half of the moiety each;
>
> *g.* If no grandmother, one half of the moiety to the grandfather, or if no grandfather one half of the moiety to the grandmother; and in either case the other one half of the moiety, or if there be neither grandfather nor grandmother the whole of the moiety, shall go to the uncles and aunts on the same side, and their descendants.

If there are no heirs, the realty goes to the state. There are similar provisions to cover personal property, but they vary from state to state. So, if Tom Smith dies intestate, and leaves a minor son, his wife is cut out of realty (other than dower) and in many states, most of the personalty. This is why the law does *not* write the best will.

BY OPERATION OF LAW

Property may be acquired by the workings of common-law principles and the statutes of the state. Examples include grants by the government, adverse possession, abandonment, accession, and use.

Grants. In earlier years, the federal government granted real estate[1] to interested persons providing they met conditions. Typical requirements were that the land be staked, improved, and occupied for a prescribed period of time. Grants are not as common as they were in the 19th century, but land is still offered in remote parts of the nation including Alaska.

Today the business person has other opportunities to acquire public land for private use. The principal ways are found in the "urban renewal" and "excess land" programs.

In urban renewal, the U.S. creates laws that provide funds with which local state agencies can acquire land and buildings in "blighted areas" of our cities. These buildings are razed and the land is offered to private investors for development under guidelines set down by state law. In a sense, private land *is* taken for private use. However, the law provides provisions for competitive bidding before private interests can acquire urban renewal land.

Many times, government acquires excess land. This happened widely in the interstate road construction programs. This land can be purchased from government for private use under established guidelines.

Adverse Possession

In the years of the land grants in the American West, the "squatter" became a household word. With the squatter came "squatter's rights" — rights supposedly earned by the unlawful activity of occupying land that was claimed, or owned by others. Squatters had no legal rights in fact and many were driven from the ranges of mid-America by force.

However, at common law, a rule developed that permitted persons to acquire the real estate of others by the possession of it — but much more was required than mere "squatting" upon the land. It was called "adverse possession." If one occupies real estate under some "color of title" (a deed, will, or other written claim) and does so "openly, adversely, and notoriously" for the time period prescribed by state law, that person will gain legal title to the realty possessed. The time period varies, but 10, 15, or 20 years are typical. It is a policy of the law to "quiet title" and if one

---

[1] 160 to 640 acres being typical.

meets the requirements, that person owns the land. The law presumes the grant that gave it has been lost — the "lost grant" presumption. Therefore, the mere "squatting" upon the land of another without "color of title" is *never enough* to ripen into legal ownership.

The long time periods in adverse possession safeguard the true owner, and gives one an opportunity to reclaim the land. But if one fails, even if merely negligent, others may acquire title to the realty. Utility companies, railroads, and private businesses, periodically inspect their property lines in search of encroachments. It was, and still is, a common practice on farms and ranches, to "ride the line" for the same reason.[2] If encroachments are found, fences are erected or signs installed. In some cases, suits are brought to stop the unauthorized use.

Adverse possession is used today to clear up boundary disputes or to gain ownership of parcels of land, the owners of which have vanished. The lawyer prepares a deed, pays back taxes, and has the client fence the parcel. If the statutory period passes, the client has acquired realty, and is free to deed or will it to others in the future. But it should be pointed out that adverse possession in most states will not run against land owned by the state. Nor will it run against properties of the federal government.

Abandonment

Most states have laws that govern personal property that has been abandoned by former owners. If the statutory requirements are met, which usually includes some payment to the state, one may acquire title to abandoned personal property. However, hazards accompany such activities and legal counsel should always be sought. The laws of the "high seas" contain provisions that cover "derelicts" and other abandoned products of shipping.

Accession

Property may be acquired by "accession," meaning that property has been added to other property. In river country, the silt is often washed from one bank and deposited on another, causing loss of realty to one and addition to realty of the other. If a tenant makes permanent additions to an apartment, the improvements become the property of the landlord.

User

All states have laws, common or statutory, that permit one to acquire a right to *use* property under certain conditions. Some states call it the right of "user" or the right of an easement — the right to use as distinguished from ownership. It arises where one uses another's realty for right-of-way purposes and the use continues uninterrupted for a prescribed period of time. Unauthorized railroad crossings are marked by

---

[2] In the days of Colonial America, this was known as "beating the bounds."

a sign that states, "Warning – private property – no public crossing – ." The sign prevents an easement from being gained by those who use the crossing over a long period of time.

FORFEITURE OF PROPERTY

In certain cases, a property owner will forfeit rights to property – both real and personal. When this is done, others will acquire the property in due course. It happens most frequently where one fails to pay taxes or defaults in the terms of secured obligations.

Failure to Pay Taxes. Each state, through taxing authorities, levies and collects taxes on real and personal property. Once the assessment becomes final, the taxes levied may be paid by a specified date and the property owner receives a discount. If the discount is not taken, the net amount must be paid by a second date. If that date passes without payment, a penalty begins to accrue. If nonpayment continues, the forfeiture period begins to run. A legal notice is placed in local papers identifying those whose taxes are delinquent. If payment, penalty, and publishing costs are not paid, the property is sold. One who purchases property at a "sheriff's sale" does not obtain good title at first. The states by law prescribe a time period in which the owner has a right to redeem. If redeemed, the owner must pay taxes, all costs, plus interest to the buyer. If the property is not redeemed, title passes to the new owner.

A Real Estate Example

The statute of an eastern state provides the following schedule for the payment of taxes: If the real estate taxes are paid for the first half of the year (January to June 30) by August 1, a discount of 4 percent is granted. From August 1, to September 1, the net amount is due and no discount is allowed.

If the taxes are not paid by May 1 of the following year, the name of the titled owner is added to the assessor's list for publication. On May 15, the list is published in a newspaper of general circulation in the county where the real estate is located.

On the 3rd day of October of that year, a public sale is held at which time all real estate that is still delinquent is sold to the highest bidders. From the date of sale, the owners of the real estate have 18 months within which to redeem the land by paying the back taxes, all costs including publication, plus 9 percent interest to the successful bidder. If not redeemed by the deadline, the buyer is given a deed by the county.

The process is slow and the owner has ample time within which to redeem. However, as a matter of good business and personal practice, it is wise to keep one's name off of delinquent tax lists for credit and other purposes.

Foreclosure

Those who buy homes and personal property, frequently do so by financing the purchase at a lending institution. If default occurs, and if not corrected, the lender will "foreclose" on the home, or "repossess" the personal property. Public sale follows and the buyer has acquired property because of the foreclosure.

SALE AND PURCHASE

The most common manner in which property is acquired—both real and personal—is by sale and purchase. The one selling gives up what is sold, and the buyer acquires it. In the majority of sales the buyer finances the purchase through a lender, giving what is bought as security for the loan. Lenders may require supplemental security in the form of collateral, co-signers on notes, down payments, or other assurance that the loan will be repaid promptly—with interest.

For a full discussion of financing personal property under Article 9 of the U.C.C., see chapter 37. Documents used in real estate sales will be examined in detail in chapter 24.

One of the losses sometimes suffered by those in business arises when one believes that one is dealing with personal property when in fact it is real property.

A Case Example

In this case, standing timber and a product of standing timber—turpentine—were involved. When turpentine is removed from trees and placed in containers, it is clearly personal property. But what is it before it is removed from the trees? That is the legal issue in this case. Note how the Uniform Commercial Code became involved in the litigation.

Newton v. Allen.[3] Allen entered into a written agreement with Newton and others as follows:

I, Mrs. Miriam N. Allen, do lease all of my workable timber to C. Newton, Jr., for a period of five years for a percentage of 30 percent of each and every dipping. Plus payment for cups all ready (sic) up. To include government payment of timber already cut.

Signed this 6th day of January, 1964.
Witness: Georgia M. Newton

s/s Miriam N. Allen_____ (L.S.)
Miriam N. Allen
s/s Jack C. Newton, Jr.
Jack C. Newton, Jr.

Defendants began using Allen's land for turpentine purposes and Allen advised them that she did not recognize the agreement as legal and binding and demanded that defendants cease further trespass. Allen offered restitution for expenses incurred, but defendants ignored

---

[3] 200 Ga. 681, 141 S.E.2d 417 (1965).

her demand and continued to remove turpentine. Allen then filed a petition against defendants, charging invalidity of the above agreement and asked for three things: (1) temporary and permanent injunction; (2) an accounting for gum taken; and (3) monetary damages.

Defendants demurred (claimed there was no cause of action), stating that the petition did not set out a cause of action and claiming the above instrument to be valid. The court overruled the demurrer and defendants appealed.

Georgia law states that

> . . . leases of standing timber must describe the land upon which the timber stands, with sufficient certainty for identification or give a key by which it may be identified, *Clarke Brothers* v. *Stowe,* 132 Ga. 621(3), 64 S.E. 786.

The court continued,

> The fact that the use is limited to turpentine purposes does not reduce the interest transferred to a mere usufruct[4] where there is no indication that the parties so intended. (*Warehouses, Inc.* v. *Wetherbee,* 203 Ga. 483, 490–491, 46 S.E.2d 894.) This instrument, then, purported to convey an estate for years in standing timber, which is realty.

Georgia Code, 20–401(4), requires that ". . . Any contract for the sale of lands, or any interest, or concerning them . . . ," must be in writing. Thus, the question of whether the description ". . . all lands owned or controlled by me . . ." meets these requirements, was before the court for decision. The court answered this question in the negative, holding that ". . . the language in the instant document was insufficient to convey any interest to the defendant Newton."

Defendant's contention that the instrument here purported to lease or sell only turpentine and thus constituted a contract for the sale of personalty under the Uniform Commercial Code, Ga.L. 1962, p. 156 et seq.; Code Ann. Title 109A, (U.C.C. 2–107), prompted the court to hold

> . . . This writing purported to lease the *trees* (italics by the court) themselves, not merely the products thereof, and therefore was a lease of realty. . . . The Uniform Commercial Code does not purport to change the law relating to instruments which transfer an interest in land.

This is well and good so far—but what about U.C.C. 2–107(1) that states:

> A contract for the sale of timber, *minerals or the like* . . . is a contract for the sale of goods . . . if they are to be severed by the seller. . . .

Subsection (2) of 2–107 continues:

> . . . A contract for the sale apart from the land of growing crops or other things attached to realty and capable of severance without material harm thereto but not described in subsection (1) is a contract for the sale of goods

---

[4] The right of enjoying the thing, the property of which is vested in another, and to draw from the same all the profit, utility, and advantage which it may produce, provided it be without altering the substance of the thing.

within this Article whether the subject matter is to be severed *by the buyer or by the seller* even though it forms part of the realty at the time of contracting, and the parties can by identification effect a present sale before severance. (Emphasis added.)

The court chose to resolve this conflict by looking to prior Georgia case law. It could be argued that "minerals or the like" includes turpentine. At the same time turpentine can be removed without material harm to the trees and can be identified with certainty. The result is probably correct, although it worked a hardship on business persons who thought they had a binding contract in operation.

No doubt Allen would have signed a proper lease as quickly as she would have signed the above agreement, and the defendants will use proper leases in the future, at least in the state of Georgia. However, it is submitted that this court *could* have arrived at an opposite conclusion had it been so inclined.

The *Newton* case permits us to arrive at two conclusions:

1. Even courts have difficulty at times deciding if property is or is not "real" property, and
2. As a matter of sound business judgment, if one is not certain, the subject matter should be treated as real property to avoid the result in the *Newton* case.

REVIEW QUESTIONS

1. Name an example of forfeiture.
2. How can someone be in possession of something that is not in his or her actual possession?
3. Do you have personal knowledge of gifts made in your family? If so, how were they made?
4. Why should a man who has small children have a will? Who does it protect?
5. True or False. Under the feudal system of land tenure, one owned land just as we do today.
6. A contract for the sale of 10 gallons of turpentine in cans would not have to be in writing. Why? What about turpentine worth $600?
7. A contract for the sale of timber from which turpentine can be extracted should be in writing and contain a legal description of the real estate. Why?
8. Apparently Mrs. Newton wrote the contract in the Newton case. Point out three errors that were made in it.
9. The chapter contains two examples of accession as a means of acquiring real estate. Name another example.
10. Why do we have statutes of descent and distribution?

Words and Phrases

Write out briefly what they mean to you.
1. Intestacy.
2. Causa mortis.
3. "Grants."
4. Adverse possession.
5. Abandonment.

Coverage:	An analysis of legal documents that are widely used in real estate transfer and litigation.
What to Look for:	The function these documents perform.
Application:	The business person makes constant use of real estate documents and should understand the nature of them.

24 Real Property Documents

Those who work with real estate, such as the realtor, are well acquainted with the purposes and functions of the wide range of legal documents used daily in thousands of transactions concerning realty. These range from the transfer of property from father to son by will to purchases of commercial buildings. But the size of the transaction or the value of the property does not change the nature of the legal documents whereby the "deal is closed." For example, if A buys a vacant lot in a rural community for $2,000 and finances it through a local bank, the same documents will be used that would be required to finance the purchase of a multimillion dollar shopping center.

Of primary importance in real estate transactions is the "plat" or picture of the realty involved. While one can go on a 40-acre tract and look it over, one still cannot see what is there in fact. This is true because things of a *legal nature* may affect or burden the land, and there will be nothing on the land that will spell these out. However, a visual inspection of realty will provide information about overhead lines and buried gas lines that are marked above the surface. Also, an accurate survey will locate the tract upon the ground – yet, the visual inspection and the survey still do not disclose the full picture. The true picture of real estate can come only from the plat of the land backed up by an "abstract of title" or a title report. First, a look at a real estate plat. (Examine Figure 24-1.)

FIGURE 24–1
Sample of a "Metes and Bounds" Survey*

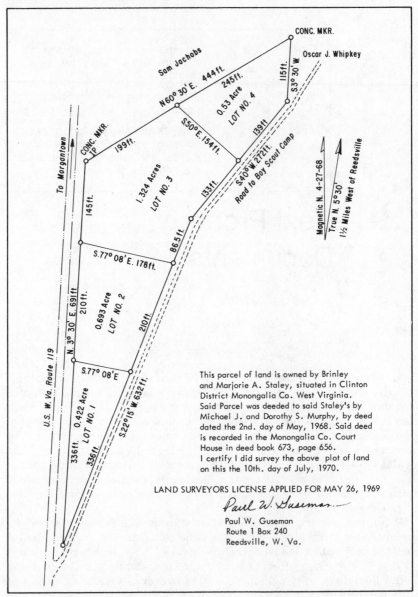

This parcel of land is owned by Brinley
and Marjorie A. Staley, situated in Clinton
District Monongalia Co. West Virginia.
Said Parcel was deeded to said Staley's by
Michael J. and Dorothy S. Murphy, by deed
dated the 2nd. day of May, 1968. Said deed
is recorded in the Monongalia Co. Court
House in deed book 673, page 656.
I certify I did survey the above plot of land
on this the 10th. day of July, 1970.

LAND SURVEYORS LICENSE APPLIED FOR MAY 26, 1969

Paul W. Guseman

Paul W. Guseman
Route 1 Box 240
Reedsville, W. Va.

* "Metes" are the *directions* of each line of survey, and "bounds" are the *length* of these lines.

REAL ESTATE PLATS

Plats or maps of land perform an important function in our society. By them we have a means of identifying and isolating portions of the earth and tying the land to its owners. Without plats, chaos could follow as one tries to identify realty so that a factory may be constructed, while another lays claim to a portion of the same land. An orderly process in home, industrial, and business construction would be impossible without an accurate system of land platting. Before a plat is examined, it is important to recognize that two systems of survey exist in the United States. First, is the system of "metes and bounds" and next the "rectangular" or "government survey" system.

Metes and Bounds

This system is based upon directions and distances which in effect draw a picture of the land. The system is followed in the original 13 states; the other New England and Atlantic Coast states; plus, Texas, Tennessee, Kentucky, and West Virginia. Florida is the only exception on the East Coast. The system has weaknesses. It is not uncommon in metes and bounds states to find that surveys made of adjoining tracts overlap

FIGURE 24–2

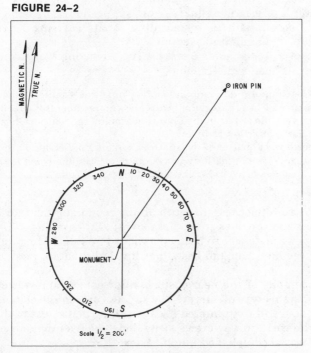

The drawing illustrates a call of N. 35° 0′ E. 800′.

at one or more points. In the early years of our nation, the surveys were made independently of each other and corner markers were lost or so poorly identified that the surveys were started from wrong points. It can be appreciated that a small error in a starting point might cause serious variations in a survey that might cover 1,000 acres and contain hundreds of "metes and bounds." In the earlier years, the "rod" or "perch" was the standard of measurement, being 16½ feet in length. It has been replaced in modern surveys by the "foot," but all property in metes and bounds states contains rod or perch measurements in their "claim of title."

The directions in metes and bounds surveys are based upon 360° and are recited in terms of "N," "S," "E," or "W," so many degrees (°), so many minutes (') in a certain direction. (Examine Figure 24-2.)

Government or Rectangular Survey

On April 26, 1785, the federal government adopted the rectangular survey system. It is noted that the adoption date was *after* American Independence and therefore came too late to be applied to the original states. The system is in use in 30 states, including Alaska. Rather than permitting a portion of land to be divided in metes and bounds, the rectangular survey divides the lands into squares which in turn are subdivided into smaller squares until a single lot is reached. Thus, the single lot is portion X of a larger square, which is portion Y of the next larger square, and so on, with each suceeding square carrying a name such as "township," "range," and "section."

Example of a Rectangular Survey. The following was taken from a deed conveying real estate in Ohio:

> ... [The Grantors] do grant and convey unto the [Grantees] the following parcel of real estate, together with the improvements thereon, situated in the Township of Lee in the County of Monroe and State of Ohio, and more particularly described as follows:
> The north west quarter of the south east quarter of Section 11 in Township 2 of range 4 containing Forty acres, more or less, and being the same real estate that was conveyed to the Grantors by deed from. . . .

Examine Figure 24-3.

The lines running north to south on the rectangular survey are "meridian" lines and the ones from east to west are "base lines." Under this system, further division can be accomplished by subdividing the squares created by the meridian and base lines into subsquares and divisions as mentioned.

The topography of the near eastern, midwestern, and western states lends itself to this type of survey. The success of it in the colonies would have been doubtful if attempted because of the denseness of the forests in which the early survey crews struggled. The eventual survey of the open west was accomplished much easier.

FIGURE 24–3

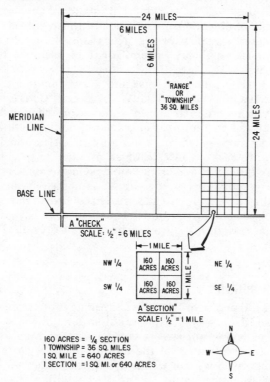

160 ACRES = ¼ SECTION
1 TOWNSHIP = 36 SQ. MILES
1 SQ. MILE = 640 ACRES
1 SECTION = 1 SQ. MI. or 640 ACRES

A Change Is Coming

An important question being debated by the land surveyors is whether surveys of the future should be in the "meter" instead of the "foot."

A "meter" is one-ten millionth of the distance from the Equator to the North Pole and forms the unit of measurement of the "metric system."

France was the first nation to adopt the system and did so in 1795. The United States has remained on the English system which is based upon the inch, foot and yard.

This double standard means that an American manufacturer who wants to compete in the world market must tool up to meet both standards. This is particularly true where machines are involved since almost all nations of the world use the metric system on machine threads. This problem will be solved in the next few years by the adoption of the meter as a unit of measure in the United States. But this still leaves unanswered the question raised above. What about land surveys and legal descriptions?

It is natural for conversion to be resisted – but there is precedent for a change of system of measurement in surveys. As discussed previously, at the turn of this century, the unit of measure used by lawyers and surveyors, was the "rod" or "perch." This standard gave way to the yard and foot in spite of objections raised back in those times.

The "kilometer" (1,000) meters) has made it's appearance on the American interstate highway system. It can be assumed that it will be used in other areas.

When conversion comes in legal and survey matters, "metes" will remain in degrees but "bounds" will be in meters. Conversion would be relatively easy in rectangular survey states. And when conversion does come, the prior and current *uses* of plats will not be disturbed.

Under either survey system, especially in cities and housing subdivisions, lots are laid out in rectangles in order to permit the orderly construction of buildings and other land developments. Once these plats or drawings are completed, perpetual use is made of them by the business person, the citizen, and the lawyer. This is true in metes and bounds as well as government survey states. It is helpful to have a working understanding of plats, how they are created, what they disclose, and how they are used.

Who Creates Plats?

It has been the practice since the earliest days of colonial exploration to run and record "surveys." This was first done in the settlements for the purposes of laying out streets and lots. Later, rough surveys were made during the exploration of the interior of America. The hardships of the early survey crews can well be imagined as they toiled in the vast wilderness of the new nation, doing battle with the elements, wild beasts, and inadequate equipment. These early surveys were crude by modern standards, and yet when viewed in light of the times in which they were made, were amazing accomplishments. The surveys were reduced to drawings, often crude and frequently showing a colony extending far beyond its true boundaries. One early survey pictured California as an island! In time they were revised and improved and became very accurate.

Today, as surveyors run lines on city lots or acreage for developments, they reduce their work to plats or maps which are placed to use by those who have need for them.

What Do They Disclose?

First, the typical plat carries a "scale" as illustrated in Figure 24-4. By this scale, careful measurements may be made on the plat itself, and preliminary estimates can be made in business and personal affairs.

Example of Use.   Assume that Executive X has an option to purchase an industrial tract of land that measures 100' × 200'. X needs to construct a warehouse that will contain 12,000 square feet. At the same time X must meet zoning requirements as they relate to width of side yards and off street parking. Can X construct a building that meets the business requirements and at the same time meet zoning requirements?

FIGURE 24-4

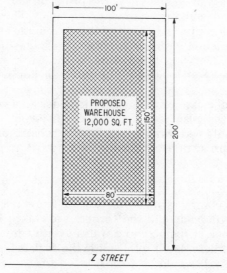

A helpful way to proceed is to create a scale drawing of the tract of land. Then a drawing of the building can be made to the same scale on a separate piece of paper. (See Figure 24-5.)

In this way, the plat can be tested against the zoning requirements by placing a simulated building upon the plat.

After this is done, an appointment should be made with the proper

FIGURE 24-5

|← 100' →|

PROPOSED
WAREHOUSE
12,000 SQ. FT.

180

200'

80'

Z STREET

Scale: $\frac{1}{2}'' = 40'$.

city official and at that meeting, the zoning requirements can be reviewed. If violations will probably occur, the plan can be changed to comply.

While the business executive is quite able to proceed without the assistance of counsel, if the application is turned down arbitrarily and without good reason, legal advice should be sought.

More on the Plat

The plat discloses the width of street right-of-ways. Many persons have been surprised to find that part of what they believed to be their front yard was in fact the street. The size of adjoining lots is set out. The "legend" names the engineer and the date of the survey, providing a source of additional information. In some instances – but not all – a plat may disclose buried gas and water lines as well as power lines and other matters that burden the land. However, most of these matters will be uncovered in the "chain of title." Once a plat is completed, it is usually recorded in the county where the realty is located. The recording serves two purposes: it gives notice of what is found on the plat and it serves, in most states, as a "dedication" of the streets. This means that the public can rely upon the streets remaining located as identified. Once a plat is on record, it is indexed so that it may be found by those who are interested. Plats are indexed in the name of the subdivision and are found in indexes under "plats" or "maps."

How Are They Used?

Plats serve many useful functions and the business person and citizen make frequent use of them. They are used in real estate developments, investments, and home construction. They are of perpetual interest to bankers, investors, and others. They are a principal source of information for taxing authorities and governmental agencies. They provide the cohesion by which a community may be structured into an orderly pattern so that it may function with a minimum of disputes between property owners. In short, plats are the picture of the earth and its divisions, available for use by all who are interested in finding out what they contain.

However, a real estate plat standing alone does not complete the picture of the land. One also needs to know the history or "pedigree" of the land and it can only be obtained from a title "chain" or "abstract" that sets forth the chain of title and related data.

CHAIN OF TITLE

Assume that A contracts in writing to sell B one acre of vacant land for $5,000. A survey is made and the corners are staked by the engineer. B takes a close look at the acre and walks over it carefully. Everything appears to be in order. May B safely close the deal and take title to land? Some reasons why B would be foolish to do so include the following: (1) A may have borrowed money against the land and someone else holds security in it; (2) there may be judgments of record against A that would be liens (encumberances) against the land; (3) the mineral rights may have been sold in prior years and someone else has the right to enter the land for drilling or mining purposes; (4) there may be restrictions (outside of zoning) upon the use of the land; (5) there may be easements, buried pipe lines, and other burdens that would prevent B from using the land for the purpose for which B is buying it; (6) taxes or paving assessments may be unpaid; and many other things may burden the land.

FIGURE 24-6

January 15, 1976–

PRELIMINARY TITLE REPORT

To: The Farmers' and Merchants' Bank
        466 High Street
        Dixon, Illinois

SUBJECT: Proposed Conveyance to Deward B. Wilson
          Lots Nos. 13 and 14, Beauty Terrace Addition

I have examined the records in the Office of the Clerk of the County Court of King County, insofar as they are correctly indexed up to 11:10 A.M., June 1, 197– and submit the following report:

Chain of Title

1. Subject property was acquired by John W. Kiles, who made the following conveyances: On September 5, 1902, John W. Kiles and wife conveyed Lot No. 13 to D. C. Coffman by Deed of record in said Clerk's Office in Deed Book 68 at page 462.

2. On April 23, 1924, D. C. Coffman, single, conveyed Lot No. 13 to C. I. Saffel by Deed of record in Deed Book 197 at page 158.

3. On the same day, April 23, 1924, Alex C. Hoffman, single, conveyed to C. I. Saffel, ". . . that certain parcel of ground located in the Fourth Ward of the city of Dixon, and being a section of Lot No. 14, in Block 'W,' in the Beauty Terrace Addition, 10 feet wide, off of the West side entire length, extending from Stewart Street to Lorentz Avenue of the lot above named." This deed is of record in Deed Book 197 at page 159.

4. On February 17, 1941, C. I. Saffel and Anna C. Saffel, husband and wife, conveyed Lot No. 13 and the 10 foot strip of Lot No. 14 to Frank Fisher, Jr. by Deed of record in Deed Book 313 at page 451.

5. On July 30, 1902, John W. Kiles and wife conveyed Lots No. 14 and 15 to D. C. Coffman, by Deed of Record in Deed Book 68 at page 459.

6. On November 9, 1912, D. C. Coffman, widower, conveyed Lots No. 14 and 15 to Alex C. Hoffman, by Deed of record in Deed Book 123 at page 120, the description of the Lots being: "All those two certain lots or parcels of land, situated in said Fourth Ward of the city of Dixon, fronting 120 feet and 1 inch on Lorentz Avenue and 137 feet and 6 inches on Stewart Street, and being known and designated as Lots Nos. 14 and 15 in Block "W" in North Dixon as laid out and surveyed for J. W. Kiles and Russel L. Morris Civil Engineer, and being the same real estate conveyed to the said grantor . . ." (As set out above in item 5.)

FIGURE 24-6 (continued)

---

7. Alex C. Hoffman then made the conveyance of the 10 foot strip as set out in item 3 above.

8. Alex C. Hoffman died testate and his holographic will was admitted to probate on May 24, 1941, after being properly attested to by two witnesses. The pertinent part of his Will reads as follows: "It is my wish that all of my possessions both real and personal be given to my wife Nellie Weltner Hoffman . . ."

9. On February 5, 1946, Nellie Weltner Hoffman, widow, conveyed to Frank Fisher, Jr., Lots Nos. 14 and 15, excepting, however, the 10 foot strip of Lot 14 conveyed to C. I. Saffel as set out in item 3.

10. The conveyances placed title to Lots Nos. 13 and 14 and 15 in Frank Fisher, Jr. On July 10, 1953, Mr. Fisher and wife conveyed Lot No. 15 to Frank K. Repair by Deed of record in Deed Book 499 at page 1.

Land Books

Subject property is assessed on the Land Books for the Fourth Ward of the city of Dixon for 1976 as follows:

>Fisher, F. Jr. 4th Ward
>Bl. W. Pt. 14, Stewart Street
>Bl. 2, 13, Pt. 14 Beauty Terrace

Assessed Value

This land is assessed at $520 and the building at $6,630, the assessments being 50% of the appraised value.

Prior Taxes

Taxes have been paid on the property since 1936. However, part of Lot 14 was sold to the State in 1928, in the name of Alex Hoffman, and Lot 13 and part of 14 were sold to the State in 1930 in the name of C. I. Saffel. All back taxes have been paid.

Current Taxes

Taxes for both halves of 1975 have been paid. Taxes for the first half of 1976 have not been paid. The fire fee must also be paid for the first half of 1976 at the rate of 30¢ per $100 assessed valuation on the building at $6,630.

Plat

A plat of subject property is of record in said Clerk's Office in Deed Book 195 at 276½. This plat is not the original as stated on the plat.

Reservations

In Deed Book 68 at page 459, as set out in item 5 above, the Grantors reserved the right to exempt certain lots in the Addition from the building restrictions that are contained in the Deed as set out in the following item.

It is imperative that B obtain the "pedigree" of the land before purchase. This is done by a "title search" by a lawyer hired for that purpose. A title report made to a bank that is contemplating lending Deward B. Wilson $20,000 with which to purchase the property described is shown in Figure 24-6. The report speaks for itself.

FIGURE 24-6 (concluded)

Restrictions

In Deed Book 68 at page 459, the following prohibitions were set out on the use of said Lots: "No slaughterhouse, smithshop, forge, furnace steam engine, brass, nail iron or any other factory, manufactory of gun powder, glue, varnish, vitriol, ink, turpentine, tannery and so on. No house to be constructed less than 2 stores and neither story to be less than 9 feet in height the foundation to be of solid stone brick or tile all the way around said building roof to be either slate or tile with at least three gables, house to have at least eight rooms square box cornice with gutter on top of same, and that he [Grantee] will not erect without the written consent of the grantor herein any dwelling house or building nearer than 20 feet to any street or pavement nor any barn stable or other outhouse on said Lot." There are other restrictions in the Deed that are unimportant at this time, but attention is called to them just the same.

Out Conveyances

On June 16, 1944, as found in Deed Book 352 at page 450, Joseph M. Smith and wife and Frank Fisher, Jr. and wife made the following conveyance to the City of Dixon ". . . do grant and convey unto the said grantee a right of way for a sewer line or sewer lines along the line dividing lots Nos. 12 and 13, in Block W, of the North Dixon Addition, known as Wiles Hill, situate in the Fourth Ward of the City of Dixon" . . . said Frank Fisher, Jr. and wife being the owners of said Lot No. 13. Said sewer line or lines shall extend from Lorentz Avenue to Stewart Street; and together with said right of way the said grantee shall have the right to go on, upon, under and over said land for the purpose of constructing, maintaining, repairing, and replacing said sewer line or lines."

Liens

None of record

It is my opinion that, subject to the matters set out above and below, Frank Fisher, Jr. and wife have good and marketable title to subject real estate, subject to the following:

1. The rights of any tenant in possession.
2. Those items above.
3. What a visual inspection of the premises would disclose.
4. An accurate survey.
5. The correctness of the records in said Clerk's Office.

Dated at Dixon this 1st day of June, 197–

s/s John Eagle
John Eagle
Attorney at Law

In review, the true picture of real estate requires four things: a visual inspection, a survey, a plat, and a title report. In the commercial setting, a survey might not be needed in the case of a building that had been constructed many years ago. But where construction is contemplated, a survey is mandatory.

Turning from the "picture" of real estate, it is helpful to become acquainted with the basic ways by which real estate may be acquired. There are three principal documents by which one may acquire real estate: by deed, by lease, and by will. The deed and lease are the most common realty documents encountered in business.

ANALYSIS OF A DEED

A deed is an instrument executed under formalities whereby title to real estate is transferred from one person or firm to another person or firm. The deed may convey the entire estate; if so, it is called a "fee simple" deed; or, it may convey less than all of the estate. For example, the mineral rights may be reserved. A deed contains within it certain legal promises called "warranties."

Warranties

A deed may warrant the title of the property to the buyer and all those who succeed the buyer in title. This would be a "general warranty" deed. The grantor in a general warranty deed covenants (promises) to defend the title to the property against the claims and demands of all persons forever. The warranty runs from the grantor and the grantor's heirs and personal representatives to the grantee, the grantee's heirs, personal representatives, and assigns. A "special warranty" deed is one in which the grantor warrants the title to the buyer only. In a special warranty deed the grantor covenants (promises) to defend the property against the claims and demands of the grantor and all persons claiming by, through, or under the grantor. But the warranty runs only to the buyer or buyers. A third type of deed in wide use is the "quit-claim" deed. It is used to clear title and often the one making the conveyance has no legal claim in the land. This type of deed is usually made without any warranties at all — or at best, "a special warranty."

All or Part?

A deed conveys whatever interest is the subject of the deed, even though the interest is less than fee simple. For example, the grantor may convey coal that underlies a tract of land together with mining rights, even though the surface is owned by others. Or, a conveyance may be of the surface only where others have title to all minerals under the land plus the right to remove them by drilling or mining. (Review Figure 22–1.)

Form of a Deed

A deed follows standard form and the one analyzed below would be satisfactory to convey title to property in Virginia, West Virginia, and most states. It is divided into it's main parts.

THIS DEED, Made this 9th day of December, 1975, by and between John Smith and Mary Smith, husband and wife, Grantors and parties of the first part, and John Eagle and Elizabeth Eagle, husband and wife, Grantees and parties of the second part.

This is the "parties clause" of a deed. The Grantors (the persons granting the property) are husband and wife. If John Smith had this property conveyed to him individually, the signature of his wife would still be required since she has "dower" interest in the property by virtue of their marriage. Dower is a provision in the law that provides a widow the use of the lands of her husband for support and maintenance where he dies without a will. Dower, by common law, consisted of a life time interest of one third of the lands of which the husband died "seized." "Seisin," at common law, imported a feudal investiture of title by equitable possession. It has the force of possession under some legal title or the right to hold.[1]

If Mary Smith failed to join in this conveyance, she would maintain title to her dower interest in the property described and a defect would exist in the title received by Mr. and Mrs. Eagle.

Consideration Clause

WITNESSETH: That for and in consideration of the sum of Ten ($10.00) Dollars and other good and valuable consideration, receipt of all of which is hereby acknowledged . . .

This is the consideration clause. Traditionally, an amount less than the actual sum is set out, and undoubtedly the practice had its origin in the rule that consideration does not have to be adequate. In law, consideration is not treated as the inducement to a contract, but the price which causes a party to enter into a contract. It contemplates something of value between the parties. It should not be confused with "motive" or "inducement." Inducement moved Mr. and Mrs. Eagle to buy this property, but "consideration" is what they gave for it. At common law, one dollar was sufficient to support the conveyance of property worth thousands of times that value.

Words of Conveyance

. . . the Grantors, John Smith and Mary Smith, husband and wife, do grant and convey onto the Grantees, John Eagle and Elizabeth Eagle, husband and wife, to have and to hold . . .

These are the words of conveyance which operate to set title over to the Eagles. The last five words are called the "Habendum Clause."

The Warranty

. . . with covenants of General Warranty . . .

This deed is a "general warranty" deed because those words are used.

Survivorship

. . . jointly and equally with the right of survivorship as provided by the laws of this state, all of which is done at the request of the Grantees . . .

---

[1] *Ford* v. *Garner*, 29 Ala. 603 (1900).

By virtue of this provision, Mr. and Mrs. Eagle hold title jointly and equally and, not as "tenants in common." Upon the death of either, the property vests in the survivor just as though it had been conveyed to the survivor in the beginning. In most instances, a husband and wife will take title in this manner. Otherwise, if they were "tenants in common," upon the death of one, that person's interest in the land would pass to the deceased person's heirs.

Description

> ... the following real estate, together with the improvements thereon, situate, lying, and being in Morgan District, King County, Typical State, and more particularly bounded and described as follows ...

Here would follow a legal description of the property which could be by block and lot number or by metes and bounds, depending upon the survey system in use. The attorney will draft the description and will use prior deeds as a guide.

Usually the deed contains mention of restrictions or reservations contained in prior deeds. However, if mention is *not* made, Mr. and Mrs. Eagle will still be bound by reservations or restrictions contained in the chain of title. They are on "constructive notice" of the facts.

The True Price

> ... DECLARATION OF CONSIDERATION. Under the penalties of fine and imprisonment as provided by law, the Grantors certify that the total consideration for the property herein conveyed is Fifteen Thousand ($15,000) Dollars ...

It is a legal requirement in some states that the true price be declared within the deed or by a separate certificate attached to the deed. This is called a "Declaration of Consideration" and gives one a means of finding out what was paid for realty.

Signatures

> WITNESS THE following signatures and seals:
>
> <u>s/s John Smith</u>   (SEAL)
> John Smith
> <u>s/s Mary Smith</u>   (SEAL)
> Mary Smith

Acknowledgment. Some states require that the name and address of the person preparing the deed be placed at the end of the document. Following the signatures would be an acknowledgment taken before a notary public who would certify that the signatures of the grantors, Mr. and Mrs. Smith, were executed in the notary's presence. In England as well as in some of our states, the requirement of an acknowledgment has been abolished.

A LEASE

A companion document of the deed is the lease. While the deed serves to transfer title to realty, the lease is a "rental document." The one giving the lease is the "lessor" – the one to whom it is given, the lessee. A lease for less than one year is generally binding if made orally. If for more than one year, it must be in writing. Leases for "99 years" are not uncommon in the business community and almost have the legal effect of an outright conveyance. Following is a lease used in the rental of student apartments in Anytown.

THIS LEASE, Made this 3rd day of November, 197– by and between Virginia Anderson, Lessor, and John Student, Lessee.

WITNESSETH, That the Lessor, for an in consideration of the rents, covenants and agreements hereinafter contained, and on the part of the Lessee to be paid, kept and performed, has granted, demised, and leased to the Lessee, and the Lessee does hire from the Lessor, that certain Apartment No. 15 in the house located at 832 Gat Avenue, Anytown, together with the furnishings therein contained, said Apartment being located on the first floor.

TO HAVE AND TO HOLD the described Apartment onto the Lessee for a term of Twenty-four (24) months, commencing on the 1st day of December, 197–, and terminating on the 30th day of November, 197– or until terminated sooner as hereinafter provided.

AND the Lessee shall yield and pay to the Lessor, her successors and assigns, for the leased Apartment, the sum of One Hundred ($100.00) Dollars for the first 30 day period after this lease commences, in advance, and the sum of One Hundred ($100.00) Dollars for each successive month, in advance, payable to the Lessor on the 1st day of each month.

The Lessee has leased the herein described apartment for a student dwelling and agrees not to use the same for any other purpose.

The parties hereto further agree as follows:

1. The Lessee shall have in and out privileges by way of the front door of said dwelling house.

2. The Lessor shall pay gas, water, electric, garbage, and TV cable service and will furnish said Apartment.

3. The Lessee will carry insurance on his personal property in such amounts as to protect his interest.

4. If the Lessee must leave school due to any reason beyond his control, the Lessor will accept a 30 day notice in writing of intention to terminate this Lease.

5. The Lessee shall make a breakage deposit of Fifty ($50.00) Dollars in advance at the time of entering into this Lease, which sum shall be returned by the Lessor at the termination of this Lease, minus any sum expended to repair damage caused to the premises by the Lessee or his guests.

6. The Lessee shall keep the Apartment free of trash and other material so as not to create a fire hazard.

7. Upon the termination of this Lease, the Lessee shall vacate the Apartment and leave it in as good a state of repair as he found it including said furnishings, subject to normal wear and tear.

WITNESS the following signatures and seals:

<u>s/s Virgina Anderson</u>   (SEAL)
Virginia Anderson
<u>s/s John Student</u>   (SEAL)
John Student

Leases of this type would not be acknowledged because it is not customary to place them on record. Commercial leases, however, are normally notarized and placed on record because they are for long time periods such as five or ten years, or longer.

Occasionally a *"last will and testament"* becomes important in the commercial setting, particularly if commercial property is transferred by that document.

It must be recognized that personal property is also transferred by a will.

Once a will is admitted to "probate," it is placed on record and becomes part of the chain of title of real estate transferred by it. At that point it has many of the characteristics of a deed.

ANALYSIS OF A WILL

As the will is examined, keep in mind that it is an instrument by which real estate may be transferred—but it does not become legally operative until the death of the "testator" occurs:

> I, Jane Hutchinson, of 1008 Pineview Drive, Anytown, King County, Typical State, and a resident and citizen of Typical State, being of sound and disposing mind and memory, and desiring to make such disposition of my worldly estate as I deem best, do hereby make, publish, and declare this to be my Last Will and Testament, hereby revoking any and all former Wills and Codicils by me at any time heretofore made.

The above paragraph identifies the testator and contains preliminary matters.

> FIRST: I do hereby nominate and appoint my husband, James Hutchinson, a resident and citizen of Typical State, to be the Executor of this, my last Will and Testament, with full power and authority to execute the same according to its true and intended meaning, and having perfect confidence in his judgment and integrity, I direct that he shall not be required to give security.
>
> PROVIDED, HOWEVER, that if my Executor is unable or unwilling to serve, or predeceases me, then I hereby nominate and appoint Daniel J. Brown, Route 1, Sunset, Other State, as my Executor, with full power to execute this, my last Will and Testament, according to its true and intended meaning, I direct that said Executor shall not be required to give security.

In this paragraph, the executor and alternate executor is named and the decision on bond is made. Either will serve without bond, meaning that they will not be required to post bond before they assume their duties.

> SECOND: I direct that all my just debts, funeral expenses, and the costs of the administration of my estate be paid by my Executor out of the moneys coming into his hands and available therefor.
>
> THIRD: I direct that all inheritance, transfer, estate, succession, or any other taxes assessed by the United States Government, or any State of the Union, or any legal political subdivision thereof, shall be paid out of my residuary estate.

These clauses dispose of two important matters: debts and taxes. Providing for these first reduces the inheritance and estate tax burden on the estate.

FOURTH: I do hereby give, devise and bequeath all the rest, residue and remainder of my estate, real, personal, mixed and of every kind whatsoever, wherever located, to my beloved husband, James Hutchinson, in fee simple, absolutely, to do with and to dispose of in any manner he deems best. PROVIDED, HOWEVER, that in the event my husband, James Hutchinson, shall die before me or simultaneously with me, then I do hereby give, devise and bequeath all the rest, residue and remainder of my estate, real, personal, mixed and of every kind whatsoever, wherever located, to my children, including any child or children born of my marriage subsequent to the date of this, my Last Will and Testament, to be divided evenly and equally between them, share and share alike.

If any of the children born of my marriage shall predecease me, and my husband, shall die before me or simultaneously with me, then it is my express wish and desire that my estate shall be divided evenly and equally between my surviving children and living issue of any deceased child share and share alike.

This section spells out who is to inherit and includes unborn children, the contingency of simultaneous death and also the contingency of a child being deceased leaving living "issue" (child or children).

As an example to explain this provision, if, at my death, my husband shall also be deceased, and I have 3 living children and one deceased child, and the deceased child leaves a living child or children, then one fourth ($\frac{1}{4}$) of my estate shall go to each of my (3) living children and one ($\frac{1}{4}$) of my estate shall go to the child or children of my deceased child; and if said deceased child leaves no living issue, then my estate would be divided among my living children each receiving one third of my estate.

By use of the explanation the testator has provided a means whereby a dispute may be avoided in the future between her heirs.

If my husband shall predecease me or die simultaneously with me, and if any of my surviving children are under the age of 18 years at such time, then it is my express wish and desire, and as provided by the laws of Typical State, I do hereby nominate and appoint as Guardian for said children, Daniel Hutchinson, Route 1, Sunset, Other State, and having perfect confidence in his integrity and ability, it is my express wish and desire that he be immediately placed into possession of the income payable to said infant children or be given advances upon the principal payable just as soon as my Executor shall determine such payment may safely be made, it being my express desire that the necessities of any of my infant children as beneficiaries under my Will be relieved without waiting for the administration of my estate.

If my husband shall die before me or simultaneously with me and I leave no children or deceased children with living issue, then it is my express wish and desire that my estate be determined and then divided as follows: An equal share to each of the living children of the brothers and sisters of Janet Hutchinson and James Hutchinson, share and share alike. For example, if there be 15 living children of said brothers and sisters, then $\frac{1}{15}$th share will go to each child.

These provisions take care of other contingencies.

> FIFTH: It is possible that I may decide to leave certain personal items of jewelry to certain friends. If so, I will leave a list in the envelope attached to this Will, in my own handwriting, and it is my express wish that my Executor shall treat this list as though it were contained herein. In no event will the supplementary list make mention of or dispose of any of my real estate.
>
> IN WITNESS WHEREOF, I have hereunto affixed my signature and seal to this my Last Will and Testament wholly contained on 6 sheets of paper, the attestation being contained on the 5th Sheet, and the affidavit on the 6th Sheet, and without interlineation, and on the signature line of this sheet, and the margin of the other sheets, I have affixed my signature for the proper identification thereof, all of which is done on this 1st day of May, 197-.
>
> <u>s/s Jane Hutchinson</u>   (SEAL)
>   Jane Hutchinson

The Fifth provision makes it possible for the testator to leave certain personal items without having to amend the will. The "witness" clause is the official statement of the testamentary act of the testator.

> The above signature of the Testator, Jane Hutchinson, was made, and the foregoing will acknowledged to be her last Will and Testament by the Testator in the presence of us, two competent witnesses, present at the same time; and we, the said two witnesses, do subscribe the Will on the date given below in the presence of the Testator, and of each other, all being present at the same time, and at the request of the Testator who was then of sound and disposing mind and over the age of Eighteen Years.
>
> Given under our hands this 1st day of May, 1976.
>
> <u>   s/s Emmett Fisher   </u>
> <u>   s/s John Polo   </u>

This is the "attestation clause" and it is self-explanatory. In most states, the attorney uses an affidavit so that the signatures of the witnesses may be notarized. The will may then be admitted to probate in "solemn form" — without the witnesses having to swear to their signatures. Some states require two witnesses, others three.

REVIEW QUESTIONS

1. Do you or your friends have a lease? What type is it? Is it in writing? If so, what does the lease contain?
2. Might there be a tax advantage of leasing commercial property rather than buying it? What might it be?
3. What type of survey is used in platting land in your state?
4. Use the drawing of the compass to plat a call of "S.10°E, 600'." Use the scale on the drawing and do it by laying a piece of paper over the drawing. (See Figure 24-2.)
5. True or False. A "rod" and a "perch" are types of fishing equipment.
6. What legal function does the "attestation clause" in a will perform?
7. True or False. A "warranty" in a deed is a promise.
8. State three times that a business person would want to have a survey made of business property.

9. The land surveyors made the change from the "rod" to the "foot." Would conversion to the "meter" be more difficult? (The rod was widely used at the turn of this century.)

10. True or False. The rectangular survey system is a matter of locating successively smaller squares within squares.

Words and Phrases

Write out briefly what they mean to you.

1. Lessor.
2. Abstract of title.
3. Declaration of consideration.
4. Restrictions.
5. Reservations.

Coverage:	The ways to encumber real estate.
What to Look for:	The legal effect of these procedures.
Application:	You are attempting to collect a debt due you. (Legal advice is in order in applying these procedures.)

25 Liens against Real Estate

There are many ways that a "lien" or claim can be placed against real estate. This in turn creates an encumberance which prevents the sale or transfer of that real estate. The business person should have an understanding of the legal procedures involved for three reasons: First, to avoid having these procedures used against the business persons own real estate. Next, one in business often has occasion to encumber the realty of debtors as a collection device. And third, the business person will want to voluntarily place liens against real estate as security for loans for use in the business.

BASIC LIENS

The legal procedures involved include mechanics or laborers liens, "lis pendens" notices, recording techniques, affidavits of claim, and voluntary liens created to secure loans.

Mechanics Lien (or Laborers Lien)

At common law there was no way that the seller of building supplies or the supplier of labor could reach the real estate of one whose property was improved by the materials or labor. The remedy of the supplier or laborer was limited to an action against the buyer of the goods or services. In many cases the buyer became insolvent or left the jurisdiction, leaving the person(s) whose property was improved free from the claims of others. This inequity was corrected by statutes which permit a lien to be filed against the real estate (land or buildings or both) that are improved by the materials or labor of others. For example, A hires B to construct a home. B purchases building supplies from C and hires D to do carpenter work. If B fails to pay C and D, they may file a lien against the realty of A, making A's property subject to the debts of B. Most states call such a lien a "mechanics" or "laborers" lien.

The remedy is harsh because an innocent person may suffer in the end. For this reason, the lien will be lost if it is not timely perfected. The time limit is measured from the time that the last improvement is made to the realty and is usually 60 to 90 days. Once a lien is perfected, time limits are imposed by statute in which the realty may be sold, with six months being representative.

The mechanics and laborers liens forces one who has construction work done to do two things: first, deal with reputable persons, and second, not make payment for labor and materials until certain that those who have money due are paid.

Lending institutions follow two practices when making construction loans. First, they determine that construction has not been started before their security papers are recorded (deed of trust or mortgage). Second, before disbursements are made to the borrower, they require proof that suppliers and laborers have been paid. If not, the lender will disburse directly to them.

Construction Lenders Technique.   Those who make loans for construc-

FIGURE 25–1

Courtesy of Elizabeth Ann
Paugh and the Farmers' and
Merchants' Bank.

tion purposes, will often send two employees to the construction site. One will pose at the site holding the front page of that days local newspaper. The other will then take a photo of the first employee. See Figure 25–1. This photo and the front page of the paper are filed with the loan papers and will constitute proof if needed later, that no construction had been started on that particular day. This will prevent one who begins work later at that site, from claiming a right to mechanics lien that is superior to the lender. (In a few states by statute, the lien *is* superior to the lender.)

Following is a sample of a mechanics lien. One copy is served on the landowner; one copy is posted at the construction site; and one is placed on record.

Copy Served on Landowner

NOTICE OF MECHANICS LIEN

To: Mr. and Mrs. Wilford Hartford
      No. Q-17
      Anytown, Typical State

YOU WILL PLEASE TAKE NOTICE THAT the undersigned King Company, Inc., a Corporation, by its authorized agent, H. J. Heart, President, under authority duly given, has furnished and delivered to Steven Egg, Next Town, Typical State, doing business at Egg's Plumbing and Heating, Anytown, Typical State, who was contractor for you for the installation of one 720 Boiler as was set out on Exhibit A, attached and made a part hereof by reference, which was installed in the following real estate for the improvement thereof, situated in the Village of Anytown, Valley District, King County, Typical State, designated as Lot No. Q-17, containing 5.494 acres as shown on a map entitled "Map of Anytown Community, Valley District, King County, Typical State, Resettlement Administration," recorded in the Office of the Clerk of the County Court of King County, Typical State, in Deed Book 236 at page 473, to which map reference is made for a more complete description of said land and including the improvements thereon, specifically the house in which said boiler was installed, and being the same real estate conveyed to Wilford Hartford, by deed from Golding Silver Company, a corporation, dated Sept. 1, 1954, of record in said Clerk's Office in Deed Book 315 at page 255, and the said materials were of the nature and were furnished on the date and in the quantity and at the price showing on Exhibit A, and repeated as follows: 1 each 720 PER Boiler (Sold October 30, 1976) at $2,000.

YOU ARE FURTHER NOTIFIED that the undersigned (by its lawful agent) has not been paid the sum of $2,000 and it claims a lien upon your interest in the real estate described above and upon the buildings, structures and improvements thereon to secure the payment of said sum.

KING COMPANY, INC., A
Typical State Corporation
By ____s/s H. J. Heart____
     By H. J. Heart, Its President by Authority Duly Given and by Corporate Resolution

---

Copy Posted at Construction Site

TYPICAL STATE,
COUNTY OF KING:

I, John J. O'Hara, a Notary Public in and for the County and State aforesaid, do hereby certify that H. J. Heart, President of King Company, Inc., A Corporation, whose name is signed to the above mechanics lien, has this day before me in my county, acknowledged that said mechanics lien was and is the act and deed of said corporation under authority duly given.

Given under my hand this 14th day of December, 1976.

My Commission expires April 12, 1980.

s/s John J. O'Hara

Notary Public

This Mechanics Lien was prepared by John Eagle, Attorney at Law, 1330 University Avenue, Anytown.

Copy on Record

TYPICAL STATE,   *RETURN*
KING COUNTY

Served the within Notice of Mechanics Lien upon the within named Mr. and Mrs. Wilford Hartford, by posting a copy of said Mechanics Lien at the usual place of abode of Mr. and Mrs. Wilford Hartford in King County on the 18th day of December, 1976, and by posting a copy at the front door of the courthouse, King County.

David K. Jansen, Deputy for   s/s Clyde Barton

Clyde Barton, Sheriff
King County, Typical State

SOLD TO: Egg's Plumbing and Heating, Anytown,
DATE OF SALE: October 30, 1976

Quantity	Catalog No.	Description	Price
1	720	PER BOILER	$2,000.00

RECEIVED BY: PAY THIS AMOUNT: $2,000.00
  Steven Egg

EXHIBIT A

One who permits accounts receivable to go uncollected for long periods of time, will lose the right to use the mechanics or laborers lien. In addition, as a matter of business reality, the accounts due are less likely

FIGURE 25–2

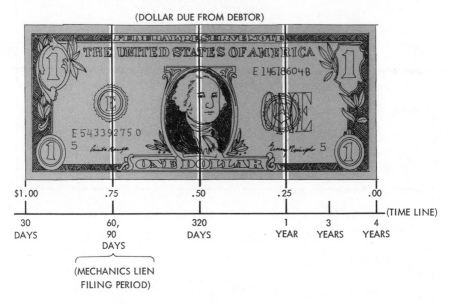

THE DOLLAR "RECEIVABLE"
(OR "WHERE DID MY DOLLAR GO?")

(DOLLAR DUE FROM DEBTOR)

to be collected at all the older they become. Figure 25–2 illustrates the legal as well as the business principle involved.

The mechanics lien cannot be used however, by one who sells goods or furnishes services to another, that are not related to real estate. In those instances, if other security was not taken by the seller or the one furnishing services, the remedy is limited to a civil suit against the debtor.

A Constitutional Taking? A mechanics lien does not deprive the debtor of the use of the property pending suit to enforce the lien. Thus the debtor is not deprived of property without due process and the lien is not unconstitutional.[1]

It is not uncommon for one who owes money to others for goods or services, to attempt to place real estate beyond the reach of creditors, and particularly at the time that suit is threatened. Most states, by statute, permit creditors to "tie up" the debtor's realty by the use of a "notice of pending litigation" — called the "lis pendens" notice at common law.

Lis Pendens Notice

The time lag between the time a suit is filed and the date a judgment is obtained may span many months. The states, by varying laws, permit a "hold" to be placed upon realty of the debtor "pending litigation." The laws require that notice of the suit be filed in the county where the real

---

[1] *Spielman-Fond, Inc.* v. *Harison's Inc.*, No. 73–1391, U.S. Supreme Court (May 1974).

NOTICE OF LIS PENDENS

KNOW ALL MEN that I, Jack Turner, Plaintiff in the hereinafter-styled cause, do give Notice of Lis Pendens by this memorandum filed with the Clerk of the County Court of King County, the 30th day of January, 1976 and state as follows:

There is now pending in the Circuit Court of King County, a Civil Action, the title of which is

Jack Turner	Plaintiff,	
v.		Civil Action #1300
Howard Hose	Defendant,	

the names of all parties to this Civil Action are Jack Turner and Howard Hose; the nature of the lien, right, or interest that may be enforced in the future against real estate owned by the Defendant Howard Hose will be in the nature of a judgment against Howard Hose arising out of the above Civil Action; the property to be affected by said judgment would be real estate owned by Howard Hose in his own right or jointly, with others, that may be located within the confines of King County, and expressly including real estate or other property acquired after the date of this Notice of Lis Pendens.

WITNESS my hand this 30th day of January, 1976.

s/s Jack Turner
Jack Turner

COUNTY OF KING, to wit:

I, John Eagle, a Notary Public in and for said county and state, do certify that Jack Turner, whose name is signed to the writing above, bearing date on the 30th day of January, 1976 has acknowledged the above Notice of Lis Pendens to be his own act and deed.

Given under my hand this 30th day of January, 1976.

My commission expires February 21, 1980.

s/s John Eagle
Notary Public

This Notice of Lis Pendens was prepared by
    John Eagle
    Attorney At Law
    1300 University Avenue

---

estate is located. One buying the real estate in the interim is subject to the outcome of the litigation. See the sample lis pendens notice.

The lis pendens notice gives the creditor time to file suit, obtain judgment, and levy execution against the real estate of the debtor.

A third technique available to creditors to assist in collecting bad debts, is to place the judgments on record.

Recording Judgments

The final pronouncement of a court is the "judgment" entered in favor of the prevailing party. It may be appealed from, but in the end becomes a final act upon which "execution" may be issued.

Executions are frequently returned by the sheriff or deputy marked "no property found." Sometimes this happens because the attaching officer "has a heart" and conveniently fails to find property of the debtor that is actually there. This means that the judgment creditor must look for other means to collect the judgment—or forget the matter. One way to turn a judgment into cash (although it may take years) is to record it in any country in which the judgment debtor may acquire realty in the future. If realty is acquired later, the judgment becomes a lien against the after acquired property. This is effective in practice and the careful creditor will see that "uncollectible judgments" are recorded as indicated. In all states, the life of a judgment is limited; ten years is typical, but it may be renewed for successive periods by reissues of the execution. Thus, the recorded judgment could remain in effect indefinitely.

CLAIMS BY AFFIDAVIT

Most states, by statute, permit a creditor to record an "affidavit of lien." This document contains the names of the creditor and debtor; a statement of how the debt arose and the balance due.

Once the affidavit is recorded, it becomes a lien against the real estate of the debtor in that it creates a "cloud on title." If an attorney doing a title search for a buyer confronts such an affidavit, the attorney will insist that a release be prepared and recorded. This forces the debtor to come to the creditor to obtain the release.

Caution is in order, however, in recording such an affidavit. For example, if the debt is controverted and it is later determined that the debtor did not in fact owe the sum in the affidavit, the creditor may be sued for damages. A good rule of thumb is to have the affidavit prepared and recorded by counsel.

All of the above methods of creating liens against real estate, have one thing in common: documents must be recorded in order to make these procedures work. Recording *other* documents will also create liens against real estate.

RECORDING OTHER DOCUMENTS

Frequently, one in business, as well as the citizen, will record legal documents that give certain legal rights, such as options to buy, contracts to buy, and powers of attorney. By doing this, others are placed on notice of what these documents contain. Therefore, the legal rights granted in those documents cannot be cut off by third parties. For example, A gives B a six month option to purchase certain real estate. If B does not record the option, A can sell the same real estate and pass good title to C because C will have no notice of the option. While B will have a cause of action against A for breach of contract, the real estate will be lost to B.

A final technique in constant use is the voluntary creation of liens against real estate to provide security for loans.

LIENS AGAINST REAL ESTATE AS A "SECURITY INTEREST"

Banks, savings and loans, credit unions, insurance companies, and other corporate and individual lenders, are quite willing to lend large sums of money to be used to purchase real estate. The principal concern of the lender is simply that the real estate (collateral) have enough value to cover the loan in the event repayment of the loan is not made.

How Is It Carried Out? First, the lender will have an appraisal made by a qualified person. The potential debtor will pay the cost of this appraisal. The appraiser will arrive at a market value by using "comparisons," square footage, or other form of real estate appraisal. After this, the lender will apply it's "percentage" to the appraised value. For example, many lenders will loan 80 percent of the appraised value of real estate. If the appraisal has been set at $50,000, the lender will loan $40,000 against the real estate. This percentage will vary from time to time and from lender to lender. It is sometimes as low as 60 percent— often in the 75 percent range and rarely over 90 percent. (Government-secured loans such as those made under the G.I. Bill, can be 100 percent loans).

This means that the borrower must make up the difference out of other resources. In our example, if the purchase price is $52,000 and the appraisal $50,000, the debtor-buyer must pay $12,000 plus closing costs out of other assets.

How Is the Lender Protected? After the decision has been made to make the loan, certain legal formalities must be met including meeting federal disclosure requirements. (See Chapter 35). The buyer will "tie up" the real estate by contract or option if this has not already been done. Next the buyer will have counsel make a title search or will purchase title insurance or both. The lawyer will then prepare the legal papers. (See Index for further information on contract, option, and title search.)

At the Closing. A date is set to "close" the transaction. The sellers will deliver the deed to the buyers, and the buyers will sign a note covering their obligation to the bank. (See Figure 29–4 for an example). The buyers will sign a deed of trust or mortgage creating a lien in favor of the lender and against the real estate. Truth in Lending and Real Estate Settlement Procedures Act disclosures will be made (see the Index) and other items will be disposed of. If new construction is involved, steps will be taken to protect the lender and the buyers as discussed previously.

Closing Statement. A statement of the closing will be prepared in advance and once the mathematics are correct, the lender will disburse the funds.

Who Is Paid What? Attorney fees and costs of the seller will be paid out of proceeds including realtor's fee. (The buyers will normally pay their legal costs direct.) Prorated taxes will be paid to the buyers. Thus when the taxes come due later, the buyers will pay them for the full year in which the transaction was closed. The sellers may owe the lender money on a previous obligation—often the obligation by which the real estate was purchased originally. The lender will pay this to itself. If there are other liens of record against the realty, such as those discussed, these must be paid and releases obtained. Recording fees will be paid out of proceeds. The balance, which has shrunk considerably by now, will be paid to the sellers. Counsel will record all documents and give the bank and the buyers a final title report certifying that the "realty is free from all liens or claims."

Where Are We Now? The buyers now have all of the rights and duties of real estate owners subject, however, to the security interest of the bank. The sellers have been paid and all liens against the realty have been paid. The lender holds a "first mortgage" against the property. The buyers are bound to the lender under the terms of the note.

The bank may keep the note and receive the payments from the buyers, or it may negotiate the note and assign the mortgage to others. In this event, the buyers will make their payments to the new holder of the note. This latter activity is known as "wholesaling" or "warehousing mortgages."

In the event of default, the owner of the note may order the real estate "foreclosed." This means that the realty will be sold at public sale. The proceeds will be applied in payment of the note and costs of foreclosure. If there is an excess after foreclosure sale, it will be paid to the makers of the note.

REVIEW QUESTIONS

1. Real estate can be burdened legally in many ways. Name one reason why it is susceptible to this.
2. Name three *legal* reasons why accounts receivable shrink in value as time passes. What effect does inflation have?
3. Name two reasons why construction lenders must use care in making their loans.
4. A mechanics lien notice must be recorded. Why is this true?
5. What practical effect does a notice of pending litigation have upon a prospective buyer?
6. A recorded judgment has stronger legal effect than one that is unrecorded. Why is this so?
7. Explain the legal effect of recording an affidavit that states that another owes you money.
8. What is an "execution"? How can it be used to keep judgments alive?
9. True or False. Mechanics liens are available in almost all types of sales situations.
10. Why is it conceded that the mechanics lien is a "harsh" remedy?

Words and Phrases

Write out briefly what they mean to you.
1. Levy of execution.
2. Recording judgments.
3. Lis pendens.
4. Keeping judgments alive.
5. Photos of construction sites.

Coverage:	The ways in which the use of real estate is controlled.
What to Look for:	The nature of controls that can be placed on realty.
Application:	Think in terms of buying real estate and what you must look for. The controls are often unknown in fact, even to those who own the realty controlled.

26 Control of Real Estate

Each parcel of land upon the earth is unique because no two parcels are the same. Because of this fact, a conflict often arises between opposing interests as they relate to the same parcel of land. For example, a farmer wants to plant corn in a field across which the state wants to construct a highway. Or a rancher wants to pasture animals in a field that a homeowner nearby wants unused. Or A wants to build a service station between the expensive homes of B and C — and B and C object strenuously.

Because of conflicts such as these, it has long been a policy of the law to allow controls, restraints, or restrictions to be placed upon realty. The manner in which these controls come into being depends upon who exercises the control. Control over land can arise by acts of government, by use of the contract, and by the "use" of the land itself.

BY GOVERNMENT

The federal and state governments have title to vast quantities of land in the United States. Much of it has been developed into state and national parks and to that extent is available for use by the public. But in the final analysis, when land is owned by government, its use is restricted and thus controlled, with the government setting the terms of its use. "This roadside park closes at 9 P.M.," is one example.

In addition to the right to own and control land, the federal and state governments have the power of "eminent domain" — the right to take private property for public use. This right, exercised frequently in road building and other governmental projects, is another control over land. That is, no private landowner is ever free from the contingency that land may be taken for public use. When such taking occurs, a fair price must be paid. If the landowner cannot agree with the governmental agency on price, the landowner is entitled to have commissioners or a jury set the price after hearing. Such hearings are called "condemnation proceedings." The most common way that land is controlled by government is through "zoning."

Zoning

In the early years of our nation, each property owner could (and did) use real estate in any manner that he or she thought best. In rural areas where farms were widely spread, little harm came from that system. But as America began going urban, with large concentrations of persons centering in the growing cities, it became desirable to control the use of land. The early attempts to do so, which came at the beginning of this century, were limited to restrictions imposed by landowners by contracts. As time passed, local and state governments began to place controls upon the use of land by means of statutory law which permitted "zoning" laws to be created on a local level.

What Is Zoning? In the simplest sense, zoning is the process whereby a city, borough or county, is divided into sections or districts, with limitations being placed upon the use of land within those districts.

The early zoning laws were met with cries of disapproval. And after the laws were enacted they were challenged as being unconstitutional— a taking of property without due process of law. However, while a few courts struck down the early zoning laws, most upheld them as constitutional under the "health, wealth, and welfare" clause of the U.S. Constitution or similar provisions of the state constitutions.

Today, by the use of districts or zones, factories can be grouped, retail stores and shopping malls can be centralized, and high-quality homes can be protected from intrusions by business that might be undesirable when located within such neighborhoods.

The sample zoning map in Figure 26-1 divides the city into five different districts. The R-1 districts are reserved for single family dwellings; R-2 for two family dwellings and R-3 for multiple family dwellings. The commercial zone is set apart as indicated. The "neighborhood business" zones reflect the businesses that existed before the zoning became law. They have the right to continue in business under certain conditions as will be discussed. This is true even though some of them exist in an R-1 zone. This does not mean that others could qualify for a new neighborhood business after the zoning law went into effect. In most instances, an application to open a neighborhood business in a residential area will be rejected by the city government. The applicant is then forced to seek a "variance" as will be discussed.

Once zoning is in effect, the use of land is restricted to the use specified—at least until an exception or "variance" is granted—and thus controlled.

Zoning Appeals. The typical zoning ordinance provides for a board or commission that has the power to hear applications for, and to decide if,

FIGURE 26–1

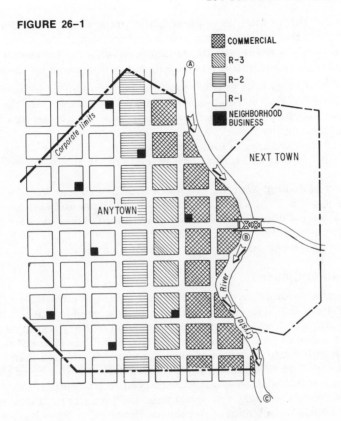

"variances" will be granted. If one wants to construct a duplex in a "single family" zone, that person must apply for a "variance." Or if one desires to construct a shopping center in an R–3 zone, *that person* must apply for a variance. It is usually done in the following manner.

First, an application is made for a building permit. After the application is reviewed by the person or board that has authority to grant or deny the permit, it is denied as "nonconforming." The applicant has now fixed the right to appeal to the proper board and this is done by a petition accompanied by payment of the required fees.

The board or agency appealed to advertises that the application has been received and sets a date for a public hearing on the matter. This is done by legal notice.

If there are no protests at the hearing, the variance is usually granted without further delay. If there are protests, then the burden is upon the petitioner to prove those facts that are required to entitle a variance to be granted as a matter of law. Typically the petitioner must prove the following:

1. That if denied the variance, petitioner is being denied a use that is enjoyed by others in the same area.

2. That if the petition is approved, the project will not reduce land values in the adjacent area.
3. That petitioner will provide the required off-street parking.
4. That congestion in the streets will not be increased by the project.

If the petitioner fails in this proof, the petition will be refused by the board. The decision of the board may then be appealed into the courts that have appellate jurisdiction over the administrative agencies of the state, county, or city.

Procedures such as these discussed above, give the zoning laws "flexibility" in that the zoning *can* be changed in the ways provided in the laws.

Theory of Zoning. Zoning promotes the "health and welfare" of the citizens since it results in a separation of industrial and commercial interests from dwelling areas. It tends to maintain values of property, particularly where single family dwellings are protected from the hazard of commercial interests developing on the lot next door.

Grandfather Clauses

Most zoning ordinances were enacted after the cities had been developed. Established land uses could not be destroyed by the new zoning laws because of the "ex post facto" provision of the Constitution. The problem was met by the enactment of "use" or "grandfather" statutes, which permit a use to continue even if located in an area restricted to another use. The neighborhood grocer often found that he or she was zoned in a residential area, but was allowed to continue in the present use. And he or she could sell or transfer the property to others and the right to continue in business remained. However, most state laws provide that if the use is discontinued for a specified period of time (one year is typical) then the old use is lost and zoning reverts to that of the surrounding area.

The chart, shown in Figure 26–2, is part of the zoning law of a midwestern city. It contains data of importance to one who is considering the purchase of land in that city.

FIGURE 26–2
Residential Uses and Requirements

	Type of Residential Use	
Requirements	*Single-Family Dwelling*	*Two-Family Dwelling*
District in which use is permitted	R1,R2,R3,B1,B2, & B3	R1*,R2,R3,B1,B2, & B3
Minimum lot size in square feet per dwelling unit in districts indicated	R1 ....7,200 R2 & B2 ....6,000 R3,B1, & B3...5,000	R1 ....5,000 R2 & B2 ....3,000 R3,B1, & B3...2,500

FIGURE 26-2 (continued)

Requirements	Type of Residential Use	
	Single-Family Dwelling	Two-Family Dwelling
Minimum lot width in feet in districts indicated	R1 .... 60 R2 & B2 .... 50 R3,B1, & B3... 40	R1 .... 70 R2 & B2 .... 50 R3,B1, & B3... 40
Maximum building height in feet in districts indicated	R1 & B2 .... 25 R2,R3,B1, & B3.................. 35	R1 & B2 .... 25 R2,R3,B1, & B3.................. 35
Minimum front yard in percent of average depth of lots in block	20 but not to exceed 25 feet	20 but not to exceed 25 feet
Minimum side yard (one) in percent of lot width†	10	10
Minimum side yards (both or two) in per-cent of lot width	20	20
Minimum rear yard in feet	20	15
Minimum ground floor building size in square feet in districts indicated	R1‡ .... 960 R2 & B2 .... 768 R3,B1, & B3... 672	R1 ....1,250 R2 & B2 .... 960 R3,B1, & B3... 672
Minimum number of parking spaces to be provided on the lot	One	Two
Maximum lot coverage in percent of lot	35	35
Vision clearance on corner lot	Yes	Yes

* May be permitted as a conditional use in accordance with the requirements specified in 19.

† One side yard shall be not less than ten (10) feet in the R1 district and not less than five (5) feet in all other districts.

‡ In an R1 district the minimum ground floor building size in square feet for a two-story building shall be nine hundred (900) square feet and for a one-story structure nine hundred and sixty (960) square feet.

An indirect governmental control is exercised by the cities through the requirement that "building permits" be obtained before repairs or new construction may be undertaken.

Building Permits

It is common for municipalities to have as a part of their zoning laws, a requirement that those who desire to construct buildings, or who want to repair old structures, must apply for a permit to do so. Such permits are "regulatory" in nature and give the city the opportunity to control the building of new structures as well as supervise repairs of old ones. Larger cities use a "building inspector" for this purpose, whose duties

FIGURE 26–3

BUILDING PERMIT

TO WHOM IT MAY CONCERN: ___March 16___ 19 _76_

    This is to certify that ___John Sterling___

_427 Mildred Street_____ (Avenue/Street), having made application and filed plans and specifications as required by the ordinances, and said plans and specifications conforming to the requirements of the Building Code of the City of Morgantown, and said application having been approved, a permit is hereby granted

h._im_ to ___remodel gasoline service station and convert to offices.___

Front wall of building to be _same_ feet from street line; distance to line of adjoining lots _same_ feet. Size of

building to be _____. Materials to be used __all new electric service, asphalt tile.__

Located on Lot No. __Pt. 25__ Block, _Old Town Plat, 1300 University Avenue_ (Avenue/Street)

in the __Third__ Ward of The City of Morgantown. Estimated Cost $__1,000.00__

        VOID After _September 23, 1976_.   THE CITY OF MORGANTOWN
Building Inspector must be notified twenty-four
hours before construction is started.   _Elmer W. Prince_
Telephone 296-4423   City Manager
    Permit Must Be Posted At Site Of Construction

                                                    Elmer W. Prince

---

include prepermit inspections, and visits during construction to see that building codes and other laws are complied with.

Where applications are made for permits to repair buildings that are unsafe, the permit is denied and the matter is referred to the proper state official for further action. The state has the power to condemn and often does so where deterioration has reached a point where the structure might endanger the lives of those who would occupy it. The state orders the owner to destroy the building and to remove the debris at the owner's expense. If the owner refuses to do so, the state will complete the destruction and sue the landowner for the costs.

The early challenges against building permits were dismissed by the courts, which held that building permits are within the constitutional powers of the cities. See Figure 26–3.

A recent and direct control on land by government is found in a 1969 federal statute.

Interstate Land Sales Full Disclosure Act[1]

It has been the practice of many land developers to misrepresent their offerings, usually by failing to disclose important facts such as swampy conditions, undermining, backfilling, and the like. In many cases, unsuspecting buyers have not learned about such defects until it came time to build upon the land.

In addition, many developers have assured buyers of such "fringes" as swimming pools, golf courses, and shopping centers which they do not intend to provide.

To counter such activities, Congress enacted the Interstate Land Sales Full Disclosure Act which became effective on April 28, 1969.

Under the act, anyone who offers for sale – in interstate commerce – 50 or more parcels or lots of unimproved land, must comply with this federal statute.

To obtain a summary of this law, send a self addressed and stamped envelope, to The Office of Interstate Land Sales Registration, Department of H.U.D., Washington, D.C., 20411. Request *HUD-15 F* (2), *August, 1970*. There is no charge.

Turning from governmental control of land, it is important to recognize that the individual person or private corporation also has the power to regulate the use of real estate.

RESTRICTION BY CONTRACT

Those engaged in real estate development will be intimately acquainted with zoning ordinances. Their activities will be geared to the zoning and they will work within the law or seek "variances." Outside of a city or town or a zoned county, the developer is at a disadvantage, particularly if engaged in the construction of quality homes or the sale of lots out of a quality subdivision. A lot may be sold to one who refuses to maintain the standards of the homes around the buyer, or may be sold to one who decides to erect a service station, or who decides to engage in the raising of animals or poultry on the property. The developer's "tool" is the use of "restrictive clauses" in the deeds of lots sold.

What Do They Say?

A typical restrictive clause in a deed does the following:

1. Establishes the location on a lot within which a house may be constructed.
2. Sets a minimum price to be paid for any house constructed.
3. Prohibits commercial interests.
4. Prohibits farming and animal or poultry raising.
5. Spells out the type of roof (slate, for example).

---

[1] Title XIV of Public Law 90-448, 82 Stat. 590, 15 U.S.C. 1701 through 1720, 15 U.S.C.A. Sections 1701 through 1720 (1973, Pocket Part).

6. Requires that a connection be made to the sewer provided.
7. Provides for changes in the restrictions by vote of all persons involved — or a percentage of them.

The Legal Effect

A purchaser of a home or lot so restricted must conform with the restrictions. Failure to do so will result in others in the subdivision going to court seeking an injunction to stop the prohibited use. The result is "private zoning" — and it works well. The guarantees afforded by restrictions in deeds help to maintain property values. If violations occur, the courts tend to uphold the restrictions or "covenants" (promises) under contract principles — although the facts will be examined carefully by the court in each case that comes before it as the *Marrone* case illustrates.

Marrone v. *Long et al.*[2] These two actions were brought by owners of lots in a subdivision to enforce restrictive covenants allegedly applicable to all lots in the subdivision but contained only in the deed to one of the plaintiffs. The cases were consolidated for trial. The parties waived a jury and stipulated the following facts:

Prior to June 22, 1965, E. B. Aycock and wife owned a 15-acre tract of land in Monroe Township, Union County. On that date they conveyed to plaintiffs Marrone a portion of the tract, a lot 200 feet x 200 feet, fronting on U.S. Highway No. 74 and a '60-foot wide proposed subdivision street.' The lot was described by metes and bounds without reference to map or lot number. The deed contained the following provisions:

THIS CONVEYANCE IS MADE SUBJECT TO THE FOLLOWING RESTRICTIONS, WHICH SHALL RUN AS COVENANTS WITH THE LAND, VIOLATIONS OF WHICH RESTRICTIONS SHALL BE EXPOSURE TO SUITS FOR DAMAGES BY ANY AND ALL ADJOINING PROPERTY OWNERS, who shall be defined as the Grantors herein or any of their subsequent Grantees who might acquire any portion of the original 15 plus acres tract:

1. Property shall be restricted to residential uses only, and no residence shall have more than one detached outbuilding.
2. Exterior construction shall be not less than 1,500 square feet of heated living area.
3. Exterior construction shall not have any exposed concrete, cinder or solite block.
4. No more than one dwelling improvement shall be constructed on any one lot, as originally sold by the Grantors herein.
5. No construction improvements shall be erected nearer than 30 feet to an adjacent street or road right-of-way, nor nearer than 8 feet to any other property line.
6. No sign of greater size than 3' x 5' shall be displayed for any purpose.

Thereafter, the Aycocks subdivided the 15 acres into streets and lots numbered 1 through 27, as shown by the 'Map of Boulevard Park,' surveyed September 27, 1965 by Ralph W. Elliott, R. L. S. This map was duly recorded in the office of the Register of Deeds on October 1, 1965. The land previously

---

[2] 176 S.E.2d 762 (1970).

conveyed to plaintiffs Marrone was designated on the map as lot No. 1. The remaining lots in the subdivision (2 through 27) were subsequently conveyed by deeds which contained no restrictive covenants and made no reference to the deed from Aycock to Marrone. On October 5, 1965 the Aycocks conveyed lots 7, 8, 9, and 12 to plaintiffs Charles F. Helms and wife. On the same day lots 2, 3, 4, and 5 of the subdivision were conveyed to Robert O. Helms and wife. On December 10, 1968, Robert O. Helms and wife conveyed lots 2, 3, 4, and 5 to defendant Charles E. Long. Only lot No. 5 is involved in this controversy.

Defendant erected upon lot No. 5 a residence containing approximately 1,000 square feet of heated living area. Plaintiffs, contending that the restrictions contained in the deed to Marrone apply to all lots in the subdivision and that defendant's dwelling is in violation of Restriction No. 2, which requires not less than 1,500 square feet of heated living area for a residence, instituted these actions. In each suit they seek damages and a mandatory injunction requiring defendant either to remove his building from the subdivision or to bring it into compliance "with the covenants and restrictions in effect upon the subdivision."

The parties agreed that the only question raised is whether the restrictions in the Marrone deed apply to defendant's lot. Judge Crissman ruled the restrictions inapplicable and dismissed the actions. Plaintiffs appealed, and, in a decision by Judge Vaughn and Chief Judge Mallard, the Court of Appeals affirmed the decision of the trial court. Judge Morris dissented and plaintiffs appealed as a matter of right to this Court.

The deed to plaintiffs Marrone imposed restrictions *only* upon the land *conveyed* to them and provided in clear language that any violation of those restrictions would subject the Marrones or their grantees to suit by E. B. Aycock and wife or any of their subsequent grantees who might acquire any portion of the original 15-acre tract of which the Marrone lot was a part. When the Aycocks sold the remaining lots in the subdivision by number, no restrictions were imposed upon any of them, either specifically or by reference.

Although the Marrone lot was described by metes and bounds and not by a lot number, the reference to a "60-foot wide proposed subdivision street" indicates that the grantors had already plotted the Boulevard Park Subdivision. The map of Boulevard Park, which was subsequently recorded, is part of the record. It shows the Marrone property to be the largest lot in the subdivision and to have a frontage of 200 feet on three public thoroughfares. No other lot provided such an attractive site for a filling station or some other business which might not have been welcome in the area. No other lot was so apt to be subdivided. Thus, it is plausible to assume that the grantors had reasons not applicable to the other 26 lots for restricting lot No. 1. In any event, had the grantors intended to impose the Marrone restrictions upon the remaining 26 lots, it is inconceivable to us that they would have failed to include them specifically. We concur in the reasoning of the majority opinion of the Court of Appeals.

Affirmed.

Caution

Buyers of lots in privately zoned subdivisions, must exercise a certain amount of care and caution. The reasons are illustrated in the following example.

A developer laid out a parcel of land as set out in Figure 26–4. As lots were sold, restrictions similar to those above, were used. In each deed, reference was made to the source of the title. All of the lots were sold except Lots Nos. 1 and 2. Homes in the $50,000 range had been constructed on all of the other lots.

It came as a shock to the homeowners there to discover that a franchised hamburger chain had purchased Lot No. 1 and was in the process of constructing a carry-out, quick food, restaurant.

As it turned out, the parcel that contained the restrictions had been obtained from one source, while the developer had obtained Lots 1 and 2 from another source. The parcel containing Lots 1 and 2 was not included in the parcel that contained the restrictions. The lot owners were not able to stop the construction of the restaurant.

FIGURE 26–4

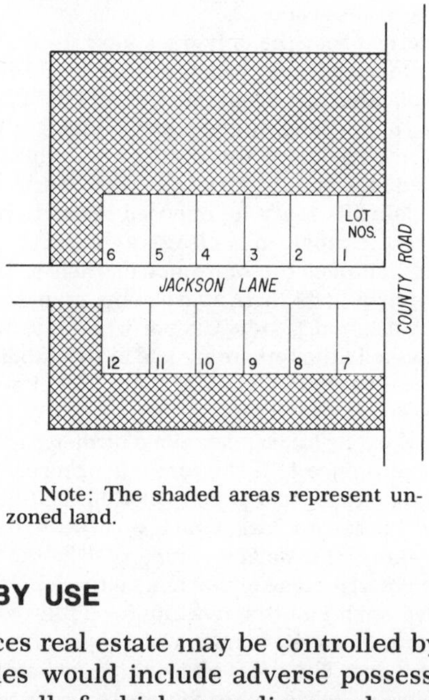

Note: The shaded areas represent un-zoned land.

RESTRICTIONS BY USE

In a few instances real estate may be controlled by the mere use of it by others. Examples would include adverse possession, easements, or the right of "user"—all of which were discussed previously.

Realty may be controlled by others in many ways. The homeowner, the business person, and the investor must recognize this simple fact and conduct their affairs in realty accordingly.

REVIEW QUESTIONS

1. Should an abstract of title contain detailed information about zoning restrictions? Why?
2. Why do you think zoning laws were challenged as being "unconstitutional"?
3. How would you describe "zoning by contract" to another?

4. What would "service business" consist of?
5. True or False. The zoning laws will be upset by the courts in the near future.
6. Can you see the legal problems that would confront the lot owners in the "franchise case" if they try to stop construction of the restaurant?
7. It was unethical for the developer to do what was done in the franchise case, but was it illegal?
8. Does the franchise case mean that a title report should include the status of *adjoining lands* in some instances?
9. What does it cost for a building permit in your home town? How can you find this out?
10. What building codes do you know of in your home town?

Words and Phrases

Write out briefly what they mean to you.
1. Private zoning.
2. Use.
3. Control of land.
4. Eminent domain.
5. Grandfather clauses.

Coverage:	The settlement of an estate.
What to Look for:	The procedural steps required to transfer property by will.
Application:	Think in terms of planning your own estate.

27 Administration of Estates—A Property Role

The purpose of this chapter is to examine in some detail how property is transferred from one to another by being included in the estate of a decedent.

The word "estate" ordinarily means all of the property that a person owns upon death including real and personal property, wherever located. It describes both the specific property as well as the extent of the ownership in that property, which can vary from absolute ownership to bare possession.

TESTATE OR INTESTATE?

One's estate comes into focus at death and the first question that arises is "did the decedent leave a will"? If so then the decedent died "testate"—that is, with a Last Will and Testament. If not, or if a will is not found, the decedent is considered to have died "intestate." The difference is often significant to the heirs. For example, one who dies intestate may leave a large number of heirs many of whom may be unknown. This causes serious problems in estate administration.

TAXATION OF ESTATES

Two types of taxation are encountered in the settlement of estates: "inheritance" taxes and "estate" taxes. The first is a tax levied against those who *receive* property by inheritance, the latter is levied against the estate itself.

Some states have both an inheritance and an estate tax, while others have only one. The federal government levies an estate tax on estates above the specified exemption.

Exemptions

The federal government allows a $60,000 exemption before the federal estate tax applies. In the states, the exemptions vary, but are usually based upon the relationship of the heirs to the decedent. For example, one state allows a $15,000 exemption for the wife or husband, a $5,000 exemption for the father, mother, and each child, and a $2,500 exemption for each grandchild.

Rates of Tax

The rates of tax vary with the exemptions and with the amount of the gross estate, and no attempt will be made to set them out here. However, the tax schedule from one state that has an inheritance tax will serve as an example: on all estates up to $50,000, (less the applicable exemptions) the rates are as follows: father, mother, husband, wife, child, stepchild, descendents of a child, 3 percent; brother or sister, 4 percent; all blood relations further removed, 7 percent; all others not entirely exempt, 10 percent of the taxable estate. On larger estates, the tax rate progresses upwards.

The federal rates will not be set out but they are quite high and can be as much as one-fourth of a taxable estate above $200,000.

Discounts are provided if taxes are paid promptly and penalties are provided if they are not.

ESTATE PLANNING

Because of the nature of estate taxation, it is essential that one have some idea of what one's estate is facing in taxes so that provisions can be made during lifetime for funds with which to pay these taxes. A good technique is to consult a Chartered Life Underwriter (C.L.U.) or other qualified person who can make an estimate of net worth and probable tax. One means of providing funds for estate taxes is to buy term life insurance for this specific purpose. If funds are not available on death, the estate is liable for the taxes and this may require liquidation of a business or sale of a home.

As one's estate grows, the need for the advice of experts in estate planning increases. The law permits us to take all steps necessary to minimize the tax burden. However, it may not be wise to defer taxation. Because when we defer taxes we may face higher rates later.

HOW IS AN ESTATE ADMINISTERED?

For purposes of discussion, let's assume the following facts: John S. Faulkner was a resident of Saulk County of a state that has an "inheritance" tax.

Mr. Faulkner's wife predeceased him, leaving her interest in their home, one vacant lot and all personal property to him. The wife's estate had been properly settled.

Several years back, Mr. Faulkner had created a "holographic will" (meaning that it was entirely in his own handwriting), leaving his estate equally to the following children:

William A. Faulkner,	son
James B. Faulkner,	son
Jerry C. Faulkner,	son
Samuel D. Faulkner,	son

Samuel was killed during the Korean War, leaving as *his* heirs, the following persons:

Nancy B. Faulkner,	daughter
Joanne C. Smith (now married),	daughter
Robert D. Faulkner,	son

Samuel's estate was not settled.

Due to an oversight on the part of John S. Faulkner, he did not change his will after Samuel's death.

John S. Faulkner passed away on the 21st day of January, 1974. At law, his heirs under the will were his three living sons and the wife and the children of the deceased son. Fortunately, the three children of the deceased son were all over the age of majority (18 in some states, 21 in others).

As of the date of his death, all of his assets, including bank account and saving account, became "frozen." In estate practice, this is a "holding" stage or time of inactivity. This is true because the banks will not release funds of the decedent once they learn of the death, and until someone qualifies to represent the estate, there is no legal way the estate can transact business.

Probate

In due course the will was tendered to the proper county official and entered into the records.

The will named William A. Faulkner as executor and provided that he serve without bond. After certain formalities, William received his "Letter of Administration." Examine Figure 27–1. With this "letter," William went to a local bank and opened an account in the name of the "John S. Faulkner Estate, William A. Faulkner, Executor." The funds in the decedent's checking and savings account were transferred into the estate account. The Executor now had the means of paying the debts and expenses of the estate which he proceeded to do.

At the time that William qualified as executor, he named three appraisers who then made an appraisal of Samuel's estate (see Figure

FIGURE 27-1

ESTATE OF James S. Faulkner

LETTER OF ADMINISTRATION

UNITED STATES OF AMERICA
COUNTY OF SAULK:

I, Tom Jackson, Clerk of the County Court of Saulk County, do hereby certify that William A. Faulkner was on the 26th day of January, 1974, appointed by the Clerk of this County Court as Executor of the Estate of James S. Faulkner, deceased, and duly qualified by taking oath prescribed by law, and by giving approved bond in the sum of One Hundred ($100.00) Dollars as provided by law.

NOW THEREFORE, be it known that said appointment is now in full force and effect and that full faith and credit are due and should be given to all the acts of the said William A. Faulkner as such Executor as well as in Courts of Judicature, as elsewhere.

IN WITNESS WHEREOF, I have hereunto set my hand and affixed this seal of the said County Court, at my office in said County, this 26th day of January, A.D. 1974.

SEAL
ss Tom Jackson
_____

27-2). An examination of the appraisal forms discloses the assets of the decedent. It is mandatory that all assets be listed and a value set upon them as of the date of death. If this is not done, the procedure may have to be repeated later to include the undisclosed assets. In practice, the appraisers have a tendency to keep the real estate values low believing this will assist the heirs. However, the error in this reasoning is this: by keeping the value low for estate purposes, the "basis" of the real estate is also kept low. This means that upon later sale of the real estate, the amount received above the basis is income which is always taxed at a higher rate than an estate.

In the state being discussed, a "Commissioner of Accounts" system is used. Under this system, the estate is referred by the county court to the commissioner who serves in the capacity of a "watch dog" as the administration progresses. One of the commissioner's first duties is to advertise the estate in the legal notices. Examine Figure 27-3. All creditors of the decedent must file their claims by the deadline. If they fail to do so, they will be excluded from the final settlement and the heirs will take the estate free from creditors claims.

In the estate being discussed, one creditor filed a claim for a note dated October 1, 1945. The Commissioner found that the note was barred by the statute of limitations and disallowed the claim.

Another creditor filed a claim for $100.00 for work done on the home of Mr. Faulkner prior to his death. The creditor proved this claim by a written contract and the commissioner allowed it. Estate claims must be "verified" – signed under oath.

FIGURE 27–2

NOTE:
No relative or immediate member of the family of the deceased should be named as appraiser to appraise estates. Appraisements must be impartial and based upon facts. All property including government bonds and treasury certificates must be appraised. *The appraisal must be completed and filed within sixty days after death.* If no property is to be reported under any particular appraisement item the word None should be entered. (In recording, omit these instructions and those at the bottom of the last page.)

A P P R A I S E M E N T

STATE OF

County of.....Saulk.., To-wit:

We, the undersigned, duly appointed appraisers, do solemnly swear that we and each of us will diligently, faithfully, and impartially seek to ascertain the true and actual value of the property, real and personal, of whatever character and wheresoever situate, including moneys, credits, investments, annuities, insurance policies, judgments and decrees for moneys, notes, industrial bonds, securities of the United States or of any State, County, District or Municipality, or of any foreign state or country, accounts receivable and all other evidences of debt whether owing to the decedent by persons or corporations in or out of the state,

and all tangible personalty of every character, or any interest therein, belonging to the estate of.....John S.............

.....Faulkner...deceased, and a late resident of......James.........district

.....Saulk County...............County,   ; and to place thereon, after careful examination, what, in our judgment, is true and actual value of each item of property so listed and examined, together with the aggregate value thereof, and to submit the same as our findings as provided by law.

Vera L. Watring.............Appraiser	Address.....128 Jones Avenue.....Fee $......00
Frank Fisher.............Appraiser	Address.....Route 1, Box 36,.....Fee $......00
Michael Paugh.............Appraiser	Address.....636 Madison Avenue.....Fee $......00
...............................Appraiser	Address.............................Fee $........
...............................Appraiser	Address.............................Fee $........

Subscribed and sworn to before me this.....30th.....day of.....January........................., 19.74..

John Eagle

....
My commission expires.............March 15,.............. 19.80.   Notary Public

---

INVENTORY

Item No. 1. **Real estate or any interest in real estate in this or any other state.**
   Do not extend values of out of State real property.

	Assessed Valuation	Appraised Valuation
House and lot, Lot No. 2, Block Z, North Hills Addition, Saulk County	$8,000.00	$16,000.00
Vacant lot, Lot No. 17, Block X, North Hills Addition, Saulk County	500.00	2,000.00
Totals	**$ 8,500.00**	**$ 18,000.00**

FIGURE 27-2 *(continued)*

Item No. 2	Tangible Personal Property of every kind.

Personal effects and household goods	$450.00
Total	**$ 450.00**

Item No. 3	Government bonds and securities of every kind. (Show date of purchase, serial numbers, etc.)

None	0.00
Total	**$ 0.00**

Item No. 4	Shares of corporate stock of every kind.

No. Shares	Certificate No.	Name of Company	Par Value	Market Value
None				0.00
			Totals $	**$ 0.00**

FIGURE 27-2 (continued)

Item No. 5	Money, certificates of deposit, notes, accounts receivable and all other evidences of debt. (Show dates of notes, etc.)	
	Checking Account, Farmers' and Merchants' Bank	$775.19
	Savings Account, " "	1,000.00
	Total	**$ 1,775.19**

Item No. 6	All other assets not hereinbefore mentioned including insurance payable to the estate.	
	Insurance payable to estate, Prudential Insurance Company Policy # 175839	$1,498.93
	Total	**$1,498.93**

Item No. 7	Gifts, Annuities, Jointly held property. Acquisition dates must be recorded. Name of Co-Owners and Blood Relationship.	Assessed Valuation (Full Value)	Appraised Valuation (Full Value)
	None		0.00
	Totals	**$**	**$ 0.00**

RECAPITULATION OF ALL PROPERTY, Excluding Item No. 7	$ 21,724.12
Item No. 1 Real estate or any interest therein	$ 18,000.00
Item No. 2 Tangible personal property of every kind	$ 450.00
Item No. 3 Government bonds and securities of every kind	$ 0.00
Item No. 4 Shares of corporate stock of every kind	$ 0.00
Item No. 5 Money, certificates of deposit, notes, accounts, etc.	$ 1,775.19
Item No. 6 All other assets not hereinbefore mentioned	$ 1,498.93
GRAND TOTAL, Excluding Item No. 7.	$ 21,724.12

IF DECEASED DIED TESTATE, COPY OF WILL MUST ACCOMPANY THIS FORM.
Will there be Federal Estate Tax Liability? ....

FIGURE 27–2 (*concluded*)

After diligently performing our duties as appraisers under the aforesaid oath, the foregoing is respectfully submitted as our report and findings for recordation in the County Clerk's office of said County, and a true copy to be transmitted to the tax commissioner

Given under our hands this...30.th.day of......January............., 19.74....

Vera L. Watring............................Appraiser   *Michael Paugh*...........................Appraiser

Frank Finder...............................Appraiser   ....Appraiser

DATE OF DEATH OF DECEASED......January 21, 1974......DID DECEDENT HAVE A WILL?......Yes........

NAME OF BENEFICIARY	Relationship	NAME OF BENEFICIARY	Relationship
William A. Faulkner	Son		
James B. Faulkner	Son		
Jerry C. Faulkner	Son		
Nancy B. Faulkner	Granddaughter		
Joanne C. Smith	Granddaughter		
Robert D. Faulkner	Grandson		

I hereby accept the foregoing as the true and lawful appraisal of all the assets of the estate of......John S.

Faulkner..., deceased.   Execut...or.........

(Signed) *William A. Faulkner*.........Administrat........

          William A. Faulkner

Address of fiduciary......1300 James Lane,.................................(......William A. Faulkner

                                                    TYPE NAME

I, ...Donald E. Price................... Commissioner of Accounts of....Saulk....................County,

, to whom the estate of......James S. Faulkner..., deceased, was referred, do hereby approve the foregoing appraisement of such estate.

Given under my hand this.....15th day of.........November...................., 19..74..

                               Donald C Price

                               Commissioner of Accounts

The appraisers should inquire of the executor or administrator and of members of the family whether there is any joint bank account, jointly held stocks, bonds, notes or other personal or real property held jointly by the decedent and any other person, with right of survivorship, and if the decedent made any gift or conveyance without adequate money consideration and whether he purchased any annuity payable to himself or any other person, and list every item in Item No. 7, giving the names of all parties involved, and the value of such items at the death of the decedent. The foregoing items are *not* part of the decedent's estate but they are required by law to be appraised.

Do not forward to State Tax Commissioner until Clerk has attested to recordation.

PLEASE TYPE NAME OF ADMINISTRATOR OR EXECUTOR UNDER THE SIGNATURE.

FIGURE 27–3

006230   June 23–30

CREDITOR'S NOTICE

To the Creditors and Beneficiaries of the estate of John S. Faulkner, deceased.

All persons having claims against the above estate, whether said claims are due or not, are notified to exhibit the same with the voucher thereof legally verified, to the undersigned at his offices on the Third Floor of Citizens Building, 265 High Street, Saulk County, on or before November 31st, 1974, otherwise they may by law be excluded from all benefit of said estate. All beneficiaries of said estate may appear on or before said date to examine any claims that may have been filed and otherwise protect their interests.

Given under my hand this 24th day of June, 1974.

Donald E. Price
Commissioner of Accounts

Calculation of the Tax

The status of the estate was now as follows:

Income

Real estate (house and vacant lot) (a buyer was found who was willing to pay this amount subject to proper settlement of the estate)............................	$18,000.00
Personal property..	450.00
Life insurance payable to the estate (If this insurance had been payable to a named beneficiary, it would not have been included)..........................	1,498.93
Savings and checking accounts	1,775.19
Estate...	$21,724.12

Expenses

Funeral expenses...	$2,000.00	
Commissioner of Accounts......................................	150.00	
Attorney fee..	298.00	
Creditor claim...	100.00	
Taxes, utilities on house...	51.00	
Total..	$2,599.00	
Taxable estate..		$19,125.12

The rate of tax was 3 percent since all of the heirs fell into this category. The exemptions of $5,000.00 for each heir cancelled the tax to the state and none was due. However, the tax form had to be completed, approved by the commissioner of accounts and forwarded to the state tax commissioner for approval.

After being satisfied that no tax was due, the state tax commissioner issued a release which was placed on record in the county where the real estate was located. Examine Figure 27–4.

FIGURE 27-4

RELEASE

OFFICE OF THE STATE TAX COMMISSIONER:

I, Charles H. Haden, II, State Tax Commissioner, pursuant to authority vested in me, do hereby certify that the Estate of John S. Faulkner, Saulk County, File No. 150447, William A. Faulkner, Fiduciary, is not subject to inheritance tax to this State for the reason that the estate is less than the exemptions allowed by statute, and hereby release any and all claim of this state against said estate by reason of inheritance tax.

Given under my hand this 24th day of February, 1975.

s/s Charles H. Haden, II
State Tax Commissioner

This Release was prepared in the office of the State Tax Commissioner by Charles H. Haden, II, State Tax Commissioner.

After the end of the period of publication, the executor prepared and submitted his "Final Settlement" to the Commissioner of Accounts. This settlement set forth the above figures and also specified that the estate was to be distributed as follows:

William A. Faulkner ($^1/_4$th) $4,781.28
James B. Faulkner ($^1/_4$th) $4,781.28
Jerry C. Faulkner ($^1/_4$th) $4,781.28
Heirs of Samuel D. Faulkner
  Nancy B. Faulkner ($^1/_3$rd of $^1/_4$th) $1,593.76
  Joanne C. Smith ($^1/_3$rd of $^1/_4$th) $1,593.76
  Robert D. Faulkner ($^1/_3$rd of $^1/_4$th) $1,593.76

The commissioner advertised by legal notice that the final settlement was presented for approval. No complaints or objections were filed and the estate became final.

The estate was now clear and the real estate was sold for the agreed $18,000.00. Distribution was made as above which closed the estate. This also closed the bank account and the executor was discharged from his duties.

It should be noted that estate representatives are entitled to a fee for their services–5 percent being typical, but the executor in this case decided against charging a fee. The appraisers also did not request a fee.

REVIEW QUESTIONS

1. Might there be a personal income tax reason for the executor in the Faulkner case refusing to charge the estate a fee of 5 percent? What is it?
2. A will standing alone, does not complete the "chain of title" in real estate. What other documents are required?

3. Explain why creditors should carefully screen estate notices in newspapers.
4. True or False. One should upgrade his or her will from time to time.
5. Explain why the bank would hesitate to release Mr. Faulkner's funds to a member of his family.
6. What would the estate tax have been if Faulkner's total net assets had been $25,000.00?
7. $50,000.00?
8. What problems might have arisen if one of Samuel's children had been under 18 years of age as of the death of John S. Faulkner?
9. If John Faulkner had owned corporate stocks in his name, why would the corporation's transfer agent refuse to transfer the stocks without a release from the state tax commissioner?
10. What is the difference between an "executor" and an "executrix"?

Words and Phrases

Write out briefly what they mean to you.
1. Estate administration.
2. "Freezing of assets."
3. Qualifying as representative of estate.
4. Appraisals.
5. Intestacy.

Coverage:	The basics of trusts.
What to Look for:	The distinction between contracts and trusts.
Application:	Think in terms of planning your own estate.

28 Trusts—A Property Role

At law, a "trust" is a "confidence" imposed by one person in another for some private or public purpose. A trust creates an "equitable" as distinguished from a "legal" interest in the property involved. That is, while the legal title remains in one person, giving that person absolute dominion over the property, the income and benefits from the property belong in whole or in part, to others. See Figure 51–1 for a diagram of a trust. The property in a trust can be real or personal or a combination of both.

A "SOPHISTICATED" DEVICE

In everyday financing, credit extention, risk – shifting, settling of disputes and other business and personal affairs, the primary tool is the contract. As a means of business organization, the laws of partnership and corporation are in almost universal usage. However, these tools are frequently too "coarse" for those situations that are too novel or "delicate" to be entrusted to them. This void is filled by the trust.

CLASSES OF TRUST

Trusts can be classified into the functions they perform.

A Vested Trust

This is a trust in which someone has an *existing* legal right to the subject matter of the trust.

An Executory Trust

Here, something must yet be done before one gains a vested interest in the subject matter of the trust.

An Active Trust

The trustee (the one who administers the trust) is not a mere depository for the property in question. Rather the trustee has active duties to perform. The duties are specified by the one who creates the trust.

Passive Trust

The trustee is a mere depository for the property of the trust and has no active duties to perform.

Support and Maintenance Trust

In this type of trust, the legal right to the property is vested in the trustee, but the beneficiary of the trust, called the "cestui que-trust," is entitled to have the rents and profit from the property.

Charitable Trusts

As the name implies, these are trusts created to benefit churches, the poor, medical societies, and other charitable organizations.

"Spendthrift" Trusts

Persons of wealth may hesitate to make large sums of money available to their children. This is true because of the danger of the younger person squandering the wealth or having it taken by others. The trust is often used to provide such beneficiaries with periodic payments out of the trust fund in order to avoid such contingencies.

Express Trust

This is a trust created by words that clearly demonstrate that there was an intention to create a trust.

Implied Trust

In these trusts, there was no expressed intention to create a trust, but one is created in *equity* to make certain that the ends of justice are met. Necessarily, only a court can imply a trust. Two common types of implied trusts are recognized: the "resulting trust" and the "constructive trust."

A *resulting trust* is one that arises when property is disposed of, but all of the surrounding circumstances make it clear that the proceeds are not to be enjoyed by the holder of the legal title.

Constructive trusts are those created by a court to prevent fraud or injustice that would otherwise arise.

These classifications should be kept in mind as the following material is covered.

How is an express trust created?

EXPRESS TRUSTS

Creation of. The seventh and eighth sections of the English statute of frauds required that there be a writing to prove the creation of an express trust in land. Many of our states did not adopt these sections of the old statute of frauds and therefore the trust can be oral in some cases, but most often will be in writing. All that is required is some pronounced intention of one person (called the "settlor") having legal title to property, to place that property in the hands of a second person (called the "trustee") to hold, administer, and distribute the property as indicated to some third person at stated times (called the "beneficiary" or "cestiu que trust"). There can be more than one trustee and frequently there are numerous beneficiaries. Trusts can be created by deed, by will, by writing not under seal and by word of mouth. It is not required that precise legal words be used. It is a matter of substance — not form.

Requisites of a Valid Trust

Legality. A trust must always be for a legal purpose because a court will not enforce a trust (or a contract) for an illegal or fraudulent purpose.

Certainty. The words creating a trust must be intelligible and capable of being understood. Before a court can bring a trust into effect there must be certainty in respect to the beneficiaries and preciseness in respect to the subject matter. If not, the trust will be void. A court cannot speculate or guess about trusts. Where there is serious doubt of the meaning of a trust, upon the death of the attempted settlor, the property will pass to the heirs of the decedent.

Statute of Frauds. At common law an express declaration of a trust was enforceable without a writing. While the English statute of frauds, as mentioned, required a writing, some states did not enact that section of the English law. Thus some oral trusts are valid and can be proven by oral testimony.

However, all modern trusts *should* be reduced to written form under advice of counsel — and upon competent tax advice.

Acceptance of Trust. Unlike a contract — there is no requirement that a trust be accepted by the beneficiary. In most cases the acceptance is presumed. (However, there *is* a contract between the donor-settlor and the trustee, for the benefit of the beneficiary.)

IMPLIED TRUSTS

An implied trust is one that has *not* been created by any express words or acts, but is created in equity by a court. This includes *all* trusts that do not arise by agreement of the parties.

Implied trusts arise by operation of law—not by the intention of the parties. Their principal function is to cover situations that could not otherwise be covered by law. They can usually be proved in court by the use of oral testimony. As mentioned, the most common types are the resulting trust and the constructive trust.

Resulting Trusts

The purpose of this type of trust is to give force and effect to the *presumed* intention of the parties.

For example, if A conveys land to B, but C in fact pays for the land, a trust results in favor of C.

Another example would be where A creates a trust for B, but due to uncertainty in parts of the trust, a partial residue or remainder of the trust property arises. By law, a trust will result in the residue for the benefit of A—or A's heirs.

A third example is encountered in those situations where the money of A is used unlawfully by B for the benefit of B. To illustrate, B, a collecting agent of A, uses $100 of A's money to purchase lottery tickets in the name of B. B wins $1,000,000. A trust results in favor of A, and A is entitled to the winnings.

Constructive Trusts

If A obtains legal title to property from B through undue influence, or other means, and A should not in good conscience have and enjoy the property, a court of equity will impress the property with a constructive trust in favor of B.

If a partner, in the scope of the partnership business, takes property in the partner's own name, a constructive trust arises in favor of the firm.

THE TRUST ESTATE

A trust estate can exist in any property, real, personal, and mixed that in the eye of a court of equity, has value. The property interest can be legal or it can be equitable.

If the form of trust property is changed-property traded for other property for example—and the new property can be traced, it will continue as the trust estate.

Characteristics of Estate

The law treats the trust estate just as though the trustee was the absolute owner of it. It can be sold, devised, and mortgaged. It can be taken by others by execution. This does not impair the trust however, because if these things occur because of a breach of trust, they will be ignored by a court of equity.

Liability for Debts

The trust estate is liable for all lawful debts incurred in the administration of trust, and can be levied against by execution as mentioned.

The estate must pay all lawful taxes levied against it. If the trust estate earns income, it must pay state and federal income tax where applicable.

Investments

A trustee, in most instances, has the legal right to invest trust funds, but in doing so must conduct the affairs as would a prudent person in the conduct of that persons own affairs. One cannot gamble or otherwise speculate with trust funds, and if one does, personal liability will follow.

Sale of Trust Estate

When trust property is sold, it must be done under acceptable guidelines. Purchasers of trust property should exercise caution to make certain that the proceeds paid by them are properly applied to trust obligations. If this is not done, title to the trust property may fail as to the purchaser.

Closely related to the forms and uses of trusts, are the tax aspects of them. Three variations of express trusts are recognized, and tax consequences vary with the form. These are the revocable, the irrevocable, and the reversionary trust.

REVOCABLE TRUST

If a settlor reserves the right to revoke the trust anytime during the settlor's lifetime, it is a "revocable trust." If revoked, the trust ends and the trust property reverts to the settlor. The value of such trusts are included in the estate of the settlor upon death—even if *not* revoked. The theory is that the settlor *could* have revoked and therefore maintained actual control until death. While the privilege of revoking may have merit in certain instances, tax advantages are lost because the trust property will be treated as part of the settlor's estate.

IRREVOCABLE TRUST

Here the settlor places the trust property beyond reach. This is a final act. Therefore tax advantages accrue to the settlor's estate since the settlor no longer owns the trust property on death.

REVERSIONARY TRUST

If a settlor creates a trust that is to revert to the settlor sometime in the future, income tax savings are possible. If the trust property will be beyond control for at least ten years, then the income from the property is shifted to the trust estate, saving the settlor taxes during the term in which the property is beyond the settlor's control.

TERMINATION OF A TRUST

Once a valid trust is in operation, expressed or implied, a court of equity will not permit it to be defeated upon trivial grounds. Rather, the court will attempt to preserve to each party their rights as they may be determined from the trust.

Generally, a trust may lawfully be terminated by acts of the parties, by agreement, and by the purposes of the trust being accomplished.

By Acts of Parties

If all of the parties to a trust agree that it should be terminated, even before its intended termination, then a court will order it done. However, no outstanding interest under the trust—no matter how slight—can be defeated by such termination. If this could happen, even though the interest is remote or contingent, the court will refuse to decree termination.

By Agreement

If the trust itself spells out the conditions under which termination will result, upon that condition being met, a court will decree termination.

Purposes Accomplished

The length of the trustee's interest in trust property is measured by the terms of the trust itself. As soon as the objectives of the trust are realized, the trust estate ends and the corpus vests in the beneficiary. This happens by operation of law and there is no need for conveyance of the trust property. However, all questions involving termination of trusts should be examined by counsel.

REVIEW QUESTIONS

1. Explain why a trust is a "confidence" by one person in another.
2. It has been common practice among the wealthy to create a variety of trusts. Name reasons for this.
3. Business person X has three children. One is incapacitated by a birth defect and the other two are pursuing successful careers in the professions. How might X utilize a trust?
4. Explain why a trust is not the same as a "sale of goods" under Article 2, U.C.C. (Refer to Chapter 20.)
5. Compare the requirements of a trust with the requirements of a conventional contract. In what ways are they similar?
6. Resulting and constructive trusts are forms of "fictions." Explain why.

7. True or False. A trust is usually taxed on income that it earns.
8. Distinguish a "revocable" from an "irrevocable trust."
9. Could a trust be created that would last "forever?"
10. The courts treat "trusts" as being more "dignified" than contracts. State one reason for this.

Words and Phrases

Write out briefly what they mean to you.
1. Reversionary trusts.
2. Passive trusts.
3. Trusts with spendthrift provisions.
4. Trust liability for debts and taxes.
5. "Cestui que."

Coverage:	An introduction to the documents that are "negotiable" under Article 3 of the U.C.C.
What to Look for:	The "concept of negotiability."
Application:	The material here is essential to an understanding of Chapter 30.

29 Introduction to Commercial Paper

At common law, "commercial paper" included promissory notes, bank checks, bills of exchange, and other instruments for the payment of money that were recognized by the "law merchant" as being "negotiable."[1] In the United States today, commercial paper is that type of paper or document recognized as negotiable by statutory law. The principal statutory law is Article 3, Uniform Commercial Code, which carries the title, "Commercial Paper." While Article 8, U.C.C., recognizes stocks and bonds as being negotiable, we are only concerned here with the coverage of Article 3 as it relates to four types of paper: notes, certificates of deposit, drafts, and bills of exchange. Before examining the four types of instruments, what does the word "negotiable" mean?

The word "negotiable" is an adjective that describes certain types of documents that are in fact contracts, which represent credit or serve as a substitute for money. The prefix "neg" means "not"; the root "otium" means "leisure"; and the suffix "able" means "capable of." Translated literally, the word means "not capable of leisure" — describing its "nomad quality" of being able to wander through the business world as a "bachelor traveling alone" or a true free agent.

Negotiable paper consists of documents that have a "transferable quality" and represent credit or serve as a substitute for dollars and coins. That is, they are documents that can pass freely from one to another free from claims of others. To illustrate, A hands B a $1 bill in payment

---

[1] "Negotiable" means "capable of being transferred by indorsement or delivery so as to pass to the next person the right to sue in that persons name free from claims of others."

of a debt. The bill was stolen in a bank robbery in California six months ago—but B has no way of knowing this. B is free of claims of others and can do with the bill as B wishes. Therefore, a dollar bill has "negotiable quality"—but we must hasten to add that it is not commercial paper under Article 3, U.C.C. because it is actual payment—not a "promise to pay."

The most common type of commercial paper is the check.

CHECKS

A check is a document that creates a contract between the one who draws it and the one to whom it is given, and which brings into play a contract that already exists between the one who draws it and the bank (see Figure 29–1).

FIGURE 29–1

In our example, Dave Zinn has promised Henry Everly that he will be paid $100, or that he may use the check to pay $100 to others. This is the first contract. The second contract, which is already in existence between Zinn and the bank, is activated. While the words are not used, Zinn has said to the bank, "Take $100 of the money that I have deposited with you and pay it to Everly, or to anyone that he should order you to pay it to."

The check is a three-party document and each party has a precise legal name. The one who "draws" the check (he or she literally "draws" the money from the bank) is called the "drawer." The bank is the "drawee" and the person to whom it is payable is the "payee." There may be more than one payee.

Traveler's Checks

A specialized form of check offered to the public is the "traveler's" check. (See Figure 29–2.) The traveler's check is essentially the same as

FIGURE 29–2
Traveler's Check

an ordinary check except for the following: Dual signatures are required by the user; one when the checks are bought and the second when each is cashed. This prevents the use of traveler's checks that are lost or stolen. It is quite difficult for the best forger to duplicate a signature while standing in front of the person who is going to cash the check. The second difference is that traveler's checks are issued by a bank that agrees to honor them. That is, while the bank does not sign the checks, the bank guarantees them. In all other respects these checks are the same as conventional checks.

When traveling, these checks are much preferred over cash – which can be lost or stolen – and regular checks which many business establishments will not accept.

If traveler's checks are lost the owner can go to a bank that honors the checks and have them replaced. To facilitate this, the receipt of purchase would be retained and carried separate from the traveler's checks. See Figure 29–3.

FIGURE 29–3
Receipt

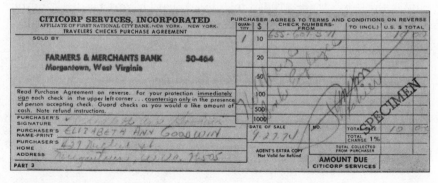

NOTES

The second instrument encountered – but not as often as the check – is the "note" and it is a "credit device." That is, by its use one allows another to have cash or goods now, but is permitted to repay the obligation in the future. Examine Figure 29–4. King has loaned Brooks $100 for one year and Brooks will owe $108 on March 3, 1977. Credit has been extended, a promise has been made – and the instrument is negotiable. Therefore, if King needs money before March 3, 1977, he may indorse the note and deliver it to the one who buys it. The buyer (who normally buys at a discount) will present the note on the due date and be paid $108.

FIGURE 29–4

Promissory Note

$100.00   March 4, 1976

One (1) year after date, I promise to pay to the order of George King, One Hundred ($100.00) Dollars at 206 North Street, Anytown, plus interest thereon at the rate of 8 percent per annum.

FINANCE CHARGE $8.00
ANNUAL PERCENTAGE RATE   8 percent

Albert Brooks (SEAL)
Albert Brooks

It should be noted at this point that the check is an *order to pay*, while a note is a *promise to pay*. The first substitutes for dollars and coins – the second is a contract of credit. But they are both negotiable.

The third class of paper under Article 3 is a "saving device" and has only two parties to it.

CERTIFICATE OF DEPOSIT

John Doe has $1,000 that he wants to place into savings – and he expects to be paid interest. He goes to the Farmers' and Merchants' Bank in Morgantown and deposits $1,000 with the cashier, who in turn issues a certificate of deposit. Examine Figure 29–5.

The instrument is a promise by the bank that it will pay John Doe the sum of $1,000 (principal) plus $55 (interest) on March 3, 1976 – or that it will pay the sum of $1,055 to anyone that Doe *orders the bank to pay*. This means that Doe can discount it to a buyer by indorsing it and delivering it. The buyer can present the instrument on the due date and be paid $1,055. In addition, the owner of the certificate of deposit can use it as collateral for a loan. Most lenders will take possession of the certificate and hold it until the loan is repaid thus making it a "pledge." In

FIGURE 29–5
Certificate of Deposit

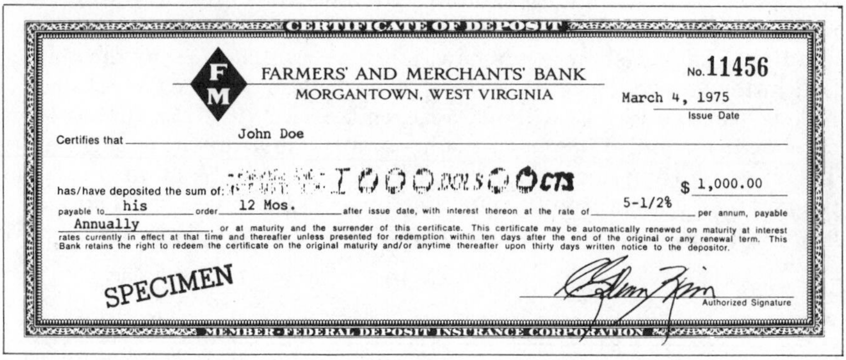
CERTIFICATE OF DEPOSIT

FARMERS' AND MERCHANTS' BANK
MORGANTOWN, WEST VIRGINIA

No. 11456

March 4, 1975
Issue Date

Certifies that John Doe

has/have deposited the sum of: 1000 DOLS 00 CTS $ 1,000.00

payable to his order 12 Mos. after issue date, with interest thereon at the rate of 5-1/2% per annum, payable Annually, or at maturity and the surrender of this certificate. This certificate may be automatically renewed on maturity at interest rates currently in effect at that time and thereafter unless presented for redemption within ten days after the end of the original or any renewal term. This Bank retains the right to redeem the certificate on the original maturity and/or anytime thereafter upon thirty days written notice to the depositor.

SPECIMEN

Authorized Signature

MEMBER–FEDERAL DEPOSIT INSURANCE CORPORATION

these pledges, some form of pre-indorsement is required so that upon default in the loan, the lender may convert the certificate to cash and apply the proceeds to the loan.

Some courts have held that a certificate of deposit may have a "security interest" perfected in it by the workings of Article 9 of the U.C.C.[2] Here the certificate is treated the same as any other item that is given as security in a secured transaction. (For an expanded discussion of Article 9 security interests, see Chapter 37.)

The certificate of deposit is a two-party instrument: the bank that issues it and the one to whom it is issued, the payee.

Many certificates of deposit state that they are "not subject to check." This simply means that checks cannot be drawn against them thus distinguishing them from a regular bank deposit.

The fourth negotiable instrument is the bill of exchange. It is not encountered frequently in the small business but it is in the large. It is the granddaddy of the check—and it is one of the oldest of the four types.

BILLS OF EXCHANGE

Bills of exchange, commonly called "drafts," are three-party instruments used to "exchange" obligations between three parties. They operate much like checks, but there is no bank involved. It is helpful to examine bills of exchange in their historical setting.

Historically

While negotiable instruments were used widely in Europe following the Norman Conquest, they did not find extensive use in England until centuries later. When they began to be used, only the bill of exchange was

[2] *Southview Corporation* v. *Kleberg First National Bank*, 512 S.W.2d. 817 (Texas 1974).

recognized as being negotiable. And when used, they "shifted obligations" between the parties involved.

To illustrate, A owed B 100 pounds sterling, and B owed C 100 pounds sterling. A resided in London; B lived 100 miles away—but C was planning to travel to the city and wanted to use the funds there. B did not have the funds, and if B did, it would have been foolish for C to travel across the countryside by coach carrying this sum of money. How could B pay C the debt due, but use the debt due B by A to do it—and how could it be done without B making the trip? It could be done by a transfer of obligation by the use of a bill of exchange.

```
          TO A
PAY TO THE ORDER OF C,
100 POUNDS STERLING.
                  – B
```

C carries the draft to A and if A honors it, A will "accept" it, pay the sum stated, and retain the document as proof that A paid the debt due to C. Thus, A has paid the debt to B, B has paid the debt to C, and it was done by the use of few words, on the face of a piece of paper. In addition, the document was negotiable and C could have negotiated it to others by indorsement and delivery to settle other obligations.

Today, if a seller of goods desires to extend credit to a buyer of goods, a "time" draft (meaning it is payable in the future) is used. The buyer must "accept" the draft before it is legally effective and this is done by writing the word "accepted" across the face of the document, followed by the name of the buyer.

A bill of exchange and a note have similar features but are easily distinguishable. The note has two parties to it—the maker and the payee. The bill of exchange has three parties—the drawer, payee, and drawee. The note *creates* a debt—the bill of exchange *shifts* debts that are already in existence.

Following is a summary of the four types of commercial paper under Article 3, showing the principal characteristics of each:

1. *Check*—a substitute for money.
2. *Note*—a credit device.
3. *Certificate of Deposit*—a savings device.
4. *Bill of Exchange*—a debt-shifting device.

All four are negotiable *if* they meet legal requirements.

In the business community, the word "draft" is often used to mean the same thing as a check. There is Code authority for the use of this word, U.C.C. 3–120, which relates to the use of "drafts payable through." These are instruments that are similar to checks but they are drawn on banks in which there is in fact no deposit on hand to cover them. This would be the "through" bank and they would be covered when the through bank receives them. The purpose of this is to avoid the loss of interest due to the "float" time of checks being in circulation and the cash being on deposit waiting for the checks to arrive.

In addition to the four types of commercial paper, there are two important categories into which the four types may be classified. These are "time" as contrasted to "demand" instruments.

DEMAND VERSUS TIME

Negotiable instruments can be classified into "demand" and "time" categories. If they are demand, they are payable now—if time, they are payable in the future. Checks and drafts that have been accepted are demand instruments, because they are payable now. However, if they are dated ahead, they are time instruments. Notes and certificates of deposit are almost always time instruments.

Next, it is helpful to examine an Article 3 case. By doing this we can gain more insight into the subject. The case chosen involved an unusual set of facts.

RACEHORSES AND COMMERCIAL PAPER[3]

This was an action by J. P. Leonard against The National Bank at Wheeling, to recover money withdrawn from his account in payment of an alleged forged check. The lower court entered judgment for Mr. Leonard in the sum of $3,000 and the bank appealed. The Supreme Court of Appeals, Judge Berry, held that the negligence of Mr. Leonard was the cause of a raised amount being paid by the drawee bank, and his actions in drawing the check constituted negligence as a matter of law since he had written the check in such a manner that it could be altered without difficulty. The court further held that this negligence entitled the bank to a directed verdict in its favor. The plaintiff below, J. P. Leonard, will be referred to as "Leonard," and the defendant below, The National Bank at Wheeling, will be referred to as the "bank."

Leonard opened a checking account with the bank on June 1, 1959, and maintained a balance between $10,000 and $30,000. Checks as high as $6,500 had been drawn on the account and cashed by the bank without question. In the early part of September, 1961, while looking through his monthly statement, Leonard discovered a check cashed by the bank and charged to his account in the sum of $3,600. The check was drawn to the order of "Martin Mattson," was dated August 3, 1961, carried the signature of Leonard as drawer and also the signature of Leonard as the last indorser in blank—that is, Leonard signed his name without further words being added. A second indorsement was found on the back of the check above the indorsement of Leonard and it was that of "Martin Mattson." Examine Figure 29–6.

Leonard complained to the bank because he had never written such

---

[3] *J. P. Leonard* v. *The National Bank of West Virginia at Wheeling, etc.*, 145 S.E.2d 23 (1965).

FIGURE 29-6

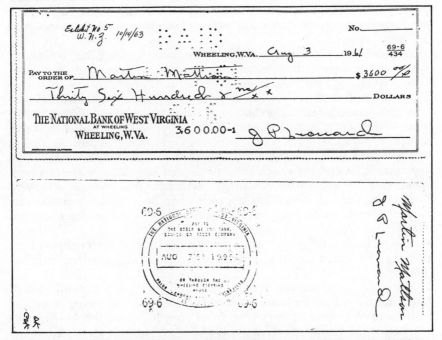

The above is a photocopy of the actual check involved in the 'racehorse' case, taken from the court file.

a check, and an investigation was made. The bank refused to credit his account for the sum of $3,600, and Leonard filed suit, claiming the check was a forgery. The bank defended, stating that Leonard was barred from recovery by reason of his negligence in drawing the check. The check had been drawn by Leonard; it was indorsed by Leonard in blank, and the check was not a forgery—facts that the bank proved ultimately. The case was given to the jury on the questions of whether there was forgery or negligence. The jury found that the check had been raised but was not a forgery and gave Leonard a verdict in the sum of $3,600. The bank appealed.

During the course of the trial, Leonard admitted that he had written a $600 check; that he had signed the check in the capacity of drawer; that he had indorsed the check in blank so that a man by the name of "Santo" could get it cashed at the race track; that he gave the check to Santo in final payment of two racehorses purchased for the sum of $1,200, a previous payment of $600 having been made; that the words "Six Hundred" looked like his writing; and that the signature and last indorsement looked like his writing.

Leonard further stated at the trial that he did not make the check out for $3,600; that he did not know "Martin Mattson"; that he did not write the word "Thirty" in front of "Six Hundred," which was misspelled and read "Thrity"; that he had not filled in the date on the check; that he had not named a payee; and that the "$3,600" opposite the dollar mark was not his writing.

Evidence introduced on behalf of the bank showed that when the check was presented to a teller, identification was required; but these details were not available at the trial. Leonard's account was checked at the time to see if he had sufficient funds to cover the check. In addition, the person presenting the check for payment was referred to the vice president of the bank. Leonard's signature was checked against the signature card and were found to correspond. The vice president then wrote "OK C. E. K." on the lower corner of the back of the check. The signature card and the check were presented as evidence, and the jury found that the signatures of Leonard as drawer and indorser were not forged, and further found that the check had been raised from $600 to $3,600. Several questions were thus presented to the higher court for decision.

1. Was Leonard barred from recovery because of his negligence in drawing the check in such a manner that it could be altered without difficulty?

The court reviewed the manner in which the check was drawn and found that Leonard had not filled in the name of the payee; that the amount of the check opposite the dollar sign had been left blank; that the words "Six Hundred" were written one and one-half inches from the left side of the check; that the indorsement of Leonard was written one inch from the top; and that the blank spaces had been filled in by unknown persons in a careful manner matching Leonard's writing as closely as possible.

The court stated that the general rule in regard to raised checks is that the drawee bank pays such check at its own peril and can only debit the drawer's account for the amount of the check as originally drawn. The exception to the rule is where the altering or raising of the check is due to the negligence of the drawer and in such cases the drawee bank cannot be held liable. The exception is generally based upon negligence or estoppel, depending upon the court.[4] The court held that the negligence on the part of Leonard was such that if it were the only negligence involved, Leonard would be barred from recovery as a matter of law. The court now looked to the negligence of the bank, if any.

2. Was the bank negligent in not having the person who presented the check for payment identified as Martin Mattson since he was the named payee and first indorser?

The court reasoned that there was no evidence that the person who presented the check was *not* Martin Mattson, and there was no evidence to lift the "prima facie" rule that Mattson had authority to assert his name as payee in the blank so provided.[5] The court further reasoned that

---

[4] 10 Am.Jur.2d, Banks, secs. 616, 617; Annot. 39 A.L.R.2d 641, at page 651.

[5] West Virginia Code, Ch. 46, Art. 1, Sec. 14 (Michie 1961).

whether the bank was negligent in not identifying Mattson was immaterial since there was no evidence that the check was forged.

3. Was the bank negligent in failing to have the person who presented the check for payment indorse it under the signature of Leonard?

The court said that by leaving so much space above his signature on the back, the bank could not be charged with negligence on this point, since Leonard's signature in blank made the check "bearer" paper,[6] that is, it could be negotiated by delivery alone.

4. Did the misspelling of the word "Thirty," which read as "Thrity," place the bank on notice of the alteration of the check?

The court said that the writing of the word "Thrity" was very similar to the words "Six Hundred," which the jury found to be the handwriting of Leonard and that this fact relieved the bank of negligence in failing to recognize that the word "Thirty" was misspelled.

5. Was the vice president negligent is not making a closer investigation before placing his "OK" on the back of the check?

The fact that the teller checked the signatures on the check against the signature card and found them to correspond was enough to satisfy the vice president—and the Court as well.

6. Was the bank negligent in that its agents failed to follow local practices of identifying the person presenting the check for payment?

Several witnesses were called at the trial and some testified that they would have required the person presenting the check to indorse it below the indorsement of Leonard and present suitable identification; some said they would have called Leonard to determine if he had written the check; others said they would have had a third party identify the person presenting the check; and one witness testified that if he could have identified the person he would not have called Leonard.

The court reasoned that if Leonard's indorsement was forged and the bank had paid the money to the third party, then Leonard could have recovered as a matter of law. The court answered question 6 in the negative, stating that the jury had found that the signatures of Leonard were *not* forgeries.

The court concluded

> . . . the evidence in this case clearly indicated that the drawer is the party responsible for the defendant Bank paying the amount of the altered check and that his actions were the proximate cause of the payment thereof, and such acts on his part constitute negligence as a matter of law . . . and . . . the Court (below) should have directed a verdict in favor of the defendant Bank.

The verdict was set aside and the case reversed and remanded.

Compare Figure 29-6, with Figures 29-7 and 29-8. It is interesting to note that the same mistake was being made 100 years ago. (Let's hope that Joe Pownall did not get caught like J. P. Leonard.)

---

[6] West Virginia Code, Chapter 46, Article 1, Section 9 (Michie, 1961).

FIGURE 29–7
Front of Wells Fargo Draft

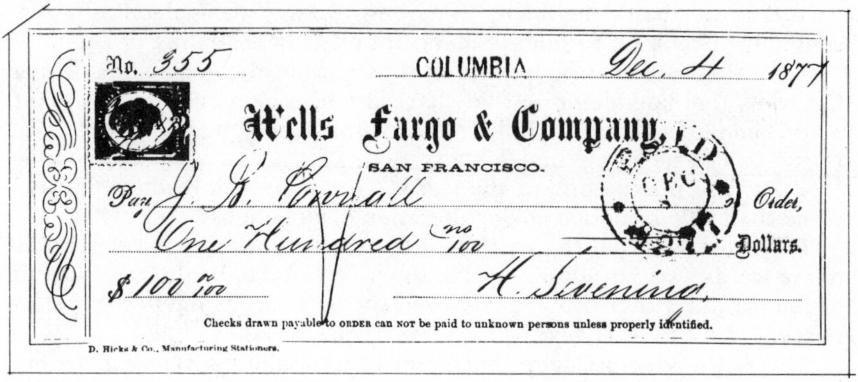

FIGURE 29–8
Back of Wells Fargo Draft

From the author's collection.

REVIEW QUESTIONS

1. Write down the four basic commercial paper documents. Write out how many parties are involved in each.
2. Write after each, one characteristic of the document.
3. Distinguish an "order" from a "promise" to pay.
4. Why is a check dated next month a "time" document?
5. True or False. A note is an order to pay.
6. Write out the principal features of a note.
7. A bill of exchange.
8. Examine Figures 29–7 and 29–8 closely and you will observe what appears to be a hole under the word "Pay" and in the bottom of the date stamp. What do these two perforations indicate to you?
9. Compare the three documents in Questions 6, 7, and 8 above.
10. "Negotiability" is of prime importance in the business community. Why?

Words and Phrases

Write out briefly what they mean to you.
1. Negotiation.
2. Acceptance.
3. Forgeries.
4. "Shifting obligations."
5. Indorsement.

30 Creation of Commercial Paper

The "racehorse case" is a striking example of the type of problems that may arise in the creation of commercial paper. Admittedly, the circumstances of that case were unique — yet, the law books contain many cases where the drawer of a check later learned that something went wrong causing a loss. Because of this, it is essential that one learn the basics of the creation of commercial paper, first, to be knowledgeable, and second, for defensive purposes. As will be seen, the creation of negotiable paper requires that both legal and practical form be met.

The creation of proper commercial paper is, in the simplest sense, a matter of meeting "form." Those instruments that meet the practical and legal form are negotiable. They can serve in the marketplace as a substitute for money or as a credit device. If the practical or legal forms are *not* met, the instrument may fail the test of negotiability. It may also fail in a court action to see whose negligence caused the loss on the instrument. This is why the practical form is so important.

PRACTICAL BUSINESS FORM

Recently an elderly lady visited a lawyer's office complaining that her bank owed her $45. She had cashed a check for $5 at a grocery store three months previously. She did not write in the name of the payee because she believed the store manager would stamp the name of the store on the line — but it was not done. By leaving the payee line blank, she created "bearer paper," and the check became as negotiable as a $5 bill.

The store manager used the check, along with others, to pay a produce account with a wholesale distributor. From that point on, no one recalls what happened to the check. When it finally reached the drawee bank, the payee line contained the name of a business in a neighboring state — and the check had been raised to $50, which the bank paid. The bank refused to make up the difference.

What could the lawyer tell the distraught drawer? The lawyer could only explain that it was her negligence that permitted the check to circulate without indorsements until it fell into the hands of the one who "kited" (raised) it. If the payee had been named, an indorsement would have been required before the check could have been used to pay the produce bill. The one who received the check would have been required to indorse it, leaving a record on the back of those whose hands it went through. But this was not done. Happily for the lady, the one who raised it decided upon $50 instead of $500.

Statistically, over $1,750 is being removed each *minute* from bank accounts in the United States by "kiting." This is probably the easiest major crime to commit because it can be done in the privacy of one's home or a motel room.

As the banks turned to automation, lawyers and others expressed hopes that losses like the one discussed would be reduced. Unfortunately, the opposite has been the truth. The "magnetic ink character recognition" (MICR) numbers found on modern checks were created to permit the automatic posting machines to read the account number, thus directing the check into the proper channel in the bank. Since the machines read the *numbers* and not the *signatures*, forgeries are easier to get through the banks today. In many cases checks are clearing the banks with no signature on them at all!

In a recent burglary, the thieves apparently did nothing but rummage through the drawers in the office of a midwestern manufacturing concern because the office manager could find nothing missing. In about six weeks the company was overdrawn at its bank by some $40,000. The thieves had taken checks from the center of the company checkbook so that they would not be missed. These checks had in turn been forged as payroll checks and passed all over the Southwest with no one the wiser — especially the machine that was reading the magnetic numbers.

After the overdrawn bank account became known, an audit of the account disclosed what had happened. The manufacturing company raised the defense of "forgery" as discussed in Chapter 32. By this, they were claiming that they were not responsible for the checks since they were in fact forged.

But what about the negligence of the company in failing to discover the missing checks? If they had made a diligent search immediately after the breaking and entering, the theft of the checks would have been discovered. The bank in turn would have been alerted to the obvious intent of the thieves.

FIGURE 30-1

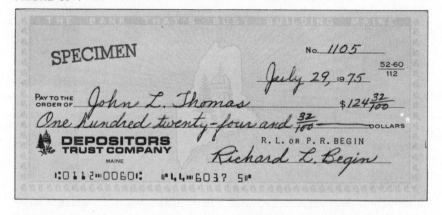

On the other hand, when checks are merely *lost,* notification of the loss is enough because this alerts the bank to the possibility of forgeries. If the bank pays a forged check under these circumstances, they must bear the loss—not the depositor. When checks are *stolen,* however, common sense tells us that extra care and caution should be exercised. Now, how *should* we fill in our checks to meet the "practical form"?

Some Techniques

First, as a matter of practice, *all* blanks on a negotiable instrument should be filled in, including the name of the payee, the date, and the amount for which the instrument is drawn. Next, all dollar amounts should be closed up to prevent one word from being changed to another, or to prevent the insertion of another word, as occurred in the racehorse case. For example, the word "seven" can be changed to "seventy" very easily if a small amount of space is left after the word. Figure 30–1 is an example of how one can "close up" a check written in ink.

FIGURE 30-2

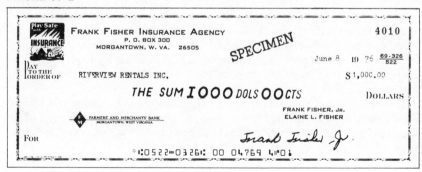

It is good business practice to use a "check writer" because it is virtually impossible to alter a check written on one of these machines. Examine Figure 30-2.

One should develop a clear, strong signature and use it carefully on all instruments. The clearer a signature the harder it is to duplicate. Finally, a suitable pen should be used—a pencil only invites disaster. The practical creation of a negotiable instrument adds up to common sense, yet its importance is worth noting.

The *legal* creation of commercial paper is something else.

LEGAL CREATION OF COMMERCIAL PAPER

The legal purposes of commercial paper were discussed in the previous chapter. Before documents can meet these purposes, they must meet legal form. All instruments that do are "negotiable commercial paper"—all others are not. However, if purported negotiable paper fails because it does not meet legal form, it is still a binding contract between the parties and contract rules apply. However, that type of paper does not carry with it the benefits that arise out of the use of negotiable instruments.

For a review of basic contract principles that would cover items that were *not* negotiable, see chapter 13 and chapters that follow.

The requirements of commercial paper are few but precise—and they are summarized in the following chart. After the chart follows two illustrations that show where these requirements are found on a check and a note. Following this is a brief discussion of each of the five requirements.

Requirements of Negotiability

The requirements of negotiability under Article 3, U.C.C., are:

1. The instrument must be in writing and signed by the:
   A. maker (notes), or
   B. drawer (bills of exchange or checks, sometimes called drafts).
2. Contain either:
   A. an unconditional *promise to pay* (commonly found in notes), or
   B. an *order to pay* (commonly found in bills of exchange and checks).
3. The promise or order in number 2 must be to pay a sum certain in:
   A. money,
   B. current funds,
   C. currency, or
   D. foreign currency.
   The sum certain is not altered by: (1) interest being added, (2) installments provided for, (3) costs of collection and attorney fees added, (4) different interest rates, (5) discount for early payment, (6) additional charge for late payment.
4. Must be payable either:
   A. on demand, or
   B. at a certain time.

5. Must be payable to:
    A. *order,* or
    B. *bearer.*

Assume that the following words are found upon three separate documents. Examine them against the five requirements and see what requirements are missing. (None are negotiable.)

1. "Due A, $500 for value received. Signed B."
2. "I.O.U. $500. Signed X."
3. "To John Doe. I wish you to pay $1,000 to the order of Roe. Signed Z."

A CHECK

In the following diagram, the check drawn by Fisher to the order of Ryan is marked to illustrate where the five requirements of negotiability are found on the instrument. Notice that requirement 4A is met by the instrument itself. There are no words that state when it is payable—so it is payable on demand. Examine Figure 30–3.

FIGURE 30–3

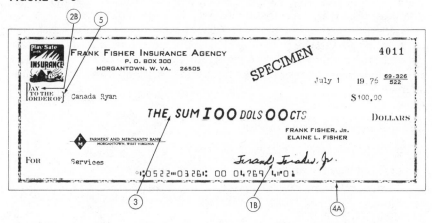

NOTE

In the note in Figure 30–4, two persons signed as makers. Therefore, they are both liable for the full amount on the due date—or either of them may be called upon to pay the full amount. If Ronald pays in full on the date due, he has the right of "contribution" from Susan.

If the note (or the check in the previous illustration) had been made payable to "bearer," or if the payee line had been left blank, then the requirement of 5B would have been fulfilled. This would have made it the equivalent of bearer paper—payable to anyone demanding payment on it.

FIGURE 30-4

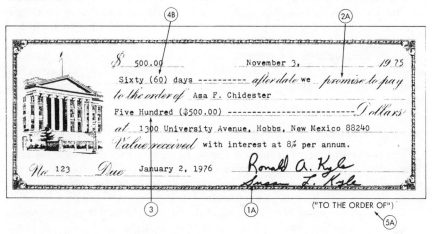

Needless to say, all negotiable instruments must be in writing, so this requirement was coupled with the requirement that the document "be signed."

THE REQUIREMENTS—SOME DETAIL

1. The Signature

The U.C.C. does not spell out formal requirements for a signature and in practice it is common for the "signature" to take many forms. It is frequently handwritten, yet just as frequently it is printed by a "signature stamp" or applied by a computer. In a few cases it may be a simple "X." A complete signature is not required and it does not have to appear at a particular place on an instrument. But good business practice dictates that a written signature be complete, clear, and written in the space provided.

2. Promise or Order

The promise or order must be unconditional—that is, it must not be qualified in any material way. "Pay" is an order—and it is unqualified. "I promise to pay" is a promise—and it is also unqualified. If checks or notes are written in a conditional manner, they fail as a substitute for money or a credit device.

However, it is permissible to place "informative" matters upon the face of notes and checks and this does not make the instrument conditional. For example, one may state upon the note the security that was given to secure it. Also many persons who hold notes will keep a record of the note payments upon the front or back of the note itself. In the case of checks, it is permissible to make a notation of an invoice paid or to include notations for business purposes. In fact most checks include a "memo" line or space for such purposes. Examine Figure 30–3. But any wording that *qualifies* payment or leads another to believe payment is qualified, might destroy the negotiability of the document. As a rule, it is best *not* to place unnecessary notations upon the face of commercial paper.

3. Sum Certain

The legal requirement here is simple: at any given time, one must be able to determine the precise sum that is due on the instrument. Therefore, adding interest, providing for payment by installments, and other items does not impair the negotiability.

The "sum certain" requirement makes it mandatory that it be a sum certain in current, domestic, or foreign medium of exchange. A check payable in "100 German marks" or "300 Swiss francs" would be a sum certain; "10 bushels of wheat" or a "truckload of coal" would not be.

4. Time of Payment

The time of payment must be "on demand" or "at a fixed time." If an instrument lacked both, its status would be so uncertain that it could not serve as a substitute for money. Most checks and bills of exchange are payable on demand. Most notes and certificates of deposit are payable in the future and serve as credit devices. Therefore, they are "time" instruments.

It has been customary to insert such phrases as "payable on sight," "payable on presentation," or "payable on demand." This usage will continue, but the necessity for these phrases is academic at best. A check dated today is a demand instrument; a note that states, "One day after date, I promise to pay" is a demand instrument tomorrow. The extra words are unnecessary.

Speeding Up a Due Date. The U.C.C., Article 3–109(1) (c), states:

> An instrument is payable at a definite time if by its terms it is payable . . . (c) at a definite time *subject to any acceleration* . . .

(Emphasis added.) This means that a negotiable document may contain a provision to the effect that time of payment may fall sooner than the document specifies. But U.C.C., Article 1–208, controls the circumstances under which this may happen. It states:

> A term providing that one party . . . may accelerate payment . . . or require collateral . . . "at will" or when he deems himself insecure . . . shall be construed to mean that he shall have power to do so only if he in good faith believes that the prospect of payment or performance is impaired.

If a note holder learns that the debtor is going to leave the state, or file bankruptcy, or place assets beyond the reach of creditors, the note holder should not be required to wait until the due date before payment is demanded.

The due date can also be *extended* by the holder of a time instrument, as well as the maker, to a limited degree. However, the practice is questionable because if an extension is permitted, any person who signed the instrument to guarantee its payment (surety) is released from further obligation.

5. Payable to Order or Bearer

The "words of negotiability" are "order" and "bearer." If an instrument lacks both, it can never be negotiable. If an instrument is "order paper," it requires an indorsement to negotiate it. If bearer paper, it does not. Occasionally one encounters the following redundancy: "Pay to the order of bearer." Under the U.C.C. this is order paper.

Figure 30–5 provides a convenient way to test the five requirements.

FIGURE 30–5

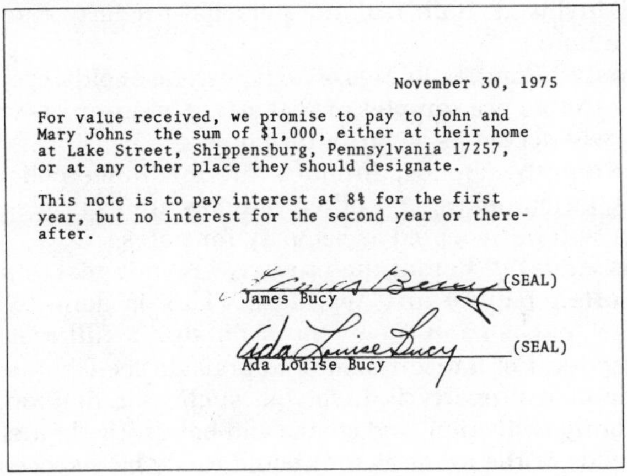

November 30, 1975

For value received, we promise to pay to John and Mary Johns the sum of $1,000, either at their home at Lake Street, Shippensburg, Pennsylvania 17257, or at any other place they should designate.

This note is to pay interest at 8% for the first year, but no interest for the second year or thereafter.

_____(SEAL)
James Bucy

_____(SEAL)
Ada Louise Bucy

Examine the document and write out the answers to the following questions:

1. Is the instrument negotiable?
2. Is it a note, bill of exchange, or neither?
3. If it is not negotiable, is it still a good contract? (For the purposes of the following questions, assume that it is negotiable.)
4. Is it for a sum certain?
5. Is it a "demand" or "time" instrument?
6. Are Mr. and Mrs. Bucy "makers" or "drawers"?
7. Are Mr. and Mrs. Johns "payees," "drawees," or "drawers"?
8. How many *parties* are there to the note?
9. If you were writing the instrument, what changes would you make?
10. Who can the Bucy's safely pay? John and Mary are divorced and the whereabouts of Mary is unknown.

(Check your responses against the answers at the end of this chapter.)

MISCELLANEOUS PROVISIONS

Many other provisions of the U.C.C. come into play in the creation of "Article 3 paper" or "commercial paper." Four of the most important follow.

1. Secured and Unsecured Notes

A note that is "unsecured" has nothing to back it except the reputation of the maker. This type is difficult to discount in the marketplace for the reason that it *is* unsecured.

Most lenders will loan money to accepted borrowers and take unsecured notes, but in limited sums. It is unusual to see an unsecured note for more than $1,000 especially when a wageearner is involved. The "secured" note is something else.

A note that is "secured" is one that is backed by "collateral." If the note is not paid, the lender can recover the loan and interest from the collateral. The one giving the collateral gives a "security interest" in the property involved. Both real and personal property can be given as security for a note.

Real Property. Land, buildings of all types, leaseholds, crops, minerals, and standing timber are samples of real estate (or interests in real estate) that lenders will accept as security for notes.

Personal Property. Bonds, antiques, life insurance policies, jewelry, coins, stocks, automobiles, and other vehicles are examples of personal property that will be accepted as security for notes.

Appraisals Made. Whether the property given is real or personal, the lender will often require an "appraisal." This is done to assure that enough "edge" exists so in the event of default, a full recovery can be had by the lender. For a discussion of appraisals see Chapter 40.

Where personal property is involved, such as a diamond ring, coin collection, stamp collection, and stocks and bonds, the lender will generally take custody of the items as they could easily be disposed of, thereby eliminating the guarantee of payment that they make. This is called a "pledge" in U.C.C. language. Once the obligation is paid, the debtor is entitled to the return of the property plus the note marked "paid in full."

2. Joint Payees

U.C.C., 3-110, states in part:

> An instrument . . . may be payable to the order of . . . (*d*) two or more payees together or in the alternative . . .

For example, a check could be made payable to "A and B and C" — two or more payees together — or to "A or B or C" — and this would be in the alternative. In the former, all three indorsements would be required; in the latter, any one of the three would be sufficient. Alternative payees are seldom used in practice; but joint payees are used routinely. For example, one writing a check to pay for joint interests in real estate should name all of the parties in interest as a payee. To illustrate, A purchased a small house and lot from B and wife, and gave them a note secured by a deed of trust (mortgage). A made the checks payable to B only because B requested it "so it would be easier to take the check to the bank." After A had paid the note in full, A requested a release (the note was secured by real estate). B's wife refused to sign the release, claiming she had not received any of the money! A was able to get the release eventually, but missed a good buy on other investment property because A was unable to use the former property of B and wife as security until the lien was cleared.

What about "A and/or B"?   It has been held that a check made payable to "A and/or B," is in the alternative and U.C.C. 3–116 (a) controls, requiring the signature of only one of the named payees. See *Lohf* v. *Warner,* 495 P. 2d 241, 10 U.C.C. Rep. 850 (1972).

3. Postdating

Dating a check ahead (postdating) is authorized by the U.C.C., Article 3–114. However, one should use caution in accepting postdated checks, especially when they take the form of a loan. For example, A owed a cement block manufacturer $1,000 for a previous purchase. A claimed to be short on cash and offered the manufacturer ten $100 checks, each dated one month ahead of the other. These were accepted. The first three checks cleared, and A requested another delivery of blocks, which were delivered. The fourth check bounced, A left town, and the block maker is $1,700 wiser about postdated checks.

4. Signing in a Representative Capacity

In recent years, many business persons have incurred considerable personal losses because of their unawareness of one section of the U.C.C., namely 3–403. It reads as follows:

> 1. A signature may be made by an agent or other representative, and his authority to make it may be established as in other cases of representation. No particular form of appointment is necessary to establish such authority.
>
> 2. An authorized representative who signs his own name to an instrument.
>> a. is personally obligated if the instrument neither names the person represented nor shows that the representative signed in a representative capacity;
>> b. except as otherwise established between the immediate parties, is personally obligated if the instrument names the person represented but does not show that the representative signed in a representative capacity, or if the instrument does not name the person represented but does show that the representative signed in a representative capacity.
>
> 3. Except as otherwise established, the name of an organization preceded or followed by the name and office of an authorized individual is a signature made in a representative capacity.

A close reading of the section makes it clear that care must be exercised when signing commercial paper in the capacity of an agent or a representative of another. The danger is in the possibility that a business or corporation may become insolvent or file bankruptcy, with a creditor bringing suit against the person who signed the check or note improperly. When this happens, the individual is often called upon to pay the instrument, plus accumulated interest if any, out of personal assets.

A Case Illustrates the Point.   Mr. George Moskowitz executed a note on behalf of the Tri-Urban Realty Co., Inc., in his capacity as president. The note was for an advance to a plasterer subcontractor who in turn, negotiated the note to others. The note had been issued for corporate business—but Mr. Moskowitz signed it as follows:

> TRI-URBAN REALTY CO., INC.
> s/s George Moskowitz

Compare this with U.C.C., 3–403(2)(b), and you will see why the New Jersey Superior Court held Mr. Moskowitz personally liable for the corporate obligation.[1]

Another Example.   This case involved 36 corporate notes. In the lower right hand corner of each was typed "S.R.S. Second Avenue Theatre Corp." Below the corporate name were two signatures as follow: "Harold Segal–George Schavan." The court held these two persons personally liable on these notes because of their failure to comply with U.C.C. 3–403.[2]

How about a Corporate Co-Signer?   A form note was executed by one corporation in favor of another as follows:

> Southdale Pro-Bowl, Inc.,
>
> *John Dorek, President*
> *Frank Buetel*

The two signatures also appeared on the back of the note as indorsements.

Southdale Pro-Bowl, Inc., filed bankruptcy and the payee wanted to hold Frank Buetel personally liable on the note pointing out that he had failed to meet the requirements of U.C.C. 403 (2) when signing the note.

The trial court held there was no "holder in due course," and *since another corporate officer had signed the note,* parol (oral) evidence could be used to determine if Buetel had signed as a corporate officer. The court ruled in favor of Buetel and the payee appealed.

The appellate court held that where there are dual signatures on a note and one is that of a corporate officer, parol evidence is admissible to determine if the other was also a corporate officer.[3]

---

[1] *O.P. Ganjo, Inc.* v. *Tri-Urban,* 7 U.C.C. Rep. 302 (January 19, 1970).

[2] *Abby Financial Corp.,* v. *S.R.S. Second Avenue Theatre Corp.,* N.Y. Sup. Ct., 11 U.C.C. Rep. 1011 (1972).

[3] *Weather-Rite, Inc.,* v. *Southdale Pro-Bowl, Inc.,* 222 N.W.2d. 789 (Minn. 1974).

Caution. It must be remembered that while Buetel prevailed, it cost him the expenses of a trial in the lower court and an appeal as well. It would have been much easier and cheaper to have complied with the law.

Examine Figure 30–6. This illustrates once again how this type of liability can be avoided. In notes 2 and 3, Doe is subject to personal liability for the reasons discussed. This means that he can be forced to pay the note out of personal assets. In note 1, Doe has complied with the statute.

FIGURE 30–6

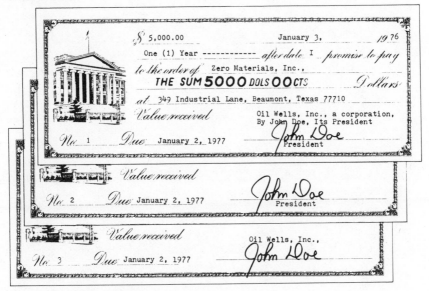

REVIEW QUESTIONS

Words and Phrases

Write out briefly what they mean to you.
1. Sum certain.
2. Acceleration.
3. "I feel insecure."
4. Joint payees.
5. "Signing checks for others."

Answers to Questions

Answers to the questions that accompany the Bucy note follow:
1. The instrument is not negotiable because the words "to the order of" or "to bearer" are missing.
2. It is neither a note nor a bill of exchange because it lacks requirements.

3. It is a good contract and contract law will govern it.
4. Yes.
5. Demand.
6. Makers.
7. Payees (joint).
8. Two.
9. Make it negotiable. Clear up due date. What else?
10. John and Mary Johns were divorced and Mary left for parts unknown. The money cannot be paid safely to either without court action.

31 Commercial Paper in Use

In the previous chapters, the nature of commercial paper and the practical and legal requirements of its creation have been examined. One should next look at the laws that govern the *use* of commercial paper in the marketplace as a substitute for money and as a credit device. A good place to begin is with "indorsements."

INDORSEMENTS

A look at a dictionary tells us that to "endorse" is the act of subscribing to or placing ones signature on a check or other commercial paper. However, the drafters of the U.C.C. chose to spell the word "indorse." To be consistent with the U.C.C. this spelling is used.

An indorsement is the act of a payee, drawee, or other holder of a negotiable document in placing his or her name in writing on the back of the document, with or without qualifying words, so that the document and the money value that it represents, can be transferred to another. An indorsement carries with it obligations or liabilities of one of two types: contractual or warranty.

Contractual Liability

Before an indorser of a check can be held to contractual liabilities, (1) the one who holds the check must present it for payment, (2) it must be dishonored, and (3) the indorser must be given notice that the check was not paid. In practice, when a bank refuses payment, the one who

FIGURE 31–1

Warranties	Maker	Drawer	Drawee (*no liability until after acceptance*)	Indorsers
Promises to pay as drawn (Primarily liable)	X		X	
Admits existence of payee	X	X	X	
Admits capacity of payee to indorse	X	X	X	
Promises instrument will be: (1) accepted or (2) paid, and if not, promises to pay it after proper present-ment, dishonor, and notice.		X		X
Admits existence of drawer			X	
Admits genuineness of drawer's signature			X	
Admits capacity of drawer to draw instrument			X	
Instrument is genuine				X
Has good title				X
All prior parties had capacity to contract				X
Knows of nothing to make worthless				X

receives the check back routinely notifies the one from whom the check was taken. This "fixes" the contractual liabilities of that person. How-ever, an indorser may limit contractual liabilities by the use of "quali-fying words" as illustrated in a moment.[1]

If the check that the bank refuses payment on has more than one indorser, the

---

[1] U.C.C., 3–414(1).

. . . indorsers are liable to one another in the order in which they indorse, which is presumed to be the order in which their signatures appear on the instrument.[2]

Warranty Liability

If an indorser escapes contractual liability by use of qualifying words, (as discussed hereafter), that person may still be held liable under the warranties found in U.C.C. 3-417. These warranties are summarized in Figure 31-1. (This chart also includes the warranties of the maker, drawer, drawee, as well as the indorser.)

The subject of warranties is complicated and, rather than spend time memorizing the chart, it is better to refer to it as the following material is examined. It should be recognized, however, that the warranties arise from the act of *negotiation* and each bank that handles a check in the collection process, makes the warranties to the next in line. The same is true of the indorsers.

The principal types of indorsements are the "blank," "special," "qualified," and "restrictive" indorsements.

1. Blank Indorsement. This type of indorsement consists of a mere signature. Once an order instrument is indorsed in blank, it becomes a "bearer" instrument: that is, it can be negotiated by delivery alone. As a rule of thumb, this indorsement should never be used unless one is standing at a teller's window ready to cash the check.

To Illustrate. Refer to the "racehorse case" check Figure 29-5. Mr. Leonard signed the check in blank and this was the principal reason for the $3,000.00 loss. In another case, a graduate student at an eastern university, received a monthly check from the finance officer, stopped by the student union on the way to the bank, and at that point indorsed the check in blank. At the bank the student discovered that the check was missing. Someone cashed it elsewhere and the graduate student was out a month's salary.

2. Special Indorsement. In this indorsement, the one to whom the instrument is to be paid is named. This means that the document can only be negotiated by that person's indorsement.

3. Qualified Indorsement. This type is encountered when one inserts qualifying words over the signature, such as "without recourse." For example, Carl Moore indorses a check as follows:

Without Recourse
s/s Carl Moore

He has in effect said, "If this instrument is not paid, do not ask me to pay it because I won't!" (He has avoided contractual liabilities – but has still made warranty liabilities. See the warranty chart.) The U.C.C.[3]

---

[2] U.C.C., 3-414(2).

[3] U.C.C., 3-205.

treats this type of indorsement as a technical "restrictive indorsement" — but it is helpful to look at it as being a separate type.

4. Restrictive Indorsement. This type prohibits further transfer of an instrument.[4] Typical restrictions are "for deposit only," "for collection," and "pay any bank." In practice, most companies and professional persons routinely apply this type of indorsement to their checks thus removing them from the market for purposes of negotiation at least as far as others are concerned.

An Illustration. A good technique is to have a stamp made such as the following:

FOR DEPOSIT ONLY
to the account of
John Sterling
Attorney at Law

As checks are received, the stamp is applied making them safe from theft or loss until they can be deposited.

For purposes of comparison, the four indorsements are set out in Figure 31–2.

OTHER FEATURES OF INDORSEMENTS

Converting Blank to Special

If one receives a check signed in blank, it can be converted to a special indorsement by writing in over the signature the person to whom it should be made payable. For example, a check signed

s/s Harvey Remington

can be converted to a special indorsement as follows:

Pay to Joseph Smith
s/s Harvey Remington

Misspelled Payee. If a name is misspelled on the payee line, it should be indorsed as follows:

Pay to Harold Fortner
x/x Omer Zewwyar
s/s Omar Zeweyer

"Reacquirer"

Occasionally one "reacquires" an instrument that that person had held and indorsed before.

---

[4] However, the one who uses a restrictive indorsement can strike it out and indorse in another manner if that person should so desire. It only restricts the instrument as to others. (U.C.C., 3–206 (1)).

FIGURE 31–2

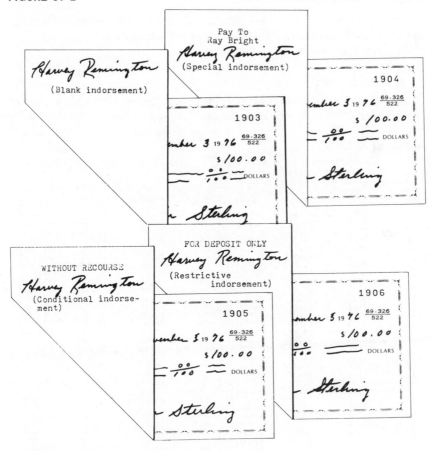

For example, a check is indorsed as follows:

Pay to James Williard
s/s Edward Alford

Pay to Elishah Liston
s/s James Willard

Pay to Paul Darnell
s/s Elishah Liston

Pay to Earl Russell
s/s Paul Darnell

James Willard reacquires the check in a business transaction. Under the U.C.C. 3–208, Williard may cancel any indorsement "not necessary to his title." This is done by drawing a line through the signatures that appear on the instrument *after* his first indorsement. Here he could strike out the signatures of Elishah Liston, Earl Russell, and Paul Darnell—and can indorse the instrument to others.

Miscellaneous Matters

Many other matters become involved in the use of commercial paper and the most important follow. Most are covered by Article 3, or Article 4, U.C.C., Bank Deposits and Collections.

1.   A Note Is Paid

Once a note is paid it is essential that the maker receive it back marked "paid in full." In a recent case, brother A gave a note to brother B for

FIGURE 31-3

ANNUAL % RATE 6.00	PAYMENT $ 100.00	LOAN $ 10,000.00	TERM: YEARS 11	MONTHS 7	PERIODS 139

Prepared by Financial Publishing Company, Boston

PAYMENT NUMBER	PAYMENT ON INTEREST	PRINCIPAL	BALANCE OF LOAN	PAYMENT NUMBER	PAYMENT ON INTEREST	PRINCIPAL	BALANCE OF LOAN
1	50.00	50.00	9,950.00	61	32.56	67.44	6,444.09
2	49.75	50.25	9,899.75	62	32.22	67.78	6,376.31
3	49.50	50.50	9,849.25	63	31.88	68.12	6,308.19
4	49.25	50.75	9,798.50	64	31.54	68.46	6,239.73
5	48.99	51.01	9,747.49	65	31.20	68.80	6,170.93
6	48.74	51.26	9,696.23	66	30.85	69.15	6,101.78
7	48.48	51.52	9,644.71	67	30.51	69.49	6,032.29
8	48.22	51.78	9,592.93	68	30.16	69.84	5,962.45
9	47.96	52.04	9,540.89	69	29.81	70.19	5,892.26
10	47.70	52.30	9,488.59	70	29.46	70.54	5,821.72
11	47.44	52.56	9,436.03	71	29.11	70.89	5,750.83
12	47.18	52.82	9,383.21	72	28.75	71.25	5,679.58
13	46.92	53.08	9,330.13	73	28.40	71.60	5,607.98
14	46.65	53.35	9,276.78	74	28.04	71.96	5,536.02
15	46.38	53.62	9,223.16	75	27.68	72.32	5,463.70
16	46.12	53.88	9,169.28	76	27.32	72.68	5,391.02
17	45.85	54.15	9,115.13	77	26.96	73.04	5,317.98
18	45.58	54.42	9,060.71	78	26.59	73.41	5,244.57
19	45.30	54.70	9,006.01	79	26.22	73.78	5,170.79
20	45.03	54.97	8,951.04	80	25.85	74.15	5,096.64
21	44.76	55.24	8,895.80	81	25.48	74.52	5,022.12
22	44.48	55.52	8,840.28	82	25.11	74.89	4,947.23
23	44.20	55.80	8,784.48	83	24.74	75.26	4,871.97
24	43.92	56.08	8,728.40	84	24.36	75.64	4,796.33
25	43.64	56.36	8,672.04	85	23.98	76.02	4,720.31
26	43.36	56.64	8,615.40	86	23.60	76.40	4,643.91
27	43.08	56.92	8,558.48	87	23.22	76.78	4,567.13
28	42.79	57.21	8,501.27	88	22.84	77.16	4,489.97
29	42.51	57.49	8,443.78	89	22.45	77.55	4,412.42
30	42.22	57.78	8,386.00	90	22.06	77.94	4,334.48

ANNUAL % RATE 6.00	PAYMENT $ 100.00	LOAN $ 10,000.00	TERM: YEARS 11	MONTHS 7	PERIODS 139

Prepared by Financial Publishing Company, Boston

PAYMENT NUMBER	PAYMENT ON INTEREST	PRINCIPAL	BALANCE OF LOAN	PAYMENT NUMBER	PAYMENT ON INTEREST	PRINCIPAL	BALANCE OF LOAN
121	9.03	90.97	1,715.10				
122	8.58	91.42	1,623.68				
123	8.12	91.88	1,531.80				
124	7.66	92.34	1,439.46				
125	7.20	92.80	1,346.66				
126	6.73	93.27	1,253.39				
127	6.27	93.73	1,159.66				
128	5.80	94.20	1,065.46				
129	5.33	94.67	970.79				
130	4.85	95.15	875.64				
131	4.38	95.62	780.02				
132	3.90	96.10	683.92				
133	3.42	96.58	587.34				
134	2.94	97.06	490.28				
135	2.45	97.55	392.73				
136	1.96	98.04	294.69				
137	1.47	98.53	196.16				
138	.98	99.02	97.14				
139	.49	97.14	97.63*				

$10,000, which he paid in full. He did not get the note back. Brother B died and the appraisers of his estate found the note and sued A for the full amount plus interest. A could not prove that he had paid the note and ultimately paid $7,000 to settle the case out of court!

As mentioned previously, it is permissible to keep a record of note payments upon the front or back of the note itself. Another technique is to have a bank create an amortization table based upon the terms of the note. See Figure 31–3.

As payments are made, they can be crossed off in pencil (being careful not to obliterate the figures), providing a perfect record of interest earned by the note holder and paid by the debtor. A running balance is also available of the amount due on the principal. Costs for these tables will vary from bank to bank, but less than $5.00 is typical.

2. Ambiguous Terms

Occasionally, ambiguities arise upon the face of commercial paper. U.C.C. 3–118 governs:

> *Ambiguous Terms and Rules of Construction.* The following rules apply to every instrument:
>
> *a.* Where there is doubt whether the instrument is a draft or a note, the holder may treat it as either. A draft drawn on the drawer is effective as a note.
>
> *b.* Handwritten terms control typewritten and printed terms, and typewritten controls printed.
>
> *c.* Words control figures except that if the words are ambiguous, figures control.
>
> *d.* Unless otherwise specified, a provision for interest means interest at the judgment rate at the place of payment from the date of the instrument, or if it is undated from the date of issue.
>
> *e.* Unless the instrument otherwise specifies two or more persons who sign as maker, acceptor or drawer or indorser and as a part of the same transaction are jointly and severally liable, even though the instrument contains such words as "I promise to pay."
>
> *f.* Unless otherwise specified, consent to extension authorizes a single extension for not longer than the original period. A consent to extension, expressed in the instrument, is binding on secondary parties and accommodation makers. A holder may not exercise his option to extend an instrument over the objection of a maker or acceptor or other party who in accordance with Section 3–604 tenders full payment when the instrument is due.

This provision will answer many questions that arise in the use of commercial paper and it was designed for that purpose.

3. Suing on a Negotiable Document

U.C.C. 3–307 makes it easy for one to sue on a negotiable instrument and recover judgment. All the holder of the document has to do is produce it, and the burden shifts to the maker or drawer to deny the signature. In practice it is rare when one fails to obtain judgment on an unpaid negotiable instrument. (Of course, one may have valid "legal defenses" to an instrument known as "real" and "personal" defenses, but these are beyond the scope of our discussion here.)

4. Acceptance Varying Draft

U.C.C. 3–412 spells out the rules that govern when the one to whom a draft is addressed accepts it, but changes the terms. For example, A draws a draft on B for $1,000 payable to C. C presents it to B, but B "accepts" it for the amount of $900 only. The holder may refuse the acceptance and treat the draft as dishonored. If the holder agrees and the drawer and any indorsers disagree, they are discharged from liability. If all agree, the draft is effective for the adjusted amount. If one is confronted with a similar situation in the business setting, and the sum involved is large, legal advice should be sought.

5. Lost, Destroyed, or Stolen Instruments

If one loses a negotiable instrument and the one who drew or made it refuses payment, what then? The one who lost the instrument can sue on the instrument. That person must prove in court the ownership of the instrument and the facts surrounding it's loss. The court then can order payment for the amount of the instrument. However, to protect the maker or drawer, the court may require the one who lost the instrument to post a bond to protect the other in case the instrument should be presented for payment by others later.

6. Stopping Payment

One may stop payment on a check by giving notice to the bank of the check number, the payee, and the amount. The stop payment may be made by phone and is good for 14 calendar days. If reduced to writing within the 14 days, it is effective for six months. A stop payment can also be renewed. But how do officers in banks react to such intrusions upon their banking operations?

An inquiry about oral stop payments directed to the vice president of a medium size mid-western bank, brought this reply: "When we receive an oral stop payment, we are naturally concerned with whether the caller is the person who drew the check in question. If the caller can give us the check number, the date, and the account number, we will place a temporary hold on the check. However, we inform the caller that he or she must come to the bank immediately so we can verify the facts. Once he or she shows, we ask that person to reduce the "stop" to writing. This protects us as well as the depositor."

"If the one who holds the check comes to the bank before the drawer arrives, we discretely ask him or her to talk with one of our loan officers who explains what has happened. In many instances, this results in the parties confronting each other at the bank and you would be surprised how quick they work it out right there."

To back up the six month stop payment rule, the U.C.C. provides that the bank has no obligation to pay a check more than six months after its date[5]—called a "stale" check in the business community.

Because of the "stop payment" and "stale" provisions of the U.C.C., an interesting question arises when a bank makes payment on a check in spite of them.

Paying on a "Stop." If a bank pays a check on which a "stop" has been placed, is it responsible for the amount that was paid? The U.C.C. provides:

> The burden of establishing the fact and the amount of loss resulting from the payment of an item contrary to a binding stop payment order is on the customer.[6]

The bank is only responsible for any proven loss.

Paying a "Stale" Check. The U.C.C. 4–404, states that a check "presented more than six months after its date . . ." does not have to be paid by the bank. If however, the bank *does* pay such a check, it must do so in good faith. "Good faith" is defined in the U.C.C. as "honesty in fact."[7] In a New York case the court held that the bank only had to be "honest" in the payment of a stale check and that was enough to relieve the bank of liability.[8]

The court (judge) that decided this case was very liberal. Other cases can be found that would hold otherwise.

A Word of Caution. A stop payment does not relieve the drawer of the check (or indorsers upon it) from liability upon the "underlying debt." It only does what its name implies—it stops payment. If A gives a check to a grocer for $30, uses the groceries and stops payment with the intention of depriving the grocer of the $30, it would be a criminal act. It would be the same as if the $30.00 had been stolen. It would also be a breach of contract.

In some states, specific statutes control the use of stop payment orders. In Missouri, for example, it is unlawful to stop payment on a check that has been given for automobile repairs. Also, it is unlawful to stop payment without good cause being shown for doing it.

7.   Unauthorized Signatures

When a depositor receives a bank statement and cancelled checks, two periods of limitation begin to run. First, the depositor has one year in which to report "any unauthorized signature" (forgery) or an alteration on "the front or back" of the instrument, and second, three years in which to discover and report unauthorized indorsements. If the time periods pass without notification, the depositor "is precluded from assert-

---

[5] U.C.C. 4–404.

[6] U.C.C. 4–403(3).

[7] U.C.C. 2–103(1)(*b*).

[8] *Advanced Alloy, Inc.* v. *Sergent Steel Co.*, Queens County Civil Ct., 11 U.C.C. Rep. 1230 (New York, 1973).

ing against the bank such unauthorized signature or indorsement or such alteration."[9]

Some banks go the U.C.C. one better and spell out in the depositors contract a time period different than that set forth in Article 3. The Manufacturers Hanover Trust of New York, has a provision in its depositors contract that unless the depositor notifies the bank *in writing within 30 days after receipt of the cancelled checks* of any forgery, the balance shall be treated as correct and the bank will not be liable for any charge made to the depositors account. This provision has been upheld as a valid matter of contract by a New York court.[10]

8. Reconciling Bank Balances

Quite often in business, the first indication that one has that someone has been forging checks or making unauthorized withdrawals, is when a shortage is found in the account. As surprising as it may sound, the typical business person is often not able to spot shortages by examining the balance furnished by the bank. And looking at the cancelled checks is not enough either.

It is mandatory that an accounting be made of the checks returned; the checks outstanding; and all deposits made in the interim period. Figure 31–4 can be used for this purpose and it is self explanatory. (Most banks furnish a similar form when cancelled checks are returned to the drawer.)

9. The Holder in Due Course Doctrine

An ancient rule of commercial paper is that one who takes commercial paper without notice of defects or defenses or claims arising out of the paper itself, is free from such defenses or claims. This simply means that one who signs a note for example, must pay the holder in due course even if the signer never received the consideration for which the note was signed in the first place. (The doctrine is illustrated by a specific example in Chapter 33.) The hardships and losses that have resulted from the application of the doctrine have in most instances fallen upon the shoulders of the wage earning consumer. Most of the losses have occurred in retail sales contracts that were backed up with a note which in turn was "discounted" with a bank or finance company.

Congress of the United States and many of the states are eliminating the doctrine as part of commercial paper law—at least as it relates to consumer purchases. (It does have legitimate uses in the business community between business persons.) The act of the New York legislature that follows illustrates the change that is taking place:

> The assignee of a retail installment contract or obligation shall be subject to all claims and defenses of the buyer against the seller arising from the

---

[9] U.C.C. 4–406(2).

[10] N.Y. *Credit Men's Adjustment Bureau, Inc.* v. *Manufacturers Hanover Trust Co.*, 343 N.Y.S.2d. 538, 12 U.C.C. Rep. 717 (1973).

sale nonwithstanding any agreement to the contrary, but the assignee's liability under this subdivision shall not exceed the amount owing to the assignee as of the time the claim or defense is asserted against the asignee. Rights of the buyer under this section can only be asserted as a matter of defense to or setoff against a claim by the assignee.

There are limitations placed upon the New York law in the application, but it illustrates the trend away from the HDC (holder in due course) doctrine.

FIGURE 31–4

CHECKBOOK RECONCILIATION

THIS FORM IS FURNISHED TO HELP RECONCILE YOUR CHECKBOOK.

1. Compare all checks and deposits with statement postings.

2. Check all checks and deposits against your stubs or check register.

3. If your statement shows a service charge or other miscellaneous charges, deduct these from the balance in your checkbook.

4. List below the number and amount of each outstanding unpaid check and any deposits not credited. Add each column.

CHECKS OUTSTANDING

Date or Number	Amount
TOTAL	

ENTER

Balance this Statement $ _____

ADD   _____

Recent Deposits
(not credited on
this statement)   _____

TOTAL   _____

SUBTRACT

Checks Outstanding   _____

BALANCE $ _____

Should agree with your checkbook balance after deducting charges and adding credits included on this statement but not shown in your checkbook.

Please report any discrepancies within 14 days.

It should be noted that there is a difference between a retail install-ment contract and a promissory note. In a true retail installment contract, the doctrine of the HDC never had any application except insofar as 9–206 of the U.C.C. applied. Under new consumer legislation in the various states, the HDC does not apply to the note any more than it does to the installment contract. The law will vary from state to state, how-ever.

10.   New Developments in Checks

American banks are constantly seeking ways to improve their systems of banking and new developments are appearing daily. Some examples follow.

A. "Flexible Checks."   Many businesses use checks that permits the *payee* to fill in the amount. These checks are issued in multicarbons and after the payee inserts the amount of the order, a carbon of the check is returned to the drawer for posting on its check stub. In short, the drawer permits the payee to draw the check! For example, a company that pur-chases books for libraries uses a three-copy precarboned check. The check is addressed to the bookseller, but the amount and discount is not filled in. The payee bookseller fills in the list price of the books ordered, deducts the discount, and figures the total. The original copy is deposited to the payee's account after indorsement. The second carbon is returned to the book buyer. The third carbon is a mailing label and is used to ship the books. One of these checks examined recently had the following words on the face: "Not good for over $25.00. Not good 30 days after date." Wider use will be made of flexible checks in the future. They make good sense because of the savings possible to both the buyer and the seller. Those who use a system as the one described report zero loss due to others filling in the checks for larger amounts. It has been found that many merchants provide an *extra* discount when orders are accom-panied by this type of check.

One of the major aluminum companies makes all of its purchases up to $1,000 in this manner, with the seller filling in the amount for the goods it supplies to the company.

B. The "Supercheck."   The supercheck contains the name of the drawee bank, the magnetic numbers of the drawer's account and the drawer's name printed over the signature line. But it is not the same as an ordinary check: it has lines for as many as 50 payees!

The drawer fills in each payee line with the name and amount to be paid to each. The check is then sent to the bank and the accounts of the payees are credited in due course as ordered upon the supercheck. The system was originated by the First National Bank of Arizona and seems to be working well at the present time.

It is advisable however, not to pay premiums on insurance policies by this type of check. This will avoid the contingency of a policy lapsing in the event the payment does not reach the payee insurance company by the end of the grace period. A personal check or money order, mailed direct to the insurance company is in order. If one makes an insurance payment *during* the grace period, a bank money order or cashiers check should be used.

C. Photos on Checks. For a modest fee, many banks will print a photo of the depositor, and spouse if requested, upon checks. Such checks have practical use: there is almost no way that another person can cash such a check unless the twin of the depositor. Also, many business persons are satisfied with this as a means of identification. If such a check should bounce, the drawer has supplied authorities with a photo for use on the wanted poster. See Figure 31–5.

FIGURE 31–5

Courtesy of Louisiana National Bank, 451 Florida Street, Baton Rouge, Louisiana 70801, Jerry D. Turk, marketing director.

D. New Identification Techniques. Most stores will accept personal checks for the amount of the purchase but identification is required by all of them. Some require two items of identification such as a drivers license and a credit card. Others have gone to new techniques.

Some require that the one who cashes the check place a thumb print upon the back of the check. This is done by use of a special stamp pad with ink that leaves no marks on the depositors thumb. If the check is a forgery or bounces, the store can issue an arrest warrant. The prosecutor has the evidence on the check by which the person may be identified and prosecuted.

Others use voice tapes which must be matched up by the voice of the one cashing the check. Some businesses require that those who cash "doubtful checks," be photographed holding the check under their face. The result is a "mug photo" along with the check showing the signature of the one that signed it. If the check bounces, the defense lawyer does not have much of a chance to defend that person – especially if the check was forged.

11. Who Besides the Banks?

It is not uncommon for private companies and even governmental agencies to be involved in money transfers by "paper." While the two examples involved here are not "commercial paper," they still serve useful business needs.

Postal Money Orders. Examine Figure 31–6. These can be purchased at any post office and are readily accepted in business as a means of "paying the bills."

Western Union? "Twink" and Mike were honeymooning in Florida when the transmission went out of their automobile. The repair garage wanted $300 and would not accept a check. A phone call to Dad up north resulted in a Western Union Money Order being sent in the amount of the repairs. Mike went to the nearest office where a draft was drawn to his order in the amount wired, and the vacation continued without mishap. Fees for money transfers by wire approximate 3 percent of the sum wired.

12. Disclosures on Consumer Notes

The C.C.P.A. Title I, Truth in Lending, requires two disclosures to be made on consumer notes (by this we mean notes given when a consumer

FIGURE 31–6

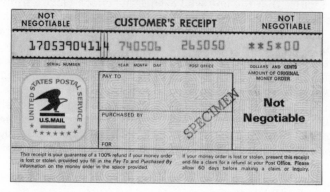

is buying "consumer goods" as contrasted to goods that will be used in a business), or on a separate form that accompanies consumer notes. First, the lender or the one extending credit, or the one who arranges to extend credit, must disclose the *annual percentage rate*. Second, the *finance charge* must be disclosed and both must be *conspicuous*. For an expanded discussion of these requirements see Chapter 35.

One final matter involves a case decided by the Supreme Court of Virginia. It illustrates the surprises that can arise in the everyday use of commercial paper. For want of a better title, it has been called a "Banker's Nightmare."

"A BANKER'S NIGHTMARE"

One who holds a properly drawn check has three means of realizing the benefits from the instrument: (1) indorse it in blank or specially[11] and negotiate it to another in full or part settlement of an existing obligation; (2) cash the check after indorsing it or (3) deposit it. The end result is the same: the payee gains the benefit of the sum of money for which the check was drawn. While each option finds use depending upon the circumstances, the majority of checks are disposed of by deposits to named accounts. Banks and their branches assume little risk in the handling of the vast number of checks processed as deposits each business day.[12] A check that is deposited is "conditional payment" only, and ultimate payment by the bank controls. This fact, backed up by the warranties of the drawer, the payee, and subsequent indorsers, makes this so.

But when a bank *cashes* a check rather than taking it in a deposit, the risks multiply. This is so because when an item is paid in cash, it constitutes "final payment."[13] There are exceptions that involve forgeries of indorsement, fraud or bad faith, but these are rare in practice. One who deposits a check, makes the warranties of a depositor.[14] One who cashes it, does not; and it is as simple as that.

What happens when a check "bounces" and a dispute arises between the payor bank (who claims that it was deposited) and the payee indorser (who claims that it was cashed)? The parties go to court.[15]

A Check Is Written

A dredging company, by its agent, W. R. Wood, drew a check on the First and Merchants' Bank, Virginia Beach, Virginia, payable to William J. and Margaret Kirby in the sum of $2,500. On December 30, 1966, Mrs. Kirby handed the check, properly indorsed, to a teller at a branch

---

[11] U.C.C., 3–204(1) and 3–204(2).

[12] Americans are writing more than 70 million checks daily and over 20 billion annually, a "billion dollar drag."

[13] U.C.C., 4–213.

[14] U.C.C., 3–417(1) and 4–207(1).

[15] *Kirby et. al.* v. *First and Merchants' National Bank*, 210 Va. 88, 168 S.E.2d 273 (1969).

of the main bank. The check was accompanied by a deposit slip showing that $2,300 was being deposited to her account. The teller gave Mrs. Kirby $200 because she was "short and needed some cash." The bank credited her account with $2,300 on January 3, 1967, which, because of intervening holidays, was the "next business day." On January 4, the bank discovered that the check had been drawn against insufficient funds. Rather than giving written notice to the Kirby's, a bank officer called and asked them to make the check good. At first they agreed — and later changed their minds. On January 10, $2,500 was charged to the Kirby account creating an overdraft of $543.47. (The Kirby's had a balance of $1,956.53 at the time.) The Kirby's refused to make up the overdraft and eight days later the bank filed suit for that sum.

The Trial

The trial was held without a jury and only one witness (a bank officer) was called. The following question was asked of him: "Did you (the bank) cash the check before you credited (the amount to the deposit)?" He answered, "Yes, sir." At the conclusion of the hearing, the court entered judgment for the bank. The Kirby's appealed. (See Figure 31–7).

FIGURE 31–7

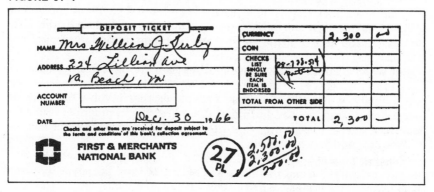

The High Court Acts

The Supreme Court of Virginia had before it four questions that had to be answered. First, was the check "cashed" or was it "deposited"? The court held that the evidence showed that it had been cashed and, therefore, the check had been "finally paid." Second, were the Kirby's liable to the bank for breach of their warranties of indorsement?[16] The court said "not so," pointing out that an indorser contracts to pay an instrument *only if it is dishonored*. Therefore, since the bank had finally paid the check, it had not been dishonored!

---

[16] U.C.C., 3–417(1) and 4–207(1).

The bank in desperation turned to its depositor contract, which stated ". . . all items are credited subject to final payment." Thus, the third question had to be answered: Did the bank have a "contract right" to charge the sum back regardless of whether or not the check was paid in cash on December 30? The court reminded the bank that its depositor's contract did not change the workings of the following Uniform Commercial Code Provision: A bank has the right to charge an item back if, before the "midnight deadline,"[17] the bank, "(*a*) returns the item; or (*b*) sends written notice of dishonor or nonpayment if the item is held for protest or is otherwise unavailable for return."[18] The bank did neither—and the court closed door number three.

As a last resort, the bank demanded that it be given its common-law right to recover the payment since it had been made by mistake. The court replied: "The rule that a drawee who mistakenly pays a check has recourse only against the drawer," has been adopted by the Uniform Commercial Code and therefore "the defense is not available to the bank." Thus, all four exits were effectively closed—and the Kirby's were home free. This left the bank with one recourse: to go after the drawer on his warranties (apparently, something the bank knew would be a useless act).

A strong dissent was filed by two justices who pointed out that, regardless of what was said about it, the check had been deposited rather than cashed.

> There is nothing in this record from which it could possibly be deducted that Mrs. Kirby walked into the bank and cashed the Neuse check for $2,500. That is, she presented the check and demanded and received $2,500 in cash, and afterwards redeposited $2,300 of it in currency. This simply did not occur, and the evidence does not reflect it. While the bank officer does refer to "cashing the check," the evidence and records of the bank show that it was not cashed, but was accepted for deposit and clearance as any other check.[19]

In addition, the dissent points out that in the past there had been a close relationship between the bank and the Kirby's. So when they promised the bank officer that they would "cover the check," the bank was justified in not giving the required written notice. Therefore, the dissent continues, the Kirby's should not be permitted to use the defense of lack of written notice when this had been caused by their own oral assurances to the bank: an estoppel situation.

The bank made two efforts to assist the Kirby's: first, by handling the deposit as it did; and second, by calling the Kirby's and alerting them to the fact that the check was drawn against "insufficient funds." There is nothing inherently wrong with the practice followed by banks who accommodate their established customers—and most make it a business policy to do so. But when a bank suffers a loss simply because it does,

---

[17] U.C.C., 4–104(1).

[18] U.C.C., 4–212(3) and 4–301.

[19] *Kirby et. al.*, page 353.

changes can be expected in customer relation practices. And when this happens, as it already has in Virginia, the depositors — not the banks — will be the losers in the end.

REVIEW QUESTIONS

1. You hold a check payable to your order. Why should you *not* indorse it in blank until you arrive at the teller's window?
2. Sketch a sample supercheck. What practical problems might arise in the use of such a check?
3. Distinguish a check from the charge slip that is given to the customer after use of a credit card at a restaurant.
4. What specific business use can you think of for a "flexible check"?
5. True or False. The HDC (holder in due course) doctrine has been a blessing to lenders.
6. You are the owner of a retail business called "Blue's Shoes." You have decided to order a rubber stamp so that the checks you take in each day can be restricted by indorsement. How would you tell the stamp maker to make the stamp?
7. Name two tax reasons for both the maker and payee of a note keeping an accurate amortization table of payments as they are made?
8. The text discusses "stop payments" and "stale checks." What might the consequences be if a bank pays a stale check that has a valid stop upon it?
9. Why does "handwriting" control typing?
10. Get in the habit of reconciling your personal bank account when the cancelled checks are received. Most banks provide a form for this purpose with the checks. Figure 31-4 is a standard form. What is the legal reason for reconciliation? The practical reason?

Words and Phrases

Write out briefly what they mean to you.
1. Holder in due course.
2. Ambiguous terms.
3. Indorsement.
4. "You have paid your note in full."
5. Warranties of an indorser. (Review chart.)

Coverage:	The various ways in which Article 3 paper is used to misappropriate funds of others.
What to Look for:	Ways to discourage this in business.
Application:	The business person must anticipate the matters discussed here.

32 Misuse of Commercial Paper

Emblers de gentz[1]

Each year in the United States, more than 200 million dollars is being taken from individuals and businesses through the misuse of commercial paper. In addition to this, 1.4 billion dollars is being extracted by fraudulent means. In most of the fraudulent schemes, commercial paper provides the vehicle by which the fraud is carried out.

These annual loses are six times the sum of money that is being stolen by robberies and other thefts. The Federal Bureau of Investigation reports that arrests for these activities have doubled in the last decade and is currently on the rise. The purpose of this chapter is to see just how these losses are possible. Four activities will be examined: "Kiting," forgery, "embezzlement," and the "cash sales trick."

"KITING"

A criminal act encountered frequently in banking arises when one who holds a check issued by the drawer "raises" the sum of money for which the check was drawn. Thousands of "kited" checks are paid by the banks each year. The classic example is the "racehorse" check discussed in Chapter 29 (see Figure 29–6 for a copy of the check involved

---

[1] "A stealing from the people." The phrase is found in the old rolls of England's Parliament. For example, "Whereas murders, robberies, *emblers de gentz,* arson are committed . . .", emphasis added.

in that case). The check had been drawn in a negligent manner making it quite easy to raise it from $600 to $3,600. This negligence of the drawer forced him to bear the loss.

Another example of kiting involved a woman in Ohio who received a workmen's compensation check in the sum of $84.36. She erased this sum, typed in $200,984.36, and the bank cashed the check! This was true in spite of the fact that the check had the amount of $84.36 printed on its face and had visible signs of erasures.[2]

Guarding against Kiting

As discussed in Chapter 30, the best protection against kiteing is to use a check writer, a commercial product, or a personal check stamp available in most office supply shops. In the absence of these devices, the next best protection is to "close up" the check (see Figure 29–1 for an example).

It must be remembered that if a bank pays a raised check because the drawer was negligent in creating it, the drawer must bear the loss. And in addition, the law holds the drawer of the instrument "responsible" for the "original tenor of the instrument."[3] If the drawer was negligent, the loss falls upon that person.

The second way that misuse of Article 3 paper occurs is through forgeries.

FORGERIES

A "forgery" occurs when an unauthorized person places another's signature on some document. Forgeries are *not* limited to commercial paper and have occurred on deeds, wills, receipts, letters, bills of lading and numerous other documents. Forgery is a felony in all states and carries severe penalties upon conviction.

One court defined forgery as:

> A fraudulent making and alteration of writing to prejudice of another man's right, or a false making, a making *malo animo*[4] of any instrument, for the purpose of fraud or deceit.[5]

A forgery is distinguished from "counterfeiting" which is the fraudulent imitation of paper money or coins.

Forgeries are frequently encounted in business and the principal law that governs is found in U.C.C. 3–401:

> (1) No person is liable on an instrument unless his signature appears thereon. (2) A signature is made by use of any name, including any trade or

---

[2] *U.S. News & World Report*, March 12, 1973, p. 54.

[3] U.C.C., 3–407.

[4] "With Evil Mind" or bad purpose or intention.

[5] *Iberville Trust & Savings Bank* v. *City Cafe*, 143 So. 73 (1932), emphasis added.

assumed name, upon an instrument, or by any word or mark in lieu of a written signature.

The rationale behind this rule is that a person, John Doe for example, is only liable on Article 3 paper when he has placed his name upon it himself or by someone to whom he gave permission to affix his signature. Until that time he has done nothing at law and cannot be held to any liability on the instrument. If a bank pays on a forgery, the bank must, as a general rule, recredit the account of the drawer. This is of course subject to the drawer giving the bank notice of the forgery within the applicable time limits. (See chapter 30 for a discussion of this.)

However, a drawer who by "his negligence substantially contributes" to a forgery, "is precluded from asserting the alteration or lack of authority against a holder in due course or against a drawee or other payor who pays the instrument in good faith and in accordance with the reasonable commercial standards of the drawee's or payor's business."[6]

Guarding against Forgeries

Care in the drawing of checks and safeguarding blank checks and check books are primary means of protecting against forgeries. But the most important technique is the prompt reconciliation of bank statements and careful personal examination of cancelled checks. Alterations or unauthorized signatures must be reported to the drawee bank at once.[7]

Forgeries have been widely used in embezzlement schemes.

EMBEZZLEMENT

Embezzlement has been defined as ". . . the fraudulent appropriation of property by a person to whom it was entrusted, or to whose hands it has lawfully come."[8] This crime is distinguishable from "larceny" or theft because larceny requires *criminal intent* at the time of the taking. Embezzlement arises when one criminally appropriates property of another that *lawfully came to his or her possession*—a legal distinction. "Property" can include stocks, bonds, goods—and checks, notes, bills of exchange, and certificates of deposit.

The definition makes it clear that embezzlement can only occur in situations where one entrusts property to another. This requires trust and confidence such as found in employer–employee, husband–wife, master–servant, principal–agent relationships.

The one who suffers embezzlement loss in these relationships must by logic, bear much of the blame. After all, that person is the one who trusted the embezzeler. Because of this, the U.C.C. has a special forgery rule where embezzlement is involved.

---

[6] U.C.C., 3–406.

[7] U.C.C., 4–406.

[8] *American Life Ins. Co.*, v. *U.S. Fidelity & Guaranty Co.*, 261 Mich. 221, 246 N.W. 71, (1933).

The "Embezzlement Forgery Rule"

Under the old Uniform Negotiable Instruments Law, instruments that were forged in the course of embezzlement were treated as "bearer paper" — even if they were not. When an employee forged an indorsement and the employer attempted to force the bank to recredit its account, the bank would refuse. If the bank was sued, the court generally held that the forged indorsement was *not necessary* and the company was stuck. Its recourse was against the embezzling employee.

The old rule was a "fiction" and has been abandoned by the U.C.C. However, the U.C.C. has substituted a new fiction for the old one. U.C.C. 3–405, provides:

1. An indorsement by any person in the name of a named payee is effective if
   a. an impostor by use of the mails or otherwise has induced the maker or drawer to issue the instrument to him or his confederate in the name of the payee; or
   b. a person signing as or on behalf of a maker or drawer intends the payee to have no interest in the instrument; or
   c. an agent or employee of the maker or drawer has supplied him with the name of the payee intending the latter to have no such interest.
2. Nothing in this section shall affect the criminal or civil liability of the person so indorsing.

Two case examples illustrate the embezzlement forgery rule in operation.

The Padded Payroll

In this scheme, an employee has checks issued to some unsuspecting person whose name is added to the payroll. The checks are then intercepted; the indorsements forged, and the checks are deposited to the account of the embezzling employee.

In a Mississippi case,[9] an employee created a fake policy loan on "Lester O. Becker," an actual policy holder with the company, and 20 checks were issued aggregating over $24,000. The employee took the checks to "deliver to Mr. Becker," forged Becker's name and deposited the checks to his own account.

The employer, upon discovery of the embezzlement, demanded that the money be recredited to its account. The bank refused and suit followed. The court applied U.C.C. 3–405 (1), holding that the indorsement by the employee "... in the name of a named payee (Becker) (was) effective ..." The employer lost the case.

Another form of embezzlement is the "fictitious payee" scheme.

Fictitious Payee

In most of these cases the employee has open access to company checks and is often in charge of drawing the checks for the employer.

---

[9] *Delmar Bank of University City* v. *Fidelity & Deposit Co.* v. *Young*, U.S. Dist. Ct. E. D. Miss., 300 F. Supp. 496, 6 U.C.C. Rep. 1060, (1969).

The employee prepares a check or checks in the name of a nonexistent person, indorses and keeps the proceeds.

Again, if the bank is called upon to make good on the check or checks, it can rely upon U.C.C. 3–405. The indorsement in the name of the payee is effective – even if fictitious.

Guarding against Embezzlement

Many techniques can be used by employers to avoid or discourage embezzlement. Included are spot audits, reconciliation of bank accounts by outside personnel, splitting of check writing duties, and other internal checks and controls. The main point is to avoid any situation in which one person has unrestricted access to the checkbook.

"Fictitious Payee" – A Variation

Zero Bank made a loan to a customer in the sum of $3,200 with which the customer was to purchase a 1970 Ford XL Coupe Serial No. OEG106235. The bank took this car as security for the loan and all of the necessary papers were filled out and the financing statement was properly filed at the filing point. The check with which to purchase the car was delivered to the customer – but it was made payable to both the customer and the car dealer. The check was indorsed by both and in time, cleared the bank. All seemed to be in order, that is, until the customer failed to make the first payment on the note.

At that time, the bank decided to foreclose upon the auto – only to discover that no such automobile had been sold by the dealer to the customer! The bank had simply been taken by two persons who worked a new variation of an old con game upon it.[10]

A final misuse of Article 3 paper has occurred in a reverse manner: One leads another to believe that payment by check will be acceptable – and then when it is advantageous to do so, payment is refused. This became known as the "cash sales trick."

CASH SALES TRICK

Assume that seller X contracts to deliver to buyer Y, by noon on Saturday, July 2, 10,000 bags of sugar at a price of $1.50 per bag. On Friday, July 1, sugar is bringing $2.00 per bag and seller X wants out of the contract. The technique applied in the past was to get the *buyer* to breach the contract. Here's how it worked.

The seller would deliver the goods as close to the deadline as possible, say at 11:50 A.M. in our example. As the buyer tendered payment by a $15,000 check, the seller would refuse, demanding the "common law" right to be paid in cash. Business persons do not keep this quantity of cash around – and by that time the banks were closed.

---

[10] *Welcome Credit Union* v. *Capital Bank & Trust Co.*, 14 U.C.C. Rep., 804, Boston Municipal Court, App. Div. (1974).

The seller would declare the buyer in breach of contract, load up the goods and sell them on the market for $20,000.

This misuse of Article 3 paper has fallen victim to the U.C.C. which provides that ". . . tender of payment is sufficient when made by any means or in any manner current in ordinary course of business *unless the seller demands payment in legal tender and gives an extension of time reasonably necessary to procure it.*"[11]

This is a good example of how a statute can "plug a legal loophole." But as surprising as it may sound, the cash sales trick is still with us. So it becomes a job of the courts to discourage its use. A 1972 Georgia case illustrates how our courts treat this violation of law after it is recognized that it is being used.

A Modern Cash Sales Trick Case

Mrs. Barnes missed the first installment on her car. The "chaser" for Chrysler Credit Corp., demanded possession of the car. Mrs. Barnes explained that the check had been mailed and must have been delayed at the post office. She then offered to write another check but was told "cash or the car." At that time, the banks were closed and Mrs. Barnes did not have access to $129.99 in cash. The car was repossessed.

The next day Mrs. Barnes tendered cash—but Chrysler Credit refused to accept it claiming default had occurred which permitted them to accelerate the entire debt. Chrysler proceeded to sell the auto to cover the debt.

The Georgia court looked to U.C.C. 2–511 (2), and held that if Chrysler wanted cash, they had to give Mrs. Barnes a reasonable time in which to obtain it.[12] The drafters intended to bring an end to the "cash sales trick" by this section. However, as the case illustrates, some persons still feel that they can rely upon this old time "seller's way out of a contract."

REVIEW QUESTIONS

1. Why is "embezzlement" not the same as a "forgery"?
2. "Kiting" almost never involves a forgery. Why is this?
3. What does "malo animo" mean? How about "maladjustment," "malnutrition," "malady," and "malingerer"?
4. Give an example of "counterfeiting." Distinguish it from "forgery."
5. It is a general principle of law that one is not bound on an instrument unless that persons name appears upon it. Why?
6. Outline the prior forgery rule and the current rule. They are different but how do they accomplish the same objective? Both are legal "fictions."
7. Distinguish "forgeries," "larceny," "embezzlement," and "counterfeiting."
8. State a common sense reason for the "embezzlement forgery rule."
9. Name two ways of avoiding embezzlement in the business setting.
10. What are the penalties for embezzlement in your state?

---

[11] U.C.C., 2–511 (2) (emphasis added).

[12] *Chrysler Credit Corp.* v. *Barnes*, 126 Ga. App. 444, II U.C.C. Rep. 274, 191 S.E.2d 121, (1972).

Words and Phrases

Write out briefly what they mean to you.
1. Forgery.
2. Counterfeiting.
3. Embezzlement.
4. Larceny.
5. Fraud.

part three
Consumers and Credit

Coverage:	An introduction to "consumerism" and the problems of the consuming poor.
What to Look for:	The types of laws that can discourage these activities.
Application:	Apply the consumer laws in coming chapters to the "business setting" here.

33 The Citizen as a Consumer

One of the ironies of our society is that those who need to know the most about our laws – the consumers – are the ones who usually know the least. In this chapter, we will test the truth of this statement by examining some of the problems faced by all of us as consumers – and especially those that can be classed as the consuming poor.

Until retirement, each of us will be an employee, or employer, or professional person, and at the same time we will be a consumer. As the years go by, we will perhaps advance to a position as an executive in the business community. When this happens, our living conditions will improve, our salary will increase, and our standing in the community may improve; but we will still be a consumer – a status shared by all of us, rich, poor, impoverished, young, and old. To begin with, what exactly is a "consumer"?

CONSUMERS

A "consumer" is one who consumes or utilizes goods and services for personal, family or household use, as contrasted with a person or firm who sells or provides such goods and services to others.

"Consumer goods" are goods that directly satisfy the human needs and wants of those who are consumers. The precise number of consumers at each minute of the day is the total of all human beings who are using the vast quantities of goods and services available to them.

The importance of the consumer to the manufacturer, distributor, and retailer is obvious when one thinks about it. When A purchases a carton of soft drinks, A absorbs all of the costs incurred in the distributive chain – from the items used to produce the flavor to the production of the package in which it is sold – and A absorbs the profits made all down the line. This simple economic fact would lead a reasonable person to the conclusion that because of this importance, the consumer, would always be provided good quality, fair prices, and safety in products for consumption – and would not be cheated in the process. In addition, it would be assumed that if a consumer is injured by a defective product, the consumer would find adequate compensation in the courts; that if one applied for a loan, that person would be treated fairly; and that if an agency furnished credit information about one it would be accurate. Unfortunately, what a reasonable person might believe is often not the way it is in practice. The path of the consumer contains many traps or "pitfalls."

Kinds of Problems

A serious problem, in the form of advertising, confronts all consumers. Quite often, it is of the "hard sell" or brainwash variety. Examples include loud commercials, ads implying sex, or that exaggerate the nature of the products offered. Some are just plain fraudulent. Steps have been taken to protect the consumer from the effects of misleading and fraudulent advertising with the Federal Trade Commission being active in this area.

Another perpetual problem is the item that will not work. It might be a toaster that will not toast, a refrigerator that will not refrigerate, or a color TV that has no color. The law has fallen short of providing proper remedies to the buyer in such instances. The controlling law has been that of "warranties," but warranty law can only be effectively applied in court – and this is the problem. The consumer with a defect in a toaster cannot always afford legal services – and the lawyer is usually not interested in the case, anyway.

Another problem area has been the home improvement swindle. Such swindles include home repairs that are defectively completed, substandard equipment for the home that often will not work, or the sale of equipment which is overpriced. Positive steps have been taken here – as will be seen – and the consumer who knows his or her rights can reduce losses in such matters in the future.

Another problem for the consumer has been in determining how maximum value may be obtained for the buying dollar. For example, in installment buying, it is difficult to determine the true price of what is purchased because of interest and carrying charges. In the supermarket, it is almost impossible to determine if the 1 lb. 3½ oz. box of soap powder is a better buy than the one with 2 lbs. 5½ oz. at a higher price. Comparison shopping is a difficult matter for any consumer. New pricing laws are helping to solve this problem.

Finally, making effective use of credit poses constant problems. The consumer has become increasingly dependent upon credit in obtaining needs and wants. In recent years, the use of credit has increased at a fantastic rate. By 1960, more than $40 billion in American consumer credit debts were outstanding daily. Ten years later, that figure was $120 billion and going up.

With this explosion came concern. For example, uninformed use of credit often led the consumer into financial chaos when obligations were undertaken that could not be met. The result was a sharp rise in personal bankruptcies. In 1960, 89,639 working persons filed personal bankruptcy. By 1967, personal bankruptcies had gone to 174,205 and the upward trend continued into the 1970s. The consumer problems identified are representative. More specific ones will be identified in the discussion of the "consuming poor."

THE CONSUMING POOR

A large number of Americans can be classified as part of the consuming poor. In this capacity they must face not only the routine problems of the marketplace, but other problems that are directly related to the environment in which they exist. They represent one of the major problems of our society. And in this fact is found the reason that the solution to their problem—which is in turn our problem—should be of major concern to each of us.

The Ghetto Society

Society tends to breed a class of persons who for one reason or another can be called "unfortunate." It can happen for hereditary reasons such as mental sickness or disease, or it can result from poverty itself. It can follow from sickness that develops accidentally or for self-imposed reasons such as drug addiction or alcoholism. Poverty attracts poverty, and each city, large or small, ends up with slum areas or ghettos. One who visits the ghetto areas of the larger cities, such as New York, Chicago, and Philadelphia, is struck by the contrast between the affluent and the poor who often exist side by side. On one side of a street may be a modern office building—on the other, a slum tenement structure. Those who live within these ghettos are faced with constant problems: lack of proper sanitation, poor garbage disposal, poor heat in cold weather, lack of proper storage for food, and—the biggest problem of all—inability to acquire the consumer goods needed to sustain life in a decent manner.

Lack of Mobility

The head of the ghetto household has no car—such ownership is a luxury reserved for the fortunate. Instead, such a person has the choice of three means of transportation: the buses, the subways, or feet. Since the first two are expensive, resort is made to the latter. For this reason, the area in which one can shop is restricted. In fact, it is almost restricted to the block in which he or she lives. Because of this, one must be satisfied with what is found in that neighborhood.

The stores available are often owned and operated by neighbors. The selection of goods is scanty, prices are high, and the merchandise is frequently of poor quality. In addition to the regular food shops, many of which are respectable but poor, the ghetto shopper must shop in stores that are operated for the express purpose of exploiting the buyer.

It is common knowledge that certain merchants seek out the poor areas of a city in which to conduct their business, and for good reason. The consuming poor are a better credit risk than at first seems possible. Their lack of mobility means that they will be there month after month. And while their income is restricted, it is regular because the welfare checks arrive on set days of the month. Thus, if the ghetto consumer can be enticed to purchase merchandise on time, the seller will eventually be paid for what was purchased.

In addition, since the consuming poor cannot alter their life style by moving to a better section of the city, or by joining a club, or by buying a new car, it is logical for them to want to upgrade their immediate surroundings; and this is done most easily by the purchase of new furniture. It is not uncommon to find large numbers of furniture stores inside the ghetto areas of the cities. The majority of unscrupulous sales activities reported involve the sale of furniture. What can happen to a buyer in a furniture store?

Bait and Switch

The ad reads: "Three rooms of furniture, $198, easy terms—this week only." Mrs. X, who is on welfare and has four children to support, sees this ad and believes that if the monthly payments are small enough she can work it into her budget. After all, the children would appreciate something to replace the scanty furniture that they now have. For example, the older children must wait at the breakfast table until the young ones have finished with the two chairs that she owns.

Mrs. X visits the store and is shown a nice arrangement of furniture. She signs the papers and the furniture dealer tells her the goods will be delivered later in the week. In the meantime, the dealer discounts the note at the bank.

When the furniture arrives Mrs. X discovers that it is not what she had been shown and is a collection of items of poor quality. What can she do?

Back to the Store.   The salesperson who sold the furniture assures her that she was shipped what she bought and the manager backs this up. "You mean that furniture there on display? Why, the price on that set is $699, you only wanted the $198 grouping." Mrs. X is told that the matter is no longer in their hands since the note has been sold to the bank, and the suggestion is made that she talk to the bank about it. At the bank, they will not discuss the matter since they had no part in the sale of the furniture. They only bought the note. What can Mrs. X do?

In the Past

For many years the "bait and switch" game has been used to reap large profits for the unscrupulous. And the buyer always lost by not being able to afford a lawyer to handle the matter. Worse, if a lawyer did take the case, the burden of proof was on the buyer – not the seller – and the burden was difficult to carry. In the usual case, the buyer paid for the furniture in the end and did without what that person tried to get in the first place – better furniture.

Today

The above is one of the most common complaints heard in the legal aid offices in the ghettos. The lawyers who staff these offices are able to do some good for the consumer, but the problem is far from being solved.

Sharking

Another practice is that of making loans to the consuming poor at high interest rates. Since there is a constant need for money, the poor are logical targets for loans. The loans are freely made for the reasons suggested previously, and are made at exorbitant interest rates.

All states have laws prohibiting the charging of interest in excess of a set amount. These are called "usury laws"; therefore, to charge more interest than the law permits is "usury." In spite of the laws, the practices of charging exorbitant rates (sharking) continue. The problems that face the person stuck with high interest on a loan are similar to those confronted by one caught in a "bait and switch" sale.

Extortion

A "big brother" to sharking is extortion. While not confined to the consuming poor, the provisions of federal legislation may be brought into play to assist the ghetto consumer who has been "taken" on a loan. Extortion is "the act or practice of wresting money away from a person by force, threats, misuse of authority, or by an undue exercise of power. It is sometimes applied to the exaction of too high of a price." The purposes of the federal extortion law are spelled out in the findings of Congress:

> Organized crime is interstate and international in character. Its activities involve many billions of dollars each year. It is directly responsible for murders, willful injuries to person and property, corruption of officials and terrorization of countless citizens. Extortionate credit transactions are characterized by the use, or the express or implied threat of use, of violence or other criminal means to cause harm to person, reputation or property as a means of enforcing payment.[1]

---

[1] Consumer Credit Protection Act, Title II, Section 201 (*a*).

The penalties for violation of the federal extortion law, which is Title II of the Consumer Credit Protection Act, are severe. The act reads

> Whoever makes any extortionate extension of credit, or conspires to do so, shall be fined not more than $10,000 or imprisoned not more than 20 years, or both.

The language of Congress is broad, and a careful reading brings one to the conclusion that the loan does not have to be between a top figure in the underworld and a member of the World Bank. Rather, it could be a loan between a ghetto consumer borrower and a ghetto lender. Perhaps the problem of loan sharking of the poor will be solved by strict application of the federal law.

While the poor have routinely been subjected to exorbitant interest rate loans, they have just as routinely been denied legitimate credit at reputable stores. This has compounded their problems. All of the factors discussed present a poor picture.

WHAT CAN BE DONE?

Federal laws discussed in coming chapters have begun to provide some of the answers. Laws such as these are justified when it becomes obvious that there are no other solutions. For example, the Consumer Credit Protection Act is now providing relief to many consumers in areas where no help was available in the past.

The state consumer laws that have been passed, and those that will be passed in the future, will provide further relief—that is, if they are enforced. It is common knowledge that state consumer laws are seldom enforced with vigor. The opposite seems to be the case with federal laws.

Another possible solution to the problems of the consuming poor is twofold: First, the chain stores should be encouraged to open branches close to the problem areas of the cities; and second, credit in these stores must be made available to the poor. Drawing upon precedent it is unlikely that the major clothing and food stores will rush headlong into the poverty-stricken areas of the city—unless it can be shown that it will be economically beneficial for them to do so. In the Watts area of Los Angeles, prior to the riots of 1965, of some 16 stores counted in one portion of the ghetto area, only one could have been remotely identified with anything that resembled a chain store. The decision to open branches in the slum areas will become one for management. And it is suggested that if living standards of the poor were upgraded, the increased buying power would benefit each of us. Some steps have been taken to extend credit to the poor.

Credit for the Poor

The National Welfare Rights Organization (NWRO) has been working with representatives of national chain stores on the question of whether they will provide credit to those on welfare. Some chains have agreed to extend credit in small amounts to those who are recommended by the NWRO. This is a step toward ultimate relief for the poor. Others are carrying out programs in education. (See Chapter 36, Equal Credit Opportunity Act, also.)

Education for the Poor

An immediate method that can be used to assist those who are in need is through education. Job training, consumer buying assistance, and basic orientation into the law are suggested topics.

The problems that exist with the consuming poor will not be solved in a few months – or even years. And the law as such will not be able to provide all of the answers. It will take an increasing awareness of the problem on the part of each of us, and a willingness to give a hand in any way we can. The citizen cannot afford to ignore the problem because if this is done, the problem will multiply. And if it does, each of us will pay for it in some manner in the long run.

REVIEW QUESTIONS

1. Do you believe that the problems of the consuming poor are problems of society? If so, why? If not, why?
2. What argument could you make for locating a legitimate store in or near a slum area?
3. In what ways could a *merchant* assist the poor consumer?
4. What is the practical result of the lack of "consumer mobility"?
5. True or False. The average buyer has an indirect voice in the production of what he or she consumes.
6. Give an example of extortion not discussed in the text.
7. The FTC in 1974, charged Sears and Roebuck with using "bait and switch" tactics. Sears denied this strenuously. How might such charges have arisen?
8. Is the seller of consumer goods also a consumer? What relevance might this have in business?
9. Name three reasons for the growth of consumer credit.
10. Name three reasons why personal bankruptcies have been on the increase in recent years.

Words and Phrases

Write out briefly what they mean to you.
1. Sharking.
2. The affluent society.
3. Pricing.
4. Consumer laws.
5. The "ghetto society."

Coverage:	Facts and the law as they relate to credit cards and electronic money.
What to Look for:	The "contracts" involved.
Application:	Compare "cash" shopping with card shopping and identify good points of both.

34 Consumers, Credit Cards, and Electronic Money

In 1900, the bulk of the wealth in the United States was concentrated in the hands of a priviledged few. In addition, little if any credit was extended to those who made up the working class. These two factors made it extremely difficult for those on the lower rungs of society to improve their standard of living. The credit system as we know it today was not even visualized at that time. As a result of this, the typical working person—and the children of that worker, were "locked" into a fixed financial strata, and had little or no chance to accumulate wealth.

CONSUMERS

In the decades between World War I and II, changes began to occur that contributed materially to our present day credit system. First, labor began to organize into effective unions once their right to bargain collectively had been upheld by the Supreme Court of the United States. This in turn led to increasing levels of personal wealth for the worker because of better pay. As a result of both of these factors, the working person became a better credit risk and lines of credit opened up that had been closed before.

CREDIT CARDS

Following this primary change in credit practices came a revolutionary development that struck the credit industry in the 1950s and 60s. It was the "credit card." A credit card is simply another method by which credit is offered to the public and it's wide acceptance opened up horizons of credit unheard of even in 1960. By the end of 1969, the personal credit outstanding on credit card accounts was $2.5 billion. By 1976, this had risen to over $9 billion or an increase of about 250 percent in just six years.

Today this trend continues as more and more persons are found acceptable to the credit card companies. This should continue to be true in the future in spite of changes that have been occurring in the credit card industry. Many of these changes are occurring because the card companies are developing new computer techniques and are placing into effect new card practices. The main goal of all card companies today is to build and maintain "quality accounts" and to do this, high standards of card payments are required – and demanded.

As might have been expected, an entirely new concept in the extension of credit occured about 1970. This development can be attributed to the success of the credit card and is being referred to as "electronic money" or "electronic transfers." This development will be examined before we look at credit cards in their conventional forms.

ELECTRONIC MONEY

In a short time, almost all transfers of money will be made through the use of electronic impulses as they operate through computers. Computers have been mentioned briefly in the processing of checks, but we are talking about the use of computers *without* checks being used at all. The impact of this change will be staggering to the banks, to others who process loans, and to the law itself. It has been suggested that the change will be so far-reaching that banking as we know it today may not exist ten years from now. It has also been suggested that the "dollar" may become a mere "concept" rather than something that is actually used in the marketplace as a medium of exchange. For example, we can tell our children about "silver dollars" and "silver halfdollars," but it is virtually impossible to show them either. Electronic money is not another offshoot of science fiction – it is a reality at the Mellon Bank of Pittsburgh, the First National City Bank of New York, the Bank of Delaware in Wilmington, and many others.

This new concept in the transfer of money has been picked up by the U.S. Treasury Department and is being used to transfer money directly to the banks of the recipients of Social Security. In addition, the concept has been given statutory backing by Congress. On October 29, 1974, Public Law 93–495[1] was enacted. Title II of this law established the National Commission on Electronic Transfers.

How Does It Work?

Assume that executive A of Zero Corporation decides to bank the "electronic way." A's monthly salary minus the standard deductions

---

[1]H.R. 11221, 93rd Cong. 2nd Sess.

(income tax, social security, and others) will be programmed on the computer used by the bank. The corporation will at any time during the month —by day, by week, or by month—deposit to A's account the amount due for salary, and this is also done electronically. The computer will then pay out of A's account, reoccurring bills that have been programmed. To illustrate, the corporation deposits $2,000 to the account and the bank pays the car payment, house payment, insurance, and other bills to the proper accounts elsewhere. If the executive runs short, the bank can make a loan at interest, and will deduct payments in the coming months. At stated times, A receives a statement of deposits and payments—a perfect record of the financial transactions.

Routine, everyday purchases can be worked into the system by the use of an identification card. If A buys a pair of shoes, the sale is literally "rung up" on A's account by a deduction, with credit being made to the shoe store account.

FIGURE 34–1
Front and Reverse of an American Express Credit Card

Courtesy The American Express Company.

The current drag on the market caused by the use of checks will give way to the widespread use of electronic money and credit cards. Americans are writing about 75 million checks a day, and the cost of handling these checks is staggering. And when one considers that most of these checks are sent to others by mail, it can be appreciated that the benefit to the post office system would be considerable.

In the meantime, credit cards are being widely used and an examination of them is in order.

The typical card is a plastic device with raised letters and account numbers measuring $2\frac{1}{8}''$ x $3\frac{3}{8}''$, which has been adopted as standard. Credit cards are issued in all phases of business, from banking to department stores, from service stations to bookstores. (See Figure 34–1.)

HOW DOES THE CREDIT CARD SYSTEM WORK?

In use, the card is placed against a multicarboned sales slip. Pressure is applied by machine as it rests upon the carboned paper. The amount of the purchase (tip, if desired) and tax is filled in. The result is an imprint upon the carboned paper which is signed by the purchaser. The buyer receives a copy, giving an instant receipt. The seller retains the other copies and forwards them for processing. The buyer is invoiced the amount of the purchase. Examine Figure 34–2.

A New Concept

Credit card law is relatively new, since credit cards did not find nationwide acceptance until the 1960s. The big use of them began when the oil companies flooded the nation with cards at no cost. Their theory was that those who received cards would purchase their oil, gas, and related items such as tires and automobile accessories. By 1976, 70 million Americans held credit cards of one sort or another.

The Banks Join the Wave of Plastic

Between 1967 and 1970, the major banks of America joined in the credit card activity. Bank of America, number one in the nation in size, has issued its "BankAmericard" over extensive areas of the nation. The next three largest banks have issued the following cards: Chase Manhattan Bank, "UniCard"; First National City Bank, "Master Charge"; and Manufacturers Hanover Trust, "Master Charge." A review of the top 20 banks in America discloses that of the other 16, ten have issued credit cards, with "Master Charge" appearing most often on the list.

Usual Practices

Many credit cards are issued free of charge and are "nonexpiring," meaning that they can be used until replaced by another card. Other cards are issued for a yearly fee and expire each year.

Most credit card companies require that the balance each month be paid in full, but some permit monthly payments to be used to reduce the

FIGURE 34-2

indebtedness. Some cards have limits on the amount that can be charged and this is usually part of the card number.

Avoiding Interest

Most card holders can avoid interest charges by payment in full within 25 or 30 days from date of billing. Where payment is not made in the designated time period, interest is charged as agreed.

Loans

Some of the bank card companies permit loans to be made by card. Such loans usually carry an interest charge of 1 percent per month or

FIGURE 34–3

Example 1
Purchase of Goods or Services

If you were to buy a set of tires on sale on October 1 for $100, and if you chose to pay $60 the first month and $40 the second month, it would work like this:

October 1:	You purchased and began using your $100 tires.
October 15:	You receive a statement for $100.
November 1:	You make your first payment of $60.
November 15:	You receive a statement for $40 plus 60¢ interest.
November 30:	You make your final payment of $40.60.
Total Interest	$0.60.

Example 2
Cash Advance

If you decide to get a $100 cash advance on October 1 and if you decide to pay for it in 30 days, it would work like this:

October 1:	You received a $100 cash advance.
October 15:	You received a statement for $100 plus 15 days interest (October 1–15) of 50¢.
November 1:	You make your first payment of $100.50.
November 15:	You receive a statement showing the balance paid off but interest owed for 15 days (October 15–30) of 50¢.
Total Interest	$1.00

12 percent on an annual basis. Two examples are shown in Figure 34–3: the first is based upon a purchase of goods and services, the second upon a cash advance.

THE CREDIT CARD CONTRACTS

Three contracts are involved in the use of a credit card. First, when a company tenders a card to a potential card holder (usually by mail), the company has made an offer. (Unsolicited offers will be discussed later.) The person who receives the card is under no obligation to accept the card and has no obligation to do anything at all. However, as a practical matter, one who receives a credit card who does not want to keep it, should cut it into three or four pieces and return it to the issuer with a statement that the card is not wanted.

To Use or Not?

If the recipient takes possession of the card with the intention of placing it in use, then an acceptance has resulted and a contract exists between the holder and the issuer. If the holder does not use the card, no further contract obligation results. Where the issuer invites the holder to ask for the card, the issuer has made an offer for a contract. When the holder requests the card and it is delivered, a contract has resulted.

The Second Contract

The second contract arises when the holder tenders the card to third parties in exchange for goods, or services, or both. Third parties widely advertise that it (or he or she) will accept card "so and so." If the card holder uses the services or buys goods on the strength of that assurance, then a second contract has resulted between the holder and the third party. The third party must then honor the card. This is subject, however, to the right to determine two things: first, that the holder is, in fact, the lawful owner, and second, that the card has not been cancelled. A significant legal question arises when the third party unduly delays the holder in the attempt to determine the facts. The delay might result in embarrassment to the holder, and a subsequent claim of mental anguish or something similar might arise.

The Third Contract

The third contract follows when the third party tenders a copy of the receipt for goods or services to the issuer or its agent. At this point, two legal things happen: first, the issuer (or its agent) is bound to pay the third party the sum due, less any percentage for handling, and second, the card holder is obligated to pay the issuer the sum charged. The contractual relationship described is unique since, in fact, a card holder binds the issuer without the issuer knowing that it has been bound until the charge slip is received.

SERVICES OFFERED

Originally, credit cards were limited to specific uses such as purchase of goods (notably oil, gas, and auto products) and for services such as motel, hotel, and dining. But with increasing use came an almost unbelievable expansion of available services. An Ohio bank has arranged for customers who use the 1040 Form to pay their income tax by credit card. The same bank permits county taxes to be paid in the same manner. Some companies allow college tuition, books, room and board to be paid by card. Others have a plan whereby checks are issued (and charged against the card) to pay income tax, license fees, donations, and a "coverall check" is added for the card holder to use for unusual expenses. The highway patrol of one state has been authorized to accept a named credit card for payment of traffic violations, thus avoiding the necessity of taking the violator to an arraigning magistrate or justice of the peace. Such an arrangement would necessitate an agreement between the issuer and the state—for obvious reasons. If the alleged highway offender demands a hearing (which one has the right to do), the card can be used for bail. Some issuers allow political contributions to be made by credit card.

UNSOLICITED CARDS

The consumers of America were taken by surprise when they became aware that most oil companies were not only sending credit cards without charge, but were also sending duplicates for use by the husband or wife. Many of these cards were labeled "nonexpiring." The apparent small misuse of these unsolicited cards is a tribute to the honesty of the American public. But complaints arose swiftly. Companies which had hesitated to enter the card business were complaining that mass mailing of unsolicited credit cards amounted to unfair competition. Many consumers began to complain of the flood of cards being issued when they had no intention of using them.

The Federal Trade Commission Acts

The Federal Trade Commission entered an order effective May 18, 1970, forbidding the mailing of unsolicited credit cards. The ruling stated in part:

> The mailing by marketers of products or services or by others of unsolicited credit cards constitutes an unfair method of competition and an unfair trade practice in violation of Section 5 of the Federal Trade Commission Act: Provided, however, that nothing in this rule should be construed to prohibit the mailing of credit cards which are renewals, substitutions, or replacements of cards expressly requested, expressly consented to, or accepted prior to the effective date of this rule through use by the holder.

Following the order, the complaint arose that those who had already entered the field were now handed a monopoly since the competition was cut off.

Others Followed

The U.S. Senate followed with a bill reinforcing the F.T.C. ruling which included common carriers and banks. The bill states that should a card holder find a card stolen or misused, the liability would be limited to $50 per card—an obvious attempt to discourage the issuance of unsolicited cards. This in turn had the desired effect of protecting the hapless card owner who lost the card.

The States Act

Several states legislatures enacted laws against unsolicited cards. In 1969, Virginia, Vermont, Rhode Island, Pennsylvania, and others considered legislation to ban or restrict issuance of cards not requested. In Delaware, it is a misdemeanor to distribute a card unless two-week advance notice is given, or unless the holder requests the card. The Kansas legislature relieved the card holder of any obligation if the card was lost or stolen—thus presenting an effective deterrent to the issuance of unsolicited cards. And more state laws are certain to follow. Two patterns have developed in the legislative acts: the holder will be relieved of liability if the cards are lost or stolen, or issuance of an unsolicited card will be a criminal offense.

Other states have enacted laws to regulate the use of credit cards that supplement the federal law. For example, in Minnesota, if a customer complains about a charge to a card account, the company must reply within 30 days. If they do not, the customer can sue for actual damages suffered by the refusal and add attorney fees as well. If a charge is made in error in that state and the card company harrasses the card holder, the card holder can again sue for further damages plus attorney fees.

The pattern in Minnesota is very similar to the Fair Credit Billing Act. For a discussion of that law, see Chapter 36.

DUTIES AND LIABILITIES OF CARD HOLDERS AND ISSUERS

After acceptance of a credit card, the holder has a duty to safeguard the card (or cards) and to pay the account as agreed. If this is not done, finance charges will accrue—and the issuer may demand surrender of the card, or cancel the privilege of using it.

The card holder must keep an accurate record of the card numbers and report the loss or theft in the manner and form suggested by the issuer. If this is done, then by law, the card holder is only liable for unauthorized use of the card until the date of notice. However, by operation of federal law, the limit on liability is $50. To illustrate, X loses a Diner's Club card and fails to notice its loss for a few days. If another charges $20 against the card before notice of loss is given, X will be responsible for the $20 loss. If notice is *not* given however, the limit on liability of X is $50. This provision of the federal law was designed to protect the consumer who fails to give notice of loss on a card upon which hundreds and often thousands of dollars in unauthorized charges are made. This law raised a related question—are *business* card holders also entitled to the $50 limit on liability?

What about Business Cards?

On November 2, 1974, the Federal Reserve Board issued a ruling making the $50 credit limit applicable to business cards as well as consumer cards. This ruling makes it clear that the $50 limit on liability shall apply to *each* card that may be lost or stolen. ($50 times each card).

To clear up further uncertainties, in Title IV of Public Law 93–495, discussed above, if a business takes 10 or more cards from one issuer, the parties can agree to a higher loss ratio. Thus, while business card holders were able to claim a benefit that was intended for consumers originally, a way is open for issuers to place a higher loss risk on business card holders. In addition, this law makes it clear that a company cannot pass losses along to employees who use business cards for business purposes.

Under these laws and rulings, issuers must do two things: First inform all card holders of the duty to report the loss or theft of cards; and second, provide each card holder with a form upon which this can be done.

Failure to do these two things removes the card holder from any liability at all.

Errors

Occasionally, the issuer will "cross accounts," thus charging A for charges of B. This sometimes happens where one card holder has a name similar to another. For this reason, it is good business for the holder to screen the charge slips as they come and check the signature on each slip.

CONSUMER DATA

It is only a matter of time until computerized credit data of all card holders is compiled at a central location. The groundwork has been laid for this. When it becomes a reality, it will permit the instant checking of the credit standing of a card holder and should sharply reduce the unauthorized use of lost or stolen cards—and about 300,000 are being stolen annually.

AS THE ISSUER SEES THE SYSTEM

From the point of view of the issuer, the operation of an effective credit card system requires several things: first, that quality be maintained in the selection of those who become card holders. Because of the volume involved, difficulty is encountered in screening applicants. The older methods of applying to a credit bureau for a $5 report is too expensive and time-consuming. Next, the issuer must be "lawsuit conscious." Too many chances exist for card holders to claim undue harrassment where accounts have been billed in error—or credited to other accounts. Another requisite is that the issuer comply with the disclosure provisions of Truth in Lending as well as state laws that prohibit usury.

Usury

An unanswered aspect of the credit card industry is that of usury— the charging of more interest than the law allows. The prevailing credit card interest charges range from 12 percent to 18 percent on an annual basis and apparently violate the usual state maximum interest statutes, which run between 6 percent and 12 percent. This is an area of potential danger from the issuer's point of view. It has been noted that several credit card companies have lowered their interest rates to match the state requirements.

ARE FINANCE CHARGES DEDUCTIBLE?

For many years the federal government refused to permit as a deduction for income tax purposes the total amount of finance charges paid to credit card companies. While these charges often averaged 18 percent, only a portion could be used as a deduction, which was approximately 6 percent.

By Revenue Ruling 71–98 in 1971, a change in position has been made—at least in part. When one uses a credit card to purchase goods or services, the card company will pay the business person the amount charged, less a fee of 4 to 6 percent for the service. Thus, the card company has been paid for its service. Therefore, when the card company invoices the customer and makes a finance charge for late payment, a situation analogous to a loan occurs. For this reason, the rule has been changed, giving recognition to the fact that a credit card finance charge is in fact interest and may be deducted accordingly. Since the Internal Revenue Service now recognizes certain credit card finance charges as interest, it seems logical for the courts to adopt the same view which will give effect to the usury laws.

It has been noted that some companies include on the January statement, a recap of all interest charges collected the previous year. This is helpful to the card holder in preparing tax returns for the previous year.

THE FUTURE?

The likelihood of more controls, both federal and state, seems certain. But this in itself will not slow the expansion and use of plastic money. The only real fraud has been practiced against the issuers, not by them. This fact lends confidence to the card users.

The future contains the need for centralized credit data, easier and faster methods to stop unauthorized use, and easier collection methods for those who default. Probably most important of all, the card revolution will lead to a national communications network for use by all credit card companies. Such an installation could also be used for other purposes such as tracing missing persons, locating dishonest debtors, those who fail to pay local and federal taxes as they should, and those who refuse to support their families. It could also be used for many forms of invasion of privacy.

REVIEW QUESTIONS

1. Name the three credit card contracts.
2. What constitutional argument will probably be made *against* a national credit center?
3. What explanation can you give for the sudden growth of credit cards?
4. Name two reasons why the law began to regulate the issuance of cards.
5. True or False. The banks were the first companies to enter the credit card business.
6. Name three reasons why a nationwide credit card system would have been impossible in 1900. How about 1930?
7. If you compare different credit cards, you will find them to be identical in outside size. Why is this true?

8. Examine the charge slip in Figure 34–2. Why do these make a good income tax record?
9. How does a credit card differ from a personal check?
10. Since the energy crisis began, many businesses have refused to accept credit cards. Name three reasons for this.

Words and Phrases

Write out briefly what they mean to you.
1. Plastic money.
2. Issuer.
3. Limit on card liability.
4. Unsolicited cards.
5. Duties of issuer.

Coverage:	The basics of Title I of the federal Consumer Credit Protection Act,
What to Look for:	New requirements placed upon those in business.
Application:	In all credit situations, ask this question: "Does Title I of the C.C.P.A. apply?"

35 Truth in Lending and Credit Advertising

TRUTH IN LENDING

At common law there was no requirement that lenders (and others who extend credit) disclose to their customers the true costs and interest rates on loans or other credit extended. As a result of this, consumers often knew the exact amount of the loan, or the precise price of the commodity purchased, but were totally ignorant of the amount of the finance charge and the true interest rate. Further, in spite of the usury statutes, when interest rates were disclosed consumers (with some exceptions), still did not know the true interest charged to them. For example, a $5,000 loan with payments of $108.33 per month for five years, was called a "6 percent loan." In this example the true annual interest rate is 10.75 percent. This is true because the customer does not receive the full use of the $5,000 for the five-year period of time since part is repaid each month. That is, the customer does not have $5,000 for five years.[1]

Congress, however, began to reason that if consumers are entitled to safe cars, pure food, and other products free from dangerous defects, they should also know what these products cost them in terms of finance charges and annual interest rates. Therefore, at the heart of Title I, Con-

---

[1] The total repayment would be $6,499.80, which would provide a total of $1,499.80 for interest. This in turn would be $300.00 for each year and thus the reason for the "6 percent." But the debtor does not have the full $5,000 for the full five years.

sumer Credit Protection Act,[2] is the basic concept: consumers should know what they pay for credit.

The problem that confronted the consumer in the past is illustrated by the following excerpt from a bank payment book. The payments were $72 per month on a loan of $8,500. Payments were made on different days of each month, which caused a variable interest charge. The interest was deducted from each payment and the balance was applied to principal. It took 22 payments of $72 each to reduce the principal by $671.26–a total of $1,564 in payments. Could an average person calculate the interest that was being paid on this loan?

Date	Interest	New or Renewal	Payment		Balance
Aug 15 68		M*8,500.00			**$8,500.00
Sep 23 68	*43.91		H*	72.00	**$8,471.91
Oct 24 68	*42.36		G*	72.00	** 8,442.27
Nov 23 68	*43.62		G*	72.00	** 8,413.87
Dec 23 68	*42.07		G*	72.00	** 8,383.96
Jan 22 69	*43.31		G*	72.00	** 8,355.27
Feb 21 69	*43.17		G*	72.00	** 8,326.44
Mar 24 69	*38.85		G*	72.00	** 8,293.29
Apr 22 69	*42.84		G*	72.00	** 8,264.13
May 24 69	*41.32		G*	72.00	** 8,233.45
Jun 24 69	*42.54		G*	72.00	** 8,203.99
Jul 23 69	*41.02		G*	72.00	** 8,173.01
Aug 23 69	*42.22		G*	72.00	** 8,143.23
Sep 24 69	*42.07		G*	72.00	** 8,113.30
Oct 24 69	*40.57		G*	72.00	** 8,081.87
Nov 24 69	*41.75		G*	72.00	** 8,051.62
Dec 24 69	*40.26		G*	72.00	** 8,019.88
Jan 26 70	*41.43		G*	72.00	** 7,989.31
Feb 23 70	*41.28		G*	72.00	** 7,958.59
Mar 24 70	*37.14		G*	72.00	** 7,923.73
Apr 24 70	*40.94		G*	72.00	** 7,892.67
May 25 70	*39.46		G*	72.00	** 7,860.12
Jun 14 70	*40.61		G*	72.00	** 7,828.74
Jul 24 70	*50.88		G*7,879.62		** 0.00

Dating from 1960, Truth in Lending had a long and stormy legislative history. After being bottled up in the Senate Banking and Currency Committee for seven years, it was enacted after severe alterations on May 30, 1968, and became effective in part July 1, 1969. The balance became effective on July 1, 1970. On October 28, 1974, the 93rd Congress of the United States, enacted a law that contained many revisions of Truth in Lending and the C.C.P.A. in general.[3] Federal Deposit Insurance

---

[2] Title II regulates Extortionate Credit transactions with severe criminal penalties provided for violations; Title III provides regulations on the use of garnishment and became effective July 1, 1970; Title IV establishes a National Commission on Consumer Finance and Title V contains general provisions; Title VI, enacted separarely, is "The Fair Credit Reporting Act."

[3] Public Law 93–495, H.R. 11221. The C.C.P.A., see Chapter 4, page 43.

Corporation coverage was increased from $20,000 to $40,000. This was added to Title I, C.C.P.A. Title II was amended to allow the creation of a National Commission on Electronic Transfers. The Fair Credit Billing Act discussed in chapter 36, was added to Title III. The Equal Credit Opportunity Act was added to Title V and Title VI was amended in detail with most of these amendments affecting Truth in Lending. These changes will be discussed at appropriate places in this and other chapters.

It has been said – and probably accurately – that this is the only major piece of federal legislation in recent years that no one – not even those who advocated it – is satisfied with.

Findings and Purpose

Stating first that an awareness of the cost of credit is important to the consumer, Congress found that economic stabilization and competition would be enhanced if the act became law. Realizing that any disclosure would be worthless if not understood, Congress further found that such disclosure would have to be meaningful. Therefore, the purpose of Title I, short title Truth in Lending,[4] is

> ... to assure a meaningful disclosure of credit terms so that the consumer will be able to compare more readily the various credit terms available to him and avoid the uninformed use of credit.

In short, the purpose of the act, Title I, is to assure to the consumer the benefits that will follow from the informed use of credit. Such benefits include a life free from the burdens of unnecessary financial tangles and free from forced resort to the bankruptcy courts. This legislation requires truth (where applicable), making this a legal requirement for the first time in this form.[5]

A Labeling Act

Contrary to popular belief, Title I of the C.C.P.A. does *not* establish, or even suggest, interest rates. Rather it is a "labeling act" requiring lenders and others who regularly extend credit to place a label upon what they are delivering to the consumer. (See Figure 35-1).

Distinguished from U.C.C.C.

Title I must be distinguished from the Uniform Consumer Credit Code. The U.C.C.C. was drafted by the Commissioners on Uniform State Laws and is available for consideration by the states. States that have adopted the U.C.C.C. include Utah, Oklahoma, (the first to do so), Colorado, Idaho, Indiana, Wyoming, and others. Others that are considering

---

[4] Title I, C.C.P.A., Section 101 (Act of May 29, 1968, P.L. 90–321: 82 Stat. 146 et seq.).

[5] Supplementing the act is Regulation Z and its amendments.

FIGURE 35-1

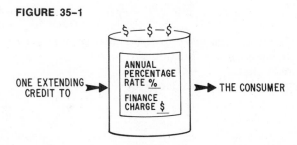

it, or who have adopted it, include Alaska, Georgia, Hawaii, Kentucky, Maryland, New York, Pennsylvania, Rhode Island, South Dakota, Virginia, and others.

Once adopted by a state, the U.C.C.C. regulates credit sales, loans, and the sale of insurance. But it will not replace the C.C.P.A. Title I completely, thus requiring dual disclosures in some instances. Under some conditions, a state can be exempt from the C.C.P.A. and Wyoming, Maine, Massachusetts, Connecticut, Oklahoma, and Idaho are examples. A number of states have rejected the U.C.C.C..

Who Is Covered?

Title I applies to all persons who in the ordinary course of business regularly extend, or offer to extend, or arrange, or offer to arrange, for the extension of consumer credit.[6] This definition is quite broad. Consumer credit is defined as

> ... credit offered or extended to a natural person, in which the money, property or service which is the subject of the transaction is primarily for personal, family, household, or agricultural purposes and for which either a finance charge is or may be imposed or which ... is or may be payable in more than four installments.[7]

Thus, the bank that makes a 30-day, one-payment loan, and collects a finance charge is covered; the lumber mill that allows a 2 percent discount on goods sold if paid in 10 days, net 30 days, but makes no finance charge, is covered (careful examination of this shows that a finance charge of 2 percent for 20 days is in fact made); the plumber who makes no finance charge but allows payments to be made in more than four installments is covered; and so is the dentist who conducts a dental finance plan. In short, the act – although federal – covers everyone who fits into the above categories unless they qualify under the exemptions.

It should be observed at this point that Truth in Lending seems to apply only where consumer credit is involved – not business credit. This is not completely true however, since the $50 limit protection on

---

[6] Regulation Z, Section 226.1(*a*).

[7] Regulation Z, Section 226.2 (*k*). This four installment rule was attacked in the courts but was upheld in *Mourning* v. *Family Publications Serv.*, No. 71–829 (U.S. April 24, 1973).

credit cards has been extended to business cards under section 135 of the 1974 amendments of the law. In addition, the 1974 changes exempted loans for agricultural purposes over $25,000 from coverage. This tells us that such loans under $25,000 are covered and these are almost always business loans.

Who else and what else is exempt from coverage?

Exemptions

Exemptions are granted to business or government credit loans (but a business loan under $25,000 for agricultural purposes would be covered), certain broker-dealer security transactions, nonreal property credit transactions that exceed $25,000, public utility loans, and minimum loans.[8] It will be noted that the exemptions are narrow and hardly warrant mention. Thus, if a finance charge is made — even on a short-term loan — or if no finance charge is made but more than four payments are provided for, the person (or firm) is covered and should be concerned about disclosure and not exemptions.

Disclosures

It is mandatory that those who are covered disclose to their customers certain information in form that complies with the law. The disclosure may be printed on the contract or security agreement and placed on the face of the note (Figure 35–2). The law also permits the disclosure to be made by a separate document (Figure 35–3). But regardless of the form, the most important concept of the disclosure is that it be truthful.

Included in the disclosure is the requirement that a precise statement of the finance charges be expressed in dollars. The act contains provisions for determining this charge[9] as does Regulation Z.[10] Such charges as interest, any sum payable under a point system, finders fees, charges for insurance where mandatory, time-price differential, and other charges must be included. Those covered must become familiar with the act and Regulation Z and its amendments to avoid stating an erroneous finance charge. The penalties can make this an expensive error.

A second major item that must be disclosed is the annual percentage rate in true percent. Again the act[11] and Regulation Z[12] spell out the manner in which this "APR" must be determined. A tolerance to the nearest quarter of 1 percent is required, spelling out caution in this calculation.[13]

---

[8] Regulation Z, Section 226.5(a)(1)(3).

[9] Title I, Section 106.

[10] Regulation Z, Section 226.5 et seq.

[11] Title I, Section 107.

[12] Regulation Z, Section 226.5.

[13] Regulation Z, Section 226.5(a).

FIGURE 35-2

PROMISSORY NOTE

$_____

_____ , _____
         (City)   (State)

For value received, we promise to pay to the order of _____,
_____ dollars ($_____) in equal _____
monthly payments of $_____ each, beginning one month from
the date hereof and continuing in the same date of each month thereafter
until paid in full. Any unpaid balance may be paid, at any time, without
penalty. In the event that maker(s) default(s) on any payment, a charge
of _____ may be assessed.

1. Proceeds... $_____
2. _____ .... $_____
   (Other charges, itemized)
3. Amount financed .... $_____
   (1 + 2)
4. FINANCE CHARGE............................ $_____
5. Total of Payments................................. $_____
   ANNUAL PERCENTAGE RATE   _____%

Signed_____

_____

_____

For this reason, reference should be made to the tables provided by the
federal government.[14] These tables simplify the calculation of the APR
and should be used in all cases where applicable.

Regulation Z sets out other disclosure requirements, thus forcing one
in business to closely examine the specific type of transaction at hand.
For example, open-end credit accounts,[15] credit other than open end,[16]
advertising credit terms,[17] and comparative index of credit cost for open-
end credit[18] are covered specifically. The business person who could be
classified under such headings would be required to become informed
of other portions of the law.

The disclosure requirements under Title I also affect the *form* of the
disclosure.

> The disclosure . . . shall be made clearly, conspicuously, in meaningful
> sequence . . . All numerical amounts and percentages shall be stated in

---

[14] Federal Reserve Board, Washington, D.C. 20051, or any Federal Reserve Bank.
[15] Regulation Z, Section 226.7.
[16] Regulation Z, Section 226.8.
[17] Regulation Z, Section 226.10.
[18] Regulation Z, Section 226.11.

FIGURE 35-3

DISCLOSURE STATEMENT
(Unsecured Loan)

_____
(Lender)

Deliver One Copy to Customer whose name is first signed below who Must Not be an Accomodation Co-Maker, Indorser, Guarantor, or Surety.

_____
(Address)

Customer(s) Name(s) _____

Purpose of Loan _____

Basic Terms of Loan Contract

1. Face amount of note _____
2. Charges paid from loan proceeds not included in finance charge:
   a. Premium credit life insurance not required by lender
   b. Premium disability insurance not required by lender
   c. Other itemized:
      _____
      _____
                            Total
                            Total
3. Prepaid finance charge (prepaid or discounted interest)
   _____
4. Amount of any add-on interest
5. Amount financed (no. 1 minus nos. 3 and 4 _____.)
6. FINANCE CHARGE:
   a. Interest (include simple, add-on, prepaid for discounted interest)
      _____ $_____
   b. Credit report
      _____ $_____
   c. Other itemized:
      _____ $_____
      _____ $_____
                 FINANCE CHARGE:
7. Total of payments (no. 5 plus no. 6)
   _____
   ANNUAL PERCENTAGE RATE

1. $_____

2. $_____

   $_____

   $_____

   $_____
   $_____
   $_____
   $_____

3. $_____

4. $_____

5. $_____

6. $_____

7. $_____

   _____%

ACKNOWLEDGMENT OF RECEIPT

The undersigned acknowledge(s) receipt from FARMERS' & MERCHANTS' BANK, of a copy of the foregoing instrument with all applicable blanks appropriately filled.

_____

Dated _____19_____   _____

figures and shall be printed in not less than the equivalent of 10 point type, or .075 inch computer type, or elite size typewritten numerals, or shall be legibly handwritten.[19]

Therefore, the finance charge, if any, and the annual percentage rate must be conspicuous—in such form that a reasonable person in the conduct of his or her affairs will or should notice them.

Under this law, the lender is required to give only one disclosure form to both husband and wife. It is assumed that both will examine the single disclosure. But what if a violation of Truth in Lending occurs in that transaction? May both husband and wife maintain an action for statutory damages and costs? A federal court in Georgia has held that they may.[20]

When Must Disclosures Be Made? After Truth in Lending became law, there was much speculation about when disclosures had to be made in real estate loan closings. One court felt that unless the disclosures were made before loan time, they would be meaningless to the debtor. This court held that the disclosures had to be made at least 10 days before the closing.[21] This decision has been modified by more recent decisions and disclosures can generally be made at the time of the closing. (However, the 1975 Real Estate Settlement Procedures Act, provides for disclosures other than Truth in Lending, that must be made one day before certain real estate closings. RESPA is discussed in chapter 36.)

Real Estate and Rescission

All transactions involving real estate loans—even in excess of $25,000—are covered and proper disclosure is required. In addition, the act permits rescission of real estate transactions under certain conditions. (See Figure 35–4.)

Where a security interest is given in the customer's home (*other* than for the purchase of the home itself), the customer has three business days in which to rescind the transaction. Certain holidays are excluded from the calculation of these three days, including Sunday.[22] Second mortgages or security interests given by the consumer in his or her home—even to provide funds for the improvement of the home itself—come within the rescission rule. In addition, the customer must not only be told of this right to rescind, but must also be provided with a form upon which this rescission can be made. But this does not apply if the loan is being made for business use—even if the debtor pledges the home for security for the loan.

If the form is signed by the customer and delivered in person or mailed to the lender by midnight of the third business day following the transaction, the customer is free from obligation under the transaction. The

---

[19] Regulation Z, Section 226.6(*a*).

[20] *Rivers* v. *Southern Dis. Co.*, Case No. 18268, Fed. Dist. Ct. (N.D. Georgia, 1973).

[21] *Bissette* v. *Colonial Mortgage Corp.*, 340 F. Supp. 1191 (D.D.C. 1972).

[22] Regulation Z, Section 226.9(*a*), footnote 14.

three day period does not begin to run until the debtor is notified of the right to rescind. Therefore, if the creditor fails to provide this notice, the right can be exercised years later. However, in Title IV of the 1974 amendments, the outside limit on rescission was set at three years or whenever the debtor sells the house, whichever occurs first. (Act 125 (f), 1974).

The effective time of the mailed rescission is when it is deposited in the United States mail. If the rescission is timely, the customer does not

FIGURE 35-4

NOTICE OF RIGHT OF RESCISSION   (Front)

_____
(Identification of Transaction)

NOTICE TO CUSTOMER REQUIRED BY FEDERAL LAW:

You have entered into a transaction on _____
                                          (Date)
which may result in a lien, mortgage, or other security interest on your home. You have a legal right under federal law to cancel this transaction, if you desire to do so, without penalty or obligation within three business days from the above date or any later date on which all material disclosures required under the Truth in Lending Act have been given to you. If you so cancel the transaction, any lien, mortgage, or other security interest on your home arising from this transaction is automatically void. You are also entitled to receive a refund of any down payment or other consideration if you cancel. If you decide to cancel this transaction, you may do so by notifying:

_____
(Name of Creditor)
at _____
(Address of Creditor's Place of Business)
by mail or telegram sent not later than midnight of _____.
                                                       (Date)
You may also use any other form of written notice identifying the transaction if it is delivered to the above address not later than that time. This notice may be used for that purpose by dating and signing below. For your protection, the use of registered or certified mail with return receipt requested is suggested.

                              I hereby cancel this transaction.

_____   _____
(Date)   (Customer's Signature)
    I, the Customer, hereby acknowledge receipt of 2 copies of the aforesaid Notice of Right of Rescission which have been given unto me this _____ day of _____, 19__.

                              _____
                                    (Customer's Signature)

See reverse side for important information about your right of rescission.

FIGURE 35–4 (continued)

EFFECT OF RESCISSION   (Back)

A customer who exercises the right to rescind under paragraph (a) of this section is not liable for any finance or other charge, and any security interest becomes void upon such a rescission. Within 10 days after receipt of a notice of rescission, the creditor shall return to the customer any money or property given as earnest money, down payment, or otherwise, and shall take any action necessary or appropriate to reflect the termination of any security interest created under the transaction. If the creditor has delivered any property to the customer, the customer may retain possession of it. Upon the performance of the creditor's obligations under this section, the customer shall tender the property to the creditor, except that if return of the property in kind would be impracticable or inequitable, the customer shall tender its reasonable value. Tender shall be made at the location of the property or at the residence of the customer, at the option of the customer. If the creditor does not take possession of the property within 10 days after tender by the customer, ownership of the property vests in the customer without obligation to pay for it.

---

have to pay fees for a title search, preparation of a deed of trust and note, and the like.[23] In addition, the act provides that

> . . . if the creditor does not take possession of the property within ten days after tender by the obligor (customer), ownership of the property vests in the obligor without obligation on his part to pay for it.[24]

This provision will assure that legitimate lenders will proceed cautiously in transactions where the customer has the right to rescind. And the illegitimate lender will probably view the right as a legal nightmare.

The right to rescind may be waived by the customer in writing for such reasons as "a personal financial emergency" or where the "health or safety of natural persons" or property might be endangered by the delay in loan closing.[25]

The rescission provision provides an effective safety valve for those who may be pressured into a contract in which their home is given as security. The right to rescind is absolute and the only exception to it is where the loan is made for the purpose of acquiring a home in which the customer will live. The purchase of a summer home with the buyer's regular residence as security would carry with it the three-day rescission period since this would not be for purposes of purchasing the customer's "home."

---

[23] Title I, Section 125.

[24] Title I, Section 125(b).

[25] Regulation Z, Section 226.9(c).

Penalties

One who willfully and knowingly fails to comply with Title I faces up to one year in federal prison or a fine of not more than $5,000 or both.[26] Where the failure to comply arises out of negligence or misinformation, and is not corrected within 15 days, the business person faces a civil penalty of double the amount of the finance charge that should have been disclosed. Since the act provides for a maximum penalty of $1,000 and a minimum of $100, even if the finance charge is less, the business person cannot afford to fail to disclose—and cannot afford to disclose erroneously. In addition to the statutory sum, court costs and reasonable attorney's fees can be recovered by the customer.[27]

This provision of the law prompted many attorneys to bring "class actions" against companies where a simple violation of the law had been repeated with all of that company's customers. This caused many companies to face the possibility of loss of millions of dollars for statutory penalties for the violation. This was considered to be unfair and an outside limit of $100,000 has been set on class action—statutory damage cases. This was done in the 1974 amendments mentioned.

Actual Damages Also. In addition to the statutory penalties, the creditor who fails to disclose properly, is subject to a civil action for all *actual* damages suffered by the debtor caused by the failure to disclose. There is no limit on these damages. Admittedly, it will be a rare case when large actual damages are caused by a failure to disclose—but it could happen.

What about Repeated Errors? If a creditor makes an error in the disclosures and repeats that error for successive monthly billings, is that creditor subject to statutory penalties for *each* month? Apparently this was the view being taken prior to the changes in 1974. Now it is law that repeated errors only entitle each debtor to recover statutory penalties once of $100 to $1,000. There is no limit on actual damages as mentioned.

Statute of Limitations. Suits to enforce violations of Truth in Lending must be brought within one year. This leaves one final question: "What court must the suits be brought in?"

Which Court? Section 130 (*e*) of Truth in Lending states that suits can be brought in any U.S. District Court ". . . or in any other court of competent jurisdiction." Does this mean that these suits cannot be brought in *state* courts? Two lower courts have so held but the highest court of Mississippi says that they can. The later is the better view.

TRUTH IN ADVERTISING[28]

Congress included in the Consumer Credit Protection Act regulations to help solve problems that fell upon consumers because of advertising.

---

[26] Title I, Section 112.

[27] Title I, Section 130. See *Lewis* v. *Delta Loans, Inc.*, 300 So. 2d 142 (1974).

[28] C.C.P.A., Title I, chapter 2.

The provision, found in Title I, C.C.P.A., along with Truth in Lending, is valuable to the consumer.

What Type of Advertising Is Covered?

Included are ads directed toward the extension of consumer credit. Catalogs are included if they include a "conspicuous table" that displays the credit terms offered. No business person can advertise that he or she will assist or aid in the extension of consumer credit unless he or she usually and customarily arranges credit payments for the time period and the amount advertised. For example, a furniture store cannot advertise "easy terms" if they do not arrange credit at all. This was often done in the past and the consumer who went into the store to make a purchase on time often ended up at the consumer credit department of a local bank, armed with a stack of papers prepared by the furniture company. Also, the business person cannot advertise that a specific down payment will be accepted unless he or she in fact customarily arranges for down payments in that amount. Thus, if one advertises "$10 down and the balance in easy terms" when in fact that sum will not be accepted, the federal law is violated. The penalties are severe as were discussed previously.

What Must the Merchant Do?

No advertisement to aid or promote consumer credit under open-end credit plans may quote specific terms unless the following are included: the time period within which the credit extended may be repaid without incurring a finance charge; the method that will be used to determine the finance charge; the way the finance charge will be calculated; and other information as required by law. This provision will discourage misleading or false advertising. Advertising of other than open-end sales is regulated and the act states that if a finance charge is quoted, the annual percentage rate must also be disclosed. The law relates only to consumer advertising.

At one time it was the practice of lenders to advertise charges that showed only the total loan and the monthly payments. These ads were misleading since the borrower did not know the interest rate and the finance charge. These ads have disappeared since the enactment of Title I and it is doubtful that they will be seen again.

SUMMARY

The increasing sophistication of organized society has produced a law that requires truth in lending as well as truth in advertising. The good faith and reasonableness concepts of the Uniform Commercial Code are thus effectively extended into a new area in the form of truth. The field of consumer credit has contained perpetual pitfalls for the consumer, but hopefully, as a result of this act, each of us will be able to cross this field in the future without facing the dangers that have befallen so many in the past.

REVIEW QUESTIONS

1. What was the "policy" that Congress attempted to establish when it enacted Title I of the C.C.P.A.?
2. Would the states have been successful in creating a law such as this one that would be the same in all states? Why?
3. What are the two basic disclosure requirements of Title I?
4. Can you establish the interest rate from the $8,500 loan chart? What do you think it was?
5. True or False. Federal law has forced those who advertise to establish guidelines in creating their advertisements that involve consumer credit.
6. How might the rescission requirement *injure* a consumer?
7. Write out why Truth in Lending is a "labeling act."
8. Why is credit that is extended to one in business not covered by T.I.L.?
9. Why must the consumer acknowledge receipt of a disclosure statement?
10. Why is the rescission requirement limited to a security interest in one's home?

Words and Phrases

Write out briefly what they mean to you.
1. Conspicuous.
2. Annual percentage rate.
3. Consumer credit.
4. Disclosure.
5. Rescission.

Coverage:	A roundup of other consumer protection laws.
What to Look for:	The impact of these laws upon business.
Application:	Think of the many types of businesses that are affected.

36 Other Federal and State Credit Laws

Title III of the Consumer Credit Protection Act (C.C.P.A.) backs up Truth in Lending and Credit Advertising and was designed to offset one of the more unfortunate statistics of our society: Between 30,000 and 120,000 wage earners were being fired each year because of wage attachments. It can be appreciated that the problems of the consumer multiply rapidly if the source of income is lost.

GARNISHMENT

Garnishment

> ... means any legal or equitable procedure through which the earnings of any individual are required to be withheld for payment of any debt.[1]

The most common example is attachment of wages of a debtor by a creditor. All 50 states have garnishment laws, although the laws vary widely and some states even expressly prohibit garnishment. In the usual situation, the judgment creditor of the debtor (suit has been brought and judgment awarded by the court) directs the clerk of the court to serve upon the employer a wage attachment. In the past, many employers summarily fired the employee, using as an excuse the extra bookkeeping required to honor the attachment.

Such a complaint is not without basis in companies that are geared to older methods of payroll payment, such as by cash. In instances where the attachments were honored, the employer looked to the state statutes

---

[1] Title III, 302(b) C.C.P.A.

to see what percentage to deduct from the earnings of an employee (if any). Assuming state law permitted garnishment, two payments were made each pay day: one to the court issuing the attachment order (which in turn paid that sum to the creditor) and the balance, less normal deductions, to the employee. The process was repeated each payday until the judgment, plus constantly accruing interest and court costs, were paid.

Many debtors found themselves facing a series of wage attachments, honored in the order served, sometimes resulting in years of wage deductions. Faced with such circumstances, the wage earner would quit the job and go elsewhere, or file bankruptcy. Either resulted in some disruption of commerce—and especially so when large numbers of employees became involved. As a part of the growing pattern of concern for consumer protection, Congress acted.

Findings

Congress found during the course of committee hearings and investigations that: (1) When garnishment of wages is not controlled properly, creditors are tempted to make ". . . predatory extension of credit." This results in excessive credit payments, thus hampering the flow of goods in interstate commerce. (2) The direct result of garnishment is often the loss of employment by the debtor. (3) The differences in state garnishment laws were so great that the uniformity of the bankruptcy laws was destroyed and the purposes of it were frustrated.

Purposes of Federal Act

Congress stated that based upon the findings, the law is necessary

> . . . for the purpose of carrying into execution the powers of Congress to regulate commerce and to establish uniform bankruptcy laws.[2]

How Does It Work?

The law, which became effective July 1, 1970, states that when a wage earner has weekly wages subjected to garnishment, the amount that can be taken from those wages must not exceed 25 percent of the "disposable earnings" for that week, or "the amount by which disposable earnings . . ." exceed 30 times the federal minimum hourly wage prescribed by section 6(a)(1) of the Fair Labor Standards Act of 1938 in effect at the time the earnings are payable."[3]

An Example

The present minimum wage law is $2.20 per hour, but it is going up. Thirty times this equals $66. If the debtor earns $78 in one week and has deductions for tax and social security of $12, the balance of $66 would

---

[2] Title III, 301(b), C.C.P.A.

[3] Section 303(a)(2), Title III, C.C.P.A.

be exempt from garnishment—leaving this sum free from attachment. Under many present state laws the $66 would be subject to an attachment ranging to 25 percent, 50 percent, 75 percent and even more in some states, leaving virtually nothing for the debtor. If disposable earnings are above $66 but less than $88 a week, only the sum above $66 can be attached. If the earnings exceed $88 per week, then 25 percent is subject to garnishment. ($88 × 25%—$66). Thus, if disposable earnings are $88 a week and 25 percent is attached, the debtor still takes home $66—the amount exempted. As the minimum wage is increased, the minimum exemption will go up, thus raising the sum subject to the 25 percent deduction. The Secretary of Labor has been given power to provide formulas to be used where the debtor is paid biweekly, semi-monthly, or monthly. (See 365 F. Supp. 583, D.N.D. 1973, for a representative case).

What Is Exempted from the Act?

The restrictions stated do not apply in the following instances: (1) where the debtor has been ordered by a court to provide support for a person; (2) where an order has been issued against the debtor by a bankruptcy court; and (3) where a debtor owes tax to a state or the federal government. In addition, wage *assignments* (see chapter 40) are not covered and thus exempt. (See 359 F. Supp. 194, S.D. W. Va. 1973).

Firing the Employee

The act prohibits the firing of an employee by reason of the fact that *one* garnishment is issued and also where there is more than one garnishment on the same debt. An employer who willfully violates this provision is subject to a fine of not more than $1,000 or a prison sentence of not more than one year—or both.

The act provides that the Secretary of Labor can enforce this provision but does not say that the debtor can. In *Simpson* v. *Sperry Rand Corp.,* 350 F. Supp. 1057 (W.D. La. 1972), an employee who was discharged because of one garnishment, tried to have the job reinstated. The court denied reinstatement. In *Andrucci* v. *Gimbel Bros. Inc.,* 365 F. Supp. 1240 (W.D. Pa. 1973), the court ordered reinstatement. The question of the employees rights is not settled on this point.

Another point that is going to have to be settled by the courts is this: what does "one garnishment" mean? One court has held that if the employer fires an employee who has two wage attachments against him *before* the first attachment is paid (the attachments are honored in the order served), the discharge is illegal. *Brennan* v. *Kroger Co.,* No. 74-1726 (7th Cir. April 9, 1975.) This decision is probably wrong because in effect, it repeals the garnishment provision.

State Garnishment Laws

State laws that are in substantial compliance with the act may be exempted by the Secretary of Labor, meaning that the state law will govern.

The act permits existing state laws to continue in force that are *more favorable to the debtor* than the federal act. To say it another way, the act supercedes any state act that is harsher to the debtor than the federal act.

Some Examples. In New York State a 10 percent limit is placed upon the amount that can be deducted from wage attachments. Therefore, since the federal law permits up to 25 percent deductions after the minimum is taken into consideration, the result is more favorable to the New York debtor under the law of that state and that law will be applied. It is presumed that the $66 minimum rule would still apply, however.

Connecticut law prohibits discharge from employment for garnishment unless *seven* garnishments are issued against a debtor within one year. Since the federal law prohibits discharge for only one garnishment, the Connecticut law will be applied in reference to discharge in that state.

In those states that prohibit garnishment, such as the head of the household residing in Florida, the federal law will bow completely to the state law. The policy reason demonstrated is to sustain the law that is the most beneficial to the debtor.

Summary

Title III of the C.C.P.A. is another example of the growing awareness of society through government of the need for protection of the consumer who works for wages in an open and competitive market. The law should bring material benefits to those who will enjoy less pressures from debts often contracted for in haste and ignorance. At the same time, there is no showing that legitimate debts will not be paid in time, but they will be paid under more equitable conditions. The result is a good compromise between harsh legal remedies and the realities of a credit-oriented society.

Following closely on the heels of the first five titles of the C.C.P.A. came Title VI, which was enacted separately. It was called "The Fair Credit Reporting Act."

FAIR CREDIT REPORTING ACT

The credit-oriented business community has had perpetual need for the services of agencies created for the purpose of accumulating and making available basic data about those who purchase goods or services on time. There is a corresponding need for data concerning those who apply for loans, insurance, or employment. The agencies that have responded to the demand have been called "credit agencies" or credit bureaus and in many instances are locally owned and operated. There are thousands of such agencies in operation throughout America.

The typical credit bureau collects, files, and makes available for a price a variety of information about the consumers that reside within the area covered by the bureau. The data is taken from newspapers, the records in the county and circuit courts, and reports of debts given to the bureau by merchants who use this method to collect bad or slow accounts. Over the years, a vast quantity of consumer information has been accumulated, much of which is out of date and some of which is just plain erroneous.

The complaints about the activities of "credit bureaus" and others who gather credit data have been increasing in recent years. The complaint heard most frequently is that detrimental data has been posted in the wrong file, resulting in the denial of credit to or loss of employment of an innocent person. In the past, if the one who was denied credit or employment demanded to see the data on file, that person was turned away, making it impossible to correct the erroneous data.

It was against this background that Congress acted.

The law enacted by Congress has been labeled "The Fair Credit Reporting Act" and became effective April 25, 1971. Known as Title VI of the Consumer Credit Protection Act, the law is of importance to credit bureaus, banks, other lenders, and those who use credit reports in the conduct of business.

What Is Covered?

The act covers credit reports (1) used to determine the extension of credit, (2) for the purpose of selling insurance, and (3) for deciding whether or not to hire one in an employment capacity. Outside of employment situations, the act primarily applies to the use of credit reports for personal, family, and household purposes. But in spite of this limitation it must be remembered that the consumer will be transacting business with a business person who in turn is regulated by the provisions of the act. Therefore, few credit transactions will *not* be covered by Title VI. A business that collects its own credit data is not covered by the Fair Credit Reporting Act, however.

Congress made the following findings before enacting Title VI.

> 1. The banking system is dependent upon fair and accurate credit reporting. Inaccurate credit reports directly impair the efficiency of the banking system, and unfair credit reporting methods undermine the public confidence which is essential to the continued functioning of the banking system.
>
> 2. An elaborate mechanism has been developed for investigating and evaluating the credit worthiness, credit standing, credit capacity, character, and general reputation of consumers.
>
> 3. Consumer reporting agencies have assumed a vital role in assembling and evaluating consumer credit and other information on consumers.
>
> 4. There is a need to insure that consumer reporting agencies exercise their grave responsibilities with fairness, impartiality, and a respect for the consumer's right to privacy.
>
> It is the purpose of this title to require that consumer reporting agencies adopt reasonable procedures for meeting the needs of commerce for consumer credit, personnel, insurance, and other information in a manner which is fair and equitable to the consumer, with regard to the confiden-

tiality, accuracy, relevancy, and proper utilization of such information in accordance with the requirements of this title.

Limits Placed on Use of Reports

The act limits the uses for which credit information may be made available to three in number. First, a reporting agency may issue a consumer credit report when ordered to do so by a court that has the power to issue such an order. Second, if the consumer requests in writing that the report be issued, the agency may make the report. It will become routine for those who extend credit to provide a form authorizing the release of credit information to them. Third, information may be released if the credit bureau has reason to believe that the report will be used in a credit transaction with a consumer; or that it will be used for employment purposes; or that it will be used to make a decision involving insurance for the consumer; or that it will be used by a governmental agency to determine the consumer's eligibility for a license or other benefit; or if the person requesting the data ". . . has a legitimate business need for the information in connection with a business transaction involving the consumer."[4] The last provision permits credit data to be released in a wide variety of circumstances. However, certain information may not be released unless the circumstances fall within the exceptions that follow.

Obsolete Data

The act provides for two periods of limitations on credit data. If the date of adjudication of bankruptcy of the consumer occurred more than 14 years prior to the request for data, the bankruptcy may not be reported. If judgments, paid tax liens, accounts placed for collection, records of arrest, conviction, parole, and other adverse information that relates to the consumer occurred more than seven years prior to the request, that information cannot be released. This provision makes it mandatory that credit agencies carefully screen all reports to make certain that obsolete data is not released.

If credit data is sought in a credit transaction that involves $50,000 or more; or if $50,000 or more in life insurance is involved; or if employment in which the annual salary may exceed $20,000 or more is at issue, the seven- and 14-year periods of limitation do not apply and a full report may be issued.

Other Requirements

Once a report is issued to one who requests it and credit is refused because of the data contained within it, the consumer must be informed that the rejection was for that reason. In addition, the consumer must be given the name and address of the agency that issues the report.

---

[4] Title VI, 604.

If a potential creditor decides to make an *investigation* of the consumer among neighbors or friends or those the consumer is associated with, the consumer must be informed of that possibility in advance. If the consumer objects to such an investigation, the application may be withdrawn. Figure 36–1 illustrates.

FIGURE 36–1

NOTICE REQUIRED BY PUBLIC LAW 91–508
(FAIR CREDIT REPORTING ACT)

Thank you for applying for insurance. Prompt consideration will be given to your application and you will be notified of our action as soon as possible.

As a part of our normal procedure for determining your insurability, an investigative consumer report may be made concerning factors affecting your insurability apart from those covered in your application. These may include information with reference to your character, general reputation, personal characteristics and mode of living, and will be obtained through personal interviews with your friends, neighbors, and associates.

Dividends to policyholders are based to a considerable degree on favorable claim experience, and this procedure will benefit you as a policyholder by providing insurance at the lowest possible cost.

You have a right to submit a written request to us for a complete and accurate disclosure of the nature and scope of the report.

Disclosure to Consumer

Under certain conditions and limitations, the consumer has a right to inspect the data on file. The consumer must present identification; give reasonable notice of the request; and the inspection must be made during business hours. The consumer may be accompanied by one person during the inspection. If the bureau should choose, it can read the report to the consumer and this satisfies the Fair Credit Reporting Act.

If the consumer claims that data on file is inaccurate, the agency must reinvestigate the facts and change data that is found to be in error. If the consumer demands that certain facts be changed, and the bureau believes them to be true as listed, the consumer has the right to file a written statement of his or her version of the facts. The statement cannot exceed 100 words and must accompany all future issues of credit reports on that consumer.

Penalties

One who is convicted of obtaining a consumer credit report under false pretenses may be imprisoned up to one year, fined $5,000, or both.

In addition, if The Fair Credit Reporting Act is willfully violated, a civil remedy of actual plus punitive damages in an unlimited sum, and attorney fees is provided. If the violation is due to mere negligence, a suit may be brought for actual damages only, plus legal costs. A limitation on actions is set at two years from the date that liability arises, or two years from the date that the fraudulent activity is discovered.

The Fair Credit Reporting Act is an asset to consumers. This is especially so when erroneous credit reports hamper them in obtaining new lines of credit and the law is working well in practice. However, there were still two voids for the consumer in the extension of credit. The first arose when errors were made in the charges assessed for credit purchases, and the second came about when lenders practiced discrimination when deciding to whom they would extend credit. Congress acted to solve these problems and the result was that two parts have been added to the C.C.P.A., The Fair Credit Billing Act and the Equal Credit Opportunity Act. These will be discussed in turn.

THE FAIR CREDIT BILLING ACT[5]

While this addition to the C.C.P.A. was passed by Congress in 1974, it did not become effective until October 28, 1975. The purpose of the delay was to give creditors an opportunity to revise their billing practices and revise them they did. In addition, the Federal Reserve Board was empowered to create new additions to Regulation Z as had been done with the original Truth in Lending Act.

What Is the Purpose of the Law?

The F.C.B.A. was designed to give the consumer a means to (1) correct errors on credit charges and (2) to allow disputed charges to be brought to the attention of the creditor in a manner that would force the creditor to give a fair hearing on the dispute.

How Does It Work?

If a consumer makes inquiry about a bill, the creditor must acknowledge receipt of the inquiry. This must be done within 30 days. The creditor must then investigate the records and correct the error or tell the consumer why there is no error. This must be completed within two billing cycles or no later than 90 days, whichever comes first. In the interim, the creditor may not inform a credit bureau or others, that the debtor is delinquent in the account.

During the time that the dispute is being investigated, the creditor may not close the consumers account. However, if the consumer has a credit limit, and the disputed charge uses up the unused credit, then further charges can be suspended while the investigation is being made.

---

[5] C.C.P.A. Title III, Sections 161 to 171, Public Law 93–945.

Failure to Comply

The creditor who fails to meet the requirements, forfeits the charge in question *even though it may have been correct!* However, the limit on forfeiture is $50. If a disputed charge is $10 and the creditor fails in the above, the $10 cannot be collected. If it is more than $50 then only $50 is forfeited. In addition, the creditor forfeits the amount in dispute up to $50 if the creditor reports the delinquency before the complaint is answered.[6]

The second of the additions to the C.C.P.A. was designed to provide equal opportunities in the extension of credit.

EQUAL CREDIT OPPORTUNITY ACT[7]

The Equal Credit Opportunity Act was passed by Congress in 1974, and became effective October 28, 1975. It was enacted as part of the C.C.P.A. but it is not part of Truth in Lending as is the Fair Credit Billing Act. The Federal Reserve Board was given power to draft regulations.

The E.C.O.A. begins as follows: "It shall be unlawful for any creditor to discriminate against any applicant on the basis of sex or marital status with respect to any aspect of a credit transaction." A close reading of the act makes it clear that the single woman and the married woman with good credit standing and independent sources of income, will benefit most from it. However, the act applies to everyone including males, business firms and others. It simply prohibits discrimination in the granting of credit. The act does not define "discrimination" leaving this to the FRB and the courts.

Penalties

Those who feel they have been discriminated against in the extension of credit may sue for both actual and punitive damages. Punitive damages however, may not exceed $10,000. If plaintiffs proceed by a class action, punitive damages are limited to $100,000 for the class, or 1 percent of the lenders net worth, whichever is less. The plaintiff can also recover costs and attorney fees. The period of limitations for such an action is one year.

Turning from the above federal credit laws, two other items will be discussed briefly. The first is an FTC ruling on door-to-door sales, and the second is yet another federal disclosure law — but in a different form.

FTC RULING ON DOOR-TO-DOOR SALES

An FTC ruling that went into effect June 7, 1974, provides a three day "cooling off period" for those who are sold encyclopedias, art lessons, magazine subscriptions, and other items by persons calling at one's

---

[6] C.C.P.A. Title III, Sections 161–162, Public Law 93–945.

[7] C.C.P.A. Title V, Public Law 93–495. This was amended by Public Law 94–240, and effective March 23, 1977, will raise the maximum to $500,000.

home. During the three day period, the buyer may cancel *if* $25 or more is involved. The ruling also requires each salesperson to inform the buyer of this right. This rule can be found in 37 *Federal Register* 22934, and 38 *Federal Register* 31828. As we will see, the states have also enacted similar laws.

The final federal law that will be discussed has an impact upon certain forms of consumer credit and once again, disclosures are involved.

REAL ESTATE SETTLEMENT PROCEDURES ACT (R.E.S.P.A.)[8]

A federal law went into effect on June 20, 1975, that regulates many secured transactions involving the purchase of consumers homes. This was the Real Estate Settlement Procedures Act and it applies to certain "federally related" loans. (There are indications that this law will be amended. It has many weak points.)

What Loans Are Covered?

Almost all secured loans on a dwelling house of one to four family units is covered. This includes condominiums and residential apartments in an apartment complex. The law covers consumer loans for the purchase of such dwelling houses or units, and loans made to buy such units for business purposes.

What Loans Are Excluded?

Loans for business purposes, other than for the purchase of those dwelling units mentioned above, loans for agriculture, manufacturing, and trade purchases are excluded.

What Lenders Are Covered?

The act speaks of "federally related" mortgage lenders as coming under the coverage so theoretically, there may be some lenders who will not be covered. But as it turns out, due to the language of the act, almost all lenders will be covered and must comply.

What Must the Lenders Do?

The law requires that each lender disclose to both the buyer and seller, all costs that will be incurred at the closing. This disclosure must be made available one day before the closing date.

All costs such as attorneys fees, credit reports, appraisal fees and other

---

[8] Public Law 93–533, 12 U.S.C. 2601 and Public Law 94–205.

costs must be itemized in the disclosure. The buyer will be free to purchase title insurance from a company of the buyer's choosing.

Sellers Disclosure

If the seller has not lived in the house and has owned it for less than 2 years, the seller must tell the buyer the price paid for it and must *list* the cost of improvements made to it. This is to assure that the buyer knows the precise nature of what is being bought.

Effect on Truth in Lending

The act supplements Truth in Lending to the extent that if there is a violation of this act and Truth in Lending as well, the buyer *cannot* recover for both violations. The buyer must sue under the Settlement Act.

Escrow Rule

In the past, lenders made the buyer pay a year's taxes in advance as well as insurance premiums. Under this law, the buyer will only be charged each month for the appropriate monthly portion for taxes and insurance. When these come due, there will be enough in escrow to cover them, but not an extra sum.

Penalties

If the disclosures are not available, the buyer can recover from the lender actual damages suffered or $500 whichever is greater. As mentioned, if there is also a violation of Truth in Lending, the buyer can sue only under the Settlement penalty.

SUMMARY

The portions of the C.C.P.A. discussed are significant laws. As will be seen, the federal law has been used as a basis for many state consumer laws. The FTC will continue its drive to assist the consumer, and new departments of "consumer affairs" can be expected in the federal government. Also, Congress can be expected to continue its efforts to create consumer laws to cover other trouble areas. But, what have the states been doing?

STATE CONSUMER LAWS

Our discussion thus far has been limited to federal laws. But the state legislatures have not been idle. State activities in creating consumer laws have increased considerably in recent years and the trend can be expected to continue.

Perhaps we will reach a point at which the desire to protect the consumer will injure the business person. If this happens, the "pendulum" will swing the other way—but that point is a long way off. Following are problem areas with a brief discussion of what some of the states have done.

Unsolicited Goods

One of the constant problems that has faced the buying public in the past is the receipt of items in the mail that have not been ordered. At first it seems foolish to think that a merchant would mail items of value to unknown persons. But this has not been a deterent and the citizen has been flooded with such items as ties, Christmas cards, miniature license plates, and sometimes books and even records. The practice apparently has been profitable since it has continued for so long.

From a strict contractual point of view, one who receives unsolicited goods has no obligation to pay for them *or* return them. Legally, the recipient simply has been made an offer by the sender and silence is not an acceptance. But if one uses the goods, then a contractual obligation arises to make payment—and this is what usually happens. In practice, the person who receives the goods feels an obligation to send them back but instead decides to pay the price and keep the items. However, the states are starting to act to protect the consumer from unsolicited goods and the following laws are typical.

Oklahoma passed a bill permitting anyone who receives unsolicited goods to keep them as gifts. In the event that the sender tries to pressure the recipient for payment, he or she can sue in court to stop the collection efforts and can be awarded costs and attorney fees as well. The law undoubtedly will stop the mailing of such goods in that state. Other states have passed similar laws, including Rhode Island, Vermont, and Michigan. The Rhode Island law makes it a *crime* to attempt to force collection for the cost of unsolicited goods.

Door-to-Door Selling

Another bother has been the salesperson who comes to the door with wares. The pressure that has been exerted on buyers has been unreasonable in case after case. In many instances, consumers agreed to contracts that were beyond their means. Local municipalities have tried to control the problem by requiring "soliciting permits" as a condition to selling door to door. But these have been ineffective since the unscrupulous are not going to obtain a permit in the first place. And if they are pressured by local law enforcement agencies, they simply go outside the city and continue their sales efforts in the county. The states have begun to enact legislation to solve the problem.

Virginia

The legislature of Virginia took a look at Truth in Lending and came up with a similar law where a citizen is sold merchandise at the door.

The buyer has three business days in which to rescind the contract and receive back the down payment – or full price if paid in full. The seller is permitted to keep up to 5 percent of the down payment as a cancellation fee. The buyer must be told of the right to rescind and be given a statement spelling out that right.

In Alaska, a similar law gives the buyer 72 hours in which to rescind – unless the sale is for a sum less than $10. The buyer can cancel orally or in writing and must send the goods to the seller. But the seller must pay the shipping costs. New York has enacted a law similar to that of Virginia but with an additional feature: the statement of the right of rescission must be in both English and Spanish.

REVIEW QUESTIONS

1. Garnishment has been a popular remedy (means of collecting a judgment) for many years. Why?
2. Congress took jurisdiction over garnishment laws because it affected "interstate commerce." What does this mean?
3. If you as an employer receive a court order to start making wage deductions from Employee X, would you seek further advice before honoring the order? Why?
4. Why was there such a wide variety of state garnishment laws?
5. True or False. The Fair Credit Reporting Act was designed to protect the consumer.
6. Name three reasons why an employer would fire an employee because of more than one wage attachment.
7. Garnishment can be a legal *or* equitable remedy. What does this mean?
8. Why did state garnishment laws help consumers in some states – and hurt them in others?
9. A "debtor" and a "judgment creditor" are different. Why?
10. Explain why garnishment is a "novation."

Words and Phrases

Write out briefly what they mean to you.
1. Unsolicited goods.
2. Credit reports.
3. Garnishment.
4. Failure to comply with T.I.L.
5. Wage attachments.

Coverage:	The credit purchase of an automobile and the documents and law involved.
What to Look for:	Ways in which credit buying can be used intelligently.
Application:	The procedures here should be reviewed when the "financing statement" is discussed.
Caution:	This chapter is technical so proceed carefully.

37 The Credit Purchase of Personal Property

A variety of durable goods are available to us on our markets. Many of the sales of these goods are carried out on a "financed" basis, with banks and other lenders advancing the funds with which the goods are bought. In this chapter, the credit purchase of an automobile will be examined in detail. However, it must be remembered that the principles, procedures, and documents discussed here are also used to finance a TV set, a washer and dryer combination, and a refrigerator.

In addition, it should be recognized that these procedures are also used by the business person to finance inventory, and one level of financing is often applied upon top of another—for example, in "floor planning."

For these reasons, this chapter has wide application in business as well as in our personal lives. Take note, however, that the chapter is *not* concerned with financed purchases of *real estate*. That topic is covered in Chapters 23, 24, and 25.

One who purchases an automobile, new or used, has two options available by which the sale may be closed: pay for the automobile and own it outright, or finance it by one means or another. The largest percentage of automobile purchases are made by the use of financing.

In the simplest sense, financing means bringing into operation a prearranged system whereby a lender advances funds to enable the buyer to obtain the automobile that the buyer desires.

TO BUY OR NOT

For three years, Mr. Brown, a single man, owned an older model automobile which served him well. Since it had been paid for in the first year, he has not had the extra burden of a car payment. However, maintenance costs have risen and he has decided to purchase another vehicle. Should it be a new or used one?

Factors which he considered included the rate of insurance on a new car, which would be higher. (Even if the law does not require insurance, the lender will require it in order to protect the security interest in the car.) He also considered the depreciation rate on a new car as compared with a used one. The depreciation rate usually exceeds the reduction by monthly payments, meaning that the auto will always have more due on it than can be realized by a trade-in or outright sale. This factor varies depending upon the amount of down payment.

Brown decided to purchase a late model used car rather than a new one. He then began to shop not only for a car of his liking, but for interest rates well. Under Truth in Lending, Brown has the right to ask lenders what the annual percentage rate will be on an auto loan. Surprisingly enough, depending upon the state, the rate will vary from a low of about 8 percent to a high of 18 percent on an annual basis. The difference can mean many dollars saved over the two- or three-year pay-back period.

TYPES OF FINANCING

If Brown has a good relationship with a bank or other lending institution, he may be able to obtain a personal loan with which to purchase the auto. If he does this, the auto will become his at the outset, free of claims of others. Of course he will owe the money borrowed.

A second type of loan is that in which the lender issues a bank check to the debtor, which may be filled in up to a preestablished amount. This is arranged in advance and the buyer can bargain with others just as though armed with cash.

The third type of financing is the "secured purchase"—the type that Brown decided to use. In this type, a lender will advance a portion of the funds needed to buy the auto, and will take security in the auto purchased to secure the loan. Before examining these procedures, an important question must be disposed of first.

WHO OWNS THE CAR?

The car on the sales lot may *not* be owned by the car dealer. In many instances another holds security in the car—often to secure the money advanced with which to purchase that car. Or the auto may be "floor planned" or "consigned" (see Chapter 21). This means that another person or firm holds legal title to the auto and retains this legal ownership until paid.

But regardless of who owns the auto on the lot, or who has a security interest in it, Brown will not be concerned since he is a "buyer in the ordinary course of business." Now, how is the transaction carried out?

The Papers

When the item being purchased is used as security to raise funds with which to buy it, three documents are used: the note, the security agreement, and the financing statement. (The federal disclosure forms in consumer loans, receipts and warranty papers are also involved as will be discussed, but the three documents mentioned provide the "security.") Examine the note.

The Note

PROMISSORY NOTE   No. A21–436

500 Magnolia Avenue   1–21–7–
(Street Address of   (City)   (State)   (Date)
Buyer)

Undersigned jointly and severally promise to pay to the order of
Scarff Car Sales, Inc.
(Corporate, Firm, or Trade Name of Dealer)

at the office of Farmers and Merchants Bank, $1,904.16 in
Twenty-four monthly installments of
(Number)

Seventy-Nine----34/100----Dollars ($79.34) each, the first installment payable one (1) month after date, balance of installments payable on even date of each succeeding month thereafter, until this note is fully paid, with interest on each installment, after maturity, at the highest lawful rate.

If any installment of this note is not paid when due, the entire amount unpaid hereof, together with interest, shall become due and payable forthwith, at the election of the holder of this note.

Presentment, demand, protest, notice of protest, and nonpayment or dishonor, and notice of the sale of any collateral security are hereby waived by all makers and indorsers hereof.

VALUE RECEIVED   s/s Rusty O. Brown   (SEAL)
                                       (Purchaser Sign Here)

SECURED BY PURCHASE MONEY
SECURITY AGREEMENT   _____ (SEAL)
                                       (Purchaser Sign Here)

The Note

This note is negotiable and it is "secured"—and it states this on its face. The document that provides this security is the "security agreement." (This document is sometimes referred to as a "chattel mortgage.")

The Security Agreement (or Chattel Mortgage)

The purposes of the security agreement are two in number: (1) to grant a "security interest" in the item being financed, and (2) to set forth the terms and conditions under which the funds are advanced.

The Security Agreement

FARMERS AND MERCHANTS BANK
PURCHASE MONEY SECURITY AGREEMENT

No. A21–436

Rusty O. Brown	500 Magnolia Avenue		
Buyer's Name	Street Address	City	State

King
County

the buyer-debtor herein, hereinafter called "Buyer," states that the foregoing address is, if an individual, his residence address or if a business firm, the address of its principal place of business in Typical State, and agrees with

Scarff Car Sales, Inc.	421 Campus Street	
Dealer's Name	Street Address	City

State

the Seller-Secured Party herein, hereinafter called "Seller," that a purchase money security interest has been retained by Seller or is hereby granted to Seller in the motor vehicle herein described, together with all parts and equipment now or hereafter attached thereto, hereinafter referred to as "Collateral," to secure the payment of the time balance stated below, evidenced by the promissory note of Buyer of even date, or any renewal note or substitutions thereof, and the performance of the terms and conditions hereof.

New/Used	Year	Make	Cyl.	Model	Body Type & Color	Serial Number
Used	1974	Pontiac	8	Catalina	4dr. Sta. Wagon	834L26065

Check All
Special
Equipment

☐Radio ☐Heater ☐Power Steering ☐Power Brakes ☐Power Seats

☐Power Wind. ☐Air Cond. ☐Describe Other:

1. Cash purchase price of motor vehicle.................................. $1,995.00
2. Cash purchase price of accessories, and installation and other services itemized as follows: $_____

$_____   + $_____

The Security Agreement (*continued*)

---

3. TOTAL CASH PURCHASE PRICE................................... $1,995.00
4. DOWN PAYMENT..CASH $ 400.00

      DESCRIPTION OF TRADE-IN
      Year Make Body Type Motor No.

      Trade-in allowance...$_____
      Less unpaid balance...$_____
      Net equity in trade-in..$_____
                 TOTAL DOWN PAYMENT.............................. $ 400.00
5. DEFERRED UNPAID BALANCE..................................... $1,595.00
6. TOTAL COST OF INSURANCE TO BE PAID BY PUR-
    CHASER... $ Outside
7. PRINCIPAL BALANCE (5 PLUS 6)............................... $1,595.00
8. FINANCE CHARGE... $ 309.16
9. TOTAL TIME BALANCE (Amount Due) EVIDENCED
    BY NOTE OF EVEN DATE HEREWITH........................ $1,904.16
    PAYABLE IN <u>24</u> MONTHLY INSTALLMENTS OF <u>$79.34</u> EACH.
    THE FIRST INSTALLMENT BECOMES DUE February 21, 197–.

Purchaser represents that he has read both sides of this contract, and that it was completely filled in at the time of signing. Purchaser hereby acknowledges receipt of a true executed copy hereof.

Said note is a negotiable instrument, separate and apart from this contract, even though at time of execution it may be temporarily attached hereto by perforation or otherwise. After thorough examination, purchaser hereby buys and accepts delivery of the foregoing chattels. Purchaser will pay said note irrespective of any imperfection in the merchandise or any breach of alleged representations. Seller and Seller's assigns are authorized to correct patent errors in said contract and other papers by undersigned in connection therewith.

If the cost of insurance is included in the motor vehicle transaction entered into by the Buyer this date, check the box below which applies to him and members of his household:

☐No Male Driver	☐Male Driver under	☐No Male Driver
under Age 25	Age 25	under Age 25
Non-Business	Business and Non-	Business and Non-
Use	Business Use	Business Use

Buyer and Seller agree that the terms and conditions on the reverse side hereof constitute a part of this Purchase Money Security Agreement and are hereby incorporated herein by reference.

| WARNING: THE INSURANCE AFFORDED HEREUNDER DOES NOT COVER LIABILITY FOR INJURY TO PERSONS OR DAMAGE TO PROPERTY OF OTHERS. | NO INSURANCE IS AFFORDED HERE-UNDER UNLESS STATED IN ITEM 6 ABOVE. |

Notice to Buyer. Do not sign this contract in blank. You are entitled to 1 true copy of the contract you sign without charge. Keep it to protect your legal rights.

The Security Agreement (*continued*)

The undersigned acknowledges receipt of an exact copy of this instrument at the time of its execution.

Executed in quadruplicate this 21st day of Jan. 197–.

Signed Scarff Car Sales, Inc.   *   Signed X Rusty O. Brown
          Seller – Secured Party   Buyer – Husband

By _____   _____
          Authorized Agent   Buyer – Wife

The *Terms and Conditions* of the security agreement follow:

Buyer warrants and agrees that: .

(1) Buyer will pay the debt secured by this security agreement according to the terms thereof. (2) Buyer is the owner of the Collateral free from any liens, encumbrances or security interests except for the security interest created hereby. (3) Buyer will keep the Collateral free of liens, encumbrances and other security interests, maintain it in good repair, not use it illegally and exhibit it to Seller on demand. (4) Buyer will keep the Collateral insured at Buyer's expense against substantial risk of damage, destruction or theft in an amount at least equal to the unpaid balance of the debt secured hereby with loss payable to Seller as its interest may appear and that Buyer will deliver all such insurance policies to Seller upon request. (5) Buyer will not sell or offer to sell or otherwise transfer the Collateral from Typical State for a period of 30 days or more, without the written consent of Seller. (6) Buyer will pay promptly when due all taxes and assessments upon the Collateral or for its use or operation. (7) At its option Seller may discharge taxes, liens or security interest or other encumbrances at any time levied or placed on the Collateral, may pay for insurance on the Collateral, and Buyer agrees to reimburse Seller on demand for any payment made or any expense incurred by Seller pursuant to the foregoing authorization.

In the event Buyer defaults in the performance of any covenant or agreement herein, or if any warranty is untrue in any material respect, the entire debt secured by this security agreement shall become due and payable immediately at the option of Seller without notice, and Seller shall have the rights and remedies of a secured party under the Uniform Commercial Code of Typical State and as provided under this security agreement, including, but not limited to, the right to require Buyer to assemble the Collateral and make it available to Seller at a place to be designated by Seller which is reasonable and convenient to both parties, the right without demand to take possession of the Collateral with or without process of law and the right to sell and dispose of the same and distribute the proceeds all in accordance with the laws of Typical State and the provisions of this security agreement. Seller will give Buyer reasonable notice of the time and place of any public sale thereof or of the time after which any private sale or any other intended disposition thereof is to be made. The parties hereto agree that the requirement of reasonable notice of sale or other disposition shall be fulfilled if Seller sends, in accordance with the provisions of the Uniform Commercial

The Security Agreement (*concluded*)

Code, such notice to Buyer at least ten (10) days prior to the date of such sale or other disposition. The parties hereto further agree that public sale of the Collateral by auction conducted either in the county in which the holder does business or anywhere in the state in which the Collateral was repossessed after advertisement of the time and place thereof in a newspaper circulated in the county, city or village in which the sale is to be held shall be deemed to be a commercially reasonable disposition of the Collateral. Buyer shall be liable for any deficiency remaining unpaid after disposition of the Collateral by holder computed according to the statute in such case made and provided, and Buyer agrees to pay the same forthwith. The computation of any deficiency or any amount required to redeem the Collateral shall include the holder's reasonable attorney's fees and legal expenses.

Prepayment and rebate of finance charges: Buyer may prepay any part or all of the time balance without penalty, and upon prepayment in full will receive a rebate of the unearned finance charge, provided the rebate amounts to $1.00 or more.

Reinstatement: Buyer has no legal rights respecting reinstatement of this security agreement or the note it secures in the event of repossession, except as may be granted by the holder hereof.

Default charges: If any installment is not paid within ten days after the due date, Seller may collect currently or may add to the final installment a default charge of 3% per month (or fraction of a month in excess of ten days) on the amount of any installment in arrears (excluding installment which would not be in arrears except for acceleration of their maturity), but this provision shall not be deemed to extend the due date or grant any period of grace.

The waiver or indulgence of any default shall not operate as a waiver of any other default or of the same default on a future occasion.

This security agreement shall be governed by the laws of Typical State.

All rights of Seller hereunder shall inure to the benefit of Seller's successors and assigns; and all obligations of Buyer shall bind Buyer's heirs, executors, administrators, successors and assigns. If there be more than one Buyer, their obligations hereunder shall be joint and several.

The car dealer indorses the note to the bank and assigns the security agreement with its security interest to secure the note. The bank then pays the $1,595.00 to the dealer. Brown will make the 24 payments to the bank which will earn the bank interest of $309.16.

The bank may take the note from the dealer "with recourse" or "without recourse." If it is "with recourse" and Brown defaults, the dealer must pay off the note at the bank and then proceed against Brown under the terms of the security agreement. If the note is taken "without recourse," the dealer is out of the picture and the bank must proceed against Brown directly.

The down payment of $400 gives the lender — or the dealer — an "edge" in the event of default. This is one of the reasons for requiring a down payment on secured purchases of personal property.

The Financing Statement

The third document is the financing statement (not illustrated). The purpose of it is to give the public notice of the existence of the security agreement and its security interest. This is done by filing it at the proper location.

Brown is a consumer and the bank is extending credit to him. Therefore, Truth in Lending disclosures must be made. The blank form below is typical of those being used today. Note the "conspicuous" ANNUAL PERCENTAGE RATE and FINANCE CHARGE. (These disclosures would not be needed in secured loans were *business persons* are the buyers–borrowers.)

The Disclosure Statement

```
                    DISCLOSURE STATEMENT OF LOAN
  Borrowers or purchasers:
  _____      Loan no._____Date_____
  _____      _____
                                            (Creditor)
  _____      _____
        (Street Address)                (Street Address)
  _____
  City      State      Zip    City        State          Zip

  Total of    FINANCE    Amount      ANNUAL        Credit Life
  Payments    CHARGE     Financed    PERCENTAGE    Insurance Charge
                                     RATE
  $           $          $                   %     $
  _____
  Disability   Property    License, Certificate,
  Insurance    Insurance   or Title or Registration Fees:
  Charge       Charge
  $            $           $
  _____
  Taxes:   Non-filing Insurance    Search, Filing, Recording
  $        (not to exceed fees if   or Releasing Fees:
           perfected):
           $                        $
  _____
  Payable in       Due Date of Payments       Amount of Payments
  Consecutive   First:   Others:    Final:   First:   Others:   Final:
  Mo. Payments:          Same Day
                         of Each
                         Month
                                             $        $         $
  _____
    (Number)    Mo/Da/Yr           Mo/Da/Yr
  PROPERTY INSURANCE, if written in connection with this loan, may
  be obtained by borrower/purchaser through any person of his choice. If
  borrower/purchaser desires property insurance to be obtained through
  the creditors, the cost will be $_____ for the term of the credit.
```

The Disclosure Statement (*continued*)

CREDIT LIFE AND DISABILITY INSURANCE is not required to obtain this loan. No charge is made for credit insurance and no credit insurance is provided unless the borrower/purchaser signs the appropriate statement below:

    (*a*) The cost of Credit Life Insurance alone will be $_____ for the term of the credit.

    (*b*) The cost for Credit Life and Disability Insurance will be $_____ for the term of the credit.

I desire Credit Life and   I desire Credit Life Insur-
Disability Insurance   ance Only

_____   _____
(Date) (Signature)   (Date)   (Signature)

I DO NOT want Credit
Life or Disability Insurance

_____
(Date)   (Signature)

REBATE FOR PRE-PAYMENT IN FULL: If the loan contract is prepaid in full by cash, a new loan, refinancing, or otherwise before the final installment date, the borrower shall receive a rebate of precomputed interest computed as follows:

_____ Rule of 78's, _____ Acturial, _____ Sum of Digits, _____ Other

DEFAULT CHARGE: In the event of default on any payment, a charge of $_____ may be assessed.

SECURITY

A. ☐This Loan is Secured by   ☐Motor Vehicle(s): Make _____
    a Security Agreement of   Serial No. _____
    Even Date covering   ☐Household Goods & Appliances of
    _____. The Secur-   the following description:
    ity Agreement will secure
    future or other indebted-   _____
    ness and will cover after-   ☐Other: (Describe): _____
    acquired property.   _____
B. ☐This Loan is Unsecured.   I/WE ACKNOWLEDGE RECEIPT OF
                                 A COPY OF THIS STATEMENT

_____   _____
(WITNESS)   (BORROWER/PURCHASER)

Depending upon the age of the auto purchased, the buyer may or may not receive a "warranty" at the time of closing of the loan. Car dealers will not normally issue a warranty on a used auto that is over three or four years old. In the event there is no warranty, the dealer will write or stamp on the papers, "AS IS AND WITH ALL FAULTS" or similar language. In that event the car is sold without warranties (promises).

If a warranty is issued. but says "50–50"—or contains words that convey the same meaning, the costs of repairs will be shared equally by the buyer and seller during the warranty period. At the end of that time, all costs of repairs fall upon the buyer. For an example of a new and used auto warranty, see Chapter 38.

In the usual transaction involving the secured purchase of an auto, the lender will transfer the title to the buyer, but will have a lien placed on the face of the new title certificate. This title is then held with the security agreement until the note is paid. At that time the financing statement is "terminated," the lien on the title is marked "paid," and the title is given to the buyer. At that point, the car is free of liens – and usually of little value because of its age.

SUMMARY

The *note* is evidence of the debt owed by the buyer. It may contain Truth in Lending disclosures – or these may be set forth on a separate document. The disclosures must be "meaningful" as well as "conspicuous."

The *security agreement* creates the "security interest" in the collateral (goods), and sets forth the conditions under which the secured party may declare default. The rights in this instrument may be assigned (set over) to another as was done in our example with Mr. Brown.

The *financing statement* is a "notice" document and gives notice of the existence of the security interest of the secured party. When a secured debt is paid on personal property, the financing statement is "terminated" by the "termination statement" on the financing statement.

FIGURE 37–1
Security Arrangements

	Real Estate Transactions	*Personal Property Transactions*
Evidence (or proof) of the Debt	Note	Note
Document by Which Transaction Is Secured (security document)	Deed of Trust (Virginia and other states) ("Mortgage" other states)	Security Agreement (U.C.C. language) (Chattel mortgage) (Personal property deed of trust)
Miscellaneous Legal Security Devices	Confession of Judgment (Recorded) (Will be unlawful in consumer transactions under FTC ruling)	Pledge Escrow
Federal Disclosures (Truth in Lending-"R.E.S.P.A.")	On the note, or a separate form unless it is a business loan	On the note, or a separate form, unless it is a business loan. (R.E.S.P.A. is not involved)

To complete the summary examine Figure 37–1 closely. In this figure the documents used in a personal property secured transaction are compared with the documents used in a real property secured transaction.

The Brown auto purchase is an example of how a car dealer can sell a car to another by use of a lenders money. It is simply a matter of A giving the money to B; B giving the auto to C; and C paying A for the amount loaned plus interest. A earns the interest; B is paid in full and makes a profit that way; and C benefits from the use of the auto. However, many other factors become involved in a personal property secured transaction and the most important are discussed in the balance of this chapter.

FILING

When security is taken in an automobile, the lender will file the financing statement in the locations provided by the laws of the state in which the transaction occurred. Some states require local filing in the county where the loan was made or where the buyer resides. Others require central filing at an office located in the capital city of the state.

The purpose of filing is to provide a way for other lenders to determine the status of collateral that is tendered to them for a loan. For example, if Brown would go to Bank B and offer the secured automobile as security, a search at the filing point would uncover the prior security interest. If Bank B made the loan without the search, their interest in the auto would be second to that of the first bank.

Title Certificate States. Most states require that a lien against a "licensed motor vehicle" be placed upon the face of the title certificate. And even in some of the "title certificate" states, the financing statement is still filed for reasons stated—although in some states it is not. As stated previously, when the note in a secured transaction is paid that involves a motor vehicle, the lien on the certificate is marked "paid" and the title is released to the buyer.

State Lines. One problem for lenders arises when the buyer takes the financed automobile across a state line. A financing statement recorded in state A in county X would be impossible for an out-of-state lender to locate, so the prior lender must refile in the new state before out-of-state lenders are placed on notice. When a motor vehicle is removed from a state, the lender has four months within which to file in the state where the vehicle is taken. The security interest relates back to the date of filing of the first financing statement and the original lender is protected.

Risk of Loss. A large body of law has developed on the question of risk of loss, meaning that in the event of fire, an accident, or other destruction, the one who "has the title" must bear the loss. Under the U.C.C. it is a matter of spelling out who will bear the loss. In the usual case, the buyer bears the risk from the time of sale forward.

POLICING THE COLLATERAL

Most lenders "police collateral" taken as security for loans. The security agreement will specify the terms and conditions of such policing.

Where warehouses of goods are financed, the lender may keep an employee on duty to prevent removal or theft of the financed goods. In car financing it is customary for an employee of the lender to take a look at the auto from time to time to make certain that it is being properly cared for.

Damage to Car

If damage occurs to the car during the time that it is financed, property damage insurance will cover the repairs. Most lenders require that the insurance policy contain a "loss payable" clause that names the lender as the one to whom proceeds will be paid. In this way the lender will avoid diversion of funds by the owner of the car.

Trading a Financed Car

These procedures are designed to protect the first lender and in practice they work well if the proper steps are followed. Does this mean that the buyer cannot use the financed auto as collateral for the purchase of a new one? Not at all. If the buyer decides to purchase a new auto, the financed auto may be used as collateral to the extent that it is unencumbered by the prior loan. The new lender will obtain a pay-off figure on the prior loan and see that it is paid out of the new proceeds. The original lender will execute the termination statement as mentioned.

The process may be thought of as "trading" with value that one has in some object.

PAYMENT OF LOAN IN ADVANCE

Frequently, one who has financed an auto (or other item of durable goods) will pay off that obligation in advance. When this occurs, the question arises, how is the pay-off figure calculated?

Example.   Zero Bank loans Debtor Jones the sum of $1,200.00 for one year at 12 percent interest, to be repaid monthly in payments of $106.50 each. The total of the 12 payments equals $1,278.00 for a total interest charge of $78.00 ($1,278.00 less $1,200.00). The note that Jones signed was for $1,278.00. The interest was on a "declining balance" at the rate of 1 percent per month or 12 percent for the year.

Assume Jones pays off this note at the end of six months. Jones should be given credit for that portion of the interest added at the beginning, that had not been earned at the time of pay-off. In our example, the interest earned by the bank at the end of six months will be $57.00 even though the interest for the full year, if the pay-off had not occurred, would have only been $78.00.

A formula is required to calculate this and it is known in many states as the "Rule of 78ths" or sometimes as the "sum of the digits." Examine Figure 37–2.

First, Why 78?   In each 12 month period, there are 78 "installment units" being the total of 1, 2, 3, 4, 5, 6, 7, 8, 9, 10, 11, and 12. This is where the rule gets it's name.

FIGURE 37–2

An Example of How One Company Discloses the Rule of 78ths

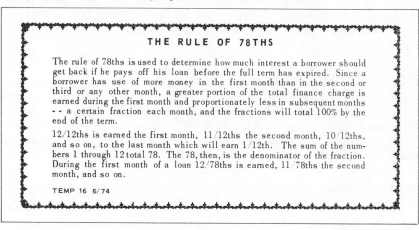

In our example, the interest for each month is calculated at 1 percent per month on the balance due. The interest for the first month would be $12.00 or 1% of the principal sum of $1,200.00. The payment for the first month of $106.50 would be applied as follows: $100.00 to principal and $6.50 to interest. The interest for the second month would be calculated on the reduced balance of $1,110.00. This would continue as payments are made until the principal plus 12 percent interest is paid. However, the payment of $106.50 per month (which will total to the correct interest for the full year plus principal) does *not* equal the amount of the interest earned for the first months of the loan. Therefore, if prepayment is made, the rule must be applied to determine the amount required to retire the note at that time. Examine Figure 37–3.

Since Jones paid off the note at the end of six months, the total amount of interest earned has not yet been paid. Jones has paid $39.00 (6 × $6.50)

FIGURE 37–3

End of Month	*Principal Balance*	*Interest Earned*	*Interest Paid*
1	$1,200.00	$12.00	$6.50
2	1,100.00	11.00	6.50
3	1,000.00	10.00	6.50
4	900.00	9.00	6.50
5	800.00	8.00	6.50
6	700.00	7.00	6.50
7	600.00	6.00	6.50
8	500.00	5.00	6.50
9	400.00	4.00	6.50
10	300.00	3.00	6.50
11	200.00	2.00	6.50
12	100.00	1.00	6.50

while the bank has earned the total of $12.00, $11.00, $10.00, $9.00, $8.00, and $7.00 or $57.00. Therefore Jones owes $18.00 additional which will be adjusted in determining the pay-off figure.[1]

The next problem that arises is where a debtor fails to meet monthly payments as they fall due. What happens then?

DEFAULT

If a debtor fails to meet obligations, the debtor is in "default." This is frequently followed by "repossession."

The U.C.C. does not define "default." Rather, it states ". . . when a debtor is in default under a security agreement . . ." the creditor has those remedies provided in the *security agreement* as well as those provided in the Code.[2] One must look to the terms of the security agreement to find what constitutes default. Some samples of default include failure to repair collateral that has been damaged; failure to provide insurance on collateral and failure to make prompt payments.

Taking Possession

Once default occurs, the secured party will, in most cases, want to take possession of the collateral as quickly as possible. However, in taking possession, the secured party must do so without committing a "breach of the peace."[3] A breach of the peace would include the use of force, threats, damage to property, or harm to the debtor. In an Ohio case, two men "surrounded" the debtor's son, who became afraid that he would be beaten, so he made no objection to their repossession of a rotary mower. The court held their actions to be a breach of the peace, even though no physical harm resulted.[4]

In all situations where the debtor resists, the secured party should proceed by legal action and obtain court process before further attempts at repossession. At common law, the action to recover possession of personal property was called "detinue"—a name still used in many courts to describe the process.

Disposing of the Collateral

Once the secured party gains lawful possession, that person ". . . may sell, lease or otherwise dispose of any or all of the collateral," provided that it is done in a commercially reasonable manner.[5] However, if the debtor has paid for 60 percent or more of the collateral and assuming that the debtor does not agree otherwise, the secured party must dispose

---

[1] The Rule of 78ths generally has no application in real estate loans where the interest is calculated monthly. In that type of loan, the pay-off is the principal balance due plus interest to day of pay-off.

[2] U.C.C., 9–501(1) (emphasis added).

[3] U.C.C., 9–503.

[4] *Morris* v. *First National*, 21 Ohio St. 2d 25 (1970).

[5] U.C.C., 9–504(1).

of the property within 90 days or become liable for conversion of the property.

The repossessed collateral may be disposed of at public or private sale and it may be sold by unit or in parcels under "commercially reasonable" terms.

The U.C.C. contemplates that the secured party will act in a reasonable manner and will take all steps necessary to assure that maximum dollar return is realized. For this reason the Act does not lay down specific guidelines. For example, the sale of repossessed perishable goods would not follow the same pattern as the sale of a piece of equipment that needed repairs.

Retaining Possession

In some cases the secured party may retain possession of the collateral in full satisfaction of the debt. Written notice of the proposal must be sent to the debtor and any other person who may have a security interest in the collateral. If no objection is received within 30 days, the secured party may keep the collateral in satisfaction of the debt and the debtor is freed from further obligation. The note would be returned to the debtor and the financing statement terminated.

Rights of a Buyer

When one purchases collateral at a lawful sale, the sale

> . . . transfers to a purchaser of value all of the debtor's rights therein, discharges the security interest under which it is made and any security interest or lien subordinate thereto.[6]

As long as the buyer has no knowledge of defects in the sale and acts in good faith, the buyer's title is free from any rights or interests, even if the sale is not conducted properly. This provision is needed to encourage purchasers to buy at foreclosure sales.

Right to Redeem

The debtor has the right to redeem before sale by paying all obligations plus expenses including costs of retaking, preparing for sale, and reasonable attorneys' fees.[7]

In the event that the sale is not conducted properly, the Code provides remedies for the debtor by way of action against the secured party, even though the buyer at the sale gains clear title.

DEFICIENCY JUDGMENTS

If the sale of the collateral brings less than the sum due to the secured party, the debtor will be expected to pay the difference. If not, suit may

---

[6] U.C.C., 9–504 (4).

[7] U.C.C., 9–506.

be filed for the deficiency. The debtor must understand what can happen in this situation, because the debtor may lose the down payment (or trade-in) plus what was paid on the note, as well as what was being bought, and still owe a sum of money in addition.

The accompanying letter, fictionalized, resulted from the repossession and sale of an automobile. The debtor lost the trade-in, over $1,000 in payments, the car that was being bought—and still owes the company $336.70! (This was taken from an actual case.)

However, the present and prior deficiency judgment practices is about to fall victim to the consumer protection movement—and probably justifiably so. In the FTC Improvement Act, P.L. 93–637, 93rd Cong., S. 356, January 4, 1975, power was given to create new rules for situa-

---

AJAX FINANCIAL AIDES COMPANY, INC.
Route 121, South
Annapolis, Maryland

September 15, 197–.

Dear Mr. Hancock:

PROTECT YOUR CREDIT AND SAVE YOURSELF MANY DOLLARS!

Your failure to redeem your car or secure a buyer to assume your liability left us no choice but to sell the car for the highest price available. The amount received from this sale did not pay your account in full.

The following figures indicate the exact status of your indebtedness:

Balance due on your contract	$969.00	
Expense of repossessing and selling your car	$_____	
Total		$969.00
Less credits due:		
Insurance settlement	$290.00	
Insurance return premium credit life	$ 4.80	
Other credits. Sale proceeds	$337.50	
Total credit allowed		$632.30
Amount you owe		$336.70

Your credit rating is one of your most valuable business assets. We are sincere in our desire to help you maintain it and for this reason we request that you contact us immediately to arrange a reasonable settlement either on a cash or monthly payment basis.

Legal action on our part will not only increase your indebtedness due to accrued interest, court costs, and attorney fees, but will also determine your future credit rating. We trust that such action on our part will not be necessary.

PLEASE TELEPHONE FOR APPOINTMENT.

Sincerely,

E. L. Shark
Credit Manager

Please contact us within a week if you are interested in making a cash settlement, whereby we will accept a lesser figure than that shown above.

tions such as that set forth above. The rule currently proposed, and the one that will probably be adopted, will require a creditor who repossesses consumer collateral, to credit the consumer with the *fair market value* of the item. This will be true even if the item brings less when sold later.

REVIEW QUESTIONS

1. Make a list of the procedural steps followed in the financed purchase of an automobile.
2. Why should a buyer read the fine print on the security agreement when financing a car?
3. It is difficult to read the legal documents in this chapter. Does this explain why so few persons know what the "fine print" says?
4. Make a list of the things that you would do before purchasing a car on credit.
5. True or False. The three principal documents used in car financing are the note, deed of trust, and security agreement.
6. Make a list of types of financing available locally for the purchase of personal property.
7. Distinguish a secured purchase of real estate from one of personal property.
8. The financing statement is a powerful legal document. Name a reason for this. (Ask your instructor to show you a financing statement.)
9. The note is the document common to both real and personal property secured transactions. Why?
10. What does "title certificate state" mean to you?

Words and Phrases

Write out briefly what they mean to you.
1. Financing statement.
2. Security agreement.
3. Refiling.
4. Security interest.
5. Note.

38 Consumers and Defective Products

The consumer is frequently confronted with problems related to the products purchased in the marketplace. There is the watch that loses a crystal the first day worn; the shelf that falls from the refrigerator door; the box of pizza that has turned bad; and worse, there is the acid in the eye wash that causes blindness, the faulty shampoo that causes loss of hair, and the automobile that kills, maims, or disfigures because of defects contained within the product.

The injuries have been many, the recoveries few and the loss in dollars, if calculated, would be staggering. It is a problem of matching up promises (warranties) of the manufacturer to the consumer who suffers loss because of products purchased. The picture as it has existed over the past one hundred years has not been a pretty one.

The fate of John Roger Horne is an example.

A Defective Heater

A 19-year-old resident of Georgia purchased a gas fired "warm-morning" heater from a major chain store. It had been manufactured by a leading stove corporation—and contained defects. As a result, the stove emitted carbon monoxide fumes the first night used, adding the name of John Roger Horne to the obituary list.

Suit was filed by Horne's estate against the manufacturer on the grounds of "breach of warranty." That is, when one makes a product, one makes promises about it including that it will be suitable for the use for

429

which it was intended. The legal steps that followed seem unbelievable, but they are true.

First, the estate had to show contract "privity," (connection) between Horne and the manufacturer. The estate failed because Horne had not bought the stove from the manufacturer. Therefore, there was no contract between them — so no privity and thus no common law warranties. Now what about statutory warranties?

The U.C.C. Article 2–318 permits warranty liability to run to certain persons stated in the law, namely one ". . . in the family or household of . . . (the) buyer or . . . a guest in his home." Since Horne was a tenant, he did not "fit into the rule."

The estate, now blocked on two fronts, turned to the Georgia law that permits recovery where death results from negligence where the product involved was

> . . . intended for human consumption or use where either knowledge of the defect or negligence by the seller is an essential element.

The court said the heater did not fit the rule because it was not made to be "consumed." The case was dismissed even though it was undisputed that the heater had caused the death![1]

THE "NEW RIGHTS" OF HUMAN BEINGS

In the days of the creation of the Magna Charta, the nature of the "rights" of human beings were in dispute and that document is ancient proof of this fact. Certainly a person in that age did not enjoy the rights claimed by the poorest in our society. As the centuries passed, "new rights" became recognized — but in looking at the progress made, the progress was painfully slow. Witness 1900 America: children in the mines and "sweat shops," no limits on working hours, and no controls on working conditions.

In the last two decades, we have become sophisticated enough to recognize that the need for clean air, pure water, unadulterated food, and safe consumer products are also part of our rights, and the reason for this is simple: recognition and protection of basic rights means very little if accompanied by bad health, disease, and death. However, these *new* rights are being ignored by some who provide us with the "goods of our time."

In numerous instances the modern consumer is being maimed, poisoned, harrassed, and in some cases killed summarily, at an unprecedented rate by the products of business. The consumer is used, abused, preyed upon, and thoroughly brainwashed in the process. And this is happening at a time when the consumer is the foundation upon which modern wealth is accumulated, the focal point about which industry revolves, and the reason for almost all economic activity.

---

[1] *Horne* v. *Armstrong Products*, 6 U.C.C. Rep. 1174, (1969).

Thus, it would seem logical that *all* modern courts would provide the protection needed to enforce these rights, but this is not always so.

Another Example

A 7-year-old lost her leg by falling in front of a power mower operated by her 11-year-old sister. The mower was inherently dangerous in that the rotary blade would be likely to injure or maim children, and although the blade appeared to be covered, *it in fact lacked a safety bar or screen. A motion for summary judgment in favor of the defendant was sustained.* Reason? The manufacturer of *this* mower had no duty to *this* plaintiff. The decision was affirmed by the Appellate Court of Illinois for the same reason.[2]

Illinois subsequently recognized this injustice and corrected it as to future consumers who become mangled by defective products. In the case of *Suvada* v. *White Motor Company*,[3] the court *held manufacturers, sellers, and others to liability* for an injury or damage caused by unreasonably dangerous products which they might place into the "stream of commerce." The case was cited and followed in a subsequent "corn picker-mangled hand" case.[4] In the mangled hand case, the court said that it would treat *defects in design* as well as *defects in manufacture* as jury questions.

The Nature of the Problem

A Connecticut court has spelled out the problem:

> The maxim "caveat emptor" has become a millstone (and a rather heavy one) around the necks of both dealers and customers. While the customer may maintain an action . . . against the retailer for breach of implied warranty, the dealer in turn must sue his supplier to recoup his damages and costs where the customer prevails. Eventually, after several separate and distinct pieces of costly litigation by those in the chain of title, the manufacturer is finally obligated to shoulder the responsibility which should have been his in the first instance.[5]

> The limitations of privity in contracts for the sale of goods developed their place in the law when marketing conditions were simple, when maker and buyer frequently met face-to-face on an equal bargaining plane, and when many of the products were relatively uncomplicated and conducive to inspection by a buyer competent to evaluate their quality.[6]

These conditions are no longer present. "The world of merchandising is no longer the world of direct contact."[7] In modern merchandising the

---

[2] *Murphy* v. *Cory Pump & Supply Company*, 47 Ill. App. 2d. 382, 197 N.E.2d. 849 (1964).

[3] 32 Ill.2d. 612, 210 N.E.2d 182 (1965).

[4] *Wright* v. *Massey-Harris, Inc.*, 68 Ill. App. 2d. 70, 215 N.E.2d. 465 (Illinois 1966).

[5] *Hamon* v. *Diglianti*, 148 Conn. 710, 174 A.2d. 294 (1960).

[6] 37 Mich.L.Rev. 1 (1963).

[7] *Lonrick* v. *Republic Steel Corporation*, 1 Ohio App. 2d. 374, 205 N.E.2d. 92 (Ohio 1965).

buyer no longer meets the maker face-to-face and in most purchases will not know where the product was made.

Further, the modern consumer is at a complete disadvantage as far as an intelligent evaluation of a product is concerned. Due to the complexity of modern products, often the only way to evaluate is through use.

The problem is thus

> . . . one of allocating a more or less inevitable loss to be charged against the complex and dangerous civilization, and liability (should be) . . . placed upon the party best able to shoulder it. The defendant (should be) . . . held liable merely because, *as a matter of social adjustment*, the conclusion is that the responsibility should be his.[8]

The purpose of this chapter is to take a look at the problem in the courts and to offer suggestions for its cure.

WARRANTIES AND DISCLAIMERS UNDER THE U.C.C.

Instead of following the basic contract principle of "privity of contract," the U.C.C. relies on the concept of "warranties." A warranty is a promise that a proposition of fact is true and warranties may be "express" or "implied."

Express Warranties

Express warranties arise by "stipulations" at the time of purchase and sale. They may take the form of an express promise; they may arise through a description that accompanies the sale; or they can come into being by the use of samples as a means of setting the standards of sale. They may further arise by conduct, custom, or usage of trade. Objective manifestations are the crucial issues, and intention of the parties is *not* necessarily relevant.[9] However, "puffing" or "mere expression of opinion" is not enough to create warranties.[10] For example, "this car could win the Indy 500" would not be a legal assurance that it would do so.

Implied Warranties

Implied warranties do not require bargaining or stipulation at the time of purchase and sale. They arise as a part of the normal sales transaction provided that ". . . the seller is a merchant with respect to goods of that kind,"[11] and are included by operation of law unless effectively "disclaimed." These warranties can be of three varieties: (1) implied warranty of title,[12] (2) implied warranty of merchantability,[13] and (3)

---

[8] Prosser on Torts, 3d ed., Chapter 14, page 509. (Emphasis added.)

[9] U.C.C., 1–313(2).

[10] *Hollenbeck* v. *Ramset Fasteners,* 267 N.C. 401, 148 S.E.2d 287 (North Carolina 1966).

[11] U.C.C., 2–314.

[12] U.C.C., 2–312.

[13] U.C.C., 2–314.

An Example of a New Car Warranty

U.S. Motor Division (hereinafter referred to as U.S.) warrants each new U.S. passenger car, chassis, and 10, 20, 30 Series truck (each being hereinafter referred to as a Vehicle) including all equipment and accessories thereon (except tires and tubes), manufactured or supplied by U.S. and delivered to the original retail purchaser by an authorized U.S. Dealer, to be free from defects in material or workmanship under normal use and service for 24 months or until it has been driven for 24,000 miles after such delivery, whichever comes first, and further warrants the power train components specifically described as the cylinder block and head and all internal engine parts, intake manifold, transmission case and all internal parts, torque converter, propeller shaft and universal joints, differential, axle shafts and rear wheel bearings on any such Vehicle, manufactured or supplied by it to be free from defects in material and workmanship under normal use and service for 5 years or until it has been driven for 50,000 miles after such delivery, whichever occurs first.

As an express condition of this warranty, once every 6 months the owner is required to furnish an authorized U.S. Dealer evidence that the engine oil, oil filter, carburetor air filter, and positive crankcase ventilator valve (and automatic transmission oil and transmission band if so equipped) have been serviced in accordance with the required maintenance schedule as stated in the applicable U.S. Owner Protection Plan booklet, and have the Dealer certify in such booklet (1) that he has received such evidence, and (2) the then current indicated mileage on the odometer.

The obligation of U.S. under this warranty is limited to repairing or replacing any part or parts which are returned to an authorized U.S. Dealer at such Dealer's place of business and which examination shall disclose to the reasonable satisfaction of U.S. to have been thus defective. The repair or replacement of defective parts under this warranty will be made by such Dealer without charge for parts and labor.

The provisions of this warranty shall not apply to any Vehicle which has been subject to misuse, negligence, alteration, or accident, or which shall have been repaired outside of an authorized Dealer's place of business in any way so as, in the reasonable judgment of U.S., to affect adversely its performance and reliability, nor to normal maintenance services (such as engine tune up, fuel system cleaning, carbon or sludge removal, brake and clutch adjustments and wheel alignment and balancing) and the replacement of service items (such as spark plugs, ignition points, positive crankcase ventilator valves, filters and brake and clutch lining) made in connection with such services, nor to normal deterioration of soft trim and appearance items due to wear and exposure.

THIS WARRANTY IS EXPRESSLY IN LIEU OF ANY OTHER WARRANTIES, EXPRESSED OR IMPLIED, INCLUDING ANY IMPLIED WARRANTY OF MERCHANTABILITY OR FITNESS FOR A PARTICULAR PURPOSE, AND OF ANY OTHER OBLIGATIONS OR LIABILITY ON THE PART OF U.S., AND U.S. NEITHER ASSUMES NOR AUTHORIZES ANY OTHER PERSON TO ASSUME FOR IT ANY OTHER LIABILITY IN CONNECTION WITH SUCH VEHICLE.

implied warranty of fitness for a particular purpose.[14] The warranties of "title" and "fitness" extend to members of the buyer's family as well as to guests in the buyer's home.[15] Implied warranties can be disclaimed, but strict rules are involved. For example, "merchantability" can be excluded only by language expressly mentioning merchantability and it must be CONSPICUOUS if in writing. Unlike the two implied warranties mentioned above, the "fitness" warranty can be excluded generally.[16] Implied warranties can further be excluded if (1) the sale is "as is" or "with all faults"; (2) if the buyer has an opportunity to inspect the goods and does not (the implied warranty would be excluded as to what his inspection *would* have disclosed); and (3) by course of dealing or usages of trade.[17] Where warranties are inconsistent and overlapping, U.C.C. 2–317 controls. Examine the new car warranty on page 433.

Give or Take? A close reading of the "warranty" shows that it is in fact a "disclaimer" because of its CONSPICUOUS provisions. The questions then arise, did U.S. give the buyer something by its express written promise—or did it take something away by its conspicuous disclaimer? A close reading of the document brings one to the conclusion that it actually *limits* the obligation of U.S. and thus is a "disclaimer."

Courts and Disfavor. Disclaimers have met with disfavor in certain courts. One judge had this to say about them:

> . . . implied warranty is more properly a matter of public policy beyond the power of the seller to alter unilaterally with disclaimers and inconsistent express warranties . . . Where there is implied in law a certain duty to persons not in contract privity, it seems preposterous that the seller should escape that duty by inserting disclaimer of which the remote injured person would be unaware . . .[18]

In that case the lessor of defective equipment was held liable to employees of the lessee who were injured because of defects in the leased equipment.

A Used Car Warranty. A used car warranty is shown on page 435. What might happen if the buyer of the car in question was injured the day after the purchase when a front wheel fell from the car causing a head-on collision with an approaching car? In all probability the buyer would be unsuccessful, regardless of whom suit was filed against. The promises made by the seller are very narrow.

A Practical Approach to the Problem. The "Restatement of Torts"—a treatise on torts—takes the following approach:

> 402A. Special Liability of Seller of Product for Physical Harm to User or consumer.
> 1. One who sells any product in a defective condition unreasonably dangerous to the user or consumer or to his property, is subject to liability

---

[14] U.C.C., 2–315.

[15] U.C.C., 2–318.

[16] U.C.C., 2–316.

[17] U.C.C., 2–316.

[18] *Greenco* v. *Clark Equipment Company*, 237 F.Supp. 427 (1965).

Example of a Used Car Warranty

USED VEHICLE WARRANTY

This warranty is hereby signed in favor of _____

No. _____

Name _____ Address _____
City _____ State _____
in connection with the purchase of the motor vehicle described as follows:
Year _____ Make _____ Type _____
Motor No. _____ Serial No. _____
Speedometer Mileage _____

1. In event of mechanical failure or defective parts, occurring in normal service for a period of 30 days from _____, 19____, or until such motor vehicle has been driven one thousand (1,000) miles, whichever shall first occur, we will furnish replacement parts and labor (except for the items listed in paragraph 2 below) necessary to keep the vehicle in operating condition under normal use at a cost of 50% of our regular list price for such items, provided the remaining 50% is paid in cash by purchaser.

2. Tires, battery, and electrical equipment are not included in this warranty. However, we will furnish replacement tires or electrical equipment at a 25% reduction from our regular list price if the remaining cost is paid in cash by the purchaser.

3. This warranty shall not apply to any vehicle which shall have been repaired or altered by anyone other than the undersigned dealer or to any vehicle which has, in our opinion, been impaired by misuse, negligence, or accident.

4. This warranty is the only warranty extended to the purchaser in connection with the sale of the above Vehicle. NO OTHER WARRANTY, EXPRESSED OR IMPLIED ON THE PART OF THE SELLER, BY ANYONE, HAS BEEN MADE OR IS AUTHORIZED.

5. This warranty must be presented with the vehicle for any and all adjustments, and the same is not transferable or assignable.

In Witness Whereof we have attached our signatures this _____
day of _____, 19____.

_____
DEALER
By _____
City _____ State _____
Signed _____
PURCHASER

for physical harm caused thereby to the ultimate user or consumer, or to his property if,

    a. the seller is engaged in the business of selling such a product, and

    b. it is expected to and does not reach the user or consumer without substantial change in the condition in which it is sold.

    2. The rule stated in Subsection (1) applies though

    a. the seller has exercised all possible care for the preparation and sale of his product, and

    b. the user or consumer has not bought the product from or entered into any contractual relationship with the seller.

The result under 402A is an implied warranty without the doctrine of "privity," disclaimer and requirements of notice of the defect. The above rule of "strict liability" in tort for products liability cases was adopted by the Supreme Court of Wisconsin.[19] Although the case was dismissed for failure to state a cause of action, the court used the opportunity to adopt the rule of 402A. The leg of a pool table had collapsed, crushing a patron's foot.

THE U.C.C. PROVISION IN OPERATION

Returning to the previous illustration, the 7-year-old girl is injured by a defect in a power mower operated by her 11-year-old sister. This defect *could not* have been discovered by inspection and an effective disclaimer was *not* in effect. The infant sues the retailer (through her father). Her grounds: breach of implied warranty of merchantability.[20] (The retailer in this illustration is a merchant with respect to goods of this kind.[21]) It is discovered that judgment against the retailer will be worthless in that the retailer has attained a "judgment proof" station in life: eligible for all unemployment, social security, and other benefits, but unable to pay legitimate obligations. Can the plaintiff bypass the retailer and sue the manufacturer? (After all, the manufacturer *built* the mower.) Traditionally the answer to this question has been "no" because the implied warranty arises only because of the sale. The manufacturer did not sell the mower to the child, or the child's parents; therefore, not being in "privity of contract" with the manufacturer, the infant has no contractual standing to demand that the manufacturer furnish merchantable goods to her.

The U.C.C. 2–318 "Myth." At first reading, UCC 2–318 seems to abolish privity as a defense in a case such as the one under discussion. However, upon closer analysis it is seen that privity is abolished only in part. The U.C.C. takes a conservative approach, leaving the final decision to the courts.

What Does U.C.C. 2–318 Say? Under UCC 2–318 the injured buyer or members of his or her family can go against the "seller" PROVIDED

---

[19] *Dippel* v. *Sciano,* 155 N.W.2d. 55 (1967).

[20] U.C.C., 2–314.

[21] U.C.C., 2–314(1). See also U.C.C., 2–104(1), comment 2. To determine if the goods are "merchantable" see U.C.C., 2–314(2).

that the sale carries an implied warranty of fitness or merchantability which is clearly breached. (The subject of disclaimer is another story.) The definition of "seller" under the UCC is *not* broad enough to encompass the manufacturer. U.C.C. 2-103(1)(*d*) states ". . . 'Seller' means a person who sells or contracts to sell goods." So in application its coverage is narrow. Witness the Horne defective heater tragedy. Some state legislatures have attempted to solve this problem.

What Some States Did. The legislatures of Virginia, South Carolina, and others ignored the uniform provision of 2-318 and drafted their own. For example, Virginia added the following language:

> . . . Lack of privity between plaintiff and defendant shall be no defense in any action brought against the manufacturer . . . if the plaintiff was a person whom the manufacturer or seller might reasonably have expected to use, consume, or be affected by the goods.[22]

The Die Is Cast. For some time the trend has been in the direction of allowing direct recovery against the manufacturer with one of three theories being used to circumvent the defense of privity: (1) On the tort theory of negligence regardless of privity. The burden is on the injured person to show negligence plus freedom from contributory negligence. Contract privity is not involved under this approach which "sounds in tort," that is, it is a tort action based on negligence. (2) Some courts simply extend the original express and implied warranties of fitness or merchantability made by the manufacturer to the injured party. (3) On the theory of "strict" or "absolute liability" in tort holding the manufacturer liable without reference to warranties, privity, or negligence. In other words, since the manufacturer constructed a defective product, let the manufacturer pay for injuries that result from its use.

The example set by the Wisconsin Supreme Court provides a realistic solution to the problem. It does not appear that any great hardship will fall upon the manufacturers of that state as a result of the action. It is probably true, however, that a duty of increased care will be forced upon the manufacturers. This will prompt a cry of "prices must go up." But such can be countered by pointing out that an increase in price in exchange for a safer product will be cheap consumer insurance in the long run.

REVIEW QUESTIONS

1. Do you understand the "contract problem" as it relates to warranties cases?
2. If not, review the facts in the Horne case. Was the result there "unconscionable"?
3. Why, as a matter of business policy, should manufacturers run quality or safety checks on the products they produce?
4. What is a "disclaimer"? Is it fair for manufacturers to use them?
5. True or False. The problems created by defective products will be resolved quickly.

---

[22] Virginia Code 8.2-318 (1965).

6. Examine U.C.C. 2–318. Why is this statute not as broad in coverage as it might have been? (Take a guess, then discuss it with your instructor.)
7. Warranties often arise out of "dickering" that occurs before a sale of goods is made. What danger can incur from this to the seller? To the buyer?
8. List two examples of writings that a court would probably hold to be "conspicuous."
9. Explain why a new or used car warranty is in fact a disclaimer.
10. Examine the new car warranty in this chapter. Why is the last paragraph in it set in capital letters?

Words and Phrases

Write out briefly what they mean to you.
1. Disclaimer.
2. Merchantability.
3. Privity.
4. Warranties
5. U.C.C. 2–318.

part four
Business

Coverage:	Regulations and restrictions that are placed upon the operation of business.
What to Look for:	The types of business decisions necessary to avoid violations of the law.
Application:	List examples of both compliance and violations of these basic regulations, drawn from your experiences as a consumer.

39 The "Ballgame of Business"

Qui jure suo utitur nemini facit injuriam.[1]

A useful analogy can be drawn between a football game and businesses that are in competition with each other. The rival ball players stage their contest on the gridiron while rival business persons seek their goals on the big, but not always so green, field of society. The competing ball teams seek what the other does its best to deny—a score by touchdown, extra point, field goal, or touchback. So it is in business when different companies seek the same market at the same time—a score by increased sales. If Company A captures more of its share of the market, then that share is denied to Company B, a competitor.

The football game is played under the observation of two classes of persons: the spectators, who follow the game by applying their concepts of the rules of the game (which they frequently know quite well); and the umpires, who look for violations, call them when they arise, and rule accordingly. The spectators apply the law of the game in a "utilitarian" manner. That is, they utilize or make use of the laws as they understand them, just as the business person applies the laws of business as he or she understands them. The umpire applies the rules as a professional just as a lawyer practices law as a professional. It follows from the analogy

---

[1] "One who uses one's legal rights harms no one."

that umpires nor lawyers can claim the exclusive right and privilege of applying the "rules of the game." The citizen as an employee, employer, or consumer also has this right and privilege, and during ones lifetime the consumer makes constant use of it. In business the game is played under the eyes of the customers and those who enforce the laws under which business is carried out.

If violations occur on the gridiron such as grabbing the face mask, personal fouls, offside, or "clipping," penalties are levied in the form of lost yardage. On the business field, violations include failure to comply with Truth in Lending, or the federal garnishment law, or the state usury laws, and many others. The penalties may take the form of reprimand, the loss of business, a fine, and, not infrequently, imprisonment. Such penalties add up to a serious loss of yards on the business field of competition.

To conclude the analogy, if one operates a business lawfully and in so doing destroys a competitor, no wrong has been committed. Neither has the linebacker who injures the opposing quarterback with a rough but lawful tackle committed a wrong. Yet, while it is true that "one who uses one's legal rights harms no one," if one does otherwise one may be called upon to pay damages to one who is injured. When business infractions occur, the result is usually a tort and occasionally a crime—and penalties follow.

A meaningful discussion of competition and the right to compete requires some basic understanding of what "freedom" means.

Freedom

The word "freedom" is difficult to define because of the nature of that to which it refers. In the simplest sense it is "the state of being free"—or the right to exist without restraint or controls. More precisely it is "the power of acting according to the dictates of the will, without check, hinderance, control or prohibition other than as may be imposed by just and necessary laws and duties of social life." Freedom is never absolute because, depending upon the sense in which it is used, it must always be qualified. An example can be found in the early business years of our nation.

After American business was freed of the tax-hungry grip of the English Crown, the business person began to make one positive demand, and directed the demand to the young government of the United States of America—"freedom of contract"—something denied by the King of England.

But freedom of contract never existed in fact, although at times the early American court decisions came close to making it so.

Bill of Rights Was Fundamental.   As the new states began their march through the 19th century, the courts started to place interpretations upon the "Bill of Rights"—the first ten amendments to the U.S. Constitution. At first, the courts recognized these amendments as a hard-won list of fundamental guarantees that *did* insure freedom of contract. That is, they permitted business to engage in lawful activity free from regulation

FIGURE 39–1

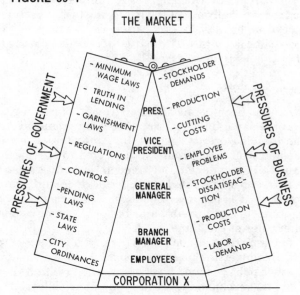

THE MARKET

PRESSURES OF GOVERNMENT

- MINIMUM WAGE LAWS
- TRUTH IN LENDING
- GARNISHMENT LAWS
- REGULATIONS
- CONTROLS
- PENDING LAWS
- STATE LAWS
- CITY ORDINANCES

PRES.
VICE PRESIDENT
GENERAL MANAGER
BRANCH MANAGER
EMPLOYEES

PRESSURES OF BUSINESS

- STOCKHOLDER DEMANDS
- PRODUCTION
- CUTTING COSTS
- EMPLOYEE PROBLEMS
- STOCKHOLDER DISSATISFACTION
- PRODUCTION COSTS
- LABOR DEMANDS

CORPORATION X

by government, and the cases of the 19th century are replete with examples.

But as time passed and the feeble voice of the worker finally began to be heard, the courts began to recognize that the Constitution also contains the words "health, wealth and welfare." The intrusion of government into American business came first at the hands of these words. Today the federal government, the states, the courts, and countless administrative agencies are perpetually engaged in the regulation of business. Needless to say, somewhere along the line "freedom of contract" went out of the window.

Today. Today, one must pursue one's goals in business keeping in mind those things that control us. First, one must be guided by moral concepts as well as the dictates of conscience. Next, one will be guided by statutory rules of the federal government and the state in which one does business. These are backed up by the court-created common-law principles laid down for almost 200 years. Finally, one must be guided by the basic concepts of what is right and wrong as they apply to the customers and the public in general. In short, the modern business person is in a "business squeeze." (See Figure 39–1.)

Kinds of Torts

The business person may commit two kinds of torts or wrongs. First are those that arise out of negligent or careless conduct. This type of tort is unintentional, and most often one does not want it to happen; however liability may still attach under general principles of tort law.

The second class of torts involves some type of "overenthusiastic efforts" on the part of one who engages in competition. This type of tort is committed intentionally as contrasted to one that is merely the result of negligence. Tort liability follows closely on the heels of competition that generates such activities. The matter here is tied closely to "competition," and examples follow.

Competition

Competition has been defined as the struggle between rivals for the same trade at the same time – the act of seeking or endeavoring to gain what another is endeavoring to gain at the same time.[2] The right to compete has become well recognized and protected in our society and is a direct outgrowth of the demand of freedom of contract. For example, Company A is free to open a retail outlet beside its rival, Company B. If in doing so Company B is destroyed, no legal wrong has been committed. The right to compete is nearly absolute, but only as long as one complies with the other rules of the game.

Freedom of competition is qualified where "public interest" operations are involved. Examples include banks, public utilities, insurance companies, and other public-related businesses. The "welfare" of the public is involved and this exception is based upon public policy, but it does not affect the general rule as it applies to competition.

Directly related to the right to compete is the right to do those things reasonably necessary to retain a fair share of a market or to recapture a share that has been lost. If Service Station A lowers the price per gallon on "regular" gasoline to 58.9 cents per gallon, Service Station B has a right to meet the lower price – or to go below it. The wisdom of "gas wars" and similar business activities is something else, but those who engage in them have the right to do so as long as the motive is for the sole purpose of competition. If the motive is to *eliminate* competition, the courts may step into the picture. As one court said, "The courts of equity should be expected to protect the legitimate businessman from unfair competition. At the same time, courts should be careful to encourage and refuse to interfere with fair competition."[3]

It often becomes necessary to take a close look at business activity to determine the true motive behind it. If it is legitimate, no one has reason to complain, but if it is not, both the one injured by it and the state have a right to have the matter reviewed. In some cases the injured party may sue for damages and the state may sue to "enjoin" or stop the activity. The state can also prosecute the offender by criminal proceedings.

SOME BUSINESS WRONGS: BOTH COMMON LAW AND STATUTORY

The following material has *not* been classified under headings of "common law" or "statutory law" because this classification would vary

---

[2] *Gibson* v. *Socony Vacuum Corporation*, C.C.A. Mass., 87 F.2d. 265, p. 270.

[3] *Crump Company* v. *Lindsay*, 130 Va. 144, 107 S.E. 679 (1921).

from state to state. That is, what is statutory in one state may exist in another by common-law provisions. The preliminary material is followed by a more precise treatment of "extortion," "price fixing," and other pure statutory material.

As the material is read, a question should be asked: Doesn't common sense and a feeling of decency tell us that these things should be avoided in the operation of a business?

"Let's Get Rid of Company A"

When one attempts to eliminate a competitor, a business wrong has been committed. It does not matter at what level of business activity the effort is made and it does not matter if the effort is made directly or indirectly. For example, Company X may deliberately try to eliminate Company Y by taking all of its business. Or it may try to reach the same result by cutting off the supply of inventory to Company Y through another company. The legal result is the same. It is difficult to prove the intention of a competitor in court because the line between legitimate and unlawful competition is thin. But once it is established, the one who engaged in the activity could be held liable for civil damages – and be subjected to criminal prosecution as well.

Stealing a Secret

When the holder of a "trade secret" trusts it to another and it is then appropriated for the use of third parties, an actionable tort has occurred.[4] This is true whether or not a patent has been granted to cover the secret. One who discloses or uses another's trade secret without the privilege to do so is liable for the damages that result and may be subject to a court restraining order. Court actions are based upon the principle that one person should not unjustly enrich oneself at the expense of another – an "equitable" rule or a "rule in equity." During the Apollo space flights one company hired a scientist from a competitor who carried with him the secret processes used in space suit manufacture. An injunction was sought by the first company and the jobhopping employee lost out in the end because he wound up with neither job.

As indicated, if there is a wrongful use of trade secrets, two courses of action are available to the injured party: First, seek an injunction to prohibit the continued use of the trade secret. Second, sue for damages and loss of profits if the wrongdoing was intentional. If it was unintentional, that person would be limited to an injunction.

Ideas that are acquired in business are an exception and do not fall under the heading of trade secrets. Restraint should not be placed upon ideas acquired while pursuing an occupation even if the ideas arise out of secret processes. The rule is based upon policy.

---

[4] *Servo Corporation of America* v. *General Electric Company*, 337 F.2d. 716. (4th Circuit, 1964).

Trademarks

A trademark is "a distinctive mark, motto, device, or implement which a manufacturer stamps, prints, or otherwise affixes to the goods he produces, so that they may be identified on the market and their origin be vouched for."[5] At common law, one who used a mark or symbol to identify a business was protected in the use of that symbol or trademark.

If one adopts the trademark of another, the buying public would tend to believe that the goods made by the former were produced by the latter, and it is this result that the law seeks to avoid. The right a business has to a particular mark arises out of its use and in its adoption. It is not the subject of property except as connected with an existing business.

Two Have the Same Symbol. If identical trademarks are created independently of each other and without knowledge of the other, both are entitled to protection, provided the original mark had been unused or abandoned by the original user.

It has been held that the owner of a trademark may enjoy an "infringement territory" to which business is not yet extended.[6] However, the existence or nonexistence of good faith on the part of the second user is a strong factor in determining whether the trademark is entitled to protection in an area where the business is identified but does not actually extend.

Registration. Registration of a trademark does not confer title to that mark if some other person has acquired a prior right by adoption and use. Registration simply constitutes "prima facie evidence," that is, evidence "on the face of it," that the registrant is entitled to the mark. The first and continual user is protected even if that user does not register the mark.

Containers. Generally, wrappers and containers used by business are not entitled to special protection unless protected by trademark or copyright or unless the wrapper has become closely identified with the trademark. The distinctive shape of a Coke bottle is an example.

Trade Names

A trade name is a name used to designate a particular individual in a business operation, or to identify the place where a business is located or to identify the kind of goods involved. Generally, a trade name, just as a trademark, is directly related to a business and its good will.

Fancy Words. Words that are "fancy" or unusual may become subject to protection as trade names. The word "Safeway" was held to be a fictional and fanciful word and eligible for protection as a trade name. Therefore, the first to coin it and connect it with a grocery operation was entitled to the exclusive use of it.[7]

Descriptive Words. A name which is merely descriptive of the ingredients, qualities, or characteristics of an article of trade cannot be

---

[5] *Trade Mark Cases*, 100 U.S. 87, 25 L. Ed. 550.

[6] *Fair Food Stores, Inc.* v. *Lackland Grocers Corporation*, 301 R.2d. 156.

[7] *Safeway Stores* v. *Suburban Foods*, 130 F. Supp. 249 (1955).

exclusively appropriated. The use of a similar name by another to truth-fully describe products is not a legal wrong. Examples include "pure," "safe," "string," and "wild." However, the words "Eagle Clothes" were held *not* to be descriptive when used in connection with the sale of men's suits, and were held to be unique and fanciful and entitled to protection as a valid statutory and common-law trade name.[8]

Proper Names.   One has a right to use his or her own name in a busi-ness operation, but will not be allowed to do so if such use tends to injure another who uses the same name in another business. In that event, one must distinguish the business in some manner from that of a competitor in order to prevent confusion and an overlapping of competitive efforts.

Geographic Names.   Generally, geographic names cannot be appro-priated to the exclusive use of one firm, the exception being where the name has acquired "a secondary meaning" so that it becomes identified with a certain product. Under these circumstances, the name *would* be protected. An example is the Elgin Watch Company, Elgin being a town in Illinois.

Proving Unfair Competition

To constitute unfair competition in respect to a trade name, two ele-ments must be present. First, the name must have acquired a secondary meaning that identifies the plaintiff; and second, the defendant must have unfairly used the name to the prejudice of the plaintiff. "Secondary meaning" has been defined as follows:

> Words and symbols used in connection with one's goods, services, or busi-nesses, or physical attributes or goods, not capable of being appropriated as a technical trademark, or determined to have acquired a secondary meaning when they have become associated in the minds of purchasers or customers with the source or origin of goods or services rather than with the goods or services themselves.[9]

In the following case the court addresses itself to the question of whether or not the name of a nation and a city has acquired a "secondary meaning" as it relates to wigs.

> *White's Wig Imports* v. *Wigmaster's.*[10] Wigmaster's Import Company, Limited, brought an action for injuction against White's Wig Imports, al-leging that Wigmaster's has been selling hair products bearing the label, "Mode de Paris, France," since about January 31, 1967, and that it learned in January, 1970, that the defendant has fradulently encroached upon its business by marketing a similar product bearing a trademark, "Mode de France." A temporary restraining order was granted, and after a hearing, an interlocutory injunction was granted, restraining the defendant from using the trademark, "Mode de France." The court discussed the legal problems as follows:
>
> "Any attempt to encroach upon the business of a trader, or other person,

---

[8] *Eagle Clothes, Inc.* v. *Frankel*, 238 F. Supp. 7.

[9] Ibid.

[10] 177 S.E.2d. 678 (1970).

by the use of similar trademarks, names, or devises, with the intention of deceiving and misleading the public, is a fraud for which equity will grant relief."[11]

"While geographical names and words which are merely descriptive are not generally the subject of exclusive appropriation as trademarks or trade names, such names and words when used so long and exclusively by a trader, manufacturer, or producer that they are generally understood to designate his business or merchandise, may acquire a secondary significance or meaning indicative not only of the place of manufacture, but of the name of the manufacturer or producer, or of the character of the product. In that event the name or title thus employed, including the geographical name and descriptive words, may be the subject of protection against unfair competition in trade and authorize equity to enjoin a newcomer competitor from the appropriation and use of a trade name or trademark bearing such resemblances to those of the pioneer as to be likely to produce uncertainty and confusion, and to pass off the goods or business of one as those of the other."

The court continued: "There is no evidence in the present record authorizing a determination that the trademark of the plaintiff, 'Mode de Paris, France,' has been used so long and exclusively that it has acquired a secondary meaning, designating the plaintiff's products. The plaintiff alleged that it had used the label approximately three years ago when it learned that the defendant was using a similar label, 'Mode de France.' There is no evidence as to the date the defendant began using its label.

"An officer of the plaintiff stated that it had invested a 'substantial amount of money' in advertising hair goods under its label, but there is no evidence indicating that this advertising for such a short period of time has made the public consider the trademark as designating the plaintiff's products. There was no evidence that the defendant had used any unfair practices to deceive the public into thinking that its goods were those of the plaintiff.

"The record shows that the wigs sold by both parties are imported from Korea. There is no evidence to show that the plaintiff has any better right than the defendant to use a label denoting that its wigs are in a style originating in France, or Paris, France, which has long had the reputation of being a fashion center."

The evidence before the trial judge did not authorize the grant of an injunction, restraining the defendant from using its label.

Judgment reversed.

Another area of danger is that of libel and slander as it applies in the business setting.

Libel and Slander

Libel has been defined as "written defamation." The courts have held that defamatory words read aloud by a speaker from a written article over radio constitutes libel. So libel includes certain spoken words.

Slander is the speaking of base and defamatory words tending to prejudice another in reputation, office, trade, business, or means of live-

---

[11] Code, 37–712.

lihood.[12] Defamation would include both libel and slander. Words that tend to injure another in trade, office, or employment are libelous or slanderous, depending upon how uttered.[13] Every unlawful and unauthorized statement spoken, written, or printed which reputes to a merchant conduct which is injurious to character and standing is libelous or slanderous as the case may be.[14]

A corporation may maintain an action to recover damages for libel or slander against it as a corporate entity if the injury affects the trade or business. The tort is complete when the publication, oral or written is heard and understood by third persons.[15] Slander is illustrated in the *Duckworth* case.

> *Duckworth* v. *First National Bank.*[16] In August, 1966, the respondent Duckworth became the manager for a middle-weight boxer named Tommy Fields. Duckworth loaned Fields various sums of money from time to time, totalling $1,000. This sum was to be paid from a check Fields was to receive for participating in a European prize-fighting tour in which he had engaged prior to Duckworth becoming his manager. Duckworth was to be made a payee, along with Fields, on the check to be recieved for such overseas fights. On April 31, 1967, a check was received purportedly drawn by *Sports Illustrated* on the Swiss Banking Corporation of Geneva, Switzerland, in the amount of $7,000, payable to Duckworth and Fields. This check was endorsed by Fields and Duckworth and deposited for collection in the Bank of Augusta, Augusta, Georgia. Four weeks later the check was returned through normal banking routine to the Bank of Augusta with notations on the front and back thereof that the check has been dishonored and was 'no good.' The dishonored check was delivered to Duckworth and thereafter, in an effort to collect the check, Duckworth and Fields went to New York and presented the check to the Swiss Bank in Rockefeller Center. It was there dishonored and the payees were advised that the check was "no good." Duckworth then delivered the check to Fields for disposition.
>
> Fields engaged a Columbia attorney to collect the check. The attorney, on May 15, 1967, deposited the check, the same bearing the endorsement of Duckworth and Fields, in his attorney account, and on May 25, 1967, he paid over from his account to Fields the sum of $6,600. Fields established a new account in his own name in the appellant bank. On May 31, 1967, in payment of his indebtedness to Duckworth, Fields purchased from the appellant bank a cashier's check in the amount of $1,000 and delivered the same to Duckworth. Duckworth cashed the check at the Washington Street office of the bank.
>
> Subsequently, on or about June 12, 1967, the Swiss Bank check in the amount of $7,000 was dishonored and returned to the bank. Thereafter, on June 16, 1967, Roy S. McBee, an assistant vice president of the bank called Duckworth at his office in North Augusta, South Carolina, advising him that the check had been dishonored and demanding that he come to the bank in Columbia. Duckworth testified that during the course of this conversation

---

[12] *Little Stores* v. *Isenberg*, 26 Tenn.App. 357, 172, S.W.2d.13, page 16.

[13] *Powell* v. *Young*, 151 Va.985, 144 S.E. 624 (1928).

[14] *James* v. *Haynes*, 60 Va. 253, 168 S.E. 330.

[15] *Thalhimer Bros.* v. *Shaw*, 156 Va.863, 159 S.E.87 (1931).

[16] 176 S.E.2d. 297 (1970).

McBee said, "We have a $7,000 check over here that you and Fields are try-ing to swindle us out of." And further said, "Well, you get over here or we will have you arrested over there." Duckworth picked up Fields and came to Columbia on the same day. When Duckworth arrived at the bank, he in-quired as to the whereabouts of Mr. McBee and was directed to his open cubicle-like office located at the rear of the bank lobby. Duckworth testified that after he and Fields were seated in the office McBee made the alleged slanderous statement: "Who are you trying to swindle? What do you think you are trying to do?" And, "Who in the hell are you trying to swindle with a $7,000 worthless check?" Duckworth testified that at the time the afore-said statement was made McBee was in a rage and "he kept shouting and hollering and going on and he got up in his chair and stood up behind his desk . . ."

There is testimony that the appellant operates a large bank with many customers entering and leaving its lobby each day and the conversation be-tween McBee and Duckworth occurred on the day of the week of the heaviest customer traffic and at the busiest hour of that day. Duckworth testified as to the presence of third parties in the bank at the time of the alleged slanderous statement made by McBee as follows:

Q.   Now, going back to the episode at the bank with Mr. McBee, were there customers around at all times within earshot of the conversation when it took place?
A.   Yes, there was.
Q.   Do you know whether or not they heard it?
A.   I know they did because they were looking, they couldn't help it.
Q.   Did you know any of the people that were there?
A.   No, sir. I don't know anyone in Columbia.

The Supreme Court, Moss, C. J., held that in light of evidence there were customers of bank around at all times and near enough to hear allegedly slanderous statement of bank officer asking Duckworth whom he was trying to swindle, whether there was publication of allegedly slanderous statement was properly for the jury, who had returned a verdict in favor of Duckworth in the trial court. (The upper court sustained the ruling of the lower court.)

So, therefore, the spoken word can cause legal injury just as effec-tively as physical harm as far as the courts are concerned.

Physical Harm

The physical mistreatment of a competitor or her customers for the purpose of gaining business has never been favored in law, and yet it has been practiced widely. In the rough and tumble alley fight days of a younger America, men and women used fists, guns, and knives to literally "capture a market." Witness the days of the cattle barons and their range wars, the great land grab from the American Indian, and the "shake-down" and "protection" days of the Twenties.

As our society advanced, business conditions changed. One who would apply 19th century strong-arm tactics to business activities of the 1970s would be a fool indeed. And yet, some holdovers still remain, but in a more subtle form. And they too are business torts.

Some Examples. Threats to customers who do not change accounts, or inducements to key personnel to change jobs, or extortion practices engaged in by underworld interests are some examples. Threats standing alone would be torts and could result in criminal prosecution.

Inducements to change jobs—while serious enough to the company who may lose a key man because of it—is the lesser of the three mentioned and usually no action follows from such activities. It is common knowledge in the retailing field that one major nationwide chain has acquired a majority of its executives from its leading competitor.

Extortion practices raise another question because of the seriousness of the activity. Congress met the problem head-on when it enacted Title II of the Consumer Credit Protection Act. The statement of "findings and purposes"[17] contains a statement of the problem and the evils that it carries with it.

> *a.* The Congress makes the following findings:
>
> 1. Organized crime is interstate and international in character. Its activities involve many billions of dollars each year. It is directly responsible for murders, willful injuries to persons and property, corruption of officials, and terrorization of countless citizens. A substantial part of the income of organized crime is generated by extortionate credit transactions.
>
> 2. Extortionate credit transactions are characterized by the use, or the express or implicit threat of the use, of violence, or other criminal means of enforcing payment. Among the factors which have rendered past efforts at prosecution almost wholly ineffective has been the existence of exclusionary rules of evidence stricter than necessary for the protection of constitutional rights.
>
> 3. Extortionate credit transactions are carried on to a substantial extent in interstate and foreign commerce and through the means and instrumentalities of such commerce. Even where extortionate credit transactions are purely intrastate in character, they nevertheless directly affect interstate and foreign commerce.
>
> 4. Extortionate credit transactions directly impair the effectiveness and frustrate the purposes of the laws enacted by the Congress on the subject of bankruptcies.

Upon the basis of these findings, Congress took jurisdiction and enacted Title II. The penalties set out testify to two things: first, the severity of extortionate credit practices; and second, the disrepute in which members of Congress hold such practices.

The penalty provision follows:

> Whoever makes any extortionate extension of credit, or conspires to do so, shall be fined not more than $10,000 or imprisoned not more than 20 years, or both.

In the past, extortion has been the source of more than one "blood bath." Since extortion is now a federal crime, it can be expected that the evils that accompany its use will be materially reduced.

---

[17] Title II, Section 201.

Problems of Pricing

One of the problems that faces each person in business is establishing prices at which merchandise – or services – will be offered. This is true whether it be at the manufacturer's, wholesaler's, or retailer's level. The following material has been drawn from both statutory and common-law principles. The discussion should find general application in most states since pricing – and its problems – has been dealt with by law for many centuries.

Price Fixing

Sometimes business persons who would normally be in competition with each other agree on the price at which they will offer their "competing products." This is done for the purpose of assuring those involved that they will receive the highest possible dollar return from their products or services. Since these agreements run between companies, they are said to be "horizontal" agreements, and when they are in operation, the buying public is deprived of the advantages that accrue from a competitive market. Those engaging in such activities violate both state and federal laws against "unreasonable restraints and monopolies," although Delaware, Pennsylvania, and Rhode Island have no monopoly provisions and Alaska, Nevada, and Oregon have no general provisions. All other states have general provisions. Also, Alaska, Delaware, Pennsylvania, and Rhode Island have no restraint of trade provisions and Nevada and Oregon have no general provisions, yet all other states do have general provisions. Severe penalties are imposed following conviction of price fixing and the practice should be avoided. Price fixing should be distinguished from price "leading," however.

Price Leading

In many industries, the principal producer of a product is a leader in establishing prices in that others follow what that company does. Frequently, identical price lists result – but there is no restraint against "leading." All competitive fields have price leaders, and this can be distinguished from price fixing by the fact that there is no agreement between the companies involved. The practice is followed widely in the explosive and oxygen and acetylene bottling industries.

Loss Leaders

A practice engaged in by retailers is the use of "loss leaders." It works like this: Certain items are offered at a low price – often below cost – and wide advertisement follows. The low prices draw buyers who will purchase other items while in the store. There is no prohibition against such practices – other than as might be found in statutes that prohibit selling below cost.

However, it is not uncommon for litigation to follow from loss leading. If it does, it becomes the job of a court to settle the dispute.

> *State* v. *National Food*.[18] In this case the court found that the defendant is engaged in the retail grocery business and had made sales and published advertisements, as alleged in the complaint, the advertisements stating, "Choice of any brand of fresh MILK–½ GALLON CARTON 39¢–LIMIT ONE ½ GAL. PER CUSTOMER PLEASE!" The court also found that the defendant so sold the milk "as a loss leader, for the purpose of attracting customers away from its competitors and luring them into defendant's stores; that the luring of said customers away from its competitors would naturally tend to harass or injure the defendant's competitors; and the court found that the sale of milk by defendant below cost was made for the purpose of injuring, harassing, or destroying competition." The court further found: "There has been a stated decrease in the number of Grade A milk producers in North Carolina in recent years. There is a growing shortage of milk in North Carolina and in the nation. Producer and consumer prices for milk in North Carolina are in line with average prices in the southeastern portion of the United States." It further found that "the widespread use of milk as a loss leader would be likely to create a chaotic condition in the marketing of milk which would be contrary to the public interest in view of the perishable nature of milk," and that "it is in the public interest for the injunction to be continued until the final hearing of this cause."
>
> An appeal was taken. The upper court stated:
>
> "We think that the record leads inescapably to the conclusion that the purpose of the defendant in selling milk below cost was not to monopolize the business of selling milk in grocery stores, or elsewhere, but was to attract customers to its stores in the hope that they would purchase there other items in sufficient volume to yield the defendant a profit from its entire operation. Since this is not a violation of G.S. 106-266.21, it was error to issue the injunction and the judgment so doing is hereby reversed."

It can be seen that the courts do permit legitimate loss leading.

Price Concessions

In both retailing and wholesaling, price concessions are often made by the seller. Two reasons for granting price concessions are quantity purchases and lower transportation charges for short hauls. Such practices are followed widely and no business wrong occurs as long as the merchant or business makes the same concessions to all others. If the seller favors one company over another, the practice is discriminatory and is a business wrong. If the practice were permitted to continue, it would be a form of price fixing in that the seller could control the sales of the buyer—at least to some degree.

Price Discrimination

Discrimination in pricing that results in competitive injury, is prohibited under Section 2 of the Clayton Act, which was amended by the

---

[18] 270 N.C. 323, 154 S.E.2d 548 (1967).

Robinson–Patman Act.[19] The Robinson–Patman Act in Section 3,[20] prohibits "area" price discrimination and sales at prices so low that the sales tend to destroy competition or eliminate competitors.

A business person cannot engage in such activities if engaged in interstate competition: has made more than one sale to different customers (one of whom is in interstate competition) and the goods sold are for use or consumption within the United States or its territories.

As a practical matter, price discrimination should be avoided in *all* sales.

In addition to the business regulations discussed, a variety of regulatory statutes face one in business in the different states. For this reason, it is important for the business person to become familiar with the laws of the state in which that person will do business. In addition, one must be aware of the federal laws that are binding, including Truth in Lending, the federal garnishment law (see Chapters 35 and 36) and minimum wage laws. How does one become familiar with state laws and local ordinances?

SOME SUGGESTIONS

A visit to the proper office at the municipal level will result in many of these questions being answered. The same is true with county officials. But this technique does not work at the federal level because of the general inavailability of federal personnel.

Another technique is to request a legal opinion from a legal firm or lawyer who represents, or will represent, the company.

Some example of state regulations follow:

Miscellaneous Samples

All states have statutes that specify the weights that units of certain commodities shall contain. The importance of such laws to the buyer is evident and the importance to the seller is in the compliance with them. A portion of one state law is set out in Figure 39–2.

The weights and measures laws also provide for inspection by persons hired for that purpose. The penalties for noncompliance are severe. For an example of such laws in operation, look at the gas pumps in a service station. The lock hook on the pump will contain a wire that has been sealed by a lead slug about the size of a dime. The inspector who tested the measuring device inside the pump sealed it to prevent alteration after departure. How else could we be certain that what a pump says on its face is in fact what went into our gas tank?

The manufacture and sale of bedding and upholstered products is regulated by statute. The nature of the business makes this mandatory since the items produced are covered and not open for inspection by

---

[19] 15 U.S.C., Section 13.

[20] 15 U.S.C., Section 13 a.

FIGURE 39–2
Regulation of Trade

Commodity	Bu. lb.	Peck lb.	Peck oz.	Quart lb.	Quart oz.	Pint lb.	Pint oz.
Apples (green)	44	11	–	1	6	–	11
Apples (dried)	24	6	–	–	12	–	6
Apple seed	40	10	–	1	4	–	10
Alfalfa seed	60	15	–	1	14	–	15
Beans (dried, shelled)	60	15	–	1	14	–	15
Beans, castor	46	11	8	1	7	–	11½
Beans (unshelled)	38	9	8	1	3	–	9½
Beans (stringed)	24	6	–	–	12	–	6
Beans (limas)	56	14	–	1	12	–	14
Beans, soy	58	14	8	1	13	–	14½
Beans, scarlet pole	50	12	8	1	9	–	12½
Beets	56	14	–	1	12	–	14
Blackberries	48	12	–	1	8	–	12
Blueberries	42	10	8	1	5	–	10½
Blue grass seed	14	3	8	–	7	–	3½
Blue grass seed eng.	22	5	8	–	11	–	5½
Broom corn seed	57	14	4	1	12½	–	14¼
Buckwheat	48	12	–	1	8	–	12
Barley	48	12	–	1	8	–	12
Bran	20	5	–	–	10	–	5
Cabbage	50	12	8	1	9	–	12½
Canary seed	60	15	–	1	14	–	15
Carrots	50	12	8	1	9	–	12½
Cement	100	25	–	3	2	–	9

buyers. For this reason, the law prohibits used mattresses being used as fill for new mattresses, and requires that labels be attached to all types of upholstered products. Examine Figure 39–3.

Other laws regulate dealers in liquids – especially flammable liquids – timber dealers, coal mine operators, and others too numerous to list.

COURTS – THEIR ROLE

Where business wrongs occur, the courts provide the forum for giving effect to the laws. It is here that injunctions can be sought as well as damages where losses result. And the courts impose penalties when necessary. The courts play one other role in the regulation of business – by placing interpretation upon the words of laws enacted by the legislatures.

Interpretation

Statutes enacted by legislatures are often subject to more than one interpretation. This is true in civil and criminal statutes. When this occurs, the court must decide what the legislature "intended" to say. To illustrate, the legislature of Connecticut enacted a statute barring "retail grocers" from conducting promotional drawings. A supermarket was

FIGURE 39-3

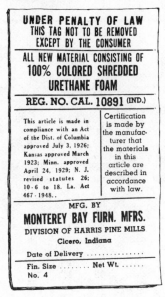

UNDER PENALTY OF LAW
THIS TAG NOT TO BE REMOVED
EXCEPT BY THE CONSUMER

ALL NEW MATERIAL CONSISTING OF
100% COLORED SHREDDED
URETHANE FOAM

REG. NO. CAL. 10891 (IND.)

| This article is made in compliance with an Act of the Dist. of Columbia approved July 3, 1926; Kansas approved March 1923; Minn. approved April 24, 1929; N. J. revised statutes 26; 10-6 to 18. La. Act 467-1948.. | Certification is made by the manufacturer that the materials in this article are described in accordance with law. |

MFG. BY
MONTEREY BAY FURN. MFRS.
DIVISION OF HARRIS PINE MILLS
Cicero, Indiana

Date of Delivery . . . .

Fin. Size . . . . Net Wt. . . . . . .
No. 4

charged with a violation of the law. The market claimed that the law did not apply to it. The Circuit Court of Connecticut, Appellate Division held that a "supermarket" is not a "retail grocer" within the meaning of the statute, thus placing a new meaning upon the law.

REVIEW QUESTIONS

1. Assume that you are a member of a group that is forming a construction company. Make a list of possible names of the company using your name, the name of your home town, and the name of your home state.
2. Analyze the names and determine if, in your opinion, others might object to them. Why might they object?
3. You suspect that B has pocketed a small item of merchandise while shopping in your store. Explain why you must be careful in what you say to B in front of others.
4. Name three legal factors to consider in establishing a price at which item X will be offered to the public.
5. True or False. Most states have restraint of trade laws.
6. Why would any business want to protect its name?
7. Write down an example of one who competes solely to gain an additional share of the market. Compare it with an example of one who competes to *eliminate* competition.
8. Why doesn't registration of a trademark give one first rights to the mark?
9. What does "prima facie" mean? Write it down. What is the importance of this ancient legal principle to one in business?
10. Write out a brief example of extortion and state the evils of it.

Words and Phrases

Write out briefly what they mean to you.
1. Extortion.
2. Proper name.
3. Geographic names.
4. Libel and slander.
5. Weights and measures.

Coverage:	An examination of legal matters encountered in routine business operations.
What to Look for:	The almost informal manner in which these matters are met.
Application:	Think in terms of how "contract" comes to the front here. Also, while the topics discussed here are routine, legal counsel should be sought in some instances.

40 Routine Legal Matters in the Business Environment

In the everyday operation of business—large or small—retail or whole-sale—service or manufacturing—a variety of routine legal matters constantly arise. In the majority of cases, the business person will respond to these without legal counsel. This is true because few businesses—even the largest—can afford the services of a lawyer to assist in doing such routine things and making such routine decisions. As it turns out, knowledgeable business persons do quite well in handling these matters, but, unfortunately, the uninformed are frequently injured because of lack of knowledge about them.

The most common of these have been assembled in this chapter and the material has been divided into two parts: first, "routine business legal documents" and second, "routine business legal matters."

ROUTINE BUSINESS LEGAL DOCUMENTS

In the operation of business, two classes of legal documents are encountered. First, are the "legal business documents," such as deeds, written contracts, financing statements, security agreements, mortgages, assignments, trusts, insurance policies, title reports, and many more. These documents should be prepared by cousel and used under professional advice. Second, are *"business legal documents"* — and these are seldom prepared by or used under guidance of counsel. Some examples include invoices, purchase orders, inventory control documents and others. These documents are available at printing supply houses and are purchased in volume. To facilitate discussion, they will be examined under the business functions they perform.

Hiring Employees

Application. It is common practice to require job applicants to fill out an application. It will contain data that will be of importance if the applicant is hired. These applications require that references be listed who in turn are questioned about the qualifications of the applicant.

Polygraph Test Reports. Many companies require that job applicants submit to a lie detector test. In addition to private businesses, the FBI, the CIA, and the City of Miami requires polygraph tests of job applicants. However, some states, such as New Jersey, have outlawed such requirements. Other courts have held them to be unconstitutional. (For a further discussion, see Chapter 42).

The information in the polygraph test report is considered along with other available information. The use of these reports is squarely within the coverage of the Fair Credit Reporting Act, and the business person must make certain that its provisions are complied with. (For an expanded discussion of the F.C.R.A., see Chapter 36).

Sales Reports. Most companies require their sales staff to submit periodic reports of travel, calls, and results. Expenses incurred must be documented, receipts retained and submitted. This has important legal overtones for many reasons; it permits the company to maintain control over the staff; it keeps the company informed of contractual commitments made by them, and it provides data needed for deductions for income tax purposes.

Many companies provide their sales personnel with credit cards. As these are used, the receipts are retained for purposes discussed. For an example of a credit card charge slip, see Chapter 34.

Ordering Goods

Inventory Control. The systems of inventory control will vary from business to business. The neighborhood grocer may keep needs listed on a scrap of paper. The chain stores will use computers. But regardless of the system, the legal importance of inventory control is to make certain that adequate stocks are maintained so that contract obligations with others can be met.

Purchase Orders. Almost all companies use a form with which to order goods from others. These forms permit orderly stocking and restocking, and facilitate control for accounting purposes. Multicarboned forms are used with copies distributed to "receiving," "inventory control," and the accounting department. Computerized cash registers perform these functions automatically as goods are sold at the checkout counter in retail outlets.

The purchase order is a contract "offer" and has important legal overtones for this reason. Most purchase orders have the terms of the contract offer printed upon them.

Telegrams and Mailograms.   These are widely used for emergency orders of goods, or to trace goods delayed in shipment. Both are treated at law as being "conspicious" and are usually given immediate attention by those who receive them. An order sent by telegram or mailogram, is an offer. Offers made by purchase orders, telegrams, and mailograms, meet the requirements of the statute of frauds because "they are in writing and signed." Even though the "signature" is typed or printed, it is still sufficient at law. See Chapter 20 for the statutory authority for this.

Shipping Goods

Acknowledgments.   Once an order is received, it is good business practice to use a written acknowledgment. Again this fulfills the requirements of the statute of frauds and gives the seller a clear opportunity to spell out the terms of the acceptance of the offer. This is also useful if the seller wants to ship goods that are different than what the buyer ordered. (See Chapter 20.)

If the seller's terms do not "match up" with the terms of the buyer, then "custom of trade" will control. Terms that are not disputed become part of the contract of sale.

Bills of Lading.   Goods are frequently shipped by "bills of lading," and stored temporarily under "warehouse receipts." This is done to facilitate financing by the buyer. These documents are treated as *being the goods themselves* and can be used as security for cash advances from a bank. Such documents are covered by Article 7 of the U.C.C.

Packing Slips.   It is customary to include a "packing slip" with each shipment of goods. This can be a copy of the acknowledgment and will contain reference to the purchase order number and date. This expedites the handling of the goods when received by the buyer. At the same time these slips perform a legal function in that they keep the goods "identified" to the contract.

Back Orders.   When goods are out of stock, the seller may hold the purchase order for later delivery. Such goods are said to be on "back order" and some notation should be sent to the buyer so the buyer will know of the delay. If the buyer objects and decides to buy elsewhere, the buyer can revoke the offer and avoid contractual obligation. In turn, this prevents a contract obligation from falling upon the seller.

Invoicing.   After goods are sold on time, an invoice will be prepared and sent to the buyer. The invoice is an important business legal document. Examine Figure 40–1. It contains quantities, price, Truth in Lending disclosures, purchase order number, terms of payment, and other legal data. If goods are shipped C.O.D. (cash on delivery) an invoice is not required since the order will be paid for upon delivery. Invoices are

FIGURE 40-1

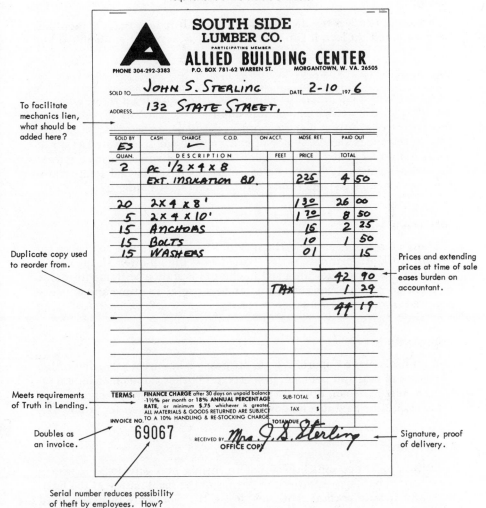

The use of a written form meets the
requirements of the Statute of Frauds.

To facilitate mechanics lien, what should be added here?

Duplicate copy used to reorder from.

Prices and extending prices at time of sale eases burden on accountant.

Meets requirements of Truth in Lending.

Doubles as an invoice.

Signature, proof of delivery.

Serial number reduces possibility of theft by employees. How?

created in multicarboned units or "no carbon required" paper. The copies
are used for inventory control, acknowledgements, packing slips, and
accounting purposes.

"Country Club" Invoicing. Many companies submit monthly statements along with copies of purchases made by each customer during
the month. This practice is acceptable as long as Truth in Lending requirements are met, and is commonly referred to as "country club billing."

MISCELLANEOUS BUSINESS LEGAL DOCUMENTS

Receipts

A receipt is a written document that acknowledges that payment has been received. At law, it can serve as proof of payment of an obligation.

Releases

A release is a document by which one *gives up* a legal right. Releases are used in the settlement of tort claims (see *Student Workbook*), in settlement of contract disputes and in many other business situations. Once a release is signed by one of contractual age, it is treated at law as being a binding contract. It is seldom that a court will set aside a release that was "knowingly" made. Releases are also used in real estate transfers (see Chapter 26) and estate settlements (see Chapter 27).

Estimates

Many companies create estimates of what they propose to charge for certain work. An estimate is *not* treated as being an offer. In the car repair business, estimates are used to obtain insurance settlements. Some repairshops charge fees for estimates because of the time and expense required in preparing them.

Appraisals

Appraisals serve important legal purposes. They are used to determine the *value* of real and personal property, and to set value on collateral offered to secure a loan. They are also used to assist a jury in deciding what value should be paid to a landowner for real estate taken for public use.

Letterheads

Surprisingly enough, business letterheads and envelopes perform legal functions. They inform third parties of the legal nature of the business and it is important that they do so. If a company misleads third parties, serious legal consequences might result. For example, stockholders in a corporation might be held to partnership liability. In addition, the courts have held that a letterhead that contains price terms and the like, can supply the "signature" needed to meet the requirements of the sales statute of frauds. See *Automotive Spares Corp.*, v. *Archer Bearings Co.*, 382 F. Supp. 513, 15 U.C.C. Rep. 590, (N.D. Ill., 1974).

Phone Logs

"Logs" should be maintained of phone calls as they are received. The log should state the time of the call, the caller, and the essence of the conversation. These are of value in proving "timing" of contract matters. Most courts will accept them as evidence, provided that they are kept in the "ordinary course of business" and preserved over a period of time.

Retaining Records

In the conduct of business, a large quantity of records will accumulate. The volume frequently becomes so great that the business executive is tempted to dispose of "last years records." But as a matter of law, it is unwise to dispose of *any* business records. Rather, all records should be retained in files and labeled so they can be found later. Pity the business person who tries to prove something in court when the proof was destroyed years ago.

How Long to Keep Them?

A good technique is to ask one's accountant and lawyer how long records should be retained. For example, federal law requires that O.S.H.A. records be kept five years. Since there is a four-year statute of limitations on U.C.C. Article 2 Sales transactions, these records should be retained for *more* than four years.

Business Documents as Evidence

A principal reason for retaining business documents is that most courts will accept them as proof of what they contain. However, they must have been kept and maintained in the "regular course of business." Most states have statutes that so provide and the Michigan law that follows, is typical.

> Any writing of record whether in the form of an entry in a book or otherwise, made as a memorandum of any act, transaction, occurrence or event shall be admissible in evidence in all trials, hearings and proceedings in any cause or suit in any court, or before any officer, arbitrators, or referees, in proof of said act, transaction, occurrence or event if it was made in the regular course of any business and it was the regular course of such business to make such memorandum of record at the time of such act, transaction, occurrence or event or within a reasonable time thereafter. . . .[1]

Turning now from business legal documents, let's examine other routine business legal matters.

OTHER ROUTINE BUSINESS LEGAL MATTERS

The first question one in business should ask is "Am I complying with *local* laws?" (The discussion will be limited to compliance with city or municipal laws. But it should be noted that counties also have laws that regulate business, and federal and state laws are in abundance.)

---

[1] M.C.L.A. § 600.2146: M.S.A. 27A 2146.

Complying with Local Laws

License Fees. Each firm must have a "license" to transact business, and these are available upon payment of the license fee. The fee will vary with the type of business. All cities have an office devoted to the collection of such fees and a visit there will permit one to comply with the license laws.

Refuse Collections. Most municipalities require that businesses utilize city sanitation services. Fees are required and must be paid in advance. Many cities base the fees upon the volume of refuse collected and the ordinances make it a misdemeanor to privately dispose of refuse.

Construction of Buildings. Before a business person can construct a building, one must first obtain a building permit. See Figure 26–3. Before the permit will be issued, architectural plans must be prepared that meet building code and zoning requirements. If the proposed structure is not in conformity with the zoning laws, a "variance" must be obtained before construction can begin. For a discussion of zoning and variances of zoning, see Chapter 26.

City Taxes. At periodic times, usually twice a year, each business must prepare and file city tax forms and pay the taxes due. This tax is frequently called the "Business and Occupation Tax," and surprisingly enough, it is a tax on gross – not net – sales. (Most states have a similar tax at the state level.)

Hauling on City Streets. In most cities, before large trucks can enter the central areas, the drivers must obtain "hauling permits." These permits control overloads on city streets and bridges. If a business person uses his or her own vehicles for supply, permits will be obtained as needed.

Business Promotions. Surprised indeed are business people who conduct a "sidewalk sale" or "down high street advertising," only to be arrested for violating city laws. Most cities have "sound ordinances" that restrict the use of loud speakers. Also, parade permits are required before traffic can be slowed in the business area. Many cities prohibit the use of sidewalks for sale purposes. Others encourage such use – but only at stated times of the year.

Other routine legal business matters are summarized in the following materials.

Paid in Full Checks

It is not uncommon for a dispute to arise in which the customer tenders a check for an amount smaller than what is due. On the check are the words "account paid in full" or words of similar effect. These checks should be treated with caution and legal advice would be in order before such a check is cashed or deposited.[2]

A matter related to paid in full checks, is the "cash refund" problem.

---

[2] *Gates* v. *Abernathy,* 11 U.C.C. Rep. 491 (Oklahoma App. 1972).

Cash Refunds

A constant problem of the retailer arises when the buyer returns merchandise as being "the wrong size," or "not wanted by the wife." All retailers will issue credit slips—providing the goods are returned in decent condition. But, must the seller make the refund in *cash* if demanded? In the absence of an established custom, or consent by the buyer *not* to demand a cash refund, the answer is "yes."

Collections

A matter of concern to all business persons is the collection of past-due accounts. While the "cash and carry" business is spared this problem, most retailers are aware that a line of credit is essential in order to capture a fair share of the buying dollars.

A Guide Line. As a matter of good business practice, the buyer should be informed of the credit terms, such as "30 days net." The seller should make certain these terms are met. After all, the business person relies upon the accounts receivable to meet the business debts. Firmness and diligence is in order. This is especially true because of the "shrinking dollar" principle discussed previously. However, *unreasonable* collection efforts should be avoided because of possibility of suit by the debtor. See the case in Chapter 3 for an example. Under FTC regulations, collection efforts must be limited to the debtor, the debtor's spouse or the debtor's attorney.

If a debtor defaults in a secured situation, repossession of the collateral is in order. However, the creditor is not permitted "to breach the peace" during the repossession. For a full discussion of this subject, see Chapter 37.

When delinquent accounts reach the point where it is obvious that they cannot be collected by reasonable means, the business person is faced with a legal problem.

File Suit or Not? Many companies have a policy *against* using the courts to collect delinquent accounts. They theorize that a reputation of being one who files suit will cost more in lost profits in the long run. Others adopt the opposite view. In the end, it is a decision for management—not the lawyer.

As a tax matter, before a bad debt can be deducted from income as a business loss, there must be evidence to satisfy the IRS that the account is uncollectible. One way of doing this is to file suit, obtain default judgment and then levy execution on the debtor. If the return is made "no property found," this is clear evidence that a loss has been sustained.

Alternatives to Court. Many businesses utilize form letters which are mailed to delinquent debtors. The effectiveness of these are questionable. In addition, a letter that threatens the debtors such as, "if not paid in 3 days your furniture will be sold on the courthouse square," (which it cannot be) might create a serious problem for the creditor. If a debtor should think such a statement to be true, and suffer a physical setback because of it, the creditor may wind up as a defendant in a court action.

Many companies use credit bureaus as collecting agents. This is effective because the debtor knows that the bureau will be providing credit information if the debtor seeks credit elsewhere in the future. For this reason, the debtor will often promptly pay the credit bureau.

A collection practice followed by most companies, is the direct call upon the debtor by a "chaser." The debtor often makes payment when requested face to face. However, collecting agents must be warned to avoid threats and other abuses for reasons discussed.

If suit is filed and a judgment obtained on a bad debt, the creditor may then decide to attach the wages of the debtor.

Wage Attachments

All states have statutes permitting a judgment creditor to attach a portion of a debtor's wages. Wage attachments will be issued through the court in which the judgment was obtained. This collection method is strictly controlled by federal statute. For a full discussion, see Chapter 36.

Related to wage attachments are "wage assignments."

Wage Assignments

Many debtors, in an effort to meet their obligations, will agree to surrender a portion of the earnings out of each pay check due them in the future. (But by FTC ruling, certain wage assignments are unlawful if used *to secure a loan.*)

Such an assignment is a contract and should be prepared by counsel and signed by the debtor. Before it becomes operative, a copy must be delivered to the employer or other money holder of the debtor, so *that* person will know of the assignment.

A weakness in the wage assignment is that the "stake holder" does *not* have to honor the assignment. If the assignment is refused, there is no way that it can be enforced. If honored, a check will be sent to the creditor for the agreed sum at the agreed times.

An important legal question in wage assignments is this: Does the federal garnishment law apply to *voluntary* wage assignments? It has been held that a merchant can sign an agreement with a customer to authorize the employer to deduct monthly bills from the worker's paychecks. Such wage assignments, says the Court of Appeals for the Fourth Circuit, are *not* garnishments in the usual legal sense. Under this ruling, the 25 percent limit imposed by Federal law does not apply to voluntary wage assignments.

Other methods of collection are available but the above are representative. One final matter related to collections arises when a creditor demands payment – but the debtor protests the sum requested.

Protested Sum

A invoices B for $10,000—but B states that only $9,000 is owed. This can arise out of innumerable circumstances. B offers a check for $9,000. After all, B admits that much is owed. The problem is that this is usually a "paid in full" check and A may refuse to accept it. This leaves the $10,000 unpaid and B may be sued for $10,000. A good technique for B is to make full payment "under protest."

Paying under Protest. If B submits a check to A for $10,000, marked "payment for invoice X under protest" or similar language, the legal position of B is vastly improved. B cannot be sued by A because the account has been paid in full. In addition, B has kept open the claim against A for $1,000. This sum can now be treated as a collection item by B.

Two final routine legal matters in the business environment will be mentioned briefly. The first is a way to create proof that a letter has been received by another. The second is the procedure that employees can use to obtain information about governmental benefits.

Return Receipt Requested

There are times when a business person will want to communicate with another in such a manner that there will be proof that the writing

FIGURE 40-2

was received by the other. A technique available to accomplish this is to use a "return receipt requested" letter.

How Does It Work? The letter is addressed to the other party and a "return receipt" is requested at the post office. The receipt is attached to the envelope and the letter is mailed to the post office in the town of the one to whom it is addressed. At the destination, the recipient must sign the receipt before the letter is surrendered. The receipt is then mailed back to the sender.

A return receipt letter can also be sent "registered mail" or "special delivery" if the circumstances warrant this. The Postal Service will not accept "RRR" letters that have cellophane tape on the front or back of the envelope. Examine Figure 40–2.

Employee Information about Benefits

The accompanying news item speaks for itself.

SS Records Are Available

Anyone eligible can get a report on the earnings credited to their social security record free of charge by calling or writing any social security office, says Joseph E. Portler, social security manager in Fairmont.

"You don't need to pay anyone to help you get a statement of your earnings," Portler said. "Just ask any social security office for a 'Request for Statement of Earnings' post card. Fill in name, address, date of birth, and social security number. Sign, stamp, and mail the card. Social security will send you a statement of earnings credited to your record free of charge."

Earnings credited to the worker's social security number build retirement, disability, survivors, and Medicare protection for workers average earnings over a period of years.

The Social Security Administration is an agency of the U.S. Department of Health, Education, and Welfare.

REVIEW QUESTIONS

1. Zero Corporation sends a purchase order to Supplier X. One of its terms states: "FOB buyer's dock." The acknowledgment reads: "FOB seller's dock." How can this be resolved and permit the contract to be performed?
2. Why is it a good business practice to use written documents?
3. Why is it good *legal* practice to use written documents?
4. Why would there be constitutional objections to the use of lie detectors on job applicants?
5. Examine the documents in Chapter 37. Are these "legal business" documents?
6. Examine the yellow pages in a phone book to see if business forms are offered for sale there.
7. Name three reasons why invoices should be numbered.
8. What does "2 percent 10 days, 30 days net" mean?

9. Truth in Lending has had a great impact on invoicing practices. See Chapter 35. Why must a seller *not* add interest to an invoice without further explanation?
10. Do you understand why a typed signature at law is treated the same as a written one?

Words and Phrases

Write out briefly what they mean to you.
1. Complying with the statute of frauds.
2. Holding orders for later shipment.
3. "Billing."
4. Reordering.
5. Supplying information to the accounting department.

41 Employers, Employees, and Agents

Qui Facit per Alium, Facit per Se.[1]

The relationship between an employer and employee comes into being by means of an "employment contract." The contract may be in writing and contain precise details that will guide the employee. The employment contract may be oral and may be created informally. Once the relationship comes into being, the employer *usually* becomes the "principal" of the employee, and the employee the "agent" of the principal. This "legal transformation" brings into play a well-developed body of law called "agency." This law creates duties and liabilities upon both the principal and agent and it is the purpose of this chapter to become acquainted with the nature of those duties and liabilities, both as they exist today and as they evolved historically.

HISTORICALLY

Agency, in one form or another, has been a part of law since history began to be recorded. The first type of agency was the master-slave re-

---

[1] "He who acts through another, acts himself."

lationship. The slave had no legal freedom and was wholly subjected to the will of the master. The slave was a mere "chattel" (article of personal property) and had no legal rights. In dealing with the master-slave relationship, the courts said, "Respondent Superior." "Let the master answer" because the master is liable in certain cases to third parties who suffered injury because of acts of the slave while the latter was acting within legitimate authority or under direct orders of the master. Thus, a relationship comparable to present-day agency came into being. As the centuries passed, this concept found its way into business and this happened relatively recently.

THE INDUSTRIAL REVOLUTION

Mass production through the use of power-driven machines prompted a transition in American industry which continues today. The owners of mills found that mass production, coupled with increasing markets, made it impossible for them to make personal contact with all of their customers to solicit sales or make deliveries. They were forced to conduct business through agents. The law of agency found its greatest development after the beginning of the industrial revolution, and therefore modern agency law is of relatively recent origin.

A review of recent agency litigation discloses that most cases can be classified under one of two headings: first are those cases in which a third party sues a principal for acts of the agent and second, those in which the question of whether an agency exists is at issue. Cases in the latter group pose a question of fact to be decided by a jury. In either type of case, the question of employment is directly involved – in other instances, though, agency problems can arise in the absence of employment.

Agency problems can also arise in a relatively small number of instances where a third party seeks recovery under agency theory where employment is *not* involved. In the majority of these cases, personal injuries arising out of automobile accidents or other personal relationships are involved. For example, A loans a car to B, her son, who negligently injures C. It is quite possible that A will be called upon to pay for the injuries of C. Similar tort liability may arise from an employment situation. In all agency cases – regardless of type – at least three parties are involved.

THE THREE PARTY CONCEPT OF BUSINESS

At the turn of this century, the economy of America was geared to shipments made by horse and buggy, steam trains, and horse-drawn canal boats. Production necessary to serve a population of 75,994,575 persons (of which 10,341,276 were foreign born) bore little relation to the present economic situation in America. While employees were used, their functions were limited. Pay was low and powers extended to employees were restricted – the employer controlled the business for all practical purposes.

Contrast 1900 with modern America, wherein 221 million persons are served by business that may be owned by persons in Florida, with production carried out in Japan, and sales concentrated in every state in the nation. Agents must be used at all stages in order to accomplish the results desired. Therefore, the goal of the three-party concept in business is simply to accomplish those things efficiently that will most benefit those involved. It follows that if one person operates for the benefit of another, one may also bind the other by his or her actions. From this, three types of liability can arise: contract, tort, and, in rare cases, criminal liability.

Contract Liability

If an agent who is acting within the range or scope of employment enters into a contract with a third person, the act binds the employer. This is a general statement and there are qualifying principles. Contract liability must be distinguished from tort liability.

Tort Liability

If, while carrying out one's duties, an agent causes injury to a third person, by carelessness, negligence, or just plain oversight, liability may attach to the principal. In the vast majority of road injuries involving employees, the employer is joined as a party to the suit and it is usually the employer-principal (or insurance carrier) who must bear the losses. The third type of liability is encountered only occasionally.

Criminal Liability

A crime of an agent generally does *not* bind the principal. There are exceptions, such as where the principal joins in committing the act or conspires in its commission, but the basic rule is firm. As a result, the chief concern of an employee is in the ways his or her acts may bind the principal in contract and tort. As a matter of common sense, an agent should avoid the commission of criminal acts in the agency relationship or outside of it.

With these preliminary thoughts in mind, it becomes important to see how agency law becomes operable. First, a word about "legal freedom."

FREE AGENTS

In our society each person occupies a position of "legal freedom" in relation to one's peers. By this we mean that the acts of one cannot force contractual or tort liability upon another. This is what is meant by "legal freedom." Distinguish this from a situation where one negligently injures another—or voluntarily enters into a contract. Here we have created duties upon ourselves—but we have not forced duties upon third parties. But one *may* create duties between a third person and another and it happens most frequently in an agency situation. Therefore, it is important to understand the nature of the "connection" or "link" that comes into legal operation in an agency situation.

The Link

The link between the principal and the agent is often created by the formation of the employer-employee relationship. Thus, the woman who is hired by a retail shoe outlet becomes an agent and the company becomes her principal. If in the course of business, the woman sells shoes to third parties, it is just as though the shoes were being sold by the company. If she signs a receipt for a shipment of new stock as part of her duties, it is just as though the company signed. If she negligently injures a customer in the store, it is just as though the injury was caused by the company. But if the salesperson steals a $20 bill from the purse of a customer, she will answer for the crime, not the company. If the woman sells shoes on credit in a cash and carry store, such acts would not bind her principal since they would be beyond the range of the authority granted. The "cash and carry" sign in the window would be notice of the restricted power of the agent and the company could demand payment in full for credit sales.

As mentioned previously, in many of the cases tried in court, the third party claims that an agency exists and the purported principal denies this. The defense is usually that the reputed agent is in fact an "independent contractor," and not an agent at all. If this is true, the acts of that person do not bind the other. The following case is a good example of what is involved in this type of situation.

The Texaco Case

A gasoline distributor of Texaco products had not complied with fire safety ordinances which required among other things that earth banks be installed around the gasoline storage tanks. The distributor did not comply and a quantity of gasoline escaped, ran under an adjoining feed mill owned by Burris. The gasoline ignited and destroyed the mill. Burris sued Texaco, claiming that the local distributor was the agent of Texaco, operating within the scope of authority, and therefore arguing that Texaco was responsible for the negligent act of its agent.

The trial court jury rendered a verdict for the plaintiff, Burris. Texaco appealed, stating that the assignment agreement with the local distributor made him an independent contractor and thereby immunized Texaco from responsibility for noncompliance with the fire safety ordinance. The court of appeals held that the local distributor, the detailed operation of which was controlled by Texaco, was, in fact, the agent of Texaco and not an independent contractor; and thereby upholding the jury verdict in the trial court.[2]

---

[2] *Burris* v. *Texaco, Incorporated*, 361 F.2d. 169 (1966).

DEFINITION—AGENCY

Agency is a personal relationship created by the mutual consent of the parties which brings into play the body of agency law. The relationship, being a personal one, places the agent in a position that requires candor and fairness with the principal. The mutual consent to create this relationship does not have to be express; it may come about by conduct of the parties.

Agency Diagram

It is helpful to think in terms of a three-party diagram in which the principal (P) grants authority to the agent (A) to bring into being, to change, and to end contracts of all sorts with the third party (C). Examine Figure 41–1. Observe the "liability flow." Any of the three parties to

FIGURE 41–1

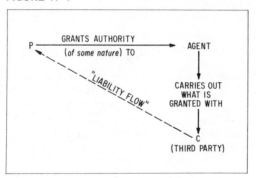

the diagram may consist of a single person or a group of persons or a corporation or a series of corporations. In addition, one agency is commonly telescoped within another.

TYPES OF AGENCIES

Agencies may be express, implied, or arise by the operation of the doctrine of estoppel.

1. Express Agency

The majority of agents receive their authority by an express understanding with their principal. Employment of a salesperson is an example. The grant of authority does not have to be in writing, and in many instances it will not be. However, if the purpose of the agency requires that the functions of the agent be carried out in writing, then the authority granted should be in writing. Authority to convey property would be an example. (See Statutes of Frauds, Chapter 12.)

The larger corporations and companies generally use preprinted employment contracts. By their use, an express agency is created. But remember, however, that agencies can arise outside of the employment situation as the following examples illustrate.

Deed of Agency. Mr. Smith, who is heavily in debt, arranges to surrender his paycheck to another who will make distribution to his creditors. This arrangement is revocable and must be entered into voluntarily. This type of agency is generally referred to as a "deed of agency" and should be in writing to protect all concerned.

Exclusive Agency. If one lists real estate with a broker under a written contract and during the life of the contract the real estate can only be sold by the broker, an "exclusive agency" has been created. Here the agent has the responsibility of finding a buyer suitable to the principal.

General Agency. A general agency is one in which the principal turns over the operation of the complete business to an agent. An arrangement of this type would require that the principal have confidence in the integrity and ability of the agent.

Power of Attorney. A common express agency is known as a "power of attorney." Examine Figure 41–2.

This is a formal document in which the person granting the authority

FIGURE 41–2

POWER OF ATTORNEY

KNOW ALL MEN BY THESE PRESENTS:

That I, John Doe, age 25, of 200 Freedom Street, Anytown, Typical State, have made, constituted, and appointed, and by these presents do make, constitute, and appoint Mary Doe of 200 Freedom Street, Anytown, Typical State, my true and lawful attorney, for me and in my name, place, and stead, to draw and indorse any check or checks, promissory note or notes on any bank, made payable to me; to deposit said checks or notes in any bank in the City of Anytown, Typical State, and to do any and all matters and things connected with my bank account in Anytown, Typical State, that I might or could do personally.

Given under my hand this __20th__ day of __May,__ 1976.

_____s/s John Doe_____ (SEAL)
JOHN DOE

TYPICAL STATE
EAGLE COUNTY

I, __Samuel Oggle__ , a Notary Public, in and for the County aforesaid in Typical State, do hereby certify that John Doe, whose name is signed to the above Power of Attorney bearing date on the __20th__ day of __May__ , 1976 has this day acknowledged the same before me in my said County.

My commission expires __April 14, 1978__ .

_____s/s Samuel Oggle_____
NOTARY PUBLIC

authorizes another to act as agent (attorney). A power of attorney is frequently placed on record to give the public notice of what it says. All powers of attorney may be revoked by the one who creates them as long as he or she has legal capacity (competency) at the time of revocation. This is true because a power of attorney is not a true contract. There is usually no consideration for them, for example. If a power of attorney is of record, then the revocation of that power must also be placed on record. This would then "release" the power of attorney.

Ratification. An express agency may be created by the ratification by the principal of an act of the agent which was unauthorized at the time performed. An unauthorized act standing alone would *not* bind the principal, however.

Ratification has been defined as an

> . . . affirmance by a person of a prior act which did not bind him, but which was done or professedly done on his account, whereby the act, as to some or all persons, is given effect as if originally authorized by him.[3]

Such ratification would revert back to the time of the unauthorized act itself, thus making the principal responsible for the act. The act must have been done for the principal's benefit. This would require that the principal had the present ability to do the act, or to have authorized it. It is for this reason that a corporation can never ratify the acts of a promoter where the acts were done prior to the creation of the corporation. The corporation can only "adopt" such acts.

Most states require that the principal know all the facts at the time of the ratification. However, if a principal fails to learn all the facts, or acts without a desire to learn the facts, ratification can still come into being. If intervening third parties might suffer by the ratification, the courts would tend to protect the third parties.

A principal must ratify the complete act of the agent and not merely those parts of the act that are to his or her benefit. The principal may not repudiate the action of an agent if unauthorized, while accepting the benefits of what the agent has done.[4]

The third party who acts with an agent whose act is not authorized initially may find oneself in a position of not wanting the principal to ratify the act of the agent. For this reason, that person may want to withdraw from the transaction. The majority view is that the third party can withdraw prior to ratification by the principal. If the principal ratifies the contract *before* the third party withdraws, most courts would hold that the third party would be bound.

An Example. A department store in Pittsburgh has a strict understanding with its department heads that all buying must be handled through a central purchasing agent. Arthur orders a series of "car coats" which, in Arthur's opinion, will be fast-moving items in the coming weeks. Arthur felt that the delay in sending a request through the pur-

---

[3] *Goldfarb* v. *Reicher*, 112 N.J.L. 413, 171 A.149, 151 (1934).

[4] *Carolina Equipment & Parts Co.* v. *Woodrow Anders*, 265 N.C. 393, 144 S.E.2d 252 (1965).

chasing department could result in loss of sales. The purchasing agent has no knowledge of the order until it is received at the warehouse and a copy of the shipping bill arrives on the purchasing agent's desk. If the purchasing agent, with full knowledge of what has transpired, accepts the order and makes no effort to alter it or cancel it, ratification has occurred.

Ratification can come about by conduct, express or implied, although the law would require that the conduct show *intention* to ratify.

If a principal (or the agent of a principal) learns of an unauthorized act of an agent which the principal does not wish to ratify, the principal should repudiate it expressly, conveying the repudiation to the third party. In those instances where the principal does not have full knowledge of what has transpired, ratification would not follow. However, as indicated above, if the principal fails to make full inquiry, or acts without a desire to make inquiry, the principal may be bound.

2. Implied Agency

The courts may imply an agency under circumstances in which the parties never created an express agency. Such an agency arises by the *acts* of the parties. It is treated the same as an express agency and has been proven by inferences or, in many cases, by deduction made from the surrounding facts. For example, a wife purchases items that are necessary for her maintenance and support and charges them to her husband. The husband has failed to provide such items. The courts might imply an agency under the circumstances. This is referred to as an agency of "necessity."

3. Agency by Estoppel — or by Operation of Law

In many instances the principal is negligent in supervising the affairs of an agent, and the agent exercises powers that have not been granted. If, under such circumstances, third parties are justified in believing that the agent has the apparent powers and they rely upon the powers to their detriment, the courts will say that an agency by estoppel has been created.

To create an agency by operation of law, the principal is "estopped" from denying the existence of the agency. The careful business person would never allow this situation to develop, although, in many situations, agency by estoppel is created where the principal has no notice of the agent's conduct. Agency by estoppel is a "fiction" applied by the courts to prevent an injustice to innocent third parties.

Closely related to agency, but falling outside of its rules, is the "independent contractor."

INDEPENDENT CONTRACTORS

In the *Texaco* case, the defendant claimed that the agreement it had with the local distributor made the distributor an independent contractor and "thereby immunized Texaco from responsibility for noncompliance with the fire safety ordinance." But Texaco failed to prove this at the trial. An independent contractor is

> ... one who exercises an independent employment in contracts to do a piece of work according to his own judgment and methods, and without being subject to his employer except as to the results of the work, and who has the right to employ and direct the action of the workmen independently of such employer and freed from any superior authority in him to say how the specified work shall be done, or what the laborers shall do as it progresses.[5]

Examine Figure 41–3. If it can be shown that the alleged agent is, in fact, an independent contractor, liability will not attach to the principal. This means that third parties who deal with an independent contractor

FIGURE 41–3

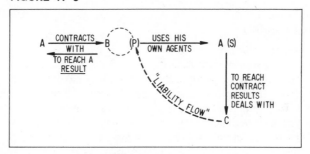

by contract or who are injured by the contractor will have to look to the independent contractor for recovery. This can be important in cases where the independent contractor is judgment proof – that is, judgment will not be collected because of his or her financial condition. Suppliers will make an effort to determine the status of the person to whom they are selling materials – although they may obtain relief by the filing of a "mechanic's lien."[6] But this is not always a satisfactory remedy. Mechanic's liens statutes require action within a specified time (for example, 90 days), and if that period passes, the right to file the lien is lost.

In cases where an independent contractor has questionable credit, other means of security should be explored by a supplier, such as making the obligation a joint one between the contractor and the persons receiving the benefit of the contract, or by taking security under Article 9 of the U.C.C.

It is possible for the employer to exercise a certain amount of control or direction over the contractor without loss of status of independent contractor. But, if the contractor is subjected to the *control* of the employer, the status would be lost and agency law would govern. Business persons

---

[5] *Johnson* v. *Asheville Hosiery Company,* 199 N.C. 28, 153 S.E. 591, 593 (1930).

[6] The term usually includes laborer's liens, materialmen's liens, and artisan's liens.

often want to maintain the status of independent contractor on the part of those doing work for them. Payroll deductions, social security obligations, group insurance coverage, and workmen's compensation are items that an employer may be faced with when the person doing work for one loses the status as an independent contractor. If the status can be maintained, the business person need not be concerned with such matters.

Frequently an infant, one under designated age, becomes involved in an agency situation.

INFANTS

Anyone who has the capacity to act for one's self may act through an agent. However, infants have legal limitations placed upon their contractual capacity because of their age. Yet infants may act through agents and be bound in any area that they would have been bound in otherwise. An infant can be the agent of an adult and the infant's actions will bind the principal. It is not uncommon to find those under legal age being employed in many capacities.

LEGALITY

The rules of unenforceable contracts also apply to agency. Therefore, the purpose of the agency must be legal. If a principal and an agent enter into a contractual situation that is illegal, or becomes illegal, the relationship and its by-products might not be enforceable.

SUBAGENTS

Once agency comes into being, it is not uncommon to find an agent employing another person to assist in carrying out the business of the principal. This "agent of the agent" is called a "subagent." A subagent is an "agent appointed by one who is an agent."[7] The principal may well be bound by the acts of the subagent. However, the subagent must be acting within the scope of the authority granted to the agent. If the principal employs an agent on the basis of personal skill and discretion, the agent is prohibited from delegating duties to a subagent. Examine Figure 41–4.

In most business situations, there is implied authority on the part of the agent to employ subagents to carry out the purposes of the agency. The manager of a supermarket is not expected to perform all administrative duties involved in the conduct of the retail food business. The manager would have implied authority to hire those persons needed to carry out the purposes of the agency. As long as the subagents act within the scope of the authority granted to the store manager, their acts will bind the principal. They can then look to the principal for payment for services —and their negligent acts may result in liability to the principal.

---

[7] Kent Comm. 633.

FIGURE 41-4

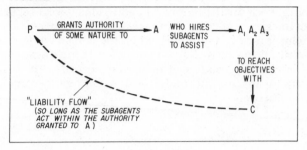

REVIEW QUESTIONS

1. An employer asks you to sign an employment contract. Name two reasons why you would want to know what the contract says. (You will be bound by it whether you read it or not.)
2. What is the purpose of having a law of agency?
3. Name a situation in which you could use a power of attorney.
4. The estoppel principle is encountered in what other areas of law?
5. True or False. A subagent always binds the principal by the subagents acts.
6. Explain why a "power of attorney" is an express rather than an implied agency.
7. The independent contractor status is popular in construction contracts. That is, the one who wants the building done, contracts with another to achieve the desired result. List two advantages to the builder. To the contractor.
8. A and B, operating independently of all third parties, can never create an agency between themselves. Why is this true?
9. Explain why the "link" creates the "liability flow."
10. Create an agency situation other than those set forth in the chapter.

Words and Phrases

Write out briefly what they mean to you.
1. Estoppel.
2. Independent contractor.
3. Master-slave.
4. Criminal liability.
5. Authority.

Coverage:	A closer look at specific duties that an agent owes to the principal.
What to Look for:	Practical ways in which these principles will be used in business.
Application:	As an agent in the future, you will place these principles into constant use.
Note:	Employers do not appreciate those who violate their basic duties as an agent.

42 The Agent—More Detail

Before the basic duties of the agent are examined, it is helpful to look at the rules that become involved in hiring an employee–agent.

HIRING THE EMPLOYEE–AGENT

The agency relationship between employers and employees, and principals and professional agents, comes into being by the creation of a contract.

The Contract

This contract usually does *not* have to be in writing. However, if it will involve conveyance of real estate or other matters that must be carried out in writing, it should be reduced to writing to comply with the statute of frauds. The contract should spell out the compensation agreement. Duties of the agent and fringe benefits should be identified. In the case of professional agents, the contract will state the results to be accomplished and will spell out the agreement for payment for services.

When employers screen applicants for jobs, they almost always turn to sources outside the company for credit and other information about the applicant. This practice has raised some interesting questions in recent years as it relates to applicants rights under the Fair Credit Reporting Act. The following is one example.

Drugs, Employers, and the Fair Credit Reporting Act

Under the F.C.R.A. (See Chapter 36 for a full discussion) guidelines are laid down to govern the distribution of consumer credit information. When requesting credit information about job applicants, employers must proceed with care and remain within the framework laid down by the federal statute.

Many employers now require that job applicants submit to a polygraph (lie detector) test as a condition precedent to being hired. When such tests are required, the question arises, "are the results of such tests under the coverage of the Fair Credit Reporting Act?" A federal case in Georgia sets out the view of one court on this question.

Job Application Made. Gary Peller filled out a job application with Robley Hats, Inc., and was told that it was company policy to require all applicants to submit to a lie detector test. Peller agreed and the test was administered by one Lincoln Zonn.

Zonn concluded in his findings that Peller had smoked marijuana. When Robley Hats, Inc., received this report, it refused to hire Peller. To make matters worse for Peller, Robley forwarded the report to Retail Credit Co., a credit reporting agency.

Peller was subsequently hired by Arthur Anderson Co., but when they received a report from the credit bureau, Peller was fired because of his alleged use of marijuana.

Peller filed suit against Robley Hats, Inc., as well as Lincoln Zonn, claiming they had violated specified sections of the Fair Credit Reporting Act.

The federal court concluded that neither of the parties were "consumer credit reporting agencies" and that their reports were not "consumer reports" and therefore they incurred no liability to Peller.[1]

The court was obviously correct as the decision related to Zonn – but may have been wrong in its ruling as to Robley Hats, Inc., because it would appear that the company was squarely under the coverage of the F.C.R.A.

New Jersey enacted a statute making an employer guilty of disorderly conduct if "it influences, requests, or requires an employee to take a lie detector test as a condition of employment or continued employment." This law was challenged as being unconstitutional but was upheld by the New Jersey Supreme Court.[2]

Other states have also outlawed or limited the use of the polygraph test for job applicants. These include Alaska, California, Connecticut, Delaware, Hawaii, Idaho, Maryland, Massachusetts, Minnesota, Oregon, Pennsylvania, Rhode Island, and Washington.

After the relationship begins, just what is expected of the agent?

BASIC CONSIDERATIONS

The principal-agent relationship requires good faith on the part of the agent, although the agent is not in a fiduciary capacity. That is, not classi-

---

[1] *Peller* v. *Retail Credit Co.,* 359 F. Supp. 1235 (N.D. Ga. 1973).

[2] *State* v. *Community Distributors,* 64 N.J. 479, 317 A. 2d 697 (1974).

fied with attorneys, guardians, trustees, or others where the highest possible standards are set, but yet the agent falls into the pattern if at a lesser
degree. Figure 42–1 illustrates.

An agent-employee should be friendly, courteous, and reasonably well
groomed—but these are not legal requirements. An agent-employee
should also be loyal, trustworthy, and obedient—and these *are* legal requirements.

When an employee leaves the services of an employer, that person
will take skills, knowledge, and abilities gained while working for the
employer. There is no restriction against the use of this type of information and skill since each person is entitled to earn a living. A former salesperson is not restricted from selling to the customers of the former employer even though that person is engaging in the same line of business

FIGURE 42–1
"Fiduciary" Requirements

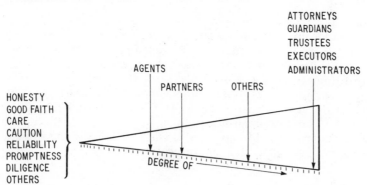

and in competition with the former employer. This is true, however, only
in the absence of a restrictive agreement between the principal and the
agent. Many employers, as part of the original employment contract,
require their employees to sign a promise (or covenant) to the effect that
if the agent leaves their employment, that person will not engage in a
similar line of business for a certain number of years and within a specified territory. "Ten years and a 125 mile radius" has been held to be reasonable in some restrictive employment contracts.

TRUSTEE'S SALE

There is an old saying that "a trustee cannot buy at his own sale."
This arises out of the duty of loyalty. The rule applies in agency and the
agent is prohibited from buying the principal's goods or wares. Frequently, however, principals give their agents the privilege of buying
merchandise at discounts. Under these circumstances the principal usually requires that the agent purchase the material through another agent.
A good example can be observed in food stores as one employee is seen
buying from another employee at the end of the workday. The rule was

developed to prevent the agent from taking advantage of the principal — which the agent is in a position to do in most instances. If the agent violates the rule and sells real estate to oneself, for example, the sale is voidable at the election of the principal. This means that the principal can set aside the sale, take back the property, and return the money paid. It makes no difference if the agent has another person buy the property for the agent. In fact, this makes the transaction more suspect. Courts are not concerned only with whether the agent personally benefited by the breach of duty, but if he or she did, the transaction can be set aside on that ground alone.

Two Masters

Matthew 6:24 reads,

> . . . No man can serve two masters: for either he will hate the one, and love the other; or else he will hold to the one and despise the other . . .

The ancient principle applies to the law of agency. Frequently an agent is in a position in which he or she has an opportunity to represent two principals in the same transaction. For example, principal number one wants to buy certain land and engages the agent to make the purchase. Principal number two, who owns the same land, asks the agent to find a buyer. If the agent accepts both employments, he or she is representing conflicting interests. Further, the agent is in a position where he or she could collect a commission for both buying and selling. If the agent buys and sells the property through a third party, conveying the same to the first principal, it is clear that the transaction is voidable and can be set aside.

Obedience

The agent must obey legitimate instructions of the principal — yet, the agent does not have to follow *all* demands. Failure to obey legitimate instructions, however, could be grounds to end the agency. Further, if loss results to the principal by failure of the agent to obey, the agent may be held liable for damages.

If detailed instructions have not been given by the principal, the agent would be expected to exercise good judgment. If an emergency should arise and the agent acts to meet that emergency, the principal would be bound by those acts.

Under certain circumstances the agent might justifiably refuse to obey instructions of the principal. One instance would be where prior instructions have become illegal. Another example would be in the event of emergencies as set out above. For example, an employer might instruct an employee to "never use the phone." If fire breaks out at the place of business, the agent is justified in disobeying the instruction.

During certain emergencies — and even during the routine operation of a business — the employee is expected to obey orders *that, in fact, have never been given.* The thought is difficult to grasp at first, but it has sound legal basis. Assume that a customer at a store has fallen and is unconscious. In all probability, the employee who reaches the injured person first has never been told what to do in such an instance. Yet, common sense dictates that the employee should notify the manager; give aid that might seem proper at the moment; and see that outside assistance is called. When the employee so responds, it is just as if those instructions had been given in advance—and thus the employee has obeyed them.

The same principle has application during the conduct of routine business affairs. For example, the employee who uses judgment in making routine decisions would in effect be "obeying orders." Replacing a typewriter ribbon, ordering office supplies as needed, sending a typist to another typewriter, or sweeping a floor that became excessively dirty would not require approval of the employer. The "nonexistent" order principle would control and the principal would be bound just as though instructions had been given to do those routine matters.

THE PRINCIPAL'S PROPERTY

An employee, in the absence of express authority, is prohibited from using or benefiting from the property of the employer. Postage machines cannot be placed to personal use; the company car is not available to drive the children to school; the office phone cannot be used for personal long-distance calls. Violations of this sort frequently result in the dismissal of the employee.

When checks and cash of the employer come into the hands of an employee, care must be exercised. First, the funds must not be used for personal purposes. If they are, criminal charges of embezzlement might follow. Second, the funds must not be "commingled" with those of the employee. If A has a quarter that belongs to the employer, it must not be put into a pocket that contains a quarter belonging to A. If it is, a "commingling" occurs. That is, the quarters are no longer identifiable because it cannot be determined which quarter belongs to the employer. The point applies where the usual commingling occurs: when an employee deposits funds of the employer into a personal account. When this occurs, the funds are no longer distinguishable. If the employee should overdraw the account—even by accident—funds of the principal have been misappropriated.

SIGNING NEGOTIABLE INSTRUMENTS

An agent who signs a contract on behalf of the principal incurs no personal liability on the contract if the principal fails to perform. The agent acted for another and the other is bound. But when an agent signs a "negotiable instrument" on behalf of a principal, such as a note or a check, a different circumstance is encountered. For an example of the nature of this problem, see Chapter 30 and the example set forth there.

This provision of the U.C.C. makes it mandatory that an agent do two things when signing negotiable, commercial paper for a principal: first, disclose the agency upon the face of the instrument, and second, state who the principal is.

REVIEW QUESTIONS

1. You are the payroll officer of Zero Corporation and it is your responsibility to sign all payroll checks. How would you want the checks printed?
2. Why is an agent not held to fiduciary responsibility?
3. What is the "evil" of commingling funds?
4. Why should one not "serve two masters"?
5. True or False. A principal always gives clearcut instructions to an agent.
6. Assume that you are the manager of a supermarket. Set out three rules that you expect your employees to follow when purchasing goods from the store.
7. It has long been a practice of some persons to use agents to accomplish things that they could not legally do themselves. At law, why is this wrong and what has been done to prevent it?
8. What effects might a collective bargaining agreement (labor-management) have on the principal-agent relationship in the giving of orders to an employee?
9. Can you identify a set of facts in which an employee, who is carrying out duties, would *not* be an agent of the employer?
10. Name three reasons why "restrictive covenants" are used in employment contracts.

Words and Phrases

Write out briefly what they mean to you.
1. Fiduciary.
2. Commingling.
3. Principal's property.
4. Obedience.
5. Lack of instructions.

Coverage:	The nature of agency as it relates to the employer and third party.
What to Look for:	What one must look for in the above capacities.
Application:	Think of the matters discussed from the employee's viewpoint.
Note:	The coverage here is detailed, so read it carefully.

43 Employers of Agents and Third Parties

The third party who is dealing with an agent, often knows that he or she *is* dealing with an agent and may know who the principal is. Such an agency is "fully disclosed." If however, the third party knows he or she is dealing with an agent but does not know the principal, the agency is "partially disclosed." If the third party does not know he or she is dealing with an agent, then the agency is "undisclosed." The legal consequences vary with the degree of disclosure. Figure 43–1 should be studied closely and then reviewed as other material is covered on agency.

FULLY OR PARTIALLY DISCLOSED AGENCY

Where the agency is disclosed or partially disclosed, the principal is a party to any contract or transaction entered into by the agent on behalf of the principal. Because of this, the principal is liable to third parties. Where the agency is fully disclosed, most courts hold that the agent is not a party to the transaction if acting within the scope or range of authority. Therefore, the agent would not be liable to the third party on any contract entered into on behalf of the principal.

If the agency is partially disclosed, the agent may be liable to the third party unless it is understood that the agent is not to be. In this type of agency, the third party is dealing with an unknown principal. The principal may be an infant or lack legal status for other reasons and not be re-

FIGURE 43–1
Agency Chart

Diagram	Liability of P to C	Liability of A to C	Writings
Disclosed Agency P——→ A ↓ C ↓ (C knows both)	Liable to C	Not liable	A binds P
Partially Disclosed Agency ?——→ A ↓ C ↓ (C knows one)	Liable to C	A may be liable	A binds P
Undisclosed Agency -----→ A ↓ C ↓ (C knows neither)	Not liable at common law Liable if: 1. A acts for P 2. A acts within scope of authority	Is liable if elected. Pennsylvania says they are jointly and severally liable	?

sponsible for the acts of the agent. For this reason the agent is considered to be a party to the contract in order to protect the third party.

UNDISCLOSED AGENCY

Where the principal operates through an agent with the relationship being unknown to a third party, different results are encountered. For example, an agent who makes a contract without disclosing that he or she is acting as an agent, or without identifying the principal, will be individually liable on the contract.[1] This rule is for the protection of the third party. At common law, the principal was not liable under such circumstances because the principal was not a party to the contract. Today the laws of agency make the principal liable, however, if the agent acts within the scope of the authority granted.

The undisclosed agency arrangement is widely used where options are taken on land or where different parcels of adjoining land are being purchased by private interests for real estate development. Private industry does not have the power of "eminent domain,"[2] which means that they must negotiate to buy private property. (See Figure 43–2.)

It is clear in such situations that the agent is liable to the third party.

---

[1] *Chambliss* v. *Hall,* 113 Ga. App. 96, 147 S.E.2d 334 (1966).

[2] The power to take private property for public use.

Negotiable Instruments – Sealed Instruments	Rights of C	Liability of P for Negligent Acts of A	Liability of P for Willful Acts of A	Liability of C
P liable if named	Can go after P	P liable	P not liable unless done in carrying out authority of P	P can sue C
P liable if named	Can go after A or P	P liable	P not liable unless done in carrying out authority of P	P can sue C
?	Go after A or P if disclosed	P liable	P not liable unless done in carrying out authority of P	Generally: P can sue C if skill of A is not involved. P takes subject to *all* defenses C has against A

After all, the third party dealt with the agent, not knowing of the undisclosed principal and was willing to accept the terms offered by the agent. A claim of unfair dealing on the part of the third party would be without basis since that person contracted with the person intended. Once the principal is disclosed, or uncovered, the third party has a right to look to the principal for performance of the contract. In effect, once disclosure has been made, the third party has two persons to look to – since rights against the agent are still retained. However, some states require that the third party elect one or the other for performance. Other states allow the third party to join the agent and principal as "joint obligors" and look to them jointly for performance. Recovery from one, of course, would bar recovery from the other. If the agent must pay, the agent would have an action against the principal for compensation.

FIGURE 43–2

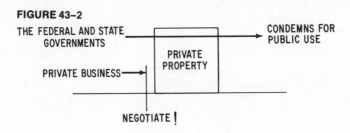

Frequently the principal, before disclosed, closes out accounts with the agent. In real estate transactions, the agent conveys the real estate acquired from third parties to the principal and all obligations are settled *between* the principal and the agent. The third party, upon learning of the existence of the undisclosed agency, may wish to look to the now disclosed principal for settlement of any obligation due. One view is that the principal would not be liable to the third party after accounts are settled with the agent. The view is unsatisfactory. Most states hold that the principal, once disclosed, is liable to the third party if the third party decides to look to the principal for performance.

A Case

A construction firm with offices in Tennessee was exploring the possibilities of building a high-rise dormitory at State University. It had been brought to their attention that a housing shortage existed there and that such a venture would be a good investment. An employee of the firm visited the university, gathered some data from the housing director, and began seeking a site for the proposed building. It was his opinion that a city block in the Third Ward would be an ideal location since it was central to the main parts of the campus. Examine Figure 43–3.

The block was bounded by four streets; an alley passed through the middle and each lot contained a single-family home. The block was zoned R-1, which meant that it was reserved for single-family residences.

FIGURE 43–3
Block A, Lots 1 through 8, Third Ward, Anytown

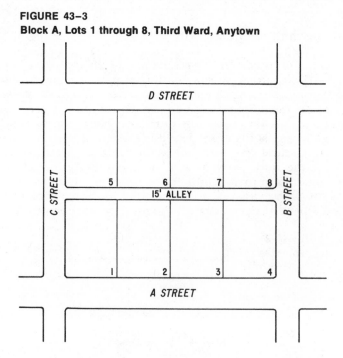

How did the Tennessee firm go about constructing the dormitory that now houses 300 students on block A in the Third Ward of Anytown?

First, preliminary cost estimates were made. The limit on land acquisition was set at $180,000. If the eight homes could be purchased for this sum or less, the project was to proceed. If not, the project was to be abandoned. The firm retained an attorney in Anytown to obtain options on the eight homes. The attorney was *not* told the purpose of the options and this is not uncommon. The eight options were obtained for prices that ranged from $18,000 to $25,000 for each house. The "option money" paid to each homeowner ranged from $1 to $600. If the options were exercised, the option money was to be applied to the purchase price. If not, the homeowner was to keep the option money. The attorney assigned the eight options to the firm and the firm gave notice to the homeowners of their intention to exercise the options. In due course the land was conveyed and paid for. The firm then applied to the city for a change of zoning as well as annulment of the alley. In due course, both were granted and the building was constructed. Governmental agencies can condemn private property for public use. This case illustrates how the private sector must rely upon the undisclosed agency, the option, and assignments in order to get the results government can by eminent domain.

SIGNED WRITINGS

Where the agency is fully or partially uncovered, the agent, acting within the authority granted, can bind the principal by signing written documents. The agent should identify the principal when signing the written contracts, documents, and negotiable instruments. If the principal is not identified on a negotiable instrument such as a check, note, or bill of exchange, the undisclosed principal is not bound by the instrument.[3] This is true even though the instrument may have been issued in behalf of the principal under express authority given to the agent. In such an instance, the third party would lose the benefit of being able to sue the principal on the negotiable instrument. The only alternative of the third party would be to "waive the instrument" and sue on the debt that gave rise to it. The third party can sue the agent upon the instrument since it carries the agent's name.

CLAIMING BENEFITS

Once the agency is uncovered, the principal may claim the benefits of the transaction with the third party. But the principal must assume the entire transaction, however, and not just those parts that are beneficial. An exception would be where the contract between the agent and the third party was entered into because of some particular skill or talent

---

[3] U.C.C., 3–401 (1). See *Ness* v. *Greater Arizona Realty, Inc.*, 517 P. 2d 1278 (Arizona App. 1974).

possessed by the agent. In this instance, the principal could not come forward and demand performance based upon skill possessed by the agent.

DEFENSES OF THIRD PARTY

After the agency is disclosed, the principal must take the contract subject to all defenses the third party may have against the agent. The third party may have some claim against the agent and this fact may have been what motivated the third party to deal with the agent. For example, the agent owes the third party the sum of $500 on an obligation that is unrelated to the business of the principal. If the principal comes forward and takes the benefit of the contract, the principal is subject to the claim of $500 against the agent.

THIRD-PARTY POSITION OF PERIL

Since third parties deal with agents at their own peril, they should first establish that there is an agency. After this, they must exercise care, even though there is no requirement that third parties inquire into all details of the agency. When confronted by an agent who demands some type of performance, such as delivery of merchandise, it is sufficient if the third party determines that the agent has authority to take possession of the goods. There is no responsibility on the part of the third party to establish every minute detail of the authority granted to the agent or to search for secret limitations placed upon the agent by the principal. Common sense prevails.

If a third party has an account payable to a principal and is confronted by an agent who demands payment, the third party must exercise caution. Custom and prior conduct of the agent may give some assurance that the agent has the authority to collect. For example, the agent may have been following a similar course of conduct for a number of years – and the principal has never objected. But if the third party is in doubt, two steps should be taken: First, the payment should be made by check payable to the order of the principal. Second, the check should be mailed to the office of the principal. Legitimate collecting agents are satisfied with this arrangement.

AGENT'S AUTHORITY EXPANDED

The authority of an agent is usually only wide enough to encompass the authority granted by the principal. Only under extreme emergencies or unusual circumstances will the law allow the authority of an agent to be expanded. For example, if the principal is not available and an immediate expenditure is necessary in the principal's business, the agent's authority would be expanded to cover a loan necessary to prevent the loss. The loan would become the responsibility of the principal. However, the agent could not make the principal liable for more money than necessary to meet the emergency. See Figure 43–4.

FIGURE 43–4
Effect of an Emergency

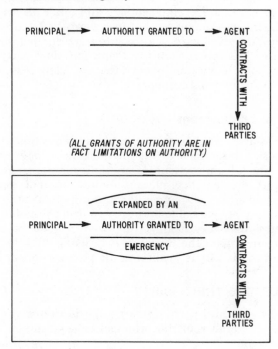

RESPONSIBILITY FOR AGENT'S WRONGS

It is not enough for the principal to be concerned with responsibilities as they relate to the *contractual* acts of the agent. There remains the problem that arises when the agent commits harm to the person or property of a third party. Such harm may come about while the agent is in the pursuit of the principal's activities or it may come about otherwise. It is not uncommon to find third parties suing principals for compensation for harm caused by agents. (See the Complaint Chapter 8).

In examining this aspect of agency, we must distinguish between a willful act that results in injury to others and a tortious act which likewise results in injury to others.

A willful act may be described as one done intentionally, knowingly and purposely, without justifiable excuse as distinguished from an act done carelessly, thoughtlessly, heedlessly, or inadvertently.[4]

If the act of the agent is willful and results in harm to others, the principal is not liable.

However, the principal may be held liable for the other torts of the agent, as discussed previously. For example, an agent transporting a load

---

[4] *Lobdell Car Wheel Company* v. *Subielski*, 125 A.462, 464 (1924).

of merchandise from one town to another, owes a duty to all third parties to drive within the speed limits; to remain on the proper side of the road; and to use ordinary care at intersections and other places where third parties may be in a position of peril. If injury results because of a breach of these duties, the third party may look to the principal for recovery of damages caused by the wrong of the agent. The third party must prove first that there is an agency and second that the agent was acting within the scope of the principal's authority.

Not Limited to Employment

It has been stated that "properly speaking, agency relates to commercial or business transactions."[5] But the doctrine of agency is not confined to commercial transactions. If an adult maintains an automobile for the comfort, convenience, pleasure, entertainment, and recreation of the family and allows a member of the family to use the automobile, that person might be held liable for injury caused by the family member to third parties. Recovery has been allowed in such cases under the doctrine of agency upon the theory that in using such an automobile, the member of the family is furthering the purposes of the adult.[6]

LIABILITY OF THE THIRD PARTY

Occasionally the third party refuses to perform and the question of the third party's liability to the principal arises—and in some cases, liability to the agent.

If the agency is disclosed or partially disclosed, the principal can look to the third party for recovery under any contract made by the agent on his or her behalf. This is true even though the contract was made in the name of the agent.

Where the agency is undisclosed, the principal still has the right to look to the third party for performance. There are exceptions such as where the contract involves skill or discretion on the part of the agent and where the undisclosed principal takes the benefits of a contract subject to a defense the third party may have against the agent.

DUTIES OF THE PRINCIPAL TO THE AGENT

The principal owes four basic duties to the agent: to compensate, to reimburse, to provide a safe place in which to work, and to provide education and guidance.

To Compensate

There is an obligation on the part of the principal to pay the agent for duties performed. The rate of pay will be determined by what was agreed

---

[5] *Humble Oil* v. *Bell*, 172 S.W.2d., 800, 803 (1943).

[6] *Jones* v. *Cook*, 90 W.Va., 710 (1922).

upon. If there was no agreement, the law would presume that the agent is entitled to a reasonable rate for the services rendered. In a few instances the agent acts without compensation but this does not change the fundamentals of the relationship.

The duty to compensate the agent may be contingent. It is not uncommon for an agent to be paid a weekly "draw" and a percentage of the sales made during the month.

To Reimburse

Reimbursing an agent is not the same as compensating him or her. In the former, the agent incurs out-of-pocket expenses for the benefit of the principal; in the latter, a wage or salary is involved.

The principal's duty to reimburse requires that the agent be "made whole" by the principal—spoken of as "indemnification." A salesperson who buys a new tire for the company automobile, for instance, would be entitled to have the cost returned. An agent can abuse the right to be reimbursed and if so (such as "padding" the expense account), would be subject to dismissal.

Safe Place to Work

In 1900, employers paid little or no attention to the physical surroundings in which their employees had to work. Witness the unsafe conditions of the coal mines, the overhead leather power belts with the deadly brass clasps, and the unguarded grinding wheels.

After the Federal Employers Liability Act became law, (F.E.L.A.), state employers became concerned because they knew that such laws would follow on the state level. These are now known as workmen's compensation laws and are discussed in detail in Chapter 44. Such laws forced the employers to improve working conditions because of what it cost them if they did not.

But surprisingly enough, it wasn't until the 1970s that safety on the job became a legal requirement—and again, the federal government took the lead when it enacted the Occupational Safety and Health Act. This act, called O.S.H.A. for short, is examined in detail in Chapter 45.

Education and Guidance

A principal should: conduct training sessions in the area in which the agent operates; discipline the agent through directives; require the agent to submit regular reports on collections, sales progress, travel expenses, and accidents; supervise the agent; expose the agent to the basic rules of libel, slander, and tort; and provide basic instructions on how the agent should sign commercial paper in the representative capacity. Other suggestions can be thought of. In addition to education and guidance, the principal should carry adequate insurance to protect all concerned.

TERMINATION OF AGENCY

The agency relationship can be ended just as it was created – by agreement of the parties. Or one or the other may violate the agreement, thus bringing the relationship to an end. For example, the agent may refuse to work or the principal may refuse to compensate the agent as agreed. In some instances, the agency agreement itself will spell out the time at which the relationship will end. A change in the circumstances of the parties may also end the agency. Some examples are bankruptcy, death, or insanity of either. Changes in business and other conditions may cause the relationship to terminate.

Once the relationship is ended, it is good practice for the principal to make this known. In the normal business when an employee quits or is fired, the principal does not publicize this fact – but it *is* customary to run a newspaper ad announcing the appointment of the new manager or salesperson as the case may be. This gives the public notice of the change. Direct notice by letter should also be given to regular customers. In the case of more informal and short-lived agency relationships, formality of notice is usually unnecessary.

REVIEW QUESTIONS

1. Make a list of three ways that an employer can guide and educate employees.
2. What use can you think of for the undisclosed agency other than the one discussed?
3. Why does government have the power to condemn realty, but private business does not?
4. What would you require your traveling sales personnel to place upon their weekly reports?
5. Name one argument for and one against a weekly draw plus a percentage of sales as a means of paying an agent.
6. When an emergency arises, an agent is not justified in using it as a reason to expand the authority in a blanket manner. Explain why.
7. Examine Figure 43–4. What is the legal message of the drawing?
8. Some companies require their employees to promise in writing to pay for charges on company credit cards if the company goes bankrupt.[7] Discuss the reasonableness of this as a company policy.
9. Perhaps the largest percentage of agencies are the partially disclosed agencies. Why is this true?
10. What effect might the "family purpose doctrine" have on car insurance policies sold to a "head of household"?

Words and Phrases

Write out briefly what they mean to you.
1. Undisclosed agency.
2. "Third party position of peril."
3. Paying agents (remuneration).
4. "A safe place to work."
5. Option.

---

[7] *American Express Co.* v. *Geller,* 169 N.Y.L.J. No. 93 (May 1973).

Coverage:	A look at the legal steps involved when an employee is injured or becomes unemployed.
What to Look for:	The matters involved as illustrated by the documents.
Application:	Think in terms of the effect the proceedings here could have on the operation of a business.
Note:	It is necessary to read the documents closely since they tell the story.

44 Unemployed, Injured, and Retired Employees

In the last three chapters, the principles of agency as they apply to the employer-employee relationship were discussed in detail. After the relationship becomes operative, many side developments flow from the employment. For example, the employee may not perform adequately on the job; or perhaps is caught in an act of embezzlement or violates other duties owed to the employer. When these things happen, the employer must take suitable action. The most frequent occurrences arise when an employee is injured on the job or is laid off from lack of work, or begins to accumulate retirement "credits."

THE UNEMPLOYED EMPLOYEE

One who is unemployed and who is qualified may draw weekly payments during the unemployment. The payment is called "unemployment compensation," and should be distinguished from "workmen's compensation," which is payment for injuries received on the job. Unemployment compensation is a form of insurance and is usually managed jointly by the states and the federal government.

Qualifications

The qualifications vary but the following are representative. The employee must be off the job for at least one week; be available for work for which fitted by "prior training or experience;" be willing to take a job that is similar to the prior job, provided that it pays a similar rate of pay; must not have quit the job without cause and must not have been fired for misconduct. If the unemployment is due to a labor dispute in which one is actively participating, one usually is disqualified.

Signing Up

Once employment ends, the employee must sign up for benefits. The employee will be questioned and if facts are uncovered to warrant it, the application may be refused. If it is, the employee is given a copy of the findings, which tells certain facts (see Figure 44–1).

FIGURE 44–1

TYPICAL STATE DEPARTMENT OF EMPLOYMENT SECURITY
DEPUTY'S DECISION

Local Office Anytown-16

S.S.	Date of	Date of
Number 234–66–9555	Claim May 6, 1976 NC	Decision 5–23–76

CLAIMANT'S NAME AND
ADDRESS

Royce D. Davis
Box 981
Next Town, Typical State

EMPLOYER'S NAME AND
ADDRESS

O'Hara and Martin
Box 407
Anytown, Typical State

FACTS AND COMMENTS: (If additional space is needed, use reverse side.)

The Claimant was last employed over thirty working days from January 11, 197– to April 29, 197– by O'Hara and Martin.

The employer released the Claimant for not giving the required production – there was a slow down on the work that he had been performing.

The Claimant's slowing down on his work is simple misconduct; therefore, the employer discharged the Claimant on April 29, 197– for simple misconduct and the Claimant is disqualified as shown below.

The Deputy applied the Unemployment Compensation Law to the circumstances described above to arrive at the decision(s) checked below. Only checked items pertain to this claimant. The section of the Law covering any checked decision (except "Other") appears on the reverse side.

☐ CLAIMANT ELIGIBLE AS OF

_____

1. ☐ Able to work.
2. ☐ Available for full-time work for which fitted by prior training or experience.
3. ☐ Other. See item 22, below.

☐ CLAIMANT INELIGIBLE

From_____To_____

1. ☐ Not able to work.
2. ☐ Not available for full-time work for which fitted by prior training or experience.
3. ☐ Other. See item 22, below.

FIGURE 44–1 (continued)

☐ CLAIMANT NOT DISQUALIFIED

7. ☐ Left work voluntarily with good cause involving fault on the part of the employer.
8. ☐ Discharged but not for misconduct.
9. ☐ Failed with good cause to (apply for) (accept) suitable work.

10. ☐ Did not fail to apply for suitable work.
11. ☐ Work offered not suitable.
12. ☐ Other. See item 22, below.

☒ CLAIMANT DISQUALIFIED

13. ☐ Left work voluntarily without good cause, involving fault on the part of the employer.
14. ☐ Discharged for misconduct.
15. ☐ Failed without good cause to (apply for) (accept) available suitable work.
16. ☐ Voluntarily quit employment to marry.
17. ☐ Voluntarily quit employment to perform _____ _____ duty.

18. ☐ Voluntarily quit employment to attend to personal business or affairs.
19. ☐ Voluntarily quit employment because of pregnancy.
20. ☐ Discharged or laid off because of pregnancy.
21. ☐ Other. See item 22, below.

☒ Disqualified from April 28, 1976 to June 15, 1976. Maximum benefits reduced by SIX times weekly benefit rate of $45.00. Total reduction $270.00.

☐ Disqualified until claimant returns to covered employment and has been employed in covered employment at least thirty working days.

---

22. OTHER. Explanation of item 3, 6, 12, or 21, if checked.

THE LAST DAY ON WHICH AN APPEAL FROM THIS DECISION MAY BE FILED IS May 31, 1976. SEE REVERSE SIDE FOR EXPLANATION OF APPEAL RIGHTS.

s/s C.E. Hoffman

Signature of Deputy

Appeals

If the employee is not satisfied with the findings of the deputy, notice of the intent to appeal must be given by the deadline specified in the decision. If timely notice is given, a hearing will be granted before an examiner. The notice of the date and time of the hearing will be accompanied by a statement of the rules that will be followed at the hearing. See Figure 44–2.

FIGURE 44–2

BOARD OF REVIEW
TYPICAL STATE DEPARTMENT OF EMPLOYMENT SECURITY

P
A   Claimant: Name   Royce D. Davis   S.S.No.   234–66–9555
R   Address   Box 981, Next Town, Typ. State
T   Employer: Name   O'Hara and Martin
I   Address   Box 407, Anytown, Typ. State
E
S   The Commissioner of Employment Security.

A. Case No. 68–686

NOTICE OF HEARING

THE ABOVE PARTIES will take notice that the Claimant has appealed from the decision of C. E. Hoffman, Deputy Commissioner of the Department of Employment Security at Anytown dated 5/23/76 which held:

Discharged for misconduct

I   _____

S   _____

S   _____

U   _____

E

THE ABOVE PARTIES are further notified that a hearing will be held on the appeal on Monday, June 10, 1976 at 2:30 P.M., at Employment Office, 601 Low Avenue, Anytown, Typical State.

IMPORTANT INFORMATION TELLING ALL PARTIES OF THEIR RIGHTS AND DUTIES, AND THE MANNER OF HOLDING THIS HEARING WILL BE FOUND ON THE ATTACHED SHEET.

BOARD OF REVIEW
TYPICAL STATE DEPARTMENT OF
EMPLOYMENT SECURITY
By_____   s/s Tom Rock
Examiner

Date Issued   6/3/76
Page 2:

INFORMATION TO CLAIMANT AND EMPLOYER: Any *individual* party (claimant, employer, or commissioner) must, to present his case, appear *in person* before the Examiner at the time and place specified. Any party may be represented by an attorney to help him present his case. Be prepared at the hearing to testify under oath (or affirmation) from personal knowledge or your records and to introduce all written evidence you desire to present, bearing on the issue as noted. Therefore, bring with you any written material that has bearing on this claim. Failure to introduce material written statements such as doctors' certificates, earning statements, absentee records, etc. at the hearing will result in their not being considered when a decision is later made. While evidence will ordinarily be confined to the issue as noted, it may appear at the hearing that other related issues must be inquired into, and you should, so far as possible, be prepared to present evidence on any issue that may arise. *Under the law, the Examiner and the Board of Review may only consider the evidence offered at the hearing before the Examiner.*

FIGURE 44–2 (*continued*)

If witnesses are needed to produce evidence in your behalf, you must arrange for them to appear at the hearing. If an important witness is absolutely necessary and will not appear voluntarily, ask the local deputy of the Department of Employment Security to have a subpoena issued to compel his appearance, or to compel production of necessary papers. *If you do not request a subpoena five days before the hearing, it may be impossible to get your witness there.* Board of Review Regulations provide that, except in labor dispute cases, only two witnesses for each party may be summoned at expense of State. Any above two must have their witness fees and mileage paid by party summoning them.

A decision will be made by the Examiner as a result of this hearing, and appeal can then be made to the Board of Review. Upon further appeal from the Examiner, the case will be reviewed and decided on the evidence presented before the Examiner. No additional testimony will be ordered taken by the Board except for proven *good cause* as to why such evidence was not presented before the Examiner.

If any party cannot be present at the hearing for reasons beyond his control, he must, himself, immediately ask the local office of the Employment Security Department how to attempt to secure a postponement of the hearing. Failure to appear if a postponement is not granted will result in your appeal being dismissed or in a decision being made without consideration of your evidence.

The appeal procedure is conducted under Article 4 and 7 of Chapter 21-A of the Code of Typical State as amended. If you do not fully understand the law or your rights, confer with your attorney, or the local deputy of the Department of Employment Security.

TO THE CLAIMANT: Fees charged a claimant by an attorney are subject to approval by the Board of Review. Do not pay such fee until the Board has approved it.

We make an effort to set this as near to your home as we can considering that we usually can hold hearings at only one place in each county or at the nearest large city outside your county. If through error this hearing is set in some city which is an unreasonable distance away, you should immediately write your local deputy to ask if he can arrange for the hearing to be held near your home. He will advise you before the hearing if he is able to make such arrangements. If you do not hear from him, make every effort to appear where the hearing is set.

(*SPECIAL NOTE TO MULTISTATE CLAIMANTS:* If your claim is against some state other than Typical State, we send your evidence to that state which will make the decision.)

The Hearing

The hearing is conducted much the way a case is tried before a judge. The employee has the right to be represented by counsel and can call witnesses. The employer has the same right and will often attempt to prevent the employee from qualifying for benefits, especially if the employee was discharged for misconduct.

After the hearing, the proceedings are transcribed and the examiner makes a ruling. Either party has the right to appeal from the decision and the appeal is to the appeal board of the state. Most unemployment cases, however, are settled at the examiner stage.

Directly related to normal unemployment is unemployment resulting from a job-related injury.

THE INJURED EMPLOYEE

At the turn of the present century, one who was injured while working was required to pay one's own medical bills and related expenses. In addition, loss of wages had to be absorbed by the employee. The result was an extreme hardship upon the worker and family. At that time there was little attention given to the employee by the employer. It was reasoned that there was no responsibility upon the employer to assist the employee.

The federal government made one of the first moves toward relief of the injured employee in 1908 when the Federal Employers Liability Act became law. The act applied only to one who was injured while engaged in interstate commerce, however, so its application was limited. The pattern set by the federal act soon spread into the states as various legislatures began creating state laws to permit state employees to be covered.

A problem that is frequently encounted in the states arises when an employer fails to place employees under workmen's compensation coverage.

Failure to Cover Employees

If an employer fails to pay into the fund, the common-law defenses of contributory negligence, fellow servant rule, and assumption of the risk will be lost. This means that an employee injured on the job will be able to file suit directly against the employer for the injuries and the employer will be stripped of means with which to defend the suit. For this reason, employers *must* provide coverage. Failure to do so can be costly—and it defeats the purposes of these laws.

Purpose of the Law

Workmen's compensation statutes provide compensation for one who is injured on the job, and the question of who was at fault will not enter the picture. The exception would be in a case of self-inflicted injury. Most state laws also provide that if the injured employee was intoxicated at the time of the injury, he or she will be barred from recovery. A related question arises when an employee claims to have been injured on the job—but the employer denies this.

On the Job or Not?

A number of cases are heard each year in state courts on the question of whether the injured employee was in fact "on the job" when injured. If not, one cannot recover from the compensation fund. In the case that follows, the court found that the employee was not entitled to be covered because he was not "on the job" within the meaning of the state law.

Ferguson v. *City of Macon.*[1] PANNELL, Judge. "An injury arises 'in the course of employment,' within the meaning of the Workmen's Compensation Act, when it occurs within the period of the employment, at a place where the employee reasonably may be in the performance of his duties, and while he is fulfilling those duties or engaged in doing something incidental thereto."[2]

"An accident arises 'out of' the employment when it arises because of it, as when the employment is a contributing proximate cause. This and the condition stated above must concur before the act can apply."[3]

"If the work of an employee or the performance of an incidental duty involves an exposure to the perils" of handling a firearm, "the protection of the Compensation Act extends to the employee while he is" handling the firearm in the performance of his duties.[4]

Where, as in the present case, a compensation claimant is employed as a deputy clerk in a recorder's court, and his duties consist, among other things, of taking guns to or from court as required in a particular case being heard, and he was on duty in an early morning hour, and a police officer came in and exhibited to the clerk a small .22 caliber derringer pistol, and the clerk undertook to examine the weapon, cocked the firing mechanism and attempted to unbreach the weapon, and it accidentally fired, injuring the clerk's left hand, such injury did not arise out of the employment, for the reason that the examination of and the cocking of the firearm by the employee claimant out of which the injury arose was not incidental to any of the duties of the employee, nor did such cocking of the firearm constitute a casual connection between the conditions under which the employment was performed and the resulting injury, such as might have been the case if a police officer or other person on the premises had accidentally discharged the firearm and injured the claimant,[5] but it was solely for the gratification of the claimant's own curiosity. The mere moving of a weapon out of the way so that one may engage in the duties for which he is employed is not involved here. The evidence was sufficient to authorize the finding of facts hereinbefore set forth, and the award of the Board of Workmen's Compensation denying compensation to such clerk claimant, if supported by the evidence, must be affirmed; and this is true even though the evidence might have also supported a contrary award. Accordingly, the judge of the superior court did not err in affirming the award of the Board of Workmen's Compensation. Judgment affirmed.

---

[1] 173 S.E.2d 227 (Ga. 1970).

[2] *New Amsterdam Casualty Co.* v. *Sumrell,* 30 Ga.App. 682, 118 S.E. 786 (1923).

[3] Ibid.

[4] Ibid.

[5] See *U.S. Fidelity & Guaranty Co.* v. *Phillips,* 97 Ga.App. 729, 104 S.E.2d 542 (1958). and *Fidelity & Casualty Co. of New York* v. *Barden,* 79, 54 S.E.2d. 443 (1949).

If Eligible

Once it is determined that one is entitled to compensation, the employee will be paid a portion of regular wages as long as he or she remains off the job. The finding of a commissioner is shown in Figure 44–3.

FIGURE 44–3

WORKMEN'S COMPENSATION FUND   359189

Administered by
STATE COMPENSATION COMMISSIONER
CAPITOL CITY

February 3, 1976   Refer to File No.

Charles G. Hardy   69–217890
Commissioner

Golden Faucet Company
Anytown, Typical State
Gentlemen:

It has this day been determined that the above entitled claim is compensable, and payments will be made to the claimant at the rate of $70.00 a week, upon a total temporary disability basis until he has returned to work or been certified by his attending physician for employment.

Either party has thirty days within which to file objection with the Commissioner to this finding. However, check for the amount due, at the above rate, is enclosed for delivery to the claimant, and by the delivery and acceptance of the enclosed check both parties agree to this order. The claimant's acceptance of the enclosed check does not waive his right to an increased rate upon the filing of additional earnings. If a claimant's lost time is less than twenty-two days, under the law, he cannot be paid for the first week.

Very truly yours,
s/s Charles G. Hardy
Commissioner

John A. Stonewell
Box 273
Anytown, Typical State
cc: Employers Service Corp.

Permanent Injury

An employee who has suffered a permanent disability, upon proper proof, will be entitled to additional compensation. The amount will be based upon the findings of a doctor who establishes the percent of disability. Once the percent is established, the statutes will be used to fix the amount of compensation.

After the percentage of disability is established, it is applied to the rate of pay of the employee and a single sum is determined. This is done usually by use of statutory formulas. This larger sum is then divided and paid to the employee over an established period of time. In some circumstances, an employee might successfully petition to have the entire sum released at once.

Notice of Injury

An employee who is injured on the job must give "timely" notice to the employer and the commissioner of the fund. All state compensation laws have a statute of limitations on claims which means that if one fails to give notice within the prescribed time period, rights under the law will be lost. A typical time period for the notice is "within one year." One who finds that a prior injury has become aggravated must give notice in order to reopen the matter. A typical time period for reopening is three years. The following documents serve as illustrations. The three letters (Figure 44-4) are followed by a "percentage of loss" statute (Figure 44-5).

FIGURE 44-4

February 3, 1976

State Director of Workmen's Compensation
811 Calcutta Avenue
State Building Number 2
Capitol City, Typical State

Attention: Commissioner

Re: Claim No. 69-217890
John A. Stonewell
Anytown, Typical State

Gentlemen:

This letter is an application for an adjustment of the above claim as provided in Typical State Code 23-4-16.

Mr. Stonewell has continued to lose the use of the small finger of his right hand as a result of his injury of December 3, 1975.

In spite of his recent operation, the finger is frozen at the middle joint and is drawing inward. His doctor is speaking of removing the finger.

There appears to be aggravation and progression of the original injury and the Commissioner did not consider this aggravation and progression when he made his previous award.

If this claim is reopened, the claimant will be entitled to greater benefits than he has received up to now.

Your attention to this matter will be greatly appreciated.

Sincerely,

s/s John Eagle
John Eagle
Attorney-at-Law

FIGURE 44–4 (continued)

WORKMEN'S COMPENSATION FUND

Administered by
State Workmen's Compensation Commissioner
Capitol City

February 9, 1976

Charles G. Hardy
Commissioner
J. R. Cutwell, M.D.
602 Masonic Building
23 Madison Avenue
Next Town, Typical State

Re: Claim No. 69–217890
John A. Stonewell
Box 273
Anytown, Typical State

Dear Dr. Cutwell:

Date of Injury: December 3, 1975

Diagnosis: Compound comminuted fr. of the proximal phalanx of the rt. 5th digit and lac. across the palmar surface of the hand to the dorsum of the proximal phalanx (8cm.)

We are directing the claimant, who has been paid $7^2/_7$ weeks compensation, to report to you when you notify him of an appointment, for the purpose of an examination to determine:

1.   Does the claimant need treatment? If so, what?
2.   Has the claimant reached maximum degree of improvement?
3.   If so, what, in your opinion, is the percentage of permanent partial disability?

Should your examination disclose that the claimant should undergo further studies under your direction or if you believe he should be referred for examination by another specialist, THIS IS YOUR AUTHORIZATION for carrying out such studies and for arranging for such examination by the specialist you deem it wise to have him examined.

Such reports of examinations, ANSWERING ITEMS 1, 2, AND 3, to be made in quadruplicate.

Very truly yours,
s/s James Fargo
James Fargo
Assistant Director
Medical Division

Jf:nr
CC: Golden Faucet Company
Anytown, Typical State
H. E. Winters
John Eagle

FIGURE 44–4 (concluded)

J. R. CUTWELL, M.D., F.A.C.S.
Diplomate American Board Orthopedic Surgery
602 Masonic Building
Next Town, Typical State

RE: Claim No. 69–217890
               John A. Stonewell
               Box 273
               Anytown, Typical State

INJURED: December 3, 1975

EXAMINED: March 16, 1976

HISTORY:

Patient has the history of sustaining a right-hand injury when he caught his right hand between the head and stop of a molding machine, while working for the Golden Faucet Company. He sustained a compound fracture of the proximal phalanx of the right 5th finger and laceration across the palmar surface of the hand. He, apparently, had an operation on the finger and was off work for over seven weeks. At the present time, he is working in the coal mines, as a roof bolter. He complains that his 5th finger is stiff and he cannot move it and it hurts him.

ORTHOPEDIC EXAMINATION:

Reveals a 24-year-old, white male who is 6 feet, 3 inches in height and weighs about 175 pounds. Examination of the right hand reveals that the disability is confined to the 5th finger. He has good circulation of the hand. He has good wrist motion. The 5th finger reveals that he has a 90 degree finger with no motion perceptible of the flexor extensor tendons of the finger. It is held at 90 degrees in the proximal interphalangeal joint, about 45 degrees of the metacarpal phalangeal joint of the right 5th finger. Feeling is present. There is practically no passive motion in the joint area. He makes a fist but the finger stays fixed.

X-RAYS: Taken March 16, 1976. Next Town General Hospital.

RIGHT HAND: Multiple views of the right hand reveals moderate deformity of the proximal phalanx of this 5th digit, due to a healed fracture. There is also approximately 90 degrees flexion at the PIP joint of this digit, no doubt due to soft tissue and tendon injuries with cicatrix formation.

No other abnormalities can be seen.

DIAGNOSIS:

Compound fracture of the 5th finger, right hand, healed with stiffness and flexion deformity of the 5th finger.

DISCUSSION:

The finger has been injured for a long period of time. I do not know of any satisfactory operation that would restore the motion of the finger. I think, since it is held in flexion, that, at least, he can grip with it and it is not in his road as much as if it were held in extension. He might be sent to Doctor Smith, hand surgeon, and see if there is any surgery that would be worthwhile trying to improve the motion of this finger, but I doubt it very much.

DISABILITY: 5 percent.

                              s/s J. R. Cutwell
                              J. R. Cutwell, M.D.

JRC:dma

FIGURE 44-5
Percentage of Loss Statute

The loss of a foot shall be considered a thirty-five percent disability.
The loss of leg shall be considered a forty-five percent disability.
The loss of thigh shall be considered a fifty percent disability.
The loss of thigh at hip joint shall be considered a sixty percent disability.
The loss of little or fourth finger (one phalanx) shall be considered a three percent disability.
The loss of little or fourth finger shall be considered a five percent disability.
The loss of ring or third finger (one phalanx) shall be considered a three percent disability.
The loss of ring or third finger shall be considered a five percent disability.
The loss of middle or second finger (one phalanx) shall be considered a three percent disability.
The loss of middle or second finger shall be considered a seven percent disability.
The loss of index or first finger (one phalanx) shall be considered a six percent disability.
The loss of index or first finger shall be considered a ten percent disability.
The loss of thumb (one phalanx) shall be considered a twelve percent disability.
The loss of thumb shall be considered a twenty percent disability.
The loss of thumb and index finger shall be considered a thirty-two percent disability.
The loss of index and middle finger shall be considered a twenty percent disability.
The loss of middle and ring finger shall be considered a fifteen percent disability.
The loss of ring and little finger shall be considered a ten percent disability.
The loss of thumb, index, and middle finger shall be considered a forty percent disability.
The loss of index, middle, and ring finger shall be considered a thirty percent disability.
The loss of middle, ring, and little finger shall be considered a twenty percent disability.
The loss of four fingers shall be considered a thirty-two percent disability.
The loss of hand shall be considered a fifty percent disability.

Complications that arise after that period of time are presumed to have no relation to the job-incurred injury.

While workmen's compensation laws are designed to compensate employees who are injured "on the job," the federal Occupational Safety and Health Act was designed to *prevent* injuries, illness, and death in the work area. This topic is examined in depth in Chapter 45.

The final topic of this chapter is of recent origin although the need for this law has been apparent for 100 years. It concerns the 1974 federal law that regulates the funds paid by employees toward retirement or pension plans.

EMPLOYEE PENSION PLANS

In the past decade serious problems have arisen between employers and employees in relation to pension or retirement plans. Often, the employee made contributions to a plan for many years, only to find that the company went out of business before one could begin drawing the pension. Or, as a variation, the employer collected retirement funds and simply misappropriated them so that the employee would draw nothing at the time of retirement.

Such activities often resulted in criminal prosecutions against the defaulting employer — but that was little consolation to the employee who could not have the benefit of what had been paid over so many years.

Congress worked on these and related problems, and on September 2, 1974, the federal Employee Retirement Income Security Act became law. While this law comes under federal jurisdiction, there are few businesses in the United States that escape its coverage. This law places duties upon covered employers and provides protection for employees who pay into pension plans. First, who is covered by this law?

Coverage

The Act does not require employers to establish pensions. It only regulates those that do. Therefore, coverage still remains an option of the employer.

If there is a pension fund available, it must cover all employees who have worked for a minimum of one year and who are over 25 years of age.

One who is over 25 years of age when becoming employed, cannot be excluded from coverage unless that person is within five years of retirement age. An employer may require a minimum of three years employment before one is eligible — but in that event, benefits must "vest" 100 percent at the end of three years.

What Is Vesting?

A pension "vests" when it can no longer be forfeited — or taken from the employee. An employer must choose one of three vesting options under the Act:

1. After five years of service, the employee is entitled to 25 percent of the "accrued credits." These credits must increase to 50 percent after 10 years and 100 percent after 15 years.
2. The pension becomes nonforfeitable after 10 years of service, or,
3. An employee with five or more years of service will gain a 50 percent vested right when his or her age plus years of service equals 45. After that, 10 percent additional will vest in each of the following years.

How Must Pension Funds Be Handled?

Strict rules are laid down to govern the use of pension funds. For example, not more than 10 percent may be invested in any single security (stocks or bonds). Those who administer the funds must conduct themselves in a "prudent manner" and cannot profit personally from the fund.

What if Funds Are Misused or Lost?

The Act creates a governmental agency, the Pension Benefit Insurance Corp. (P.B.I.C.) that provides federal insurance coverage for pension funds. This solidifies the long-needed protection for the employee.

Disclosures Required

Each employer must:

1. Give an annual accounting to employees.
2. Permit each covered employee to be informed in writing of the standing of the pension fund.
3. Provide an annual accounting to the U.S. Department of Labor – or the Social Security Administration in some instances.

An employee who is denied benefits, must be given reasons why in writing. The employee then has access to the federal courts if it is justified.

REVIEW QUESTIONS

1. You are about to discharge an employee because of what you have decided to be misconduct on the job. Name one factor that unemployment compensation might have on the final decision you make.
2. What might the policy reason be for specifying a time period in which an appeal may be taken in an unemployment compensation case?
3. The states are beginning to place limits upon the percentage that a lawyer may charge in a workmen's compensation case. What reason might you give for this?
4. As a *practical* matter, why would it be foolish for an employer to fail to cover employees with workmen's compensation?
5. How would the percentages in the workmen's compensation statutes be converted to dollars?
6. How might an employer suffer a large loss by failure to cover an employee with workmen's compensation?
7. Many employees abuse both workmen's compensation and unemployment compensation laws. How can this be done?
8. Must an unemployed employee take *any* job that is offered? Why?
9. In an unemployment appeal, what must the claimant do to make certain that his or her witnesses are present at the hearing?
10. Explain the "rule of 45" under the federal pension law and set forth an example.

Jeff Hertrick
296-3766

Sun Morning

Gary Britton
296-6626
11/15   10:00

Mary Ellen Mabe
5:30 pm Thurs
599-9144

Barb Keefer
598-0376 after 2:00
Fri.

David Williams
293-2525
1 passenger

SAM WOLFF
296-4614
16 - 4:00

... System Fare Card you have received should provide access to the transportation provided by the PRT if used and cared for properly. The card is coded to provide for valid use during this semester only and will not be valid after issuance of next semester's cards.

CARE OF THE FARE CARD

The Fare Card is durable but not indestructible and should not be used for purposes other than riding the PRT (such as removing ice from windshields, washing and drying it with your clothes). Store the card flat in your wallet or purse. DO NOT EXPOSE THE CARD TO HIGH MAGNETIC FIELDS AS THEY WILL ERASE THE CARD AND MAKE IT UNUSEABLE.

USE OF THE FARE CARD

Select a gate whose illuminated status (green) panel reads "INSERT CARD OR 25¢ IN COIN". Hold the card with the printed side up and the arrow pointing toward the gate. Insert the card all the way into the card slot and withdraw it quickly. The "SELECT STATION" panel and station names (on top of the gate) should illuminate. Press the button for your destination. The green "ENTER" panel should then illuminate. Proceed through the turnstile.

If, on withdrawal of your card, the yellow panel labeled "INVALID FARE" illuminates, the gate has not obtained the proper information from your card. This can be caused if:

(a) The card has been withdrawn too slow, too fast, or in a jerky fashion.

(b) The card was inserted upside down or backwards.

(c) The card is not for the current semester.

(d) The card has been erased by a strong magnetic field.

(e) The card has excessive warpage due to improper storage or care of the card.

Check card position and gate status and try again. If your card will still not work in a gate that is accepting other people's cards, your card is probably faulty or damaged. If necessary, contact the PRT Central Operator for assistance using the platform telephone located in the vicinity of the entry gates. Contact the PRT Office to have your card checked for properly encoded data.

To avoid any service charge this card must be returned for recoding when you obtain your next semester's card.

Words and Phrases

Write out briefly what they mean to you.
1. Percentage of disability.
2. "On the job."
3. Examiner.
4. Misconduct.
5. Reporting the injury.

Coverage:	The basic principles of O.S.H.A.
What to Look for:	What employers must do to comply with this law.
Application:	Think in terms of compliance in your own business.
Note:	The penalties for violations are severe.

45 Occupational Safety and Health Act[1]

At the beginning of this decade, a statistic gave us some frightful facts: 55 persons were being killed and 8,500 injured *each day* doing nothing but working at the jobs that provided them their livelihoods! It was against these facts that the Congress of the United States decided that it was time to stop the slaughter in the work places of America.

On May 29, 1971, the initial standards of the Occupational Safety and Health Act became effective. By July 16, 1972, over 100 revisions had been made in the standards and the revisions continue today.

During the first three years of O.S.H.A. enforcement, inspectors issued over 91,000 citations charging almost a half million violations of the act. More than 138,000 businesses were inspected in arriving at these violations.

Today, O.S.H.A. in action takes two forms: first, on-the-job inspections, and second, voluntary compliance in the elimination of job hazards.

EXAMPLES OF HAZARDS

When the law became effective and inspections began, the list of work space hazards was appalling. Conditions found in the most modern businesses included: improper stacking of inventory; open pits; unguarded scaffolds; defective electric wiring; unmarked exits; safety guards removed; accumulation of debris; fire extinguishers in inacces-

---

[1] United States Code Annotated, Title 29, chapter 15. (The material presented here is in part, verbatim from *"Recordkeeping Requirements,"* U.S. Department of Labor, with permission of the Secretary of Labor.)

sible locations, and countless others. The list continues to grow daily as the *causes* of job injuries and deaths are reported under O.S.H.A.

First, some general observations.

GENERAL OBSERVATIONS ON O.S.H.A.

The act does *not* include employees of the federal government or any state government. Federal employees are covered by "executive order."[2] State workmen's compensation laws are not affected, but there is a direct tie in between compensation laws and O.S.H.A. The Act provides that if a state accident report contains all of the information found on O.S.H.A. form 101, then the state report can serve both federal and state reporting purposes.

Certain industries and types of health hazards were "targeted" by the act.

Target Industries

The industries that were causing the most injuries and deaths, in the order of severity, were: roofing and sheet metal; meat products; lumber and wood products; miscellaneous transportation equipment; and marine cargo handling.

Target Health Hazards

The target health hazards in their order of severity were: asbestos, cotton dust, silica, lead, and carbon monoxide.

With this preliminary material in mind, let's examine O.S.H.A. in more detail. To begin with, what did Congress say was the purpose of the act?

PURPOSE OF THE LAW

The Congressional purpose and policy of the Act is "to assure so far as possible every working man and woman in the nation safe and healthful working conditions and to preserve our human resources."

COVERAGE

The provisions of the law apply to every employer engaged in a business affecting commerce who has employees.[3] The law applies in all 50 States, the District of Columbia, Puerto Rico, the Virgin Islands, American Samoa, Guam, the Trust Territory of the Pacific Islands, Wake Island, the Outer Continental Shelf Lands, Johnston Island, and the Canal Zone. Federal, state and local government employees are specifically excluded

---

[2] Executive Order 11612.

[3] O.S.H.A. is being modified to exclude from its coverage any business with three or less employees.

from coverage, but they are covered by equally effective requirements by executive order as mentioned.

In addition, the Act provides that its terms shall not apply to working conditions protected under other federal occupational safety and health laws (such as those under the Federal Coal Mine Health and Safety Act; and the Atomic Energy Act of 1954, as amended, including state agreements under that Act).

DUTIES OF EMPLOYERS AND EMPLOYEES

Each employer has the duty to furnish employees places of employment free from recognized hazards causing, or likely to cause, death or serious physical harm; and the employer has the specific duty of complying with safety and health standards under the Act. Each *employee* has the duty to comply with these safety and health standards, as well as all rules, regulations, and orders issued pursuant to the Act which are applicable to the employee's own actions and conduct.

ADMINISTRATION

Administration and enforcement of the Act, is vested primarily in the Secretary of Labor and in a new agency, the Occupational Safety and Health Review Commission, a quasijudicial board of three members appointed by the President. Research and related functions are vested in the Secretary of Health, Education and Welfare whose functions are carried out by the National Institute for Occupational Safety and Health established within HEW.

The Secretary of Labor is responsible for promulgating and enforcing job safety and health standards. Occupational safety and health inspections are made by inspectors located in communities throughout the country.

OCCUPATIONAL SAFETY AND HEALTH STANDARDS

In general, job safety health standards consist of rules for avoidance of hazards which have been proven by research and experience to be harmful to personal safety and health. They constitute an extensive compilation of wisdom which sometimes applies to all employees. An example of this would be fire protection standards. A great many standards, however, apply only to workers while engaged in specific types of work— such as handling compressed gases.

Two of the many thousands of occupational safety and health standards follow:

One Typical Standard. Aisles and passageways shall be kept clear and in good repair, with no obstruction across or in aisles that could create a hazard.

Another Typical Standard. In operations such as chipping, caulking, drilling, riveting, grinding, and pouring babbit metal, in which the eye hazard of flying particles, molten metal, or liquid chemical exists, employees shall be protected by suitable face shields or goggles.

It is the obligation of all employers and employees to familiarize themselves with those standards which apply to them and to observe them at all times.

The Act also contains provision for standards which may require: (1) That no employee dealing with toxic materials or harmful physical agents will suffer material impairment of health or functional capacity, even if such employee has regular exposure to the hazard dealt with by such standard for the period of his or her working life; (2) Development and prescription of labels or other appropriate forms of warning so that employees are made aware of all hazards to which they are exposed; (3) Prescription of suitable protective equipment; (4) Monitoring or measuring employee exposure to hazards at such locations and intervals and in such manner as may be necessary for the protection of employees; and (5) Prescription of the type and frequency of medical examinations or other tests for employees exposed to health hazards. At the request of an employee, the examination or test results shall be furnished to the employee's physician.

COMPLAINTS OF VIOLATIONS

Any employee (or representative thereof) who believes that a violation of a job safety or health standard exists which threatens physical harm, or that an imminent danger exists, may request an inspection by sending a signed written notice to the Department of Labor. Such a notice shall set forth with reasonable particularity the grounds for the notice and a copy shall be provided the employer or agent. The names of the complainants need not, however, be furnished to the employer. If the Secretary finds no reasonable grounds for the complaint and a citation is *not* issued, the Secretary is required to notify the complaintants in writing of the determinations or final disposition of the matter. Also, the Secretary is required to set up procedures for informal review in a case where a citation is not issued.

Enforcement

In enforcing the standards, Labor Department safety inspectors may enter without delay, and at reasonable times, any establishment covered by the Act to inspect the premises and all pertinent conditions, structures, machines, apparatus, devices, equipment, and materials therein, and to question privately any employer, owner, operator, agent, or employee. The Act permits the employer and a representative authorized by the employees to accompany the inspector during the physical inspection of any workplace for the purpose of aiding such inspection. The Secretary of Labor also has power, in making inspections and investigations under the Act, to require the attendance and testimony of witnesses and the production of evidence under oath. The Secretary of Health, Education and Welfare is also authorized to make inspection and question employers and employees in order to carry out those functions assigned to HEW under the Act.

Where an investigation reveals a violation, the employer is issued a written citation describing the specific nature of the violation. All citations shall fix a reasonable time for abatement of the violation and each citation (or copies thereof) issued by the Department of Labor must be prominently posted at or near each place where a violation referred to in the citation occurred. Notices, in lieu of citations, may be issued for de minis[4] violations which have no direct or immediate relationship to safety or health.

No citation may be issued after the expiration of six (6) months following the occurrence of any violation.

Notification of Proposed Penalty

Within a reasonable time after issuance of a citation, the Labor Department shall notify the employer by certified mail of the penalty, if any, which is proposed to be assessed. The employer then has 15 working days within which to notify the Department that he or she wishes to contest the citation or proposed assessment of penalty. If the employer fails to notify the Department within such time of the intention to contest the citation or proposed assessment of penalty, the citation and the assessment shall be final, provided no employee files an objection to the time allowed for abatement.

Failure to Correct Violation within Allowed Time

Where time for correction of a violation is allowed but the employer fails to abate within such time, the Secretary of Labor shall notify the employer by certified mail of such failure and of the proposed penalty. Such notice and assessment shall be final unless the employer contests the same by notice to the Secretary within 15 days.

Penalties for Violations

Willful or repeated violations of the Act's requirements by employers may incur monetary penalties of up to $10,000 for each violation. Citations issued for serious violations incur mandatory monetary penalties of up to $1,000 for each violation, while penalties in the same amount may be incurred where nonserious violations are cited. A serious violation exists where there is a substantial probability that death or serious physical harm could result. An employer who fails to correct a violation for which a citation has been issued within the period prescribed may be penalized up to $1,000 each day the violation persists.

---

[4] At common law, a writ used when a person was threatened with personal violence, or harm to one's property, to force the other to keep the peace.

A willful violation by an employer which results in the death of any employee is punishable by a fine of up to $10,000 or imprisonment up to six months. A second conviction doubles these criminal penalties.

Criminal penalties are also included in the Act for making false official statements and for giving unauthorized advance notice of inspections to be conducted under the Act.

RECORDKEEPING REQUIREMENTS

In order to carry out the purposes of the Act, employers are required to keep and make available to the Labor Secretary (and also to the HEW Secretary) records on certain employer activities under the Act. Employers are also required to maintain accurate records (and periodic reports) of work-related deaths, injuries, and illnesses. Minor injuries requiring only first-aid treatment need not be reported but a record must be made if it involves medical treatment, loss of consciousness, restriction of work or motion, or transfer to another job. (O.S.H.A. forms 100, 101, and 102 are found in the *Student Workbook.*)

IMMINENT DANGERS

Conditions or practices in a place of employment which are such that a danger exists which could reasonably be expected to cause death or serious physical harm immediately or before the imminence of such danger can be eliminated through normal enforcement procedures, may be restrained by order of a United States District Court upon petition of the Secretary of Labor. If the Secretary arbitrarily or capriciously fails to seek action to abate an imminent danger, a mandamus action to compel action may be brought in the U.S. District Court by any employee who may be injured by reason of such failure. A Labor Department safety inspector who concludes that such imminent-danger conditions exist in a place of employment is obligated to inform the affected employees and employers of the danger and recommend to the Secretary of Labor that relief be sought.

PROTECTION AGAINST HARASSMENT

No person shall discharge or in any manner discriminate against any employee who exercises any right under the Act or files a complaint or other proceeding or because one testifies or is about to testify in any proceeding under the Act. Any employee who believes that he or she has been discharged or who has been discriminated against in violation of this provision may, within 30 days of such illegal action, file a complaint with the Secretary of Labor. The Secretary is authorized to investigate the matter and to bring action in the U.S. District Court for appropriate relief, including rehiring or reinstatement of the employee to the former job with back pay. The Secretary must notify the complaintant of the action on the complaint within 90 days of its receipt.

WORKMEN'S COMPENSATION

The Act does not affect workmen's compensation law or enlarge or diminish or affect the common law or statutory rights, duties, or liabilities of employers and employees under any law with respect to injuries, diseases, or death of employees arising out of, or in the course of, employment.

ADDITIONAL INFORMATION

Additional information concerning this law may be obtained by contacting the Acting Regional Administrator, Occupational Safety and Health Administration, U.S. Department of Labor, with appropriate jurisdiction, or by contacting the Office of Information Services, Occupational Safety and Health Administration, U.S. Department of Labor, Washington, D.C. 20210.

REVIEW QUESTIONS

1. Other than those exceptions stated, what other types of businesses might *not* be covered by O.S.H.A.?
2. How can the yearly reports be used to reduce industrial injuries and deaths?
3. Why have so many changes been made in the safety standards under O.S.H.A.?
4. Outline a safety program that might be placed in use in a steel mill.
5. Several periods of limitations are set out in O.S.H.A. What time periods are involved?
6. "Imminent dangers" are given priority under the act. What are the "policy" reasons for this?
7. What effects will O.S.H.A. have on state workmen's compensation laws?
8. Why does this act have wider national coverage than the U.C.C.?
9. List safety hazards you observe where you eat lunch. How about at the field house and the football stadium?
10. What is the main difference between O.S.H.A. and state workmen's compensation laws?

Words and Phrases

Write out briefly what they mean to you.
1. Reducing job related injuries and death.
2. Target industries.
3. Target health hazards.
4. Standards.
5. Harassment.

Coverage: Introduction to the partnership.

What to Look for: The general nature of a partnership.

Application: Answer this question: Did the partnership develop accidentally or because there was a need for it?

46 The Partnership

The principal forms of business in use in America today are the partnership and the corporation. Between the two the corporation is predominant in production, size, and number of persons employed, and yet the partnership is in evidence in every community, town, and city.

A partnership is a form of business in which two or more persons, or firms, pool their capital and labor—or capital or labor—and carry on business activity as co-owners, with the intention of making a profit. In terms of complexity a partnership would rank above the one-man proprietorship, but well below the corporation. The ease of formation is one of the main features and this attracts many persons to it. In addition, it provides a means by which a business person who needs assistance can obtain it relatively easily.

Frequently one in business needs assistance from others in some form other than a mere employer-employee relationship. For example, one who has the ability to conduct a certain type of business may need financial backing on some basis other than a loan. Or, two or more persons may find that collectively they possess business talents which they lack as individuals. When such persons combine forces for the purposes of conducting a business with the hope of making a profit over a continuing period of time, a partnership situation is encountered. A partnership may arise out of an expanding proprietorship or more than one proprietorship; it may be chosen initially by two or more persons as a way to conduct business or it may come into being by operation of law where two or more persons conduct themselves so that they create a partnership in fact.

Still Basic

While the largest percentage of modern manufacturing, distributing, buying, and selling is carried out by corporations acting through their

519

agents, the partnership is still a basic way of conducting business today. In 1975 over one million partnerships filed federal income tax returns. The dollar value of those returns was about 16 billion dollars. The returns came from the neighborhood grocery store, other "family" enterprises that dot the nation, and professional offices of all types. Individuals and other business persons make daily contact with these organizations. For this reason, and others, one who would have a broad understanding of the legal nature of business should have a corresponding understanding of the nature of partnerships and the laws that govern them. First, a brief look at the history of the partnership.

SOME HISTORY

In ancient times, business persons recognized that cooperation between themselves and others was required to assure that their business goals were reached efficiently, profitably, and with safety from the dangers of adverse activities of outsiders. The partnership provided a workable solution.

These early partnerships were guided by rules of law which were known in the earliest years of recorded history, such as the rules found in the ancient Code of Hammurabi. The principles of partnership law became so well established over the centuries that by 529 A.D. the Justinian Code or Codex Justinianeus which was published in that year, defined a partnership in almost the same words that are used in the Uniform Partnership Act today.

While there is little evidence to support the statement, partnership law undoubtedly evolved over the centuries prior to the earliest times that we may read of today, making the principles of partnership law of ancient, obscure origin.

As the centuries passed, the partnership became a standard way of conducting business and found widespread use, the ease of formation and the informality of operation being contributing reasons for its popularity. During the Middle Ages the bulk of business was carried out by this form. The continued use gave rise to a corresponding need for a means to settle the disputes that grew out of the operations of partnerships. That need was met by the development of the Law Merchant or Lex Mercatoria—a system of laws adopted by all commercial nations.

Lex Mercatoria

The Law Merchant was a court that spanned many centuries as an institution in many nations. Thus, no precise period of time can be spelled out in which it controlled the activities of merchants and traders. While the Law Merchant is usually associated with England, it is known that every commercial nation developed a system of laws and controls to guide the merchants and traders as they pursued their activities with themselves and the buying public. These laws were part of the "law of the land" and were frequently based upon customs and usages developed over the centuries.

In England in the days following the Conquest of 1066, it was the practice to buy, sell, and trade at merchant fairs organized for that purpose. The gathering of merchants facilitated the business process, especially so where delivery of goods was involved. It was customary at the fairs to name a "law merchant"—a person cloaked with the power to hear and decide disputes that arose between the merchants. These courts were called "Courts of Piepoudre"[1] and, as the name indicates, were very expeditious. It was said that "dust settled upon the boots of the litigants as justice was dispensed."

Appeals of rulings of the law merchant in England were to the courts at Westminster. The law-merchant system eventually merged with the common law and made contributions to many areas of modern law, including the law of commercial paper, partnerships, and contracts. The modern-day equivalent of the law merchant would be the small claim and magistrates' courts.

FIGURE 46-1

The American colonies continued to use the principles of the law merchant and at the time of American Independence adopted the English common law insofar as it was suitable for use in the fledgling nation.

As the early years of the new nation passed, the states altered, amended, and even replaced some of the ancient rules of partnership by legislation adopted for that purpose.

The most recent step in the long evolution of partnership was the creation of the Uniform Partnership Act—the work of the National Commissioners on Uniform Laws. At the present time the act has been adopted by more than 40 states. In time it may find unanimous acceptance thus reducing the law to a pure statutory status. Until that time, the common-law rules will be applied in seven states.

It is helpful to think of a partnership as a "legal conduit" through which two or more persons do business with third parties. Examine Figure 46-1. As A, B, and C transact business, the laws of partnership apply since their acts pass *through* the conduit.

It should be noted that their acts as partners run direct to the third parties and therefore, as a matter of law, there is no immunization from

---

[1] "Piepoudre" – "dusty boots."

liability between themselves and the third parties. (An exception to this will be noted later under the "limited partnership.")

IS IT AN "ENTITY"?

A partnership is not a legal entity, although it is treated as one in some instances. More precisely it is an "aggregate" of its members. In short, it is not a legal "something" that has existence apart from the members. In most states, a suit filed against a partnership must be brought in the names of the individual partners—although there are probably statutory exceptions to this. For this reason, and others that will be discussed, a general partner assumes risks when joining a partnership.

PARTNERSHIP COMPARED WITH A CORPORATION

General partners face unlimited liability where insolvency of the firm occurs. A stockholder's liability in a corporation is usually limited to any unpaid portion of the stock issued to him or her. A partnership is dissolved upon the death, incapacity, or bankruptcy of a partner. Such events have no effect upon the life of a corporation. A partner cannot transfer that person's ownership without causing a dissolution of the firm. A stockholder's interest in a corporation may be freely transferred by the sale of stock unless transfer is restricted. A corporation is created by a formal act of the state—the issuance of a charter. A partnership may be created informally—and even by implication. A partnership does not pay income tax upon the earnings of the firm, but a partnership informational return must be filed. The income of partners is taxed to them as individuals. In a corporation, a stockholder is faced with double taxation: once as the corporation pays tax upon its earnings, and secondly as the stockholder receives dividends from the corporation, which is personal income. The Internal Revenue Service regulations provide for modifications of these rules.

It is usually easier to raise capital in a corporation than in a partnership. It is done by the sale of authorized stock or by amendment of the charter to allow a subsequent issue of additional stock. Problems are raised when additional funds are needed in a partnership. A partner may or may not be willing to make additional contributions to capital. While loans may be made to the partnership and a partner who is a creditor of the firm gains some additional protection, in most cases, the only way to raise additional capital is to take in a new partner. This causes problems for many reasons: the partners may not be able to agree; if a new partner is taken in, it causes a dissolution of the firm; a dispute may arise in reference to who owes what debts; and the incoming partner will be reluctant because under the Act the new partner's capital contribution immediately becomes subject to the existing debts of the firm.[2]

---

[2] U.P.A., Section 17.

REVIEW QUESTIONS

1. Name a company in your home town that you believe to be a partnership. Can you think of reasons why they should incorporate? (Usually a company name that is *not* followed by "Co." "Inc." or "Corp.," indicates a partnership.)
2. Name a reason why a state would refuse to adopt the Uniform Partnership Act.
3. What code was published in 529 A.D.?
4. Why are there so many partnerships in the United States?
5. Why has it been necessary to have merchants courts in an organized society?
6. Liability generally flows direct to partners. Why is this so?
7. Why can't a partner's interest in the firm, be freely transferred to others? Take a guess.
8. A partnership may choose to be taxed as a corporation. Why might this choice be made?
9. You have been asked to become a partner in a going firm. Why might you *not* be interested?
10. List three disadvantages of a partnership. Three advantages.

Words and Phrases

Write out briefly what they mean to you.
1. U.P.A.
2. Law Merchant.
3. "Dusty boots."
4. A new partner.
5. Pooling capital.

47 A Partnership Case

Preliminary Case

A owned 36 acres of marketable timber but had no means of cutting and shipping it to a suitable market. B was experienced in timber production and owned equipment for this type of work. After negotiations, the following agreement was prepared:

> I, A and wife, for and in consideration of One ($1.00) Dollar and in further consideration of the mutual promises set forth below, do sell, assign, and transfer to B, all of our right, title, and interest to all of the standing timber (above a certain diameter) located (here follows a legal description of the realty) . . .
>
> The terms of this agreement are as follows: (1) B and his agents shall have full and free access to the above timber with the right to (construct roads and so on.) (2) In consideration of this, B shall pay A and wife Five ($5.00) Dollars per every 1,000 feet of timber cut.
>
> As additional consideration, B shall pay A and wife $\frac{1}{3}$ of profits made by B as a result of the sale of the timber from the above property. (Profits were then defined as any sum realized by B *after* $21.00 per 1,000 feet was deducted to cover costs of production. The contract had other provisions for restoration of the land, care of existing roads, and clean up of debris. It was signed by all parties.)

B purchased $5,000 worth of supplies from C, and began cutting timber. In less than one year, B filed a petition in bankruptcy listing A and C as creditors. C seeks to hold A responsible for the $5,000 debt of B, claiming that A and B were partners. If the court finds that there was in fact a partnership, A and wife will be forced to pay the debt of B in full. What then is a partnership and were A and B partners?

DEFINITION

A partnership is "a voluntary contract between two or more competent persons to place their money, effects, labor, and skill, or some or all of them, in lawful commerce or business, with the understanding that there shall be a proportional sharing of the profits and losses between them."[1] The Uniform Partnership Act defines a partnership as "an association of two or more persons to carry on as co-owners a business for profit."[2]

The requirement of "carrying on" a business contemplates continuity of business transactions over a period of time with the objective of making continuing profits. When persons engage in a series of transactions for the purpose of making a single profit, the requirement of "carrying on" a business might not be met.

Two or more persons may be co-owners of property and still not be partners.[3] For example, if two persons own rental property jointly and share profits from rental income, this arrangement standing alone would not be enough to establish the existence of a partnership.[4] They would not be "carrying on a business" within the definition of the Act. In agricultural regions of our nation it is not uncommon for farmers to rent or jointly purchase machinery to be used at harvest time, commonly called a "cooperatus." They combine labor and move from farm to farm until the harvest is complete. This arrangement meets the requirement of being joint or co-owners but falls short of "carrying on a business for profit" within the meaning of the definition.

Further, the definition contemplates ownership of a business that may not have tangible property. For example, A and B, two lawyers, form a partnership to engage in the practice of law. A owns the office building as well as all of the office equipment, including books and fixtures. B understands and agrees that the ownership of these items is to remain with A. Although the partnership does not have any real or personal property, A and B are still co-owners within the meaning of the definition—they are co-owners of the practice of law.

The first definition above speaks of "competent persons." This indicates that problems may arise in a partnership where infants, insane persons, and those under other legal disabilities desire to become a partner.

Under the Act, "person: includes individuals, partnerships, corporations, and other associations."[5] Applying this provision literally, it would be possible for an individual to be a partner with a corporation or with another partnership. However, state law would have to be examined to see if such an arrangement would be legal.

At common law a rule developed that "statutes in derogation of com-

---

[1] *Black's Law Dictionary*, 4th ed.

[2] U.P.A., Section 6(1).

[3] U.P.A., Section 7(2).

[4] U.P.A., Section 7(3).

[5] U.P.A., Section 2.

mon law" shall be strictly construed. In application, this rule means that when a state amends, repeals, or alters common-law principles by legislation, the courts will, in later court contests involving the statute, resolve doubt *against* the statute and in favor of the common law. It might be thought of as "youth bowing to age." However, the Act provides that the rule shall have no application under the Act,[6] so it does not help in the timber case.

The law of estoppel[7] and agency[8] *does* apply under the Act and, as it will be seen, this provision provides the courts with a broad brush with which to paint. Rather than being concerned at this point with the application of estoppel and agency, let's examine the usual ways in which a partnership comes into existence.

CREATION OF A PARTNERSHIP

A partnership, just as a contract, may be created by express wishes of the partners; it may be implied from the acts of the parties; or it may arise by operation of law, which is called an "estoppel."

Express Creation

A written partnership agreement is desirable although not legally necessary, and should be prepared by counsel.

When a buy-and-sell agreement is created as part of a partnership agreement, it should be funded by life insurance so the survivor will have funds with which to purchase the interest of the deceased partner. In addition, it should be made clear that the survivor *must* buy the interest. If not, the survivor may refuse to purchase the interest and divert the insurance proceeds to personal use.

In most partnerships, the ages of the partners will not be the same and this will cause a variation in the premiums paid on the policy. Examine Figure 47–1 and answer the question that accompanies it. (Assume that A, B, and C are forming a partnership).

A few life insurance companies offer "joint policies" in which two persons are covered by one policy. The premium is based upon the average age of those covered. This provides one means of handling the problem of variable ages.

Related to the funded buy-and-sell agreement is the problem that might arise if one partner should become disabled.

Disability of an active partner would work a dissolution of the firm just as death because it would be a "change in the relations of the partners." The agreement could provide that a certain sum would be paid to the disabled partner for the first six months of disability. If the partner returns to the firm, there has been no interruption of the business. If the dis-

---

[6] U.P.A., Section 4(1).

[7] U.P.A., Section 4(2).

[8] U.P.A., Section 4(3).

FIGURE 47-1
$100,000 Term Life

Partner	Age	Annual Premium
A	27	$ 873.00
B	33	$1,051.00
C	42	$1,500.00

What problems might the above facts cause in a buy-and-sell agreement funded with life insurance? How might the problem be met?

ability continues, the agreement can provide for a sliding schedule of benefits which would ultimately phase out the disabled partner. The agreement might also provide that if disability continues for one year, the remaining partners have the right to buy out the disabled partner.

When a firm is created expressly but there is no written agreement, general law applies. For example, the Act provides that the sharing of profits and losses shall be equal and they (the partners) shall ". . . contribute toward the losses . . . according to his share in the profits."[9] This provision could work an unexpected hardship upon a partner who does not realize that the law says what it does. In the timber case there was no written partnership agreement between A and B, although there was a written contract that covered the removal of the timber. A second way that a partnership may be created is by "implication."

Implied Creation

If two or more persons conduct themselves in such a manner that they meet the requirements of a partnership, partnership liability may attach by "implication." Implication has been defined as "an inference of something not expressly declared but arising from what is admitted or expressed." Those engaging in performance contracts with others should avoid arrangements that might lead others to believe that a partnership exists. The insolvency of one presents the problem because if a third person can prove loss from reliance upon the existence of the "apparent" partnership, and if the requirements of a partnership are met, the other may be faced with liability as a partner. The creation of a partnership in this manner comes close to the facts in the timber case.

A third way in which a partnership can be formed is by an estoppel.

Creation by Estoppel

The creation of a partnership by estoppel requires some conduct on the part of one who allows another to represent him or her to a third

---

[9] U.P.A., Section 18(*a*).

party, who in turn relies upon the representation and suffers a loss because of it. When this happens, the law will "close the mouth" of the party who allowed the representation. The result could be a jury trial based upon partnership law in which the defendant is not permitted to tell the jury that there was no partnership. In such cases there is no partnership in fact. Rather, the courts indulge in a "fiction" by saying that a partnership exists in order to protect an innocent party. If the defendant is found guilty at trial, liability is the same as if the defendant had been an actual partner.[10] If partnership liability does not result (a not-guilty verdict for the defendant), joint liability still remains with the other person who consented to the contract or representation that incurred the liability, otherwise separately.[11] As one court said about estoppel, "a man's own act or acceptance stops or closes his mouth to allege or plead the truth."[12] The estoppel principle is most commonly used to prevent "unjust enrichment."

Still referring to the timber case, does the Act provide other provisions that might help us solve the problem?

DOES A PARTNERSHIP EXIST?

The Act spells out certain tests for determining if a partnership exists. For example, those who are not partners to each other will not be partners to others. If a person receives a share of the profits of a business, this is "prima facie" evidence that that person is a partner. Prima facie means "on the first appearance or on the face of it." This means that a "presumption" has been raised that indicates that there is a partnership. The Act makes it clear that payment of a debt by installments, payment of wages to an employee, or payment of rent to a landlord does not give rise to the presumption. This is true even if the payments vary according to the success of the business involved.[13] For example, if a salesperson is paid a commission based upon the gross earnings of the company, there would not be a presumption that a partnership exists between the salesperson and the employer. Joint or common ownership where co-owners share profits from the use of property, standing alone, is not enough to determine the existence of a partnership. This is true if other gross returns are shared by such common owners. (Test the timber case with these points.) One final type of business that is closely associated with a partnership must be examined before the decision in the timber case is disclosed.

A JOINT VENTURE

A joint venture involves an undertaking where there is a "community of interest" in the objectives. One court defined a joint venture as ". . . a

---

[10] U.P.A., Section (1)(*a*).

[11] U.P.A., Section 16(1)(*b*).

[12] *Williams* v. *Edwards*, 163 Okl. 246, 22 P.2d. 1026 (1933).

[13] U.P.A., Section 7(4).

commercial enterprise undertaken by several persons jointly; a limited partnership—not limited in a statutory sense as to the liability of the partners, but as to its scope and duration."[14]

The parties to a joint venture have an equal right to govern the conduct of each other and have a voice in the control or management. Such relationships are distinguished from a partnership, although they are similar. The same rules govern both relationships, although a joint venture is usually limited to one transaction. Third parties who deal with those in a joint venture are generally held to be on notice of the limited scope of the business and should exercise caution. While the law of partnership governs the relationship, the law does *not* govern the rights of third parties. For this reason, the parties to a joint venture might not have unlimited liability as far as third-party creditors are concerned.

The material discussed demonstrates the factors that must be reviewed by the court in deciding the timber case.

THE DECISION

The court ruled that a partnership did *not* exist in the timber case. There was no community of interest in the venture; there was no common voice in the management; and there was no sharing of the profits and losses within the meaning of partnership law. The court came to the last conclusion by reasoning that the sum to be deducted from the receipts to cover costs was arbitrary and bore no relationship to the actual costs of production. Therefore, the payments made under the agreement were not in fact a "sharing" of profits and losses.

Even though the owner of the timber avoided partnership liability, the costs of the court action must have been considerable. The message of the case is that business persons (and citizens) must use care and caution in their dealings with others. The possibility that a court might find that a partnership exists—even though the parties believed otherwise—is all too real.

REVIEW QUESTIONS

1. A, B, and C are seniors at Zero University and are members of the university band. Each Saturday night they play as a group at various motels. A provides a V.W. van to carry the instruments and B takes care of the booking arrangements. After expenses are paid, they divide the balance equally. They do not have a written agreement. Are they partners?
2. In Problem 1, A and B are over the age of majority but C is under 18 years of age. What bearing might this have?
3. A, B, and C call their group "The Zero University Three." They have legal problems because of this name. What might that problem be?
4. True or False. A partnership agreement must always be in writing.
5. Name one reason for using a buy-and-sell agreement in a partnership.
6. How would you cover the contingency of disability in your partnership?

---

[14] *McDaniel* v. *State Fair*, Tex.Civ.App. 286 S.W. 513, 517 (1926).

7. Why does the law say that a partnership can be created by implication?
8. Describe an "estoppel."
9. Distinguish a joint venture from a true partnership.
10. Name two other provisions that could have been included in the timber cutting contract.

Words and Phrases

Write out briefly what they mean to you.
1. Estoppel.
2. Implication.
3. Buy-and-sell agreement.
4. Funding with life insurance.
5. Disabled partner.

Coverage:	An analysis of the nature and extent of partnership property.
What to Look for:	The peculiar manner in which partners hold firm property.
Application:	Think in terms of lending money to a partnership which offers its property as security.
Note:	If you fail to understand what "specific partnership property" is, ask for help.

48 Partnership Property

The key to an effective understanding of the partnership is a working knowledge of the property of the firm. This is true because the property is the substance around which the firm revolves.

This subject is of concern to creditors of the firm because they are entitled by law to look first to the assets of the firm for satisfaction of debts due them. Individual creditors of the partners look first to the individual assets of each partner for payment and if not fully satisfied, they may *then* look to partnership assets.[1] However, they will not have any claim on assets classified as partnership property. Disputes constantly arise between the two classes of creditors in reference to what is or is not partnership property. The final decision in such a dispute usually benefits one class of creditors and not the other for the simple reason that one often gets paid and the other does not.

WHAT CONSTITUTES PARTNERSHIP PROPERTY?

Generally all property brought into the firm originally with the intention of making it partnership property, and all property later acquired on behalf of the firm, is partnership property.[2] Property acquired with funds of the firm is logially included unless a contrary intention appears.[3] The first type of property that comes into a partnership comes from contributions to capital.

---

[1] U.P.A., Section 40(1)(I).

[2] U.P.A., Section 8(1).

[3] U.P.A., Section 8(2).

531

Partnership Capital

The capital consists of contributions made by the partners which must be returned to them upon the winding up and termination of the business. Included would be initial contributions and additional permanent investments made in the partnership. Temporary investments, such as loans and unwithdrawn profits would not be partnership capital and therefore would not be partnership property. For this reason individual creditors of the partners would have first call upon this type of asset in satisfaction of obligations due them.

Contributions to capital may be in some form other than money. One partner may contribute a truck and another may deed a building to the firm. When this occurs, a value would be placed upon the items and that amount would be credited to the capital account of the contributing partner. Contributions of property which are made in good faith and made prior to any interest of third parties attaching to them, would be partnership property. Because of this, the property would be beyond the reach of individual creditors of the partners, at least as far as direct suit is concerned. Closely associated with firm property are the *rights* that the partners have in the property.

PROPERTY RIGHTS OF A PARTNER

"The property rights of a partner are (1) rights in specific partnership property, (2) interest in the partnership, and (3) right to participate in the management."[4] The definition lends itself to a diagram (Figure 48–1). Three persons, A, B, and C, form a partnership by express agreement. The firm is made up of three parts: the "base," which represents the "hot plate" of management, and a two-part container into which the initial capital contributions are "poured." The first level of the container represents the "specific firm property" and includes initial and later permanent contributions. The second level represents the "interest" in the firm, which arises from the use of firm property as business is conducted. In short, if the firm makes a profit, interest is generated. This level will go up and down depending upon the success of the firm. The level will go down as the partners withdraw their interest.

The interest in a partnership is comparable to the retained earnings of a corporation. It is the interest in the firm that is distributed to the partners at agreed times.

Now examine Figure 48–2. The figure illustrates the sources of recovery for the two classes of creditors. Individual creditors of the partners will look to the individual assets of A, B, and C but will be limited to the *interest* of A, B, and C in the firm. The specific firm property is beyond the immediate reach of individual creditors of the partners. A closer look at the nature of specific partnership property will make the diagram more meaningful.

---

[4] U.P.A., Section 24.

FIGURE 48-1

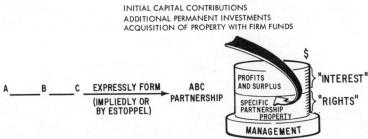

INITIAL CAPITAL CONTRIBUTIONS
ADDITIONAL PERMANENT INVESTMENTS
ACQUISITION OF PROPERTY WITH FIRM FUNDS

Specific Partnership Property

At common law a "tenancy in common" was a status of ownership in which "several and distinct titles by unity of possession were held without either knowing his own severally, and therefore they all occupy promiscuously."[5] For example, if two persons owned an acre of land as tenants in common, each owned an undivided one half of the whole. If a question arose regarding the ownership of a certain portion of the acre, the answer was that each owned one half of the portion in question. The characteristics of the tenancy in common have been applied to the partnership by the Uniform Partnership Act and partners hold specific partnership property as "tenants in partnership." Therefore, each partner owns an undivided interest in the whole. For this reason, personal creditors of an individual partner cannot reach that partner's interest in specific firm property. (The reverse was true at common law, and the act of taking a partner's interest in specific firm property caused the destruction of the partnership. The drafters of the Act sought to avoid this result.) Today, under the Act, if a truck is owned by a firm made up of A and B, the creditors of B cannot reach B's ownership in that particular piece of equipment. And further, A and B have equal rights to use the truck for firm purposes.

The right in specific partnership property is exempt from attachment or executions issued as a result of judgments obtained by individual creditors. The reverse is true with firm creditors, however, and they can attach, or otherwise reach such rights in order to satisfy firm debts. Where this happens, the partners cannot claim the benefits of rights that they may have under homestead or exemption laws.[6]

When a partner dies, that person's rights in specific firm property does not pass to the estate or heirs as does other real and personal property. Rather, it vests in the surviving partner or partners, for firm purposes. For this reason, a partner's right in specific property is beyond the reach of "dower," "curtsey," or allowances to widows, heirs, or next of kin.[7]

---

[5] *Fullerton* v. *Storthz*, 77 S.W.2d. 966, 968 (1935).

[6] U.P.A., Section 25(2)(c).

[7] U.P.A., Section 25(2)(e).

FIGURE 48–2

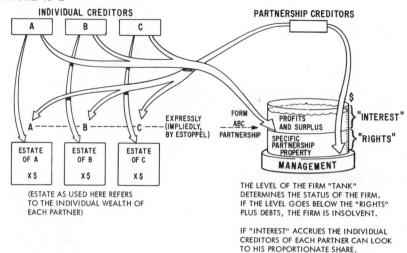

THE LEVEL OF THE FIRM "TANK"
DETERMINES THE STATUS OF THE FIRM.
IF THE LEVEL GOES BELOW THE "RIGHTS"
PLUS DEBTS, THE FIRM IS INSOLVENT.

IF "INTEREST" ACCRUES THE INDIVIDUAL
CREDITORS OF EACH PARTNER CAN LOOK
TO HIS PROPORTIONATE SHARE.

Interest in the Firm

A partner's interest in the firm is that partner's share of the profits and surplus. This interest is personal property and can be looked to by individual creditors of each partner.[8] The interest can be assigned but the assignee would only receive the rights to proceeds as they accrue.[9]

A partner's interest also extends to funds that he or she would be entitled to upon termination. Since a partner's interest in the firm is personal property, one would have the protection of the exemption and homestead laws. Examine Figure 48–3.

The "charging order," which will be discussed later, can be used by an individual judgment creditor of a partner to reach the interest in the firm. Upon application a court will appoint a receiver to take the interest of the judgment debtor partner as it accrues and pay it to the creditor.

The third property right is the right to take part in the management of the business.

Management of the Firm

The right to take part in the management of the firm is a property right, and each partner, in the absence of a contrary agreement, has an equal voice and vote in the management. This is true regardless of the amount of the capital contributions of each partner. The equal vote and voice provision arises from the fact that *each partner is considered, at law, to have made an equal contribution regardless of whether one*

---

[8] U.P.A., Section 26.

[9] U.P.A., Section 27(1).

FIGURE 48-3
"Who Can Reach What?"

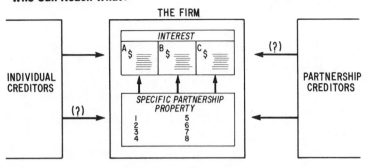

contributed more than the other. This concept will be explored under "sharing profits and losses."

TITLE TO PARTNERSHIP PROPERTY

"Title" in the broad sense is the means by which the owner of property has the legal right to what is owned and it is more than mere evidence of ownership. For example, the title certificate to an automobile can be destroyed, but this in no way disturbs the ownership. Legal title is enforceable in a court of law and does not carry with it any "beneficial interest" in the property in question. It is title that is complete so far as the rights of ownership and possession are concerned.

On the other hand, "equitable title" involves a beneficial interest in one person whom a court of equity might consider as the owner even though at the same time legal title is vested in another. Any discussion of partnership property requires mention of both legal and equitable title, and such property may be real, personal, or mixed.

Real Property

At common law, title to real property (the earth and everything permanently attached to it) could *not* vest in a partnership. A partnership was a mere "aggregate" and therefore the firm could not take title to real property. Under the Act, a partnership is considered to be an entity for the purposes of holding title to real estate.[10]

If real property is acquired in the firm name, a subsequent conveyance must also be in the firm name.[11] One partner may convey such property to others as long as the deed is executed in the firm name.[12] But the partner must be acting within authority duly given.[13] The buyer must be

---

[10] U.P.A., Section 10.
[11] U.P.A., Section 8(3).
[12] U.P.A., Section 10(1).
[13] U.P.A., Section 9(1).

FIGURE 48–4
Partnerships and Real Property

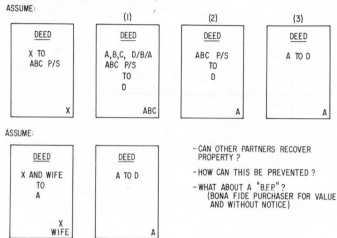

careful and determine if the partner in fact had the authority to convey the property. The careful buyer would require all partners to join in the deed.

A more difficult problem is presented where title to real property is in the firm name and a conveyance is executed by one partner in his or her own name. Such a deed will pass equitable title provided the conveyance is ". . . apparently carrying on in the usual way the business of the partnership."[14] If not, the firm can recover the property. A buyer should never accept a deed made out in that manner.

If real property is held in the name of one or more, but not all, of the partners, the named partner (or partners) can convey title. A good-faith buyer is protected and may keep what has been conveyed. The rule also extends to the assignee of the good-faith buyer.[15]

"A conveyance to a partnership in the partnership name, though without words of inheritance ("habendum et tenedum" — "to have and to hold"), passes the entire estate of the grantor (seller) unless a contrary intent appears."[16] (Use the above in conjunction with Figure 48–4.)

Upon the death of a partner, rights in firm property pass to the surviving partner, or partners. They can convey title in the firm name if done for purposes of carrying on the partnership business — or winding up and terminating the affairs of the firm.

Real Property at Common Law. At common law if real property was conveyed to partners in their own name (it was useless to convey to the firm in its name), they held title as tenants in common. If real property

---

[14] U.P.A., Section 9(1).

[15] U.P.A., Section 10(3).

[16] U.P.A., Section 8(4).

was conveyed to one partner on behalf of the firm, title vested in that partner but as a trustee for the firm. The common-law rule still applies in seven states.

Personal Property

The personal property of a partnership would be all property of the firm other than real property. Title can be taken in the firm name and this presents no problems. Each partner has the right to possess and use such property, but only for firm purposes. Upon the death of one partner, the interest in personal firm property passes to the survivors and not to the heirs of the deceased partner.

Many partnership disputes are in the books that grew out of litigation after the death of a partner. In most of these disputes, the matter could have been avoided if the partners had created a buy-and-sell agreement funded with life insurance.

PARTNERS AND LIFE INSURANCE

By the very nature of a partnership, the effective use of life insurance can mean the difference between a firm that continues to operate after the death of a partner and one that is forced to liquidate.

Insurable Interest

Partners have an insurable interest in the lives of each other. To have an insurable interest, one person must benefit from the continuance of the life of another rather than benefit from its ending.

If partners decide to insure their lives as partners, an agreement must be prepared to spell out how the proceeds of the life insurance will be applied upon death. The agreement should be in writing, signed by the partners, and should be prepared by counsel. The following case illustrates the problems that can arise where partners purchase life insurance but fail to make it clear how the funds are to be applied upon death.

Insurance Case. A, B, and C formed a partnership for the purpose of carrying on a business as soft line, retail merchants. Their total capital contributions came to $16,000, of which A contributed $10,000, B, $5,000, and C, $1,000. The partnership agreement was silent on how profits and losses were to be shared, so they shared them equally as provided by the Act.

The partners purchased insurance on the lives of each other in the sum of $50,000 each. This figure was based upon the estimated amount that would be needed to buy out one partner. A buy-and-sell agreement was prepared and signed, but, unfortunately, details were not spelled out. Premiums for the insurance were paid by the firm.

A died and by will left his estate to his widow. At the time, partnership assets totaled $200,000. The figure did not include the $50,000 payment received from the insurance policy but did include the cash surrender value of the other two policies.

Liabilities were $100,000 not including capital contributions, leaving $100,000 in assets (on paper). After making allowance for the $16,000 capital contributions, the net assets of the firm came to $84,000.

The sum of $10,000 was to be returned to the widow of A since this was A's contribution to the firm. The problem arose when it came time to apply the proceeds of the life insurance. It was suddenly discovered that the parties saw the situation two different ways.

The Survivors' Contention. The surviving partners wanted to pay the widow $10,000 plus one third of the net assets of $84,000. This would be $28,000 for a total payment of $38,000. The $50,000 would be available for this purpose and the assets of the firm would be left untouched, allowing the surviving partners to continue the business.

It is obvious that the contention of the survivors, if carried out, would result in a windfall of $22,000 for the survivors in that their interest in the firm would be increased in this amount.

The Widow's Contention. The widow contended that the proceeds of the insurance should be added to the assets of $84,000, making a total of $144,000. One third of this sum ($48,000) would then be paid to her in addition to the $10,000 capital contribution.

In the absence of a clear buy-and-sell agreement, most courts would be inclined to sustain the contention of the widow. One reason is that when insurance premiums are paid by the firm, there is a presumption that the partners intended the proceeds to be firm property. The widow's case illustrates the need for a clear buy-and-sell agreement.

LIABILITY AND INDEMNITY INSURANCE

In addition to life insurance, the firm should carry insurance to protect the members from the negligence of each other (torts) and other losses such as fire and wind damage. The purchase of such insurance is routine and will not be discussed further. However, the questions of how premiums are to be paid and who is to receive the proceeds requires mention. These details are worked out at the time of the application for insurance, but it should be made clear that the proceeds of indemnity policies will be *firm property* and not individual property. Otherwise, difficulties might arise as seen in the life insurance case.

One effective method of paying insurance premiums is by prearrangement with the bank and the insurance company. Under these plans, the company draws a draft for the sum of the premium and sends it to the bank. The bank charges the amount to the account of the firm, marks the draft paid, and returns it to the firm with the cancelled checks.

THE FIRM NAME AND GOODWILL

The name chosen for the firm is partnership property and is entitled to the same protection extended to other firm property. This means that one partner cannot use the firm name for personal gain any more than one may use other firm property. Such unauthorized use has resulted in many lawsuits.

Any discussion of the firm name must be accompanied by mention of "goodwill." Goodwill is "the favor which management of a business wins from the public." It involves the hope of continued business from satisfied customers. Goodwill is also firm property and gains legal protection just as other partnership property. Unauthorized use of the firm name would normally impair the goodwill of the firm. When a firm is sold, the buyer expects to receive the goodwill. For this reason, the buyer would acquire the right to own and use the name of the firm.

The question of how a partnership can be sold and the problems that face both the buyer and sellers will not be discussed. Such sale raises problems about the rights of the individual creditors of the partners and the rights of partnership creditors. Advice of counsel would be in order by both parties to a sale and purchase.

REVIEW QUESTIONS

1. A friend asks you what "specific" partnership property is. How would you explain it?
2. Why is a partner's "interest" in the firm personal property?
3. You and a friend have decided to form a partnership. You mention a buy-and-sell agreement and your friend says there is no need for one. What might you say that would change his or her mind?
4. What was the problem at common law in taking title to partnership property?
5. True or False. The partner who makes the largest contribution to capital has the biggest voice in the management.
6. Partners are treated as "legal counterparts" of each other because of the law of agency. Name two reasons why they are also treated as "legal equals."
7. "Interest" converted into additional contributions to capital, would become specific partnership property. Explain the legal effect of this.
8. Explain why the drafters of the U.P.A. created "specific partnership property."
9. Which class of creditors has first call on "interest" in a firm.
10. Name two times when a note should be used in a partnership.

Words and Phrases

Write out briefly what they mean to you.
1. Partnership property.
2. The rights of a partner.
3. Management.
4. Capital contribution.
5. Life insurance.

Coverage:	Legal factors that control the relationship between partners and others.
What to Look for:	Guidelines for being a good partner.
Application:	Think of ways that disputes could arise between partners.

49 Being Partners

The relationship that exists between those who become partners is a highly personal one. This is so because the law changes the legal nature of the partners from that of individuals who are "free agents" to persons who become the legal counterparts of each other. This happens because the law of agency applies to partnerships.[1] It follows that duties come into being between the partners and between them and third parties. Included are those that are specifically spelled out in the partnership agreement, those provided by law, and those that can be implied from the nature of the partnership itself. The absence of a written agreement makes no difference because the courts will apply the general rules of partnership law, both legal and equitable.

Within legal limits, partners may choose by contract between themselves to increase or decrease the burdens imposed by law. For example, the partners may agree to share profits on some basis other than equally. But partners cannot change the duties that they owe to those outside of the firm such as creditors of the partnership or those who are injured by the negligence of an employee of the firm. Their duties to third parties are fixed by law and are thus beyond any contract that they may make between themselves.

HOW TO DECIDE DUTIES

One of the problems that faces those who expressly create a partnership is in drawing the lines that spell out duties and responsibilities. It is never possible to provide for all contingencies that arise in the operation of the firm. In addition, general law such as the U.P.A. is never extensive

---

[1] U.P.A., Section 4(3).

enough to cover all situations that may arise. Therefore, the U.P.A. provides that "in any case not provided for . . . the rules of law and equity, including the law merchant, shall govern."[2] This provision sends the lawyers to the case books when partnership cases arise that are not covered by the U.P.A.

Each partner has the power to bind the other partners in both contract and tort. This means that each has the power to create duties on the part of the others. Because of this, the relationship requires confidence, care, and good faith between the partners. The rules that have developed have been based upon these requirements which include simple honesty. The principles involved will be discussed under the headings of "money," "records," and "accounting."

Money

When a partner makes a contribution to a firm in whatever form, that partner is granted a "license" or right by which he or she can expect certain benefits in return. For example, he or she receives the right to share equally in profits and surplus and to be repaid any contributions when the firm is dissolved, "wound up," and terminated. But with the "license" goes the duty to contribute toward losses in the same manner in which one shares profits. In short, if profits are shared equally, one must share losses equally.[3]

Sharing of Profits and Losses—An Example. Three persons formed a partnership but the agreement was silent on sharing of profits. Therefore, the Act controls and they share profits equally.[4] This means that they also share losses equally. Their contributions to capital were uneven, but the rule on how they share profits remains unchanged. The contributions were as follows:

A	$20,000
B	12,000
C	4,000
Total	$36,000

The capital was used to rent a building and to purchase the beginning inventory. The capital contributions and the inventory purchased with it made up the partnership property—that is, the "specific partnership property." Part of the capital was deposited in the bank to cover operating expenses and the firm then opened its doors for business.

The First Year. After all taxes and other operating expenses were paid, a profit of $6,000 remained. The sum of $2,000 was credited to the capital account of each partner. The firm filed a partnership informational federal income tax return, but no tax was paid by the firm. Each partner simply had an addition of $2,000 to personal income for the year.

---

[2] U.P.A., Section 5.

[3] U.P.A., IV. Section 18(*a*).

[4] Ibid.

In summary, the $36,000 worth of "specific partnership property" had been used to generate $6,000 of partners' "interest" in the firm.

Dissolution Occurs. After a few years of operation, the nature of the market changed, profits fell, and it became apparent that the firm was in difficulty. The death of A occurred, causing dissolution. Working in conjunction with the executor of A (named by A in A's will), B and C carefully liquidated the business. After paying all partnership debts, $15,000 remained. How was it distributed?

Operating Loss. Since the firm began business with $36,000 and ended with $15,000, an operating loss of $21,000 resulted. This meant that the firm did not have enough funds to return to A's estate and to B and C what had been contributed initially. In short, the $21,000 loss had to be adjusted so that the loss was shared equally. Since there was no agreement to the contrary, the three shared the loss equally—$7,000 each. Since A contributed $20,000 initially, A's estate had the right to have $13,000 returned to it. Since B contributed $12,000, B was entitled to a return of $5,000, making the loss the same as that of A.

The contribution of C was only $4,000, so it was C's legal obligation to contribute an additional sum of $3,000 to make the loss equal to the others. The following distributions were then made:

Funds Available		Distributed to	
$15,000	remaining in assets	A's estate	$13,000
3,000	from C	B	5,000
$18,000			$18,000

The effect of the distribution was that each partner was treated as if the capital contribution of each had been as follows in the beginning:

A..................	$12,000
B..................	12,000
C..................	12,000
	$36,000

If each had in fact contributed $12,000 in the beginning, then based upon the above facts, each would have received $5,000 from the $15,000, making their losses equal. The law treats them as equals in the end—even if they are not so in the beginning. It is for this reason that they have equal votes and voices in the management of the business.

If C could not pay the additional $3,000, A's estate and B would divide the loss between them, with each receiving $1,500 less than the previous figure.[5]

Indemnification. If one partner incurs expenses out of pocket for the benefit of the partnership, that partner is entitled to be repaid such sum—called "indemnification." In short, one is legally entitled to be returned to the position one enjoyed prior to the expenditure. Indemnification is not the same as "remuneration."

---

[5] U.P.A., Section 40(d).

Remuneration. A partner is *not* entitled to be paid wages for carrying out partnership business unless it is so agreed between the parties.[6] The reason for the rule is clear: The nature of the partnership is such that monetary benefits follow from the sharing of profits and not from the payment of wages. However, a surviving partner is entitled to reasonable compensation for services rendered while winding up the partnership affairs.

Interest. As a basic rule, a partner is *not* entitled to be paid interest upon capital contributions. It is assumed that any return upon the investment will come in the form of profits from the business. Therefore, an investment in the partnership is not the same as a deposit in a savings account or a loan made to another. However, if a partner makes advances to the partnership in some amount *above* capital, he or she would be entitled to interest on the advance. In addition, a partner is entitled to interest on capital contributions from the time that it should have been repaid but was not.[7] This often occurs where a partnership has been dissolved by death and the survivors and the representative of the estate of the deceased disagree on "who gets what" — not an unusual situation.

Records

Partners are under a duty to give true and accurate information of all matters concerning the partnership upon demand by other partners or representatives of deceased partners.[8] This would extend to demands made for information contained in the partnership books.

Each partner has the right to inspect and copy the books of the partnership, which are usually kept at the principal place of business.[9] This can be important where questions arise about the conduct of one of the partners in reference to use of partnership funds. The right cannot be taken from a partner simply because one partner claims the books are his or her responsibility and under his or her control.

The right to inspect the books carries with it a question of "When and where may the right be exercised?" A suggested rule of thumb is "at a reasonable time and place." If the records of a partnership are computerized, the same rule should be applied to prevent inconveniences to the operation of the business.

Accounting

Partners are in a relationship that makes each a fiduciary of the other. A fiduciary is a "person having a duty created by the undertaking to act for the benefit of another. Such a relationship is always founded upon trust and confidence."[10] Therefore, partners must conduct themselves accordingly.

---

[6] U.P.A., Section 18(*f*).

[7] U.P.A., Section 18(*a*)(*b*)(*c*)(*d*).

[8] U.P.A., Section 20.

[9] U.P.A., Section 19.

[10] *Black's Law Dictionary*, 4th ed.

A partner cannot enter transactions that involve partnership property which benefits one personally, and cannot use partnership property for personal benefit.[11] To do so would violate the duty as a fiduciary. The duty likewise applies to legal representatives of a deceased partner who are engaged in the liquidation of the partnership.

A partner is prohibited from competing with the partnership. If one does, a duty would arise to account for profits made.

Forcing an Accounting. A partnership accounting is initiated by filing a complaint or petition in a court of competent jurisdiction. The action is on the equity side of the court since a breach of fiduciary relationship is involved. For this reason, the matter would be heard by the court without a jury. This action is often taken when one partner has reason to believe that another partner has wrongfully diverted funds.

A partner is entitled to an accounting under certain specified conditions as follows: if one is wrongfully excluded from the partnership business; if one is denied possession of partnership property by other partners; if one is denied a right existing under the partnership agreement; and under such other circumstances that would make it seem just and reasonable to a court that one should be entitled to an accounting.[12]

If the jurisdiction of a court is invoked for a "petty" or "incidental" accounting ("A took $10 more from the partnership than A should have"), the courts will dismiss the petition as being trivial. The courts will not act as a referee for minor partnership disputes.

PARTNERS AND OTHERS

An operating partnership touches the lives of many persons—and in different ways. For example, a company selling to a partnership is a creditor of the firm. One who buys from the firm is a customer. If a firm truck negligently strikes a pedestrian, a tort situation has arisen. Finally, a firm may conduct itself in such a manner as to give rise to a criminal charge against the partners. Therefore, partners must have a basic understanding of the duties that are placed upon them as those duties relate to third persons.

As Agents

As stated, each partner is an agent of his or her partners and the law of agency governs. The acts of one partner that are reasonably necessary to carry out the purposes of the partnership become the acts of the other partners. One partner may place the partnership name on an instrument and that act binds the partners if it was done inside the scope of the authority granted.[13] But acts of a partner that are not in the scope of authority do not bind the partners.[14] Generally, a partner does not have the

---

[11] U.P.A., Section 21(1).

[12] U.P.A., Section 22.

[13] U.P.A., Section 9(1).

[14] U.P.A., Section 9(2).

right to dispose of the goodwill of the business, waive a judgment, or do any other act which would make it impossible to carry out the ordinary business of the partnership.[15] These matters directly affect the partnership and would require unanimous consent of all partners before they could be done.

Admissions

Any admission or representation concerning the affairs of the partnership made by one partner, may be used as evidence against the partnership.[16] The admissions, however, must have been made within the scope of authority of the partner making the admissions before they can be used in court.

Notice

When one partner knows of a fact which should be communicated to the other partners, that knowledge operates as notice to all of the partners whether or not the others have notice of it.[17] This places a duty upon each partner to communicate notice or knowledge acquired in dealing with third parties which may be material to the interests of the partnership. Therefore, notice and knowledge should always be passed on. A popular technique is the use of carboned memos which are distributed to the other partners after the information is filled in.

Wrongful Acts

When a tort is committed by one partner in the conduct of the partnership business which results in injury to the body or property of a third person, the partnership is liable for the damages. Any breach of trust by a partner involving misapplication of money or property of a third person binds the partnership to make good the loss. However, the partner must have held the money or property within the scope of the partnership business.[18]

Partners are jointly and severally liable for the torts and other wrongful acts of partners that are chargeable to the partnership. In cases of breach of contract, the partners are jointly liable. In other words, in the event of a wrongful act, the injured third party would look to all the partners or to any one of them for full recovery.[19] But, if there is a breach of contract, the partners would be held jointly liable, and the third party would have to look to them collectively and could not necessarily have full recovery from any one partner.[20]

---

[15] U.P.A., Section 9(3).
[16] U.P.A., Section 11.
[17] U.P.A., Section 12.
[18] U.P.A., Section 14.
[19] U.P.A., Section 13.
[20] U.P.A., Section 15.

Individual Creditors

A partner's "rights in specific property" is not assignable unless all other partners join in the assignment of the property.[21] However, a partner's "interest in a partnership" may be assigned and such assignment does not dissolve the partnership. The assignee cannot interfere in the management of the partnership business. The assignee could not claim the rights of a partner such as the right to inspect the books or the right to an accounting. The assignee of a partner's interest in a partnership would be entitled to receive the profits of the assigning partner as they accrue.[22]

REACHING THE INTEREST OF A PARTNER

At common law, an individual creditor of a partner could sue one partner, obtain judgment, and then levy upon the total assets of the partnership in order to obtain the sum due. That action would force the other partners to pay the judgment to save the business, or result in the liquidation of the firm. Since the interest of one partner could not be determined without the liquidation of the interest of all, the business was often destroyed.

The drafters of the Act made an effort to change the common law to prevent this result in modern cases. This is the reason for the U.P.A. rule that specific partnership property is beyond the direct reach of attaching creditors of one partner.[23] In short, the holdings of the other partners in the firm cannot be disturbed simply because one of the partners is in financial difficulty. Therefore, under the Act, an attaching creditor must look to the "interest" of the debtor, and the method provided is by use of the "charging order."

Charging Order

A judgment creditor of a partner has the right to apply to a court of proper jurisdiction for a "charging order" against the interest in the partnership of the judgment debtor. The act permits the court to appoint a "receiver," who will receive the interest of the debtor as it comes due in the partnership. The receiver in turn pays the amount to the creditor, retaining a portion for a fee. In this way, the creditor is paid without disturbing the rights of the other partners.

The law permits the other partners to pay off the debt of the debtor partner and avoid interference from the court.[24] Partnership funds may be used for that purpose as long as all of the partners agree—and so long as the payment does not render the firm insolvent.[25]

---

[21] U.P.A., Section 25(*b*).

[22] U.P.A., Section 27.

[23] U.P.A., Section 25.

[24] U.P.A., Section 28(2)(*a*).

[25] U.P.A., Section 28(2)(*b*).

If the interest of a partner is "charged," that partner would be entitled to protection under law such as the right to a homestead exemption[26] or rights that one might have under the minimum deductions of the Federal Garnishment Law.[27]

RATIFICATION[28]

As stated, the laws of agency govern, and the partnership may ratify an unauthorized act of a partner provided that the partner, at the time of committing the act, held out as being a partner. The ratification would relate back and cure the lack of authority.

IMPLIED POWERS

Each partner has implied powers to do all acts reasonably necessary to advance the purposes of the partnership. However, third parties should be careful in attempting to interpret the implied powers of a partner. An act committed outside of apparent authority may well be outside of implied powers and the third party could be injured because the other partners would not be bound.

Some partnerships engage in buying and selling as part of their routine operation. Here, in the absence of notice to the contrary, each partner has implied power to buy and sell the merchandise of the partnership. Each partner would thus have implied power to borrow money, sign notes to carry on the purposes of the partnership, and the acts would bind the others.

However, in manufacturing partnerships where buying and selling is not a part of the routine operation of the business, the powers to borrow money or to sell are not implied. Third parties dealing with nonselling partnerships deal at their own risk. Inquiry should be made by the third party to determine the exact authority of the partner with whom they are dealing.

CRIMES

Generally a partnership cannot be held liable for the criminal acts of one partner. An exception would be if the partnership collectively participated in the criminal act. Crimes generally involve *intention,* and intention can only be manifested by a human being. A partnership, not being a legal entity, could never form intention to commit a crime. But the partners could conspire to fix prices, for example, and be held collectively for the crime.

---

[26] U.P.A., Section 28(3).

[27] See Chapter 36.

[28] Subsequent approval of an act unauthorized when done.

A NEW PARTNER

If an existing partnership takes in a new partner, he or she is liable for all of the debts of the partnership incurred before admission, just as though that person had been a partner from the beginning. On the surface, this appears unjust, but the liability can only be satisfied out of partnership property.[29] This means that if X becomes a member of an existing partnership and contributes $5,000 in capital, X may immediately have the $5,000 subjected to the payment of outstanding obligations of the partnership. However, X would not be personally liable beyond $5,000 for debts incurred prior to admission to the partnership. It would rapidly become impossible to separate capital contributions of new partners from those of partners who existed prior to admission, and the rule was developed for this reason. See Figure 49–1.

FIGURE 49–1

Note: The contribution of D is immediately subject to X debts. D is also liable for Y debts.

When a firm takes in a new partner, this causes a dissolution of the business within the meaning of that term. However, in practice a new partner seldom creates the problems that are encountered when one partner dies, files bankruptcy, or leaves the firm.

REVIEW QUESTIONS

1. You and your partner are considering taking in a third partner. What would be one factor that you would consider?
2. Why does the law treat partners as legal equals?
3. Why are partners normally not paid wages?
4. Name a crime that a partnership might commit.
5. True or False. Courts will honor all petitions for a partnership accounting.
6. Give an example of how a court may imply a partnership power.
7. Why does the law hold *all* partners liable in contract? Is this a "policy" matter?
8. Name a time when a partner might want to force an accounting.
9. Discuss the impact of computers upon the "right to inspect" the firm "books."
10. How would you want "indemnification" handled in your firm?

---

[29] U.P.A., Section 41(7).

Words and Phrases

Write out briefly what they mean to you.
1. Records.
2. Sharing profits.
3. Wages.
4. Interest.
5. Implied powers.

Coverage:	A study of dissolution, winding up, and termination.
What to Look for:	Ways in which a firm can continue after dissolution occurs.
Application:	Apply this chapter to what you know about a buy-and-sell agreement.
Note:	Dissolution does not end a partnership.

50 End of the Partnership Road

Dissolution of a partnership can be caused by insanity, or bankruptcy of a partner; imprisonment of a partner who was active in the firm; the refusal of a partner to carry out his or her share of the agreement; and many other reasons. But "dissolution" in the legal sense is not synonymous with "termination."

DISSOLUTION

Dissolution is ". . . the change in the relation of the partners caused by any partner ceasing to be associated in the carrying on as distinguished from the winding up of the business."[1] Once dissolution occurs, the Act spells out the steps that must be taken. First, the affairs of the partnership must be "wound up," including the performance of existing contracts, the avoidance of new contracts, and the ultimate liquidation of all assets of the firm. Next, the debts must be paid, and if enough funds are not available, the partners must contribute the amount needed from their individual assets. Finally, funds remaining, if any, are distributed to the partners as provided by law. Therefore, when "dissolution" occurs, the partnership is not "dissolved" but it continues until the winding up is completed and capital is returned.[2] Examine Figure 50-1.

---

[1] U.P.A., Section 29.

[2] U.P.A., Section 30.

FIGURE 50–1
The Three Steps to "The End of the Partnership Road"

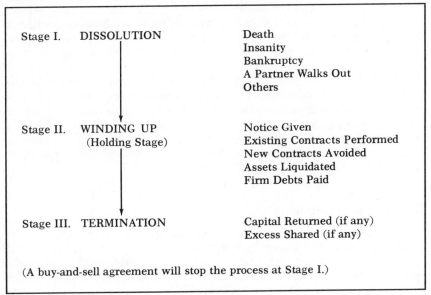

Stage I.   DISSOLUTION

- Death
- Insanity
- Bankruptcy
- A Partner Walks Out
- Others

Stage II.   WINDING UP
            (Holding Stage)

- Notice Given
- Existing Contracts Performed
- New Contracts Avoided
- Assets Liquidated
- Firm Debts Paid

Stage III.   TERMINATION

- Capital Returned (if any)
- Excess Shared (if any)

(A buy-and-sell agreement will stop the process at Stage I.)

Specific Examples of Dissolution

Many partnership agreements provide for a definite term and upon the expiration of the specified time, the partnership would be dissolved. Or a partnership may have been formed originally to complete a specified undertaking. The partnership would be dissolved upon the completion of the undertaking. Any partner may dissolve the partnership at will, provided that no definite term or particular undertaking is involved. However, all partners must be in agreement, and this cannot be done if a partner has assigned his or her interest in the partnership. Further, it cannot be done if a charging order has been placed against the partnership.

The mutual dissolving of a partnership may come about before or after a specified term or before or after a particular undertaking is completed. If a partner is removed from the business under "bona fide" power existing in the partnership, this will also dissolve the partnership. The Act provides that one partner can dissolve the partnership by withdrawing where dissolution is not permitted otherwise. In other words, a partner has the *power* to dissolve a partnership by walking out, although, strictly speaking, one may not have the *right* to do so.

Illegality that intervenes in the operation of a partnership would dissolve it. For example, if partners were involved in an undertaking which becomes prohibited by act of a legislature, dissolution follows.

Under certain circumstances, a court may decree a dissolution. This could happen where a partner has been declared of unsound mind by proper proceedings; where a partner otherwise becomes incapable of carrying out a part of the partnership; where the conduct of a partner has been such as to prejudice the carrying on of the business; where a partner's conduct with the other partners is such that it is not practical to carry on the business; and where it is shown that further operation of the partnership will cause a loss.

The assignee of a partner's interest or a judgment creditor who has placed a charging order against a partner's interest, may apply to a court to decree dissolution where the partnership existed initially for a specified term or a particular undertaking. The assignee or judgment creditor may petition a court for dissolution at any time if at the time the interest was assigned, or when the charging order was issued, the partnership existed at will.[3]

Notice of Dissolution

After dissolution, a partner may bind the firm by any transaction that would bind it if dissolution had not taken place, *if* the third party had extended credit to the partnership prior to dissolution and has no notice or knowledge of dissolution.[4] If the third party had not extended credit prior to dissolution but knew the partnership existed, the same result would follow if that person did not receive notice.

It is important for a withdrawing partner to make certain that notice is given to creditors of the partnership to avoid continuing partnership liability on his or her part. This notice is also important to keep a withdrawing partner from binding the others by acts with third parties who do not know that that person has withdrawn. Notice of dissolution should be given to those who extended credit to the firm prior to dissolution, and this notice should be given by direct means such as a letter or phone call. General notice to the public can be given by a legal notice published in a newspaper of general circulation in the area in which the partnership business had been carried on.

CONTINUING THE BUSINESS

If proper steps are taken, a partnership may be continued by surviving partners, even in the absence of a buy-and-sell agreement. Legal advice should be sought if this is desired.

Creditors of the original partnership remain creditors of the continuing partnership. Third parties may find themselves in a difficult position as a result of the dissolution of the firm, and for this reason the law protects the creditors of the partnership. This is true regardless of the manner in which dissolution occurs.

---

[3] U.P.A., Section 32(2)(*b*).

[4] U.P.A., Section 35(1)(*b*).

WINDING UP

Any partner who has not wrongfully dissolved a partnership has the right to wind up its affairs. The legal representative of the last surviving partner has the same right, assuming the last survivor was not bankrupt. Any partner, legal representative, or assignee may obtain the power of winding up by court decree, assuming that proper cause is shown for it.

Upon winding up, partnership property must be applied to the liabilities of the firm. Surplus is paid to the partners. Where a partner wrongfully causes dissolution, the surviving partners may be entitled to damages if any resulted from the breach of the agreement. In cases where the dissolution is caused by a violation of the agreement, the remaining partners may continue the business and process the partnership property for this purpose. However, they must post bond approved by a court or pay to the partner who caused the dissolution, a sum of money equal to that person's interest minus damages the continuing parties may be entitled to.

The continuing parties must indemnify the other partner against present and future liability. Under these circumstances, a problem might arise in determining the dollar value of the partner's share in the partnership. The Act provides that in determining the value of the partner's interest, the value of the goodwill shall not be considered.[5] The provision seems fair in that the person who wrongfully causes the dissolution of the partnership, which is then continued by the others, would be punished to this extent.

Fraud or Misrepresentation. Fraud or misrepresentation of a partner would be reason for the other partners to ask that the partnership be wound up. The innocent partners would have a lien on any surplus of partnership property to secure any sum paid for the purchase of an interest in the partnership or for capital or advances contributed to the partnership.

Rights of the Retiring or Estate of Deceased

When any partner leaves the partnership or dies, provision is made for termination of the interest in the partnership. The payment is made as it is determined. That person's liability would continue and present creditors would still have the right to look to his or her personal estate if necessary for satisfaction of obligations due them. A retiring partner would be entitled to interest upon the share of the partnership if he or she chooses not to withdraw it.[6]

TERMINATION

The assets of a partnership are (1) partnership property and (2) contributions that any partner may be called upon to make in order to pay liabilities. This provision in the Act creates unlimited liability.

---

[5] U.P.A., Section 38(2)(*c*)(II).

[6] U.P.A., Section 42.

Order of Payment. The liabilities of the partnership shall be paid in the following order: (1) those owing to creditors other than partners; (2) those owing to partners other than for capital and profits; (3) those owing to partners in respect of capital; and (4) those owing to partners in respect of profits.[7]

If a partner has become bankrupt or is insolvent, the claims are ranked as follows: (1) those owing to separate creditors; (2) those owing to partnership creditors; and (3) those owing to partners by way of contribution. The remaining partners must pay the bankrupt or insolvent partner's share of liabilities out of their personal funds. Where individual creditors take the assets of the insolvent partner, the contributing partners may find themselves without a means of recovery.

Sample Distribution. For many years, A, B, and C operated a partnership. On December 31 of the previous year, the partnership business showed a profit of $3,000, and the sum was distributed to the partners equally since they had no agreement for sharing of profits and losses.

In June of the following year, A died and B and C decided not to continue the partnership. There was no buy-and-sell agreement and no life insurance on the lives of each other.

For purposes of simplicity, the estate of A will be referred to as "A" below. After careful liquidation of all partnership property, which required two months, the assets came to $20,000. The partnership creditors were owed $30,000. Firm creditors rank first in the order of distribution and they are entitled to be paid first—and will be paid so long as any of the partners remain solvent.

The individual assets of the three partners at the time were as follows:

> A.......................... $65,000
> B.......................... $10,000
> C.......................... $ 3,000

Under the law of distribution, individual creditors have a right to look to individual assets before partnership creditors. The individual obligations of the three partners were as follows:

> A.......................... $10,000
> B.......................... $ 5,000
> C.......................... $ 9,000

Partner C is insolvent because the amount of C's personal assets will not pay off the individual creditors.

The original capital contributions were as follows:

> A.......................... $20,000
> B.......................... $20,000
> C.......................... $10,000

for a total of $50,000. Since the three partners started with $50,000 and ended up owing $10,000 to partnership creditors, there was a total loss

---

[7] U.P.A., Section 40(*b*).

of $60,000. The loss must be shared equally between the partners in the sum of $20,000 each.

A's individual creditors will be entitled to $10,000, leaving A with $55,000 in assets. B's individual creditors will be paid in full, leaving $5,000 in B's assets. C's individual creditors will share the $3,000 on a 1 to 3 ratio, which leaves C still owing them $6,000. In short C is literally out of business and can pay nothing on the partnership debt.

Since A contributed $20,000 initially, A is entitled to be repaid nothing, and this makes A's share of the loss $20,000. B, who contributed $20,000 initially, is also even. C is legally obligated to pay $10,000 since C's initial capital contribution was $10,000, but this cannot be paid because of the insolvency. If it were possible for C to make the payment, the $10,000 would be paid to the partnership creditors. However, C is insolvent and cannot pay, so A and B must pick up the tab and must do so equally—if they are financially able to do so.

In the example, A would pay $5,000 above the initial $20,000 and B would also pay $5,000 (the total of individual assets). The partnership creditors would receive the $10,000. A and B each would have the right to sue C for $5,000. If the payments are eventually realized by them, each partner will have lost $20,000 in the partnership.

Because of the unlimited liability encountered in a general partnership, it is helpful to know that most of our states provide a means by which this liability can be limited.

LIMITED PARTNERSHIP

A limited partnership is composed of one or more limited partners and one or more general partners. The liability of the limited partner is restricted to the amount of contribution to the capital of the partnership. There is no limit upon the liability of the general partners as illustrated above.

Such an agreement is in "derogation of common law"[8]—and, therefore, there must be statutory authority for the creation of such a partnership. Most states have adopted the Uniform Limited Partnership Act along with the Uniform Partnership Act. The Limited Partnership Act is similar to those statutes that provide for incorporation of a business.

To gain limited liability, it is necessary for the limited partner to give notice that personal assets will not stand behind the partnership obligations. This is done by filing in the county in which the partnership is to do business, a notorized certificate that contains the necessary information. The information includes the name of the limited partner, the purpose of the business, the amount of capital that person is contributing, and other information such as the location of the business.

As of the time of the recording, third parties have "constructive notice" of the limit of liability of the limited partner and they cannot complain later that they did not in fact know. One with limited liability in a partnership cannot take active part in the firm since the limited liability

---

[8] In all other respects a limited partnership is the same as a general partnership.

might prompt carelessness. Unnecessary risks by the one with limited liability could result in unlimited liability on the part of the others. The law does not contemplate such a result.

Therefore, in exchange for limited liability, the limited partner gives up the right to have his or her name used in the business, and cannot take part in the operation of the partnership. If these provisions are violated, the limited partner will lose the status as a limited partner and will be held liable as a general partner. However, it has been held that a limited partner can *advise* the unlimited partner in time of crisis without losing the unlimited status. See *Trans-Am Builders, Inc.*, v. *Woods Mill, Ltd*, 210 S.E.2D 866 (1975).

Any business that can be carried on by a partnership can be carried on by a limited partnership. One with a large personal estate who desires to invest in an existing partnership should consider doing so under the Limited Liability Act.

REVIEW QUESTIONS

1. True or False. The Uniform Partnership Act, being a state statute, replaces the rules of the law merchant "in toto."
2. Name one reason why an understanding of basic partnership law is important to the business executive.
3. Name one reason why a buy-and-sell agreement should be considered by partners.
4. True or False. The U.P.A. treats partners as being equals unless they agree otherwise.
5. Define "operating loss" in a partnership.
6. Dissolution problem:

   A, B, and C operated a partnership for ten years. They had agreed to create a buy-and-sell agreement funded with life insurance, but failed to have the necessary papers prepared. A died, causing a dissolution of the firm.

   The heirs of A steadfastly refused to discuss continuation of the business. Instead, they demanded that they be paid the share of A in the business.

   As a result, all assets of the firm were reduced to cash, bringing a total of $101,000. The debts of the firm, plus capital contributions, were as follows:

1.	Due firm creditors	$60,000.00
2.	Due C, who had made a loan to the firm......	10,000.00
3.	Capital contributions:	

A...	$10,000.00
B...	6,000.00
C...	3,000.00

   Apply the "order of payment" as set out in the Act, and match the amounts to the questions.

1.	3,000
2.	1,000
3.	14,000
4.	12,000
5.	6,000
6.	4,000

   1. What total sum will go to the estate of A? _____
   2. What part of the sum in question 1 is in respect to profits? _____
   3. How much will be paid to B? _____
   4. How much will be paid to C? _____

7.   9,000
8.   10,000
9.   13,000
10. 17,000

5. What was the total sum divided as profits?

    _____

6. If the total assets had been $90,000, what would the profits have been? _____

Words and Phrases

Write out briefly what they mean to you.
1. Limited liability.
2. Order of payment.
3. Continuing partner.
4. Withdrawing partner.
5. Dissolution.

Coverage:	A brief history of the corporation; comparison with other forms of business and preliminary characteristics.
What to Look for:	The basic characteristics of this form of business.
Application:	Choose a major business with which you are familiar and apply the basic characteristics to it.
Note:	Get in mind at the outset that a corporation is a "fiction"—that is, it only exists because of law.

51 Introduction to the Corporation

The predominant form of business in the United States today is the corporation. Through its use the greatest proportion of goods and services provided to the American public are created, distributed, and ultimately sold to the buying public. Many American corporations are true giants, some having annual budgets that exceed those of the smaller states. Many are international in scope of operation, while others are operated on a purely local basis.

A recent issue of the *Statistical Abstract of the United States*, published by the U.S. government, discloses that over 1,400,000 corporation income tax returns are being filed yearly. Of this figure, over 27,000 are engaged in agriculture, forestry, and fisheries; over 13,000 in mining; over 113,000 in construction; over 185,000 in manufacturing; and the greatest number, over 440,000, are engaged in wholesale and retail trade. The total number of corporations is impressive, especially so when one realizes that the average number per state exceeds 28,000 firms.

In the *Dartmouth College* v. *Woodward* case,[1] the corporation was defined as ". . . an artificial person or legal entity created by or under the authority of the laws of the state or union." It should be recognized at

---

[1] Wheat 518, 4L.Ed. 629.

the outset that the corporation is a *fiction* and only exists in the minds of those that think about it—an accurate concept, but one that is difficult to accept at first. This concept arose as the corporation evolved historically.

HISTORICALLY

The idea of conducting business through the use of a fictitious being or entity was recognized quite early. The early English corporations were created by the grant of a charter from the king or queen or Parliament. These early corporations, being created by government, operated under sanction and the will of that government. The same is true today, and charters are created and issued by each state, through the proper official, usually the Secretary of State.

A charter is an instrument emanating from the sovereign power in the nature of a grant assuring certain rights or powers. A charter is not the same as a constitution since a constitution is an instrument by which a state is created. After the state is in being, it can issue charters which create corporations.

In ancient precorporation centuries, one accumulated "wealth" by exercising physical control over tangible items of goods and livestock. The "wealthier" one became, the more immobile that person became because increased holdings of goods and livestock burdened one to a standstill. So as a practical matter, high levels of wealth were limited for practical reasons. One who needed grain, traded cattle; if one needed linen, that person traded some other commodity—a system of "barter" or exchange.

As the centuries passed, and after suitable quantities of precious metals became available, the barter system gave way to a monetary or coin system of exchange. When this happened, wealth could be accumulated because the metal could be stored, exchanged, and used to purchase goods and services.

It was at this point in history that the search for a safer way of conducting business began, and the reason was simple. If A had accumulated 1,000 gold coins, A might be quite willing to risk 100 of them in a new business venture. And yet A would hesitate if the form of business contemplated might result in unlimited liability with the subsequent loss of the 900 coins.

One of the early attempts at placing a limit upon liability was through the use of a contract between the business partners. In the contract, A would agree that the limit of liability upon B would be 100 gold coins and B would agree to the same thing for A. Between A and B, the agreement was effective and the liability of each was limited. However, if during the course of business A and B caused injury or contract loss to C, the agreement was not effective because C was not a party to the contract. If C sued A and B and obtained a judgment of 2,000 gold coins, C would enforce the judgment against A and B or either, and their contract was useless. The attempt to limit liability by contract created a "joint-stock company." While it found widespread use, it contained the weakness mentioned.

Another early attempt at limiting liability was by use of a "trust." A and B would place their business assets in the hands of C, who operated the business. If loss occurred, third parties were limited in recovery to the assets held by C. The weakness of the trust was that A and B lost their right to manage and control the business. As it turned out, the corporate fiction provided the answer to the search that started many centuries ago.

At the time of American independence, business was developing rapidly in the United States. Great opportunities existed but the risks were high, and the corporate device was used as a means of limiting liability. In 1811, New York passed the first general corporation-for-profit statute, making the formation of corporations statutory. Other states followed with similar laws. In those years it was natural for the courts as well as creditors to be suspicious of those who transacted business by means of a fiction. They were giving the world notice that they did not intend to subject their personal wealth to the hazards of unlimited liability. Today this thought rarely enters the minds of those who deal with corporations, and all states have corporation-for-profit statutes — some being more liberal than others.

It was not until 1855 that England — if not the mother of the corporation at least the mother of the American colonies — by act of Parliament, reduced their common-law principles of corporations to statutory form. This act was called the Limited Liability Act and today in Great Britain and Canada the use of the word "Limited" or the abbreviation "Ltd." following a business name tells one that the business is a corporation.

COMPARISON

A brief comparison of the main features of a corporation for profit with other forms of business provides a helpful basis from which to take a further look at the concept.

Proprietorship

Many businesses in the United States are operated by means of the simplest form — the one person, unincorporated proprietorship. In these businesses the owner will hire employees to assist in the conduct of the business. In some of them, the owner does not take an active part in the business. In either situation, the liability of the owner runs directly to the customers and others doing business with the proprietorship.

The nature and extent of the legal liability of the owner is determined by general principles of contract, tort and agency law. The sole proprietorship is totally removed from the corporation as far as comparison is concerned.

Partnership

A partnership is created by agreement of the partners, while a corporation is created by an act of a state. A partnership is not considered to be a legal entity with an existence separate from its members. A corporation is a legal entity and is treated as a separate legal person. Any number of causes such as death or bankruptcy will dissolve a partnership, while the life of a corporation can be perpetual.

In the absence of a limited partnership, partners have unlimited liability. The liability of stockholders in a corporation is limited to any unpaid portion of initial stock subscriptions. A share of ownership in a partnership cannot be transferred without dissolving the firm, while ownership in a corporation is freely transferable in the absence of some restriction upon transfer.

Each partner is an agent of the partners, while stockholders are not agents of their corporations. Capital is raised in a corporation by a sale of securities, while in a partnership it must come from capital contributions, loans from the partners, or from a subsequent increase in capital contributions.

Limited Partnership

Partnerships in which the liability of one or more partners is limited was not known at common law. For this reason, a statute permitting limited liability is required before one can become a limited partner. A limited partner is in much the same position as a stockholder in a corporation. Yet that person loses the right to take part in the management and must give up the right to use his or her name in the partnership. Therefore, while one enjoys limited liability, one loses other rights which are enjoyed by the stockholder.

Civic Association

Civic associations are voluntary organizations formed for charitable or recreational purposes and are usually nonprofit organizations. Only those members who actually enter into contracts on behalf of the association incur liability. The remaining members of the association would not be liable unless they voluntarily agreed to be.

Joint-Stock Company

This form of business had many characteristics of a corporation for profit, but its operation was awkward and is not in use in the United States today. As mentioned, it was an attempt to use the contract to limit liability. It frequently failed in practice because liability to third parties could not be disposed of by a contract between two or more persons independent of the third person.

Business Trust

A business trust is a way of doing business in which assets of a business are transferred to a trustee who manages the business for the benefit of the beneficial owners. In some states it is called a "Massachusetts Business Trust" because of the wide use of it in that state. The "settlor" creates the trust by conveying assets to the trustee. Those who receive the benefit of the trust are called the beneficiary or "cestui que trust" and are frequently the settlors. See Figure 51–1.

FIGURE 51–1

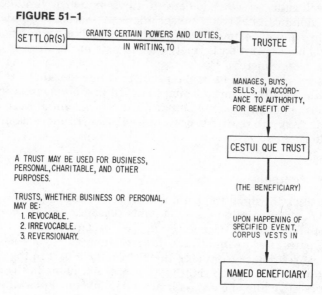

The ownership in the trust is evidenced by certificates which are given to the settlors by the trustee. This form of business requires a written contract between the settlors and the trustee. The trustee has a seal and is governed by bylaws. The beneficiaries are able to avoid liability because they do not own the business—the trustee does. Some states refuse to recognize the business trust as a way of doing business. Others say that if the certificate holders exercise control in the trust, it is a partnership. While a business trust has centralized management and limited liability, the uncertain status of the certificate holders makes it a less desirable form of transacting business than the corporation.

FURTHER CHARACTERISTICS OF A CORPORATION

The principal feature of a corporation for profit is that it has a legal existence separate from those who own it. It is a legal "person," a resident of the state that creates it and of the state in which it operates. Therefore, it is subject to taxation and amenable to service of process. It is a "person" entitled to various "guarantees" of the U.S. Constitution.

However, corporations are not entitled to the "privileges and immunities" guarantee of Article IV, Section 2, U.S. Constitution, which states:

> The Citizens of each State shall be entitled to all Privileges and Immunities of Citizens in the several States.

Amendment XIV, 1, provides:

> All persons born or naturalized in the United States, and subject to the jurisdiction thereof, are citizens of the United States and of the State wherein they reside. No State shall make or enforce any law which shall abridge the privileges or immunities of citizens of the United States; nor shall any State deprive any person of life, liberty, or property, without due process of law; nor deny to any person within its jurisdiction the equal protection of the laws.

A close reading of the two provisions discloses that a corporation cannot be a citizen because it was not "born or naturalized." It cannot vote, for example, and would be without means to do so. Since it is not a "citizen," it is not entitled to the privileges and immunities of citizens of other states. For example, if the speeding fine in New York is $100, a resident of Pennsylvania arrested there cannot be charged more than that sum for speeding. Since corporations do not have the protection of this portion of the Constitution, they are often taxed more out of their state of incorporation than domestic corporations. An example of this can be observed on the back of tractor trailers.

```
This Vehicle Pays
    $4,975.33
Road Taxes Each Year
```

Also it has been held that a corporation does not have 5th Amendment protections where disclosure of what corporate documents contain is involved.

A corporation can sue and be sued, own and convey real estate, enter into contracts, and do any other act of a natural person. But being a fiction, it must act through agents since it has no way to operate otherwise.

The stockholders own the corporation but they do not have title to its assets because title is in the corporation. For this reason stockholders do not incur personal liability for losses caused by the corporation since third persons must look to it and its assets for recovery. Any recovery would normally be limited to corporate assets, and the individual assets of the stockholders would not be involved.

The stockholders elect those who run the corporation, and therefore the corporation has centralized management. Other forms of business have some of these characteristics, but no other one has all of them. Turning from characteristics, it is helpful to see how corporations may be classified.

CLASSIFICATION OF CORPORATIONS

Corporations are classified according to the activities they pursue and the purposes of their existence. A fuller understanding can follow once one becomes aware of the differences. For example, the motorist is often unaware of the meaning of the road sign that announces "City Limits, Anytown, Unincorporated." A look will be taken first at historical classifications, followed by several modern classifications.

At common law, corporations were classified as "ecclesiastical" or "lay" corporations.

Ecclesiastical Corporations

In English law an ecclesiastical corporation was one organized for spiritual purposes or for administering property held for religious use. Examples included bishops and their services and other dignitaries of the church and, in older times, abbeys and monasteries.

Lay Corporations

Corporations composed of laypersons, created for secular or business purposes, were called lay corporations. They would be called "corporations for profit" today. The distinction between ecclesiastical and lay corporations is not recognized today in American law. While corporations exist for purposes of owning and administering real and personal property for religious use, they are lay corporations in the sense of the English law.[2] Another common-law classification was that of "eleemosynary" as contrasted to "civil" corporations.

Eleemosynary Corporation

An eleemosynary corporation was one created for the distribution of alms or species of relief bestowed upon the poor. Also it was one for the distribution of charities or for purposes of charity in its widest sense, including hospitals and asylums.

Civil Corporation

A civil corporation was one organized for purposes of transacting business for the profit or advantage of its members,[3] and included corporations which related to "temporal police." Examples include the incorporation of cities and companies organized for the advancement of commerce, agriculture, colleges, and universities. Religious corporations are those whose establishment relates only to religion.[4]

---

[2] *Robertson* v. *Bullions*, 11. N.Y. 243.

[3] *Dartmouth College* case.

[4] Civ. Code La. Art. 431.

One further historical classification was that of a "sole" corporation as compared to an "aggregate" corporation—a classification still in use today.

Sole and Aggregate

A sole corporation is one consisting of one person only and an English example was the "Bishop Sole." The equivalent today would be a corporation that has only one stockholder. An aggregate corporation has a number of stockholders and is the most common type found today. Some modern classifications follow.

Domestic–Foreign

A domestic corporation is one created and organized under the laws of a given state. That is, it is domestic to that state but it would be foreign to all other states. Therefore, a foreign corporation is one that has been created by the laws of one state but which is operating in another. As indicated previously, each state has the power to place burdens upon corporations who are foreign to their state provided that they are "doing business" in the other state. The question of whether a corporation is or is not doing business in another state is directly related to the degree of activity in the other state. Most state courts require that a foreign corporation transact more than "casual business" in a state before it will be held to be doing business in that state. This determination can be of importance where one attempts to sue an out-of-state corporation.

In addition, if a corporation does business in another state, it may find its personal property being assessed for tax purposes in that state and that it must pay other state taxes such as a business and occupation or "privilege" tax.

Profit–Nonprofit

A corporation for profit is one formed with the aim of an eventual return coming to the stockholders in the form of dividends and other distributions of profits. Frequently a corporation for profit does not make a profit—but this does not make it a nonprofit corporation. A nonprofit corporation is one formed with the express purpose of *not* engaging in business activity for the purpose of a return on the dollar invested. Some examples include flying clubs, racing clubs, rifle ranges, and other activities in which there could be a high risk potential. The corporate entity safeguards the members from the liability that might flow to them as individuals in a partnership. The provisions for the formation of a nonprofit corporation are similar to those for profit, but in most instances, stock is not issued to the members. In some states, it takes more incorporators to form a nonprofit corporation than it does to form a corporation for profit. Many charitable organizations are nonprofit corporations.

Public–Private

A public corporation is one created to act as an agency in the adminis-tration of civil government, generally within a described territory. They are usually invested with local powers of legislation and examples in-clude counties, cities, towns, or school districts. They are also sometimes called "political corporations."[5] Private corporations are those founded by and composed of private persons for private purposes. The public corporation is organized for governmental purposes, the private corpora-tion is not. Another distinction is that the former are not voluntary as-sociations and the latter are. There is no contractual relationship between the government and the public corporation or between the individuals who compose it.[6]

In stock market language, private corporations are said to "go public" when their stock is offered on the exchanges. Nevertheless, they are still "private" as the term is used here.

Close–Open

A corporation in which the directors and officers have the power to fill vacancies in their own membership without the stockholders having any choice, is a close corporation. A corporation in which all the members have a vote in the election of directors and officers is an open corporation.

Parent–Subsidiary

The parent-subsidiary classification arises in a "holding company" situation. A holding company is a corporation created for the purpose of owning and holding shares of stock in other corporations. The share-holders of the subsidiary receive shares in the parent corporation in exchange for their shares of stock.

A court defined a holding company as

> A super corporation which owns or at least controls such a dominant interest in one or more other corporations that it is enabled to dictate their policies through voting power; a corporation organized to hold the stock of other corporations; any company, incorporated or unincorporated, which is in a position to control or materially influence the management of one or more other companies by virtue, in part at least, of its ownership or se-curities in the other company or companies.[7]

Dejure–Defacto

If a corporation is formed in full compliance with the corporation-for-profits statute, it is a "dejure" or legally correct corporation. But as frequently happens, corporations are sometimes created with some

---

[5] *Goodwin* v. *East Hartford,* 70 Conn. 18, 38 A. 876 (1897).
[6] *Ibid.*
[7] *Cities Service* v. *Koeneke,* 137 Kan. 7, 20 P.2d. 460.

defect occurring in the incorporation. A frequent oversight is the failure to record the charter within the time period prescribed by law. Does such a defect render the corporation subject to attack and place the stockholders in jeopardy of losing the corporate protection?

As a matter of policy, the defacto principle was created to cover the situation. If (1) there is a law or charter authorizing such a corporation, (2) an attempt in good faith is made to comply with law authorizing its incorporation, (3) an unintentional omission of some essential requirements of the law or charter is made, and (4) the corporation in good faith functions under the law or charter, the corporation will be held to be a defacto corporation and the stockholders maintain their corporate protection.[8] To say it another way, the law states that if the above test is met, the corporation is *substantially* a valid corporation and entitled to the protection extended to the dejure corporation.

If a corporation is formed in a negligent manner, it may be less than a defacto organization and the stockholders will be treated as partners.

Regular and Conglomerate

In recent years a new term has gained prominence in the corporate world: "conglomerate." There is some question whether it is in fact a new corporate form—or whether it is simply a new corporate term. But as it is spoken of currently, it is a corporation that has characteristics not observed in the "normal" corporation. The chief characteristic is aggressive growth by acquisition of other corporations and businesses. Common manufacturing and distribution facilities are utilized, but management is not centralized. Profits are up due to acquisition and there is continuity of earnings. Some suggest that it is a mere holding company or parent-subsidiary organization in which one company holds controlling interest in the stock with voting rights in another, with each corporation maintaining a separate existence.

The conglomerate presents problems for the investor. For example, A Corporation, which is earning $2 million per year, acquires B Corporation, which is earning $1 million per year. If the profits of A Corporation jump to $2,750,000, are profits in A up $750,000—or are they down $250,000?

The conglomerate form creates internal problems, also. For example, will the corporation report by each division for accounting and tax purposes or as a unit? Further, antitrust implications are also indicated.

Merger Distinguished from Consolidation

Related to the conglomerate situation is the distinction between a "merger" and a "consolidation." In a merger, there is a combining of two corporations in which one survives. For example, X and Y Corporations merge and become Y Corporation. In a consolidation there is a

---

[8] *Richmond* v. *Town of Largo*, 155 Fla. 226, 19 So. 2d. 791, 793 (1944).

combining of corporations in such a manner that both lose their identities. For example, X and Y become Z Corporation. In a merger or consolidation, legal requirements must be met including stockholder approval, notice to creditors, approval of the state that granted the original charter, and in some instances, approval of the Department of Justice of the United States.

A Corporation Not Taxed as a Corporation

Under the Internal Revenue Service code, if a corporation has ten or less stockholders and has little investment-type income, it can probably qualify as a Subchapter S corporation and avoid income tax at the corporate level. The election to be so taxed does not cause a loss of other advantages of incorporation including limited liability. The election must be timely made and cannot be reversed within specified time periods. Where this choice is made, a new corporation classification results: the "Subchapter S" corporation as distinguished from a regular taxed corporation. Finally, a point of interest.

The Secretary of State of a medium size east coast state provided the author with the following statistics: since the state was organized in 1863, 100,000 corporations have been formed within the state. Of these, 26,000 are still active. The active corporations are broken down as follows: 16,000 are domestic corporations; 5,000 are foreign corporations; and 5,000 are nonprofit organizations. That state receives and processes between 8 and 15 applications for corporate charters each day.

REVIEW QUESTIONS

1. What similarities do you observe in the history of the partnership and the corporation?
2. You have been asked to justify the use of a fiction—the corporation—in the business setting. What reason would you argue in favor of it?
3. Why may states place extra burdens on foreign corporations?
4. Write down the name of a corporation that you know of. See how many of the classifications apply to it.
5. True or False. A nonprofit corporation is one that has a bad year and loses money.
6. Why is it difficult to limit liability by use of the contract?
7. Why is a corporation a "legal entity?"
8. Define a "limited partnership."
9. A settlor can be the beneficiary of the settlor's own trust. Why?
10. Why doesn't a corporation have all constitutional rights of an individual?

Words and Phrases

Write out briefly what they mean to you.
1. Defacto.
2. Holding company.
3. Fictitious person.
4. "The search for the corporation."
5. Conglomerate.

52 Converting to and Forming Corporations

CONVERTING BUSINESSES

When one business is converted to another, many basic factors must be taken into consideration. This is true whether a corporation is converted by merger, consolidation, or by acquisition as part of a conglomerate. It is also true when a proprietorship or partnership is converted to a corporation.

A Going Partnership Converts to a Corporation

Since partners face the hazards of unlimited liability, it is logical for them to become interested in gaining the protection offered by the corporation. This is especially so as the business grows and expands its operations—and obligations.

An important question at the outset is this: Do *all* of the partners understand what is being contemplated and do they all agree that the change should be made? If not, a successful conversion will be impossible. Next, what are the possible effects on license fees and taxation? For example, will license fees have to be paid that are not being paid now? What effect will there be on personal state and federal income tax, and income taxation of the business?

Next, will the partners be compatible with a form of business in which strict formalities must be observed? In many partnerships an informal pattern is followed in the operation of the firm. Major decisions are made by phone and few, if any, records are kept of what has been agreed upon. These practices can be deadly in the operation of a corporation since a corporation – just as a court – speaks only through its records. Therefore, proper records must be kept of all actions taken, including giving notice of meetings and keeping minutes and resolutions, which must be drafted, attested to, and maintained in a minute book. These and other formalities must be met and if they are not, the stockholders may find themselves liable as partners – the very thing they intended to avoid by the formation of the corporation.

The status of the contracts of the existing firm must be looked at carefully. Will the conversion result in the loss of any contractual right that exists in the name of the partnership? For example, if the partnership has a franchise, the franchisor may refuse to reexecute the contract in the corporate name. Also, trademarks, patents, or trade names registered in the name of the firm must be considered.

If the partnership has a security interest that has been perfected by the filing of a financing statement, refiling might cause a loss of priority in the collateral secured. Other factors to be considered include title to realty of the firm as well as insurance coverage. A change in business form would require retitling of realty as well as a change in the name on the insurance policies.

Procedure. After the decision to convert to a corporation has been made, someone who acts as a "promoter" must carry the conversion to a conclusion. Creditors of the old firm must be notified of the change to assure that they know that further dealings with the business will be on a corporate basis. The public should also be given notice by a legal or other ad published in a newspaper of general circulation in the area in which the firm does business. This is necessary in order to prevent partnership liability to creditors who later claim that they had no knowledge that the partnership is no longer in existence. The conversion is completed by making application for a corporate charter.

Converting a Corporation to a New Corporation

Once the stockholders of the firm are in agreement, it is relatively easy to convert one corporation to another. A proper notice is required of the meeting at which the motion to reorganize will be made. The minutes of the meeting must reflect favorable action on the motion and a resolution authorizing the change will be prepared. The resolution is forwarded to the proper official of the state of incorporation, accompanied by fees and a petition asking that the charter of the firm be amended. Notice must be given to existing creditors and the general public for the reasons mentioned previously.

Transfer of Ownership in a Corporation

Rather than convert a corporation, ownership may be transferred to others in whole or in part, and this is common in practice. In larger corporations the transfer will be complex, while in smaller corporations it may be routine. In either, the same requirements must be met. (Consideration may also be given to the sale of the assets of the corporation as opposed to the sale of the stock. Tax advantages may be gained by doing this and the decision should only be made after professional advice is sought.) The following case illustrates the problems that can arise in the sale of the stock of a corporation.

Case.   Zero Homes, Inc. was granted a charter in January, 1964. The incorporators, A, B, C, and D, subscribed to the common stock of the firm as follows: A, 1 share; B, 1 share; C, 25 shares; and D, 26 shares, for a total of 53 shares. They commenced business with $5,300, being $100 per share which was fully paid. The total authorized capital was set at $25,000. In February, 1964, A and B sold their shares to D, giving D 28 shares as compared with the 25 shares of C.

Early in 1975, X offered C and D $150,000 for the business. The buyer specifically wanted to maintain the corporate name as it stood, thus ruling out a sale of the assets of the firm. After advice was sought, they decided to proceed by sale of the stock. While the transfer seemed simple enough at the outset, problems arose. First, it was discovered that the charter had not been recorded within the six-month period required by the laws of the state of incorporation. The franchise that covered the home constructed by the firm had been issued in the name of one of the stockholders. Without the franchise the assets of the corporation were practically worthless. The stockholders had failed to keep minutes of the stockholders' and directors' meetings. All of the equipment of the corporation, including the real estate, trucks, and office equipment, was in the name of one of the stockholders.

In addition, two weeks pay was due the employees, the funds for social security were in the bank in a special account, and the corporation had accounts receivable and payable on the books. To complicate the matter, X wanted assurance that C and D would not reenter the same business in the same part of the state for a reasonable period of time. What appeared to be a simple transfer at the outset became a difficult situation for the lawyer who handled the transfer. (The sale was successfully accomplished in time.)

When the corporate form is chosen at the outset as the means of transacting business, the complexities that accompany the conversion of a business do not follow. It is just a matter of complying with the corporate statutes of the state, the other laws of the state, and of the federal government where applicable. However, even when the decision is made to incorporate at the outset, certain questions must still be answered.

SHOULD WE INCORPORATE?

While the corporate form is predominant, it is not exclusive. In many instances the proprietorship or partnership will serve well as a business "vehicle" and should be considered. In some cases a business may be conducted on a temporary basis as a partnership with conversion to follow later. Taxation and license fees are factors to be considered as well as size and type of the business. If the company is to operate locally, serving a small market, the decision might be one way. If it is to engage in interstate buying, selling, and distribution, the decision may be the other. Once the decision has been made to incorporate, a second question arises.

WHERE TO INCORPORATE?

Incentives, such as lower fees or gifts of land for building sites may be avilable in one state and not another. Corporate and other taxes – such as "value added" on goods produced – should be carefully weighed. If the main office must be close to the market, this should have weight. If not, the main office may be located in any state. At one time a factor in choosing the state of incorporation was that of avoiding service of process. If by incorporating in state A and transacting business in state B, suits could be avoided in state B, then there was an advantage (underhand of course) of incorporating in state A. The "long-arm statutes," which apply to corporations in or out of a state in which they do business, have rendered this factor moot. That is, this factor is no longer of business importance. Today over 40 states plus the District of Columbia permit a foreign corporation to be sued by service upon the Secretary of State or other designated official of the state where suit is brought. The states with such laws include:

Alabama	Louisiana	Oregon
Alaska	Maine	Pennsylvania
Arkansas	Maryland	Rhode Island
California	Massachusetts	South Carolina
Colorado	Minnesota	Tennessee
Connecticut	Mississippi	Texas
Delaware	Montana	Utah
District of Columbia	Nebraska	Vermont
Florida	Nevada	Virginia
Georgia	New Hampshire	Washington
Hawaii	New Mexico	West Virginia
Indiana	North Carolina	Wisconsin
Iowa	North Dakota	Wyoming
Kansas	Ohio	
Kentucky	Oklahoma	

The *Goldman* case illustrates the long-arm statutes in use.

Goldman v. Parkland of Dallas, Inc.[1] The law of North Carolina provides in part:

> Every foreign corporation shall be subject to suit in this State, by a resident of this State . . . , whether or not such foreign corporation is transacting or has transacted business in this State and whether or not it is engaged

---

[1] 277 N.C. 223, 176 S.E.2d 784 (1970).

exclusively in interstate or foreign commerce, on any cause of action arising as follows:

(1) Out of any contract made in this State or to be performed in this State.

The court stated:

> In the instant case the contract in question clearly met the requirement of "substantial connection" with North Carolina. It was made in this State. Plaintiff, under the terms of the contract, solicited business in thirty or more North Carolina cities and towns for the purpose of creating and expanding a market for appellant's dresses in North Carolina. He devoted a larger part of his time to promoting defendant's business in North Carolina than in any other state and did in fact sell a quantity of dresses manufactured by the defendant to customers within this State. The other essential requirements set out in *Byham* v. *National Cibo House Corp.,* supra, are also met; that is, the form of substituted service adopted by North Carolina gives reasonable assurance that the defendant would be given actual notice —in fact, there is no contention on the part of the defendant that it did not receive actual notice; by entering into a contract made in North Carolina and to be performed in part in North Carolina, the defendant availed itself of the privilege of conducting its business in this State thus invoking the benefits and protection of its laws, and clearly the North Carolina Legislature, by the express words of the statute authorizing such service on a foreign corporation when the contract was made in North Carolina, sought to give to its courts the power to assert jurisdiction over nonresident defendants to the full extent permitted by the due process requirement.
>
> The court's assumption of in personam jurisdiction over defendant in this action fully meets the requirements of due process under the decisions of the United States Supreme Court and the decisions of this Court. The judgment below is
> Affirmed.

After the decision is made on the place of incorporation, a final question arises: How is the corporation formed?

HOW TO INCORPORATE

The formation of a corporation requires action by one who promotes the incorporation—commonly called the "promoter." The promoter may be a lawyer or a law firm retained for that purpose, or may be one of the incorporators.

The promoter occupies a unique legal position. The promoter is not an agent because there is nothing to be an agent of, or a trustee for the same reason. He or she is, in short, a person entering into certain preincorporation contracts that are personally binding. Contracts for attorney fees, tax advice, printing expenses, and other costs, remain personal obligations even after the corporation comes into existence. At that time, the corporation may *adopt*—not ratify—the obligations of the promoter. In practice, the promoter assumes few actual risks.

After the preliminary groundwork has been laid, the first formal step is the creation of the application for a charter. The form shown in Figure 52-1 spells out the data that must be submitted to the state.

FIGURE 52–1
The Application

APPLICATION FOR A CERTIFICATE OF INCORPORATION

I. The undersigned agree to become a corporation by the name of (1) Brook Cable Co., Inc.

II. The principal Office of Place of Business of said corporation will be located at (1) No. __123 X__ Street, in the city (2) town, village of __Anytown__, in the county of __King__ and of __Typical State__. Its chief works will be located (3) in __the same town and elsewhere in the state__.

III. The objects for which this corporation is formed are as follows:

(They would be spelled out here in detail.)
(See certificate that follows.)

IV. The amount of the total authorized capital stock of said corporation shall be __$20,000.00__ Dollars, which shall be divided into __2,000__ shares of the par value of __$10.00__ Dollars each.

The amount of capital stock with which it will commence business is __$10,000.00__ Dollars being __1,000__ shares at __$10.00__ Dollars.

V. Name (5) and P. O. Address (6) – Write plainly, typewrite if possible; – the full names and addresses, including street and street numbers, if any, and the city, town or village, of the incorporators, and if a stock corporation, the number of shares subscribed by each. (See Certificate.)

VI. The existence of this corporation is to be perpetual.

WE, THE UNDERSIGNED, for the purpose of forming a corporation under the laws of Typical State do make and file this Agreement; and we have accordingly hereunto set our respective hands this __1st__ day of __January__, 1976.

s/s Edward Johnson
s/s Fred Wright
s/s Joseph Newhouse

CERTIFICATES

__Typical State__ County of __King__, to wit:

I, __John Eagle__, A Notary Public in and for the County and State aforesaid, hereby certify that Edward Johnson, Fred Wright, Joseph Newhouse, whose names are signed to the foregoing agreement bearing date of the __1st__ day of __January__, 1976, this day personally appeared before me in my said county and severally acknowledged their signatures to the same.

Given under my hand an official seal this __1st__ day of __January__, 1976.

(SEAL) _____ s/s John Eagle _____
                                         Notary Public

My commission expires on the __21st__ day of __February__ 1979.

Granting of Charter

If the official of the state of application (usually the secretary of state) approves the application – and if the proper fees are paid – the charter is granted. The corporate life begins as of the date of the charter. Figure 52–2 shows the charter granted to the TV Cable Company.

Charter Mailed

After the charter is granted, it is mailed to the promoter. At this time a unique situation exists: a new corporation has been formed but there is no board of directors, no stockholders, and no guidelines to be followed by the corporation. Other matters must now be taken care of.

FIGURE 52–2

TYPICAL STATE
CERTIFICATE OF INCORPORATION

I, JACK T. TURNER, Secretary of State of Typical State, hereby certify that an Agreement, duly acknowledged, has been this day filed in my office, which agreement is in words and figures following:

I. The undersigned agree to become a corporation by the name of

Brook Cable Co., Inc.

II. The principal Office of Place of Business of the Corporation will be located at 123 X Street, in the city of Anytown, in the county of King and Typical State. Its chief works will be located in King County, Typical State, and elsewhere in said State.

III. The objects for which this Corporation is formed are as follows: To provide cable television service to customers in and around Anytown, Typical State, and other municipalities, towns, and villages in Typical State; to provide cable television service in communities by exclusive franchises and contracts with the governing authorities of such municipalities; to service, sell, distribute, repair, replace, and generally deal in television sets, radios, aerials, electric equipment, antennaes and parts, replacements and allied merchandise; to build community antennaes for use of customers of cable television service, to own, lease, purchase, sell, and rent real estate, easements, and rights-of-way for laying, stringing, connecting, repairing, replacing, and installing television cable, transformers, electrical and electronic equipment for the transmission of pictures by television from a television sending station by means of community television cable into homes of customers purchasing the service; to wholesale and retail television sets, radios, repair parts, and generally deal in radio and television sets, radios, repair parts, phonographs, and combinations thereof. To purchase, sell, and trade the articles named herein and all other equipment, service, and goods necessary to effect the purposes herein stated, and, in general, to do any and all things necessary and convenient for the successful operation of a television cable company, including service, sale, and repair of television sets and installation thereof.

FIGURE 52–2 (continued)

IV. The amount of the total authorized capital stock of said corporation shall be Twenty Thousand Dollars ($20,000.00), which shall be divided into Two Thousand shares of the par value of Ten ($10.00) Dollars each.

The amount of capital stock with which it will commence business is Ten Thousand ($10,000.00) Dollars being One Thousand (1,000) shares Ten Dollars ($10.00) each.

V. The names and post office addresses of the incorporators and the number of shares of stock subscribed for by each are as follows:

Name	Post Office Address	No. Shares of Common Stock
Edward Johnson	Route 6, Anytown, Typ. St.	499
Fred Wright	Schubert Place, Anytown Typical State	500
Joseph Newhouse	281 High Street, Anytown, Typical State	1
	Total Shares	1,000

VI. The existence of this corporation is to be perpetual.

WE, THE UNDERSIGNED, for the purpose of forming a Corporation under the laws of Typical State do make and file this Agreement, and we have accordingly hereunto set our respective hands this 8th day of January, 197–

> Edward Johnson
> Fred Wright
> Joseph Newhouse

WHEREFORE, the incorporators named in the said Agreement, and who have signed the same, and their successors and assigns, are hereby declared to be from this date a Corporation by the name and for the purposes set forth in the said Agreement, with the rights of perpetual succession.

(The Great Seal of the State)

Given under my hand and the Great Seal of the said State, at the city of Capital, this Eleventh day of January, Nineteen Hundred and Seventy-Six.

(Signed) _____ Jack T. Turner
Secretary of State

Recording of Charter

The formation of the corporation has been "ex parte" to this point. That is, other than the group that has been involved in the incorporation, no one else has knowledge of its existence. The notice to others is provided by recording of the charter in those places where the corporation is to do business. The purpose of recording is to provide a means whereby those who are interested may obtain the facts contained in the charter. As a business moves into a new state to transact business, it must comply with the recording requirements of the new state. Some require recording in the counties where business is to be transacted; some states require recording at the state capital; some require both.

Most states by statute set a period of time in which a corporate charter must be recorded, and a typical period is six months. After the charter is recorded, other steps must be taken to complete the incorporation.

Organizational Meetings

Three meetings are required after the charter is received. The incorporators must meet and take care of preliminary matters including the issuance of stock. The second meeting is that of the stockholders since the incorporators are not stockholders at the time of the first meeting. The stockholders will elect the first board of directors, who will then hold the first meeting of the board. Minutes of the three meetings must be prepared and maintained for future reference and bylaws must be drafted.

Bylaws are regulations or rules of conduct adopted by a corporation for its "government." In England the term "bylaw" includes any order, rule, or regulation made by any local authority or statutory corporation subordinate to Parliament. A resolution is not necessarily a bylaw, although a bylaw may be in the form of a resolution. In short, bylaws are rules of conduct for a corporation. These are usually drafted in broad terms and must not violate the laws of the state. They can be amended by the stockholders, or the board of directors if the board controls the corporation. However, if the stockholders limit the authority of the board in the bylaws, then the limitation of authority could not be changed by the directors.

The usual bylaws contain the date and place for the annual meeting; how special meetings are to be called; how voting will be carried out at the stockholders' meeting; the number of stockholders needed to constitute a quorum; the duties of the directors and officers; provisions for dividends, amendments, and other rules to be followed by the corporation in the conduct of it's business. For sample bylaws and corporate minutes, see *Student Workbook*.

REVIEW QUESTIONS

1. Reread the facts in the Zero Homes, Inc. case. Make a list of what must be done to complete the sale of stock. Do not be concerned with *how* it will be done.
2. It is customary for directors to review the bylaws before declaring a dividend. What is the reason for this?
3. Could Brook Cable Co., Inc. go into the car radio-phone business or would their objectives have to be redrafted to permit this activity?
4. Why must the purposes or objectives of a corporation be set forth in the application for a charter?
5. True or False. Stockholders are elected at the annual meeting of the board of directors.

6. List three hazards of converting one business to a new form.
7. What *harm* could "long-arm" statutes do to a corporation?
8. Why does the state want full names and addresses of incorporators? Why might the IRS be interested in these names in the future?
9. How difficult would it be for one to remain anonymous yet still own a corporation?
10. Might it be a criminal act to do what is stated in Question 9?

Words and Phrases

Write out briefly what they mean to you.
1. Long-arm statutes.
2. Bylaws.
3. Application for a charter.
4. Minutes.
5. Restrictions on transfer of stock.

Coverage:	A detailed look at what is covered in an application of incorporation.
What to Look for:	The manner in which each part of the chapter relates to the application in Chapter 52.
Application:	You are an employee of a corporation. How can the information here assist you in doing a better job for your company?

53 Analysis of the Agreement of Incorporation

The procedures followed in the formation of a corporation were discussed in Chapter 52. The statutory requirements will vary but the material there is representative. In this chapter, the most important parts of the application for a charter will be examined in detail. These include selecting a name, stating the objectives, setting the authorized capital, designing the stock, and deciding on the length of corporate existence.

NAME

The name chosen must have a suffix such as "Association," "Incorporated," "Company," "Corporation," "Inc.," or "Co." to identify the company as being incorporated. This will vary from state to state. The name becomes related to the future success of a company and care should be used in the selection. Many court fights have erupted over names and the right to use them. The name must not be similar to or the same as the name of any corporation organized in the state or authorized to do business there. Applications are carefully screened and if the proposed name conflicts with one in existence, the application is returned with the request that another be selected. Most states permit a name to be reserved for a period of time prior to application. This can be done by making a request by letter or phone. If another application with a similar name arrives at the office of the state official, the new application will be deferred to the first one. Once a name is selected, the statement of purposes or objectives must be formulated.

OBJECTIVES

A corporation must have clearly defined guidelines to follow. These guidelines will identify the business in which the corporation will engage. This is of importance to investors and those who will extend credit because they need to know the nature of business the corporation will engage in. A person buying stock in a plastics operation is entitled to know that the investment will not be risked in oil speculation. A lending institution that makes a loan to a corporation engaged in dry-cleaning does not want its loan jeopardized in an unrelated venture. The guidelines are referred to as "corporate purposes," and they are arrived at by an elimination process. For example, a corporation formed to build houses does not need to mine coal. So unnecessary objectives are eliminated. Once the objectives are selected, acts of the corporation that goes beyond those spelled out are "ultra vires," or beyond power. Such acts violate the corporate contract with the state. Once corporate objectives are set out, they form the powers of the corporation.

Diagram

Assume for a moment that all possible legal, corporate objectives or purposes exist within a circle. Those objectives selected by a corporation would be a slice out of the circle. By selecting certain objectives all others are eliminated. In addition, corporate objectives are enlarged by implication and by the statutes of the state. Examine Figure 53-1.

In the diagram, all powers outside of those selected (or coming into play by implication or statutes) would be "beyond powers" or "ultra vires."[1]

In summary, there are three sources of corporate power: those selected in the statement of objectives, those provided by statute, and those that can be reasonably implied from the objectives stated.

The state must approve the objectives and if they are for clear legal purposes, no problems will arise. If an agreement states illegal or immoral objectives, it would be refused. The objectives are, in short, a promise to the stockholders, creditors, and the state that the scope of business will be limited to the matters specified.

Powers from Statutes

The laws of each state spell out those powers that can legally be used by corporations formed under the laws of that state. For example, all

---

[1] Acts beyond the scope of the powers of a corporation, as defined by its charter or act of incorporation. *State ex rel* v. *Holston Trust Co.*, 168 Tenn. 546, 79 S.W.2d., 1012, 1016.

FIGURE 53–1

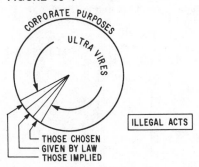

states allow a corporation to have a name, to issue a seal, and to own and transfer property used in its business. It can enter into contracts and can sue others in its own name.

The English language is subject to interpretation, and therefore a statement of corporate objectives is much like a statement of power to a general agent. Frequently the purposes of a corporation must be interpreted because of doubt as to what they in fact mean.

Implied Powers

Most states give a corporation the implied power to do those acts reasonably necessary to advance its purposes. The courts apply the rules of statutory construction when interpreting purposes set out in a charter. The courts will generally give liberal interpretation to the stated corporate objectives, but where there is doubt, they will construe the language in a light that is most favorable to the interests of third parties.

CAPITAL

As the phrase is used in the agreement of incorporation, capital refers first to the total amount of stock authorized and second to the amount of stock with which the corporation will begin business, and in both cases it is expressed in dollars.

Total Authorized Capital

The incorporators must decide at the outset the amount of the total authorized capital of the corporation. Ordinarily this has nothing to do with the amount of capital with which they will begin business.

Annual license fees are generally based upon the total authorized capital, even though the amount they commence business with is much less. If the sum set in the application is too high, the corporation will pay an unnecessary annual license fee. (See Figure 53–2.) On the other hand, if the sum is too low, the corporation may find that it must petition the

FIGURE 53-2
Capital to Commence Business Contrasted with Total Authorized Capital

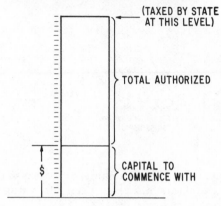

state to increase its authorized capital stock so that additional stock can be issued. Problems often arise upon the increase of authorized capital stock and the subsequent issue of stock. This is usually caused by a demand of present stockholders for their "preemptive" right in the new issue.

The Amount of Capital with Which to Commence Business

All states set a minimum amount of capital with which a corporation must begin business. This assures the creditors that at least that much will be available for security to them in their transactions with the corporation. The sum is as low as $500 in some states with Missouri requiring that sum.

Generally the liability of the stockholders will be limited to the amount with which the corporation begins business. For this reason, it may be desirable to keep the sum low. On the other hand, creditors may hesitate to extend a line of credit if the amount of capital is too low. Figure 53-2 distinguishes total authorized from starting capital.

SECURITIES

A corporation is financed in one of two ways: by the use of retained earnings and by the sale of corporate "securities." The word "security," as defined in Article 8 of the Uniform Commercial Code, means ". . . an instrument which (*i*) is issued in bearer or registered form; and (*ii*) is of a type commonly dealt in upon securities exchanges or markets or commonly recognized in any area in which it is issued or dealt in as a medium for investment; and (*iii*) is either one of a class or series or by its terms is divisible into a class or series of instruments; and (*iv*) evidences a share, participation, or other interest in property or in an enterprise or evidences an obligation of the issuer."

The most common types of securities are stocks and bonds. A wide variety of them can be created and it is the job of management to decide what types and kinds to issue as well as when they should be issued. The creation and issuance of a security places obligations upon the corporation. Many factors must be considered, and probably the most important is that in time the corporation will want to retire outstanding securities — or at least part of them. As a rule of thumb, a security should be looked at as a long-term debt. When securities are "structured" or created, they can be designed to allow for their retirement in the future. First, a look at stock.

Stock

The terms "share of stock" and "stock certificate" are often confused. A share of stock is that intangible part of the corporation that a stockholder owns. It includes the right to participate in the corporate business and is intangible personal property. The stock certificate is written evidence of the share of stock, and one certificate may represent more than one share of stock. The stock certificate may be destroyed without disturbing the underlying ownership of the share. The shareholder would be entitled to have a new certificate issued under regulations prescribed by law. Related to stock is the "capital" of the corporation.

The capital of a corporation is sometimes called "legal capital," "stated capital," or "capital stock." Sometimes the words "stock," "capital," and "capital stock" are used synonymously. Capital is the net assets of the corporation and includes all gains and losses. Capital stock is what was received by the corporation from the shareholders in cash, services, or property in payment for shares issued. Capital stock is represented by certificates for the number of shares owned by the stockholders and is dedicated to use in the business. It is not changed by profits and losses.

Further, it is the amount retained for the protection of the creditors and is often called the "creditors cushion." Capital stock takes the place of the individual liability of the shareholders, and creditors who deal with the corporation have every right to expect that it be there for their protection. The balance sheet of a corporation will show capital stock as a liability since it is an obligation that a corporation owes to its shareholders. Upon dissolution, the corporation would be under an obligation to return its capital stock to the respective shareholders of record.

Generally a corporation may not pay dividends or buy its own outstanding stock if such acts would reduce assets below the total of outstanding liabilities plus capital stock. In other words, dividends or funds for the purchase of stock must come from "surplus." Surplus is the excess of assets above capital stock plus liabilities. For example, if a corporation has $100,000 assets, capital stock of $50,000, and liabilities of $25,000, its surplus would be $25,000. If a corporation spends more than it has in surplus its capital stock is impaired—that is, there is not enough remaining to return the capital intact.

A Diagram

In Figure 53–3, the right-hand column represents the liability side of the corporation while the left-hand column is the asset side. On the right-hand side of the diagram is a dollar scale. As capital stock is paid in, the liability side rises to equal the amount of capital stock and this causes a corresponding rise on the asset side.

FIGURE 53–3
Balance Sheet

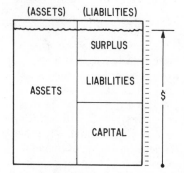

FIGURE 53–4
A Corporation with Impairment of Capital

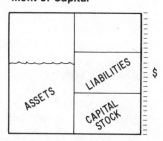

It is from the assets that the corporation will purchase its initial inventory as it begins to do business. As the corporation incurs further liabilities, this causes a rise on the liability side. If there is no corresponding rise on the asset side, the corporation is insolvent because it is not able to meet its obligations.

If the asset side rises to equal the total of liabilities and capital stock but goes no higher, then the corporation is solvent but has no surplus. If the asset side rises above capital stock plus liabilities, the excess amount is surplus. It is from surplus that the corporation may pay dividends or buy its outstanding stock. Surplus can take different forms. "Paid-in" surplus, for example, results from the sale or exchange of corporate stock at a price above par. (Compare Figure 53–3 with Figure 53–4.)

BUYING STOCK

One who buys a share of common stock is purchasing a part of the business. The share of stock entitles the holder to vote for the directors and to share in profits and assets. One who buys "preferred" stock, owns a part of the business but generally has no right to vote. An investor's money is safer in preferred stock because one will be paid sooner in the event of insolvency of the corporation. Regardless of the type of stock purchased, each investor is interested in the "yield" of what is purchased.

Yield. The ratio of what one spends for stock compared to what is received from it by dividends is called "yield." For example, if X purchases one share of Oil Wells, Inc. for $37.50, that sum must be divided into the dividend declared in order to determine the yield. Assume the directors of Oil Wells, Inc. decide to pay a dividend of $1 per share. The sum of $37.50 is divided into $1, giving a yield of .0266 or 2.66 percent. Assume the corporation is prosperous and dividends increase to $3 per year, but due to the success of the business, one share now costs $100. What happens to the yield? Divide $3 by $37.50 paid for the original share and the yield is 8 percent, but new investors who are paying $100 per share are getting a yield of only 3 percent. This illustrates why the yield from stock tends to remain relatively constant.

Rule of Thumb. To decide if the price of stock is right, divide the price of one share by the earnings per share. If one pays $37.50 for a share when it is earning $2.50, the price-to-earnings ratio is 15 (divide $37.50 by $2.50). Investors are willing to pay between 10 and 20 times the earnings of the stock.

A Share of Stock

A share of stock is intangible personal property. Upon the death of its owner it does not pass to ones heirs. Rather, it goes to the legal representative of the deceased. If a person dies leaving a will, the stock goes to the executor. If one dies intestate (without a will), it goes to the administrator. Therefore, a person who wants heirs to have the stock intact should make arrangements for its distribution prior to death.

A share of stock represents a unit of interest in a corporation and entitles a stockholder to an "aliquot"[2] part of the corporation. It gives the stockholder the right to participate in the control of the corporation through the vote at regular and special meetings. A share of stock gives its holder the right to share in surplus through dividends, and the right to have the capital contribution returned and to share in assets, if any, on dissolution.

Upon purchasing a share of stock, the shareholder obtains in addition to those rights above, all rights spelled out in the charter, the state statutes, and in the bylaws. Since bylaws are not readily available to shareholders additional rights contained in the bylaws can be set out on the face of the stock certificate. The second classification of securities are bonds.

Bonds

Bonds are obligations of the corporation owed to creditors who have extended value to the corporation, usually in the form of a loan. The bond

---

[2] "Aliquot" – "contained in something else an exact number of times."

is evidence of the debt just as a certificate of stock is evidence of the underlying share of stock. When corporate assets are pledged as security for payment of bonds, they are "secured bonds." On some occasions, loans are made to the corporation with the lender accepting unsecured bonds which are called "debentures."

Bondholders are creditors of the corporation, while stockholders are not. Interest payable on bonds is a deductible business expense and reduces income on which corporate income tax is payable. Dividends paid on stock, on the other hand, are not deductible since they are merely dis-

FIGURE 53–5

From the author's collection.

tributions of surplus to which the shareholders are already entitled. Frequently, corporations will issue bonds instead of stock in order to raise working capital, thus taking advantage of the interest deduction. Figure 53–5 is the front of a bond issued in pre-war Germany, and Figure 53–6 contains the coupons for that bond.

FIGURE 53–6

From the author's collection.

KINDS OF STOCK

Two basic kinds of stock are encountered: common stock and preferred stock. A third class found in English corporations is "deferred stock." Deferred stock must wait for other classes to be paid before it will receive payments. The term "deferred stock" is not commonly used in the United States, although where a corporation has preferred stock, its common stock is in a sense deferred.

Common Stock

One who holds common stock shares in the profits and assets in proportion to the amount owned—and in common with other common shareholders. For example, if one share of common stock is held in a corporation having 500,000 common shares outstanding, and a $500,000 dividend is declared, the holder would be entitled to $1 dividend. The common shareholder shares in surplus and assets on dissolution in proportion to the amount owned, and takes the biggest risk as far as possible loss is concerned—but is usually in a position to make the biggest gain if the corporation is successful. Common shareholders normally control the corporation since in most instances only the common stock has voting rights.

Preferred Stock

A preferred shareholder is entitled to a prior claim on dividends when declared and, in most cases, a prior claim to assets on dissolution of the corporation. In the latter case, the preferred shareholder will be paid even if nothing is left for the common shareholders. This type of stock is usually created by placing it in the application for incorporation. If this is not done, then it can be created only by authority of the existing shareholders. In most cases, it would require unanimous consent because it has prior claims on dividends and assets on dissolution and would thus make the common shareholders subordinate to it. This class of stock is usually created for the purpose of attracting investments in the corporation without allowing control to be taken from the common shareholders. Preferred stock can be created in a variety of forms and combinations.

Cumulative Preferred. The dividend on cumulative preferred stock accumulates each year until funds are available for the payment of dividends. If one holds one share of $1 cumulative preferred stock and the dividend is not paid in the current year, a $1 credit accrues to the shareholder and the sum must be paid when dividends are declared. If five years go by before a dividend is declared, the shareholder would be entitled to a cumulative dividend of $5 before common shareholders received payment. Cumulative preferred stock is attractive because the stock gains value each year whether or not the board of directors declares a dividend.

Noncumulative Preferred. This class of stock is entitled to preferential payment out of current surplus if a dividend is declared. If the directors decide not to pay a dividend in a stated year, a holder of this stock would lose the right to a dividend for that year. However, the preference would be retained on a dividend declared the following year or in subsequent years.

Participating Preferred. Participating preferred stock is entitled to a full share of a current dividend, and after common has had a share, it participates on a stated basis in any additional sum remaining. Generally, common shareholders are entitled to a full share before there is additional participation. For example, if one common shareholder and one shareholder of fully participating preferred stock of $1 preference has $3 available between them, distribution would be as follows: The preferred stockholder would take the first dollar. Common would be entitled to an equal share of $1. This leaves $1 for distribution. Since the preferred is fully participating, the extra dollar would be shared equally between them for an additional 50 cents or a total of $1.50 to each. Different variations of distributions are possible and it depends upon the way it is established initially.

Nonparticipating Preferred. Nonparticipating preferred stock is entitled to a dividend at a fixed amount but does not share in additional profits. It receives the share specified but that is all.

FURTHER STOCK CLASSIFICATIONS

The vast variety of stock issues that are in use today involve common stock or some variety of preferred stock. While the combinations or forms of stock issues possible are large, there are just two types. However, as these basic forms are placed into use, other classifications or categories emerge. The ones most frequently encountered are "bonus stock," "founders" or "promoters stock," "watered stock," "no par," and "treasury" stock.

Bonus Stock

When shares (of whatever type) are issued as a bonus to encourage the purchase of stock, such shares are called bonus stock. For example, a certain percentage of common stock may be given to one who buys a prescribed number of shares of preferred stock. In effect, this is a sale of stock at a discount since the buyer is paying less than if the bonus had not been given. If a regular stock issue exceeds the surplus available, "bonus stock" results. Holders of bonus stock are liable to subsequent creditors of the firm for a sum equal to the par value of the stock that they hold. The laws of many states make the issuance of bonus stock illegal or require that the buyer of it be held liable for the par value in the event of insolvency of the corporation.

Founders or Promoters Stock

In some corporations the promoter or founder is issued stock in payment for services in the incorporation. The phrase "founders stock" is widely used in English law and is similar to American promoters stock. Such stock is sometimes referred to as "management" or "deferred" stock, and in many cases has resulted in a windfall to the promoter where the corporation has outstanding growth.

Watered Stock

When stock is issued as fully paid when in fact the full amount of the par value has not been paid, it is said to be "watered." This happens frequently when new corporations sell stock below par in order to encourage investors to buy. Most states have statutes regulating the sale of stock below par, and some states prohibit it. Others permit the sale but prescribe by law the steps that must be followed in doing it. In all states, an innocent person who suffers a loss because of watered stock would have access to the courts to seek recovery for the loss.

The phrase "watered stock" apparently evolved from an old cattle drover's trick used the day before sale. The animals were given quantities of salt and water during the night. The result was an increase in weight—and thus a higher price at the sale. Later, shrinkage would occur and the animals would return to normal proportions. Whether or not this situation is the true origin of the phrase "watered stock," it presents a good analogy of what the phrase means as it relates to corporate stock.

If one share of stock of $100 par value is sold for $75, the capital structure of the corporation is "watered." The assets underlying the share are short $25. In effect, the sale at less than par cuts the asset value of all other shares of stock which have been fully paid for. If the practice becomes extensive, the reduction of the asset value of the corporation could become dangerous to creditors. For this reason, creditors can usually enforce payment of the balance of watered stock.

Examine Figure 53–7. A contracted to buy one share of $1,000 par stock for $750. After the stock was issued, creditor X extended credit to the corporation, relying upon the $1,000 value. If the corporation becomes insolvent and cannot pay creditor X, X would have the right to sue A for the $250 or that part of it that is due. The corporation cannot enforce the payment of the $250 since it had contracted to sell the stock for $750. If A sells the share of stock to B, who buys it without notice that the stock is watered, B would be protected since B would be a bona fide purchaser for value and X could not look to B for recovery. This is true even if B paid A less than $1,000 for the stock.

Once a shareholder owns a share of stock that was fully paid for initially, it can be sold at any price one can obtain and the buyer incurs no liability under the watered theory. The stock would not be watered since the full amount had been paid initially.

When the watered condition occurs, the states permit recovery for the innocent creditor under one of two theories. First, when a buyer of the initial issue of stock pays less than par for it, one has shorted the capital of the corporation, which is a "trust fund" for the creditors. Second, recovery is permitted in some states on the theory that it is wrong to "hold out" funds that appear to have been paid in—a fraud type approach.

FIGURE 53-7
Zero Corp., Inc. Balance Sheet

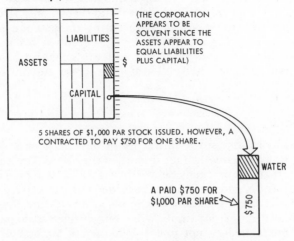

Creditor X believes the level of capital is $5,000; thus X
has been misled. X can look to A up to the sum of $250.

Trust Fund.   The courts that allow recovery on the trust-fund basis
hold that the capital of a corporation is a trust fund for the protection of
the creditors. For this reason, such courts engage in a fiction and imply
a promise on the part of the initial shareholder to pay the difference if it
is ever needed by the corporation. The result is a contract implied in law
to prevent an injustice.

So, as a matter of law, a shareholder's liability is limited to the amount
paid for stock but liability also extends to the unpaid portion of stock
purchased at a discount. The Underwood case illustrates the "trust
fund" theory as applied in court.

> *Underwood* v. *Stafford.*[3] "The pleadings and evidence tend to show that
> the corporation was insolvent and inactive, and that the property of the
> corporation had been divided among or purchased by the directors and
> stockholders for an undisclosed consideration. Under the circumstances,
> the corporation should be made a party to the action, and the appointment of
> a receiver would be appropriate. North Carolina adheres to 'trust-fund
> doctrine,' which means, in a sense, that assets of corporation are regarded
> as a trust fund, and officers and directors occupy fiduciary position with
> respect to stockholders and creditors, so as to charge officers and directors
> with preservation and proper distribution of corporation's assets.
>
> "Without dealing with the merits of the case, the judgment below is
> vacated and the case is remanded to the end that further proceedings may
> be had consistent with this opinion."

Fraud or "Holding Out."   States that allow creditors to recover under
this theory base the action on the "wrong" or on fraud. These courts say
that holding out that the corporation had $5,000 capital when, in fact,

---

[3] 270 N.C. 700, 155 S.E.2d 211 (1966).

only $4,750 was there, constituted an intentional misstatement of a material existing fact upon which creditors relied to their detriment — the legal elements of fraud. Under the fraud theory, only a creditor who, in fact, relies upon the stock as representing the actual capital paid in can ask for recovery. Creditor X who extends credit *before* watered stock is issued would not be able to recover under this theory because X could not show that he or she had relied upon a larger amount being in the capital.

No-Par Stock

One who looks at a stock certificate of one share of $100 par stock cannot know what value in fact underlies the share. The share may be worth more than par or it may be worth less. In 1912, New York enacted the first statute permitting stock to be issued without stating a par value. The purpose of the legislation was to avoid misleading those who buy stock that has a stated par value. When one purchases no-par stock and pays $100 for it, it does not matter whether 5, 50, or 500 shares are given in return. Each share would be worth 1/5th, 1/50th, or 1/500th of the $100 as the case may be. One who purchases the stock later could not be misled because that person would know that behind each share is part of the total assets of the corporation that applies to the stock, unexpressed in money.

For purposes of sale, no-par stock must have a stated value. The value is decided by the shareholders or the board of directors, but regardless of who makes the determination, the decision must be made in good faith. For taxation and annual license fee purposes, most states place a stated value upon no-par stock. For example, in West Virginia no-par stock is valued at $25 per share for taxation purposes. The law was created to close what could have been a true "loophole."

It is not possible to have watered, no-par stock for the reason set out above. Upon sale of no-par stock to a shareholder, the decision must be made of what part of the proceeds goes to the capital account and what part (if any) goes to surplus. Again the matter rests with the directors and they must exercise good faith in making the decision. If directors place a fraudulent value upon the portion to go to capital stock in order to create a surplus for dividend purposes, it would be an unlawful act and could result in criminal liability.

Treasury Stock

Treasury stock is stock that has been reacquired by a corporation by gift or purchase or otherwise, and which had been fully paid for originally. Upon repurchase or upon being reacquired, it can be held for future sale or it can be retired. If resold, it can be sold at any price that it may bring — even if the price would be below par.

Reissued treasury stock is different than watered stock even if sold below par. During the time it is held in the corporation, dividends are not paid on it and no one is allowed to vote it. If the stock is retired, it loses the classification of treasury stock.

RESTRICTIONS ON TRANSFER

Right to Preference upon Increase of Stock

Once a corporation is organized, the total authorized capital cannot be increased unless there is consent of the shareholders. If consent is given, application is made to the proper official of the chartering state who would approve or disapprove the increase.

Once an increase has been authorized, each shareholder may have a "preemptive right" to a proportionate share of the new issue. The rule developed at common law to enable each shareholder to retain "relative control" in the corporation, and in effect, is a restriction upon transfer of that stock to others.

Preemptive Right Analyzed

Zero Corporation has total authorized capital stock of $100,000. The stock was fully issued in 1,000 shares of $100 par value. A purchased 100 shares, which represented a 1/10th control of the corporation. After consent of the shareholders and application to the state, the corporation was authorized to increase its capital stock by 500 shares. If the additional 500 shares would be purchased by others, A would have 100/1500 or 1/15 control in the corporation. At common law, A had a preemptive right to 50 of the additional 500 shares. If A purchased them, it would give A 150/1500 or 1/10 control of the corporation. Thus, A is returned to where A was initially in terms of relative voting control in the corporation.

One may give up the preemptive right at the time of the purchase of stock. Yet, the right is good to retain in a small corporation. Some states preserve the right by statute; but inquiry should be made at the time of incorporation to determine the exact status in any given state.

It is also important to know whether the preemptive right is to be at par value, market value, or book value. For example, if A had a preemptive right in an additional 50 shares at $100 par value, A could purchase them for $5,000. It is quite possible that the market value of the shares at that time might be in excess of $5,000, and A would receive a windfall. On the other hand, the market value could be considerably less and A must pay more for the stock than it is worth, or face the alternative of losing "relative control" in the corporation.

The preemptive right does not apply to a reissue of treasury stock because each shareholder retains relative control in the corporation regardless of what happens to treasury stock. This is true even though, during the period that treasury stock lies dormant, a shareholder's voting power may *increase* because of the smaller amount of voting stock outstanding. The preemptive right is one method of controlling the transfer of stock. Another is by use of the option.

Option

An option is a privilege existing in one person for which one has paid money or other consideration, which gives the right to buy specified securities or other items from another person at any time within a specified time period and at a specified price. An option may involve the sale of securities to another person at an agreed price and time. A "call" is an option that gives a choice of buying or not. A "put" is the choice of selling or not selling. If an option is a combination of both "call" and "put," it gives the privilege of buying or selling or not and is called a "straddle" or "spread eagle."

Stock options are often used as an inducement to attract management to a corporation. If the corporation prospers and the value of the stock increases, the option could then be exercised. An option is, in essence, a continuing offer which is held open for a stated period of time and which is a contract within itself. It restricts the transfer of stock as long as the option is in effect. The strongest legal way to restrict transfer is by use of a restrictive clause.

Restrictive Clauses

In small corporations, it is wise to place restrictions on the sale of stock before it is issued. This provides the shareholders an opportunity to buy outstanding stock if the owner desires to sell. These restrictions are upheld if they are reasonable. But a restriction that prohibited the sale of stock to anyone but the corporation would be invalid as being an unreasonable restraint upon the alienation of property. A restriction that gave the corporation an option to buy for a reasonable period of time before the stock could be sold to third parties would be valid. Most restrictions take this form. The restrictions are spelled out in the charter or an amendment of the charter or in the bylaws. It is a legal requirement under the U.C.C. that restrictions be placed on the stock certificates in conspicuous form. (Review the bylaws, *Student Workbook*.)

The next part of the agreement requires the names and addresses of those who are forming the corporation.

THE INCORPORATORS

Number

The number of incorporators needed varies from state to state and sometimes depends upon the type of corporation being formed. Nevada statutes provide that any number of persons, no less than three, may associate to form a corporation and there are no requirements that they be residents of the state or that they subscribe to stock. Michigan provides that one or more natural persons, partnerships, or corporations, may incorporate. No less than three incorporators, however, are required in that state for a nonprofit corporation. Louisiana permits three or more natural persons of full age (or emancipated) to form a corporation for any lawful business purpose except the businesses of banking, insurance, homesteads, and building and loan associations.

In a Closely Held Corporation

In a closely held corporation the incorporators, after they become stockholders, may serve as directors as well as officers. In many instances they also serve as employees. In other words, those who own a small corporation can make up the board, split the duties of the officers, and hire themselves as employees. They do not lose their corporate protection by doing this as long as they meet corporate formalities of regular meetings, the keeping of minutes, and other statutory formalities.

Straw Men

In the formation of small corporations, it is not uncommon for a "straw man" or "dummy" to be used as an incorporator. For example, if John Zero wants to be a "one person corporation," he may use two others to meet the requirements of three incorporators. Once the corporation is formed, and stock issued, the other two will sell their stock to him.

Many states now permit one person to incorporate in the beginning, thus placing the straw man into virtual retirement in those states.

EXISTENCE OF CORPORATION

Most states require that the application contain a statement of the life or term of the corporation. Two choices exist: perpetual existence or for a stated period of time.

Perpetual Existence

One of the features of a corporation is that since its life is separate from those who own it, and since it has no physical existence, it can (theoretically) last forever. In most instances, all that is required to obtain unlimited life is to state in the application that the corporate life is to be "perpetual."

Set Term

In some cases it might be desirable to form a corporation that is to have a life of a set period of time. This is frequently done where investors want to engage in one activity, such as building an apartment complex, but once the job is completed, they intend to end all business relations. The corporate form will give protection during the building phase, and there would be no need for the corporation to have perpetual existence.

REVIEW QUESTIONS

1. Name the three sources of corporate power.
2. Explain why so many Americans are stockholders.
3. Using the various classifications, create a type of preferred stock that would be an attractive investment.
4. What practical effect does a restriction on transfer have when it is on the face of the stock certificate?
5. True or False. The premptive right is present in all corporations.
6. Name three reasons why careful consideration should be given to the selection of a corporate name.
7. Why should incorporators avoid making objectives too broad?
8. In your own words, distinguish "ultra vires" acts from "illegal" acts.
9. Name two reasons why corporations have powers beyond those set forth in their charters.
10. In construing doubts about corporate powers, why do courts tend to favor third parties?

Words and Phrases

Write out briefly what they mean to you.
1. Watered stock.
2. Bonus stock.
3. Impairment of capital.
4. Total authorized capital.
5. Preemptive right.

Coverage:	The stockholder in action.
What to Look for:	The importance of a basic understanding of the nature of stock.
Application:	Would it have made a difference (in each item discussed) if the stock had been structured differently in the beginning?

54 Stockholders

ACQUIRING STOCK

A person becomes a member of a corporation by acquiring shares of stock in that corporation in one manner or another. The customary way is to purchase stock. In buying stock, one must pay what another is willing to accept, plus a broker's commission if the stock is listed and sold on the exchanges. On a stock purchase of $100 or less, the commission is approximately 6 percent. On purchases above $500, the commission drops to about 2 percent.

However, these are only approximate fees because the Security and Exchange Commission ordered that all broker fees must be subject to negotiation between the buyer and the broker. This ruling became effective in May, 1975, and has been referred to as "Mayday." Because of this ruling, there has been a tendency for brokers to "unbundle" their fees, and make separate charges for services that were formerly contained within the standard fixed fees.

The stock exchanges operate a monthly investment plan and stock can be purchased in this manner. Another way is through a mutual fund. Advantages of such funds include diversification, professional management, and the right to sell shares back to the fund at current value, thus avoiding a handling charge. Detailed analyses of individual corporations are published in *Moody's Handbook of Common Stocks, Standard and Poor's Listed Stock Reports,* and others.

Some potential shareholders of a corporation enter into a contract to buy stock. These contracts are called stock subscriptions and are entered into before or after incorporation.

Stock Subscription before Incorporation

An offer to buy stock in a corporation being formed takes the form of a continuing offer. Under strict rules of contract, an offer can be revoked any time before acceptance. In this situation, since the corporation is not yet in being, it cannot accept the offer. After the corporation comes into being and is properly organized, the offer can be accepted. If a stock subscription is entered into and the corporation is defectively formed, the subscriber would not be bound by the subscription.

Sometimes stock subscriptions are made subject to "conditions precedent." For example, A may subscribe to 100 shares of $100 par value stock in X Corporation that is being formed, provided that at least 1,000 shares are subscribed to by others at the same price. Under such circumstances, the offer of A would be cancelled if the prescribed number of additional shares were not subscribed to—that condition being a "condition precedent."

Stock Subscription after Incorporation

Once a corporation comes into being and one subscribes to a stated number of shares at a stated price, it is a binding contract. However, the distinction between a "present subscription" and a "contract to purchase" can be important.

Present Subscription. When A contracts for stock in X Corporation under a present subscription, A becomes immediately liable for full payment of the stock. Under these circumstances A would not be able to breach the contract to buy since A has become a stockholder, even though the stock has not yet been received.

Contract to Purchase. Where a contract to purchase exists, the subscriber could breach the contract and be liable only for damages sustained by the corporation. Under a contract to buy, dividends are paid to the stockholder of record—which would not be the one who has contracted to buy the stock.

ACQUIRING STOCK FROM A STOCKHOLDER

Stock may be acquired from a stockholder by gift or by purchase.

By Gift

Where a gift of stock is involved, the burden of proof is upon the donee (the one receiving the stock) to prove, first, the intention of the donor (the one making the gift) to make the gift so as to divest the donor of all right and title to, and control of, the stock; and, second, that there has been delivery, actual or constructive, of the stock certificate properly indorsed by the donor. It has been held that where stock was kept for the donee in a safety deposit box in a bank, and the donee had a key to the box, that this was sufficient evidence to show delivery of the certificates to the donee.[1]

By Purchase

The most common way to acquire ownership in a corporation is to purchase stock from an individual stockholder or from the stock exchanges. At common law, stock was transferred from one person to another by an assignment. Under the laws of assignment, the assignee only gets those rights that the assignor has. If the owner of the stock held it subject to a claim by a third party, one to whom it was transferred would hold the stock subject to the same claim. Under the Uniform Commercial Code, corporate stock and bonds are treated as being negotiable. An instrument is "negotiable" when the legal title to the instrument may be transferred from one person to another without a formal assignment. It is negotiated by indorsement and delivery or by delivery alone. Where a share of stock is negotiated to a buyer, the purchaser can get better rights than the seller had. The requirements for transfer depend upon the type of security.

In the transfer of stock, the blue-sky laws of the state must be complied with and, if the stock is offered on the exchange, the transfer must comply with the Securities and Exchange Acts of 1933 and 1934. The term "blue-sky laws" is a popular one for acts that provide for regulation of the sale of investment securities. The purpose of such laws is to protect the investing public from acts of fraudulent corporations and those who operate them.

Article 8 of the Uniform Commercial Code covers investment securities. The article is divided into four sections: title and general needs; purchase; issue; and registration. Article 8, in short, provides the rules for making transfers of securities. It does *not* replace the blue-sky laws of the states and the federal government.

Mechanics of a Transfer. Stock is intangible personal property and the certificate is mere evidence of ownership in the corporation. Under the Uniform Commercial Code, a stock certificate is treated as tangible property having the value of the shares it represents. Conveyances of stock are called "transfers" and three steps are involved: (1) the stock must be properly indorsed; (2) it must be delivered to the buyer; and (3) the issuer will register the transfer upon the transfer books of the corporation. The issuer would not register the transfer if the stock was improperly indorsed or if there was any question as to whether the indorsements were genuine.

The issuer must register the transfer if it has been made to a "bona fide purchaser." Under these circumstances, the issuer is liable to the person presenting stock for registration for loss resulting from unreasonable delay in registration, or from failure or refusal to register the transfer.[2]

---

[1] *Snidow* v. *First Nat. Bank,* 178 Va. 239, 16 S.E.2d 385 (1941).

[2] U.C.C., 8–401.

Example of Transfer. By an agreement before incorporation, A contracts to purchase 100 shares of $100 par, common stock in X Corporation. After X Corporation is formed, A purchases the 100 shares. Later, A has an opportunity to sell 50 shares to B. On the back of A's stock certificate of 100 shares is an assignment form which is filled in as follows.

> For value received, I hereby sell, assign, and transfer unto B Fifty (50) shares of the Capital Stock represented by the within Certificate and do hereby irrevocably constitute and appoint John Eagle Attorney to transfer the said Stock on the books of the within named Corporation with full power of substitution in the premises.
>
> Signed _____ "A" _____
> Dated _____ 1–1–76 _____
> In presence of
> _____ James Pickett _____

The stock certificate is then presented for transfer on the stock transfer books. Two new certificates will be issued by the corporation; one to A for 50 shares and the second to B for the 50 shares purchased. The handling of the transfer would normally be done through a broker. The transfer could be done by a separate assignment form. (See Figure 54–1).

Indorsements in Blank or Special. Under the Uniform Commercial Code,[3] an indorsement may be in "blank" or "special." An indorsement in blank is one in which the transferee (buyer) is not named and also includes an indorsement to "bearer." Such a certificate could be transferred by delivery and no indorsement would be required. A special indorsement is one that names the person to whom the stock is to be transferred. This indorsement is preferable in almost all transfers and avoids the possibility of the certificate falling into the hands of a third party who might make improper use of it.

The holder of a stock certificate indorsed in blank may convert it to a special indorsement. For example, one could insert one's own name into the document. This would prevent improper transfer if the certificate were lost or stolen.

"Street certificates" are bearer stocks or bonds which have been indorsed in blank. They can be transferred by delivery alone because of their form. A "registered" bond or stock certificate, on the other hand, is one that requires indorsement before it can be transferred.

Effect of Transfer upon the Corporation. The rights of a corporation are not affected by transfer of stock certificates until they are presented for transfer and registration. For this reason, prior to transfer, the registered owner is treated as having the rights to vote and to receive dividends. This often creates problems. The buyer may find that dividends are being paid to the seller. The seller may be called upon for assessments or "calls" since the seller is still the registered owner as far as the corporation is concerned.

---

[3] U.C.C., 8–308(2).

FIGURE 54–1

```
     1817                ASSIGNMENT SEPARATE     Branch | Account No. | Type
                         FROM CERTIFICATE       |      |            |     |
 Blake & Co.                                    |      |            |     |
 Incorporated


 FOR VALUE RECEIVED, I, Peter Cupp, do _____

 hereby sell, assign and transfer unto  Leonard Largin  _____


 _____

 One Hundred------------------( 100 ) Shares of The  Common

 Capital Stock of the    Zero Corporation    _____

 standing in   the above   name on the books of said

 corporation and _____ represented by Certificate No.

  S231589          herewith and do hereby irrevocably

 constitute and appoint     Kent Forman    _____

 attorney to transfer the said stock on the books of the

 within named Company with full Power of Substitution in the

 premises.


     Dated  January 5, 1976

                                    _____
                                         s/s Peter Cupp

 IN PRESENCE OF

   s/s Thurmond Clawges  _____


 FORM 2095      | Date Requested |
                |                |
                |                |
```

Duty of the Corporation to Make Transfer. If an instrument is properly indorsed and all other requirements are met, the corporation has a duty to make the transfer when the instrument is presented to it or its transfer agent.[4] The corporation has a right to make reasonable inquiry, which might delay registration.[5] Otherwise, if the corporation fails to make the

_____
[4] U.C.C., 8–401 (1).
[5] U.C.C., 8–403.

FIGURE 54–2

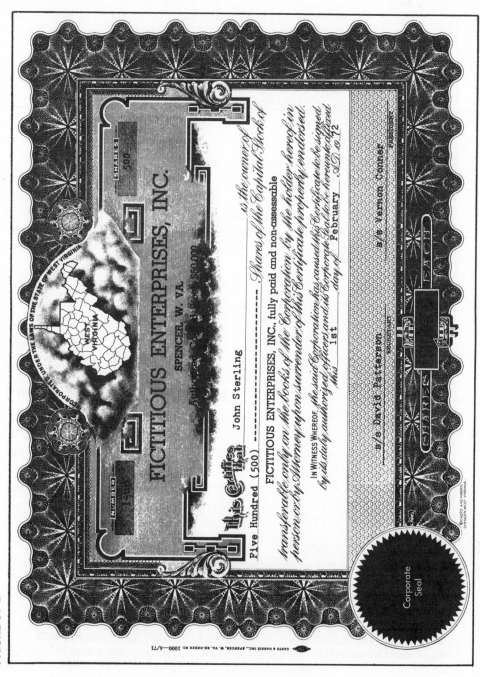

See Figure 54-6, for an example of a computerized stock certificate. Compare it with the above.

FIGURE 54-3

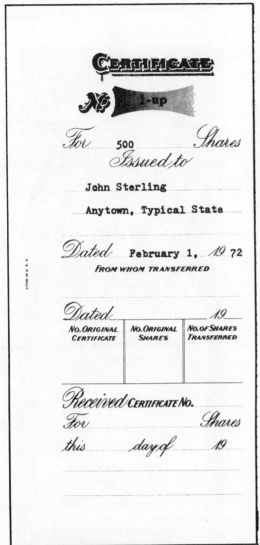

Certificate No. 1 for 500 shares of $100 par value stock was issued to John Sterling on February 1, 1972.

George Candem has offered to purchase 100 shares from Sterling at a figure agreeable to both.

Figure 54-4 illustrates how Sterling will fill out the assignment on the back of the stock certificate. He may use the separate assignment as illustrated in Figure 54-1.

The corporation will issue two new certificates: one to Candem for 100 shares the other to Sterling for 400 shares.

The old certificate will be marked "cancelled" and filed with the original stock stub.

The stock stub for the original certificate for 500 shares will be completed as indicated on the stub. This will provide a record of the transfer.

(This process illustrated here is costly and time consuming. Computerized stock certificates ease this burden).

transfer, it could become liable for loss that might result from delay in registration or from refusal to register the transfer.[6] Illustrated are sample forms of stock certificates, stock book stub, and affidavit of nonresidency. Examine Figures 54-2, 54-3, 54-4, and 54-5.

Duty to Make Inquiry. There are two times when a corporation *must* make inquiry before stock is transferred. First, when the corporation has

---

[6] U.C.C., 8-401 (2).

FIGURE 54–4

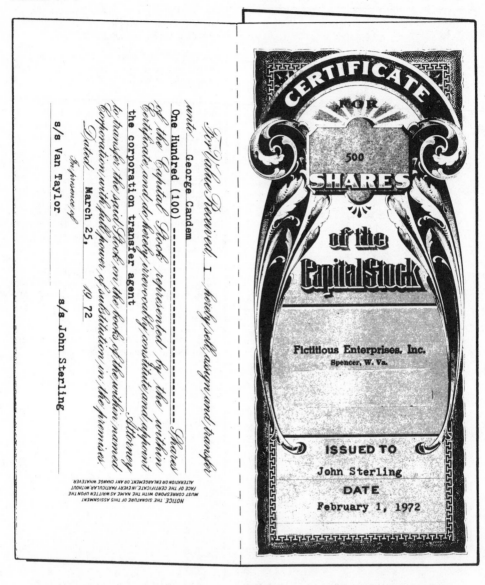

received written notification of an "adverse claim," it must not make a transfer to the person(s) to whom its attention has been brought.[7] Second, the issuer is charged with notice of an adverse claim when restrictions are found on the front or back of the certificates offered for transfer.

---

[7] U.C.C., 8–403.

FIGURE 54-5

AFFIDAVIT OF NON-RESIDENCE (NEW YORK)

TYPICAL STATE   S.S.:
COUNTY OF KING

   JAMES GRAHAM   being duly sworn, deposes and says: I
am a duly appointed and acting Executor of the estate of
NATHAN METHENY , who died on the_1st_ day of _January_ ,
19_72_ ; that at the time of his death, the domicile (legal
residence) of the said decedent was at _200 Freedom Street_ ,
County of _King_ , _Typical State_ ; and the said decedent was
not a resident of the State of New York and did not reside,
dwell, or lodge in the State of New York for the greater part
of any twelve consecutive months during the twenty-four
months immediately preceding his death and did not by any
formal statement executed within one year of his death, or
by his Last Will and Testament declare himself to be a resident of the State of New York. This affidavit is made for
the purpose of securing the transfer of the following
described property owned by said decedent at the time of his
death:

_1,000_ shares of the _common_ stock of _Zero Motor Company_ a

Typical State corporation.

The physical situs of these shares at the time of the death
of the decedent were located at _200 Freedom Street_ County
of _King_ , _Typical State_ .

                       s/s James Graham (LS)
                       (Signature of Depodent)

Subscribed and sworn to before
me this _15th_ day of _March_ , 19_72_.
My Commission expires April 20, 1974.
    s/s Elisha Liston
(Affix Seal)

Either will cause the issuer and its agent to hold up the transfer. But
if the matter stopped here, the issuer would be caught in the middle.
Therefore, the U.C.C. permits the issuer to discharge the duty to make
inquiry in one of two ways. First, the issuer can notify the one who sent
notice of the adverse claim that the transfer will be made in 30 days
unless the complaining party files suit in a court of competent jurisdiction or obtains a restraining order to the issue. Second, the issuer may

demand that the complaintant issue an indemnity bond in a sum sufficient to protect the issuer if later it should be determined that the issuer should have made the transfer in spite of the complaint. In either way the issuer is protected.

Liability of Issuer. The issuer is not liable to any person who may suffer a loss because of registration if the issuer did not have notice of adverse claims and if the necessary indorsements were on the security.[8]

If the issuer registers stock when it should not have been done, the true owner can demand that the issuer deliver a like issue, unless this would cause an overissue.[9]

Transfer from the Corporation's Point of View. In a small corporation the transfer is carried out by using the stubs to which the stock certificates were originally attached. The stub is marked with the name of the person to whom the shares are transferred together with the number of shares transferred. A new stock certificate will be issued. In large corporations, the transfers are handled by professional transfer agents. The "books" of other days have given way to computers. Even the traditional stock certificates are being replaced with computer cards. (See Figure 54–6).

Lost, Stolen, and Destroyed Certificates. If securities are lost, stolen, or destroyed, the stockholder must notify the issuer immediately. If one fails to do so within a reasonable time, and if the issuer transfers to another, the issuer incurs no liability. The issuer is entitled to notice as well as an indemnity bond for its protection.

Stockholders Meetings

Stockholders must act at meetings called for the purposes stated in the notice of the meeting. In the absence of this, the acts of the stockholders may be held to be invalid. This might result in directors being held individually liable for acts that the stockholders later refuse to ratify. It can also cause an unsettling of corporate activities since a minority of the stockholders will have legal grounds to attack corporate functions not authorized at properly called meetings.

Notice

The stockholders cannot lawfully function in a meeting unless all of them have been given notice and an opportunity to be present and protect their interests. The procedures for giving notice are set out in the by-laws and should be complied with.

The bylaws will prescribe a definite date for the annual meeting and will spell out how special meetings are to be called.

A stockholder may "waive" the right to attend a meeting once one knows the purposes of that meeting. However, a stockholder cannot

---

[8] U.C.C., 8–401.

[9] U.C.C., 8–404.

FIGURE 54–6

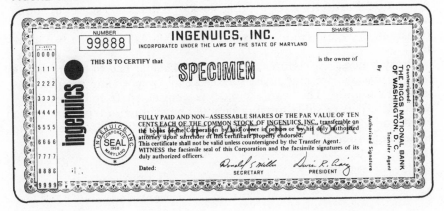

waive rights concerning matters that one does not know will be brought before a meeting.

If all stockholders attend a meeting and proper notice has *not* been given, a waiver of notice could be prepared and signed by the attending stockholders. This would cure the lack of notice.

Voting

A stockholder can generally vote at a stockholder's meeting on any issue, even those in which he or she has a personal interest. A stockholder is not a trustee for the other stockholders and one can represent one's own interests as one sees best. The owner of stock as shown on the stock transfer book of the corporation is the person entitled to vote. However, the personal representative of a deceased stockholder can vote stock without having it transferred to that representative.

Problems can arise in voting where a transfer of stock is contemplated, or under way, but not yet completed. The stockholder of record can vote, and innocent third parties will be protected on contracts arising out of such voting. Careful consideration should be given to this fact by the purchaser of stock. It can be handled by contract between the parties, thus assuring the buyer the right to vote the stock.

Special voting privileges may be conferred upon preferred stockholders by the charter of the corporation. If the charter is silent, most state statutes say that preferred stock cannot be voted. The stock voting rules have evolved over a long period of time.

Historical Transition of Voting

At common law each shareholder had one vote regardless of the amount of stock held. The rule probably grew out of the common-law partnership principle that each partner has an equal voice in the management—regardless of the size of the capital contribution. Today, one vote is permitted for each share of voting stock. If A holds 100 shares of voting stock, A has 100 votes. If B has 1,000 shares, B has 1,000 votes. The transition of voting from the common-law rule is illustrated in Figure 54-7.

Proxy Voting. At common law, the stockholder had to be present to vote. Provisions are now made for voting by "proxy," and the power is given by statute. The word "proxy" is contracted from "procuracy," which is a person substituted or deputed by another to represent or act for the other, particularly at a meeting or public body. It also refers to the instrument containing the appointment of such a person.

FIGURE 54-7

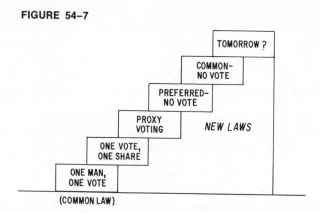

The proxy should be issued with authority that states how it is to be voted. When this is not done, some courts have held that the proxy is void. The laws of agency govern a proxy so the authority of the holder of the proxy (agent) can be revoked before the authority is exercised. The life of a proxy is limited in some states by statute. In one state a proxy that is not revoked expires after three years. Other state statutes say that a proxy expires after the next annual meeting after it is given.

A proxy can be voted after the death of the one giving it if the holder of it has no knowledge of the death. The rule is designed to safeguard actions taken at proper meetings which are carried out in good faith.

Cumulative Voting. The statutes of most states provide for voting for directors by cumulative voting and one state by constitution requires that "directors shall not be elected in any other manner." The minority stockholders cannot control the board but such stockholders are entitled to have representation on the board. Examine Figure 54-8.

Where cumulative voting is allowed, or required, the number of shares held by each stockholder is multiplied by the number of offices to be filled. The voter can spread the votes or cumulate them on one candidate. For example, if A holds 10 shares in Oil Wells, Inc., and three directors are to be elected, A has 30 votes to cast. A can cast 30 votes for one person or spread the votes. Also, A may "pool" the votes with other stockholders to gain representation among the board members.

Generally, notice must be given if one intends to cumulate votes. The reason for this is that cumulative voting is designed to give the minority representation—not control. For example, A has 300 shares in a corporation and B has 200. Five directors are to be elected and the total stock outstanding is held by A and B. A has 1,500 votes and B has 1,000, the number of shares held by each times the directors to be elected. B can be assured of representation on the board. But what if A spreads 1,500 votes over five persons, giving them 300 votes each. If B spreads the

FIGURE 54–8

votes over three, or 333⅓ votes to each, B has elected three of the five officers! Cumulative voting was not designed to permit this to happen.

Another Example. Zero Corporation has 2,600 votes outstanding, and five directors are to be elected by cumulative voting.

Smith	$1,000 \times 5 = 5,000$
Jones	$700 \times 5 = 3,500$
Brown	$500 \times 5 = 2,500$
Green	$100 \times 5 = 500$
Pickett	$300 \times 5 = 1,500$

Picket and Green seem to be out as far as electing even one director, and especially if all of the other votes are present and are voted in person or by proxy. What might they do in order to gain representation on the board? Two suggestions follow.

Voting Pools. In a voting pool, minority shareholders "join forces" and use their votes in a block. Such arrangements are legal as long as they are used for a proper purpose. The weakness in voting pools lies in the fact that one or more stockholders can withdraw their votes prior to the time they are cast and the remaining voters in the pool can do nothing about it.

Voting Trusts. The trust arrangement discussed in Chapter 51 can be used for voting purposes in some states. The states that allow voting trusts generally require that they be limited in time. West Virginia says ten years, but Virginia by case law has upheld voting trusts for as long as 25 years. This type of arrangement separates ownership of stock from the control of it and this is often stated as a reason for not allowing them. In a voting trust, there is an actual transfer of stock to the trustee who becomes the shareholder of record. The trustee votes the shares according to the purposes of the trust and receives the dividends as they are paid. The dividends are held for the "cestui que" (beneficiaries) who are paid from time to time under provisions of the trust. The former owners of the stock receive certificates or some evidence of their "beneficial ownership" of the shares. The trustee is the legal owner—the beneficiaries are the equitable owners. Upon the completion of the trust, the trustee has a duty to transfer the shares back to the original owners or their heirs or assigns.

Closely related to voting is the requirement that a quorum be present at stockholders meetings.

Quorum. A quorum is "such a number of members of a body as is competent to transact business in the absence of the other members."[10] When the required number of persons goes into session as a body, votes of the majority are sufficient as a binding action. Once a meeting is legally constituted, the fact that a number of those present leaves the meeting does not render the actions of the remainder ineffective. The rule is designed to prevent obstruction by dissenters. At common law a majority of the shareholders made up a quorum. The bylaws usually prescribe the number needed and a number more than a simple majority may be prescribed for designated types of business. In most states a quorum would be at least a majority of all shares entitled to vote. A quorum of directors would be at least a majority of the total number of the board. This can be changed by bylaws as pointed out.

Certain motions require more than a simple majority of those present to carry and some types of business require unanimous consent of all stockholders.

Unanimous Vote. In certain instances the unanimous vote of all shareholders is required. Examples would include a contemplated change in the structure of the corporation, the dissolution of a going concern, or the creation of a class of stock that would take benefits away from present shareholders. When unanimous vote is required, a minority shareholder has great power in that one vote can stop a contemplated action no matter how many votes are present.

STOCKHOLDERS SUITS

Stockholders have the right to bring suit under certain circumstances. Three classes of suits are recognized: minority suits, individual suits, and "derivative" suits.

---

[10] *Morton* v. *Talmadge*, 166 Ga. 620, 144 S.E. 111 (1928).

Minority Suits

If the majority stockholders use their voting power in such a manner that it causes injury to the minority, a cause of action exists. For example, if dividends are arbitrarily withheld because the majority stockholders elect board members who consistently refuse to declare dividends, the minority would have a right to file suit in an attempt to correct the situation. The burden of proof would be on the minority since they would be the plaintiffs.

Individual Suits

In rare cases an individual shareholder is injured personally in some manner by the corporation. For example, shareholder X may be engaged in a contract with the corporation which is breached, causing loss. Or, X may be injured by the negligence of an agent of the corporation. In either case, X would have the right to file suit in an attempt to recover the losses. The distinction between a minority and an individual suit is that in the former one is injured as a shareholder, in the latter as an individual.

Derivative Suits

The word "derivative" is defined as "coming from another." A derivative suit is one brought by a shareholder to enforce a *corporate* cause of action. The corporation must be a party to the suit and if a judgment or decree is obtained against a third party, it must be in favor of the corporation and not the shareholder. Before a derivative suit can be brought, certain preliminary conditions must be met.

First, there must be an injury to the corporation. For example, the board of directors might be making unlawful expenditures, causing loss. Next, the interested shareholder must "exhaust remedies;" that is, take all reasonable steps necessary in an attempt to allow the directors to correct the problem. Since the shareholder will be a volunteer, the requirement seems unrealistic. Yet it is founded upon the simple principle that a court will not hear and decide something if there is another remedy available. In the situation suggested, a demand must be made of the directors to stop making the unlawful expenditures. If the efforts fail, the shareholder then has standing to sue.

At one time certain "shady" individuals were engaged in the practice of buying a share or two in a corporation, looking for problems in the corporation, which they often found, and then filing a derivative suit. Later they would attempt to settle the case in return for an agreed sum of money. These suits were labeled "nuisance suits" and led the states to adopt minimum stock requirements before one has standing to bring a derivative suit. One state requires that 10 percent of the outstanding stock of the corporation in question be held individually or accumulated by "pooling" stock with others, before a derivative suit can be filed.

One of the hardest fought derivative suits was that of *Rogers* v. *Hill et al.* The following language is that of the court.

Rogers v. *Hill* et al.[11] The American Tobacco Company is a corporation organized under the laws of New Jersey. The petitioner, plaintiff below, acquired in 1916 and has since been the owner of 200 shares of its common stock. He also has 400 shares of common stock B. In accordance with bylaw XII, adopted by the stockholders at their annual meeting, March 13, 1912, the company for many years has annually paid its president and vice-president large amounts in addition to their fixed salaries and other sums allowed them as compensation for services.

	Salary	Cash Credits	Bylaw
Hill (vice president)			
1921			$ 89,833.94
1922			82,902.61
1923			77,336.54
1924			88,894.26
1925			97,049.38
Hill (president)			
1926	$ 75,000.00		188,643.45
1927	75,000.00		268,761.45
1928	75,000.00		280,203.68
1929	144,500.00	$136,507.71	447,870.30
1930	168,000.00	273,470.76	842,507.72
Neiley (vice president)			
1929	33,333.32	44,897.89	115,141.87
1930	50,000.00	89,945.52	409,495.25
Riggio (vice president)			
1929	33,333.32	45,351.40	115,141.86
1930	50,000.00	90,854.06	409,495.25

Plaintiff maintains that the bylaw is invalid and that, even if valid, the amounts paid under it are unreasonably large and therefore subject to revision by the courts. In March, 1931, he demanded that the company bring suit against the officers who have received such payments to compel them to account to the company for all or such part thereof as the court may hold illegal. The company, insisting that such a suit would be without basis in law or fact, refused to comply with his demand. He brought suit in the supreme court of New York against the president and some of the vice presidents to require them so to account, and joined the company as defendant. The case was removed to the federal court for the southern district of New York. In May, 1931, plaintiff brought suit in that court against Taylor, a vice president, not a defendant in the earlier suit, to require him to account, and made the company defendant. The cases were consolidated, plaintiff filed an amended complaint, and defendants answered. The officers of the company now before the court are Hill, the president, Neiley, Riggio, and Taylor, vice presidents. The answer, after admissions, denials, and explanations, asserts several separate defenses.

The only payments that plaintiff by this suit seeks to have restored to the company are the payments made to the individual defendants under the bylaw.

---

[11] 289 U.S. 584 (1932).

We come to consider whether these amounts are subject to examination and revision in the district court. As the amounts payable depend upon the gains of the business, the specified percentages are not per se unreasonable. The bylaw was adopted in 1912 by an almost unanimous vote of the shares represented at the annual meeting and presumably the stockholders supporting the measure acted in good faith and according to their best judgment. The tabular statement in the margin shows the payments to individual defendants under the bylaw. Plaintiff does not complain of any made prior to 1921. Regard is to be had to the enormous increase of the company's profits in recent years. The 2.5 percent yielded President Hill $447,870.30 in 1929 and $842,507.72 in 1930. The 1.5 percent yielded to each of the vice presidents, Neiley and Riggio, $115,141.86 in 1929 and $409,495.25 in 1930, and for these years payments under the bylaw were in addition to the cash credits and fixed salaries shown in the statement.

While the amounts produced by the application of the prescribed percentages give rise to no inference of actual or constructive fraud, the payments under the bylaw have, by reason of increase of profits, become so large as to warrant investigation in equity in the interest of the company. Much weight is to be given to the action of the stockholders, and the bylaw is supported by the presumption of regularity and continuity. But the rule prescribed by it cannot, against the protest of a shareholder, be used to justify payments of sums as salaries so large as in substance and effect to amount to spoilation or waste of corporate property. (The stockholder prevailed.)

OTHER RIGHTS OF SHAREHOLDERS

It has been traditional at common law to give the shareholders the right to inspect and copy the "books" of the corporation, and especially so where one can show good cause for the request. For example, a shareholder who is seeking office as a director would have good cause to ask for a list of shareholders' names and addresses for use in seeking proxies. Most courts have held that an inspection must be done at a reasonable time and under reasonable conditions. A "split of authority" (the courts have ruled both ways) has developed on the question of whether a shareholder has a right to inspect the books out of mere curiosity. Some states permit it—some do not.

The right to inspect the books was abused and, as a result, most states have minimum-stock requirements that must be met by the one (or the group) making the request. If the request is refused, the stockholder has the right to proceed by petition in court in an attempt to obtain an order from a judge ordering the corporation to produce the books for inspection.

Today, with more and more corporations using computers for recordkeeping purposes, new regulations will develop regarding the right of shareholders to inspect "books."

REVIEW QUESTIONS

1. A, a stranger, offers to purchase your 1,000 shares of Ford Motor Company stock and tenders a personal check in the sum that you have asked for the stock. Should you surrender the stock at that time? Why?

2. What is the inherent danger in a blank indorsement on a stock certificate?
3. You have lost a certificate for 500 shares of U.S. Communications Company stock. What must you do? The serial number of the certificate is 2962821.
4. In the *Rogers* v. *Hill* case, Mr. Hill spent about $25,000 in fees to win the case. Does it surprise you to learn that he had to pay this out of his own pocket? (A later board of directors reimbursed him for the expenditure.)
5. True or False. The one who casts a vote by proxy is an agent and the stockholder is the principal.
6. Why is a broker's commission usually lower for larger purchases of stock?
7. Distinguish a "present stock subscription" from a "contract to buy."
8. Define a "condition precedent."
9. What is the legal problem with an offer to buy stock in a corporation that has not yet been formed?
10. Why is a stock certificate "mere evidence of ownership" in a corporation?

Words and Phrases

Write out briefly what they mean to you.
1. Cumulative voting.
2. Notice of meeting.
3. Minority suit.
4. Derivative suit.
5. Quorum.

Coverage:	Duties of corporate officials.
What to Look for:	Things to avoid while serving as a director or officer.
Application:	Look for points that would help make decisions at the time of incorporation.

55 Directors, Officers, and Dissolution

Directors are elected by the stockholders at the annual meeting, although a special meeting may be called to fill a vacancy. Once a quorum is present, the stockholders vote by oral vote or written ballot. If cumulative voting is mandatory or provided in the bylaws, each stockholder will multiply the voting shares times the offices to be filled and proceed as discussed in Chapter 54. Directors should be elected upon the basis of business experience, skill, and judgment, but, as might be expected, frequently they are not.

Some states require that at least one member of the board be a stockholder, otherwise they do not have to be. Most boards have at least three members and in large corporations the number will be many times that figure.

After the directors or their replacements have been elected, they constitute the board. The board must operate under guidelines of the bylaws, the laws of the state, and the dictates of common sense.

The board represents *all* of the stockholders and not just those whose votes placed them in office. For this reason the board members must exercise independent judgment and not be influenced by the will of the majority of the stockholders. If the board should ignore the interests of the minority stockholders, this would be an abuse of discretion and a minority suit could follow. Unless there is an abuse of discretion or negligence on the part of the board, the courts will refuse to interfere in the management of a corporation. Even when the courts entertain petitions of complaining stockholders, they seldom substitute their judgment for that of the board.

Management

It is the function of the board to manage the business affairs of the corporation. They do this at their meetings, which will be recorded in properly kept minutes.

Voting

Each member of the board is entitled to one vote on any matter that lawfully comes before the directors. They are not permitted to vote by proxy. If they are absent from a meeting in which a lawful vote carries, they are bound by that vote provided that a quorum was present. Directors are prohibited from voting on any matter in which they have a "personal interest." That is, an interest other than as a member of the board. For example, if Zero Corporation is considering the purchase of land owned by the family of Director X, X would have a personal interest in the transaction. A director who has personal interest in a pending matter, directly or indirectly, should do three things. First, disclose the interest. Next, let the record show this action. Last, leave the meeting and not be present when the business is voted on. By taking these steps, the director is disqualified and the record discloses this. If one fails to do this, one may later be accused of improper conduct or possibly fraud.

Quorum

A quorum of the board is usually one more than one half of the number serving. For example, in a corporation with 17 directors, 9 would constitute a quorum. If this number is present, the meeting may proceed. If only eight show, the meeting would be adjourned from day to day until the prescribed number appears. If a director attends a meeting and finds that his or her presence is needed to make the quorum, that person cannot leave and defeat the purposes of the meeting. Most courts hold that the initial presence (if only for a moment) served to constitute the quorum and the balance of the board may transact business by majority vote of the remainder. In practice, directors seldom fail to attend meetings.

Scheduled Meetings

Directors operate at regular or scheduled meetings and the dates and times are spelled out in the bylaws. They may meet at special meetings if notice is given as specified in the bylaws. There is a tendency for directors in small corporations to meet informally without proper notice or waiver of notice. This is a mistake and should be avoided. There is always the risk of incurring partnership liability because of informality in the management of the business. In larger corporations, the necessary formalities are routinely met.

Who Presides?   The officer who presides at directors meetings is the chairperson of the board or the president of the corporation, depending upon the structure of the business.

Minutes. A corporation, just as a court, speaks through its records. All corporations, large and small, through agents, must keep and preserve minutes. Failure to do so may result in future liability of the directors when they are unable to prove that actions taken by them were done under corporate authority. The minutes should be safeguarded from theft, fire, loss, or alteration.

The minutes should contain the time and place of the meeting, the names of those present, the motions that were made, and the outcome of votes taken. Minutes do not have to contain each word spoken at the meeting, but should contain enough detail that someone reading them in the future can tell what took place at the meeting without having to consult other sources.

At the next meeting of the board, the presiding officer should present the minutes from the last meeting for approval. There is a tendency among directors, to move that the reading of the minutes be dispensed with. This is foolish because the directors are waiving their right to correct errors or to amend the minutes. If copies of the minutes are distributed prior to the meeting, then the motion would be in order. After the minutes are approved, they must be signed by the appropriate officers and filed in the minute book.

The minutes of corporations provide a valuable source of information about the history of the firm and it is not uncommon for researchers to turn to the minutes of previous decades to reconstruct historical fact. (For a sample set of minutes, see *Student Workbook.*)

Executive Sessions

For many years it has been a practice in corporations, as well as city, state, and federal governments, for the managing or law-making body to hold closed sessions, frequently called "executive sessions." These meetings are used to arrive at an agreement that will later be "rubber stamped" at a regular meeting. In corporations, this procedure is frequently used by a majority of the board to prearrange decisions so that minority members of the board can be kept out of the final determination.

The executive session is a deadly weapon if used effectively, and especially so in governmental activities. Opposition has been growing to the practice and changes are occurring by statutory law or other regulations. For example, a corporation could create a regulation in its bylaws to prohibit closed or executive sessions of the directors. Many states have enacted "sunshine laws" to force open meetings of governmental bodies. However, these laws usually recognize that certain matters, such as preparing to accept bids on contracts, cannot be held in open session and thus the laws have exceptions.

How Long Do Directors Serve?

Directors hold office until their successors are elected, or until they become incapacitated or die, or until they are replaced by action of the stockholders. In the event the term of a director ends and no replacement has been named, the old director continues to hold office until the successor is elected and that person would have full power to act at meetings in the interim. This "holdover" provision prevents a break in the board's structure. In addition, it is customary to "stagger" the terms of board members to assure continuity of operation.

Standard of Care and Liability

A director is held to that standard of care that would be possessed by one of his or her training and experience—or to that standard of experience that one holds out as having. A director who exercises reasonable skill and judgment will generally not incur personal liability. In short, one is not held responsible for "honest errors" or good-faith errors in judgment.

One who is *negligent* in doing something or in failing to do something that should have been done, may be held liable for the resulting loss. The corporate entity protects the stockholders, but the directors are "legally naked."

As Agents

Directors are agents of the corporation—not the stockholders—and the rules of agency control. In a partial sense they are trustees of the corporation, but not in the strict sense. They cannot act on a matter in which they have a personal interest, and if they do must account to the corporation for profits made because of it.

While they are not agents of the stockholders, questions arise in dealing with shareholders. Must they answer questions put to them? May they buy stock from stockholders without disclosing "inside knowledge" that they have? Must they disclose pending action contemplated by the corporation? Historically, directors owed no duties to stockholders that they did not owe others, but this is changing. As a basic guide, directors should act in good faith with all shareholders at all times. As to disclosures, the question should be raised at a meeting called for that purpose. A legal opinion should be sought. Directors should avoid treating stockholders as though they have no interest in the business. Also, directors must not violate the Securities and Exchange Acts of 1933 and 1934.

ULTRA VIRES ACTS

Directors must operate within the bounds of the stated purposes, the bylaws, and state law that is binding upon the corporation. If they engage in activities beyond the limits prescribed, their acts are "ultra vires."

> The term has broad application and includes not only acts prohibited by the charter of a corporation, but acts which are in excess of powers granted but not prohibited.[1]

---
[1] *State* v. *Cook*, 234 Mo.App. 898, 136 S.W.2d. 142, 146 (1940).

In short, ultra vires acts are ones that are beyond the powers of a corporation.

Not an Illegal Act

An ultra vires act is not an illegal act—the reverse is true. If the directors of Zero Corporation enter into an agreement to construct a shopping mall for Smith, when the purpose of the corporation is to bottle soft drinks, the contract would be ultra vires although there would be nothing illegal about it. If the same directors engaged in a price-fixing agreement with a competitor, that agreement would be illegal as well as ultra vires.

What May Happen?

The danger inherent in ultra vires acts is that the corporation may not be bound by what the directors have done. In that event the directors would be held personally liable by third parties who may be injured. Therefore, directors must make certain that their acts are within the scope of the authority of the corporation, expressly, impliedly, or as may be granted by state law. If a director is in doubt about the status of pending board action, inquiry should be made. If still not satisfied, the director should dissent if a vote is taken and have the negative vote recorded. Most states provide by statute that if an illegal or ultra vires act is performed by a board of directors, all members present when the action was taken are personally responsible *even if they voted "no."* However, if the record shows the "no" vote, they are relieved of liability.

Third parties who deal with a corporation must also exercise care. Regardless of what they may be told by others, it is still their responsibility to make certain that the corporation, who is dealing with them by its agents, has the power to do that which is contemplated. If the corporation does not, third parties may lose the benefits of their contract or business arrangement. If in doubt, independent inquiry should be made and a legal opinion sought. Since all corporations must record their charters, the information upon which a decision can be based is usually close at hand.

Who Can Complain?

The stockholders have every right to complain about ultra vires since these acts divert their investments into directions not contemplated initially. They would have a right to demand that such acts be discontinued, and if not, they would have standing to use the derivative suit to enjoin the action by the directors. The attorney general of the state of incorporation also has a right to complain of ultra vires acts because the statement of purposes in the application was a promise that the corporation would operate within the purposes stated. Many suits have been brought by the states to enjoin ultra vires acts or to force the forfeiture of corporate charters for noncompliance.

Who Pays?

If a corporation suffers losses because of ultra vires acts, the directors or officers, if involved, will be called upon to make good the losses. As a rule, third parties cannot complain of ultra vires acts because of the duty placed upon them to determine the purposes of corporations with which they transact business. If they fail to inquire and suffer loss, it is due to their *own* carelessness.

If directors commit ultra vires acts that result in physical injury or property damage to a third party, the result is different. The corporation may avoid contract liability for the acts of its agents committed beyond authority—but it cannot avoid tort liability because the law of agency governs the relationship of the directors with the corporation. Therefore, if a third party is injured because of the negligence of an agent, the principal (corporation) may be called upon to answer for the damages—a fundamental rule of agency.

Generally speaking, a corporation would not be held responsible for *crimes* committed by a director. A corporation, being a fictitious being, would be incapable of forming intention, which is an essential element in most crimes. However, a corporation may be held liable where directors violate statutes that have criminal penalties attached to them, such as the price fixing or restraint of trade laws.

DIVIDENDS

A dividend occurs when a corporation divides appropriate funds and distributes a share to the shareholders. Whether or not dividends are declared and paid is a decision that must be made by the board of directors. The board is permitted to exercise independent judgment and the final decision is left to the sound discretion of the board. Very seldom will a court substitute its judgment for that of directors unless arbitrariness or capriciousness is involved in their refusal to declare a dividend.

From What Funds?

A dividend must be paid from legal funds. For example, if a corporation has $100,000 in assets and $100,000 in liabilities, a cash dividend could not be declared because distribution of funds would render the corporation insolvent. Each state has laws that spell out the conditions that must be met before a cash dividend can be paid. Some states permit dividends to be paid out of net profits for any year, even though losses may have occurred in prior years. Other states permit the payment of dividends only after all prior losses are made up, and then dividends may only be paid out of "surplus." Surplus for dividend purposes has been defined as "an excess of the aggregate value of all assets of a corporation over the sum of its entire liabilities, including capital stock."[2] The definition lends itself to a diagram. (See Figure 55–1.)

---

[2] *Branch* v. *Kaiser*, 291 Penna. 543, 140 A. 498, 500 (1928).

to the amount of such dividends severally received by them, to reimburse the directors for any sums which they may be compelled to pay as such to the creditors of the corporation under the provisions of this section. Such liability may be enforced in equity on a bill filed by any creditor or director.

A reading of both statutes—which are typical—leads one to the consion that this state is a surplus state and not a net profit state. In short, dividend may be declared and paid in that state which would impair capital, that is, reduce the total of assets below the total of capital ck plus liabilities.

ds of Dividends

The principal types of dividends are cash and stock dividends. Ocionally a corporation will issue a dividend in bonds, property (such the product of the corporation), or some "right" that gives the shareders an option to buy a portion of a future issue of stock.

Property dividends are treated as income in the year in which they are eived and are valued at "fair market value." Most states permit shareders to refuse a property dividend and demand that they be paid in h. For example, a dividend of the products of a distillery might be ensive to certain stockholders—but not to others.

Bonds may be issued as dividends, but existing rights of creditors ist not be harmed nor may the capital of the corporation be impaired. ere "rights" are used as dividends, they often take the form of "stock rrants." The holder of the warrant has the right, within a prescribed riod of time and at a set price, to surrender it for the stock represented it. The warrants themselves often look like stock certificates and are netimes traded on the market.

Cash Dividends. Seldom is a "cash" dividend paid in cash. It is routine the payments to be made by computerized checks. The "cash" idend is different from those mentioned since it may be used as a dium of exchange to pay debts of the stockholder or to purchase other urities. In almost all instances, an announcement of a cash dividend reflected in the price that such shares are traded for on the market. r this reason, once a cash dividend is declared and made public, the m is committed to that dividend. The directors would not have the right revoke it.

Distribution Example. Zero Corporation has the following number d types of shares outstanding, and all shares have been issued.

	Par	Shares Out
Common stock	$10	5,000
Cumulative, preferred, fully participating, 4 percent......................	$10	2,000

By the term of the preferred stock contract, each share is to receive a percent preference and any additional sum available is to be shared ually with each share of common. Dividends passed over will "ac-

FIGURE 55–1
Surplus for Dividend Purposes

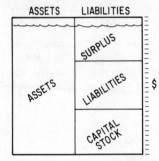

Net Profit Approach

As long as a profit is realized in the current year, a
paid out of those profits in states that follow this rul
created by "writing up" the value of corporate assets (a
surplus could not be used for dividend purposes. It
"paper profit" – even if accurate – and would not be a p
for that year.

Surplus States

A typical statute follows:

> *Dividends; Deduction of Indebtedness; Determinat*
> *Exploitation of Wasting Assets.* The board of directors
> time, declare and pay dividends of so much of the net p₁
> plus arising from a reduction of capital pursuant to sec
> this article as they deem it prudent to divide. If any stock
> to the corporation, his dividend, or so much thereof as is
> applied to the payment of such indebtedness if then due

At first, one might conclude that the state from which
taken is a "net profit" state. However, a companion statu
sidered.

> *Liability of Directors and Stockholders for Unlawfu*
> board of directors shall declare and pay any dividend wh₍
> is insolvent, or any dividend the payment of which would :
> or would diminish the amount of capital, the members p
> action is taken shall be jointly and severally liable to th
> corporation for the amount of dividends so declared and ₁
> the debts of the corporation then existing; but any dire
> dissents from such action and causes his dissent to be ent₍
> of the proceedings shall not incur any liability. The direc
> proceeded against separately or jointly. Every stockholder
> any such dividend shall be liable to the creditors for the ar
> by him. The stockholders shall be jointly and severally liab]

cumulate." The directors declare a $10,000 dividend to be paid in June, 1976. No dividends were paid in 1975 or 1974.

		Preferred	Common
Distribution	1974	$800	.00
	1975	$800	.00
	1976	$800	
Additional sharing		$3,800	$3,800
Total		$6,200	$3,800
Each share receives		$3.10	$1.90

The cumulative feature coupled with the 4 percent preference enables the preferred shareholders to capture a larger percentage of the dividend.

Stock Dividend. A stock dividend occurs when the directors decide to convert surplus or retained earnings to capital and issue additional shares to evidence the transfer. Such a "dividend" is, for practical purposes, not a dividend but a "capitalization" of the funds represented in the transaction. The increased number of shares now held by the shareholders will equal the value in the corporation that the smaller number of shares represented. Because of this fact, most states will not permit the expenses of a stock dividend to be deducted for tax purposes. Conversely, the Internal Revenue Service does not treat a stock dividend as a taxable event since it is merely a division of the value of the corporation. The stockholder's "equity" remains unchanged. There is legal authority that a stock dividend may be revoked after it is declared, for the reasons discussed.

One who receives a stock dividend gains an advantage: That person has a means of reaching the underlying assets of the corporation by selling the new shares. However, by so doing one proportionally reduces voting power one may enjoy in the corporation.

Two practical advantages to a corporation follow from the use of a stock dividend. First, it tends to reduce the market price of stock. For example, if the stock has a current market value of $10 and a 100 percent stock dividend is declared, the market price (theoretically) is reduced to $5. Second, the use of the stock dividend spreads the ownership, and control of the corporation may be maintained by one who holds a smaller number of shares.

Distinguished from a Stock Split. A stock split is not the same as a stock dividend. In the stock dividend there is a change in surplus or retained earnings. In a stock split there is not, and the existing capital remains unchanged, although it equals a new number of shares. For example, the directors might decide to change 1,000 shares of $10 par common to 2,000 shares of $5 par common. Or they might decide to convert 2,000 shares of $5 par common to 1,000 shares of $10 par—a "reverse split."

Stock splits have various uses, but the most common is to reduce the market price of stock after it rises to a level that tends to discourage investors from purchasing it.

While the decision to split stock is one of financial judgment, legal steps must be followed before the change can be made. A resolution of the directors (or stockholders) is required; an application for an amendment of the corporate charter must be made; and the state of incorporation must approve the change. Figure 55–2 illustrates the distinction between a cash dividend, a stock dividend, and a stock split.

Liquidating Dividend. A "liquidating" dividend is an "act or operation in winding up the affairs of a firm or corporation, a settling with its debtors or creditors, and an appropriation and distribution to its stock-

FIGURE 55–2

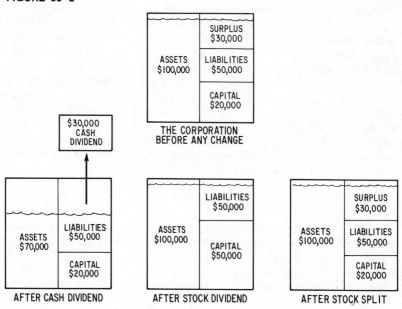

holders ratably of the amount of profit and loss."[3] The statutes require that a shareholder be informed when a liquidating dividend is received. Since it is only a return of capital, it is not subject to income taxes. A liquidating dividend occurs when a distribution is made of funds that have been set aside as a reserve for depreciation and when a corporation returns to its shareholders the capital assets of the firm after it has been dissolved.

Ex Dividend. If the seller of stock is going to keep dividends declared but not yet paid, the seller will sell "ex dividend"—without the dividend. The buyer takes the stock subject to the right of the previous owner to receive the dividends already declared.

---

[3] *Hellman* v. *Helvering*, App.D.C., 68 F.2d. 763, 765 (1934).

REMOVAL OF DIRECTORS

The stockholders have the power to remove directors, and the bylaws will spell out the circumstances under which removal may be carried out. It may be "for cause" or "without cause." If the director to be removed was elected to the board by a certain class or type of stock, then the director may only be removed by shareholders of that class or type. In rare occasions, the removal of a director may impair an existing contract. In that event the removal might require reconsideration.

The Model Business Corporation Act contains a unique provision: a director may not be removed from office if the votes *against* removal would, if cumulated, be enough to reelect the director to office.[4]

A vacancy caused by removal is filled by a majority vote of the remaining members of the board. The new director will serve out the term of the old or until the successor is elected at the next meeting of the shareholders.

OFFICERS

Officers of a corporation are hired or appointed by the board and may be members of the board. The officers include the president (and vice presidents), secretary, and treasurer. In some states the president must be a director. One person may hold dual offices such as secretary-treasurer. The president should not hold dual offices.

THIRD PARTIES

Those who transact business with a corporation may treat it as a "person." If a contract is breached, or if the third party is injured by the negligence of an agent of a corporation, the third party may sue the corporation. Service of process could be made upon an officer or agent of the corporation. In the case of a nonresident corporation, the long-arm statutes are used.

Execution may be levied upon corporate property and attachments placed against corporate assets. In short, the corporation must answer to third parties just as an individual must.

AMENDING THE CHARTER

The corporate charter is a contract with the state that issued it. It may be amended with the approval of the state, provided the proper legal steps are followed.

DISSOLUTION

In the usual case of dissolution, the incorporation procedure is reversed. Publication is required to give creditors an opportunity to file

---

[4] Model Business Corporation Act, Section 36A.

claims. Upon proof of compliance, the state will retire the charter. In rare cases, the state, acting through the attorney general, may force a corporation into involuntary retirement.

REVIEW QUESTIONS

Reexamine the dividend distribution example above.

1. Would the common shareholders in Zero Corporation be interested in a long-range plan to retire the preferred stock? Why?
2. Name one reason why the common shareholders might *not* want to retire the preferred.
3. Name one reason why the common shareholders may not be able to legally retire the preferred even though they decided to do so.
4. Distinguish a cash dividend from a stock dividend.
5. True or False. A director who votes "no" at a meeting will never incur personal liability on that particular transaction.
6. Create an example of how a quorum dispute may arise.
7. Name two reasons why minutes should be kept accurately.
8. How could a director who is serving a one year term, legally serve for two years without being reelected?
9. Why are directors not agents of the stockholders?
10. Explain why an ultra vires act is usually not an illegal act.

Words and Phrases

Write out briefly what they mean to you.

1. Surplus.
2. Stock split.
3. Personal interest.
4. Executive sessions.
5. Stock dividend.

Appendixes

A Selected Portions of the Uniform Commercial Code

1. The Overlooked Article—Article 1

Introduction. The Code calls for liberal administration of its sections.[1] The courts are complying and the Review Board has not had to intervene by arguing for this in court. Contracting parties may adopt provisions different from those in the code, but they cannot contract away

> good faith,
> diligence,
> reasonableness, and
> care.

Further, they can set the standards to be applied to their contracts, but what they adopt must not be "manifestly unreasonable."

Does Not Have All of the Answers. The Code does not have all of the answers. Therefore the rules of the law merchant, principal and agent, capacity to contract, estoppel, fraud, duress, coercion, and mistake still apply.[2] Further, since the Code is not a federal law, it does not have any effect upon federal statutes. For example, the bankruptcy act presents serious problems on the questions of "voidable preferences" and "priorities" under secured transactions. The cases in these areas are beginning to develop fully in the courts.

Conflict of Laws. Modern business transactions almost always involve two or more states. Under the Code the parties may choose the law that will be binding upon them.[3] But the law they choose must bear a "reasonable relationship" to the facts involved in the transaction. In drafting contracts it is essential that a "reasonable jurisdiction" be chosen. There have been decisions where a court has held that the jurisdiction chosen was not reasonable, thus applying the law of another state. This is what is meant by "conflicts of law."

Waiver or Renunciation. After there has been a breach of a sales contract, there may be a "waiver" or "renunciation," and consideration

---

[1] U.C.C., 1–106.
[2] U.C.C., 1–103.
[3] U.C.C., 1–105.

is not necessary to make it binding—that is, a party may waive or re-nounce rights under the contract. However, such waiver or renunciation must be in writing and signed, and it is good business practice to have a copy signed by the other party as proof.[4]

Captions Part of Code.   The captions are a part of the code but the comments are not. The captions are helpful in locating applicable parts of the code and are essential for an in-depth study.[5]

Definitions.   Forty-six (46) basic definitions are found in U.C.C., 1–201. It is essential to look here to see if a term has been defined. If it has, the definition governs. But there are problems in definitions. For example, "agreement" is defined, but the term does not mean what it says. Under the Code the courts may apply three factors in determining what a word means: (1) language, oral or written, (2) course of dealing, and (3) usage of trade. For this reason the terms on the face of a written contract cannot be relied upon completely. The word "agreement" is not only what the parties *say* but what they *do*. Thus, a contract may be found in the way one acts as contrasted with what one "promises" to do.

The definition of "conspicuous" is important. Whether something is conspicuous or not is for the determination of the court. The Code tells us that any term contained in a telegram is conspicuous—but what about a restriction on transfer of stock typed in small type on the back of a stock certificate? That type of restriction should be placed on the certificate in bold type or colored ink.

The old "fungible" concept of law has been altered by definition. The parties may agree that things that are not fungible in the old sense are in fact fungible. This can be applied to warehousing by using an average value on the items as they go in and out. This procedure was followed in former times but the code gives it statutory backing.

The Code definitions U.C.C., 1–201 (25) through (27) require that the business person establish a routine to assure that notice is routed within the organization. And further, it requires that one be able to prove that the system is in operation.

Third-Party Documents.   Third-party documents such as insurance policies are *"prima facie"* evidence of what they say. Therefore, there is no need to bring someone into court to lay the foundation for their introduction into evidence.[6]

Heart of the Code.   "Every contract or duty within this act imposes an obligation of good faith in its performance or enforcement."[7]

New Statute of Frauds.   A $5,000 level is established above which the sale of personal property must be evidenced by a writing.[8] This section does not apply to other sections setting out statutes of frauds, namely

---

[4] U.C.C., 1–107.
[5] U.C.C., 1–109.
[6] U.C.C., 1–202.
[7] U.C.C., 1–203.
[8] U.C.C., 1–206.

U.C.C., 2–201 (Sales), U.C.C., 8–319 (Securities), and U.C.C., 9–203 (Security Agreements).

"I feel insecure": The insecure language is preserved by the Code.[9] But it is not enough to feel this way; the Code requires that one state some basis for it.

2.   Article 2 — Some Observations

The Reason for the Unconscionable Clause.   Article 2 makes up 25 percent of the Code, having 100 of the 400 sections. It is the most radical of all sections and alters basic contract rules. Simple contract rules did not work well in commercial sales. The unilateral contract with the power of revocation caused most of the problems. In decisions under the Uniform Sales Act, the courts tried to reach a just result and had to "twist" the law to do so. The unconscionable clause was inserted to provide a means of reaching just results without having to alter basic contract rules. "Unconscionable" goes to oppression or surprise.

How Is a Sales Contract Formed under the Code?   The question seems complex, but the answer is not too difficult: simple contract rules are used, coupled with U.C.C., 2–201 through U.C.C., 2–210.

The "Privity Myth" Article 2.   At first reading, U.C.C. 2–318 seems to abolish "privity" as a defense to those who manufacture products that cause injury to consumers because of defects. Closer reading of the section shows that privity as a defense is only abolished in part. The drafters of the Code chose the conservative approach and left the matter to the courts and "the developing body of case law." Some states considered this a mistake and re-drafted U.C.C., 2–318, eliminating privity as a defense. The Virginia Code provides a good example. (See Chapter 38.)

Under the standard version of U.C.C., 2–318, the buyer or members of the buyer's family who are injured can go against the seller provided that the sale carried an implied warranty of fitness[10] or an implied warranty of merchantability[11] which are breached. The effect of disclaimers on the privity problem is another story. However, disclaimers must be "conspicuous." See Chapter 38 for an example.

3.   Article 3 — Some Misunderstandings

The Key.   The key section of Article 3 is U.C.C., 3–104(1), which spells out the requirements of negotiable instruments. (See Chapter 30.)

How to Try a Negotiable Instruments Case.   U.C.C., 3–307 is a "procedural" section and is followed carefully in law suits on negotiable instruments. Once the signature is established, the mere production of

---

[9] U.C.C., 1–208.

[10] U.C.C., 2–315.

[11] U.C.C., 2–314.

the instrument entitles the plaintiff to recover unless a defense is asserted. The signature is established unless it is denied, making it hard to defend a negotiable instruments suit.

A Misquote. One misquoted section is U.C.C., 3–805. Article 3 applies to the rights of parties including transfer and defenses even though the instrument is *not* negotiable. (But there can be no holder in due course of such an instrument.) What has happened is this: two laws could be applied to instruments not payable to order or bearer—(1) contract law and (2) negotiable instruments law. The Code simply states that negotiable instruments law is applied—it does not make such instruments negotiable.

A New Jersey Case. In *Unico* v. *Owen*,[12] a company sold a series of record albums to Owen but failed to deliver them. Unico was the financing agent of the company and purchased the paper signed by Owen. Records were not shipped, and Unico sued on the note, claiming the status of a holder in due course. (There was a failure of consideration—but this is a personal defense.)

> Held: (at page 417)
>
> For the purposes of consumer goods transactions, we hold that where the seller's performance is executory in character and when it appears from the totality of the arrangements between dealer and financier that the financier has had a substantial voice in setting standards for the underlying transaction, or has approved the standards established by the dealer, and has agreed to take all or a predetermined or substantial quantity of the negotiable paper which is backed by such standards, the financier should be considered a participant in the original transaction and therefore not entitled to holder in the due course status.

See Chapter 31 for a further discussion.

Miscellaneous. Certain words may be added to negotiable instruments as spelled out in U.C.C., 3–105. "Pay to" coupled with the name, is all that is needed for a special indorsement under Article 3. There is no need to say "pay to the order of" in the indorsement.[13]

4. Observations on Article 4

The law of stop payment has been changed by U.C.C., 4–403. A bank must honor an oral stop payment up to 14 days. If the stop payment is reduced to writing, the period is extended to six months—and can be renewed.

A check is an "order from the drawer to the bank" and if the bank does not pay as ordered, it cannot charge what it pays to the account of the drawer. This is why forged checks normally cannot be charged to an account. For a classic exception, see *J. P. Leonard* v. *National Bank,* Chapter 29.

The Code gives a drawer three years to check indorsements and one

---

[12] 232 A.2d 405 (New Jersey, 1967).

[13] U.C.C., 3–204.

year to notify the bank of any forgery. The Code has further placed a duty upon the bank to act in good faith.

5.   Article 6—One Observation on "Bulk Sales"

If a seller is in doubt whether one is selling a "major part" of the business the doubt should be resolved and proceed under Article 6. The "notice" and other requirements of that article should be complied with carefully. However, Article 6 applies only to a business that sells from inventory—manufacturers and service businesses are not covered.

One side point: the Code speaks of "creditors" in Article 6, and this probably means *all* creditors. To be safe, the seller of a business should pay all creditors from the proceeds of the sale.

Article 6 also covers auctions.

6.   A Confusing Area—Article 7

The drafters of the U.C.C. intended that Article 7 (Warehouse Receipts, Bills of Lading, etc.) be used to create a piece of paper that represents the goods in question. So transfer of the paper is in effect a transfer of the goods. It therefore takes priority in the hands of those to whom it is negotiated. If it is negotiated, it takes preference over a warehouse lien. If not negotiated, this is not true.

7.   Placing Security into Investment Securities

Not a Stock Transfer Law.   Article 8, Investment Securities, was not intended to be a new corporation law. It does not provide for issuing stock and it is not a security law. It is a negotiable instruments law for investment securities. At common law there was no accurate place for investment securities because they did not meet the test of negotiable instruments, but they were something more than mere contracts. The scope of the article is set out in U.C.C., 8–102.

Stock is a medium of investment, issued in a class or series, and the stock instrument evidences a share in or a debt of the corporate entity. The main purpose of Article 8 is to make the investment security as freely transferable as possible.

Liens of Issuer or Restrictions on Transfer Must Be "Conspicuous." A lien of the issuer must be noted on the face of the instrument "conspicuously." Restrictions on transfer must also be noted "conspicuously."[14]

Article 8 makes it easy to transfer stock out of an estate. However, the issuer is liable if a transfer is unlawful and must be careful for this reason. The Code spells out what the issuer may require.

Duty to Issue.   The duty of the issuer is set out in U.C.C., 8–401. The issuer must issue if the security is indorsed by an "appropriate person"

---

[14] U.C.C., 8–204.

and the issuer has reasonable assurance that the signature is genuine.[15] The issuer can avoid "adverse claims" by use of the 30-day notice rule discussed in Chapter 54.

8. "Insecurity under Secured Transactions" — Article 9

Prior to the Code there were a variety of security devices such as conditional sales contracts, chattel mortgages, factors liens, trust receipts, pledges, and the like. All had two things in common: a debt and security for the person who extended the credit. These have been replaced by the "security interest" of the Code. Certain secured transactions are exempt from the Code, including real estate secured transactions.[16]

Surprisingly enough, it is not always easy to determine if a transaction is one that falls under Article 9. Normal sales transactions would be covered by Article 2 and, yet, some Article 2 sales fall within Article 9. Doubt should be resolved by treating it as a secured transaction under Article 9.

From Security Interest to Priorities.   Article 9 can be divided into five areas: (1) creation of the security interest, (2) the execution of the security agreement (the Article 9 statute of frauds), (3) attaching of the security interest, (4) perfection of the security interest, and (5) priorities.

The following chart provides a means of becoming oriented to Article 9.

The Five Steps of Article 9

1. The "security interest" must arise first, but it is worthless standing alone.[17]
2. The "security agreement" must be entered into. This is a Code statute of frauds. It must be in writing, signed by the debtor, containing a description of the collateral and reference to the debt secured. If the collateral concerns crops, or oil, gas, or minerals to be extracted, or timber to be cut, a description of the land is necessary.[18] This description should be legally sufficient.[19]
3. The "security interest" must "attach" and three steps are required (although they do not have to occur in any particular order):
   a.   There must be a "security agreement."
   b.   Value must be given (a trap for the "floating lien").
   c.   The debtor must have "rights" in the collateral.[20]
4. The "security interest" (which has "attached") must now be "perfected." It is "perfected" when it has:
   a.   "Attached" (see above) and
   b.   All steps required for "perfection" have been taken. There are three types of perfection.[21]

---

[15] U.C.C., 8–308.

[16] See U.C.C., 9–104 for the full list.

[17] 151 S.E.2d 464 (1966) and 154 S.E.2d 886 (1967).

[18] U.C.C., 9–203.

[19] See *ABLJ*, Volume 6/1, Spring, 1968, page 484. But see U.C.C., 9–110. What the code says and what the courts say are two different things.

[20] U.C.C., 9–204(1).

[21] U.C.C., 9–303(1).

(1) Possessory perfection. No written "security agreement" is needed in these cases.[22] Example: A debtor hands the lender a valuable ring to secure a loan. Possession is enough to "perfect."[23] Where field warehousing is involved, see U.C.C., 9–394(2) and (3).

(2) "Perfection" without filing or possession. Examples are purchase money security interests in consumer goods and farm equipment. "Attachment" is all that is necessary.[24] However, this type of perfection still leaves open the question of priorities. See below.

(3) Perfection by filing.[25]

   (a) *What do you file?* The "security agreement" can be filed if both sign and add their addresses, otherwise the "financing statement" is filed.[26]

   (b) *Where do you file?* This depends upon the option selected by the state in question.[27]

   (c) *How soon do you file?* As soon as possible in most cases but there is a 10-day "relation back" in purchase money, consumer goods, situations, and a four-month period when cars cross state lines.

5. PERFECTION IS NOT PRIORITY. Priorities comprise the fifth step. The "floating lien" of Article 9 must be considered. It is possible to "perfect" by the "attachment" of the "security agreement" and yet not have "priority." For example, the creditor might still lose because of a preference in bankruptcy. See after acquired property, U.C.C., 9–204(3); future advances, U.C.C., 9–204(5); processing of collateral, U.C.C., 9–315 (the security interest continues in spite of processing); security interest continues into proceeds of collateral, U.C.C., 9–306.

The Power of the Financing Statement. The financing statement is the bedfellow of the security agreement and is used to give the world "notice" of the security agreement. It does *not* take the place of the security agreement. The financing statement is a powerful document and a close study of Article 9 makes this apparent. In the chart "Five Steps to Article 9," it is pointed out that perfection can arise by possession or by filing. The financing statement is used where filing is required. The form has been standardized and is not complicated – but its legal effect is.

U.C.C., 9–402 sets out requirements for the financing statement. It must have the signatures and addresses of the secured party and the debtor. A description of the property given as security by type or item is needed but can be general. If fixtures or crops are involved, a description of the real estate is required.

Filing the Financing Statement Is a "Notice" Concept. When a financing statement is filed, this is "waving the red flag" for a five-year period. This does not create a security interest but rather provides notice that

---

[22] U.C.C., 9–302(1)(*a*), 9–304(1), and 9–305.

[23] U.C.C., 9–203(1)(*a*).

[24] U.C.C., 9–302(1)(*c*) and (*d*), 9–304(4) and (5), and 9–307(2).

[25] U.C.C., 9–203(1)(*b*), 9–304, and 9–304(1).

[26] U.C.C., 9–402, 9–403(2), and 9–110.

[27] U.C.C., 9–401.

there is one. The security agreement can be filed if it contains the above requirements.

Filing Location. The location of the filing point depends upon the options adopted by each state. Some have central filing and others have local filing.

The Stampede to Record. Where loans are involved, the financing statement should be filed as quickly as possible. (See the example below.) But in a "purchase money" situation involving an interest in consumer goods, the Code provides a ten-day period in which to file and the filing relates back to the time of sale. The filing is good for five years and the security interest is retained for that period. If a maturity period is stated, then the filing is good for 60 days after the maturity date.[28]

The Consumer Goods Test. The test to determine if goods are "consumer goods" is this: for what will the goods be used? If a business person buys a chair for the office, the chair is *not* consumer goods. If purchased for the home, it would be.

Perfection without Filing. A "purchase money" security interest in consumer goods is "perfected" without filing and would protect the seller in the event of bankruptcy of the debtor. But what happens if the buyer of consumer goods (involving the purchase money situation) sells to another for use in the home and the third party has no actual notice of the security interest because the original seller did not file?[29]

Loan Example. A borrower offers a car for security for a loan. The records are checked by the lender and nothing is found. The lender cannot safely make the loan because other interests may be in effect. One example is the purchase money "relation back principle" mentioned above and its ten-day period. A second example is found under the conflicts-of-laws provision, which provides a four-month period to record where a car has been moved across state lines. And there are others.

Filing the Financing Statement Fixes the Priorities. The Code makes it clear that priorities depend upon the time of filing the financing statement. Some lenders are taking financing statements from potential borrowers and recording them before the decision is made to make the loan. If the loan is made, the security interest dates back to the time of filing.

---

[28] U.C.C., 9–403.

[29] U.C.C., 9–307(2).

B A Criminal Prosecution

Certain constitutional provisions have become so well established in the criminal courts that they are traditional. These will be examined first.

In all criminal prosecutions, the indicted person has the right to a speedy, impartial, and public trial by a jury of the state in which the alleged crime has been committed. The accused is entitled to be clearly informed of the charge; to be confronted with the witnesses for the prosecution; entitled to the assistance of counsel; and to have compulsory process for obtaining witnesses who will testify in one's favor.[1] The court cannot set excessive bail or inflict cruel and unusual punishments after a finding of guilty.[2] The 5th Amendment guarantees have been "absorbed" through the 14th Amendment and made applicable to the states. Therefore, the guarantees of the 5th Amendment are applicable to state prosecutions.

The accused shall not be twice placed in jeopardy of life or limb nor be compelled in any criminal case to be a witness against oneself. One shall not be deprived of life, liberty, or property without due process of law. One's private property cannot be taken for public use without just compensation.[3] The states are prohibited from making or enforcing any law which will abridge the privileges or immunities of the citizens of the United States. The state shall not deny any person equal protection of the laws.[4] The trial of all crimes must be by jury and the trial must be held in the state where the crime has been committed.[5]

These basic guarantees or "rights" were a long time in the making and their roots can be traced to the Great Charter of 1215, the Charter of the Forest of 1217, and subsequent acts of the early English parliaments.

THE MAGNA CHARTA

The word "charta" in Latin means the grant of liberties and privileges to the nation as a group, or to a group of private individuals — such as the grant of a charter to a corporation. Thus, the Magna Charta — the

---

[1] U.S. Constitution, 6th Amendment.
[2] U.S. Constitution, 5th Amendment.
[3] U.S. Constitution, 5th Amendment.
[4] U.S. Constitution, 14th Amendment.
[5] U.S. Constitution, Article III, Section 2.

Great Charter—was a grant to the people of England as a nation. On June 15, 1215, King John met with the representatives of the barons, clergy, and the people on a small island in the River Thames. The site of the meeting was a meadow known as Runnymeade—today the site of a memorial to John F. Kennedy. Out of this meeting came a remarkable document—the Great Charter. The Charter, although said to be inviolable as to what it contained, was confirmed more than 30 times by subsequent kings, thus raising a question as to its effectiveness. Within the Great Charter in its 38 sections, are provisions for the regulation of justice; specifications upon the limits of taxation; details of the rights of the church in reference to the state; and a declaration—for the first time—of the rights of the common person and one's property. It has been said that when King Henry III confirmed the Great Charter in Parliament in 1225, he placed it upon the English books, and every act of the English legislature since that time is only an amendment of the Charter.

"Law of the Land"

Found within the Charter are the words "by the law of the land." The document states:

> No free man shall be taken or imprisoned or disseised, or outlawed or exiled, or in anywise destroyed; nor shall we go upon him, nor set upon him, but by the lawful judgment of his peers or by the law of the land.

When Henry III reissued the Great Charter in 1217 and 1225, the words "of his free hold or liberties or free customs" were added after the word "disseised." The United States Constitution does not contain the words "by the law of the land" but by interpretation, the words "due process" in the 5th Amendment mean the same thing. The words "due process" are also found in the 14th Amendment as well as in most state constitutions.

The concept of the Great Charter was that the individual possesses natural rights and that these rights are secured by fundamental law— even against the king. It is difficult to understand the Great Charter today because we tend to place current meanings upon words that are almost 700 years old. For example, the Charter speaks of "existing liberties, property rights, and customs" that were to be protected from the king. Law was to be administered impartially by judges who were not only bound to obey the law but be "such as know the law and mean duly to observe it." Thus, the law was to be supreme over the judges who administered it: no official, judge, or king or queen or lord was to be above the law—but what did those words mean in those times?

Separation of Powers

The sections on taxation (12 and 14) spell out the basic idea of separation of government as exemplified by the United States Constitution in the first three articles: namely, the executive, judicial, and legislative branches. Further, Section 14 stated that all merchants

. . . shall have safe and secure conduct to go out of, and come into England, and to stay there, and to pass as well by lands as by water for buying and selling by the ancient and allowed customs.

In other words, a common market where no one enjoyed a monopoly was insured. The use of the words "ancient and allowed customs" provides evidence that at this period of time law was part of the common knowledge of the people – merchants in particular – but it would be impossible to identify those customs today.

CHARTA DE FORESTA

The Charter of the Forest was granted in 1217, which was early in the reign of Henry III that began on October 28, 1216. It was the "sister document" of the Great Charter and was designed to be applied to the "forest population" of England. This indicates that the application of the Great Charter was limited to certain persons. It has been stated: "Magna Charta et Charta de Foresta sont apeles les 'dues Grandes Charters" – that is, "The Great Charter and the Charter of the Forest are the 'two great charters.' "

The Statutes of Westminster of 1354 continued the trend started by the two charters. The Norman French of the act of Parliament states: "Saunz estre mesne en respons par due proces de lei" – "No person should be condemned without first being brought to answer without due process of law." This is the earliest known use of the words "due process of law." The act was passed during the reign of Edward III.

An important act of Parliament in 1369 provided a principle that an American Supreme Court justice was to draw upon centuries later to establish an important principle of American constitutional law. The act stated that

. . . the Great Charter should be Holden and kept in all points, and if any statute be made to the contrary, that shall be holden for none.

In short, if a law violates the Great Charter, it is void. In *Marbury* v. *Madison*, Chief Justice John Marshall stated that any act contrary to the United States Constitution is void. From the beginning, the courts and society moved in the direction of fully protecting the rights of those accused of crimes – but the progress has been painfully slow. It should be recognized that the status of our criminal procedures – and civil procedures, for that matter – are simply in an advance stage of development.

A CRIMINAL PROSECUTION

Before the criminal law process begins to operate, a "criminal" act must occur. For an act to be labeled as a "crime," it must be a "crime" in the jurisdiction where it occurs. The determination is based upon what the legislative body of the state (or Congress) says is a crime, or upon what has been considered criminal at common law. The legislatures of a state and the federal government have the power to define—and redefine —what is or is not a crime.

For example, the "national experiment" of prohibition was reversed by the subsequent amendment to the U.S. Constitution legalizing the sale of a product previously declared to be unlawful. Examples of redefinition of criminal acts at the state level include the legalizing of horse racing, abortions, and the sale of fireworks. Once a crime has been defined, and one breaks the law—or where there is reason to believe that the law has been broken—arrest follows.

Arrest

Arrests can be of two types, "citizen's arrests" and arrests by authorities. If a crime is committed in the presence of a citizen, one has the right at common law to "arrest" the one who commits the act. But as a practical matter, since the citizen is usually lacking in training and unarmed, the effort may prove foolish. However, the citizen should immediately report the crime to the authorities so that action may be taken by them.

Arrest by authorities comes about in one of three ways. First, the arrest may occur at the scene of the crime. This seldom occurs other than in the case of mob actions or similar occurrences. Second, most arrests are made after a warrant is issued. The warrant names the person sought, and is directed to the authorities for action. Once a warrant is issued, the one to whom it is directed must, as a legal duty, make every effort to arrest the person named. A warrant is obtained by "swearing it out" before the proper official, often a justice of the peace or magistrate. A third time at which arrests are made is upon warrant issued after a person is indicted by a grand jury. In price fixing and conspiracy cases, presentments are often made to a grand jury without the accused knowing about it. Once the indictments are returned, arrests upon warrant follows.

Miranda Rights[6]

Once an arrest is made, the arresting officer has a duty to inform the suspect of his or her constitutional rights. There is no requirement that this be done instantly and it is often impractical to do so in cases where the arrest has been resisted and the suspect has been subdued by force. But the suspect must be informed of the rights before any "material step" is taken that may prejudice the accused. Most law enforcement officers carry a "Miranda Card," which is read to the suspect. Examine Figure B–1.

The practical value of this requirement is open to question. It is not uncommon in criminal practice for an accused to swear under oath that he or she had not been informed of the "rights"—only to find from testimony of eye witnesses that the rights had in fact been given.

---

[6] *Miranda* v. *U.S.* 384 U.S. 456 (1966).

FIGURE B–1

MIRANDA WARNING   (Front)

1. You have the right to remain silent.
2. Anything you say can and will be used against you in a court of law.
3. You have the right to talk to a lawyer and have him present with you while you are being questioned.
4. If you cannot afford to hire a lawyer, one will be appointed to represent you before any questioning, *if* you wish one.

WAIVER   (Back)

(After the warning and in order to secure a waiver, the following questions should be asked and an affirmative reply secured to each question.)
1. Do you understand each of these rights I have explained to you?
2. Having these rights in mind, do you wish to talk to us now?

Courtesy of Fred R. Elig, Probation officer, 17th Judicial Circuit, West Virginia.

Business Application

Surprisingly enough, the Miranda warning is being read to thousands of persons each year who in fact have not committed a crime – but who may be suspected of having done so. This came about when Internal Revenue Special Agents found that criminal acts uncovered in routine audits could not be used in court if the information had been obtained without informing the accused of his or her rights.

It is now routine in almost all tax audits for the taxpayer to be informed of the rights before being questioned in any manner.

CONFESSIONS

It has been the practice of arresting authorities to take a confession from the suspect immediately following arrest. Surprisingly enough, one who has been arrested is usually willing to give and sign a complete confession. Considerable law has developed in recent years regarding the use of confessions in trials. The accused may enter a "not guilty" plea and then argue that the confession had been taken at a time when one was not fully informed of the rights. The courts tend to uphold confessions if the state can show that they were obtained after the accused was fully informed of the rights.

ARRAIGNMENT

Within a reasonable time following arrest, the authorities must give the suspect a preliminary hearing – referred to as "booking," and this is often done before a magistrate or justice of the peace. The Supreme Court has ruled that the arraignment is a "critical step." Therefore, the suspect must have counsel available at this point. The hearing is informal since there is no requirement of positive proof at this time. The hearing is brief and in many cases the suspect "waives" to the grand jury, meaning that one agrees to do away with a hearing at that time.

If the suspect does not waive to the grand jury, one of two things occur: after a hearing, the magistrate finds cause to hold the suspect for grand jury action, or finds there is insufficient evidence and orders the suspect to be freed. The assistance of counsel at the arraignment gives one a better chance of being freed—or of being booked on a lesser charge. It is not uncommon for one who is arrested on a grand larceny warrant to be booked for petty larceny after the preliminary hearing.

Bail

If the crime is other than murder, the magistrate will set the amount of bail for the suspect. The amount is in the discretion of the magistrate, but in most cases is geared to the severity of the crime charged. For example, one picked up for shoplifting may have bail set as low as $50, while one accused of armed robbery may have bail set at $25,000. If the suspect can "make bail," he or she is permitted to go free until further action is taken in the case. Bail is posted by cash or posting of bond. If the suspect posts cash bail, he or she is entitled to a receipt for the funds. The authorities will hold the money until final disposition of the case.

Most nations of the world practice "preventative detention" meaning that upon arrest, the accused is jailed until trial. The U.S. system of bail is thus unique.

Bonds are often used as bail in the United States.

Bonds

Bonds are used in civil and criminal matters, and represent the most common type of "bail." The purpose of bail, bond or cash, is to assure that the accused will appear for future hearings. The bail system works well and most suspects show with regularity at hearings. Only in rare cases does a suspect "jump bail." The consequences make that action a foolish move. The bail system has been criticized by many who feel that once a suspect is arrested, that person should be confined without bail until trial. One who takes this position ignores the fact that the U.S. Constitution clearly provides for "reasonable bail."

Types of Bonds. In minor criminal cases, magistrates will release an accused "on ones own recognizance." The suspect signs a document that states that if he or she fails to appear later he or she will forfeit a certain sum of money. The accused, in fact, advances nothing—unless one later fails to appear. In that event, one will owe the sum of money specified.

In cases where a definite sum of money is specified as bail, a monetary, surety bond is often used. The bond spells out the amount of bail and is signed not only by the accused but by a surety acceptable to the state— usually a bonding company. If the accused jumps bond, the state will recover from the surety. In most cases, professional bond sellers sign bonds for their companies and receive a fee from the accused for doing so. In rare instances, a property owner signs as surety for the accused.

EXTRADITION

Where one has been arrested on a warrant issued by another jurisdiction, such as another state, problems arise. These warrants are commonly called "fugitive warrants" and permit authorities in other states to arrest and detain those who are named in the warrants. Following the arrest, the problem of getting the suspect to the state where the crime occurred arises. No state has jurisdiction beyond its borders and has no authority to surrender an accused person to another state. A precise process must be followed before a transfer can occur called "extradition."

Extradition Hearing. The authorities of the state seeking custody must prove three things: first, that a criminal act has been committed in the state seeking custody; second, that the accused was in the other state when the crime occurred; and third, that the accused fled from the other state. Strict proof is required and in some cases, a suspect is able to avoid extradition. If one has not committed a crime in the holding state and the other state fails in its proof, that person must be set free. Extradition proceedings are carried out by formal documents between the governors of the states involved and time limits are provided by statute.

If an accused flees international borders, the matter becomes even more complex. If treaties between the nations involved permit extradition, then they control. If there are none, an accused felon may be granted "asylum" in the other nation. If asylum is refused, the accused will be requested to leave that nation.

Waiving Extradition. One accused of a crime in another state may "waive extradition"—in other words, agree to the transfer to the other state. The court will first make certain that the accused knows the consequences of what he or she is doing and he or she will be surrendered to authorities of the state seeking custody. In cases where extradition is not involved, if the suspect is unable to raise bail, one will be imprisoned by local authorities until further action is taken by the state. In cases involving a charge of first-degree murder, the courts often set bond so high that it cannot in fact be posted.

THE PROSECUTOR STEPS IN

The prosecuting or state's attorney must take up the matter and investigate the facts. After this investigation, the prosecutor must decide if the case will be presented to a grand jury. In some cases, this investigation discloses legal reasons why further action is not warranted and the matter is dropped.

If the state's attorney is satisfied that the matter should proceed, the case will be prepared for presentation to the grand jury. If it is federal matter, the case will be presented to a federal grand jury by the United States attorney.

THE GRAND JURY ACTS

If a "true bill" or indictment is returned, it means that the jury has found "probable cause" to believe that the accused committed the crime and the accused stands formally charged at that time.

As a matter of practice, indictments are drafted by the state's attorney —in advance of the grand jury session. If the grand jury votes to indict, they will examine the document to see if it agrees with their findings. If so, the foreman of the grand jury signs the document and delivers it to the state's attorney. This practice is used because of the legal language requirements of both statutory and common-law indictments. An indictment is a strange document when read by a layman. An example is shown. This indictment contains more than one "count." Multiple counts are used for a practical reason: If the court holds one count defective for technical reasons, the state can proceed on an alternative count.

Plea Day

Following grand jury action, the court schedules a day for the entry of pleas. Those who are imprisoned are brought before the court and those free on bond are expected to appear. If they do not, upon motion of the state's attorney, bond may be forfeited and a fugitive warrant issued. An accused free on bond occasionally becomes confused about hearing dates and times. In these cases, the judges are liberal in setting future dates for the entry of pleas.

"A Critical Stage."   An accused who stands before a judge for purposes of entering a plea to an indictment is at "the crossroads of the prosecution." If a court permits a plea of "guilty" to be entered under questionable circumstances, any sentence will almost always be set aside when reviewed by a higher court. The classic error in the past was the failure of the state to let the record show that the accused was represented by counsel. A court only speaks through its record, and if the record is silent on this point, the defendant will be freed by a reviewing court. For this reason, judges use great caution today. Following is testimony from the transcript of proceedings in a criminal court. The defendant is in court but has not yet retained counsel. (He did not know he was being indicted.)

State's Attorney: Next, the state calls Felony No. 123 – State against John Doe, defendant. Is the defendant present in court?
Defendant: Yes, sir.
Judge: Do you have a lawyer?

Example of a Grand Jury Indictment

Typical State, King County, to wit:
In the Circuit Court of Said County

The Grand Jurors of Typical State, in and for the body of the King County, upon their oaths present that John France on the 15th day of February, 1974, in the said King County, a certain storeroom, beer garden, and building, commonly known as Bob's Place, of Bob Jones, said storeroom, beer garden, and building not then and there being a dwelling house or outhouse adjoining thereto or occupied therewith, situated in the County aforesaid, unlawfully and feloniously did break and enter, with intent the goods and chattels of the said Bob Jones in the said storeroom, beer garden, and building then and there being, then and there unlawfully and feloniously to steal, take, and carry away; and then and there, in the said storeroom, beer garden, and building, one (1) gold watch of the value of One Hundred Twenty-Five Dollars ($125.00), three (3) watches of the value of Thirty Dollars ($30.00), and Twenty-One Dollars ($21.00) United States currency of the value of Twenty-One Dollars ($21.00) the denominations of which are to the Grand Jurors unknown, and of the total and aggregate value of One Hundred and Seventy-Six Dollars ($176.00), of the money, goods, effects, and property of the said Bob Jones, in the said storeroom, beer garden, and property, in the County aforesaid, then and there being found, then and there unlawfully and feloniously did steal, take, and carry away; against the peace and dignity of the State.

Second Count: And the Grand Jurors aforesaid, upon their oaths aforesaid, further present that John France, on the 15th day of February, 1974, in the said King County, a certain storeroom, beer garden, and building, commonly known as Bob's Place, of Bob Jones, said storeroom, beer garden, and building not then and there being a dwelling or outhouse, adjoining thereto or occupied therewith, situated in the County aforesaid, unlawfully and feloniously did enter, without breaking, with intent the goods and chattels of the said Bob Jones, in the said storeroom, beer garden, and building, then and there being, then and there unlawfully and feloniously to steal, take, and carry away; and then and there, in the said storeroom, beer garden, and building, one (1) gold watch of the value of One Hundred Twenty-Five Dollars ($125.00), three (3) watches of the value of Thirty Dollars ($30.00), and Twenty-One Dollars ($21.00), the denominations of which are to the Grand Jurors unknown, and of the total and aggregate value of One Hundred and Seventy-Six Dollars ($176.00), of the money, goods, effects, and property of the said Bob Jones, in the said storeroom, beer garden, and building, in the County aforesaid, then and there being found, then and there unlawfully and feloniously did steal, take, and carry away; against the peace and dignity of the State.

Found upon the testimony of

Lieutenant William Jones
Anytown Police Department
of King County, Typical State, duly
sworn in open Court to testify the
truth and sent before the Grand Jury,
this the
10th day of March, 1976

Joseph Smith
Prosecuting Attorney

Defendant: No, sir.

Judge: Do you intend to retain one?

Defendant: Your honor, I do not have any funds.

Judge: Do you know anyone who will assist you financially?

Defendant: I have no family at all.

Judge: Very well, the court appoints Attorney Smith to represent you. (In "court appointment" states, the accused must file a paupers affidavit plus a second affidavit stating that the attorney is representing the accused. This permits the appointed attorney to be paid the statutory fee by the state).

Attorney Smith (who happens to be present at the bar): Your honor, may I have this hearing continued so that I may confer with the defendant and also investigate the matter?

Judge: The matter is continued to _____.

(At the delayed hearing, the following took place.)

State's Attorney: The State calls Felony No. 123 against John Doe. Your honor, please let the record show that the defendant is present in open court in person and is accompanied by his court-appointed counsel, Attorney Mary Smith.

Judge: The record may so state. John Doe, the grand jury of this county has indicted you on the following charges: (Here follows a reading of the indictment and its counts.) Have you received a copy of the indictment?

Defendant: Yes, sir.

Judge: Have you read it and do you understand it?

Defendant: Yes, sir.

Judge: Has your attorney explained the indictment to you?

Defendant: Yes, sir.

Judge: Mr. State's Attorney, will you please state to the defendant the penalty that might accompany a plea of guilty or a finding of guilty by a jury under this indictment?

State's Attorney: The offense charged carries an indeterminate prison sentence of 1 to 10 years and a fine not to exceed $5,000, in the discretion of the court.

Judge: If your plea is "not guilty," you are entitled by law to an impartial trial of 12 jurors selected at random from this county. Do you understand that?

Defendant: Yes, sir.

Judge: What is your plea?

In most cases, the plea entered is "not guilty" to all counts. Counsel for the defendant will reserve the right for the defendant to change the plea. If the defendant is on bond, the court will continue the bond and the defendant is free to leave. If not on bond, the defendant will be taken to jail. In either event, the case will be scheduled for trial on the earliest possible criminal docket—within 90 days in federal courts.

On rare occasions at plea day, a defendant will plead "guilty" and place oneself at the mercy of the court.

Plea Bargaining. For many years, state's attorneys and defense counsel have privately discussed the defendant's case after a plea of not guilty. The state may have an "iron-clad" case—and yet the not guilty plea requires the state's attorney to prepare for trial, thus increasing the court load. The defendant's lawyer is naturally interested in knowing what the state's attorney will recommend to the court if the defendant changes the plea. In the past this type of "bargaining" has been done privately and the judge is assured at the time the plea is changed "that no promises have been made to the defendant." An example is the agreement by the prosecutor to drop a more serious count in an indictment in exchange for a guilty plea to the lesser count. There is a growing tendency to treat plea bargaining as a legitimate part of the criminal process, thus permitting it to be carried out in open court.

Bar associations are experimenting with "open plea bargaining" in which the state's attorney and defense lawyer reduce to writing what each is willing to do. This is done out of the presence of the judge. In the event the judge does not accept the recommendation of the state's attorney, the accused has the right to change the plea and stand trial. A typical compromise in a criminal case would be the reduction of a felony to misdemeanor in exchange for a guilty plea. If approved by the court, the defendant serves less time in prison—and a court docket is not further congested by another jury trial. (It should be noted however, that such bargaining has been severely criticized by many persons and groups.)

Trial

It is the practice of all courts to set criminal cases for trial as quickly as possible. This is done for two reasons: first, the U.S. Constitution requires a "speedy trial" and second, it is easier to dispose of cases once a docket is set. In addition, the accused is frequently in jail and an injustice would occur if one had to wait a year or more for trial. Criminal cases are "docketed" much in the fashion of civil cases.

There are basic differences between a criminal prosecution and a civil action. For example, the accused has a right to remain silent in a criminal case. If one does, the fact that the accused may have a record is not permitted to go to the jury. The burden is on the state to prove guilt beyond a reasonable doubt. There is no burden on the accused to prove innocence. If the accused does not testify, then the state's attorney is prohibited from making comment to the jury of that fact. In addition, the accused is entitled to an instruction that failure to testify must not be construed as evidence of guilt.

Once a judge gives a criminal case to a jury, the procedure followed is much the same as discussed in Chapter 10. The verdict of the jury is announced in open court and in the presence of the accused. If the verdict is "not guilty," the case is ended and the accused is free. The state has no appeal in such case. If the verdict is "guilty," the accused may continue free pending an appeal if on bond. If not on bond, the accused will be remanded to jail pending appeal.

Sentencing

After a jury finds guilt, the court will pronounce the sentence—even if the defendant intends to appeal the verdict. But a request for probation where it is requested, is usually considered before sentence is imposed.

Probation.   If the nature of the crime is not serious, or if a first offense is involved, the defense lawyer routinely requests that the defendant be considered for probation. If the state's attorney does not resist the motion, the judge will refer the matter to the proper officer of the court — usually called the "probation officer." The probation officer will investigate the background of the defendant and if the report is favorable, the judge *may* grant probation — but only after sentence is imposed. In a recent criminal case, the following took place:

> It is the duty of the court at this time to pass judgment upon you. It is the judgment of the court that you serve one to ten years in the state penitentiary with credit to be given for the time served in jail in this county. However, upon the recommendation of the probation officer, I suspend the sentence and place you on probation for a period of three years.

The terms of probation usually include the following: the defendant must (1) keep a full-time job; (2) not leave the county without permission of the court; (3) report to the probation officer at regular times; and (4) pay all costs of the prosecution within a designated time period. The social purpose of probation is obvious; it keeps one productive while at the same time that person is punished for the crime committed. As a matter of policy, probation is not granted where a person has a prior conviction or a prior plea of guilty to another offense. Also, in most states, one convicted of first degree murder, even if it *is* a first offense, is prohibited from being considered for probation.

Form of Sentence.   Sentences are of one of two types: determinate or indeterminate. A determinate sentence is one for a prescribed number of years, such as "life" or "20 years." An indeterminate sentence is one for a number of years between two numbers, such as "one to ten." In the indeterminate type sentence, the convicted person has the opportunity for early release for good behavior and evidence of rehabilitation. The social purpose is to encourage the convicted person to make an effort in prison to rehabilitate oneself through study, cooperation, good attitude, and productiveness.

HABITUAL CRIMINAL STATUTES

Most states have enacted "recidivist statutes" — laws directed toward the person who continues to commit crimes. A typical statute provides that if a person is convicted of a second felony (a prior plea of guilty is counted as a conviction), then five years shall be added to the sentence for the second offense. If the same person is convicted of a felony a third time — "a three-time loser" — that person is sentenced to life imprisonment. A special hearing must be held to "invoke the statute" and the burden is upon the state to prove that the defendant is the same person who was convicted of the prior felonies.

PAROLE SYSTEM

Contrary to popular belief, no sentence is final under the American criminal law system. Each state and federal institutions maintain "parole boards." The function of the boards is to review sentences from time to time to see if a defendant should be permitted to return to society on "parole." It is not uncommon for one who was sentenced to a flat term of 30 years to be paroled in eight or ten years. An imprisoned person who knows that he or she may go free by demonstrating rehabilitation, will usually tend to work toward that goal. In some states however, by statutory law, if one is convicted of first degree murder and the jury does not recommend mercy, that person must serve a life sentence without ever being eligible for parole.

C Glossary

A

Abstract of title. A "history" or record of real property.

Acceleration. Speeding up the due date of commercial paper.

Acceptance. Agreeing to be bound by the terms of a bill of exchange. Also agreeing to the terms of an "offer" in a contract setting.

Acceptance varying draft. Agreeing to be bound by a bill of exchange—but on terms different than set out on the document.

Accession. Adding to something, such as a new room to a house.

Accord and satisfaction. The tender of substitute performance in a contract situation which is accepted by the other party.

Acknowledgment. A formal statement attesting to the genuineness of a document or signature. Usually performed by a notary.

Adjudicate. To decide or render a decision in a lawsuit.

Adjuster. An agent of an insurance company who investigates claims and attempts to settle them out of court.

Adverse possession. A method of acquiring title to real property that requires open and continued possession for a statutory time period.

Affidavit. A formal written statement made under oath.

Agency. A relationship in which a "principal" grants specified authority to an "agent."

By estoppel. An agency created by operation of law. A "fiction."

Express. An agency created by stated words, either spoken or written.

Implied. An agency created by acts of the parties.

Ambiguity. Subject to more than one interpretation.

Answer. The legal document used to reply to a "complaint" filed in court.

Appellant. One who takes an appeal.

Appellee. One against whom an appeal is taken.

Area of compromise. A "gray area" encountered in compromise attempts.

Argument. Statements of counsel advanced orally in court to support their view of a case.

Arraign. To "bring before" or hold a preliminary hearing for one suspected of a crime.

Assign. To set over some legal right to another.

Assignee. The one to whom an assignment is made.

Assignor. The one who makes an assignment.

Attachment. A legal step used to "tie up" something that is usually in the hands of another. Example: a wage attachment.

Attestation. The result of acknowledging or placing a seal on a document.

Award. The findings of an arbitration panel.

B

Bail. Bond required to permit one to remain free pending further criminal proceedings.

"Bait and switch." An unscrupulous business practice that results in one receiving inferior merchandise.

Bankruptcy. A federal law that permits a systematic distribution of the assets of an insolvent debtor.

Bar. To block or stop. Also, the nonexistent place in a court where the attorneys practice.

Barter. To trade in kind or to exchange for something else.

Bearer paper. A negotiable instrument that can be negotiated without any indorsement.

Beneficiary. One who gains an ultimate benefit, such as in a trust.

"Benefit of clergy." An ancient concession extended to those charged with a crime upon proof of their literacy.

"Beyond a reasonable doubt." The degree of proof required of the state in criminal proceedings.

Bids. Legal offers extended in reply to invitations for them.

Bill of exchange (draft). One of the four types of commercial paper under the U.C.C.

Bill of Rights. The first 10 amendments to the U.S. Constitution.

Bill of sale. A legal document listing the items of personal property sold by one to another.

"Blue-sky" laws. State and federal laws designed to regulate the issuance of stocks and bonds.

Bond. In criminal law, a document binding one to a sum of money to assure the appearance of another. Bail.

Brief. A legal document that sets forth the legal authorities one relies on in court.

Business wrongs. Torts committed in the business setting.

Buy-and-sell agreement. Widely used in partnerships to spell out how one partner can buy out another.

Bylaws. The rules of conduct of a corporation.

C

Call. In corporation law, a demand by the board of directors upon subscribers for payment of a portion or installment from each subscriber.

Causa mortis. In contemplation of death.

Caveat emptor. Let the buyer beware.

Caveat venditor. Let the seller beware.

Certificate of deposit. One of the four types of commercial paper, used as a savings device.

Certificate of incorporation. A grant of powers by a state to a corporation. Frequently called a "charter."

Certificate of service. A statement of service of papers used in "civil action" states.

Change of venue. Moving a trial from one location to another.

Charging order. A means of reaching a partner's "interest" in a partnership.

Charta de Foresta. The Charter of the Forest, issued in 1217, in England.

Charter. A grant of powers from a state. A corporate charter, for example.

Chattel. An item of personal property.

Check. One of the four types of commercial paper under · the U.C.C.

Circuit. Referring to courts, a grouping of courts.

Circumstantial evidence. Evidence based upon inferences rather than what someone saw or heard.

Civic association. A voluntary grouping of persons for civic, nonprofit purposes.

Civil action. Private litigation between persons or firms.

Clerk of the court. The court official charged with receiving and preserving all court records.

Code of Professional Responsibility. American Bar Association guidelines for the practicing attorney.

Coercion. Forcing someone into something against his or her will.

Collateral. In secured transactions, personal property given as security for a loan.

Proceeds of. Funds realized from the sale of secured personal property.

Products of. Secured personal property that is used to create new property. Example: secured lumber used to construct kitchen cabinets.

Commingling. Mixing up or joining so as to lose former identity. For example, coal of A and B dumped into a common coal tipple.

Commercial paper. The subject of Article 3, U.C.C.

Compensatory damages. A money award to compensate one for an injury or other loss.

Competency. Full legal capacity.

Complaint. The first paper filed in a civil action.

Compromise and settlement. Adjusting and paying off a disputed claim or matter.

Condemnation. The taking of private property for public use by government.

Conflicting interests. In the attorney-client relationship, a state of affairs that casts a lawyer into a position where by seeking to aid one client, the lawyer goes against the interests of another client.

Consideration. In contract law, the "reason for enforcing promises."

Consignee. The one to whom goods are left "on consignment."

Consignment. A contractual arrangement by which one person deposits goods with another for resale, with payment to be made at time of resale.

Consignor. One who consigns goods.

Consolidation. To bring together or to group into one.

Conspicuous. Of such form or style that one should have noticed it. Examples: bold type, red ink.

Constructive notice. Knowledge that a person should have because it is available. (The person may, in fact, not have the knowledge.)

Contempt of court. A proceeding brought against one who refuses to obey a lawful order of a court.

Contingent fees. Fees that are to be paid out of future recovery.

Contract. An agreement.

Bilateral. An agreement based upon mutual promises.

Express. A stated agreement.

Implied:

In fact. An agreement assumed because of the acts of parties in dealing with each other.

In law. A fiction used by the courts in which they find an agreement where none exists.

Oral. An agreement that arises from spoken words only.

Sales. An agreement between merchants for the purchase and sale of commodities of all types.

Written. An agreement that is written or typed.

Unilateral. An agreement in which one makes a promise in exchange for an act of the other party.

Conversion. To wrongfully appropriate the personal property of another.

Conveyance. The transfer of real estate from one to another. The delivery of something to another.

Counseling. In law, the giving of advice by a lawyer.

Counteroffer. A reply to a contractual offer that varies the terms of the offer.

Court.

Appellate court. A court to which appeals are taken.

Circuit court. A trial court.

County court. An administrative court charged with handling administrative matters of a county.

Court appointment. The assignment of a lawyer by a court to an indigent person who is accused of a crime.

Court interpretation. The judicial process of deciding the meaning of the words of a legislature.

Court martial. A body of military officers convened to hear and decide a criminal charge against a military man.

Police court. The judicial body of a municipality.

Trial court. A "court of record" where juries hear and decide cases.

Covenant. Promise.

Cross-examination. Asking questions of one who has just given direct testimony in court.

D

"Day in court." A lawyer's phrase to describe the right each person has who is involved in a dispute.

Debentures. Unsecured bonds.

Deceit. An underhand, unscrupulous action.

Deed. A legal document widely used to convey real estate.

Reservations. Clauses in deeds that "hold back" or reserve a portion of what is conveyed.

Restrictions. Clauses in deeds that place limitations upon what real estate can be used for.

General warranty. A deed containing promises to defend title to real estate to all future owners.

Special warranty. A deed containing a promise to defend title to real estate to the immediate buyer only.

Deed of trust. A security device by which equitable title to realty is conveyed to a trustee. Called a "mortgage" in some states.

Defacto. "In fact" or "almost so." At law, a sufficient status to qualify as being "legally correct."

Default. To break terms of an agreement.

Defendant. The one against whom legal action is brought.

Deficiency judgment. A court order for a sum of money yet owing on an obligation.

Degree of proof. The extent of evidence required in court.

Dejure. "Correct" or "just."

Deliberations. Discussions by jurors about a pending verdict.

Demurrer. A legal challenge to the sufficiency of a legal pleading.

Deposition. The oral statement of one taken under oath and before a court reporter.

Derivative suits. A lawsuit, the cause of action for which accrues from or is "derived" from a corporation.

Descriptive words. Words that illustrate the nature of products.

"Designate the record." Selecting those portions of the record that one wants a higher court to see.

Detinue. An action to recover personal property.

Direct examination. Questioning one's own witness on a witness stand.

Directed verdict. A verdict returned by a jury in the manner and form given them by a judge. A "judge's verdict."

Directors. Those who run a corporation.

Disaffirmance. To repudiate or reject.

Disclaimer. To deny responsibility such as for warranties.

Disclosure statement. A form re- required under Truth in Lending and R.E.S.P.A. containing pre- scribed matters.

Discovery. Under civil practice acts, those means of obtaining information about the other side of the case.

"Dispatch and discipline." Re- quirements found in the *Code of Professional Responsibility,* re- lating to a lawyer's actions in court.

Dissenting opinion. An opinion of an appellate judge that disagrees with the majority opinion of the same court.

Dissolution. To dissolve or break up, or the act of doing such things.

Dividend. A division of corporate funds, usually profits.

  Cash dividend. A dividend paid by cash or check.

  Ex dividend. Without dividend.

  Liquidating dividend. A return of capital assets — not a true dividend.

  Property dividend. A division of the products of a corporation.

  Stock dividend. A capitalization of earnings evidenced by new certificates.

Docket. The schedule of trials.

Donee. The one to whom a gift is made.

Donor. The one who makes a gift.

Dower. The common law right of a wife to use and occupy real estate upon death of the husband.

Drawee. The one on whom a bill of exchange or check is drawn.

Drawer. The one who draws a bill of exchange or check.

Dual court system. Each state maintains its own court system — and so does the federal government.

Due process. A phrase generally understood to mean "full protec- tion of our laws and unqualified access to our courts."

Duress. A condition of mental stress created by threats or other pressure.

E

Easement. Legal recognition of one's right to cross over real estate at a designated point or route.

Ejectment. A common-law form of action used to throw someone off of real property.

"Electronic money." A phrase at- tached to the growing field of "electronic banking."

Embezzlement. The taking of an- other's money with the intention of permanently depriving that person of it.

Eminent domain. The power of condemnation held by govern- ment.

Employment contract. An agree- ment between an employer and employee covering wages, du- ties, and the like.

Enabling legislation. Statutory law that permits some other law to be passed.

Endowment. In life insurance, a policy payable in whole or monthly payments, when the in- sured reaches a certain age. Used to supplement retirement income.

Enfeoffment. The common-law method of passing title of real estate from one to another.

Equity. The branch of the courts devoted to equitable matters as distinguished from legal matters.

Escheat. The passing of property to the state because of a failure in the line of heirs.

Estoppel. To stop or "close one's mouth to admit the truth."

Eviction. The legal process used to force one from rented prem- ises.

Evidence. That which is elicited from the testimony of witnesses in court.

Ex contracto. "In contract."

Ex delicto. "In tort."

Ex post facto. "After the fact."

Execution. A legal process used to collect assets of a judgment debtor and to apply them to the judgment.

Executive sessions. Closed meetings of members of a board of a corporation.

Executor. A person who administers the estate of a deceased.

Extortion. Forcing money or related matters from one under threat of bodily harm or death.

Extradition. The process whereby an accused felon is removed from one state to another where the alleged crime occurred.

F

Fair-trade laws. Laws designed to permit prices at retail to be established by the manufacturer.

Fancy words. Unusual words associated with a business or product which are entitled to trade-name protection.

Fee simple. Absolute title in real estate. The best title one can have in realty.

Fee splitting. The unlawful practice of lawyers on opposite sides of litigation sharing fees in exchange for concessions.

Felony. A classification of crime severe in nature, and punishable by imprisonment in a state penitentiary or death.

Fiduciary. Of Roman origin, and when used as a noun means one in a high position of trust and confidence.

Financing statement. The "notice document" used under Article 9, U.C.C.

"Fixing damages." Establishing the actual loss caused by a breach of contract.

Fixtures. Items of personal property that become part of real estate after installation. Example: a water heater.

"Flexible checks." A slang phrase referring to checks that serve other purposes than the payment of money.

Foreclosure. To execute legal rights after default in a secured transaction.

Forfeiture. To give up property rights, usually for failure to pay taxes.

Forgery. A signature of A written by B with the intent to steal from or defraud A by that signature.

Franchise. A contract given by one to another authorizing a certain activity in a certain area.

Fraud. An intentional misrepresentation of a material fact that misleads another.

"Freedom of contract." A theoretical privilege that we have to contract as we wish. In practice the right is restricted.

Freehold. An estate comprised of land and buildings owned by the "freeholder."

Fugitive warrant. A court order demanding the arrest of one who has fled the jurisdiction of the court.

Fungible goods. Goods that are incapable of being separated once commingled. Example: wheat in a grain elevator.

G

Garnishment. A legal process whereby the goods or money of one is attached while in the hands of another.

Geographic names. Names that contain the name of a town, county, or state.

Gift. The passing of property from one to another at no charge or cost.

"Going business." A firm that is successfully pursuing a profitable course of business activity.

Good faith. "Honesty in fact."

Government or rectangular survey. A system of survey in which land is divided into blocks or rectangles.

"Grandfather's clauses." Statutes that permit property uses in violation of zoning laws to continue in the future.

Grantee. The one to whom a grant, such as a deed, is made.

Grantor. The one who grants something such as one who deeds property to another.

H

Habitual criminal (recidivist) statutes. Statutes that add years of imprisonment for repeated criminal acts. Witness, "a three-time loser."

Hearing. The taking of testimony before a court, administrative agency, or other tribunal for the purpose of making findings from the testimony.

Hearsay evidence. Testimony based upon the statements of one who is not in court.

Holder in due course. In commercial paper, a preferred position that is free of certain defenses.

Holding company. A company that holds stock in another company.

I

Implied. Inferred.

Indemnification. To make whole.

Independent contractor. One who agrees to complete work free of control of another.

Indictment. A finding of probable cause by a grand jury or the paper upon which the finding is placed.

Indorsement. Commercial paper, Article 3, U.C.C. The act of signing one's name with or without additional words.

Blank. A signature only.

Qualified. A signature accompanied by qualifying words.

Restrictive. A statement limiting the use of commercial paper. Example: "For deposit only."

Special. An indorsement accompanied by the name of another person to whom the instrument is to be paid.

Indorser. One who indorses.

Information. A proceedings by which a prosecutor brings matters before a grand jury or a judge.

Injunction. An equitable remedy used to cause one to refrain from a designated activity or action.

Instruction to the jury. A statement by the judge to the jury of the applicable law.

Insurable interest. That which one person has in the life of another when that person stands to gain from the continuance, rather than the loss, of that life.

Interlocutory injunction. A temporary order stating that one is to refrain from a certain activity until further hearings are held on the matter.

Interrogatories. Written questions directed to one in litigation that must be answered under oath.

Intestate. One who dies without a will.

Investment securities. Article 8, U.C.C., Stocks and bonds.

J

Joint payees. More than one person who has the same negotiable instrument payable to them.

Joint stock company. An early attempt to limit liability in business by the use of the contract.

Joint venture. An undertaking in which one or more persons combine labor and capital to achieve a single result.

Judgment by default. A court order entered when a defendant fails to set up a defense within the prescribed time period.

Judicial review. The power of the courts to review legislative acts and to rule them unconstitutional if necessary.

Jurati. Latin. "The sworn."

Jurisdiction. The power that courts have under prescribed circumstances to hear and decide disputes and to impose sentences.

> **Limited.** Limited power in courts.
>
> **Obtaining.** The process of acquiring power in the courts.

Jury. A panel of persons who hear matters and render decisions. Sometimes called "a panel of peers."

> **Advisory jury.** A panel called for the sole purpose of advising a judge who must render a decision in a dispute.
>
> **Alternate juror.** An extra juror who will serve if a regular panel member cannot continue in a case.
>
> **Coroner's jury.** A panel called to make inquiry into the cause of death of a person.
>
> **Deadlocked jury.** A panel that, while deliberating, is unable to agree on a verdict.
>
> **Grand jury.** A panel chosen to make inquiry into possible crimes and find "probable cause."
>
> **Hung jury.** Another phrase for a "deadlocked" jury.
>
> **Jury commissioners.** Officials, usually appointed, who select names of those from whom jury panels will be called.
>
> **Jury duty.** A service that each citizen is obligated to perform if called upon.
>
> **Petit jury.** A trial jury.
>
> **"Polling" the jury.** After a verdict is returned, asking each juror individually if the juror agrees with the verdict.
>
> **Striking the jury.** Reducing an initial panel down to the jury that will hear and decide a case.

K

Kiting. Raising the amount of a negotiable instrument.

L

Law. That body of legal and related sanctions which can be enforced in a court.

> **Administrative.** Rulings of non-judicial agencies created by law.
>
> **Common.** Historically, the law of England. Today, the rulings of courts in the states.
>
> **Constitutional.** Principles that relate to what the constitution means in application in the courts.
>
> **Private.** That body of legal principles that controls disputes that arise between individuals.
>
> **Procedural.** The "machinery" of the law or the steps involved in litigation in the courts.
>
> **Property.** That body of legal principles that relates to real and personal property.
>
> **Public.** That body of legal principles that relates to the public interest. Example: criminal and administrative law.
>
> **Statutory.** Those legal principles created expressly by acts of law-making bodies.
>
> **Substantive.** That which makes up the substance or body of the law; the law itself.

Law Merchant (Lex Mercatoria). An early English court created to decide the disputes of merchants.

Lawsuit. The process whereby one litigates against another in court.

Leading question. In trial work, a question to a witness that suggests the answer desired.

Lease. A contract between a landowner and a lessee, spelling out rights of both.

Legal entity. Something that has a separate existence in contemplation of law. Example: a corporation.

Legal notice. An advertisement, published in newspapers of general circulation, concerned with legal matters.

Lessee. The one to whom real estate is leased.

Lessor. The one who leases real estate to a lessee.

Liability. As used in law, "responsibility."

Absolute. Responsibility without permitting a defense.

Contract. Responsibility for failure to keep promises.

Criminal. Responsibility for commission of a crime.

Joint. Responsibility that rests upon two or more at the same time.

Joint and several. Responsibility that can be laid upon two or more or any one of them.

Limited. Responsibility that is restricted in amount. Found in partnership and corporate law.

Tort. Responsibility for wrongful damages to another's person or property.

Unlimited. Responsibility that has no limits. In partnership law.

Libel. Written defamation.

License. A right or privilege granted to one by another.

Lien. A claim against real estate, usually arising out of some court action.

Lis pendens notice. A claim, recorded as provided by law, giving notice of a pending lawsuit, which results in a "lien" against any real estate of the defendant.

Long-arm statutes. Laws that permit service of process beyond state borders.

Loss leading. Selling items at low prices to attract customers into a store.

M

Magna Charta. The Great Charter issued in 1215 in England.

Majority opinion. Relating to appellate courts, the holding of the court upon which the vote is not unanimous.

Maker. Commercial paper. The one who creates a note and signs it.

Mechanics lien. A statutory claim against real property for services or material furnished to that property.

Merger. Corporations. A joining of firms.

Metes and bounds. Property law. Directions and distances.

Minor. Contract law. One under the age of majority.

Minority suits. Corporations. Litigation instituted by stockholders.

Minutes. Corporations. Written records of meetings.

Miranda rights. Criminal law. Those basic rights that one must be informed of soon after arrest.

Misdemeanor. Criminal law. A class of crime less severe than a felony and usually punished by a fine or local imprisonment.

Misrepresentation. An unintentional misleading of one person by another.

Mistake. In law, a justifiable reason for setting aside a contract.

Bilateral. A mistake made by both parties to a contract.

Unilateral. A mistake made by one party only to a contract. (Usually not grounds to set aside a contract.)

Mistrial. Any state of affairs in court that causes a judge to stop all proceedings and discharge the jury.

Mitigation of damages. A legal requirement in contract law that one "keep down" the damages of the one who has breached a contract.

Model acts. Sample laws of all types created as a pattern for law-making bodies.

Model Business Corporation Act. A model act created to serve as a guide to legislatures in creating corporate statutes.

Monopoly. A business situation in which one person or a firm "captures" and controls a market to its advantage.

Morality in law. A phrase indicating that what is "moral" should guide what is "legal"—although it frequently does not.

Mortgage. An encumbrance against real estate that arises out of a secured loan obtained from a lending institution.

Motion. A spoken or printed request under parliamentary procedure addressed to a judge (or presiding officer) seeking a ruling on the point raised.

Motion to dismiss. A request to a court to strike a matter from the court's itinerary.

Motion to reconsider. A request to a court to examine a ruling already made and to consider changing that ruling.

Motion to set aside. Following a verdict in a trial, a request to a court to ignore the jury verdict by setting it aside.

Mutuality. In contract law, the state of being in agreement upon particulars.

N

Necessities. In the law of infancy, those items that one must have to maintain station in life in a decent fashion.

Negligence. Failure to exercise due care.

Contributory negligence. Failure to exercise due care that adds to injury caused by another's failure to use due care.

Negotiability. In commercial paper, that quality of transferability unhampered by any restraints.

Negotiable instruments. Those instruments covered by Article 3, U.C.C.

Net profit. Gains after all costs are taken into consideration.

Notary public. A public officer who acknowledges the signatures of others on documents.

Note. Commercial paper. A written promise to pay.

Notice. Something that brings one's mind to observe or know of something.

Actual or express. Positive knowledge of a fact.

Constructive. Opportunity to know of a fact.

Implied. Presumed knowledge of a fact.

Legal. A published advertisement relating to legal matters.

Notchel. Notice that warns others of domestic problems as they relate to credit.

Notice of appeal. Fixing the right to go to a higher court by disclosing to the other the intention to do so.

Novation. Substitution of debtors. For example, A owes B $100 and C agrees to pay B because B owes A $100.

Nuisance. A form of tort that arises out of conduct that constitutes an actionable annoyance to others.

O

Offer. In contract law, a proposal of what one is willing to do in a contract setting.

Offeree. The one to whom a contract offer is made.

Offeror. The one who makes a contract offer.

Ombudsman concept. A practice based upon Swedish principles, of authorizing someone to oversee administrative agencies.

Option. A contract that binds one to hold an offer open for a specified period of time for an agreed price.

Oral application. In appellate practice, a spoken presentation to an appeals court designed to encourage them to grant the appeal.

Ordeals. At common law, forms of "trial" based upon the principle that God would intervene and protect those who are innocent.

Order paper. Commercial paper. Negotiable instruments that must be indorsed before they can be negotiated.

Order to pay. Commercial paper. One requirement of negotiable paper usually met by the word "pay."

Ordinance. Municipal law. A law created by a city council.

P

"Parol" evidence rule. Contract law. A rule of long standing that prohibits a written contract to be changed by oral testimony.

Parole system. Criminal law. Found in the penal systems of all states and designed to permit one's release from confinement upon the meeting of specified requirements.

Partnership. "An association of two or more persons to carry one as co-owners, a business for profit."

Implied partnership. A partnership created by the acts of the parties.

Interest in the firm. One of the property rights of a partner.

Limited partnership. A firm in which the liability of one or more partners is restricted to their capital contributions.

Partnership agreement. A contract used to form a partnership.

Partnership property. That which is owned by a partnership including real and personal property.

Silent partner. A partner with limited liability who cannot take an active part in the operation of a partnership.

Specific partnership property. That which is owned by the partners as partners and thus beyond the reach of individual creditors.

Tenants in partnership. A legal phrase to describe how partners own "specific partnership" property.

Patent. A protective process provided by government to reserve to one for a stated period, the fruits of one's creations.

Payee. Commercial paper. The one to whom negotiable instruments are made payable.

Perfection. Secured transactions. That stage where one's security interest is completed to the fullest extent provided by law.

Perjury. False testimony given while under oath.

Petition. At law, a written document containing a statement of "legal position" or demands.

Petty offenses. Minor infractions of law such as jaywalking or failure to yield the right of way.

Plaintiff. One who initiates a civil action.

Plat. A drawing that depicts real estate.

Plea. Criminal law. A statement by one who has been indicted of whether that person is "guilty" or "not guilty."

Plea bargaining. Criminal law. A defense lawyer's tactic of "trading off" with a prosecutor to gain an advantage for a client.

Policies of the law. Trends or customs that develop in the law which enable one to make sensible decisions in the business setting.

Possession. Custody that is either "actual" or "constructive."

Postdating. Commercial paper. Dating a negotiable instrument ahead, usually a check, thus making it a "time instrument."

Posttrial motions. Trial work. Requests for action by a judge after a trial has ended.

Power of attorney. A formal "agency" in which the principal grants specified authority to an "agent."

Preemptive right. Corporation law. A right of stockholders to purchase a proportionate share of any new stock issues.

Preliminary hearing. Criminal law. A hearing held shortly after an arrest to decide if the one arrested should be held for further action.

Prepayment without release. A program followed by some insurance companies of making advance payment to the other party.

Preponderance of evidence. The degree of proof required in civil court trials.

Price concessions. The granting of price deductions for quantity purchases.

Price fixing. Unlawful price maintenance by firms that would normally be in competition with each other.

Price leading. A system of lawful price maintenance in which competing firms follow price raises by one of the firms.

Prima facie. "On the face of it." In trial work, evidence that is sufficient to establish a case or right of recovery.

Principal. Agency law. The one who grants authority to an agent.

Priority. Secured transactions. What one secured party has that gives it better claim to collateral than another secured party.

Privity. Contract law. The relation created when one contracts with another. The term means "closeness" in contract law.

Probable cause. Reason to believe a crime has been committed. The finding of a grand jury.

Probate. The system of administering the estate of a deceased person, including payment of debts, taxes, and fees.

Probation. Criminal law. A period of time usually granted to first offenders in lieu of imprisonment, during which they must remain on good behavior and follow specific instructions of the court.

Promise to pay. Commercial paper. A phrase required in notes.

Promissory note. Often used to describe a note created under Article 3, U.C.C.

Promoter. Corporation law. One who lays the groundwork and sees that the proper procedures are followed to create a new corporation.

Property. The earth and all property rights that exist with it.

Intangible. Property that has no physical existence. Example: a patent right.

Personal. Property that is not affixed to the earth. Example: one's watch, shoes, car, and furniture in the home.

Real. The earth and everything permanently affixed to it.

Tangible. Property that has a physical existence.

Proprietorship. An unincorporated business owned and frequently operated by one person.

Prosecuting attorney (district attorney). The state's attorney usually elected in the county served.

Proximate cause. Tort law. The actual or "real cause" of personal injury or property damage.

Proxy. Corporation law. Written authority granted by a stockholder to another to vote stockholder's stock. An agency.

Q

Quasi-judicial. "Almost judicial" but lacking some formality.

Question of fact. An unresolved question that a jury must answer. Example: "Was the defendant guilty of negligence?" or "Did the accused commit the crime?"

Question of law. An unresolved question that only a judge can decide based upon knowledge of the law.

Quitclaim deed. A conveyance of real estate in which the grantor conveys whatever interest grantor may have—which in fact may be none. Widely used to clear up doubts in real property titles.

Quorum. A prescribed number needed before business can be transacted in a meeting.

Quotient verdict. A dollar verdict based upon an average of what each juror feels a plaintiff should receive.

R

Ratification. A later adoption of an act that was unauthorized when committed.

Reasonable person. The ordinary person acting in the conduct of personal affairs. A measuring stick used widely in court.

Rebate. A "kickback" or return of part of a purchase price of goods or services.

Record. The written transcript of evidence given and proceedings in a court or administrative agency.

Recording. The act of reducing court testimony to a written transcript.

Redemption. The act of redeeming.

Rejection. Refusing or casting off. In contract law the refusal of an offer made by another.

Release. A contract designed to free one from further legal claims of another.

Remuneration. Wages or payment for services.

Repossession. Secured transactions. The act of retaking secured collateral because of default in payment on a loan.

Rescission. Cancelling or taking back.

"Respondent superior." Latin. "Let the master respond."

Retainer. A fee paid in advance for services to be performed.

Reversal. The ruling of an appellate court that upsets the verdict of a lower court.

Reversed and remanded. The ruling of an appellate court that upsets the verdict of a lower court and sends the case back for further consideration.

Revocation. The cancelling of an offer after it has been made but before it has been accepted.

Right of appeal. The right that one has after an adverse verdict; ruling, or finding in court or other agency or tribunal.

Right of way. A legal right granted by an owner to another to cross or use a portion of one's land.

Right to compete. An inherent right of all merchants in our competitive business community.

Right to trial by jury. A right that exists in certain types of cases to have the decision made by a jury of one's peers.

Rules of evidence. Principles of law that regulate the taking of testimony in court.

S

Secondary meaning. Trade-name law. A word or words that have become identified with a firm or its products so as to become entitled to trade-name protection.

Secured transactions. That body of law spelled out in Article 9, U.C.C., as well as secured loans made where real estate is used as security.

Securities. Stocks and bonds.

Security or collateral. That which is used as assurance that a loan will be repaid.

Security agreement. A legal document used under Article 9, U.C.C., to grant a security interest and to spell out terms of the loan.

Security interest. That which is granted to a lender as security in collateral used in a loan situation.

"Seisin." Common law. The status of owning or being vested of a legal interest in real estate.

Sentence. The announcement by a judge of the penalty one must pay following a conviction or guilty plea where a crime is involved.

Separate note of argument. A brief containing a typed argument in an appeal.

Separation of powers. A doctrine of dividing responsibilities in government to prevent a concentration of power.

Service. Court procedure. The process of giving notice to one that a suit has been filed against him or her.

    Personal. Suit papers handed directly to the defendant.

    Substitute. Suit papers handed to a member of the defendant's family.

Settle out of court. Compromising a dispute.

"Sharking." An unscrupulous practice of making loans at excessive rates of interest.

Sheriff. The chief executive officer of a county. The chief conservator of the peace.

Slander. Spoken defamation.

Small claims court. Tribunals created to decide small disputes.

Soldiers' and Sailors' Civil Relief Act. A federal law created to protect military personnel from civil court action.

Specific performance. Contract law. A remedy in equity designed to force one to keep contract promises.

Standard of care. The level of caution that one should exercise.

"Stare decisis." Latin. "Let the decision stand."

Statute of frauds. Acts of legislatures that require certain contractual matters to be in writing and signed by the person to be charged by them.

Statute of limitations. Acts of legislatures stating time limits within which suits may be brought.

Statutes of descent and distribution. Acts of legislatures that spell out how the estate of a deceased should be distributed when no will is left.

Stay of execution. The delay of confinement in a criminal case or a delay in further civil proceedings while an appeal is taken.

Stock. Corporation law. That which is owned by shareholders and which represents a unit of interest in the firm.

    Bonus stock. Stock given as an incentive to purchase stock in a firm. Sometimes the phrase refers to an unlawful overissue of stock.

    Capital stock. The issued stock of a corporation and the value received by the sale of the same.

    Common stock. Stock held in common with others. The most predominant type of stock.

Founders (promoters) stock. Stock used to pay for the services of one who creates a corporation.

No-par stock. Stock that does not have a stated value.

Preferred stock. A type of stock that has an "edge" or preference over common stock.

Cumulative. Preferred stock whose preference accumulates until it is paid.

Noncumulative. Preferred stock that loses its preference in any year the preference is not paid.

Nonparticipating. Preferred stock that is entitled to its preference but nothing else.

Participating. Preferred stock with an additional feature permitting it to share in some ratio with common stock after it receives its preference.

Share of stock. That intangible portion of ownership of a corporation.

Stock certificate. A piece of paper that is evidence of the underlying shares in a corporation.

Stock split. A redesignation of the number of shares and par value of outstanding shares of stock.

Stock subscriptions. A contract to buy stock in a corporation after it is formed.

Stock warrants. A certificate issued by a corporation giving specified rights to the stockholders.

Treasury stock. Stock that is issued and then reacquired and held by a corporation.

Watered stock. Stock that is issued for less than the par value thereof.

Stockholder. One who owns a portion of a corporation.

Stop payment. Article 4, U.C.C. The process of alerting a drawee bank and requesting that they not honor a check already issued.

Subagent. Agency law. An agent hired by one who is an agent of a principal.

Subpoena. Court procedure. A legal document that commands attendance in court at a designated time.

Subrogation. The right one acquires to file a suit which was originally the right of another. Common in insurance settlements.

Substitute debtors. Novation.

Substitute performance. Accord and satisfaction.

Sum certain. Commercial paper. An amount that is precise or can be calculated precisely at any given moment.

Summary judgment. Court procedure. A judgment entered summarily without further hearings or court action.

Summons. A court document that commands one to take certain action by a certain time.

Surety bond. A legal document by which one promises to back up a money promise made by another.

Surplus. Corporations. An excess of assets over liabilities plus capital stock.

Suspend the sentence. Criminal law. After a sentence is imposed, a court has the power to place it "in limbo" so one may be placed on probation.

T

Tenancy. The legal ownership that one has in the real property of another by virtue of being a tenant.

Tenancy at will. A tenancy that can be discontinued at any time by the landlord or tenant by giving proper notice.

Tenants in common. A legal status in which two or more persons own the same real estate at the same time.

Tenure. A legal status attained that carries with it specified rights and privileges.

Termination. To end or bring to a conclusion.

Testator. A person who leaves a will.

Title. A status that carries with it legal rights and privileges.

   Equitable. Title that is grounded in equity.

   Legal. Title grounded in law. One who holds a deed to land has the legal title.

Tolling of statutes. The stopping of the running of a time period specified by law.

Tort. A wrong committed against another or another's property.

Tort feasor. One who commits a tort.

Trademark. A distinctive mark used in business that is entitled to protection.

Trade name. A distinctive name used in business that is entitled to protection.

Treason. A crime directed against a nation itself.

Trespass. The act of going upon or over another's land without permission. Also refers to an attack upon another.

Trial. The process of settling a dispute in court.

True bill. An indictment or finding of probable cause by a grand jury.

Trust. An arrangement in which certain powers are granted to a trustee.

Trust fund. A sum of money set aside for the benefit of designated persons.

Trustee. One who serves for the benefit of designated beneficiaries in a trust.

Trustee's sale. The action of a trustee in disposing of secured property under a trust after default.

Truth in Advertising. A requirement of Title I. C.C.P.A.

Truth in Lending. A requirement of Title I, C.C.P.A.

U

Ultra vires. Latin. "Beyond powers."

Unconscionable agreement. A contract that is oppressive or "contains surprises."

Undue influence. An overactive forcing of one's will upon another.

Unemployment compensation. A form of insurance created to assist those who are without work.

Unenforceable. Cannot be enforced.

Unfair competition. In business, conduct that exceeds the normal bounds of competition.

Uniform Commercial Code. An extensive body of business laws adopted by 49 states.

Uniform laws. Written laws designed to be adopted by every state legislature without modification.

Uniform Limited Partnership Act. A uniform law designed to permit the creation of a partnership, with one or more partners having a ceiling placed on their potential liability.

Uniform Partnership Act. A uniform law to regulate partnerships in the states that adopt the law.

Unjust enrichment. The gaining of wealth in a manner that is oppressive to the one from whom the wealth is taken.

U.S. attorney. In the federal court system, the "nation's lawyer."

U.S. District Court. In the federal court system, a trial court located within a state and possessing federal jurisdiction only.

Usury. The charging of more interest than the law allows.

V

Valid. Good, effective.

Venue. The county in which a cause of action arises, or the county in which a crime occurs.

Verdict. The finding of a jury.

Void. Invalid. Worthless.

Voidable. Subject to cancellation. Good but can be avoided.

Voting. Corporations. The act of stating one's position on an issue.

Cumulative. A voting procedure that permits one's vote to be multiplied by the number of offices to be filled.

Pools. A voluntary combination of votes in an attempt to gain voting power.

Trusts. A combination of votes by the transfer of stock to a trustee who becomes the "stockholder of record."

W

Wage attachment. Garnishment. A legal proceeding used to pay off a judgment out of one's wages.

Waive. To "let go" or forego a legal right. "To waive to a grand jury."

Waiver. A renunciation or release of some legal right. "A waiver of notice of meeting."

Warrant. Criminal law. A document issued by a court upon showing of "probable cause" that one has committed a crime, which commands the authorities to arrest the one named.

Warranty. Contract law. A promise that relates to the quality of goods. Also promises made in the use of commercial paper.

Express. An express promise of the quality of goods.

Implied. An unspoken promise of the quality of goods.

Warranty liability. Responsibility that arises out of contract or commercial paper promises.

Will. A testamentary document by which one disposes of one's estate upon death.

Holographic. A will wholly in the handwriting of the testator.

Nuncuptative. An oral statement by one in mortal danger that is honored as a will. Widely used in time of war.

"Winding up." Partnership law. That stage in the life of a firm where all assets are liquidated and all bills paid.

Without recourse. Commercial paper. An indorsement by which an indorser disclaims any warranty liability.

Witness. One who observes something and is called to court to state what was observed.

Workman's compensation. A "no fault" procedure designed to compensate one who is injured on the job.

Writ. A legal document containing legal matters. A "writ of mandamus" or a "writ of prohibition" are examples.

Writ of error. A part of the appellate process by which one claims to a higher court that errors occurred in the lower court.

Writ of mandamus. A legal document that demands that a public official perform certain actions.

Writ of prohibition. A legal document that demands that a public official *not* perform certain actions.

Z

Zoning. A systematic alignment of real property and its uses, designed to protect property values.

Variances. Uses of land that deviate from the basic zoning scheme that are granted after a proper hearing.

Indexes

Index of Cases and Case References

Index of Charts, Drawings, Documents, and Photos

Index of Subjects

R

This book has been set in 9 and 8 point Primer, leaded 2 points. Part numbers are 30 point Helvetica Medium, and titles are 24 point (large) Helvetica. Chapter numbers are 24 point Engravers Roman, titles are 24 point (small) Helvetica. The size of the type page is 27 × 45½ picas.